C# and the
.NET Platform

ANDREW TROELSEN

Apress™

ISBN (pbk): 1-893115-59-3

Printed and bound in the United States of America 12345678910

Editorial Directors: Dan Appleman, Gary Cornell, Jason Gilmore, Karen Watterson
Technical Editor: Eric Gunnerson
Managing Editor: Grace Wong
Copy Editors: Anne Friedman, Beverly McGuire, Nancy Rapoport
Production Editor: Anne Friedman
Compositor and Artist: Impressions Book and Journal Services, Inc.
Indexer: Nancy Guenther
Cover Designer: Karl Miyajima

Distributed to the book trade in the United States by Springer-Verlag New York, Inc., 175 Fifth Avenue, New York, NY, 10010
and outside the United States by Springer-Verlag GmbH & Co. KG, Tiergartenstr. 17, 69112 Heidelberg, Germany

In the United States, phone 1-800-SPRINGER; orders@springer-ny.com; http://www.springer-ny.com
Outside the United States, contact orders@springer.de; http://www.springer.de; fax +49 6221 345229

For information on translations, please contact Apress directly at 901 Grayson Street, Suite 204, Berkeley, CA, 94710
Phone: 510-549-5937; Fax: 510-549-5939; info@apress.com; http://www.apress.com

The source code for this book is available to readers at http://www.apress.com. You will need to answer questions pertaining to this book in order to successfully download the code.

*To my wife Amanda for her tremendous support
during the (sometimes painful) writing process.
Thanks for encouraging me to write;
even when I am sure I have nothing at all to say.*

Brief Contents

Contents

Chapter 3   Object-Oriented Programming with C# *133*

Chapter 4   Interfaces and Collections *203*

Chapter 5   Advanced C# Class Construction
Techniques *237*

Chapter 6   Assemblies, Threads, and AppDomains *283*

Chapter 7   Type Reflection
and Attribute-Based Programming *349*

Chapter 8   Building a Better Window
(Introducing Windows Forms) *385*

Chapter 9   A Better Painting Framework (GDI+) *465*

Chapter 10   Programming with Windows
Form Controls *545*

Chapter 11   Input, Output, and Object Serialization

Chapter 14 Web Development and ASP.NET 815

Chapter 15 Building (and Understanding) Web Services 887

An Important Note About This Book

THE EDITION OF THE BOOK you are holding is a Beta 2-compliant book. As many of you may be aware, there have been dramatic changes in Visual Studio.NET between the Beta 1 and Beta 2 releases (most notably in the areas of ADO.NET, assembly configuration files and general class library organization). Therefore, understand that select topics (and the code related to said topics) will most certainly require modifications in subsequent Beta/Gold releases of .NET.

The good news is, updates and corrections to both the source code and contents of this book will be available on the Web for both future beta releases and for the final release of Visual Studio.NET! In this way, you can be confident that this book will not become obsolete as the release date nears. On a related note, be aware that future releases of this text will include additional content that I was unable to include due to the tight deadlines required for this project (you'll have to obtain your updates to see exactly what these mystery topics will be ;-)

All code listings in this book have been verified against the latest software build available to authors, and have only been verified only under Windows 2000. At the time of publication, Microsoft recommends doing all .NET development on Windows 2000. Be sure to check the Web site at http://www.apress.com or http://www.intertech-inc.com for the latest updates and corrections. Enjoy!

Introduction

At the time of this writing (shortly before the release of .NET Beta 2), the .NET platform and C# programming language are already making a distinct mark on the programming landscape. Without succumbing to marketing hype, I whole-heartedly believe that the .NET platform is poised to become the New World Order of Windows development (and possible for non-Windows development in the future).

.NET represents an entirely new way to build distributed desktop and mobile applications. One thing to be painfully aware of from the onset is that the .NET platform has nothing at all to do with classic COM. For example, as you read over this text, you will find that .NET types require no class factory, do not support IUnknown, and are not registered in the system registry. These COM atoms are not simply hidden away from view—they don't exist.

Given that .NET is such a radical departure from the current modus operandi of Win32 development, Microsoft has developed a new language named C# (pro-nounced see-sharp) specifically for this new platform. C#, like Java, has its syn-tactic roots in C++. However, C# has also been influenced by Visual Basic 6.0. In this light, you are quite likely to find a number of similarities between C# and other modern programming languages. This is of course a good thing, as you can leverage your existing skills to come up to speed on the structure C#.

The truth of the matter is that .NET is an extremely language-agnostic plat-form. You can make use of any .NET-aware language (and possibly numerous .NET aware languages) during the development of your next coding effort. In this vein, your greatest challenge is not necessarily learning the C# language, but rather coming to terms with the numerous types defined in the .NET base class libraries. Once you understand how to leverage the existing code base, you will find that the concept of "syntax" becomes a non issue given that all .NET-aware languages make use of the same base class types. This is also a good thing, given that you should be able to move swiftly between various .NET languages with minimal fuss and bother.

The purpose of this text is to provide a solid foundation of the syntax and semantics of C#, as well as the architecture of the .NET platform. As you read through the (numerous) pages that follow, you will be exposed to each major facet of the .NET base class libraries. A high-level overview of each chapter follows.

Chapter 1: The Philosophy of .NET

Chapter 1 functions as the backbone for this text. The first task of the chapter is to examine the world of Windows development as we know it today, and review the shortcomings of the current state of affairs. However, the primary goal is to acquaint you with the meaning behind a number of .NET-centric building blocks such as the Common Language Runtime (CLR), Common Type System (CTS), the Common Language Specification (CLS), and the base class libraries. Once you have a solid understanding of the .NET runtime, you take an initial look at the C# programming language, and learn how to compile applications using the stand-alone compiler (csc.exe) as well as Visual Studio.NET.

Chapter 2: C# Language Fundamentals

The goal of Chapter 2 is to showcase the core syntax of the C# programming language. As you would hope, you are introduced to the intrinsic data types of C# as well as the set of iteration and decision constructs. More important, you learn about the composition of a C# class, and make friends with a number of new .NET techniques such as boxing, unboxing, value and reference types, namespace development, as well as the mighty System.Object's role.

Chapter 3: Object-Oriented Programming with C#

Now that you can build complex standalone types, Chapter 3 focuses on the pillars of object technology: encapsulation, inheritance ("is-a" and "has-a") and polymorphism (classical and ad hoc). The chapter begins with a review of these key terms, and then quickly turns attention to understanding how C# supports each pillar. Along the way, you are exposed to class properties, the "readonly" keyword and the development of class hierarchies. Finally, this chapter examines the official and correct way to handle runtime anomalies: Structured Exception Handling. The chapter ends with a discussion of the .NET garbage collection scheme, and you see how to programmatically interact with this service using the System.GC class type.

Chapter 4: Interface and Collections

Like Java and the Component Object Model (COM), C# supports the technique of interface-based programming. Here, you learn the role of interfaces, and understand how to define and implement such a creature in C#. Once you can build types that support multiple interfaces, you learn a number of techniques you can use to obtain an interface reference from a valid type instance. The second half of this chapter examines a number of predefined interfaces defined within the .NET class libraries, and illustrates how to make use of the System.Collections namespace to build custom container types. You will also learn how to build clonable and enumerable types.

Chapter 5: Advanced Class Construction Techniques

This chapter rounds out your understanding of core OOP with C#. You begin by examining the use of indexer methods, and see how this syntactic maneuver allows you to build a container that exposes its contents using standard array like indexing. The chapter also illustrates how to overload operators, in order to allow the object user to interact with your custom types more intuitively. Next, you examine the .NET-event protocol and come to understand the use of the "delegate" and "event" keywords. The chapter wraps up with an examination of XML-based code documentation.

Chapter 6: Assemblies, Threads, and AppDomains

At this point you should be very comfortable building standalone C# applications. This chapter illustrates how to break apart a monolithic EXE into discrete code libraries. Here, you learn about the internal composition of a .NET assembly and understand the distinction between "shared" and "private" assemblies. This entails a discussion of the Global Assembly Cache (GAC), XML configuration files and side-by-side execution. To further illustrate the virtues of the CLR, this chapter also examines cross-language inheritance and examines how to build multithreaded binaries.

Chapter 7: Reflection and Attributes

Reflection is the process of runtime type discovery. This chapter examines the details behind the System.Reflection namespace, and illustrates how to investigate the contents of an assembly on the fly. On a related note, you learn how to *build* an assembly (and its contained types) at runtime using the System.Reflection.Emit namespace. Chapter 7 also illustrates how to exercise late binding to a .NET type and dynamically invoke its members. Finally, the chapter wraps up with a discussion of attribute-based programming. As you will see, this technique allows you to augment compiler-generated metadata with application specific information.

Chapter 8: Building a Better Window (Introducing Windows Forms)

Despite its name, the .NET platform has considerable support for building traditional desktop applications. In this chapter, you come to understand how to build a stand-alone main window using the types contained in the System.Windows.Forms namespace. Once you understand the derivation of a Form, you then learn to add support for top-most and pop-up menu systems, toolbars, and status bars. As an added bonus, this chapter also examines how to programmatically manipulate the system registry and Windows 2000 event log.

Chapter 9: A Better Painting Framework (GDI+)

Chapter 8 examines the guts of a Form-derived type. This chapter teaches you how to render geometric images, bitmap images, and complex textual images onto the Form's client area. On a related note, you learn how to drag images within a Form (in response to mouse movement) as well as how to perform hit tests against geometric regions (in response to mouse clicks). This chapter ends with an examination of the .NET-resource format, which as you might assume, is based on XML syntax.

Chapter 10: Programming with Windows Form Controls

This final chapter on Windows Forms examines how to program with the suite of GUI widgets provided by the .NET framework. Here, you discover details behind the Calendar, DataGrid, and input validation controls, in addition to the vanilla flavored TextBox, Button, and ListBox types (among others). You wrap up by examining how to build custom dialog boxes and come to understand a new technique termed "Form Inheritance."

Chapter 11: Input, Output, and Object Serialization

The .NET framework provides a number of types devoted to IO activities. Here you learn how to save and retrieve simple data types to (and from) files, memory locations, and string buffers. Of greater interest is the use of object serialization services. Using a small set of predefined attributes and a corresponding object graph, the framework is able to persist related objects using an XML or binary formatter. To illustrate object serialization at work, this chapter wraps up with a Windows Forms application that allows the end user to create and serialize custom class types for use at a later time.

Chapter 12: Interacting with Unmanaged Code

As bizarre as it may seem, Microsoft's Component Object Model (COM) can now be regarded as a legacy technology. As you will most certainly know by this point in the book, the architecture of COM has little resemblance to that of .NET. This chapter examines the details of how COM types and .NET types can live together in harmony through the use of COM Callable Wrappers (CCW) and Runtime Callable Wrappers (RCW). Here you see how various IDL constructs such as SAFEARRAYs, connection points, and COM enumerations map into C# code.

The chapter concludes by examining how to build .NET types that can take advantage of the COM+ runtime.

Chapter 13: Data Access with ADO.NET

To be perfectly blunt, ADO.NET has little resemblance to classic ADO proper. As you discover, ADO.NET is a data access model specifically built for the disconnected world. To begin, you learn how to create and populate an in memory DataSet, and establish relationships between the internal DataTables. The second half of this chapter examines how to make use of the OleDb and Sql managed providers to obtain access to relational database management systems such as Microsoft Access and SQL Server. Once you understand how to connect to a give data store, you learn how to insert, update, and remove data records as well as trigger logic contained within stored procedures.

Chapter 14: Web Development and ASP.NET

For the sake of completion, this chapter begins with an overview of the Web programming model, and examines how to build Web front ends (using HTML), client-side validation (using JavaScript), and requesting a response from a classic ASP Web application. The bulk of the chapter however provides a solid introduction to the ASP.NET architecture. Here you learn about Web Controls, server side event handling, and the core properties of the Page type (including the Request and Response properties).

Chapter 15: Building (and Understanding) Web Services

In this final chapter of this book (some 900 pages later), you examine the role of .NET Web services. Simply put, a "Web service" is an assembly that is activated using standard HTTP. Here you examine the surrounding technologies (WSDL, SOAP, and discovery services) which enable a Web service to take incoming client requests. Once you understand how to construct a C# Web service, you then learn how to build a client side proxy class, which hides the low level SOAP logic from view.

What You Need to Use This Book

The very first thing you must do is download the accompanying source code for this book from the Apress Web site (http://www.apress.com). As you read over each chapter, you will find the following icon has been liberally scattered throughout the text:

This is your visual cue that the example under discussion may be loaded into Visual Studio.NET for examination.

In addition to the source code, you need to have a copy of .NET Beta 2. Let me assure you that there have been some significant changes under the hood in the move between Beta 1 and Beta 2, especially in the area of ADO.NET. If you are currently running Beta 1, you are bound to find numerous explanations out of whack.

I have chosen to focus on using the Visual Studio.NET development environment in this text. Although you are free to build and compile your code using nothing more than the C# compiler (which is included with the .NET SDK) and Notepad.exe, you will find that VS.NET takes care of a number of low level details on your behalf.

Finally, although I assume no foreknowledge of C# or the .NET platform, I wrote this book with the following assumptions:

- You are an experienced software professional who has background in some modern day programming language (C++, Visual Basic, Java, etc.).

- You are unafraid to consult online Help (and do so often without shame).

Even a book of this size cannot possibly cover each and every aspect of the .NET platform. The online Help that ships with the .NET SDK is incredibly readable, and provides numerous code examples, white papers, and online tutorials. Once you have read (and understood) these 15 chapters, you will be in a perfect position to build complete .NET solutions with the C# language. At this point, on-line Help will become your faithful companion, which extends and complements the material presented here.

So, let's get on with the show! It is my sincere hope that this book will guide you safely through this .NET universe, and serve as a solid reference during your life as an author of managed code.

Andrew Troelsen
Minneapolis, Minnesota

Acknowledgments

This book was a *huge* undertaking. I am absolutely certain that this text would not be ready for prime time if it were not for the following fine people at Apress. First, thanks to Gary Cornell who was a consistent source of support during the writing of this book (I look forward to finally meeting you at Tech Ed and working together again soon). A big thanks to Grace Wong, who kept the entire project well focused, positive, and on track. Thanks to Stephanie Rodriguez, who has done a fantastic job marketing this material, posting sample chapters, and remaining patient and kind as I "kept forgetting" to deliver the cover copy. Last but certainly not least, thanks to Nancy Guenther for working with an incredibly tight deadline in order to index this material.

A mammoth amount of gratitude to the editorial staff: Doris Wong, Anne Friedman, Nancy Rapoport, and Beverly McGuire, all of whom did an outstanding job formatting and massaging the knots out of my original manuscript. Special thanks to Anne for working around the clock with me to ensure a timely delivery of this material!

I also must offer heartfelt thanks to my primary technical editor, Eric Gunnerson (Microsoft employee and general C# guru) who took time out of his extremely busy life to perform technical reviews and clarifications (especially when upgrading the manuscript from alpha to Beta 1). Additional thanks are extended to Microsoft's Joe Nalewabau, Nick Hodapp, and Dennis Angeline for helping to clarify numerous bits of content. Any remaining faux pas are my sole responsibility.

Thanks to my fellow cohorts at Intertech, Inc.: Steve Close, Gina McGhee, Andrew "Gunner" Sondgeroth, and Tom Barnaby who, while working on their own books, provided an encouraging, intense and positive environment. Finally, thanks to Tom Salonek for buying me that first cup of coffee over five years ago.

CHAPTER 1

The Philosophy of .NET

EVERY FEW YEARS OR SO, THE modern day programmer must be willing to perform a self-inflicted knowledge transplant, in order to stay current with the new technologies of the day. The languages (C++, Visual Basic, Java), frameworks (MFC, ATL, STL) and architectures (COM, CORBA) that were touted as the silver bullets of software development, eventually become overshadowed by something better or at very least something new. Regardless of the frustration you can feel when upgrading your internal knowledge base, it is unavoidable. Microsoft's .NET platform represents the next major wave of (positive) changes coming from those kind folks in Redmond.

The point of this chapter is to lay the conceptual groundwork for the remainder of the book. It begins with a high-level discussion of a number of .NET-related atoms such as assemblies, intermediate language (IL), and just in time (JIT) compilation. During the process, you will come to understand the relationship between various aspects of the .NET framework, such as the Common Language Runtime (CLR), the Common Type System (CTS), and the Common Language Specification (CLS).

This chapter also provides you with an overview of the functionality supplied by the .NET base class libraries and examines a number of helpful utilities (such as ILDasm.exe) that may be used to investigate these libraries at your leisure. The chapter wraps up with an examination of how to compile C# applications using the command line compiler (csc.exe), as well as the Visual Studio.NET Integrated Development Environment (IDE).

Understanding the Current State of Affairs

Before examining the specifics of the .NET universe, it's helpful to consider some of the issues that motivated the genesis of this new platform. To get in the proper mindset, let's begin this chapter with a brief and painless history lesson to remember your roots and understand the limitations of the current state of affairs (after all, admitting you have a problem is the first step toward finding a solution). After this quick tour of life as we know it, we turn our attention to the numerous benefits provided by C# and the .NET platform.

Life as a Win32/C Programmer

Traditionally speaking, developing software for the Windows operating system involved using the C programming language in conjunction with the Windows API (Application Programming Interface). While it is true that numerous applications have been successfully created using this time-honored approach, few of us would disagree that building applications using the raw API is a complex undertaking.

The first obvious problem is that C is a very terse language. C developers are forced to contend with manual memory management, ugly pointer arithmetic, and ugly syntactical constructs. Furthermore, given that C is a structured language, it lacks the benefits provided by the object-oriented approach (can anyone say *spaghetti code?*) When you combine the thousands of global functions defined by the raw Win32 API to an already formidable language, it is little wonder that there are so many buggy applications floating around today.

Life as a C++/MFC Programmer

One vast improvement over raw C development is the use of the C++ programming language. In many ways, C++ can be thought of as an object-oriented *layer* on top of C. Thus, even though C++ programmers benefit from the famed "pillars of OOP" (encapsulation, polymorphism, and inheritance), they are still at the mercy of the painful aspects of the C language (e.g., memory management, ugly pointer arithmetic, and ugly syntactical constructs).

Despite its complexity, many C++ frameworks exist today. For example, the Microsoft Foundation Classes (MFC) provide the developer with a set of existing C++ classes that facilitate the construction of Windows applications. The main role of MFC is to wrap a "sane subset" of the raw Win32 API behind a number of classes, magic macros, and numerous CASE tools (e.g., AppWizard, ClassWizard, and so forth). Regardless of the helpful assistance offered by the MFC framework (as well as many other windowing toolkits), the fact of the matter is C++ programming remains a difficult and error-prone experience, given its historical roots in C.

Life as a Visual Basic Programmer

Due to a heartfelt desire to enjoy a simpler lifestyle, many programmers have shifted away from the world of C(++)-based frameworks to kinder, gentler languages such as Visual Basic 6.0 (VB). VB is popular due to its ability to build complex user interfaces, code libraries (e.g., COM servers) and data access logic with minimal fuss and bother. Even more than MFC, VB hides the complexities of the

Win32 API from view using a number of integrated CASE tools, intrinsic data types, classes, and VB-centric functions.

The major downfall of VB (at least until the advent of VB.NET) is that it is not a fully object-oriented language, but rather "object aware." For example, VB 6.0 does not allow the programmer to establish "is-a" relationships between types (i.e., no classical inheritance), has no support for parameterized class construction, and no intrinsic support for building multithreaded applications (and so on).

Life as a Java Programmer

Enter Java. The Java programming language is a completely object-oriented entity that has its syntactic roots in C++. As many of you are aware, Java's strengths are far greater than its support for platform independence. Java (as a language) cleans up the unsavory syntactical aspects of C++. Java (as a platform) provides programmers with a large number of predefined "packages" that contain various class and interface definitions. Using these types, Java programmers are able to build "100% Pure Java" applications complete with database connectivity, messaging support, Web-enabled front ends and rich-user interfaces (in addition to a number of other services).

Although Java is a very elegant language, one potential problem is that using Java typically means that you must use Java front-to-back during the development cycle. In effect, Java offers little hope of language independence, as this goes against the grain of Java's primary goal (a single programming language for every need). In reality however, there are millions of lines of existing code out there in the world that would ideally like to comingle with newer Java code. Sadly, Java makes this task problematic.

On a related note, Java alone is quite simply not appropriate for every situation. If you are building a graphics intensive product (such as a 3D-rendered video game), you will find Java's execution speed can leave something to be desired. A better approach is to use a lower-level language (such as C++) where appropriate, and have Java code interoperate with the external C++ binaries. While Java does provide a limited ability to access non-Java APIs, there is little support for true cross-language integration.

Life as a COM Programmer

The truth of the matter is if you are not currently building Java-based solutions, the chances are very good that you are investing your time and energy understanding Microsoft's Component Object Model (COM). COM is an architecture that says in effect "If you build your classes in accordance with the rules of COM, you end up with a block of *reusable binary code*."

The beauty of a binary COM server is that it can be accessed in a language-independent manner. Thus, C++ programmers can build classes that can be used by VB. Delphi programmers can use classes built using C, and so forth. However, as you may be aware, COM's language independence is somewhat limited. For example, there is no way to *derive* a new COM type using an existing COM type (no support for classical inheritance). Rather, you must make use of the less robust "has-a" relationship to reuse existing COM types.

Another benefit of COM is its location-transparent nature. Using constructs such as Application Identifiers (AppIDs), stubs, proxies, and the COM runtime environment, programmers can avoid the need to work with raw Sockets, RPC calls, and other low level details. For example, ponder the following Visual Basic 6.0 COM client code:

```
' This block of VB 6.0 code can activate a COM class written in
' any COM aware language, which may be located anywhere
' on the network (including your local machine).
'

Dim c as New MyCOMClass           ' Location resolved using AppID.
c.DoSomeWork
```

Although COM is a very dominant object model, it is extremely complex under the hood (at least until you have spent many months exploring its plumbing . . . especially if you happen to be a C++ programmer). To help simplify the development of COM binaries, numerous COM-aware frameworks have come into existence. For example, the Active Template Library (ATL) provides another set of C++ predefined classes, templates, and macros to ease the creation of classic COM types.

Many other languages (such as Visual Basic) also hide a good part of the COM infrastructure from view. However, framework support alone is not enough to hide the complexity of classic COM. Even when you choose a relatively simply COM-aware language such as Visual Basic, you are still forced to contend with fragile registration entries and numerous deployment related issues.

Life as a Windows DNA Programmer

Finally there is a little thing called the Internet. Over the last several years, Microsoft has been adding more Internet-aware features into its family of operating systems. It seems that the popularity of Web applications is ever expanding. Sadly, building a complete Web application using Windows DNA (Distributed iNternet Architecture) is also a very complex undertaking.

Some of this complexity is due to the simple fact that Windows DNA requires the use of numerous technologies and languages (ASP, HTML, XML, JavaScript,

VBScript, COM(+), as well as a data access technology such as ADO). One problem is that many of these items are completely unrelated from a syntactic point of view. For example, JavaScript has a syntax much like C, while VBScript is a subset of Visual Basic proper. The COM servers that are created to run under the COM+ runtime have an entirely different look and feel from the ASP pages that invoke them. The end result is a highly confused mishmash of technologies. Furthermore, each language and/or technology has its own type system (that typically looks nothing like the other type systems). An "int" in JavaScript is not the same as an "int" in C which is different from an "Integer" in VB proper.

The .NET Solution

So much for the brief history lesson. The bottom line is life as a Windows programmer is tough. The .NET framework is a rather radical and brute-force approach to making our lives easier. The solution proposed by .NET is "Change everything from here on out" (sorry, you can't blame the messenger for the message). As you will see during the remainder of this book, the .NET framework is a completely new model for building systems on the Windows family of operating systems, and possibly non-Microsoft operating systems in the future. To set the stage, here is a quick rundown of some core features provided courtesy of .NET:

- *Full interoperability with existing code.* This is (of course) a good thing. As you will see in Chapter 12, existing COM binaries can comingle (i.e., interop) with newer .NET binaries and vice versa.

- *Complete and total language integration.* Unlike classic COM, .NET supports cross-language inheritance, cross-language exception handling, and cross-language debugging.

- *A common runtime engine shared by all .NET aware languages.* One aspect of this engine is a well-defined set of types that each .NET-aware language "understands."

- *A base class library* that provides shelter from the complexities of raw API calls, and offers a consistent object model used by all .NET-aware languages.

- *No more COM plumbing!* IClassFactory, IUnknown, IDL code, and the evil VARIANT-compliant types (BSTR, SAFEARRAY, and so forth) have no place in a .NET binary.

- *A truly simplified deployment model.* Under .NET, there is no need to register a binary unit into the system registry. Furthermore, the .NET runtime allows multiple versions of the same DLL to exist in harmony on a single machine.

Building Blocks of .NET (CLR, CTS, and CLS)

Although the roles of the CLR, CTS, and CLS are examined in greater detail later in this chapter, you do need to have a working knowledge of these topics to further understand the .NET universe. From a programmer's point of view, .NET can be understood as a new runtime environment and a common base class library. The runtime layer is properly referred to as the Common Language Runtime, or CLR. The primary role of the CLR is to locate, load, and manage .NET types on your behalf. The CLR takes care of a number of low-level details such as automatic memory management, language integration, and simplified deployment (and versioning) of binary code libraries.

Another building block of the .NET platform is the Common Type System, or CTS. The CTS fully describes all possible data types supported by the runtime, specifies how those types can interact with each other and details how they are represented in the .NET metadata format (more information on "metadata" later in this chapter).

Understand that a given .NET-aware language might not support each and every data type defined by the CTS. The Common Language Specification (CLS) is a set of rules that define a subset of common types that ensure .NET binaries can be used seamlessly across all languages targeting the .NET platform. Thus, if you build .NET types that only use CLS-compliant features, you can rest assured that all .NET-aware languages could make use of your types.

The .NET Base Class Libraries

In addition to the CLR and CTS/CLS specifications, the .NET platform provides a base class library that is available to all .NET programming languages. Not only does this base class library encapsulate various primitives such as file IO, graphical rendering and interaction with external hardware devices, but it also provides support for a number of services required by most real world applications.

For example, the base class libraries define types that support database manipulation, XML integration, programmatic security, and the construction of Web-enabled (as well as traditional desktop and console-based) front ends. From a conceptual point of view, you can visualize the relationship between the .NET runtime layer and the corresponding base class library as shown in Figure 1-1.

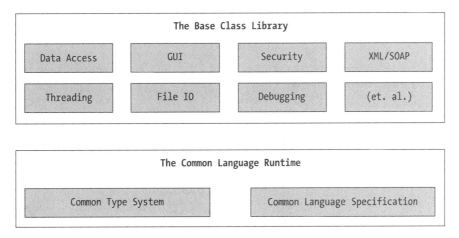

Figure 1-1. A sampling of the functionality provided by the base class libraries

What C# Brings to the Table

Given that .NET is such a radical departure from the current thoughts of the day, Microsoft has developed a new programming language (C#) specifically for this new platform. C# is a programming language that looks *very* similar (but not identical) to the syntax of Java. For example, like Java, a C# class definition is contained within a single-source code file (*.cs) rather than the C++-centric view of splitting a class definition into discrete header (*.h) and implementation (*.cpp) files. However, to call C# a Java rip-off is inaccurate. Both C# and Java are based on the syntactical constructs of C++. Just as Java is in many ways a cleaned-up version of C++, C# can be viewed as a cleaned-up version of Java.

The truth of the matter is that many of C#'s syntactic constructs are modeled after various aspects of Visual Basic and C++. For example, like Visual Basic, C# supports the notion of class properties. Like C++, C# allows you to overload operators on your custom class types (as you may know, Java lacks both of these features). Given that C# is a hybrid of numerous languages, the end result is a product that is as syntactically clean (if not cleaner) than Java, just about as simple as Visual Basic, and provides just about as much power and flexibility as C++ (without the associated ugly bits). In a nutshell, the C# languages offers the following features:

- No pointers required! C# programs typically have no need for direct pointer manipulation (although you are free to drop down to that level if you desire).

- Automatic memory management.

- Formal syntactic constructs for enumerations, structures, and class properties.

- The C++ like ability to overload operators for a custom type, without the complexity (i.e., making sure to "return *this to allow chaining" is not your problem).

- Full support for interface-based programming techniques. However, unlike classic COM, the interface is *not* the only way to manipulate types between binaries. .NET, supports true object references that can be passed between boundaries (by reference or by value).

- Full support for aspect-based programming techniques (aka attributes). This brand of development allows you to assign characteristics to types (much like COM IDL) to further describe the behavior of a given entity.

Perhaps the most important point to understand about the C# language is that it is only capable of producing code that can execute within the .NET runtime (you could never use C# to build a classic COM server). Officially speaking, the term used to describe the code targeting the .NET runtime is *managed code*. The binary unit that contains the managed code is termed an *assembly* (more details in just a bit).

.NET-Aware Programming Languages

When the .NET platform was announced to the general public during the 2000 Professional Developers Conference (PDC), several speakers listed vendors who are busy building .NET-aware versions of their respective compilers. At the time of this writing, more than 30 different languages are slated to undergo .NET enlightenment. In addition to the four languages that ship with Visual Studio.NET (C#, Visual Basic.NET, "Managed C++," and JScript.NET), be on the lookout for .NET versions of Smalltalk, COBOL, Pascal, Python, and Perl as well as many others. Conceptually, Figure 1-2 shows the big picture.

The funny thing about .NET binaries is despite the fact that they take the same file extension (DLL or EXE) as classic COM binaries, they have absolutely no internal similarities. For example, DLL .NET binaries do not export methods to facilitate communications with the classic COM runtime (given that .NET is *not* COM). Furthermore, .NET binaries are not described using IDL code and are not registered into the system registry. Perhaps most important, unlike classic COM servers, .NET binaries do not contain platform-specific instructions, but rather platform-agnostic "intermediate language" officially termed Microsoft Intermediate Language (MSIL) or simply, IL.

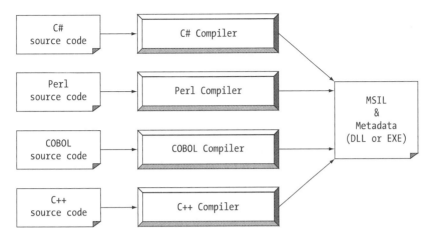

Figure 1-2. All .NET-aware compilers emit IL instructions and metadata.

An Overview of .NET Binaries (aka Assemblies)

When a DLL or EXE has been created using a .NET-aware compiler, the resulting module is bundled into an assembly. You examine the complete details of .NET assemblies in Chapter 6. However to facilitate the discussion of the .NET runtime environment, you do need to examine some basic properties of this new file format.

As mentioned, an assembly contains IL code, which is conceptually similar to Java byte code in that it is not compiled to platform-specific instructions until absolutely necessary. Typically "absolutely necessary" is the point at which a block of IL instructions (such as a method implementation) are referenced for use by the .NET runtime engine.

In addition to IL instructions, assemblies also contain metadata that describes in vivid detail the characteristics of every "type" living within the binary. For example, if you have a class named Foo contained within a given assembly, the type metadata describes details such as Foo's base class, which interfaces are implemented by Foo (if any), as well as a full description of each method, property, and event supported by the Foo type.

In many respects, .NET metadata is a dramatic improvement to classic COM type information. As you may already know, classic COM binaries are typically described using an associated type library (which is little more than a binary version of IDL code). The problems with COM type information is that it is not guaranteed to be present, and the fact that IDL code has no way to catalog externally referenced servers that are required for the correct operation of the contained coclasses. In contrast, .NET metadata is always present and is automatically generated by a given .NET-aware compiler.

In addition to type metadata, assemblies themselves are also described using metadata, which is officially termed a *manifest*. The manifest contains information about the current version of the assembly, any optional security constraints, locale information, and a list of all externally referenced assemblies that are required for proper execution. You examine various tools that can be used to examine an assembly's underlying IL, type metadata and information listed in the manifest later in this chapter.

Single File and Multifile Assemblies

In a great number of cases, there is a simple a one-to-one correspondence between a .NET assembly and the underlying DLL or EXE binary. Thus, if you are building a .NET DLL, it is safe to consider that the binary and the assembly are one and the same. As seen in Chapter 6 however, this is not completely accurate. Technically speaking, if an assembly is composed of a single DLL or EXE module, you have a "single file assembly." Single file assemblies contain all the necessary IL, metadata and associated manifest in a single well-defined package.

Multifile assemblies, on the other hand, may be composed of numerous .NET binaries, each of which is termed a *module*. When building a multifile assembly, one of these modules must contain the assembly manifest (and possibly IL instructions). The other related modules contain nothing but raw IL and type metadata.

So why would you choose to create a multifile assembly? When you partition an assembly into discrete modules, you end up with a more flexible deployment option. For example, if an end user is referencing a remote assembly that needs to be downloaded onto his or her machine, the runtime will only download the required modules. In contrast, if all your types were placed in a single file assembly, the end user may end up downloading a large chunk of data that is not really needed (which is obviously a waste of time). Thus, as you can see, an assembly is really a logical grouping of one or more related modules.

The Role of Microsoft Intermediate Language

Now that you have a better feel for .NET assemblies, let's examine Microsoft Intermediate Language (MSIL) in a bit more detail. MSIL is a language that sits above any particular platform-specific instruction set. Regardless of which .NET aware language you choose (C#, Visual Basic.NET, Eiffel, and so forth) the associated compiler emits IL instructions. For example, the following C# class definition models a trivial calculator (which is only capable of returning the sum of 10 and 84 . . .). Don't concern yourself with the exact syntax for the time being, but do notice the signature of the Add() method:

```
// We will examine namespaces later in the chapter. . .
namespace Calculator
{
    using System;

    // The calculator class contains an Add() method,
    // as well as the application's entry point, Main().
    public class Calc
    {
        // Default ctor.
        public Calc(){}

        public int Add(int x, int y)
        {
            return x + y;
        }

        public static int Main(string[] args)
        {
            // Make a Calc and add some numbers.
            Calc c = new Calc();
            int ans = c.Add(10, 84);
            Console.WriteLine("10 + 84 is {0}.", ans);
            return 0;
        }
    }
}
```

Once the C# compiler (csc.exe) compiles this source code file, you end up with a single file assembly that contains a manifest, IL instructions, and metadata describing each aspect of the Calc class. For example, if you peek inside this binary and investigate the IL instructions for the Add() method, you find the following:

```
.method public hidebysig instance int32 Add(int32 x, int32 y) il managed
{
    // Code size        8 (0x8)
    .maxstack   2
    .locals ([0] int32 V_0)
    IL_0000:  ldarg.1
    IL_0001:  ldarg.2
    IL_0002:  add
    IL_0003:  stloc.0
    IL_0004:  br.s        IL_0006
```

```
        IL_0006:  ldloc.0
        IL_0007:  ret
} // end of method Calc::Add
```

Don't worry if you are unable to make heads or tails of the resulting IL for this method. Chapter 7 examines some IL basics in greater detail. The point to concentrate on is that the C# compiler emits IL, not platform specific instructions. Now, recall that this is true of all .NET aware compilers. To illustrate, assume you created the Calc class using Visual Basic.NET, rather than C#:

```
' The VB.NET calculator. . .
Module Module1
    ' Again, Calc defines an Add() method and the application entry point.
    Class Calc

        Public Function Add(ByVal x As Integer, ByVal y As Integer) As Integer
            ' Yes!  VB.NET supports a 'return' keyword.
            Return x + y
        End Function
    End Class
    Sub Main()
        Dim ans As Integer
        Dim c As New Calc()
        ans = c.Add(10, 84)
        Console.WriteLine("10 + 84 is {0}.", ans)
    End Sub
End Module
```

If you examine the IL for the Add() method, you would find the same set of instructions (slightly tweaked by the VB.NET compiler):

```
.method public instance int32 Add(int32 x, int32 y) il managed
{
    // Code size       11 (0xb)
    .maxstack  2
    .locals init ([0] int32 Add)
    IL_0000:  nop
    IL_0001:  ldarg.1
    IL_0002:  ldarg.2
    IL_0003:  add.ovf
    IL_0004:  stloc.0
    IL_0005:  nop
    IL_0006:  br.s       IL_0008
```

```
    IL_0008:  nop
    IL_0009:  ldloc.0
    IL_000a:  ret
} // end of method Module1$Calc::Add
```

SOURCE CODE *The CSharpCalculator and VBCalculator applications are both included under the Chapter 1 subdirectory.*

Benefits of IL

At this point, you might be wondering exactly what benefits are gained by compiling source code into IL (with the associated metadata) rather than directly to a specific instruction set. One benefit of compiling to IL (with the associated metadata) is language integration. As you have already seen, each .NET aware language produces the same underlying IL. Therefore, all languages are able to interact within a well-defined binary arena.

Given that IL is platform agnostic, it is very possible that the .NET runtime will be ported to other (non-Windows) operating systems. In this light, the .NET runtime is poised to become a platform-independent architecture, providing the same benefits Java developers have grown accustomed to (i.e., the potential of a single code base running on numerous operating systems). Unlike Java however, .NET allows you to build applications in a language-independent fashion. Thus, .NET has the potential to allow you to develop an application in *any* language and have it run on *any* platform.

Again, the crux of the last paragraph is "potential platform independence." At the time of this writing, there is no official word from Microsoft regarding the platform-agnostic nature of .NET. For the time being, you should assume that .NET is only equipped to run on the Windows family of operating systems.

The Role of Metadata

COM programmers are without a doubt familiar with the Interface Definition Language (IDL). IDL is a "metalanguage" that is used to describe in completely unambiguous terms the types contained within a given COM server. IDL is compiled into a binary format (termed a type library) using the midl.exe compiler, that can then be used by a COM-aware language, in order to manipulate the contained types.

In addition to describing the types within a COM binary, IDL has minimal support to describe characteristics about the server itself, such as its current version (e.g., 1.0, 2.0, or 2.4) and intended locale (e.g., English, German, Urdu, Russian). The problem with COM metadata is that it may or may not be present and it is often the role of the programmer to ensure the underlying IDL accuracy reflects the internal types. The .NET framework makes no use of IDL whatsoever. However, the spirit of describing the types residing within a particular binary lives on.

In addition to the underlying IL instructions, a .NET assembly contains full, complete and accurate metadata. Like IDL, .NET metadata describes each and every type (class, structure, enumeration, and so forth) defined in the binary, as well as the members of each type (properties, methods, and events).

Furthermore, the .NET manifest is far more complete than IDL, in that it also describes each externally referenced assembly that is required by this assembly to operate. Because .NET metadata is so wickedly meticulous assemblies are completely self-describing entities. In fact, .NET binaries have no need to be registered into the system registry (more on that little tidbit later).

A Quick Metadata Example

As an example, let's take a look at the metadata that has been generated for the Add() method of the C# Calculator class you examined previously (the metadata generated for the VB.NET Calculator class is identical):

```
Method #2
————————————————————————————-

MethodName: Add (06000002)
Flags      : [Public] [HideBySig] [ReuseSlot]  (00000086)
RVA        : 0x00002058
ImplFlags : [IL] [Managed]  (00000000)
CallCnvntn: [DEFAULT]
hasThis
ReturnType: I4
2 Arguments
      Argument #1:  I4
      Argument #2:  I4
2 Parameters
      (1) ParamToken : (08000001) Name : x flags: [none] (00000000) default:
      (2) ParamToken : (08000002) Name : y flags: [none] (00000000) default:
```

Here you can see that the Add() method, return type, and method arguments have been fully described by the C# compiler (and yes, you'll see how to view type metadata and IL later in this chapter).

Metadata is used by numerous aspects of the .NET runtime environment, as well as by various development tools. For example, the IntelliSense feature provided by Visual Studio.NET is made possible by reading an assembly's metadata at design time. Metadata is also used by various object browsing utilities, debugging tools, and the C# compiler itself.

Compiling IL to Platform-Specific Instructions

Due to the fact that assemblies contain IL instructions and metadata, rather than platform specific instructions, the underlying IL must be compiled on the fly before use. The entity that compiles the IL into meaningful CPU instructions is termed a just-in-time (JIT) compiler that sometimes goes by the friendly name of "Jitter." The .NET runtime environment supplies a JIT compiler for each CPU targeting the CLR. In this way, developers can write a single body of code that can be JIT-compiled and executed on machines with different architectures.

As the Jitter compiles IL instructions into corresponding machine code it will cache the results in memory. In this way, if a call is made to a method named Bar() defined within a class named Foo, the Bar() IL instructions are compiled into platform specific instructions on the first invocation and retained in memory for later use. Therefore, the next time Bar() is called, there is no need to recompile the IL.

.NET Types and .NET Namespaces

A given assembly (single file or multifile) may contain any number of distinct types. In the world of .NET, a *type* is simply a generic term used to collectively refer to classes, structures, interfaces, enumerations, and delegates. When you build solutions using a .NET aware language (such as C#), you will most likely interact with each of these types. For example, your assembly may define a single class that implements some number of interfaces. Perhaps one of the interface methods takes a custom enum type as an input parameter.

As you build your custom types, you have the option of organizing your items into a namespace. In a nutshell, a *namespace* is a logical naming scheme used by .NET languages to group related types under a unique umbrella. When you group your types into a namespace, you provide a simple way to circumvent possible name clashes between assemblies.

For example, if you were building a new Windows Forms application that references two external assemblies, and each assembly contained a type named GoCart, you would be able to specify which GoCart class you are interested in by appending the type name to its containing namespace (i.e., "CustomVehicals.GoCart" not "SlowVehicals.GoCart"). You look at namespaces from a programmatic point of view later in this chapter.

Understanding the Common Language Runtime

Now that you have an understanding of types, assemblies, metadata, and IL, you can begin to examine the .NET runtime engine in a bit greater detail. Programmatically speaking, the term *runtime* can be understood as a collection of services that are required to execute a given block of code. For example, when developers make use of the Microsoft Foundation Classes (MFC) to create a new application, they are (painfully) aware that their binary is required to link with the rather hefty MFC runtime library (mfc42.dll). Other popular languages also have a corresponding runtime. Visual Basic 6.0 programmers are also tied to a runtime module or two (i.e., msvbvm60.dll). Java developers are tied to the Java Virtual Machine (JVM) and so forth.

The .NET platform offers yet another runtime system. The key difference between the .NET runtime and the various other runtimes I have just mentioned is the fact that the .NET runtime provides a single well-defined runtime layer that is shared by *all* languages that are .NET aware. As mentioned earlier in this chapter, the .NET runtime is officially termed the Common Language Runtime, or simply CLR.

The CLR consists of two core entities. First we have the runtime execution engine, mscoree.dll. When an assembly is referenced for use, mscoree.dll is loaded automatically, which then in turn loads the required assembly into memory. The runtime engine is responsible for a number of tasks. First and foremost, it is the entity in charge of resolving the location of an assembly and finding the requested type (e.g., class, interface, structure, etc.) within the binary by reading the supplied metadata. The execution engine compiles the associated IL into platform-specific instructions, performs any (optional) security checks as well as a number of related tasks.

The second major entity of the CLR is the base class library. Although the entire base class library has been broken into a number of discrete assemblies, the primary binary is mscorlib.dll. This .NET assembly contains a large number of core types that encapsulate a wide variety of common programming tasks. When you build .NET solutions, you always make use of this particular assembly, and perhaps numerous other .NET binaries (both system supplied and custom).

Figure 1-3 illustrates the workflow that takes place between your source code (which is making use of base class library types), a given .NET compiler, and the .NET execution engine.

Understanding the Common Type System

Recall that the Common Type System (CTS) is a formal specification that describes how a given type (class, structure, interface, intrinsic data types, etc.) must be defined in order to be hosted by the CLR. Also recall that the CTS defines

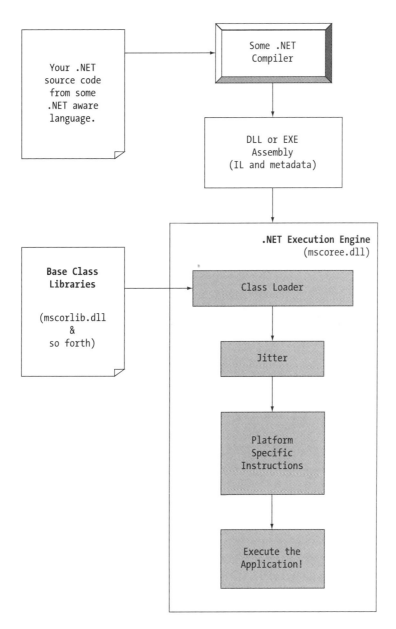

Figure 1-3. mscoree.dll in action

a number of syntactic constructs (such as overloading operators) that may or may not be supported by a given .NET-aware language. When you wish to build assemblies that can be used by all possible .NET-aware languages, you need to conform your exposed types to the rules of the CLS (mentioned in just a moment). For the time being, let's preview the formal definitions of various members of the CTS.

CTS Class Types

Every .NET-aware language supports the notion of a "class type," which is the cornerstone of object-oriented programming. A class is composed of any number of properties, methods, and events. As you would expect, the CTS allows a given class to support abstract members that provide a polymorphic interface for any derived classes. CTS-compliant classes may only derive from a single base class (multiple inheritance is not allowed for class types). To help you keep your wits about you, Table 1-1 documents a number of characteristics of interest to class types.

Table 1-1. NET Class Characteristics

CLASS CHARACTERISTIC	MEANING IN LIFE
Is the class "sealed" or not?	Sealed classes are types that cannot function as a base class to other classes.
Does the class implement any interfaces?	An interface is a collection of abstract members that provide a contract between the object and object user. The CTS allows a class to implement any number of interfaces.
Is the class abstract or concrete?	Abstract classes cannot be directly created, but are intended to define common behaviors for derived types. Concrete classes can be created directly.
What is the "visibility" of this class?	Each class must be configured with a visibility attribute. Basically this trait defines if the class may be used by external assemblies, or only from within the containing assembly (e.g., a private helper class).

CTS Structure Types

The concept of a structure is also formalized by the CTS. If you have a C background, you should be pleased to know that these user-defined types (UDTs) have survived in the world of .NET (although they behave a bit differently under the hood). In general, a structure is a lightweight class type, with a number of notable exceptions (fully explained in Chapter 2). CTS-compliant structures may define any number of *parameterized* constructors (the no-argument constructor is reserved). In this way, you are able to establish the value of each field during the time of construction. For example:

```
// Create a C# structure.
struct Baby
{
    // Structures can contain fields.
    public string name;

    // Structures can contain constructors (with arguments).
    public Baby(string name)
    { this.name = name; }

    // Structures may take methods.
    public void Cry()
    { Console.WriteLine("Waaaaaaaaaaaah!!!"); }

    public bool IsSleeping() { return false; }
    public bool IsChanged() { return false; }
}
```

Here is our structure in action:

```
// Welcome to the world Max Barnaby!!
//
Baby barnaBaby = new Baby("Max");
Console.WriteLine("Changed?: {0}", barnaBaby.IsChanged().ToString());
Console.WriteLine("Sleeping?: {0}", barnaBaby.IsSleeping().ToString());

// Show your true colors Max...
for(int i = 0; i < 10000; i ++)
    barnaBaby.Cry();
```

All CTS-compliant structures are derived from a common base class: System.ValueType. This base class configures a structure to function as a value-based (stack) data type rather than a reference-based (heap) entity. Be aware that the CTS permits structures to implement any number of interfaces; however structures may not derive from other types and are therefore always "sealed."

CTS Interface Types

Interfaces are nothing more than a collection of abstract methods, properties, and event definitions. Unlike classic COM, .NET interfaces do *not* derive a common base interface such as IUnknown. On their own, interfaces are of little use.

However when a class or structure implements a given interface in its own unique way, you are able to request access to the supplied functionality using an interface reference. When you build custom interfaces using a .NET-aware programming language, the CTS permits a given interface to derive from *multiple* base interfaces. Again, you examine interface based programming in Chapter 4.

CTS Type Members

As you have just seen, classes and structures can take any number of *members.* Formally speaking, a member is from the set {method, property, field, event}. These are examined in detail over the course of the next few chapters. However, do be aware that the CTS defines the various "adornments" that may be associated with a given member.

For example, each member has a given "visibility" trait (e.g., public, private, protected, and so forth). A member may be declared as "abstract" in order to enforce a polymorphic behavior on derived types. Members may be "static" (bound at the class level) or "instance" level (bound at the object level).

CTS Enumeration Types

Enumerations are a handy programming construct that allows you to group name/value pairs under a specific name. For example, assume you are creating a video game application that allows the end user to select one of three player types (Wizard, Fighter, or Thief). Rather than keeping track of raw numerical values to represent each possibility, you could build a custom enumeration:

```
// A C# enumeration.
enum PlayerType
{ Wizard = 100, Fighter = 200, Thief = 300 };
```

The CTS demands that enumerated types derive from a common base class, System.Enum. As you will see, this base class defines a number of interesting members that allow you to extract (and manipulate) the underlying name/value pairs.

CTS Delegate Types

Delegates are the .NET equivalent of a type safe C style function pointer. The key difference is that a .NET delegate is a *class* that derives from MulticastDelegate, rather than a raw memory address. These types are useful when you wish to provide a way for one entity to forward a call to another entity. As you will see in Chapter 5, delegates provide the foundation for the .NET event protocol.

Intrinsic CTS Data Types

The final aspect of the CTS to be aware of is that it establishes a well-defined set of intrinsic data types (i.e., boolean, int, float, char, and so forth). Although a given language may use a unique keyword used to declare an intrinsic data type, all languages ultimately alias the same type defined in the .NET class libraries. Consider Table 1-2.

Table 1-2. The Intrinsic CTS Data Types

.NET BASE CLASS	VISUAL BASIC.NET REPRESENTATION	C# REPRESENTATION	C++ WITH MANAGED EXTENSIONS REPRESENTATION
System.Byte	Byte	byte	char
System.SByte	Not supported	sbyte	signed char
System.Int16	Short	short	short
System.Int32	Integer	int	int or long
System.Int64	Long	long	__int64
System.UInt16	Not supported	ushort	unsigned short
System.UInt32	Not supported	uint	unsigned int or unsigned long
System.UInt64	Not supported	ulong	unsigned __int64
System.Single	Single	float	float
System.Double	Double	double	double
System.Object	Object	object	Object*
System.Char	Char	char	__wchar_t
System.String	String	string	String*
System.Decimal	Decimal	decimal	Decimal
System.Boolean	Boolean	bool	bool

As you can see, not all languages are able to represent the same intrinsic data members of the CTS. As you might imagine, it would be very helpful to create a well-known subset of the CTS that defines a common, shared set of programming constructs (and types) for all .NET-aware languages. Enter the CLS.

Understanding the Common Language Specification

As you are aware, different languages express the same programming constructs in unique, language-specific terms. For example, in C#, string concatenation is denoted using the plus operator (+) while in Visual Basic you make use of the ampersand (&). Even when two distinct languages express the same programmatic construct (for example, a function with no return value) the chances are very good that the syntax will appear quite different on the surface:

```
' VB function returning void (aka VB subroutines).
Public Sub Foo()
    ' stuff. . .
End Sub

// C# function returning void.
public void Foo()
{
    // stuff. . .
}
```

As you have already seen, these minor syntactic variations are inconsequential in the eyes of the .NET runtime, given that the respective compilers (csc.exe or vbc.exe in this case) are configured to emit the same IL instruction set. However languages can also differ with regard to their overall level of functionality. For example some languages allow you to overload operators for a given type while others do not. Some languages may support the use of unsigned data types, which will not map correctly in other languages. What we need is to have a baseline to which all .NET aware languages are expected to conform.

The Common Language Specification (CLS) is a set of guidelines that describe in vivid detail, the minimal and complete set of features a given .NET-aware compiler must support to produce code that can be hosted by the CLR and at the same time be used in a uniform manner between all languages that target the .NET platform. In many ways the CLS can be viewed as a *subset* of the full functionality defined by the CTS.

The CLS is ultimately a set of rules that tool builders must conform to, if they intend their products to function seamlessly within the .NET universe. Each rule is assigned a simple name (e.g., "CLS Rule 6"), and describes how this rule affects those who build the tools as well as those who (in some way) interact with those tools. For example, the crème de la crème of the CLS is the mighty Rule 1:

- **Rule 1**: CLS rules apply only to those parts of a type that are exposed outside the defining assembly.

Given this statement you can (correctly) infer that the remaining rules of the CLS do not apply to the internal logic used to build the inner workings of a .NET type. For example, assume you are building a .NET tool that exposes its services to the outside world using three classes, each of which defines a single function. Given Rule 1 the only aspect of the classes that must conform to the CLS are the member functions themselves (i.e., the member's visibility, naming conventions, parameters, and return types). The internal implementations of each method may use any number of non-CLS techniques, as the outside world won't know the difference.

Of course, in addition to Rule 1, the CLS defines numerous other rules. For example, the CLS describes how a given language must represent text strings, how enumerations should be represented internally (the base type used for storage), how to use static types, and so forth. Again, remember that in most cases these rules do not have to be committed to memory (unless you build the next generation of LISP.NET!). If you require more information, look up "Collected CLS Rules" using online Help.

Working with Namespaces

Now that you have examined the role of the .NET run time, you can turn your attention to the base class libraries. Each of us understands the importance of code libraries. The point of libraries such as MFC or ATL is to give developers a well-defined set of existing code to leverage in their applications. For example, MFC defines a number of C++ classes that provide canned implementations of dialog boxes, menus, and toolbars. This is a good thing for the MFC programmers of the world, as they can spend less time reinventing the wheel, and more time building a custom solution. Visual Basic and Java offer similar notions: intrinsic classes and packages, respectively.

Unlike MFC, Java, or Visual Basic, the C# language does not come with a predefined set of language-specific classes. Ergo, there is no C# class library. Rather, C# developers leverage existing types supplied by the .NET framework. To keep all the types within this binary well organized, the .NET platform makes extensive use of the namespace concept.

The key difference of this approach and a language specific library such as MFC, is that any language targeting the .NET runtime makes use of the *same* namespaces and *same* types as a C# developer. For example, the following three programs all illustrate the ubiquitous "Hello World" application, written in C#, VB.NET, and C++ with managed extensions (MC++):

```
// Hello world in C#
using System;

public class MyApp
{
    public static void Main()
    {
        Console.WriteLine("Hi from C#");
    }
}
```

```
' Hello world in VB.NET
Imports System

Public Module MyApp

    Sub Main()
        Console.WriteLine("Hi from VB")
    End Sub

End Module

// Hello world in Managed C++ (MC++)
using namespace System;

// Note! The .NET runtime secretly wraps the global
// C(++) main function inside a class definition.

void main()
{
    Console::WriteLine("Hi from MC++");
}
```

Notice that each language is making use of the Console class defined in the System namespace. Beyond minor syntactic variations, these three applications look and feel very much alike, both physically and logically. As you can see, the .NET platform has brought a streamlined elegance to the world of software engineering.

A Tour of the .NET Namespaces

Your primary goal as a .NET developer is to get to know the wealth of types defined in the numerous base class namespaces. The most critical namespace to get your hands around is named "System." This namespace provides a core body of types that you will need to leverage time and again as a .NET developer. In fact, you cannot build any sort of working C# application without at least making a reference to the System namespace.

As you recall, namespaces are little more than a way to group semantically related types (classes, enumerations, interfaces, delegates, and structures) under a single umbrella. For example, the System.Drawing namespace contains a number of types to assist you in rendering images onto a graphics device. Other namespaces exist for data access, Web development, threading, and programmatic security. From a very high level, Table 1-3 offers a rundown of some (but certainly not all) of the .NET namespaces.

Table 1-3. A Sampling of .NET Namespaces

.NET NAMESPACE	MEANING IN LIFE
System	Within System you find numerous low-level classes dealing with primitive types, mathematical manipulations, garbage collection, and so forth.
System.Collections	This namespace defines a number of stock container objects (ArrayList, Queue, SortedList).
System.Data database System.Data.Common System.Data.OleDb System.Data.SqlClient	These namespaces are (of course) used for manipulations. You examine each of these later in this book.
System.Diagnostics	Here, you find numerous types that can be used by any .NET-aware language to debug and trace the execution of your source code.
System.Drawing System.Drawing.Drawing2D System.Drawing.Printing	Here, you find numerous types wrapping GDI+ primitives such as bitmaps, fonts, icons, printing support, and advanced rendering classes.
System.IO	This namespace is full of IO manipulation types, including file IO, buffering, and so forth.
System.Net	This namespace (as well as other related namespaces) contains types related to network programming (request/response, sockets, etc.).
System.Reflection System.Reflection.Emit	Defines items that support runtime type discovery and dynamic creation and invocation of custom types.
System.Runtime.InteropServices System.Runtime.Remoting	Provides facilities to interact with "unmanaged code" (e.g., Win32 DLLs, COM servers) and types used for remote access.
System.Security	Security is an integrated aspect of the .NET universe. Here you find numerous classes dealing with permissions, cryptography, and so on.
System.Threading	You guessed it, this namespace deals with threading issues. Here you will find types such as Mutex, Thread, and Timeout.
System.Web	A number of namespaces are specifically geared toward the development of Web applications, including ASP.NET.

continued

Table 1-3. A Sampling of .NET Namespaces (Continued)

.NET NAMESPACE	MEANING IN LIFE
System.Windows.Forms	Despite the name, the .NET platform does contain namespaces that facilitate the construction of more traditional Win32 main windows, dialog boxes, and custom widgets.
System.Xml	Contains numerous classes that represent core XML primitives and types to interact with XML data.

Accessing a Namespace Programmatically

It is worth pointing out that a namespace is nothing more than a convenient way for us mere humans to logically understand and organize related types. For example, consider again the System namespace. From your perspective, you can assume that System.Console represents a class named *Console* that is contained within a namespace called *System*. However, in the eyes of the .NET runtime, this is not so. The runtime engine only sees a single entity named *System.Console*.

In C#, the "using" keyword simplifies the process of accessing types defined in a particular namespace. Here is how it works. Let's say you are interested in building a traditional main window. This window renders a pie chart based on some information obtained from a back end database and displays your company logo using a Bitmap type. While learning the types each namespace contains takes time and experimentation, here are some obvious candidates to reference in your program:

```
// Here are all the namespaces used to build this application.
using System;                    // General base class library types.
using System.Drawing;            // Rendering types.
using System.Windows.Forms;      // GUI widget types.
using System.Data;               // General data centric types.
using System.Data.OleDb;         // OLE DB access types.
```

Once you have referenced some number of namespaces, you are free to create instances of the types they contain. For example, if you are interested in creating an instance of the Bitmap class (defined in the System.Drawing namespace), you can write:

```
// Explicitly list the namespace...
using System.Drawing;

class MyClass
{
    public void DoIt()
    {
        // Create a 20 * 20 pixel bitmap.
        Bitmap bm = new Bitmap(20, 20);
        ...
    }
}
```

Because your application is referencing System.Drawing, the compiler is able to resolve the Bitmap class as a member of this namespace. If you did not directly reference System.Drawing in your application, you would be issued a compiler error. However, you are free to declare variables using a fully quailed name as well:

```
// Not listing namespace!
class MyClass
{
    public void DoIt()
    {
        // Using fully qualified name.
        System.Drawing.Bitmap bm = new System.Drawing.Bitmap(20, 20);
        ...
    }
}
```

I think you get the general idea: Explicitly specifying namespaces reduces keystrokes.

Referencing External Assemblies

In addition to referencing a namespace via the using keyword, you also need to tell the compiler the name of the assembly containing the actual IL. As mentioned, many core .NET namespaces live within mscorlib.dll. System.Drawing is contained in a separate binary named System.Drawing.dll. By default, the system-supplied assemblies are located under <drive>:
\WINNT\Microsoft.NET\Framework\<version>, as seen in Figure 1-4.

Depending on the development tool you are using to build your .NET types, you will have various ways to tell the compiler which assemblies you wish to include during the compilation cycle. You examine how to do so in just a bit.

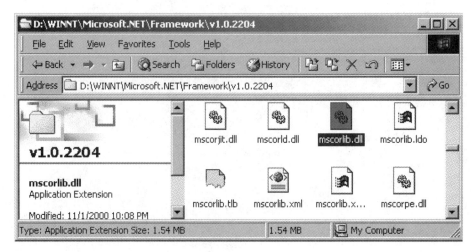

Figure 1-4. The Base Class Libraries

If you are beginning to feel a tad overwhelmed at the thought of gaining mastery over every nuance of the .NET world, just remember that what makes a namespace unique is that the items it defines are all somehow *semantically related*. Therefore, if you have no need for a user interface beyond a simple console application, you can forget all about the System.Windows.Forms and System.Drawing namespaces (among others). If you are building a painting application, the database programming namespaces are most likely of little concern. Like any new set of prefabricated code, you learn as you go.

Increasing Your Namespace Nomenclature

Throughout the course of this book, you are exposed to numerous aspects of the .NET platform and related namespaces. As it would be impractical to detail every type contained in every namespace in a single book, you should be aware of the following techniques that can be used to learn more about the .NET libraries:

- .NET SDK online documentation (MSDN).

- The ILDasm.exe utility.

- The ClassView Web application.

- The WinCV desktop application.

- The Visual Studio.NET Object Browser

I think it's safe to assume you know what to do with the supplied online Help (remember, F1 is your friend). However it is important that you understand how to work with the ILDasm.exe, ClassView and WinCV utilities, each of which is shipped with the .NET SDK. You examine the VS.NET Object Browser a bit later in this chapter.

Using ILDasm.exe

The Intermediate Language Dissasembler utility (ILDasm.exe) allows you to load up any .NET assembly (EXE or DLL) and investigate its contents (including the associated manifest, IL instruction set and type metadata) using a friendly GUI. Once you launch this tool, proceed to the "File | Open" menu command and navigate to the assembly you wish to explore. For the time being, open up mscorlib.dll (Figure 1-5). Note the path of the opened assembly is documented in the caption of the ILDasm.exe utility.

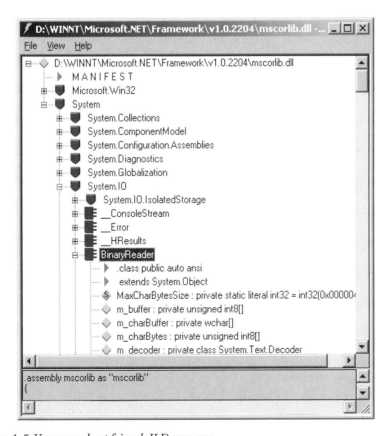

Figure 1-5. Your new best friend, ILDasm.exe

As you can see, the structure of an assembly is presented in a familiar tree view format. While exploring a given type, notice that the methods, properties, nested classes (and so forth) for a given type are identified by a specific icon. Table 1-4 lists some of the more common iconic symbols and text dump abbreviations.

Table 1-4. ILDasm.exe Tree View Icons

ILDASM.EXE SYMBOL	TEXT DUMP ABBREVIATION	MEANING IN LIFE
▶	. (dot)	This icon signifies that additional information is available for a given type. In some cases, double-clicking the item will jump to a related node in the tree.
	[NSP]	Represents a namespace
	[CLS]	Signifies a class type. Be aware that nested classes are marked with the <outer class>$<inner class> notation.
	[VCL]	Represents a structure type.
	[INT]	Represents an interface type.
	[FLD]	Represents a field (e.g., public data) defined by a given type.
	[STF]	Represents a static (e.g., class level) field defined by a given type.
◇	[MET]	Represents a method of a given type.
⑤	[STM]	Represents a static method of a given type.
▲	[PTY]	Signifies a property supported by the type.

Beyond allowing you to explore the types (and members of a specific type) contained in a given assembly, ILDasm.exe also allows you to view the underlying IL instructions for a given item. To illustrate, locate and double-click the default constructor icon for the System.IO.BinaryWriter class. This launches a separate window, displaying the IL shown in Figure 1-6.

```
BinaryWriter::.cctor : void()                              _ □ ×
.method private hidebysig specialname rtspecialname stati
        void .cctor() cil managed
{
  // Code size       11 (0xb)
  .maxstack  8
  IL_0000:  newobj      instance void System.IO.BinaryWrit
  IL_0005:  stsfld      class System.IO.BinaryWriter Syste
  IL_000a:  ret
} // end of method BinaryWriter::.cctor
```

Figure 1-6. Viewing the underlying IL

Dumping Namespace Information to File

The next point of interest with regard to ILDasm.exe is the very useful ability to dump the relational hierarchy of an assembly into a text file. In this way, you can make hard copies of your favorite assemblies to read at your neighborhood coffeehouse (or brew pub). To do so, select "File | Dump TreeView" and provide a name for the resulting *.txt file. As you look over the dump, notice that the identifying icons have been replaced with their corresponding textual abbreviations (see the previous table). For example, ponder Figure 1-7.

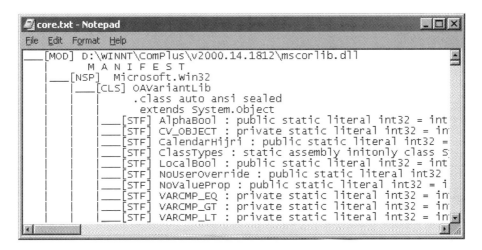

Figure 1-7. Dumping namespace information to file

Dumping IL Instructions to File

On a related note, you are also able to dump the IL instructions for a given assembly to file, using the "File | Dump" menu option. Once you configure your dump options, you are asked to specify a location for the *.il file. Assuming you have dumped the contents of mscorlib.dll to file you can view its contents. For example, Figure 1-8 shows the IL for a method you will come to know (and love) in Chapter 7, GetType().

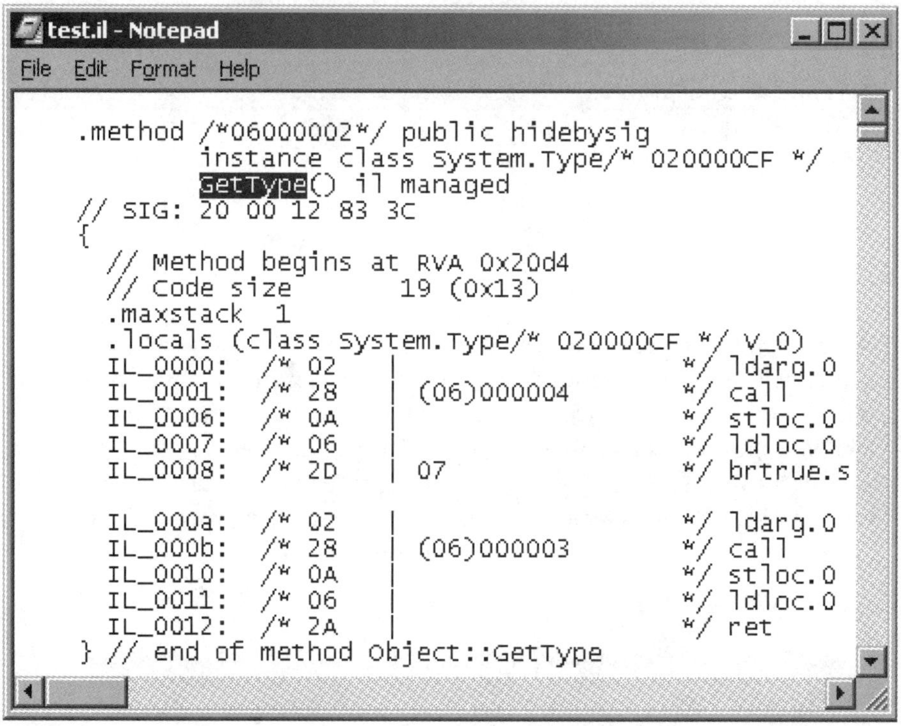


```
.method /*06000002*/ public hidebysig
        instance class System.Type/* 020000CF */
        GetType() il managed
// SIG: 20 00 12 83 3C
{
  // Method begins at RVA 0x20d4
  // Code size       19 (0x13)
  .maxstack  1
  .locals (class System.Type/* 020000CF */ V_0)
  IL_0000:  /* 02   |                  */ ldarg.0
  IL_0001:  /* 28   | (06)000004       */ call
  IL_0006:  /* 0A   |                  */ stloc.0
  IL_0007:  /* 06   |                  */ ldloc.0
  IL_0008:  /* 2D   | 07               */ brtrue.s

  IL_000a:  /* 02   |                  */ ldarg.0
  IL_000b:  /* 28   | (06)000003       */ call
  IL_0010:  /* 0A   |                  */ stloc.0
  IL_0011:  /* 06   |                  */ ldloc.0
  IL_0012:  /* 2A   |                  */ ret
} // end of method Object::GetType
```

Figure 1-8. Dumping IL to file

Viewing Type Metadata

ILDasm.exe has additional options that can be discovered from the supplied online Help. Although I assume you will investigate these options on your own, one item of interest is the "CTRL + M" keystroke. As you recall, .NET-aware compilers emit IL *and* metadata that is used by the CLR to interact with a given type. Once you load an assembly into ILDasm.exe, press CTRL + M to view the generated type metadata. Now, be aware that the larger the assembly, the longer it will take to disassemble the binary! To offer a preview of things to come, Figure 1-9 shows the metadata for the TestApp.exe assembly you create in just a bit.

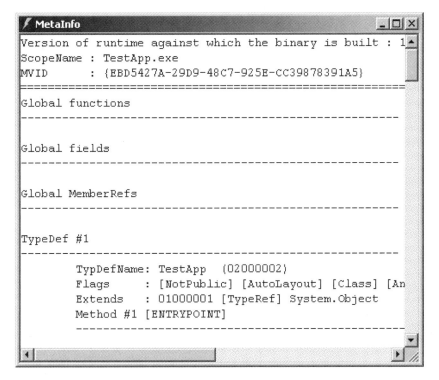

Figure 1-9. Viewing type metadata with ILDasm.exe

If you have not realized it by now, ILDasm.exe is in many ways the .NET equivalent of the OLE/COM Object Viewer utility. Oleview.exe is the tool of choice to learn about classic COM servers and examine the underlying IDL behind a given binary. ILDasm.exe is the tool of choice to examine .NET assemblies, the underlying IL and related metadata.

The ClassViewer Web Application

In addition to ILDasm.exe, the ClassViewer sample application (shipped with the .NET SDK) is yet another way to explore the .NET namespaces. Once you have installed the samples shipped with the SDK, launch Internet Explorer and navigate to http://localhost/ClassViewer/Default.aspx. This enables you to examine the relationship of various types in a more Web-savvy manner (Figure 1-10).

The WinCV Desktop Application

The final tool to be aware of is WinCV.exe (Windows Class Viewer). This application allows you to browse the underlying C# type definition in the base class libraries. The GUI of this tool is quite simple: Type in the name of the item

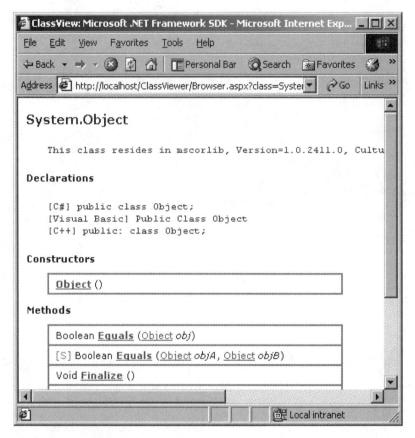

Figure 1-10. Viewing types using the ClassViewer Web Application

you wish to explore, and the underlying source code definitions are displayed on the right-hand side. Figure 1-11 shows the member set for the System.Windows.Forms.ToolTip class.

Now that you have a number of strategies that you can use to explore the entirety of the .NET universe, the time has come to examine how to build some C# applications.

Building C# Applications Using the Command Line Compiler

The first option you have as a C# developer is to compile your assemblies using the standalone compiler, csc.exe (C Sharp Compiler), which is include in the .NET SDK, and is freely downloadable from Microsoft. The goal in this section is to build a simple standalone assembly named TestApp.exe. First, you need some

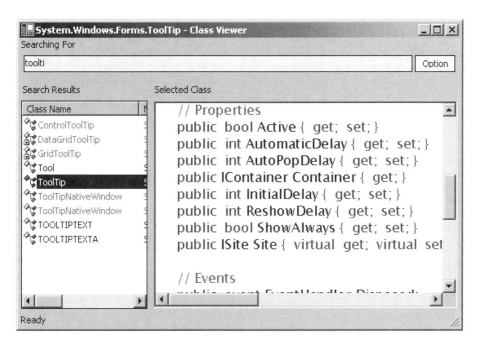

Figure 1-11. Working with WinCV.exe

C# source code. Open a text editor (notepad.exe is fine), enter the code seen in Figure 1-12 and save the file (in a convenient location) as TestApp.cs.

Now, let's get to know the core options of the C# compiler. The first point of interest is to understand how to specify the sort of output file you are interested in building (e.g. Console application, DLL, a Windows EXE application, etc.). Each option is assigned a specific flag that is sent into csc.exe as a command line parameter (Table 1-5).

```
// The first C# app of the book...
using System;

class TestApp
{
    public static void Main()
    {
        System.Console.WriteLine("Testing!  1, 2, 3");
    }
}
```

Figure 1-12. The TestApp class

Table 1-5. Output Options of the C# Compiler

FILE OUTPUT OPTION	MEANING IN LIFE
/doc	Tells the csc.exe compiler to process your source code comments into an XML file. You examine this behavior in Chapter 5.
/out	Used to specify the name of the output file (e.g., MyAssembly.dll, WordProcessingApp.exe, etc.) By default, the name of the output file is the same as the name as the input *.cs file, and thus the /out flag can be omitted.
/target:exe	This option will build an EXE console application (e.g., a DOS application). This is the default file output type, and thus may be omitted.
/target:library	This option will build a DLL assembly, with a related manifest.
/target:module	This option will build a "module" that, as you recall, is a DLL that does not contain a related manifest (used in multifile assemblies).
/target:winexe	Although you are free to build Windows based applications using the /target:exe flag, this option hides the console window that appears as the application is running.

Thus, to compile our TestApp.cs file into as a console application, you would use the following command set (note that the output flags must come *before* the name of the C# file not *after*):

```
csc /target:exe TestApp.cs
```

Be aware that the C# command line flags have an abbreviated version. Such as "/t" rather than "/target":

```
csc /t:exe TestApp.cs
```

Furthermore, given that the /t:exe flag is the default used by the C# compiler, you could also compile the TestApp.cs file simply by saying:

```
csc TestApp.cs
```

To try this out for yourself, open a command window and change to the directory containing your TestApp.cs file. Then, enter the previous command and hit return. This will build TestApp.exe, which can now be run from the command line (see Figure 1-13).

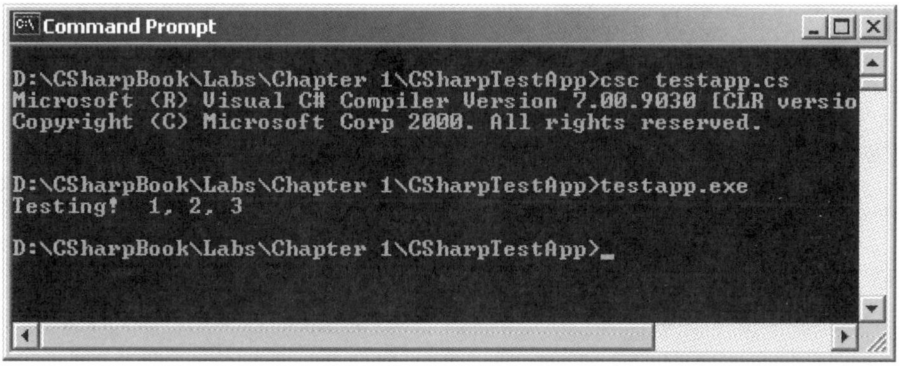

Figure 1-13. The TestApp in action

Referencing External Assemblies

Next, we need to examine how we can build an application that makes use of types defined in a separate .NET assembly. In case you are wondering how the C# compiler understood your reference to the Console class, realize that mscorlib.dll is automatically referenced during the compilation process. To illustrate referencing additional .NET assemblies, let's update your TestApp application to launch a message box. Thus, open up your TestApp.cs file and update it as shown in Figure 1-14.

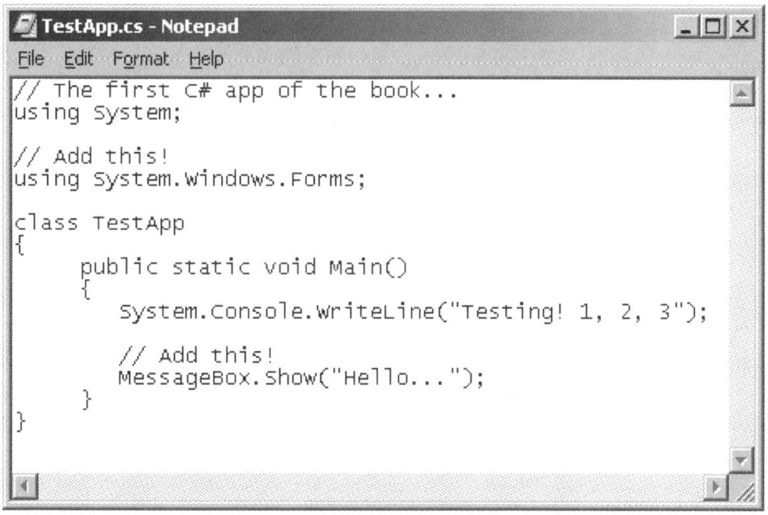

Figure 1-14. The updated TestApp.cs file

Notice we have made a reference to the System.Windows.Forms namespace ala the C# "using" directive. In order for the compiler to resolve the MessageBox class, you must specify the System.Windows.Forms.dll assembly as a compiler option using the /reference flag (which may be abbreviated to simply /r). Be aware that the /reference flag must not have a space between the colon and assembly name:

```
csc /r:System.Windows.Forms.dll testapp.cs
```

If you were to now rerun your application, you should see what appears in Figure 1-15.

Figure 1-15. Your first Windows Forms application

Compiling Multiple Source Files

The current incarnation of the TestApp.exe application was created using a single *.cs source code file (as well as a single external assembly). Of course, most projects will be composed from multiple files. To illustrate, assume you have created the additional class shown in Figure 1-16. And update your previous class to make use of this new type as shown in Figure 1-17.

We can compile this multifile application by explicitly listing each *.cs file:

```
csc /r:System.Windows.Forms.dll testapp.cs hellomsg.cs
```

When you run the program again, the output will be identical. The only difference between the two applications is the fact that its logic was split among multiple files. On a related note, the C# compiler does allow you to make use of the wildcard character (*) to inform csc.exe to add all *.cs files contained in the current directory as part of the current build. When you use this option, you must specify the name of the output file (/out):

```
csc /r:System.Windows.Forms.dll /out:TestApp.exe *.cs
```

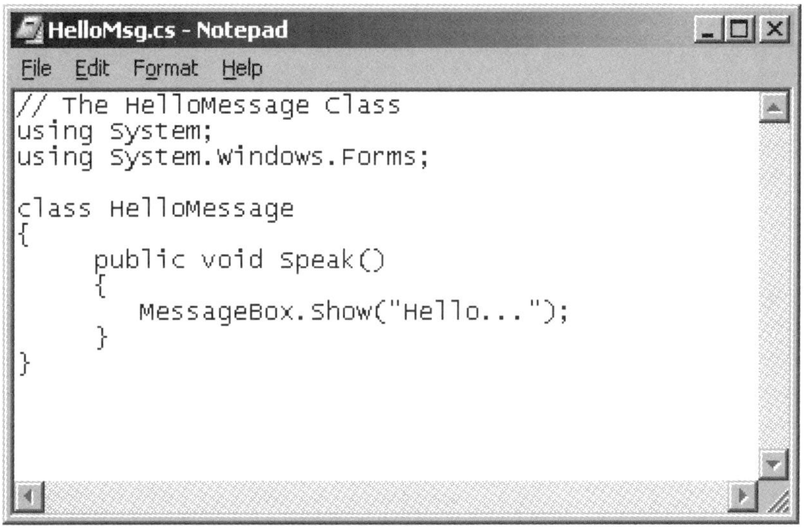

Figure 1-16. The HelloMessage class type

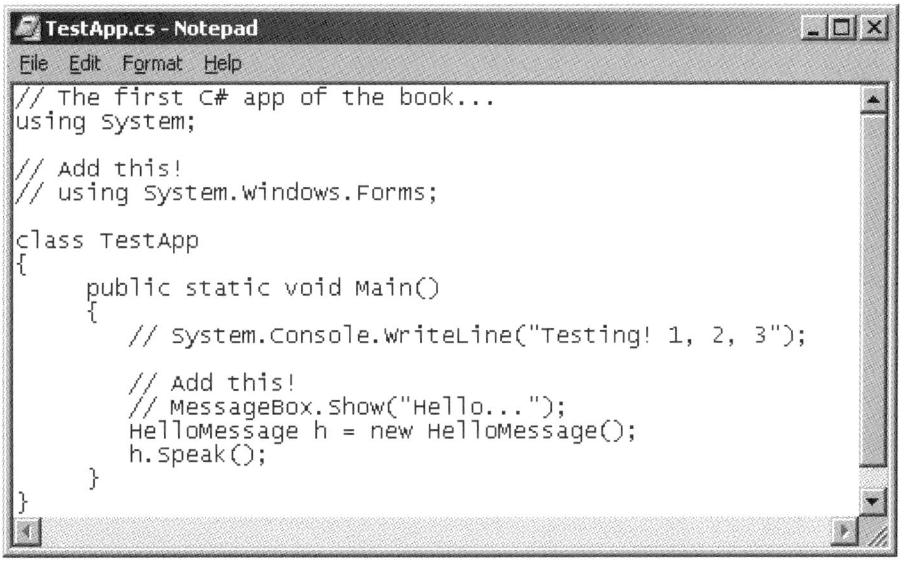

Figure 1-17. The updated TestApp.cs file

Now, what if you need to reference numerous external assemblies? Simply list each assembly using a semicolon delimited list. You have no need to do so for your current example, but here is some sample usage:

```
csc /r:System.Windows.Forms.dll;System.Drawing.dll testapp.cs hellomsg.cs
```

As you would guess, the C# compiler has many other flags that may be used to control how the resulting binaries are generated. You can explore these options on your own using online Help.

SOURCE CODE   *The TestApp application is included under the Chapter 1 subdirectory.*

Building C# Applications Using the Visual Studio.NET IDE

To close this chapter, let's take some time to examine the core features of the Visual Studio.NET IDE (the operative word being *core*). You see other aspects of the development environment as necessary throughout this text. The first thing to be aware of is that Visual Studio.NET now provides a common IDE for *all* Microsoft languages. Therefore, regardless of the type of project you are creating (ATL, MFC, C#, Visual Basic.NET, FoxPro, raw C++, etc.) you use the exact same environment.

Creating a VS.NET Project Solution

To begin, fire up Visual Studio.NET and activate the "File | New | Project" menu selection. As you can see from Figure 1-18, project types are grouped (more or

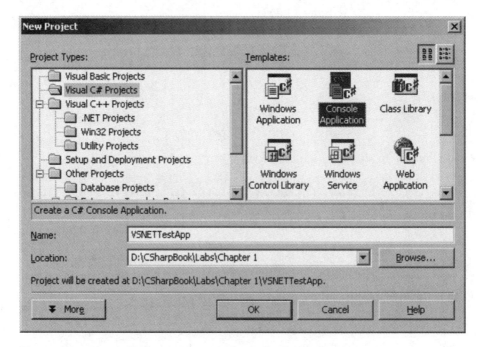

Figure 1-18. Creating a new VS.NET C# Console Application

less) by language. To illustrate, let's build a Visual Studio.NET version of the TestApp program (entitled VSNETTestApp).

The Solution Explorer Window

VS.NET logically arranges a given project using a solution metaphor. Simply put, a "solution" is a collection of one or more "projects". Each project contains any number of source code files, external references, and resources that constitute the application as a whole. Using the Solution Explorer window, you are able to view and open any such item (Figure 1-19). Notice the default name of your initial class is "Class1.cs."

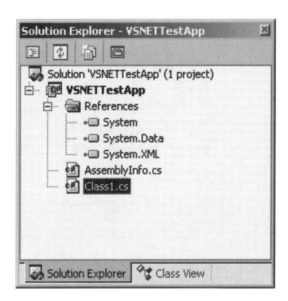

Figure 1-19. The Solution Explorer

Notice as well that the Solution Explorer window provides a Class View tab, which shows the "object-oriented view" of your project (Figure 1-20).

As you would expect, when you right click on a given item, you will activate a context sensitive pop-up menu that allows you to access a number of CASE tools allowing you to add members to your type (methods, properties, indexers, and whatnot). For an example, check out Figure 1-21.

I assume you will explore each possible option. The general approach in this book is to assume you will be writing C# code *by hand* in order to truly understand the language. However, once you have pounded out the first couple of applications, feel free to make use of these integrated tools to lessen your typing burden.

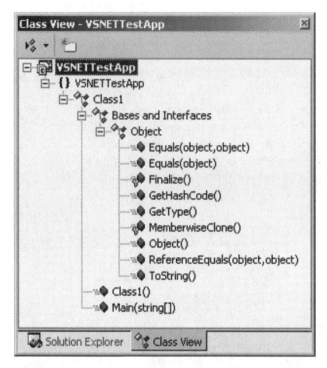

Figure 1-20. Class View

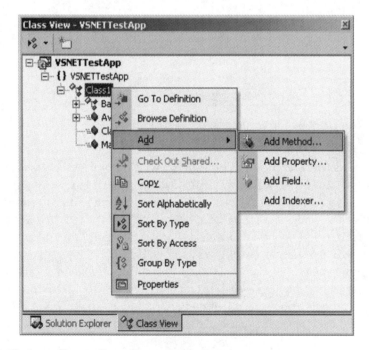

Figure 1-21. A small sampling of integrated wizards

The Properties Window

Another important aspect of the IDE is the Properties Window. This window details a number of characteristics for the currently focused item. Be aware that this item may be an open source code file, GUI widget (as you see later when you examine Windows Forms) or the project itself. For example, to change the name of your initial file, select it from the Solution Explorer and configure the FileName property (Figure 1-22).

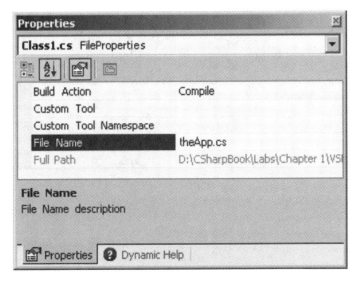

Figure 1-22. File names may be changed using the Properties Window

To change the name of the class itself, select the Class1 node from Class View and update the (Name) property (Figure 1-23). Once you do, you see that the code itself as been updated accordingly.

Outlining Your Code

One extremely helpful aspect of the code view window is the ability to show or hide a class member using the "+" and "-" icons. When you place your mouse cursor over the ellipses icon (which represents a collapsed block of code) a pop-up window gives you a snapshot of the member implementation (Figure 1-24).

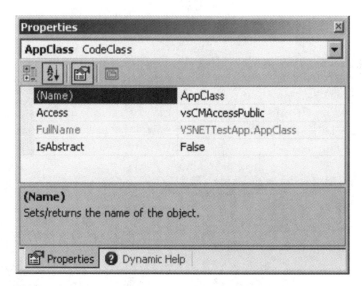

Figure 1-23. Class names may also be changed using the Properties Window.

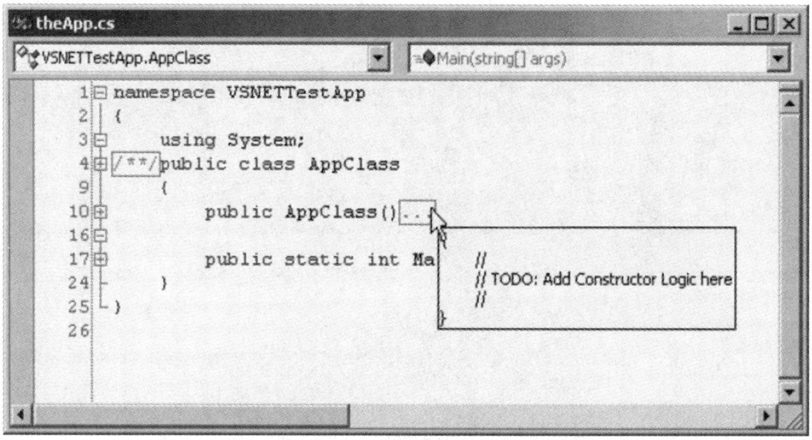

Figure 1-24. Code blocks may be collapsed to conserve screen real estate.

The code in Main() is as you would expect (print out a string and show a message box). As you type, note the improved IntelliSense support (Figure 1-25).

Referencing External Assemblies

When you need to add external references (such as System.Windows.Forms.dll) into your current project, access the "Project | Add Reference. . ." menu selection (or right-click the Assembly node from the Solution Explorer window). Either way you go, you end up with the dialog box shown in Figure 1-26.

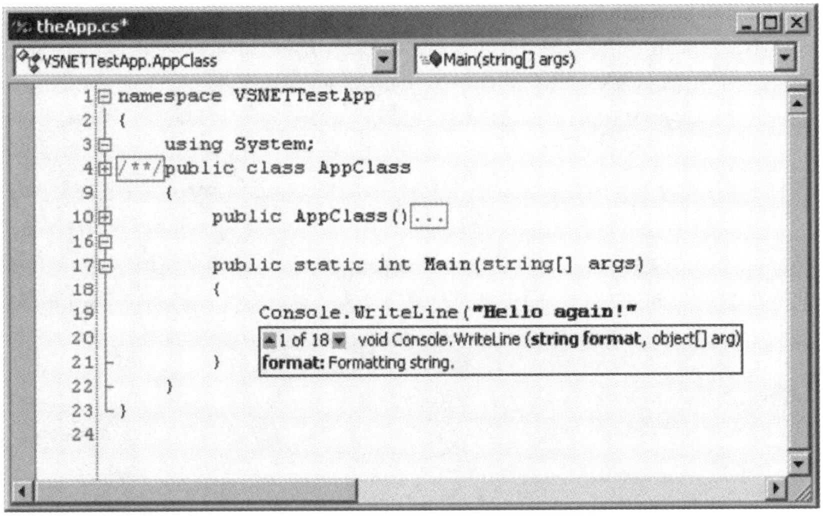

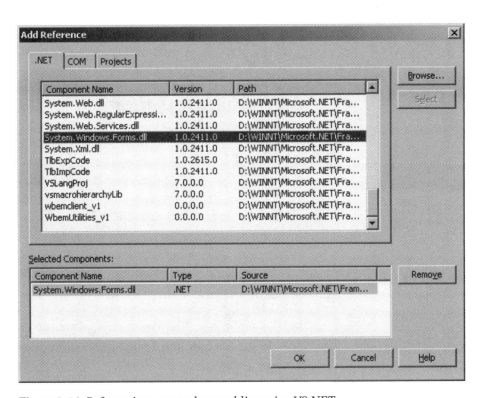

Figure 1-25. The expected IntelliSense

Figure 1-26. Referencing external assemblies using VS.NET

As you can see, this dialog box also allows you to reference classic COM servers (you examine the gory details of .NET/COM interoperability in Chapter 12). Once you have added the System.Windows.Forms.dll assembly you can compile and run your application.

Debugging with the Visual Studio.NET IDE

Like the previous versions of Developers Studio, Visual Studio.NET contains an integrated debugger. To illustrate the basics, begin by clicking in the far left gray column in the code window to insert a breakpoint (Figure 1-27).

```
theApp.cs

VSNETTestApp.AppClass          Main(string[] args)

 1 namespace VSNETTestApp
 2 {
 3     using System;
 4     using System.Windows.Forms;
 5 /**/public class AppClass
11     {
12         public AppClass()...
18
19         public static int Main(string[] args)
20         {
21             Console.WriteLine("Hello again!");
22             MessageBox.Show("Hey...");
23             return 0;
24         }
25     }
26 }
27
```

Figure 1-27. Setting breakpoints

When you initiate the debug session, the flow of execution will halt at each breakpoint. Using the Debug toolbar, you are able to step over, step into and step out of a given line of code. As you would expect, the integrated debugger hosts a number of debug-centric windows (e.g. Call Stack, Autos, Locals, Breakpoints, Modules, Exceptions and so forth). To show or hide a particular window, simply access the "Debug | Windows" menu selection.

SOURCE CODE   *The VSNETTestApp project is included under the Chapter 1 subdirectory.*

Examining the Server Explorer Window

Another extremely useful aspect of Visual Studio.NET is the Server Explorer window (Figure 1-28), which is accessed using the View menu.

This window can be thought of as the command center of a distributed application you may happen to be building. Using the Server Explorer, you are able to attach to and manipulate local and remote database (and view any of the given database objects), plug into a message queue as well as obtain general machine-wide information (running services, and view the event log).

XML-Related Editing Tools

Visual Studio.NET has integrated tools to edit XML-related data (as well as HTML files). Much of this functionality was taken from the legacy Visual InterDev IDE. Once your insert a new XML file into your application, you are then able to edit XML related files using a number of GUI design-time tools (and related toolbars). For example, Figure 1-29 shows an XML file you will generate during our discussion of ADO.NET.

Figure 1-28. The Server Explorer Window

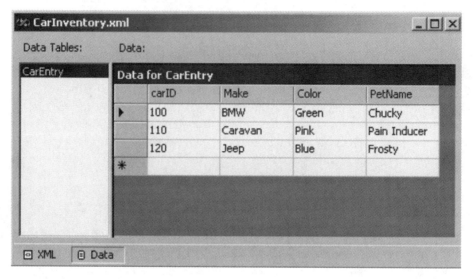

Figure 1-29. The integrated XML editor

Support for UML Diagrams

Next, Visual Studio.NET has integrated (and improved) the Visual Modeler utility that shipped previously with Visual Studio 6.0. Using this tool, you are able to diagram UML (Unified Modeling Language) relationships between the types in your application. Once you insert a new *.mdx file into your application using the "File | Miscellaneous Files | File. . ." menu selection, you will see that your Toolbox window now provides a number of UML related icons (Figure 1-30).

The Object Browser Utility

In addition to the standalone tools you examined earlier in this chapter, the Visual Studio.NET IDE also supplies an object-browsing utility. If you access the "View | Other Windows | Object Browser" menu option, Figure 1-31 shows what you will find.

Database Manipulation Tools

Integrated Database support is also part of the VS.NET IDE. As mentioned earlier in this section, once you add a data connection to your application using the Server Explorer window, you are able to open and examine any database object in place. For example, Figure 1-32 shows a view of the Cars database you will build during our discussion of ADO.NET.

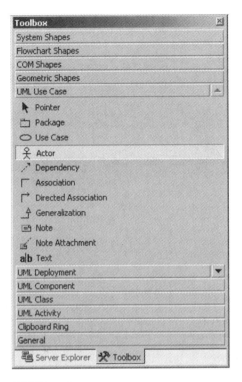

Figure 1-30. Integrated UML tools

Integrated Help

The final aspect of the IDE you should be familiar with is the fully integrated Help system. Rather than having to "ATL + TAB" between MSDN and the development environment, this version provides the Dynamic Help window, which changes its contents (dynamically!) based on what item (window, menu, source code keyword, etc.) as focus. For example, if you place the cursor on top of the Main() method, the Dynamic Help window displays what's shown in Figure 1-33.

As you would expect, if you select on one of the suggested links, you will be shown relevant information Figure 1-34.

As you can see, you have many new toys at your disposal. Now that you have a solid background on the philosophy of .NET and have seen two approaches to compile your projects, you can begin your formal investigation of the C# language and the .NET platform.

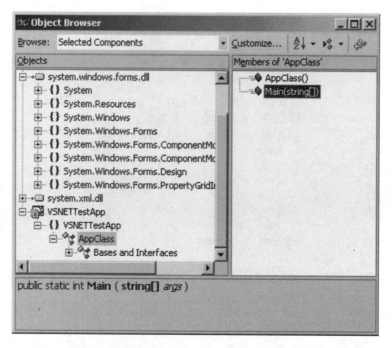

Figure 1-31. The integrated Object Browser

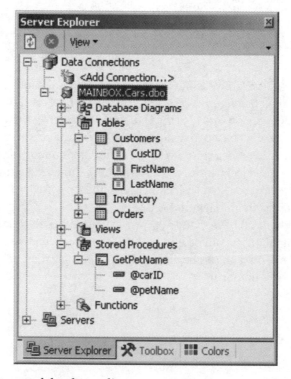

Figure 1-32. Integrated database editors

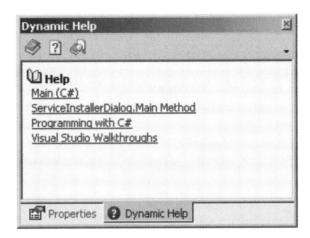

Figure 1-33. Integrated Help

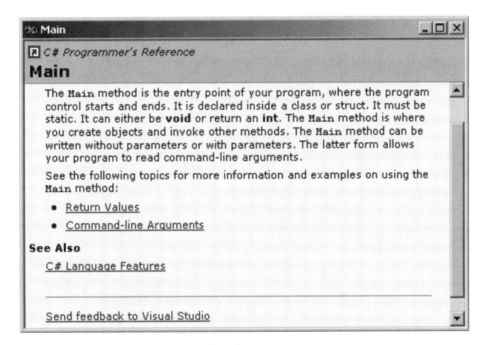

Figure 1-34. Remember, F1 is your friend.

Summary

The point of this chapter was to lay out the conceptual framework necessary for the remainder of this book. It began by examining a number of limitations and complexities found within the technologies of today, and followed up with an overview of how .NET and C# attempt to simplify the current state of affairs.

.NET basically boils down to a runtime execution engine (mscoree.dll) and base class library (mscorlib.dll and friends). The Common Language Runtime (CLR) is able to host any .NET binary (aka "assembly") that abides by the rules of managed code. As you have seen, assemblies contain IL instructions (and accompanying metadata) that are compiled to platform-specific instructions using a Just In Time (JIT) compiler. In addition, you explored the role of the Common Language Specification (CLS) and Common Type System (CTS). Finally, you learned how to build a simple application using the standalone C# compiler (csc.exe), as well as the Visual Studio.NET IDE.

CHAPTER 2

C# Language Fundamentals

THE THRUST OF THIS CHAPTER IS to introduce you to the core aspects of the C# language, including intrinsic data types (both value-based and reference-based); decision and iteration constructs; boxing and unboxing mechanisms; and basic class construction techniques. Along the way, you also learn how to manipulate strings, arrays, enumerations, and structures.

To illustrate these language fundamentals, you will take a programmatic look at the .NET base class libraries, and build a number of sample applications making use of various namespaces. Once you understand how to leverage prefabricated namespaces, the chapter closes by showing you how to organize your custom types into discrete user-defined namespaces (and explains why you might want to do so).

The Anatomy of a Basic C# Class

Like the Java language, C# demands that all program logic is contained within a type definition (recall that a "type" is a generic name referring to a class, interface, structure, and so forth). Unlike C(++), it is not possible to create global functions or global points of data using the C# language. In its simplest form, a C# class can be defined as follows (also recall that the using keyword simplifies type declarations):

```
// C# class files end with a *.cs file extension.
using System;

class HelloClass
{
    // Oddly enough, Main() can be declared as 'private'
    // if need be...
    public static int Main(string[] args)
```

```
    {
            Console.WriteLine("Hello World!");
            return 0;
    }
}
```

Here, you have created a definition for an appropriately named type (HelloClass) that supports a single method named Main(). Every C# application must contain a class defining a Main() method, which is used to signify the entry point of the application. Although it is technically possible for a single C# project to contain multiple classes defining a Main() method, you must specify (to the C# compiler) which Main() method should be used as the application's entry point, or you encounter a compile-time error.

As you can see, the signature of Main() is adorned with the public and static keywords (also note the capital "M" in Main(), which is obligatory). Later in this chapter you are supplied with a formal definition of the "public" and "static" keywords. Until then, understand that public methods are accessible by the outside world, while static methods are scoped at the class level (not at an object level) and can thus be invoked without the need to first create a new object instance.

In addition to the public and static keywords, our Main() method has a single parameter, which happens to be an array of strings (string[] args). Although you are not currently bothering to manipulate this array, it is possible that this parameter can contain any number of command line arguments (you see how to access them momentarily).

The program logic of the HelloClass is within Main() itself. Here, you make use of the Console class, which is defined within the System namespace. Among its set of members is the static WriteLine(), which as you might assume, pumps a text string to the standard console:

```
// Pump some text to the console.
Console.WriteLine("Hello World!");
```

Because our Main() method has been defined as returning an integer data type, you return zero (success) before exiting. Finally, as you can see from the HelloClass definition, C and C++ styles comments have carried over into the C# language.

Variations on the Main() Method

The previous iteration of Main() was defined to take a single parameter (an array of strings) and return an integer data type. This is not the only possible form of

Main() however. It is permissible to construct your program's Main() method using any of the following signatures (assuming each is contained within a class definition):

```
// No return type, array of strings as argument.
public static void Main(string[] args)
{
    // Process command line arguments.
    // Make some objects.
}

// No return type, no arguments.
public static void Main()
{
    // Make some objects.
}

// Integer return type, no arguments.
public static int Main()
{
    // Make some objects.
    // Return a value to the system.
}
```

Obviously, your choice of how to construct Main() will be based on two questions: First, do you need to process any command line parameters? If so, they will be stored in the array of strings. Next, do you want to return a value to the system when Main() has completed? If so, you need to return an integer data type rather than void.

Processing Command Line Parameters

Assume that you now wish to update the HelloClass to process any possible command line parameters (I examine the details behind the {0}syntax in just a bit):

```
// This time, check if we have been sent any command line arguments.
using System;

class HelloClass
```

```
{
    public static int Main(string[] args)
    {
        // Print the args!
        for(int x = 0; x < args.Length; x++)
        {
            Console.WriteLine("Arg: {0}", args[x]);
        }

        Console.WriteLine("Hello World!");
        return 0;
    }
}
```

Here you are checking to see if the array of strings contains some number of items using the Length property of System.Array (as you see later in this chapter, all C# arrays actually alias the System.Array type). If you have at least one member in the array, you loop over each item and print the contents to the output window.

Supplying the arguments themselves is equally as simple, as illustrated in Figure 2-1.

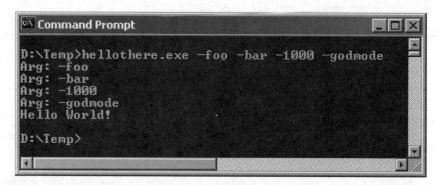

Figure 2-1. Supplying and processing command line arguments

As an alternative, you may iterate over incoming string arrays using the C# for each construct. This bit of syntax is fully explained later in this chapter. Here is some example usage:

```
// Notice we have no need to check the size of the array when using 'foreach'.
public static int Main(string[] args)
```

```
{
    foreach(string s in args)
        Console.WriteLine("Arg: {0}", s);
    . . .
}
```

Needless to say, *you* are the one in charge of determining which command line parameters your application will respond to, and what to do with them once the end user has supplied them.

Creating Objects: Constructor Basics

All object-oriented languages make a clear distinction between *classes* and *objects*. A *class* is a definition of a user-defined type (UDT) that is often regarded as a blueprint for variables of this type. An *object* is simply a term describing a given instance of a particular class. In C#, the *new* keyword is the only way to create an object instance. To illustrate, observe the following updated Main() method:

```
// Make some HelloClass objects when the static Main() method is called.
Using System;
class HelloClass
{
    public static int Main(string[] args)
    {
        // You can declare and create a new object in a single line
        HelloClass c1 = new HelloClass();

        // . . .or break declaration and creation into two lines.
        HelloClass c2;
        c2 = new HelloClass();

        return 0;
    }
}
```

The new keyword is in charge of allocating the correct number of bytes for the specified object and acquiring sufficient memory from the managed heap. Here, you have allocated two objects (c1 and c2) each of which points to an instance of the HelloClass type. Understand that C# class variables are actually a *reference* to the object in memory, not the actual object itself. Thus, in this light, c1 and c2 each reference a distinct HelloClass object allocated on the managed heap (Chapter 3 offers additional details).

As you may be aware, the previous code is making calls to the *default constructor* of the class. Every C# class is automatically endowed with a default constructor, which you are free to redefine if need be. Like C++, default constructors never take arguments. Beyond creating a new object instance, the default constructor ensures that all state data (for example, member variables of the class) is set to an appropriate default value (this is true for all constructors). Contrast this to C++, where uninitialized state data points to garbage (sometimes the little things mean a lot).

Typically, your custom classes provide additional constructors beyond the default. In doing so, you provide the object user with a simple way to initialize the state of an object at the time of creation. Here is the HelloClass type once again, with a custom constructor, a redefined default constructor, and some simple state data:

```csharp
// HelloClass, with constructors.
using System;

class HelloClass
{
    // The default constructor always assigns state data to default values.
    public HelloClass()
    {
        Console.WriteLine("Default ctor called!");
    }

    // This custom constructor assigns state data to a known value.
    public HelloClass (int x, int y)
    {
        Console.WriteLine("Custom ctor called!");
        intX = x;
        intY = y;
    }

    // Some public state data.
    public int intX, intY;

    // Program entry point.
    public static int Main(string[] args)
```

```
    {
        // Trigger default constructor.
        HelloClass c1 = new HelloClass();
        Console.WriteLine("c1.intX = {0}\nc1.intY = {1}\n", c1.intX, c1.intY);

        // Trigger parameterized constructor.
        HelloClass c2;
        c2 = new HelloClass(100, 200);
        Console.WriteLine("c2.intX = {0}\nc2.intY = {1}\n", c2.intX, c2.intY);

        return 0;
    }
}
```

On examining the program's output you can see that the default constructor has indeed assigned the internal state data to the default values (zero), while the custom constructor has assigned the member data to values specified by the object user (see Figure 2-2).

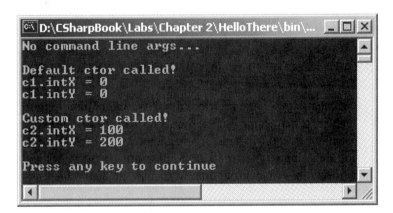

Figure 2-2. Simple constructor logic

Is That a Memory Leak?

Notice that the Main() method has no logic that explicitly destroys the c1 and c2 object instances:

```
// Leaky method?
public static int Main(string[] args)
{
    HelloClass c1 = new HelloClass();
```

```
Console.WriteLine("c1.intX = {0}\nc1.intY = {1}\n", c1.intX, c1.intY);
HelloClass c2;
c2 = new HelloClass(100, 200);
Console.WriteLine("c2.intX = {0}\nc2.intY = {1}\n", c2.intX, c2.intY);

// Hey! Did someone forget to delete these objects?
return 0;
    }
}
```

This is not a horrible omission, but the way of .NET. Like Visual Basic and Java developers, C# programmers never explicitly destroy an object instance. The .NET garbage collector frees the allocated memory automatically, and therefore C# does not support a "delete" keyword. Chapter 3 examines the garbage collection process in detail. Until then, just remember that the .NET runtime environment destroys the objects you allocate automatically.

The Composition of a C# Application

Currently, our HelloClass type has been constructed to perform two duties. First, the class defines the entry point of the application. Second, HelloClass maintains two custom data members and a few overloaded constructors. While this is all well and good, it may seem a bit strange (although perfectly legal) that the static Main() method creates an instance of the very class in which it was defined:

```
class HelloClass
{
    public HelloClass(){ Console.WriteLine("Default ctor called!"); }

    public HelloClass (int x, int y)
    {
        Console.WriteLine("Custom ctor called!");
        intX = x; intY = y;
    }

    public int intX, intY;

    public static int Main(string[] args)
    {
        // Make some HelloClass objects. . .
        HelloClass c1 = new HelloClass();
        . . .
    }
}
```

Many of my initial examples take this approach, just to keep focused on the task at hand. However, a more natural design would be to factor the HelloClass type into two distinct classes: HelloClass and HelloApp. In OO parlance, this is termed the "separation of concerns." Thus, you could reengineer the application as the following (notice you have added a new member to the HelloClass type):

```
class HelloClass
{
    public HelloClass(){ Console.WriteLine("Default ctor called!"); }
    public HelloClass (int x, int y)
    {
        Console.WriteLine("Custom ctor called!");
        intX = x; intY = y;
    }
    public int intX, intY;

    // Member function.
    public void SayHi() {Console.WriteLine("Hi there!");}
}

class HelloApp
{
    public static int Main(string[] args)
    {
        // Make some HelloClass objects and say howdy.
        HelloClass c1 = new HelloClass();
        c1.SayHi();
        . . .
    }
}
```

When you build your C# applications, it becomes quite common to have one type functioning as the application object (the type that defines the Main() entry point) and numerous other types that constitute the application at large. Furthermore, each type you create is typically placed into a separate *.cs file (to keep your code as portable as possible). Again, you make use of each approach during the remainder of this text.

SOURCE CODE   *The HelloThere project is located under the Chapter 2 sub-directory.*

Member Initialization

Because a given class may have numerous custom constructors, you may find yourself in the annoying position of having to write the same initialization code in each and every constructor implementation. This is particularly necessary if you do not wish to accept the default values assigned to your state data. To avoid this redundancy, C# allows you to assign a type's member data to an initial value at the time of declaration:

```
// This technique is useful when you don't want to accept default values
// and would rather not write the same initialization code in each constructor.
class Test
{
    private int myInt = 90;
    private string myStr = "My initial value.";
    private HotRod viper = new HotRod(200, "Chucky", Color.Red);

    . . .
}
```

As you may be aware, other object-oriented languages (such as C++) do not allow you to initialize a member in this way. In this case, OO programmers may choose to create a private helper function that can be called by each class constructor. Yet another option is to forward calls from one constructor to another "master" constructor (you see this technique later in Chapter 3 during our discussion of the "this" keyword). While each of these constructs are still valid in a C# application, explicit member initialization provides another handy alternative.

Basic Input and Output with the Console Class

The previous HelloClass type made use of the System.Console class. Console is one of many types defined in the System namespace. As its name implies, this class encapsulates input, output, and error stream manipulations. Thus, you are correct to assume that this type is mostly useful when creating console-based applications rather than GUI-based applications (as we begin doing in Chapter 8).

Principal among the methods of System.Console are ReadLine() and WriteLine(), both of which are defined as static. As you have seen, WriteLine() pumps a text string (including a carriage return) to the output stream. The Write() method pumps text to the output stream, without a carriage return. ReadLine() allows you to receive information from the input stream up until the carriage return, while Read() is used to capture a single character from the input stream.

To illustrate basic IO using the Console class, consider the following program, which prompts the user for some bits of information and echoes each item to the standard output stream. The output can be seen in Figure 2-3.

```
// Make use of the Console class to perform basic IO.
using System;
class BasicIO
{
    public static void Main(string[] args)
    {
        // Echo some stats.
        Console.Write("Enter your name: ");

        string s;
        s = Console.ReadLine();
        Console.WriteLine("Hello, {0}", s);
        Console.Write("Enter your age: ");

        s = Console.ReadLine();
        Console.WriteLine("You are {0} years old\n", s);
    }
}
```

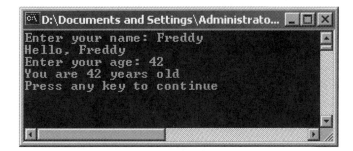

Figure 2-3. Basic IO using System.Console

Introducing C# String Formatting

During these first few examples, you have seen numerous occurrences of the tokens {0}, {1}, and the like. .NET introduces a new style of string formatting, slightly reminiscent of the C printf() function, without the cryptic "%d" "%s', " "%c" flags. A simple example follows (see the output in Figure 2-4).

```
using System;
class BasicIO
{
    public static void Main(string[] args)
    {
        . . .
        int theInt = 90;
        float theFloat = 9.99;
        BasicIO myIO = new BasicIO();

        // Format a string. . .
        Console.WriteLine("Int is: {0}\nFloat is: {1}\nYou Are: {2}",
                    theInt, theFloat, myIO.ToString());
    }
}
```

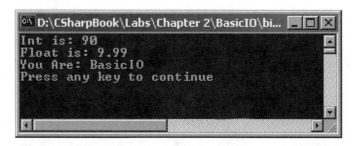

Figure 2-4. Simple format strings

The first parameter to WriteLine() represents a format string that contains optional placeholders designated by {0}, {1}, {2}, and so forth. The remaining parameters to WriteLine() are simply the values to be inserted into the respective placeholder (in this case, an integer, a float, and a string). Also be aware that WriteLine() has been overloaded to allow you to specify placeholder values as an array of objects. Thus, you can represent in any number of items to be plugged into the format string as follows:

```
// Fill placeholders using an array of objects.
object[] stuff = { "Hello", 20.9, 1, "There", "83", 99.99933 };
Console.WriteLine("The Stuff: {0}, {1}, {2}, {3}, {4}, {5}", stuff);
```

Each placeholder can optionally contain various format characters (in either uppercase or lowercase), as seen in Table 2-1.

Table 2-1. C# Format Characters

C# FORMAT CHARACTER	MEANING IN LIFE
C or c	Used to format currency. By default, the flag will prefix a dollar sign ($) to the value, however this can be changed using a NumberFormatInfo object.
D or d	Formats decimal numbers. This flag may also specify the minimum number of digits used to pad the value.
E or e	Exponential notation.
F or f	Fixed point formatting.
G or g	General. Used to format a number to fixed or exponential format.
N or n	Basic numerical formatting (with commas).
X or x	Hexadecimal formatting. If you use an uppercase X, your hex format will also contain uppercase characters.

These format characters are placed within a given placeholder using a single colon (for example, {0:C}, {1:d}, {2:X}, and so on). To illustrate, assume you have updated Main() with the following logic:

```
// Now make use of some format tags.
public static void Main(string[] args)
{
. . .
    Console.WriteLine("C format: {0:C}", 99989.987);
    Console.WriteLine("D9 format: {0:D9}", 99999);
    Console.WriteLine("E format: {0:E}", 99999.76543);
    Console.WriteLine("F format: {0:F3}", 99999.9999);
    Console.WriteLine("N format: {0:N}", 99999);
    Console.WriteLine("X format: {0:X}", 99999);
    Console.WriteLine("x format: {0:x}", 99999);
}
```

Figure 2-5 shows a test run.

Be aware that the use of the C# formatting characters are not limited to the System.Console.WriteLine() method. For example, these same flags can be used within the context of the static String.Format() method. This can be helpful when you need to build a string containing numerical values in memory and display it at a later time:

Figure 2-5. More complex format strings

```
// Use the static String.Format() method to build a new string.
string formStr;
formStr = String.Format("Don't you wish you had {0:C} in your account?",
                        99989.987);
Console.WriteLine(formStr);
```

SOURCE CODE   *The BasicIO project is located under the Chapter 2 subdirectory.*

Understanding Value Types and Reference Types

Like any programming language, C# defines a number of intrinsic data types. As you would expect, there are types to represent whole numbers, strings, floating-point numbers, and Boolean values. If you are coming from a C++ background, you will be happy to know that these intrinsic types are fixed constants in the universe. Meaning, when you create a data point of type integer (int), all .NET-aware languages understand the fixed nature of this type, and all agree on the range it is capable of handling.

Specifically speaking, a C# data type may be *value based* or *reference based*. Value-based types, which include all numerical data types (int, float, etc.) as well as enumerations and structures, are allocated *on the stack*. When you assign one value type to another, a bitwise copy is achieved. To illustrate, assume you have the following C# structure (you examine structures in greater detail later in this chapter):

```
// Structures are value types.
struct FOO
{
    public int x, y;
}
```

Now, observe the following Main() logic (the output can be seen in Figure 2-6).

```
class ValRefClass
{
    // Exercise some value types.
    public static int Main(string[] args)
    {
        // The 'new' keyword is optional when creating structures
        // using the default constructor.
        FOO f1 = new FOO();
        f1.x = 100;
        f1.y = 100;

        // Assign a new FOO type (f2) to an existing FOO type (f1).
        FOO f2 = f1;

        // Here is f1. . .
        Console.WriteLine("F1.x = {0}", f1.x);
        Console.WriteLine("F1.y = {0}", f1.y);

        // Here is f2. . .
        Console.WriteLine("F2.x = {0}", f2.x);
        Console.WriteLine("F2.y = {0}", f2.y);

        // Change f2.x. This will NOT change f1.x.
        Console.WriteLine("Changing f2.x");
        f2.x = 900;

        // Print again.
        Console.WriteLine("F2.x = {0}", f2.x);
        Console.WriteLine("F1.x = {0}", f1.x);
        return 0;
    }
}
```

Here you have created a variable of type FOO (named f1) that is then assigned to another FOO type (f2). Because FOO is a value type, you have two copies of the FOO type on the stack that can be independently manipulated. Therefore, when you change the value of f2.x, the value of f1.x is unaffected.

In stark contrast, reference types (that includes classes and interfaces) are allocated on the garbage-collected heap. Copies of a reference type result in a

D:\CSharpBook\Labs\Chapt...
F1.x = 100
F1.y = 100
F2.x = 100
F2.y = 100
Changing f2.x
F2.x = 900
F1.x = 100
Press any key to continue

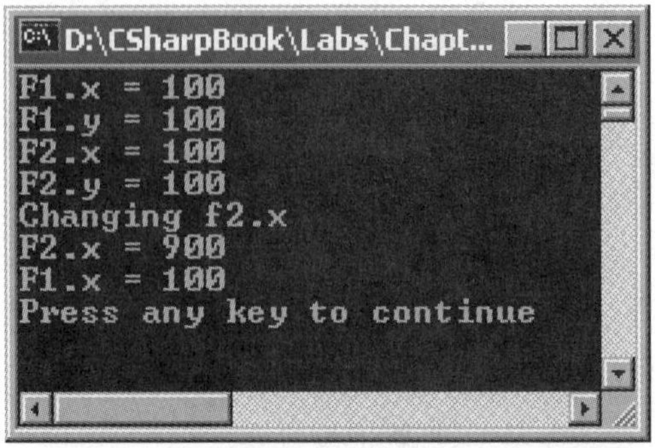

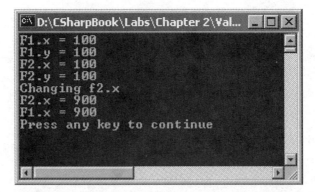

Figure 2-6. Assigning one value type to another results in a bitwise copy.

shallow copy, meaning multiple references are pointing to the same location in memory. To illustrate, let's change the definition of the FOO type from a C# structure to a C# class:

```
// Classes are always reference types.
class FOO
{
    public int x, y;
}
```

If you were to run our test program once again, notice the change in behavior (Figure 2-7). Here, you have two objects referencing the same memory location of the managed heap. Therefore, when you change the value of *x* using the f2 reference, f1.x reflects the same value.

D:\CSharpBook\Labs\Chapter 2\Val...
F1.x = 100
F1.y = 100
F2.x = 100
F2.y = 100
Changing f2.x
F2.x = 900
F1.x = 900
Press any key to continue

Figure 2-7. Assigning reference types to another results in a shallow copy.

Value and Reference Types: Further Details

To further understand the distinction between value types and reference types, ponder Table 2-2 that illustrates how each stands up against a number of "intriguing questions" (many of which are examined in greater detail throughout this text):

Table 2-2. Value Types and Reference Types Side by Side

INTRIGUING QUESTION	VALUE TYPE	REFERENCE TYPE
Where is this type allocated?	Allocated on the stack	Allocated on the managed heap
How is a variable represented?	Value types variables are local copies	Reference type variables are pointing to the memory occupied by the allocated instance
What is the base type?	Must directly derive from System.ValueType	Can derive from any other type (except System.ValueType) as long as that type is not "sealed". . . more later
Can this type function as a base to other types?	No. Value types are always sealed and cannot be extended	Yes. If the type is not sealed, it may function as a base to other types
What is the parameter passing behavior?	Variables are passed by value (i.e., a copy of the variable is passed into the called function)	Variables are passed by reference (e.g., the address of the variable is passed into the called function)
Able to override Object.Finalize()?	No. Value types are never placed onto the heap and therefore do not need to be finalized	Yes . . . indirectly (more details in Chapter 3)
Can I define constructors for this type?	Yes, but the default constructor is reserved (i.e., your custom constructors must all have arguments).	But of course!
When do variables of this type die?	When it falls out of the defining scope	When the managed heap is garbage collected

Despite their differences, value types and reference types both have the ability to implement standard (i.e., preexisting) and custom (i.e., you made them) interfaces, and may support any number of fields, methods, properties, and events. Just to solidify some of the key differences between value and reference types one more time, consider the following code:

```
// A value type.
struct PERSON
{
    public string Name;
    public int Age;
};
// A reference type.
class Person
{
    public string Name;
    public int Age;
};
class ValRefClass
{
    public static void Main()
    {
        // Create an object reference on the managed heap.
        Person fred = new Person();

        // Create a value on the stack.
        PERSON mary = new PERSON();

        // This performs a bit copy, resulting in two structures on the stack.
        PERSON jane = mary;

        // This performs a shallow copy, resulting in two references to the
        // same object in memory.
        Person fredRef = fred;
    }
}
```

SOURCE CODE   *The ValAndRef project is located under the Chapter 2 subdirectory.*

The Master Node: System.Object

In C#, every data type (value or reference based) is ultimately derived from a common base class: System.Object. The Object class defines a common polymorphic behavior for every type in the .NET universe (if you like, consider Object to be the VARIANT of .NET). In the previous HelloClass type definition, you did not explicitly indicate that Object was the base class, but this is assumed. If you wish to explicitly state System.Object as your base class, you are free to define your class definitions as such:

```
// Here we are explicitly deriving from System.Object.
// We could also write 'class HelloClass : object'
class HelloClass : System.Object
{...}
```

Like any C# class, System.Object defines a set of instance members. Note that some of these items are declared "virtual," and can therefore be overridden by a subclass:

```
// The top-most class in the .NET world: System.Object
namespace System
{
    public class Object
    {
        public Object();
        public virtual Boolean Equals(Object obj);
        public virtual Int32 GetHashCode();
        public Type GetType();
        public virtual String ToString();
        protected virtual void Finalize();
        protected Object MemberwiseClone();
    }
...
}
```

Table 2-3 offers a rundown of the functionality provided by each method.

Table 2-3. Core Members of System.Object

INSTANCE METHOD OF OBJECT CLASS	MEANING IN LIFE
Equals()	By default this method returns true only if the items being compared refer to the exact same item in memory. Thus, Equals() is used to compare object references, not the state of the object.
	Typically, this method is overridden to return "true" only if the objects being compared have the same internal state values (that is, value-based semantics).
	Be aware that if you override Equals(), you should also override GetHashCode().
GetHashCode()	Returns an integer that identifies a specific object instance.
GetType()	This method returns a Type object that fully describes the object you are currently referencing. In short, this is a Runtime Type Identification (RTTI) method available to all objects (discussed in greater detail in Chapter 7).
ToString()	Returns a string representation of this object, using the "<namespace>.<class name>" format (termed the "fully qualified name"). If the type has not been defined within a namespace, <class name> alone is returned.
	This method can be overridden by a subclass to return a tokenized string of name/value pairs that represent the object's internal state, rather than its fully qualified name.
Finalize()	For the time being, you can understand this method (when overridden) is called to free any allocated resources before the object is destroyed. We talk more about the CLR garbage collection services in Chapter 3.
MemberwiseClone()	This method exists to perform a shallow copy of the current object (for example, to create another reference that points to the same object in memory).
	This method cannot be overridden. If you need to add support for deep copy semantics (for example, to create a brand new identical object) your class needs to implement the ICloneable interface, which we do in Chapter 4.

To illustrate some of the default behavior provided by the Object base class, consider the following class definition:

```csharp
// Create some objects and exercise the inherited System.Object methods.
using System;
class ObjTest
{
    public static int Main(string[] args)
    {
        // Make an instance of ObjTest.
        ObjTest c1 = new ObjTest();

        // Pump info to console.
        Console.WriteLine("ToString: {0}", c1.ToString());
        Console.WriteLine("Hash code: {0}", c1.GetHashCode());
        Console.WriteLine("Type: {0}", c1.GetType().ToString());

        // Make some other references to c1.
        ObjTest c2 = c1;
        object o = c2;

        // Are all 3 instances pointing to the same object in memory?
        if(o.Equals(c1) && c2.Equals(o))
            Console.WriteLine("Same instance!");

        return 0;
    }
}
```

Figure 2-8 shows a test run.

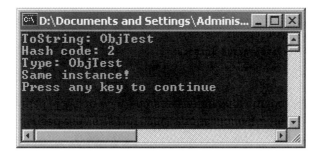

Figure 2-8. Working with select Object methods

73

First, notice how the default implementation of ToString() simply returns the name of the current type (ObjTest). In many situations, derived classes override this method to return a string representing the values of its internal state data (as you do in a moment). Now, examine the following block of code:

```
// Compare objects references. . .
public static int Main(string[] args)
{
    // Make an instance of ObjTest.
    ObjTest c1 = new ObjTest();
    . . .
    // Make some other references to c1.
    ObjTest c2 = c1;
    object o = c2;

    // Are all 3 instances pointing to the same object in memory?
    if(o.Equals(c1) && c2.Equals(o))
        Console.WriteLine("Same instance!");

    return 0;
}
```

The default behavior of Equals() is to compare two objects using *reference semantics* not *value semantics.* Here, you create a new ObjTest variable named c1. At this point, a new ObjTest is placed on the managed heap. C2 is also of type ObjTest. However, you are not creating a *new* instance, but rather assigning this variable to reference c1. Therefore, c1 and c2 are both pointing to the same object in memory, as is the variable *o* (of type object, which was thrown in for good measure). Given that c1, c2 and *o* all point to the same memory location, the equality test succeeds.

Overriding Some Default Behaviors of System.Object

Although the canned behavior of Object can fit the bill in a number of cases, it is quite common for your custom types to override some of these inherited methods. For example, assume you have retrofitted the previous Person class to define some state data representing an individual's name, social security number, and age:

```
// Remember! All classes implicitly derive from Object.
class Person
{
    public Person(string fname, string lname, string ssn, byte a)
    {
        firstName = fname;
        lastName = lname;
        SSN = ssn;
        age = a;
    }

    public Person(){}     // All member variables assigned to default values.


    // The state of a person.
    public string firstName;
    public string lastName;
    public string SSN;
    public byte age;
}
```

To begin, let's override Object.ToString() to return a textual representation of an object's state. You examine the details of method overriding in the next chapter. For the time being, just absorb the fact that you are changing the behavior of the ToString() method to work specifically with our Person class:

```
// Need to reference this namespace to access StringBuilder type.
using System.Text;

// A Person class implements ToString() as so:
class Person
{
...
    // Overriding a method inherited from System.Object.
    public override string ToString()
    {
        StringBuilder sb = new StringBuilder();

        sb.Append("[FirstName= " + this.firstName);
        sb.Append(" LastName= " + this.lastName);
        sb.Append(" SSN= " + this.SSN);
        sb.Append(" Age= " + this.age + "]");
```

```
            return sb.ToString();
        }
    . . .
    }
```

How you choose to format the string returned from System.Object.ToString() is largely a matter of personal choice. In this example, the name/value pairs have been contained within square brackets ([. . .]). Also notice that this example is making use of a new type, System.Text.StringBuilder (which is also a matter of personal choice). This type is described in greater detail later in the chapter.

Let's also override the behavior of Object.Equals() to work with *value-based semantics*. Recall that by default, Equals() returns true only if the two objects being compared are referencing the same object instance in memory. For our Person class, it would be helpful to implement Equals() to return true if the two variables being compared contain the same state values (e.g., name, SSN, and age):

```
// A Person class implements Equals() as so:
class Person
{
. . .
    public override bool Equals(object o)
    {
        // Does the incoming object instance have the same values as me?
        Person temp = (Person)o;

        if(temp.firstName = = this.firstName &&
           temp.lastName = = this.lastName &&
           temp.SSN = = this.SSN &&
           temp.age = = this.age)
                return true;
        else
                return false;
    }
. . .
}
```

Here, you are examining the values of the incoming object against the values of our internal values (note the use of the "this" keyword). If the name, SSN, and age of each are identical, you have two objects with the exact same state data and therefore return true.

Before you see the output of this new type, you have one final detail to attend to. When a class overrides the Equals() method, you should also override the default implementation of GetHashCode() (if you do not, you are issued a compiler warning). This method returns a numerical value used to identify an object in memory, and is commonly used with hash-based collections.

There are many algorithms that can be used to create a hash code, some fancy, others not so fancy. For our current purposes, let's assume that the hash code of the string representing an individual's SSN is unique enough:

```csharp
// Return a hash code based on the person's SSN.
public override int GetHashCode()
{
    return SSN.GetHashCode();
}
```

With this, here is our new Person class in action (check out Figure 2-9 for output):

```csharp
// Make a few people and play with the overridden Object methods.
public static int Main(string[] args)
{
    // Now make some people and test for equality.
    // NOTE:  We want these to be identical to test the Equals() method.
    Person p1 = new Person("Fred", "Jones", "222-22-2222", 98);
    Person p2 = new Person("Fred", "Jones", "222-22-2222", 98);

    // Equals() now uses value semantics (same hash codes).
    if(p1.Equals(p2) && p1.GetHashCode() = = p2.GetHashCode())
        Console.WriteLine("P1 and P2 have same state\n");
    else
        Console.WriteLine("P1 and P2 are DIFFERENT\n");

    // Change state of p2.
    p2.age = 2;

    // Test again (same hash codes).
    if(p1.Equals(p2) && p1.GetHashCode() = = p2.GetHashCode())
        Console.WriteLine("P1 and P2 have same state\n");
    else
        Console.WriteLine("P1 and P2 are DIFFERENT\n");

    // Get 'stringified' version of objects.
    Console.WriteLine(p1.ToString());
    Console.WriteLine(p2);          // ToString() called automatically
    return 0;
}
```

```
D:\CSharpBook\Labs\Chapter 2\ObjectMethods\bin\Debug\ObjectMet...   _ □ ×
P1 and P2 have same state

P1 and P2 are DIFFERENT

FirstName=Fred LastName=Jones SSN=222-22-2222 Age=98
FirstName=Fred LastName=Jones SSN=222-22-2222 Age=2
Press any key to continue
```

Figure 2-9. The result of value based equality testing

SOURCE CODE   *The ObjectMethods project is located under the Chapter 2 subdirectory.*

Static Members of System.Object

In addition to the instance level members you have just examined, System.Object does define two (very helpful) static members that also test for value-based or reference-based equality. Consider the following code:

```csharp
// Static members of System.Object.
Person p3 = new Person("Sally", "Jones","333", 4);
Person p4 = new Person("Sally", "Jones","333", 4);

// Do P3 and P4 have the same state? TRUE!
Console.WriteLine("P3 and P4 have same state: {0}", object.Equals(p3, p4));

// Are they the same object in memory? FALSE!
Console.WriteLine("P3 and P4 are pointing to same object: {0}",
                object.ReferenceEquals(p3, p4));
```

Here, you are able to simply send in two objects (of any type) and allow the System.Object class to determine the details automatically.

The System Data Types (and C# Aliases)

As you may have begun to notice, every intrinsic C# data type is actually an alias to an existing type defined in the System namespace. Table 2-4 lists each system data type, its range, the corresponding C# alias, and the type's compliance with the Common Language Specification (CLS).

Table 2-4. System Types and C# Aliases

C# ALIAS	CLS COMPLIANT?	SYSTEM TYPE	RANGE	MEANING IN LIFE
sbyte	No	SByte	-128 to 127	Signed 8-bit number.
byte	Yes	Byte	0 to 255	Unsigned 8-bit number.
short	Yes	Int16	-32,768 to 32,767	Signed 16-bit number.
ushort	No	UInt16	0 to 65,535	Unsigned 16-bit number.
int	Yes	Int32	-2,147,483,648 to 2,147,483,647	Signed 32-bit number.
uint	No	UInt32	0 to 4,294,967,295	Unsigned 32-bit number.
long	Yes	Int64	-9,223,372,036,854,775,808 to 9,223,372,036,854,775,807	Signed 64-bit number.
ulong	No	UInt64	0 to 18,446,744,073,709,551,615	Unsigned 64-bit number.
char	Yes	Char	U+0000 to U+ffff	A single 16-bit Unicode character.
float	Yes	Single	1.5×10^{-45} to 3.4×10^{38}	32-bit floating point number.
double	Yes	Double	5.0×10^{-324} to 1.7×10^{308}	64-bit floating point number.
bool	Yes	Boolean	true or false	Represents truth or falsity.
decimal	Yes	Decimal	10^0 to 10^{28}	A 96-bit signed number.
string	Yes	String	Limited by system memory.	Represents a set of Unicode characters.
object	Yes	Object	Anything at all. All classes derive from object. Therefore, everything is an object.	The base class of all types in the .NET universe.

The relationship between these core system types (as well as some other soon-to-be-discovered types) can be understood as shown in Figure 2-10.

As you can see, each of these types ultimately derives from System.Object. Thus, because data types such as "int" are simply shorthand notations for the corresponding system type Int32, the following is perfectly legal syntax:

```
// Remember! A C# int is really an alias for System.Int32.
Console.WriteLine(12.ToString());
```

Also notice that although C# defines a number of data types, only a subset of the whole are compliant with the rules of the CLS. When you build custom types that must work seamlessly across all languages, you must stick to this well-defined subset. The basic rule of thumb is to avoid use of unsigned types

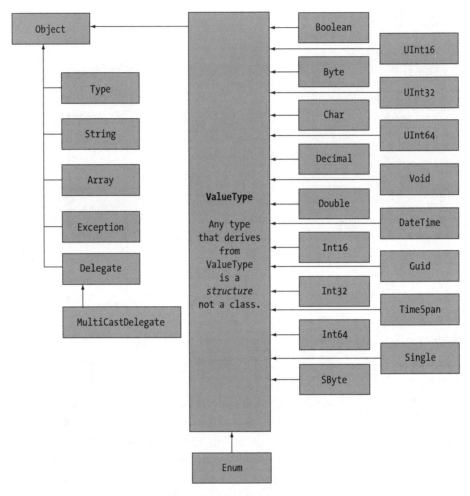

Figure 2-10. The hierarchy of System types

when defining any public member of a type definition. By doing so, you ensure that your custom classes, interfaces, and structures can be understood by any language targeting the .NET runtime. In Chapter 7, you learn about a specific assembly level attribute that you can leverage to ensure that all types are up to snuff with the CLS.

Experimenting with the System Type Classes

Most intrinsic C# data types alias a related structure derived from ValueType. Functionally, the only purpose of System.ValueType is to override the virtual methods defined by System.Object to work with value-based verse reference-based semantics. In fact, the signatures of the methods defined by ValueType are identical to those of Object. However, keep in mind that when you compare two instances, you are using value-based semantics:

```
// Test value semantics.
System.Int32 intA = 1000;        // Same as:    int intA = 1000;
System.Int32 intB = 1000;        // Same as:    int intB = 1000;

// The test succeeds! The two instances contain the same value.
if(intA == intB)
    Console.WriteLine("Same value!");
```

Every system value type (e.g., Int32, Char, Boolean, and so on) has a similar set of helpful members. While I assume you will consult online Help for full details, some points of interest are the MaxValue and MinValue properties that provide information regarding the minimum and maximum value a given type can hold. Assume you have created a variable of type System.UInt16, and exercised it as follows:

```
// Note that an implicit data type (ushort) has the same methods available as
// the corresponding wrapper (System.UInt16).
//
class MyDataTypes
{
    public static int Main(string[] args)
    {
        // Working with UInt16 as a structure.
        System.UInt16 myUInt16 = 30000;
        Console.WriteLine("Max for an UInt16 is: {0}", UInt16.MaxValue);
        Console.WriteLine("Min for an UInt16 is: {0}", UInt16.MinValue);
        Console.WriteLine("Your value is: {0}", myUInt16.ToString());
        Console.WriteLine("I am a: {0}", myUInt16.GetType().ToString());

        // Now in UInt16 shorthand (e.g. a ushort).
        ushort myOtherUInt16 = 12000;
        Console.WriteLine("\nYour value is: {0}", myOtherUInt16.ToString());
        Console.WriteLine("I am a: {0}", myOtherUInt16.GetType().ToString());

        return 0;
    }
}
```

The output can be seen in Figure 2-11.

Figure 2-11. Exercising some system data types

Minor Commentary on Select Data Types

A few system types deserve special comment. First is the System.Boolean data type. Unlike C(++), the only valid assignment a C# bool can take is from the set {true | false}. You cannot assign makeshift values (e.g., -1, 0, 1) to a C# bool, which (to most programmers) is a welcome change:

```
// No more ad hoc Boolean types in C#.
bool b = 0;          // Illegal!
bool b2 = -1         // Also illegal!
bool b3 = true;      // No problem.
bool b4 = false;     // No problem.
```

Next, it is important to note that C# textual data is represented by the string and char data types. Thus, no more nasty char*, wchar_t*, LPSTR, LPCSTR, BSTR or OLECHAR types! I am sure you agree with me that string manipulation in the COM and Win32 universe was horrifying. C# offers a very simplified view of string management, as all .NET-aware languages map textual data to the same underlying types (System.String and System.Char) both of which are Unicode under the hood.

Beyond bool, char, and string, the other intrinsic data types behave as you would expect.

SOURCE CODE   *The DataTypes project is located under the Chapter 2 sub-directory.*

Moving Between Value Types and Reference Types: Boxing and Unboxing

C# provides a very simple mechanism to convert between value types and reference types, termed *boxing*. First, assume that you have created a simple value data type of type short:

```
// Make a simple value data point.
short s = 25;
```

If, during the course of your application, you wish to convert this value type into a corresponding object reference, you would "box" the value as follows:

```
// Box the value into an object reference.
object objShort = s;
```

Boxing can be defined as the process of explicitly converting a value type into a corresponding reference type. When you box a value, essentially all you are doing is allocating a new object on the heap and copying the internal value (in this case 25) into that instance.

The opposite operation is also permitted through *unboxing*. Unboxing is the term given to the process of converting an object reference back into a corresponding value type. The unboxing operation begins by verifying that the receiving data type is equivalent to the boxed type, and if so, copying the value out of the box. For example, the following unboxing operation works successfully, given that the underlying type of the objShort is indeed a short:

```
// Now, unbox the reference back into a corresponding short.
short anotherShort = (short)objShort;
```

However, the following unboxing operation generates an InvalidCastException exception (you examine casting and exception handling in detail in the next chapter, so hold tight for now):

```
// Bad unboxing!
public static int Main(string[] args)
{
...
    try
    {
        // The type contained in the box is NOT a string, but a short!
        string str = (string)objShort;
    }
```

```
catch(InvalidCastException e)
{
    Console.WriteLine("OOPS!\n{0}", e.ToString());
}
...
}
```

Figure 2-12 illustrates the output of the boxing example.

```
D:\CSharpBook\Labs\Chapter 2\DataTypes\bin\Debug\Dat...
short s = 25
short is a: Int16

Boxed object is a: Int16

short anotherShort = 25
Unboxed object is a: Int16

OOPS!
System.InvalidCastException
    at DataTypes.MyDataTypes.Main(System.String[])
```

Figure 2-12. Bad boxing

So, you may be thinking, when would you really need to box (or unbox) a data type? In reality, you don't need to box data types all that often, if ever. In fact, most of the time, the C# compiler automatically boxes and unboxes variables when appropriate. For example, if you pass a value type into a method requiring an object parameter, boxing occurs behind the curtains:

```
// Assume the following method:      public static void Foo(object o)
int x = 99;
Foo(x);      // Automatic boxing.
```

At times, boxing and unboxing can be used explicitly to help improve the performance of your application. You revisit boxing later in this chapter when you formally examine the C# structure.

SOURCE CODE *The DataTypes project is included under the Chapter 2 sub-directory.*

Default Assignments and Variable Scope

As illustrated in this chapter, all intrinsic .NET data types have a default value.
When you create custom types, all member variables are automatically assigned
to an appropriate initial value. To illustrate, consider the following class
definition:

```
// C# automatically sets all member variables to a safe default value.
class DefValObject
{
    // Here are a number of fields. . .
    public sbyte        theSignedByte;
    public byte         theByte;
    public short        theShort;
    public ushort       theUShort;
    public int          theInt;
    public uint         theUInt;
    public long         theLong;
    public ulong        theULong;
    public char         theChar;
    public float        theFloat;
    public double       theDouble;
    public bool         theBool;
    public decimal      theDecimal;
    public string       theStr;
    public object       theObj;

    public static int Main(string[] args)
    {
        DefValObject v = new DefValObject();
        return 0;       // Set breakpoint here and check out the Autos window.
    }
}
```

If you were to now create an instance of the DefValObject class and begin a
debugging session, you would see that each member variable has been automatically assigned to a corresponding default value, as seen in Figure 2-13.

The story is very different however when you create variables within a
method scope. When you define variables within a method scope, you *must*

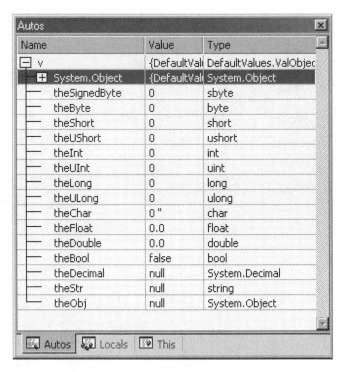

Figure 2-13. All types have a safe default value.

assign an initial value before you use them, as they do not receive a default assignment. For example, the following code results in a compiler error:

```csharp
// Compiler error! Must assign localInt to an initial value before use.
public static void Main()
{
    int localInt;
    Console.WriteLine(localInt.ToString());
}
```

Fixing the problem is trivial. Simply make an initial assignment:

```csharp
// Better. Everyone is happy.
public static void Main()
{
    int localInt = 0;
    Console.WriteLine(localInt.ToString());
}
```

There is one exception to the mandatory assignment of local variables. If the variable is functioning as an "out" parameter (examined later in this chapter) the variable does not need to be assigned an initial value. Methods that define "out" parameters assume incoming variables are assigned within the scope of the called function.

SOURCE CODE   *The DefaultValues project is located under the Chapter 2 subdirectory.*

Defining Program Constants

Now that you can create variables, you need to examine the logical opposite: Constants. C# offers the "const" keyword, like C(++), in order to define constant data types. Although it is possible to define constants within a method scope, a more beneficial use of const is to create class level constant definitions. For example:

```
// Some const data.
using System;
class MyConstants
{
    // These must be accessed at the class level.
    public const int myIntConst = 5;
    public const string myStringConst = "I'm a const";

    public static void Main()
    {
        // Scoped constant.
        const string localConst = "I am a rock, I am an island";

        // Use const data (note the class level scope).
        Console.WriteLine("myIntConst = {0}\nmyStringConst = {1}",
                        MyConstants.myIntConst,
                        MyConstants.myStringConst );

        Console.WriteLine("Local constant: {0}", localConst);
    }
}
```

If you create a utility class that contains nothing but constant data, you may wish to define a private constructor. In this way, you ensure the object user cannot make an instance of your class:

```
// Private constructors prevent the creation of a given type.
class MyConstants
{
    // Some const data.
    public const int myIntConst = 5;
    public const string myStringConst = "I'm a const";

    // Don't let the user make this class,
    // as its only purpose is to define constant values.
    private MyConstants(){}
}
```

The same end result can be achieved by marking your "constant only class" as an abstract type. You examine the use of this keyword in the next chapter. An example of its use follows:

```
// Abstract definition also prevents the creation of a given type.
abstract class MyConstants
{
    // Some const data.
    public const int myIntConst = 5;
    public const string myStringConst = "I'm a const";
}
```

In either case, if another object attempts to create an instance of MyConstants, a compiler error is generated. These techniques can be quite helpful given that C# does not allow you to define global level constants. On a final note, realize that unlike C++, you cannot use the const keyword as part of a method definition.

 SOURCE CODE *The Constants project is located under the Chapter 2 subdirectory.*

C# Iteration Constructs

All programming languages provide ways to repeat blocks of code until a terminating condition has been met. Regardless of which language you are coming from, the C# iteration statements should pose no raised eyebrows and require little explanation. In a nutshell, C# provides the following four iteration constructs:

- for loop

- foreach/in loop

- while loop

- do/while loop

C, C++, and Java programmers will no doubt be familiar with the "for," "while," and "do/while" loops, but may be unfamiliar with the "foreach" statement. Visual Basic programmers on the other hand, are in the fortunate position to be well aware of all four C# iteration statements, as VB already supports "For Each" syntax. Let's quickly examine each looping construct in turn.

The for Loop

When you need to iterate over a block of code a fixed number of times, the "for" statement is the construct of champions. In essence, you are able to specify how many times a block of code repeats itself, as well as the terminating condition. Without belaboring the point, here is a sample of the syntax:

```
// A basic for loop.
public static int Main(string[] args)
{
    // Note! 'i' is only visible within the scope of the for loop.
    for(int i = 0; i < 10; i++)
    {
        Console.WriteLine("Number is: {0}", i);
    }

    // 'i' is not visible here.
    return 0;
}
```

All of your old C, C++, and Java tricks still hold when building a C# for statement. You can create complex terminating conditions, build endless loops, and make use of the "goto," "continue" and "break" keywords. I'll assume that you will bend this iteration construct as you see fit.

The foreach/in Loop

Visual Basic programmers have long seen the benefits of the For Each construct. The C# equivalent allows you to iterate over all items within an array. Here is a simple example using foreach to traverse an array of strings that represent possible titles for forthcoming publications. Once this array has been filled, you iterate over the contents looking for a pattern match (COM or .NET) using String.IndexOf():

```
// Digging into an array using foreach.
public static int Main(string[] args)
{
    string[] arrBookTitles = new string[] {"Complex Algorithms",
                                    "COM for the Fearful Programmer",
                                    "Do you Remember Classic COM?",
                                    "C# and the .NET Platform",
                                    "COM for the Angry Engineer"};
    int COM = 0, NET = 0;

    // Assume there are no books on COM and .NET (yet).
    foreach (string s in arrBookTitles)
    {
        if (-1 != s.IndexOf("COM"))
            COM++;
        else if(-1 != s.IndexOf(".NET"))
            NET++;
    }
    Console.WriteLine("Found {0} COM references and {1} .NET references.",
                    COM, NET);
    return 0;
}
```

In addition to iterating over simple arrays, foreach is also able to iterate over system-supplied or user-defined collections. I'll hold off on the details until Chapter 4, as this aspect of the foreach keyword entails an understanding of interface-based programming and the system-supplied IEnumerator and IEnumerable interfaces.

The while and do/while Looping Constructs

You have already seen that the for statement is typically used when you have some foreknowledge of the number of iterations you wish to perform (e.g., loop until $j > 20$). The "while" statement on the other hand is useful for those times when you are uncertain how long it might take for a terminating condition to be met.

To illustrate the while loop, here is a brief look at C# file manipulation (which is fully detailed in Chapter 11). The StreamReader class, defined within the System.IO namespace, encapsulates the details of reading from a given file. Notice that you are obtaining an instance of the StreamReader type as a return value from the static File.OpenText() method. Once you have opened the config.win file, you are able to iterate over each line in the file using StreamReader.ReadLine():

```
try     // Just in case we can't find the correct file. . .
{
        // Open the file named 'config.win'.
        StreamReader strReader = File.OpenText("C:\\config.win");

        // Read the next line and dump to the console.
        string strLine;
        while(null != (strLine = strReader.ReadLine()))
        {
             Console.WriteLine(strLine);
        }
        // Close the file.
        strReader.Close();
}
catch(FileNotFoundException e)     // Again, we examine exceptions in Chapter 3.
{
        Console.WriteLine(e.Message);
}
```

Closely related to the while loop is the do/while statement. Like a simple while loop, do/while is used when you need to perform some action for an undetermined number of times. The difference is that do/while loops are guaranteed to execute the corresponding block of code at least once (in contrast, it is possible that a simple while loop many never execute if the terminating condition is false from the onset). The output of the Iteration logic can be seen in Figure 2-14.

```
// The do/while statement
string ans;
do
{
    Console.Write("Are you done? [yes] [no] : ");
    ans = Console.ReadLine();
}while(ans != "yes");
```

```
D:\CSharpBook\Labs\Chapter 2\Iterations\bin\Debug\Iter...  _ □ ×
Found 3 COM references and 1 .NET references.

Here is the contents config.win
************************************************
DEVICE=C:\WINDOWS\HIMEM.SYS
DEVICE=C:\WINDOWS\EMM386.EXE
REM To make a DOS Boot Diskette; See the file C:\D

[common]
dos=high,umb
buffers=40
; SBPCI mod: device=c:\windows\himem.sys /testmem:

rem The below DOS CD ROM driver is not required to
DEVICE=c:\cdrom\OakCdRom.SYS /D:IDECD000
************************************************

Are you done? [yes] [no] :  1
Are you done? [yes] [no] : no
Are you done? [yes] [no] : hello
Are you done? [yes] [no] : yes
Press any key to continue
```

Figure 2-14. Iteration logic

SOURCE CODE   *The Iterations project is located under the Chapter 2 subdirectory.*

C# Control Flow Constructs

Now that you can iterate over a block of code, the next related concept is how to control the flow of program execution. C# defines two simple constructs to alter the flow of your program, based on various contingencies. First you have our good friend, the "if/else" statement. Unlike C and C++ however, the if/else statement only operates on Boolean expressions (not ad hoc values such as –1, 0 and so on). Given this, if/else statements typically involve the use of the following C# operators (Table 2-5).

C and C++ programmers need to be aware that the old tricks of testing a condition for a value "not equal to zero" will not work in C#. Let's say you want to see if the string you are working with is greater than zero. You may be tempted to write:

```csharp
// This is illegal, given that Length returns an int, not a bool.
string thoughtOfTheDay = "You CAN teach an old dog new tricks";
if(thoughtOfTheDay.Length)     // Error!
```

Table 2-5. C# Relational and Equality Operators

C# EQUALITY/RELATIONAL OPERATOR	EXAMPLE USAGE	MEANING IN LIFE
==	if(age == 30)	Returns true only if each expression is the same.
!=	if("Foo" != myStr)	Returns true only if each expression is different.
<	if(bonus < 2000)	Returns true if expression A is less
>	if(bonus > 2000)	than, greater than, less than or
<=	if(bonus <= 2000)	equal to, or greater than or equal
>=	if(bonus >= 2000)	to expression B.

```
{
    // stuff. . .
}
```

If you wish to make use of the String.Length property to determine if you have an empty string, you would need to modify your conditional expression as follows:

```
// No problem.
if( 0 != thoughtOfTheDay.Length)      // Better!  This resolves to {true | false}.
{
    // Stuff. . .
}
```

An "if" statement may be composed of complex expressions as well. As you would expect, if conditionals can contain *else* statements to perform more complex testing. The syntax is identical to C(++) and Java (and not too far removed from Visual Basic). To build such a beast, C# offers an expected set of conditional operators (Table 2-6).

Table 2-6. C# Conditional Operators

C# CONDITIONAL OPERATOR	EXAMPLE	MEANING IN LIFE
&&	if((age == 30) && (name == "Fred"))	Conditional AND operator.
||	if((age == 30) || (name == "Fred"))	Conditional OR operator.
!	if(!myBool)	Conditional NOT operator.

The other simple selection construct offered by C# is the *switch* statement. As I am sure you are aware, switch statements allow you to handle program flow based on a predefined set of choices. For example, the following application prompts the user for one of three possible values. Based on the user input, act accordingly:

```csharp
// The good ol' switch statement.
class Selections
{
    public static int Main(string[] args)
    {
        Console.WriteLine("Welcome to the world of .NET");
        Console.WriteLine("1 = C#\n2 = Managed C++ (MC++)\n3 = VB.NET\n");
        Console.Write("Please select your implementation language:");
        string s = Console.ReadLine();

        // All intrinsic data types support a static Parse() method.
        int n = int.Parse(s);

        switch(n)
        {
            // C# demands that each case (including 'default') which
            // contains executable statements, must have
            // a terminating 'break' or 'goto' to avoid fall through.
            case 1:
            Console.WriteLine("Good choice!  C# is all about managed code.");
            break;

            case 2:
            Console.WriteLine("Let me guess, maintaining a legacy system?");
            break;

            case 3:
            Console.WriteLine("VB.NET:  It is not just for kids anymore. . .");
            break;
            default:
            Console.WriteLine("Well. . .good luck with that!");
            break;
        }
        return 0;
    }
}
```

Figure 2-15 shows a possible test run.

```
C:\ D:\Documents and Settings\atroelsen\Desktop\CSh...  _ □ X
Welcome to the world of .NET
1 = C#
2 = Managed C++ (MC++)
3 = VB.NET

Please select your implementation language:3

VB.NET:  It is not for just kids anymore...
Press any key to continue
```

Figure 2-15. They grow up so quickly. . .

It is worth pointing out that the C# also supports switching on character data as well (it even supports a "null" case for empty strings).

SOURCE CODE   *The Selections project is located under the Chapter 2 subdirectory.*

Additional C# Operators

C# defines a number of operators in addition to those you have previously examined. By and large, these operators behave like their C(++) and Java counterparts. Table 2-7 lists the set of C# operators in order of precedence.

Table 2-7. The Full Set of C# Operators

OPERATOR CATEGORY	OPERATORS
Unary	+ - ! ~ ++x x++ --x x--
Multiplicative	* / %
Additive	+ -
Shift	<< >>
Relational	< > <= >= is as
Equality	== !=
Logical AND	&
Logical XOR	^
Logical OR	|
Conditional AND	&&
Conditional OR	||
Conditional	?:
Assignment	= *= /= %= += -= <<= >>= &= ^= |=

The only operators that you may not be familiar with are the *is* and *as* operators. The *is* operator is used to verify at runtime if an object is compatible with a given type. One common use for this operator is to determine if a given object supports a particular interface, as you discover in Chapter 4. The *as* operator allows you to downcast between types (also seen in chapter 4). As for the remaining operators, I will make the assumption that many (if not all) of them are old hat to you. If you need additional information regarding the C# looping and decision constructs, consult the C# Language Reference using online Help.

Defining Custom Class Methods

Before going much further, let's examine how to define custom methods for a C# class. Every method you implement must be a member of a class or struct. Global methods are not allowed in C#. As you know, a method exists to allow the type to perform a unit of work. Like Main(), your custom methods may or may not take parameters, may or may not return values (of any intrinsic or user defined types) and may or may not be declared as static.

Method Access Modifiers

To begin, a method must specify its level of accessibility (see Table 2-8). C# offers the following method access modifiers (you examine the use of protected and internal methods in the next chapter during the discussion of class hierarchies):

Table 2-8. C# Accessibility Keywords

C# ACCESS MODIFIER	MEANING IN LIFE
public	Marks a method as accessible from an object instance, or any subclass.
private	Marks a method as accessible only by the class that has defined the method. If you don't say otherwise, private is assumed (it is the default visibility level).
protected	Marks a method as usable by the defining class, as well as any child class, but is private as far as the outside world is concerned.
internal	Defines a method that is publicly accessible by all types in an assembly (but not from outside the assembly).
protected internal	Protected access or internal access.

Here are the implications of each accessibility keyword:

```
// Visibility options.
class SomeClass
{
    // Accessible anywhere.
    public void MethodA(){}

    // Accessible only from SomeClass types.
    private void MethodB(){}

    // Accessible from SomeClass and any descendent.
    protected void MethodC(){}

    // Accessible from within the same assembly.
    internal void MethodD(){}

    // Internal or protected access.
    protected internal void MethodE(){}

    // Private by default.
    void MethodF(){}
}
```

Methods that are declared public are directly accessible from an object instance. Private methods cannot be accessed by an object instance, but instead are called internally by the object to help the instance get its work done (that is, private helper functions). To illustrate, the Teenager class shown next defines two public methods, Complain() and BeAgreeable(), each of which returns a string to the object user. Internally, both methods make use of a private helper method named GetRandomNumber(), which manipulates a private member variable of type System.Random:

```
// Two public methods, each using an internal helper function.
using System;
class Teenager
{
    // The System.Random type generates random numbers.
    private Random r = new Random();

    public string Complain()
```

```
        {
                string[] messages = new string[5]{"Do I have to?",
                        "He started it!", "I'm too tired. . .",
                        "I hate school!", "You are sooo wrong."};
                return messages[GetRandomNumber(5)];
        }

        public string BeAgreeable()
        {
                string[] messages = new string[3]{"Sure!  No problem!",
                        "Uh uh.", "I guess so."};
                return messages[GetRandomNumber(3)];
        }

        // Private function used to grab a random number.
        private int GetRandomNumber(short upperLimit)
        {
                // Random.Next() returns a random integer between 0 and upperLimit.
                return r.Next(upperLimit);
        }

        public static void Main(string[] args)
        {
                // Let mike complain.
                Teenager mike = new Teenager();
                for(int i = 0; i < 10; i++)
                {
                        Console.WriteLine(mike.Complain());
                }
        }
}
```

Obviously the benefit of defining GetRandomNumber() as a private helper method is that various parts of the Teenager class can make use of its functionality. The only alternative would be to duplicate the random number logic within the Complain() and BeAgreeable() methods (which in this case would not be too traumatic, but assume GetRandomNumber() contains 20 or 30 lines of code). Figure 2-16 shows a possible test run.

Note the use of the System.Random type. This class (obviously) is used to generate and manipulate random numbers. Random.Next() method returns a number between 0 and the specified upper limit. As you would guess, the Random class provides additional members, all of which are documented within online Help.

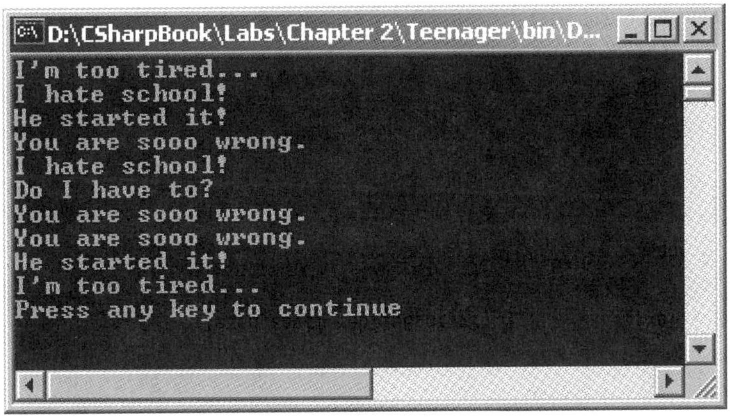

Figure 2-16. Random complaints

Static Methods and Instance Methods

As you have seen, methods can be declared "static." So, what does it mean to be a static method? When a method is marked with the static keyword, it may be called directly from the class level, and does not require an object instance. For this very reason, Main() is declared static to allow the runtime to invoke this function without needing to allocate a new instance of the defining class. This is a good thing of course, or else you would need to create an object to create an object to create an object to (. . .).

To illustrate custom static methods, assume I have reconfigured the Complain() method as follows:

```
// Teenagers complain so often, there is no need to create an initial object...
public static string Complain()
{
    string[] messages = new string[5]{"Do I have to?",
        "He started it!", "I'm too tired...",
        "I hate school!", "You are sooo wrong."};
    return messages[GetRandomNumber(5)];
}
```

Calling a static method is simple. Just append the member to the name to the defining class:

```
// Call the static Complain method of the Teenager class.
public static void Main(string[] args)
```

```
{
    for(int i = 0; i < 40; i++)
        Console.WriteLine(Teenager.Complain());
}
```

Nonstatic (instance) methods are methods that are scoped at the object level. Thus, if Complain() was *not* marked static, you would need to create an instance of the Teenager class before you could hear about the gripe of the day:

```
// Must make an instance of Teenager class to call instance methods.
Teenager joe = new Teenager();
joe.Complain();
```

SOURCE CODE   *The Teenager application is located under the Chapter 2 subdirectory.*

Defining Static Data

In addition to static methods, a C# class may also define *static data members*. Recall that a class typically defines a set of state data. This simply means that each object instance maintains an internal copy of the underlying values. Thus, if you have a class defined as follows:

```
// We all love Foo.
class Foo
{
    public int intFoo;
}
```

you can create any number of objects of type Foo and set the intFoo field to a unique value:

```
// Each Foo reference maintains a copy of the intFoo field.
Foo f1 = new Foo();
f1.intFoo = 100;

Foo f2 = new Foo();
f2.intFoo = 993;

Foo f3 = new Foo();
f3.intFoo = 6;
```

Static data, on the other hand, is shared among all object instances. Rather than each object holding a copy of a given field, a point of static data is allocated exactly once. Assume you have a class named Airplane that contains a single point of static data. In the constructor of the Airplane class you increment this data point. Here is the initial definition:

```
// Note the use of static keyword.
class Airplane
{
    // This static data member is shared by all Airplane objects.
    private static int NumberInTheAir = 0;

    public Airplane()
    {
        NumberInTheAir++;
    }

    // Get value from an object instance.
    public int GetNumberFromObject() { return NumberInTheAir;}

    // Get value from class.
    public static int GetNumber() { return NumberInTheAir;}
}
```

Notice that the Airplane class defines two methods. The static GetNumber() returns the current number of airplane objects that have been allocated by the application. GetNumberFromObject() also returns the static NumberInTheAir integer, however given that this method has not been defined as static, the object user must call this method from an instance of Airplane. To illustrate, observe the following usage:

```
// Make some airplanes are examine the static members.
class StaticApp
{
    public static int Main(string[] args)
    {
        // Make some planes.
        Airplane a1 = new Airplane();
        Airplane a2 = new Airplane();

        // How many are in flight?
```

```
                Console.WriteLine("Number of planes: {0}",
                                a1.GetNumberFromObject());

                Console.WriteLine("Number of planes: {0}", Airplane.GetNumber());

                // More planes!
                Airplane a3 = new Airplane();
                Airplane a4 = new Airplane();

                // Now how many?
                Console.WriteLine("Number of planes: {0}",
                                a3.GetNumberFromObject());

                Console.WriteLine("Number of planes: {0}", Airplane.GetNumber());

                return 0;
        }
    }
```

Figure 2-17 shows the output.

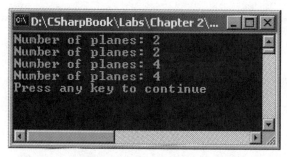

Figure 2-17. Static data is shared among all like objects

As you can see, all instances of the Airplane class are sharing (i.e., viewing) the same point of data. That's the point of static data: To allow all objects to share a given value at the class (rather than at the object) level.

SOURCE CODE   *The StaticTypes project is located under the Chapter 2 subdirectory.*

An Interesting Aside: Some Static Members of the Environment Class

Environment is yet another class defined within the System namespace. This class represents a type exposing a number of details regarding the operating system currently hosting your .NET application. Each detail is obtained using various static members. To illustrate:

```
// Here are some (but not all) of the interesting
// static members of the Environment class.
using System;

class PlatformSpy
{
    public static int Main(string[] args)
    {
        // OS?
        Console.WriteLine("Current OS: {0}", Environment.OSVersion);

        // Directory?
        Console.WriteLine("Current Directory: {0}",
                        Environment.CurrentDirectory);

        // Here are the drives on this box.
        string[] drives = Environment.GetLogicalDrives();

        for(int i = 0; i < drives.Length; i++)
            Console.WriteLine("Drive {0} : {1}",  i, drives[i]);

        // Which version of the .NET platform?
        Console.WriteLine("Current version of .NET: {0}",
            Environment.Version);

        return 0;
    }
}
```

The output can be seen in Figure 2-18.

SOURCE CODE   *The PlatformSpy example is located under the Chapter 2 subdirectory.*

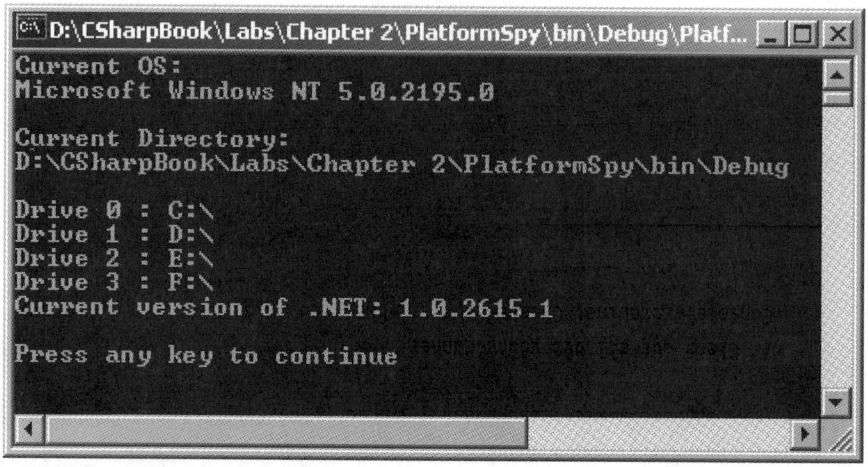

```
D:\CSharpBook\Labs\Chapter 2\PlatformSpy\bin\Debug\Platf...
Current OS:
Microsoft Windows NT 5.0.2195.0

Current Directory:
D:\CSharpBook\Labs\Chapter 2\PlatformSpy\bin\Debug

Drive 0 : C:\
Drive 1 : D:\
Drive 2 : E:\
Drive 3 : F:\
Current version of .NET: 1.0.2615.1

Press any key to continue
```

Figure 2-18. Basic environment variables

Method Parameter Modifiers

Methods tend to take parameters. If you have a COM background, you are certainly familiar with the use of the [in], [out] and [in, out] IDL attributes. Classic COM objects use these attributes to clearly identify the direction of travel (and memory allocation rules) for a given interface method parameter. While IDL is not used in the .NET universe, there is analogous behavior with the set of C# parameter modifiers shown in Table 2-9.

Table 2-9. C# Parameter Modifiers

PARAMETER MODIFIER	MEANING IN LIFE
(none)	If a parameter is not marked with a parameter modifier, it is assumed to be an input parameter passed by value. This is analogous to the IDL [in] attribute.
out	This is analogous to an IDL [out] parameter. Output parameters are assigned by the called member.
ref	Analogous to the IDL [in, out] attribute. The value is assigned by the caller, but may be reassigned during the scope of the method call.
params	This parameter modifier allows you to send in a variable number of parameters as a single parameter. A given method can only have a single params modifier, and must be the final parameter of the method. This is (roughly) analogous to a COM SAFEARRAY.

First you have the use of implicit input and explicit output parameters. Here is a version of an Add() method that returns the summation of two integers using the C# out keyword:

```
// Output parameters are allocated by the callee.
public void Add(int x, int y, out int ans)
{
    ans = x + y;
}
```

Calling a method with output parameters also requires the use of the out keyword. For example:

```
// Assume the Add() method is defined in a class named Methods.
public static void Main()
{
...

    Methods m = new Methods();
    int ans;      // No need to assign before use when a variable is used ala
out.

    // Note use of out keyword in calling syntax.
    m.Add(90, 90, out ans);
    Console.WriteLine("90 + 90 = {0}", ans);
}
```

As you are aware, this incarnation of Add() is logically equivalent to the following:

```
// A slightly more natural Add() method.
public int Add(int x, int y)
{
    return x + y;
}
```

Reference parameters are necessary when you wish to allow a method to operate (and usually change the values of) various parameters (such as a sort routine). Note the distinction between output and reference parameters:

- Output parameters do not need to be initialized before they are sent to the callee. Reason? It is assumed the method fills the value on your behalf.

- Reference parameters *must* be initialized before being sent to the callee. Reason? You are passing a reference to an existing type. If you don't assign it to an initial value, that would be the equivalent to operating on a NULL pointer!

Let's illustrate the use of the ref keyword:

```
// Reference parameter.
public void UpperCaseThisString(ref string s)
{
    // Return the uppercase version of the string.
    s = s.ToUpper();
}
```

```
// . . .meanwhile back in Main(). . .
public static void Main()
{
    . . .
    // Use 'ref'.
    string s = "Can you really have sonic hearing for $19.00?";
    Console.WriteLine("Before: {0}", s);

    m.UpperCaseThisString(ref s);
    Console.WriteLine("After: {0}", s);
}
```

The final parameter modifier is the params keyword, which is somewhat odd (but convenient) given that it allows you to send a varied number of parameters *as a single parameter.* Yes, this can be confusing. To clear the air, assume I have written a simple method defined as follows:

```
// This method has two physical parameters.
public void DisplayArrayOfInts(string msg, params int[] list)
{
    Console.WriteLine(msg);

    for ( int i = 0 ; i < list.Length ; i++ )
        Console.WriteLine(list[i]);
}
```

This method has been defined to take two physical parameters: one of type string, and one as a parameterized array of integers. What this method is in fact saying is "Send me a string as the first parameter and *any number of integers as the second.*" You can call ArrayOfInts() in any of the following ways:

```
// Use 'params' keyword.
int[] intArray = new int[3] {10,11,12};
m.DisplayArrayOfInts ("Here is an array of ints", intArray);
m.DisplayArrayOfInts ("Enjoy these 3 ints", 1, 2, 3);
m.DisplayArrayOfInts ("Take some more!", 55, 4, 983, 10432, 98, 33);
```

Looking at the previous code, you can see that the bolded items in a given invocation correspond to the second parameter (the array of integers). Of course, you do not have to make use of simple numeric value types when using the params keyword. Assume Person is now defined as so:

```
// Yet another person class.
class Person
{
    private string fullName;
    private byte age;

    public Person(string n, byte a)
    {
        fullName = n;
        age = a;
    }

    public void PrintInfo()
    {
        Console.WriteLine("{0} is {1} years old", fullName, age);
    }
}
```

Now assume that your Methods class defines another method to make use of the params keyword. This time however, you specify an array of objects, which boils down to *anything.* With this logic, you can test for an incoming Person type. If you find one, you call the PrintInfo() method. If you do not have a Person type, just dump the info to the console:

```
// What did they send me this time?
public void DisplayArrayOfObjects(params object[] list)
{
    for ( int i = 0 ; i < list.Length ; i++ )
```

```
    {
        if(list[i] is Person)        // Is the current item a Person type?
        {
            ((Person)list[i]).PrintInfo();        // If so, call some methods.
        }
        else
            Console.WriteLine(list[i]);
    }
    Console.WriteLine();
}
```

The calling logic can be seen here (the output appears in Figure 2-19):

```
// Make some objects.
Person p = new Person("Fred", 93);
m.DisplayArrayOfObjects(777, p, "I really am an instance of System.String");
```

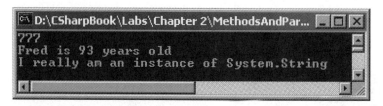

Figure 2-19. Params keyword in action

So there! As you can see, C# allows you to work with parameters on many different levels. For the C++ programmers in the world, you should be able to map the C# output and reference parameters to pointer (or C++ reference) primitives without the ugly * and & operators.

SOURCE CODE   *The MethodsAndParams project is located under the Chapter 2 subdirectory.*

Array Manipulation in C#

Mechanically, C# arrays look and feel much like their C, C++, or Java counterparts. As you'll see in just a moment, all C# arrays actually derive from the System.Array base class, and therefore share a common set of members.

Formally speaking, an array is a collection of data points (of the same underlying type), that are accessed using a numerical index. As you might assume, arrays can contain any intrinsic type defined by C#, including arrays of objects, interfaces, or structures. In C#, arrays can be single or multidimensional, and must be declared with the square brackets ([]) placed *after* the data type of the array. For example:

```
// A string array containing 10 elements {0, 1, . . ., 9}
string[] booksOnCOM;
booksOnCOM = new string[10];

// A 2 item string array, numbered {0, 1}
string[] booksOnPL1 = new string[2];

// 100 item string array, numbered {0, 1, . . ., 99}
string[] booksOnDotNet = new string[100];
```

As you can see, the first example declares the type and size of the array on two separate lines. The final two examples illustrate that you are also able to declare and construct your array on a single line (just like any object). In either case, notice that you are required to make use of the "new" keyword when you are constructing an array of an initial fixed size. Thus, the following array declaration is illegal:

```
// Need 'new' keyword when you define a fixed size array.
int[4] ages = {30, 54, 4, 10};          // Error!
```

Remember that the size of an array is established when it is created, not when it is declared. Therefore, if you choose to declare an array with a fixed initial size, you must use the new operator. However, if you would rather let the compiler determine the size of the array, you are free to use the following shorthand notation:

```
// The size of this array will automatically be set to 4.
// Note the lack of the 'new' keyword and empty [].
int[] ages = {20, 22, 23, 0};
```

Like many languages, member initialization can be achieved using curly bracket notation ({}) rather than assigning values member by member. Therefore, the following two arrays are identical:

```
// Initialize each member at declaration OR. . .
string[] firstNames = new string[5]{"Steve", "Gina", "Swallow", "Baldy",
                                    "Gunner"};

// . . .assign values member by member.
```

```
string[] firstNames = new string[5];
firstNames[0] = "Steve";
firstNames[1] = "Gina";
firstNames[2] = "Swallow";
firstNames[3] = "Baldy";
firstNames[4] = "Gunner";
```

One final difference between C(++)and C# arrays is that every member in an array is automatically set to a default value. For example, if you have an array of numerical types, each member is set to 0, arrays of objects begin life set to null, and so forth.

Working with Multidimensional Arrays

In addition to the single dimension arrays you have seen thus far, C# also supports two varieties of multidimensional arrays. The first of these is termed a "rectangular array." This type is simply an array of multiple dimensions, where each row is of the same length. To declare and fill a multidimensional rectangular array, proceed as follows:

```
// A rectangular MD array.
int[,] myMatrix;
myMatrix = new int[6,6];

// Populate (6 * 6) array.
for(int i = 0; i < 6; i++)
    for(int j = 0; j < 6; j++)
        myMatrix[i, j] = i * j;

// Show (6 * 6) array.
for(int i = 0; i < 6; i++)
{
    for(int j = 0; j < 6; j++)
    {
        Console.Write(myMatrix[i, j] + "\t");
    }
    Console.WriteLine();
}
```

The output is seen in Figure 2-20 (note the rectangular nature of the array).

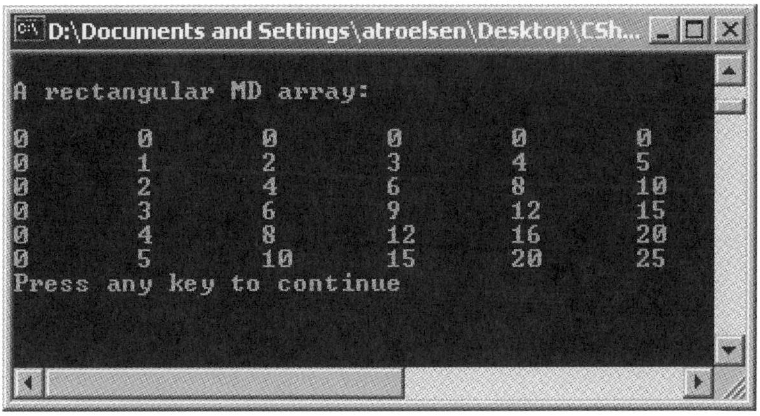

Figure 2-20. A rectangular array

The second type of multidimensional array is termed a "jagged" array. As the name implies, jagged arrays contain some number of inner arrays, each of which may have a unique upper limit. For example:

```
// A jagged MD array (i.e. an array of arrays).
// Here we have an array of 5 different arrays.
    int[][] myJagArray = new int[5][];

// Create the jagged array.
for (int i = 0; i < myJagArray.Length; i++)
{
        myJagArray[i] = new int[i + 7];
}

// Print each row (remember, each element is defaulted to zero!)
for(int i = 0; i < 5; i++)
{
    Console.Write("Length of row {0} is {1}:\t", i, myJagArray[i].Length);
    for(int j = 0; j < myJagArray[i].Length; j++)
    {
        Console.Write(myJagArray[i][j] + " ");
    }
    Console.WriteLine();
}
```

The output is seen in Figure 2-21 (note the jaggedness of the array).

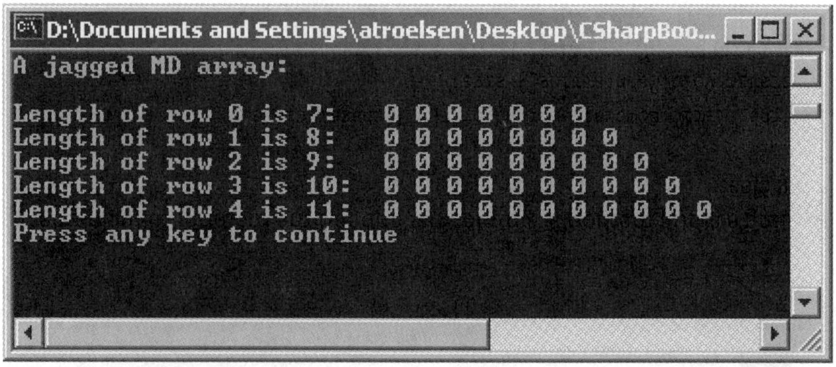

Figure 2-21. A jagged array

Now that you understand how to build and populate C# arrays, you can turn your attention to the ultimate base class of any array, System.Array.

The System.Array Base Class

The most striking difference between C and C++ arrays is the fact that every array you create is automatically derived from System.Array. This class defines a number of helpful methods that make working with arrays much more palatable. Table 2-10 gives a rundown of some (but not all) of the more interesting members.

Table 2-10. Select Members of System.Array

MEMBER OF ARRAY CLASS	MEANING IN LIFE
BinarySearch()	This static method is applicable only if the items in the array implement the IComparer interface (see Chapter 4). If so, BinarySearch() finds a given item.
Clear()	This static method sets a range of elements in the array to empty values (0 for value items, null for object references).
CopyTo()	Used to copy elements from the source array into the destination array.
GetEnumerator()	Returns the IEnumerator interface for a given array. I address interfaces in Chapter 4, but for the time being, keep in mind that this interface is required by the foreach construct.
GetLength() Length	The GetLength() method is used to determine the number of elements in a given dimension of the array. Length is a read-only property.
GetLowerBound(); GetUpperBound()	As you can guess, these two methods can be used to determine the bounds of a given dimension.

Continued

Table 2-10. Select Members of System.Array (Continued)

MEMBER OF ARRAY CLASS	MEANING IN LIFE
GetValue() SetValue()	Retrieves or sets the value for a given index in the array. These methods have been overloaded to work with single and multidimensional arrays.
Reverse()	This static method reverses the contents of a one-dimensional array.
Sort()	Sorts a one-dimensional array of intrinsic types. If the elements in the array implement the IComparer interface, you can also sort your custom types (again, see Chapter 4).

Let's see some of these members in action. The following code makes use of the static Reverse() and Clear() methods (and the Length property) to pump out some information about the firstName array to the console:

```csharp
// Create some string arrays and exercise some System.Array members.
class Arrays
{
    public static int Main(string[] args)
    {
        // Array of strings.
        string[] firstNames = new string[5]{"Steve", "Gina", "Swallow",
                                            "Baldy", "Gunner"};

        // Print out names in declared order.
        Console.WriteLine("Here is the array:");

        for(int i = 0; i < firstNames.Length; i++)
            Console.Write(firstNames[i] + "\t");

        // Flip things around using the static Reverse() method. . .
        Array.Reverse(firstNames);

        // . . . and print them.
        Console.WriteLine("Here is the array once reversed:");
        for(int i = 0; i < firstNames.Length; i++)
            Console.Write(firstNames[i] + "\t");

        // Clear out all but young gunner.
        Console.WriteLine("Cleared out all but one. . .");
```

```
        Array.Clear(firstNames, 1, 4);

        for(int i = 0; i < firstNames.Length; i++)
        {
            Console.Write(firstNames[i] + "\t\n");
        }
        return 0;
    }
}
```

The output can be seen in Figure 2-22.

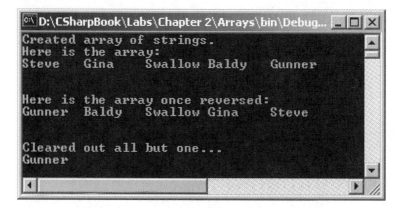

Figure 2-22. Fun with System.Array

The ability to treat arrays as objects has been a luxury long known by the Java programmers of the world (among others). With C# and the .NET platform, traditional Windows developers now have the same benefits (as a happy side note, you can forget about the horrors of manipulating the COM SAFEARRAY structure . . . at least after you have read Chapter 12).

SOURCE CODE   *The Arrays application is located under the Chapter 2 subdirectory.*

String Manipulation in C#

As you have already seen, string is a native data type in C#. However, like all intrinsic types, string actually aliases a type in the .NET library, which in this case is System.String. System.String provides a number of methods you would expect from such a utility class, including methods that return the length, find substrings, convert to and from uppercase/lowercase, and so forth. Table 2-11 lists some (but by no means all) of the interesting members.

Table 2-11. Select Members of System.String

MEMBER OF STRING CLASS	MEANING IN LIFE
Length	This property returns the length of the current string.
Concat()	This static method of the String class returns a new string that is composed of two discrete strings.
CompareTo()	Compares two strings.
Copy()	This static method returns a fresh new copy of an existing string.
Format()	Used to format a string using other primitives (i.e., numerical data, other strings) and the {0} notation examined earlier in this chapter.
Insert()	Used to insert a string within a given string.
PadLeft() PadRight()	These methods are used to pad a string with some character.
Remove() Replace()	Use these methods to receive a copy of a string, with modifications (characters removed or replaced).
ToUpper() ToLower()	Creates a copy of a given sting in uppercase or lowercase.

You should be aware of a few aspects of C# string manipulation. First, although the string data type is a reference type, the equality operators (== and !=) are defined to compare the *values* of string objects, not the memory to which they refer. The addition operator (+) has been overloaded as a shorthand alternative to calling Concat():

```
// == and != are used to compare the values within strings.
// + is used for concatenation.
public static int Main(string[] args)
{
    System.String strObj = "This is a TEST";
    string s = "This is another TEST";

    // Test for equality between the stings.
    if(s = = strObj)
        Console.WriteLine("Same info. . .");
```

```
    else
        Console.WriteLine("Not the same info. . .");

    // Concatenation.
    string newString = s + strObj;
    Console.WriteLine("s + strObj = {0}", newString);

    // System.String also defines a custom indexer to access each
    // character in the string.
    for(int k = 0; k < s.Length; k++)
        Console.WriteLine("Char {0} is {1}", k, s[k]);

    return 0;
}
```

When you run this program, you are able to verify that the two string objects (s and strObj) do not contain the same values, and therefore, the test for equality fails. When you examine the contents of newString, you will see it is indeed "This is another TESTThis is a TEST." Finally, notice that you can access the individual characters of a string using the index operator ([]).

Escape Characters and Verbatim Strings

Like C(++) and Java, C# strings can contain any number of escape characters:

```
// Escape characters (\t, \\, \n, et. al.)
string anotherString;
anotherString = "Every programming book needs \"Hello World\"";
Console.WriteLine("\t" + anotherString);

anotherString = "c:\\CSharpProjects\\Strings\\string.cs";
Console.WriteLine("\t" + anotherString);
```

In case you are a bit rusty with the meaning behind these escape characters, Table 2-12 should refresh your memory.

In addition to traditional escape characters, C# introduces the @-quoted string literal notation. Strings that support the @ prefix are termed "verbatim strings." Using verbatim strings, you are able to bypass the use of cryptic escape characters and define your literals as follows:

```
// The @ string turns off the processing of escape characters.
string finalString = @"\n\tString file: 'C:\CSharpProjects\Strings\string.cs'";
Console.WriteLine(finalString);
```

Table 2-12. String Escape Characters

ESCAPE CHARACTER	MEANING IN LIFE
\'	Inserts a single quote into a string literal.
\"	Inserts a double quote into a string literal.
\\	Inserts a backslash into a string literal. This can be quite helpful when defining file paths.
\a	Triggers a system alert.
\b	Triggers a backspace.
\f	Triggers a form feed.
\n	Inserts a new line.
\r	Inserts a carriage return.
\t	Inserts a horizontal tab into the string literal.
\u	Inserts a Unicode character into the string literal.
\v	Inserts a vertical tab into the string literal.
\0	Represents a NULL character.

The output of the string program can be seen next (Figure 2-23). Notice how the output is prefixed with "\n\t", as these escape characters are not processed in @-quoted strings.

Using System.Text.StringBuilder

One thing to be very aware of with regard to C# strings: The value of a string cannot be modified once established. Like Java, C# strings are immutable. In fact, if you examine the methods of System.String, you notice that the methods that *seem* to internally modify a string, in fact return a modified *copy* of the string. For example, when you send the ToUpper() message to a string object, you are not

```
D:\CSharpBook\Labs\Chapter 2\Strings\bin\Debug\Strings.exe
Not the same info...
s + strObj = This is another TESTThis is a TEST

        Every programming book needs "Hello World"
        c:\CSharpProjects\Strings\string.cs

\n\tString file: 'C:\CSharpProjects\Strings\string.cs'
Press any key to continue
```

Figure 2-23. Fun with System.String

modifying the underlying buffer, but are returned a fresh copy of the buffer in uppercase form:

```
// Make changes to this string? Not really. . .
System.String strFixed = "This is how I began life";
Console.WriteLine(strFixed);

string upperVersion = strFixed.ToUpper();   // Returns an uppercase copy of
strFixed.

Console.WriteLine(strFixed);
Console.WriteLine(upperVersion);
```

It can become slightly annoying to have to work with copies of copies of strings. To help ease the pain, the System.Text namespace defines a class named StringBuilder. This class operates much more like an MFC CString or ATL CComBSTR, in that any modifications you make to the StringBuilder instance affect the underlying buffer (and is thus more efficient):

```
// Play with the StringBuilder class.
using System;
using System.Text;           // StringBuilder lives here!

class StringApp
{
    public static int Main(string[] args)
    {
        // Create a StringBuilder and change the underlying buffer.
        StringBuilder myBuffer = new StringBuilder("I am a buffer");
        myBuffer.Append(" that just got longer. . .");
        Console.WriteLine(myBuffer);
        return 0;
    }
}
```

Beyond appending to your internal buffer, the StringBuilder class allows you to replace and remove characters at will. Once you have established the state of your buffer, call ToString() to store the final result into a System.String data type:

```
// Play with the StringBuilder class.
using System;
using System.Text;           // StringBuilder lives here!

class StringApp
```

```
{
    public static int Main(string[] args)
    {
        // Play with the StringBuilder class some more...
        StringBuilder myBuffer = new StringBuilder("I am a buffer");

        myBuffer.Append(" that just got longer...");
        Console.WriteLine(myBuffer);

        myBuffer.Append("and even longer.");
        Console.WriteLine(myBuffer);

        // Transfer the buffer to an uppercase fixed string.
        string theReallyFinalString = myBuffer.ToString().ToUpper();
        Console.WriteLine(theReallyFinalString);
        return 0;
    }
}
```

As you might assume, StringBuilder contains additional methods and properties beyond those examined here. I leave it to you to drill into more specifics at your leisure.

SOURCE CODE   *The Strings project is located under the Chapter 2 subdirectory.*

C# Enumerations

Often it is convenient to create a set of symbolic names for underlying numerical values. For example, if you are creating an employee payroll system, you may wish to use the constants VP, Manager, Grunt and Contractor rather than raw numerical values such as {0, 1, 2, 3}. Like C(++), C# supports the notion of custom enumerations for this very reason. For example, here is the EmpType enumeration:

```
// A custom enumeration.
enum EmpType
{
    Manager,       //  = 0
    Grunt,         //  = 1
    Contractor,    //  = 2
    VP             //  = 3
}
```

The EmpType enumeration defines four named constants, corresponding to discrete numerical values. In C#, the numbering scheme sets the first element to zero (0) by default, followed by an *n+1* progression. You are free to change this behavior as you see fit, thus:

```
// Begin with 102.
enum EmpType
{
    Manager = 102,
    Grunt,          //  = 103
    Contractor,     //  = 104
    VP              //  = 105
}
```

Enumerations do not necessarily need to follow a sequential ordering. If (for some reason) it made good sense to establish your EmpType as seen here, the compiler continues to be happy:

```
// Elements of an enumeration need not be sequential!
enum EmpType
{
    Manager = 10,
    Grunt = 1,
    Contractor = 100,
    VP = 9
}
```

Under the hood, the storage type used for each item in an enumeration automatically maps to an integer by default, however you are also free to change this to your liking. For example, if you want to set the underlying storage value of EmpType to be a byte rather than an int, you would write the following:

```
// This time, EmpType maps to an underlying byte.
enum EmpType : byte
{
    Manager = 10,
    Grunt = 1,
    Contractor = 100,
    VP = 9
}
```

C# enumerations can be defined in a similar manner for any of the core system types (byte, sbyte, short, ushort, int, uint, long, or ulong).

Once you have established the range and storage type of your enumeration, you can use them in place of so-called "magic numbers.'" Assume you have a class defining a static public function, taking EmpType as the sole parameter:

```csharp
using System;
class EnumClass
{
    public static void AskForBonus(EmpType e)
    {
        switch(e)
        {
        case EmpType.Contractor:
            Console.WriteLine("You already get enough cash. . .");
            break;

        case EmpType.Grunt:
            Console.WriteLine("You have got to be kidding. . .");
            break;

        case EmpType.Manager:
            Console.WriteLine("How about stock options instead?");
            break;

        case EmpType.VP:
            Console.WriteLine("VERY GOOD, Sir!");
            break;

        default: break;
        }
    }

    public static int Main(string[] args)
    {
        // Make a contractor type.
        EmpType fred;
        fred = EmpType.Contractor;

        AskForBonus(fred);

        return 0;
    }
}
```

System.Enum Base Class

The interesting thing about C# enumerations is that they implicitly derive from
System.Enum. This base class defines a number of methods that allow you inter-
rogate and transform a given enumeration. First, System.Enum defines a static
method named GetUnderlyingType(), which resolves (pardon the redundancy)
the underlying data type used to represent this enumeration:

```
// Get underlying type (System.Byte for our current example).
Console.WriteLine(Enum.GetUnderlyingType(typeof(EmpType)));
```

Of greater interest is the ability to extract the named constant behind the
numerical values. How many times have you had to perform transformational
logic between a C++ enumeration and the underlying strings? Using the static
Enum.Format() method, the dirty work has been done on your behalf. In the previous example, an EmpType variable named "fred" was established as a Contractor (which is mapped to the value 100) was established. To extract the corresponding string, just call Enum.Format(), specifying the type of enumeration you wish
to investigate and the desired format flag. In this context "G" marks a string value
(you may also specify the hexadecimal value (*x*) or decimal value (*d*)):

```
// The following pumps the string "You are a Contractor" to the console:
EmpType fred;
fred = EmpType.Contractor;

Console.WriteLine("You are a {0}", Enum.Format(typeof(EmpType), fred, "G"));
```

System.Enum also defines another static method named GetValues(). This
method returns an instance of System.Array. Each item in the array corresponds
to a member of the specified enumeration. Thus:

```
// Get all statistics for the EmpType enumeration.
Array obj = Enum.GetValues(typeof(EmpType));

Console.WriteLine("This enum has {0} members.", obj.Length);

// Now show the string name and associated value.
foreach(EmpType e in obj)
{
    Console.Write("String name: {0}", Enum.Format(typeof(EmpType), e, "G"));
    Console.Write(" ({0})", Enum.Format(typeof(EmpType), e, "D"));
    Console.Write(" hex: {0}\n", Enum.Format(typeof(EmpType), e, "X"));
}
```

The output is seen in Figure 2-24.

```
D:\CSharpBook\Labs\Chapter 2\Enum\bin\Debug...
VERY GOOD, Sir!
System.Byte
You are a VP
This enum has 4 members.
String name: Grunt (1) hex: 01
String name: VP (9) hex: 09
String name: Manager (10) hex: 0A
String name: Contractor (100) hex: 64
Press any key to continue
```

Figure 2-24. Fun with System.Enum

Next, let's explore the IsDefined property. This allows you to determine if a given string name is a member of the current enumeration. For example, assume you wish to know if the value "SalesPerson" is part of the EmpType enumeration:

```
// Does EmpType have a SalePerson value?
if(Enum.IsDefined(typeof(EmpType), "SalesPerson"))
    Console.WriteLine("Yep, we have sales people.");
else
    Console.WriteLine("No, we have no profits...");
```

Last but not least, it is worth pointing out that C# enumerations support the use of various overloaded operators, which test against the assigned values. For example:

```
// Which of these two EmpType variables has the greatest numerical value?
EmpType Joe = EmpType.VP;
EmpType Fran = EmpType.Grunt;

if(Joe < Fran)
    Console.WriteLine("Joe's value is less than Fran's");
else
    Console.WriteLine("Fran's value is less than Joe's");
```

SOURCE CODE *The Enum project is located under the Chapter 2 subdirectory.*

Defining Structures in C#

While you have already encountered structures earlier in this chapter, structures deserve a second look. C# structures behave very much like a custom class. Structures can take constructors (provided they have arguments), can implement interfaces, and can contain numerous members. C# structures do not have an identically named alias in the .NET library (that is, there is no System.Structure class), but are implicitly derived from ValueType. Recall that the role of ValueType is to configure the members of System.Object to work with value based semantics. Here is a simple example:

```
// Our existing enumeration.
enum EmpType : byte
{
    Manager = 10, Grunt = 1,
    Contractor = 100, VP = 9
}

struct EMPLOYEE
{
    public EmpType title;          // One of the fields is our custom enum.
    public string name;
    public short deptID;
}

class StructTester
{
    public static int Main(string[] args)
    {
        // Create and format Fred.
        EMPLOYEE fred;
        fred.deptID = 40;
        fred.name = "Fred";
        fred.title = EmpType.Grunt;
        return 0;
    }
}
```

You created an EMPLOYEE structure on the stack and manipulated each field using the dot operator. To provide a more optimized construction of this type, you are free to define additional custom constructors. Recall that you *cannot* redefine the default constructor for a C# structure, as this is a reserved member. Given this fact, any custom constructors must take some number of parameters:

```
// Structs may define custom constructors (if they have args).
//
struct EMPLOYEE
{
    // Fields.
    public EmpType title;
    public string name;
    public short deptID;

    // Constructor.
    public EMPLOYEE(EmpType et, string n, short d)
    {
        title = et;
        name = n;
        deptID = d;
    }
}
```

With this, you can create a new employee as follows:

```
class StructTester
{
    // Create and format Mary using a ctor.
    public static int Main(string[] args)
    {
        // Must use 'new' to call a custom constructor.
        EMPLOYEE mary = new EMPLOYEE(EmpType.VP, "Mary", 10);
        . . .
        return 0;
    }
}
```

Structures can, of course, be used as parameters to any member function. For example, assume the StructTester class defines a method named DisplayEmpStats():

```
// Extract interesting information from an EMPLOYEE structure.
public void DisplayEmpStats(EMPLOYEE e)
{
    Console.WriteLine("Here is {0}\'s info:", e.name);
    Console.WriteLine("Department ID: {0}", e.deptID);
    Console.WriteLine("Title: {0}", Enum.Format(typeof(EmpType), e.title, "G"));
}
```

Here is a test run of using DisplayEmpStats() (see Figure 2-25):

```
// Let Mary & Fred strut their stuff.
public static int Main(string[] args)
{
    . . .
    StructTester t = new StructTester();
    t.DisplayEmpStats(mary);
    t.DisplayEmpStats(fred);

    return 0;
}
```

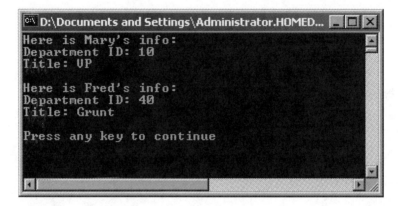

Figure 2-25. Fun with structures

(Un)Boxing Revisited

As mentioned earlier in this chapter, boxing and unboxing provide a convenient way to flip between value types and reference types. Structures in general are a way to achieve the bare bones benefits of object orientation (i.e., encapsulation) while having the efficiency of stack allocated data. To convert a structure to an object reference, simply box the value:

```
// Create and box a new employee.
EMPLOYEE stan = new EMPLOYEE(EmpType.Grunt, "Stan", 10);
object stanInBox = stan;
```

Because stanInBox is a reference-based data type, but still holds the internal values of the original EMPLOYEE data type, you can use stan whenever an object is required, and unbox as needed:

```
// Because we have boxed our value data type into a structure,
// we can unbox and manipulate the contents.
public void UnboxThisEmployee(object o)
{
    // Unbox into EMPLOYEE structure to get at the fields.
    EMPLOYEE temp = (EMPLOYEE)o;
    Console.WriteLine(temp.name + " is alive!");
}
```

Here is the calling logic and output:

```
// Send boxed employee in for processing.
t.UnboxThisEmployee(stanInBox);
```

Recall that the C# compiler automatically box values where appropriate. Therefore, it would be permissible to directly pass stan (the EMPLOYEE type) into UnboxThisEmployee() directly:

```
// Stan is boxed automatically.
t.UnboxThisEmployee(stan);
```

However, because you have defined UnboxThisEmployee() to take an object parameter, you have no choice but to unbox this reference to access the fields of the EMPLOYEE structure.

SOURCE CODE   *The Structures project is located under the Chapter 2 subdirectory.*

Defining Custom Namespaces

To this point, you have been building small test programs leveraging existing namespaces in the .NET universe. When you build real-life applications, it can be very helpful to group your related types into custom namespaces. In C#, this is accomplished using the "namespace" keyword.

Assume you are developing a collection of geometric classes named Square, Circle, and Hexagon. Given their similarities you would like to group them all together into a shared custom namespace. You have two basic approaches. First, you may choose to define each class within a single file (shapeslib.cs) as follows:

```
// shapeslib.cs
namespace MyShapes
```

```
{
    using System;

    // Circle class.
    public class Circle{  // Interesting methods... }

    // Hexagon class.
    public class Hexagon{ // More interesting methods... }

    // Square class.
    public class Square{ // Even more interesting methods... }
}
```

Notice how the MyShapes namespace acts as the conceptual "container" of each type. Alternatively, you can split a single namespace into multiple C# files. To do so, simply wrap the given class definitions in the same namespace:

```
// circle.cs
namespace MyShapes
{
    using System;

    // Circle class.
    class Circle{  // Interesting methods... }
}


// hexagon.cs
namespace MyShapes
{
    using System;

    // Hexagon class.
    class Hexagon{ // More interesting methods... }
}

// square.cs
namespace MyShapes
{
    using System;

    // Square class.
    class Square{ // Even more interesting methods... }
}
```

Now, when another application you are building wishes to use these fine objects from within its namespace, simply use the "using" keyword:

```
// Make use of objects defined in another namespace
namespace MyApp
{
using System;
using MyShapes;

class ShapeTester
{
    public static void Main()
    {
        // All defined in the MyShapes namespace.
        Hexagon h = new Hexagon();
        Circle c = new Circle();
        Square s = new Square();
    }
}
}
```

Resolving Name Clashes Across Namespaces

A namespace can also be used to avoid nasty name clashes across multiple namespaces. Assume the ShapeTester class wishes to make use of a new namespace termed My3DShapes, which defines three additional classes capable of rendering a shape in stunning 3D:

```
// Another shapes namespace. . .
namespace My3DShapes
{
    using System;

    // 3D Circle class.
    class Circle{ }

    // 3D Hexagon class
    class Hexagon{ }

    // 3D Square class
    class Square{ }
}
```

If you update ShapesTester as was done here, you are issued a number of compile-time errors, because both namespaces define identically named types:

```
// Ambiguities abound!
namespace MyApp
{
using System;
using MyShapes;
using My3DShapes;

class ShapeTester
    {
        public static void Main()
        {
            // Which namespace do I reference?
            Hexagon h = new Hexagon();
            Circle c = new Circle();
            Square s = new Square();
        }
    }
}
```

As one would hope, these errors are caught at compile time (Figure 2-26).

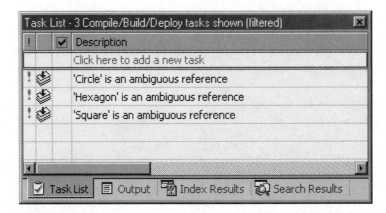

Figure 2-26. Ambiguous reference

Resolving the ambiguity is simply a matter of using "fully qualified names":

```
// We have now resolved the ambiguity.
public static void Main()
```

```
{
    My3DShapes.Hexagon h = new My3DShapes.Hexagon();
    My3DShapes.Circle c = new My3DShapes.Circle();
    MyShapes.Square s = new MyShapes.Square();
}
```

Defining Namespace Aliases

An alternative approach to resolving namespace ambiguity is accomplished through the use of aliases. For example:

```
namespace MyApp
{
using System;
using MyShapes;
using My3DShapes;

// Make an alias to a class defined in another namespace.
using The3DHexagon = My3DShapes.Hexagon;

class ShapeTester
{
    public static void Main()
    {
        My3DShapes.Hexagon h = new My3DShapes.Hexagon();
        My3DShapes.Circle c = new My3DShapes.Circle();
        MyShapes.Square s = new MyShapes.Square();

        // Create a 3D hex using a defined alias:
        The3DHexagon h2 = new The3DHexagon();
    }
}
}
```

Nested Namespaces

The final point of interest with regard to namespaces, is the fact that you are free to nest namespaces within other namespaces. The .NET base class libraries do so in numerous places to provide an even deeper level of type organization. For example, if you wish to create a higher level namespace that contained the existing My3DShapes namespace, you could update our code as follows:

```
// The Chapter2Types.My3DShapes namespace contains 3 classes.
namespace Chapter2Types
{
    namespace My3DShapes
    {
        using System;

        // 3D Circle class.
        class Circle{ }

        // 3D Hexagon class
        class Hexagon{ }

        // 3D Square class
        class Square{ }
    }
}
```

SOURCE CODE   *The Namespaces project is located under the Chapter 2 sub-directory.*

Summary

This chapter has exposed you to the core atoms of the C# programming language. The focus was to examine the constructs that will be commonplace in any application you may be interested in building. First, every C# program must have a class defining a static Main() method, which serves as the program's entry point. Within the scope of Main(), you typically create any number of objects, which work together to breathe life into your application.

As you have seen, all intrinsic C# data types alias a corresponding type in the System namespace. Each system type has a number of methods that provide a programmatic manner to obtain the range of the type.

You also peeked inside a number of classes that place an OO spin on common programming constructs, such as arrays, strings, and enumerations, and took a tour of their functionality. This chapter also illustrated the concept of boxing and unboxing. This simple mechanism allows you to easily move between value-based and reference-based data types. Finally, the chapter ends by explaining how to build your own custom namespaces, and why you might want to do so.

CHAPTER 3

Object-Oriented Programming with C#

IN THE PREVIOUS CHAPTER YOU were introduced to a number of core constructs of the C# language. Here, you will spend your time digging deeper into the details of object-based development. I begin by reviewing the famed "pillars of OOP," and then examine exactly how C# contends with the notions of encapsulation, inheritance, and polymorphism. This will equip you with the knowledge you need in order to build custom class hierarchies using C#.

During this process, you examine some new constructs such as establishing type (rather than member) level visibility, building custom properties, and designing "sealed" classes. You also gain an understanding of the use of structured exception handling to contend with runtime errors. This chapter wraps up with an examination of the "managed heap," including how to programmatically interact with the .NET garbage collector using the static methods defined by System.GC.

Formal Definition of the C# Class

If you have been "doing objects" in another programming language, you are no doubt aware of the roll of class definitions. Formally, a class is nothing more than a custom UDT (user defined type) that is composed of data (often called attributes or properties) and functions that act on this data (often called methods in OO speak). The power of object-based languages is that by grouping data and functionality in a single UDT, you are able to model your software types after real-world entities.

For example, assume we are interested in modeling a generic employee. At minimum, you may wish to build a class that maintains the name, current pay, and employee ID for each worker. In addition, the Employee class defines one method named GiveBonus(), which increases an individual's current pay by some amount, and another named DisplayStats(), which prints out the relevant statistics for this individual (Figure 3-1).

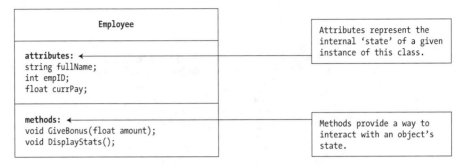

Figure 3-1. A simple class definition

As you recall from Chapter 2, C# classes can define any number of constructors. These special class methods provide a simple way for an object user to create an instance of a given class with an initial look and feel. As you know, every C# class is endowed with a freebee default constructor. The role of the default constructor is to ensure that all state data is set to an initial safe value. In addition to the default constructor, you are also free to supply as many custom constructors as you feel are necessary. To get the ball rolling, here is our first crack at the Employee class:

```
// The initial class definition.
class Employee
{
    // Private state data.
    private string fullName;
    private int empID;
    private float currPay;

    // Constructors.
    public Employee(){}
    public Employee(string fullName, int empID, float currPay)
    {
        this.fullName = fullName;
        this.empID = empID;
        this.currPay = currPay;
    }

    // Bump the pay for this employee.
    public void GiveBonus(float amount)
    { currPay += amount; }
```

```
    // Show current state of this object.
    public virtual void DisplayStats()
    {
        Console.WriteLine("Name: {0}", fullName);
        Console.WriteLine("Pay: {0}", currPay);
        Console.WriteLine("ID: {0}", empID);
        Console.WriteLine("SSN: {0}", ssn);
    }
}
```

Notice the empty implementation of the default constructor:

```
class Employee
{
    // All member variables assigned to default values automatically.
    public Employee(){}
. . .
}
```

Like C++, if you choose to include custom constructors in a class definition, the default constructor is *silently removed*. Therefore, if you wish to allow the object user to create an instance of your class such as:

```
// Calls the default constructor.
Employee e = new Employee();
```

you need to explicitly redefine the default constructor for your class. If you forget to do so, you generate compile time errors. Triggering the logic behind a constructor is self-explanatory:

```
// Call some custom ctors (two approaches)
public static void Main()
{
    Employee e = new Employee("Joe", 80, 30000);
    e.GiveBonus(200);

    Employee e2;
    e2 = new Employee("Beth", 81, 50000);
    e2.GiveBonus(1000);
    e2.DisplayStats();
}
```

SOURCE CODE   *The Employees project that we examine during the course of this chapter is included under the Chapter 3 subdirectory.*

Self-Reference in C#

In the implementation of our custom constructor, you made use of the C# "this" keyword:

```
// Like C++ and Java, C# also supplies a 'this' keyword.
public Employee(string fullName, int empID, float currPay)
{
    this.fullName = fullName;
    this.empID = empID;
    this.currPay = currPay;
}
```

This particular C# keyword is used whenever you wish to make reference to the current object instance. Visual Basic programmers can equate the C# "this" keyword with the VB "Me" keyword. C++ and Java programmers should feel right at home, given that these languages have an identically named "this" keyword used for the same purpose.

The reason you made use of "this" in your custom constructor was to avoid clashes between the parameter names and names of our internal state variables. Of course, another approach would be to change the names for each parameter and avoid the name clash altogether (but I am sure you get the point). Also, be aware that static member functions cannot access the "this" pointer. It should make perfect sense, as static member functions operate on the class (not object) level.

Forwarding Constructor Calls Using "this"

Another use of the C# "this" keyword may also be used to force one constructor to call another. Consider the following example:

```
class Employee
{
    public Employee(string fullName, int empID, float currPay)
    {
        this.fullName = fullName;
        this.empID = empID;
        this.currPay = currPay;
    }
```

```
// If the user calls this ctor, forward to the 3-arg version.
public Employee(string fullName)
        : this(fullName, IDGenerator.GetNewEmpID(), 0.0F) {}
. . .
}
```

First, notice that this iteration of the Employee class defines two custom constructors, the second of which requires a single parameter (the individual's name). However, to fully construct a new Employee, you want to ensure you have a proper Employee ID and rate of pay. Assume you have a custom class (IDGenerator) that defines a static method named GetNewEmpID() for this very purpose. Once you gather the correct set of start-up parameters, you forward the creation request to the alternate three-argument constructor. If you did not forward the call, you would need to add redundant code to each constructor:

```
// currPay automatically set to 0.0F. . .
public Employee(string fullName)
{
    this.fullName = fullName;
    this.empID = IDGenerator.GetNewEmpID();
}
```

Defining the Default Public Interface

Once you have established a class' internal state data and constructor set, your next step is to flesh out the details of the *default public interface* to the class. The term refers to the set of public members that is accessible from an object instance. From an object user's point of view, the default public interface is the set of items that are accessible using the C# dot operator. From the class builder's point of view, the default public interface is any item declared in a class using the public keyword. In C#, the default interface of a class may be populated by any of the following members:

- Methods: Named units of work that model some behavior of a class.

- Properties: Accessor and mutator functions in disguise.

- Fields: Public data (although this is typically a bad idea, C# supports them).

As you will see in Chapter 5, the default public interface of a class may also be configured to support custom events. For the time being, let's concentrate on the use of properties, methods, and field data.

Specifying Type Level Visibility: Public and Internal Types

Before we get too far along in our employee example, you must understand how to establish visibility levels for your custom types. In the previous chapter, you were introduced to the following class definition:

```
class HelloClass
{
    // Any number of methods with any number of parameters. . .
    // Default and/or custom constructors. . .
    // If this is the program's entry point, a static Main() method.
}
```

Recall that each member defined by a class must establish its level of visibility using the public, private, protected, or internal keywords. In the same vein, C# classes also need to specify their level of visibility. The distinction is that *method visibility* is used to constrain which members can be accessed from a given object instance, and *class visibility* is used to establish which parts of the system can create the types themselves.

A C# class can be marked by one of two visibility keywords: Public or internal. Public classes may be created by any other objects within the same binary as well as by other binaries (e.g., another assembly). Therefore, HelloClass could be redefined as follows:

```
// We are now creatable by members outside this assembly.
public class HelloClass
{
    // Any number of methods with any number of parameters. . .
    // Default or custom constructors. . .
    // If this is the program's entry point, a static Main() method.
}
```

By default, if you do not explicitly mark the visibility level of a class, it is implicitly set to "internal." Internal classes can only be created by objects living within the same assembly, and are not accessible from outside the assembly's bounds. As you might suspect, internal items can be viewed as "helper types" used by an assembly's types to help the internal classes get their work done:

```
// Internal classes can only be used by other types within the same assembly.
internal class HelloClassHelper
{
    . . .
}
```

Classes are not the only UDT that can accept a visibility attribute. As you recall, a type is simply a generic term used to refer to classes, structures, enumerations, interfaces, and delegates. Any .NET type can be assigned public or internal visibility. For example:

```
// Any type may be assigned public or internal visibility.
namespace HelloClass
{
using System;
internal struct X                // Cannot be used outside this assembly.
{
    private int myX;
    public int GetMyX() { return myX; } public X(int x){ myX = x; }
}
internal enum Letters        // Cannot be used outside this assembly.
{
    a = 0, b = 1, c = 2
}

public class HelloClass        // May be used outside this assembly.
{
    public static int Main(string[] args)
    {
        X theX = new X(26);
        Console.WriteLine(theX.GetMyX() + "\n" + Letters.b.ToString());
        return 0;
    }
}
}
```

Logically, the previously defined types can be envisioned as shown in Figure 3-2.

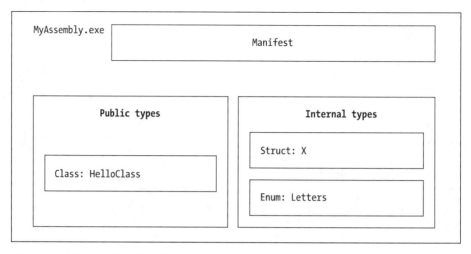

Figure 3-2. Internal and public types

Chapter 6 drills into the specifics of composing .NET binaries. Until then, just understand that all of your types may be defined as public (accessible by the outside world) or internal (not accessible by the outside world).

Pillars of OOP

C# is a newcomer to the world of object-oriented languages (OOLs). Java, C++, Object Pascal, and (to some extent) Visual Basic 6.0 are but a small sample of the popularity of the object paradigm. Regardless of exactly when a given OOL came onto existence, all object-based languages contend with three core principals of object-oriented programming, often called the famed "pillars of OOP."

- *Encapsulation:* How well does this language hide an object's internal implementation?

- *Inheritance:* How does this language promote code reuse?

- *Polymorphism:* How does this language let me treat related objects in a similar way?

Before digging into the syntactic details of each pillar, it is important you understand the basic role of each. Therefore, here is a brisk high-level rundown, just to clear off any cobwebs you may have acquired between project deadlines.

Encapsulation Services

The first pillar of OOP is called *encapsulation*. This trait boils down to the language's ability to hide unnecessary implementation details from the object user. For example, assume you have created a class named DBReader (database reader), which has two primary methods: Open() and Close():

```
// The database reader encapsulates the details of opening and closing a
database. . .
DBReader f = new DBReader();
f.Open(@"C:\foo.mdf");
    // Do something with database. . .
f.Close();
```

The fictitious DBReader class has encapsulated the inner details of locating, loading, manipulating, and closing the data file. Object users love encapsulation, as this pillar of OOP keeps programming tasks simpler. There is no need to worry about the numerous lines of code that are working behind the scenes to carry out the work of the DBReader class. All you do is create an instance and send the appropriate messages (e.g., "open the file named foo.mdf").

Closely related to the notion of encapsulating programming logic is the idea of data hiding. As you know, an object's state data should ideally be specified as private. In this way, the outside world must ask politely in order to change or obtain the underlying value. This is a good thing, as publicly declared data points can easily become corrupted (hopefully by accident rather than intent!)

Inheritance: The "is-a" and "has-a" Relationships

The next pillar of OOP, inheritance, boils down to the languages' ability to allow you to build new class definitions based on existing class definitions. In essence, inheritance allows you to extend the behavior of a base (parent) class by inheriting core functionality into a subclass (also called a 'child class'). Figure 3-3 shows a simple example.

As you are aware, Object is always the top-most node in any .NET hierarchy. The Shape class extends Object. You can assume that Shape defines some number of properties, fields, methods, and events that are common to all shapes. The Hexagon class extends Shape, and inherits the core functionality defined by Shape and Object, as well as defines additional hexagon related details of its own (whatever those may be).

You can read this diagram as "A hexagon is-a shape that is-a object." When you have classes related by this form of inheritance, you establish "is-a" relationships between types. The is-a relationship is often termed *classical inheritance*.

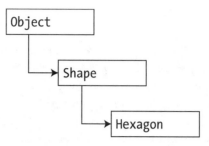

Figure 3-3. The "is-a" relationship

There is another form of code reuse in the world of OOP: The containment/delegation model (also known as the "has-a" relationship). This form of reuse is not used to establish base/subclass relationships. Rather a given class can contain another class and expose part or all of its functionality to the outside world.

For example, if you are modeling an automobile, you might wish to express the idea that a car "has-a" radio. It would be illogical to attempt to derive the Car class from a Radio, or visa versa (a Car "is-a" Radio? I think not!). Rather, you have two independent classes working together, where the *outer* (or containing) class creates and exposes the *inner* (or contained) class' functionality (Figure 3-4).

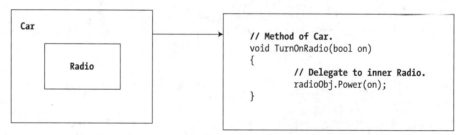

Figure 3-4. The "has-a" relationship

Here, the outer object (Car) is responsible for creating the inner (Radio) object. If the Car wishes to make the Radio's behavior accessible from a Car instance, it must extend its own public interface. Notice that the object user has no clue that the Car class is making use of an inner object.

```
// The inner Radio is encapsulated by the outer Car class.
Car viper = new Car();
viper.TurnOnRadio(false);        // Delegates request to inner Radio object.
```

Polymorphism: Classical and Ad Hoc

The final pillar of OOP is *polymorphism.* This trait captures a language's ability to treat related objects the same way. Like inheritance, polymorphism falls under two camps: Classical and ad hoc. Classical polymorphism can only take place in languages that also support classical inheritance. If this is the case (as it is in C#), it becomes possible for a base class to define a set of members that can be *overridden* by a subclass. When subclasses override the behavior defined by a base class, they are essentially redefining how they respond to the same message.

To illustrate classical polymorphism, let's revisit the shapes hierarchy. Assume that the Shape class has defined a function named Draw(), taking no parameters and returning nothing. Given the fact that every shape needs to render itself in a unique manner, subclasses (such as Hexagon and Circle) are free to reinterpret this method to their own liking (Figure 3-5).

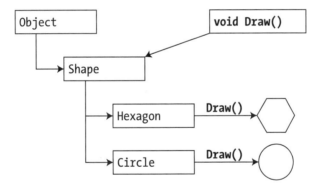

Figure 3-5. Classical polymorphism

Classical polymorphism allows a base class to enforce a given behavior on all descendents. From Figure 3-5, you can assume that any object derived from the Shape class has the ability to be rendered. This is a great boon to any language because you are able to avoid creating redundant methods to perform a similar operation (e.g., DrawCircle(), DrawRectangle(), DrawHexagon(), and so forth).

Next, you have *ad hoc polymorphism*. This flavor of polymorphism allows objects that are *not* related by classical inheritance to be treated in a similar manner, provided that every object has a method of the exact same signature (that is, method name, parameter list, and return type). Languages that support ad hoc polymorphism employ a technique called *late binding* to discover at runtime the underlying type of a given object. Based on this discovery, the correct method is invoked. As an illustration, first ponder Figure 3-6.

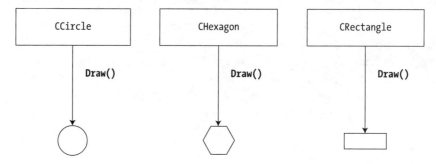

Figure 3-6. Ad hoc polymorphism

Notice how there is no common base class between the CCircle, Chexagon, and CRectangle classes. However, each class supports an identical Draw() method. To illustrate what this boils down to syntactically, consider the following Visual Basic 6.0 code. Until the advent of VB.NET, Visual Basic did not support classical polymorphism (or classical inheritance for that matter), forcing developers to make due with the following ad hoc functionality:

```
' Visual Basic 6.0 code below!
' First create an array of Object data types, setting each to an object
reference.
Dim objArr(3) as Object
Set objArr(0) = New CCircle
Set objArr(1) = New CHexagon
Set objArr(2) = New CCircle
Set objArr(3) = New CRectangle

' Now loop over the array, asking each object to render itself.
Dim i as Integer
For i = 0 to 3
    objArr(i).Draw       ' Late binding. . .
Next i
```

In this code block, you begin by creating an array of generic Object data types (which is an intrinsic Visual Basic 6.0 type capable of holding any object reference, and has nothing to do with System.Object). As you iterate over the array at runtime, each shape is asked to render itself. Again, the key difference is that you have no common base class that contains a default implementation of the Draw() method.

To wrap up this review of the pillars of OOP, recall that every object-oriented language needs to address how it contends with encapsulation, polymorphism, and inheritance. As you may already suspect, C# completely supports each pillar of object technology, including both flavors of inheritance (is-a and has-a) as well as classical and ad hoc polymorphism. Now that you have the theory in your minds, the bulk of this chapter explores the exact C# syntax that represents each trait.

The First Pillar: C#'s Encapsulation Services

The concept of encapsulation revolves around the notion that an object's internal data should not be directly accessible from an object instance. Rather, if an object user wishes to alter the state of an object, it does so indirectly using accessor and mutator methods. In C#, encapsulation is enforced at the syntactic level using the public, private, and protected keywords. To illustrate, assume you have created the following class definition:

```csharp
// A class with a single field.
public class Book
{
    public int numberOfPages;
...
}
```

When a class defines points of public data, we term these items *fields*. The problem with field data is that the items have no ability to "understand" if the current value to which they are assigned is valid with regard to the current business rules of the system. As you know, the upper range of a C# integer is quite large (2,147,483,647). Therefore, the compiler allows the following assignment:

```csharp
// Humm. . .
public static void Main()
{
    Book miniNovel = new Book();
    miniNovel.numberOfPages = 30000000;
}
```

Although we have not overflowed the boundaries of an integer data type, it should be clear that a mini-novel with a page count of 30,000,000 pages is a bit unreasonable. As you can see, fields do not provide a way to trap logical upper (or lower) limits. If your current system has a business rule that states a book must be between 1 and 2000 pages, you are at a loss to enforce this programmatically. Because of this, public fields typically have no place in a production level class definition.

Encapsulation provides a way to preserve the integrity of state data. Rather than defining public fields (which can easily foster data corruption), you should get in the habit of defining *private data*, which are indirectly manipulated using one of two main techniques:

- Define a pair of traditional accessor and mutator methods.

- Define a named property.

Additionally, C# supports a special keyword, "readonly," which also delivers a form of data protection. Whichever technique you choose, the point is that a well-encapsulated class should hide the details of how it operates from the prying eyes of the outside world. This is often termed "black box" programming. The beauty of this approach is that an object is free to change how a given method is implemented under the hood, without breaking any existing code making use of it, provided that the signature of the method remains constant.

Enforcing Encapsulation Using Traditional Accessors and Mutators

Let's return to your existing Employee class. If you want the outside world to interact with your private string representing a worker's full name, tradition dictates defining an *accessor* (get method) and *mutator* (set method). For example:

```
// Traditional accessor and mutator for a point of private data.
public class Employee
{
    private string fullName;
...
    // Accessor.
    public string GetFullName() { return fullName; }

    // Mutator.
    public void SetFullName(string n)
```

```
    {
        // Remove any illegal characters (!, @, #, $, %),
        // check maximum length or case before making assignment.
        fullName = n;
    }
}
```

This technique requires two uniquely named methods to operate on a single data point. The calling logic is as follows:

```
// Accessor/mutator usage.
public static int Main(string[] args)
{
    Employee p = new Employee();
    p.SetFullName("Fred");
    Console.WriteLine("Employee is named: " + p.GetFullName());

    // Error! Can't access private data from an object instance.
    // p.fullName;
    return 0;
}
```

Another Form of Encapsulation: Class Properties

In addition to traditional accessor and mutator methods, classes (as well as structures and interfaces) can also support *properties*. Visual Basic and COM programmers have long used properties to simulate publicly accessible points of data (that is, fields). Under the hood however, properties resolve to a pair of hidden internal methods. Rather than requiring the user to call two discrete methods to get and set the state data, the user is able to call what appears to be a single named field:

```
// Representing a person's first name as a property.
public static int Main(string[] args)
{
    Employee p = new Employee();

    // Set the value.
    p.EmpID = 81;

    // Get the value.
    Console.WriteLine("Person ID is: {0}", p.EmpID);
    return 0;
}
```

Properties always map to "real" accessor and mutator methods. Therefore, as a Class designer you are able to perform any internal logic necessary before making the value assignment (e.g., uppercase the value, scrub the value for illegal characters, check the bounds of a numerical value, and so on). Here is the C# syntax behind the EmpID property:

```
// Custom property for the EmpID data point.
public class Employee
{
. . .
    private int empID;

    // Property for the empID.
    public int EmpID
    {
        get {return empID;}
        set
        {
            // You are still free to investigate (and possibly transform)
            // the incoming value before making an assignment.
            empID = value;
        }
    }
}
```

A C# property is composed using a get block (accessor) and set block (mutator). The "value" keyword represents the right-hand side of the assignment. As all things in C#, "value" is also an object. However, the underlying type of the object depends on which sort of data it represents. In our example, the EmpID property is operating on a private integer, which, as you recall, maps to an Int32:

```
// Calls set, value = 81.
// 81 is an instance of Int32, so 'value' is an Int32.
e3.EmpID = 81;
```

To illustrate, assume we have updated our set logic as follows:

```
// Property for the empID.
public int EmpID
{
    get {return empID;}
    set
```

```
    {
        // Just to prove the point.
        Console.WriteLine("value is an instance of: {0}", value.GetType());

        Console.WriteLine("value as string: {0}", value.ToString());

        empID = value;
    }
}
```

You would see the output shown in Figure 3-7.

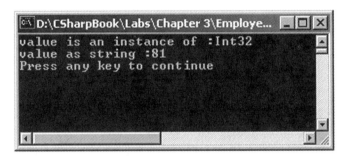

Figure 3-7. The value of "value" when EmpID = 81

Do be aware that you may only access the "value" object within the scope of a property's set block. Any attempt to do otherwise results in a compiler error.

Finally, understand that properties (as opposed to traditional accessors and mutators) make your types easier to manipulate. For example, assume that the Employee type had an internal private member variable representing the age of the employee. On his or her birthday, you wish to increment the age by one. Using traditional accessor and mutator methods, you would need to write:

```
Employee joe = new Employee();
joe.SetAge( joe.GetAge() + 1 );
```

However using type properties, you are able to write

```
Employee joe = new Employee();
joe.Age++;
```

Internal Representation of C# Properties

Many programmers tend to design accessor and mutator methods using "get_"
and "set_" prefixes (e.g., get_Name() and set_Name()). This naming convention
itself is not problematic. However, it is important to understand that under the
hood, a C# property is internally represented using these same prefixes. For example, if you open up the Employees.exe assembly using ILDasm.exe you see that
each property actually resolves to two discrete (and hidden) methods (Figure 3-8).

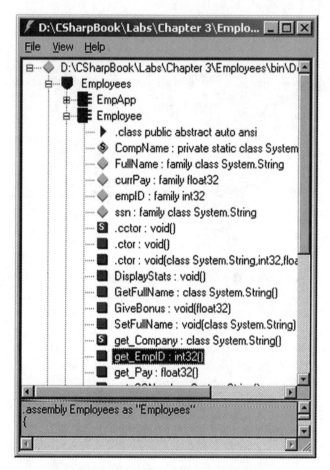

Figure 3-8. Properties map to hidden get_ and set_ methods

Given this, realize that if you were to define a class as such, you generate
compiler errors:

```
// Remember, a C# property really maps to a get_/set_ pair.
public class Employee
```

```
{
. . .
    // Another property.
    public string SSN
    {
        get { return ssn; }      // Maps to get_SSN().
        set { ssn = value;}      // Maps to set_SSN().
    }
    // ERROR! Already defined by SSN property!
    public string get_SSN() { return ssn;}
    public void set_SSN(string val) { ssn = val;}
}
```

Finally, understand that the reverse of this situation is *not true*. Meaning, if you define two methods named get_X() and set_X() in a given class, you cannot write syntax that references a property named X:

```
// Assume Foo has two methods named get_X() and set_X() but not a
// literal C# property definition.
Foo f = new Foo();
f.X = 100;                       // Error! ! Must be defined as C# property,
not set_X().
Console.WriteLine(f.X);      // Error! ! Must also be a C# property, not get_X().
```

Read Only, Write Only, and Static Properties

To wrap up our investigation of C# properties, there are a few loose ends to contend with. First, recall that EmpID was established as a read/write property. When building custom properties, you may wish to configure a read-only property. To do so, simply build a property without a corresponding set block. Likewise, if you wish to have a write-only property, omit the get block. To illustrate, here is a read-only property for our Employee class:

```
public class Employee
{
. . .
    // Assume this is assigned in the class constructor. . .
    private string ssn;

    // A read only property.
    public string SSN { get { return ssn; } }
    . . .
}
```

C# also supports *static properties.* Recall that static types are bound to a given class, not an instance (object) of that class. For example, assume that the Employee type defines a point of static data to represent the name of the organization employing these workers. We may define a static (e.g., class level) property as follows:

```
// Static properties must operate on static data!
public class Employee
{
    private static string CompName;
    public static string Company
    {
        get { return CompName; }
        set { CompName = value;}
    }
    . . .
}
```

Static properties are manipulated in the same manner as static methods, as seen next:

```
// Set and get the name of the company employee these people. . .
public static int Main(string[] args)
{
    Employee.Company = "Intertech, Inc";
    Console.WriteLine("These folks work at {0}", Employee.Company);
    . . .
}
```

Static Constructors

As an interesting sidebar, consider the use of static constructors. This may seem strange given that the "constructor" is understood as a method called on a new *object* instantiation. Nevertheless, C# supports the use of static constructors that serve no other purpose than to assign initial values to static data. Syntactically, static constructors are odd in that they *cannot* take a visibility modifier (but must take the static keyword). To illustrate, if you wished to ensure that the name of the static CompName field was always assigned to "Intertech, Inc" on creation, you would write:

```
// Static constructors are used to initialize static data.
public class Employee
```

```
{
. . .
    private static string CompName;

    static Employee()
    {
        CompName = "Intertech, Inc";
    }
. . .
}
```

If you were to invoke the Employee.Company property, there is no need to assign an initial value within the Main() method, as the static constructor does so automatically:

```
// Automatically set to "Intertech, Inc" via the static constructor.
public static int Main(string[] args)
{
. . .
    Console.WriteLine("These folks work at {0}", Employee.Company);
}
```

To wrap up our examination of C# properties, understand that these syntactic entities are used for the same purpose as a classical accessor/mutator pair. The benefit of properties is that the users of your objects are able to manipulate the internal data point using a single named item.

Pseudo-Encapsulation: Creating Read-Only Fields

Closely related to read-only properties is the notion of read-only *fields*. As you know, a field is a point of public data. Typically speaking, public data is a bad thing because the object user has a fairly good chance of making an illogical assignment. Read-only fields offer data preservation that is established using the "readonly" keyword:

```
public class Employee
{
. . .
    // Read only field (set in the ctors).
    public readonly    string    SSNField;
}
```

As you can guess, any attempt to make assignments to a field marked "read-only" results in a compiler error.

Static Read-Only Fields

Static read only fields are also permissible. This can be helpful if you wish to create a number of constant values bound to a given class. In this light, readonly seems to be a close cousin to the const keyword. The difference is that the value assigned to const must be resolved at compile time. The value of readonly static fields, however, may be computed at *runtime*.

For example, assume a type named Car that needs to establish a set of tires at runtime. You can create a new class (Tire) consisting of a number of static read-only fields:

```
// The Tire class has a number of readonly fields.
public class Tire
{
    public static readonly        Tire GoodStone = new Tire(90);
    public static readonly        Tire FireYear = new Tire(100);
    public static readonly        Tire ReadyLyne= new Tire(43);
    public static readonly        Tire Blimpy = new Tire(83);

    private int manufactureID;

    public int MakeID
    {
        get { return manufactureID; }
    }

    public Tire (int ID)
    {
        manufactureID = ID;
    }
}
```

Here is an example of working with these new types:

```
// Make use of a dynamically created readonly field.
public class Car
{
    // What sort of tires do I have?
    public Tire tireType = Tire.Blimpy;            // Returns a new Tire.
```

```
. . .
}

public class CarApp
{
    public static int Main(string[] args)
    {
        Car c = new Car();

        // Prints out "Manufacture ID of tires: 83"
        Console.WriteLine("Manufacture ID of tires: {0}", c.tireType.MakeID);
        return 0;
    }
}
```

The Second Pillar: C#'s Inheritance Support

Now that you understand how to create a single well-encapsulated class, it is time to turn your attention to building a family of related classes. As mentioned, inheritance is the aspect of OOP that facilitates code reuse. Inheritance comes in two flavors: Classical inheritance (the is-a relationship) and the containment/delegation model (the has-a relationship). Let's begin by examining the classical is-a model.

When you establish is-a relationships between classes, you are building a dependency between types. The basic idea behind classical inheritance is that new classes may leverage (and extend) the functionality of other classes. To illustrate, assume that you wish to define two additional classes to model sales people and managers. The hierarchy looks something like what you see in Figure 3-9.

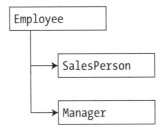

Figure 3-9. The employee hierarchy

As illustrated in Figure 3-9, you can see that a SalesPerson is-a Employee (as is a Manager—at least in a perfect world). In the classical inheritance model, base classes (such as Employee) are used to define general characteristics that are common to all descendents. Subclasses (such as SalesPerson and Manager) extend this general functionality while adding more specific behaviors to the class.

In C#, extending a class is accomplished using the colon operator (:). Therefore, you can syntactically model these relationships as follows:

```
// Add two new subclasses to the Employees namespace.
namespace Employees
{
public class Manager : Employee
{
    // Managers need to know their number of stock options.
    private ulong numberOfOptions;
    public ulong NumbOpts
    {
        get {return numberOfOptions;}
        set {numberOfOptions = value; }
    }
}

public class SalesPerson : Employee
{
    // Sales people need to know their number of sales.
    private int numberOfSales;
    public int NumbSales
    {
        get {return numberOfSales;}
        set { numberOfSales = value; }
    }
}
}
```

Notice how each subclass has extended the base class behavior by adding a custom property that operates on an underlying private point of data. Because you have established an is-a relationship, SalesPerson and Manager have automatically inherited all public members of the Employee base class. To illustrate:

```
// Create a subclass and access base class functionality.
public static int Main(string[] args)
```

```
{
    // Make a sales person.
    SalesPerson stan = new SalesPerson();

    // These members are inherited from the Employee base class.
    stan.EmpID = 100;
    stan.SetFullName("Stan the Man");

    // This is defined by the SalesPerson subclass.
    stan.NumbSales = 42;

    return 0;
}
```

Needless to say, a child class cannot directly access private members defined by its parent class. Also, when the object user creates an instance of a subclass, encapsulation of private data is ensured:

```
// Error! ! Instance of child class cannot allow access to a base class' private
// data!
SalesPerson stan = new SalesPerson();
stan.currPay;
```

Controlling Base Class Creation

Currently, SalesPerson and Manager can only be created using the default class constructor. With this in mind, consider the following line of code:

```
// Create a subclass using a custom constructor.
Manager chucky = new Manager("Chucky", 92, 100000, "333-23-2322", 9000);
```

Here, you are creating an instance of the Manager class using a custom constructor. If you look at the argument list, you can clearly see that most of these parameters should be stored in the member variables defined by the Employee base class. To do so, you could write the following logic:

```
// If you do not say otherwise, a subclass constructor automatically calls the
// default constructor of its base class.
public Manager(string fullName, int empID,
                      float currPay, string ssn, ulong numbOfOpts)
{
    // This point of data belongs with us!
    numberOfOptions = numbOfOpts;
```

```
    // Assigning values to base class data using inherited base class members.
    EmpID = empID;
    SetFullName(fullName);
    SSN = ssn;
    Pay = currPay;
}
```

Although this is technically permissible, it is not optimal. First, like C++, the base class constructor (in this case the default constructor) is called automatically *before* the logic of the custom Manager constructor is executed. After this point, the current implementation accesses four public members of the employee base class to establish its state. Thus, you have really made six hits during the creation of this derived object!

To help optimize the creation of a derived class, implement your subclass constructors to explicitly call an appropriate custom base class constructor, rather than the default. In this way, you are able to call an appropriate constructor to initialize state data, and increase the efficiency of an object's creation in the process. Let's retrofit the custom constructor to do this very thing:

```
// This time, use the C# 'base' keyword to call a custom constructor on the base
// class.
public Manager(string fullName, int empID, float currPay,
                        string ssn, ulong numbOfOpts)
                    : base(fullName, empID, currPay, ssn)
{
    numberOfOptions = numbOfOpts;
}
```

Here, our constructor has been adorned with an odd bit of syntax. Directly after the closing parenthesis of the constructor's argument list there is a single colon followed by the C# "base" keyword. In this situation, you are explicitly calling the four-argument constructor defined by Employee and saving yourself unnecessary calls during the creation of the child class. The SalesPerson constructor looks almost identical:

```
// As a general rule, all subclasses should explicitly call an appropriate
// base class constructor.
public SalesPerson(string fullName, int empID,
                        float currPay, string ssn, int numbOfSales)
                    : base(fullName, empID, currPay, ssn)
{
    this.numberOfSales = numbOfSales;
}
```

Also be aware that you may use the base keyword any time a subclass wishes to access a public or protected member defined by a parent class. Use of this keyword is not limited to constructor logic.

Regarding Multiple Base Classes

It is important to keep in mind that C# demands that a given class have *exactly one* direct base class. Therefore, it is not possible to have a single type with two or more base classes (this technique is known as multiple inheritance or simply, MI). As you will see in Chapter 4, C# does allow a given type to implement any number of discrete interfaces. In this way, a C# class can exhibit a number of behaviors while avoiding the problems associated with classic MI. On a related note, it is permissible to configure a single *interface* to derive from multiple *interfaces* (again, more details to come in Chapter 4).

Keeping Family Secrets: The "protected" Keyword

As you already know, public items are directly accessible from any subclass. Private items cannot be accessed from any object beyond the object that has indeed defined the private data point. C# takes the lead of many other modern day object languages and provides an additional level of accessibility: Protected.

When a base class defines protected data or protected methods, it is able to create a set of members that can be accessed directly by any descendent. If you wish to allow the SalesPerson and Manager child classes to directly access the data sector defined by Employee, you can update the original Employee class definition as follows:

```
// Protected state data.
public class Employee
{
    // Child classes can directly access this information. Object users cannot.
    protected    string fullName;
    protected    int empID;
    protected    float currPay;
    protected    string ssn;
...
}
```

However, as far as the object user is concerned, protected data is private. Therefore, the following is illegal:

```
// Error! Can't access protected data from object instance
Employee emp = new Employee();
emp.ssn = "111-11-1111";
```

Preventing Inheritance: Sealed Classes

Classical inheritance is a wonderful thing. When you establish base class/subclass relationships, you are able to leverage the behavior of existing types. However, what if you wish to define a class that cannot (for whatever reason) be subclassed? For example, assume you have added yet another class to your employee namespaces, which extends the existing SalesPerson type. Figure 3-10 shows what this looks like.

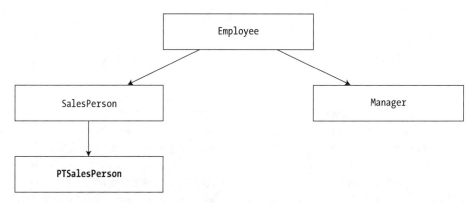

Figure 3-10. The extended employee hierarchy

PTSalesPerson is a class representing a (of course) part-time sales person. For the sake of argument, let's say that we wish to ensure that no other developer is able to subclass from PTSalesPerson (after all, how much more part-time can you get than "part-time"?). To prevent others from extending a class, make use of the C# "sealed" keyword:

```
// Ensure that PTSalesPerson cannot act as a base class to others.
public sealed class PTSalesPerson : SalesPerson
{
    public PTSalesPerson(string fullName, int empID,
        float currPay, string ssn, int numbOfSales)
            : base(fullName, empID, currPay, ssn, numbOfSales)
    {
        // Interesting constructor logic. . .
    }
```

```
        // Other interesting members. . .
}
```

Because PTSalesPerson is sealed, it cannot serve as a base class to any other type. For example, if you attempted to extend PTSalesPerson, you receive a compiler error.

```
// Compiler error! PTSalesPerson is sealed and cannot be extended!
public class ReallyPTSalesPerson : PTSalesPerson
{
    . . .
}
```

By and large, the sealed keyword is most useful when creating standalone utility classes. As an example, the String class defined in the System namespace has been explicitly sealed. Therefore, you cannot create some new class deriving from System.String. If you wish to build a class that leverages the functionality of a sealed class your only option is to make use of the containment/delegation model (speaking of which. . .).

Programming for Containment/Delegation

As noted a bit earlier in this chapter, inheritance comes in two flavors. We have just explored the classical is-a relationship. To conclude the exploration of the second pillar of OOP, let's examine the has-a relationship (also known as the containment/delegation model). Assume you have created a simple C# class modeling a radio:

```
// This type will function as a contained class.
public class Radio
{
    public Radio(){}

    public void TurnOn(bool on)
    {
        if(on)
            Console.WriteLine("Jamming. . .");
        else
            Console.WriteLine("Quiet time. . .");
    }
}
```

Now assume you are interested in modeling an automobile. The Car class maintains a set of state data (the car's pet name, current speed and maximum speed) all of which may be set using a custom constructor. Here is the initial definition:

```csharp
// This class will function as the 'outer' class.
public class Car
{
    private int currSpeed;
    private int maxSpeed;
    private string petName;
    bool dead;                  // Is the car alive or dead?

    public Car()
    {
        maxSpeed = 100;
        dead = false;
    }

    public Car(string name, int max, int curr)
    {
        currSpeed = curr;
        maxSpeed = max;
        petName = name;
        dead = false;
    }

    public void SpeedUp(int delta)
    {
        // If the car is dead (e.g., beyond the maximum speed) just say so. . .
        if(dead)
        {
            Console.WriteLine(petName + " is out of order. . ..");
        }
        else    // Not currently maxed out, so speed up.
        {
            currSpeed += delta;
            if(currSpeed >= maxSpeed)
            {
                Console.WriteLine(petName + " has overheated. . .");
                dead = true;
            }
        }
```

```
        else
            Console.WriteLine("\tCurrSpeed = " + currSpeed);
    }
  }
}
```

At this point we have two independent classes. Obviously, it would be rather odd to establish an is-a relationship between the two entities. However, it should be clear that some sort of relation between the two could be established. In short, we would like to express the idea that the Car has-a Radio. In OO parlance, a class that wishes to contain another class is termed the "parent" class. The contained class is termed a "child" class. To begin, you can update the Car class definition as follows:

```
// A Car has-a Radio.
public class Car
{
. . .
    // The contained Radio.
    private Radio theMusicBox;
. . .
}
```

Notice how the outer Car class has declared the Radio object as private. This of course is a good thing, as we have preserved encapsulation. However, the next obvious question is: How can the outside world interact with child objects? It should be clear that it is the responsibility of the outer Car class to create the child Radio class. Although the outer class may create any child objects whenever it sees fit, the most common place to do so is in the constructor set:

```
// Outer classes are responsible for creating any child objects.
public class Car
{
. . .
    // The contained Radio.
    private Radio theMusicBox;

    public Car()
    {
        maxSpeed = 100;
        dead = false;
        // Outer class creates the contained class(es) upon start-up.
```

```
            // NOTE:  If we did not, theMusicBox would
            // begin life as a null reference.
            theMusicBox = new Radio();
        }

        public Car(string name, int max, int curr)
        {
            currSpeed = curr;
            maxSpeed = max;
            petName = name;
            dead = false;
            theMusicBox = new Radio();
        }
...
}
```

Alternatively, we could make use of the C# initializer syntax as follows:

```
// A Car has-a Radio.
public class Car
{
...
    // The contained Radio.
    private Radio theMusicBox = new Radio();
...
}
```

At this point, you have successfully contained another object. However, to expose the functionality of the inner class to the outside world requires *delegation*. Delegation is simply the act of adding members to the parent class that make use of the child classes' functionality. For example:

```
// Outer classes extend their public interface to provide access to inner
// classes.
public class Car
{
...
    public void CrankTunes(bool state)
    {
        // Delegate request to inner object.
        theMusicBox.TurnOn(state);
    }
}
```

In the following code, notice how the object user is able to interact with the hidden inner object indirectly, and is totally unaware of the fact that the Car class is making use of a private Radio instance:

```
// Take this car for a test drive.
public class CarApp
{
    public static int Main(string[] args)
    {
        // Make a car (which makes the radio).
        Car c1;
        c1 = new Car("SlugBug", 100, 10);

        // Jam some tunes (which makes use of the radio).
        c1.CrankTunes(true);

        // Speed up.
        for(int i = 0; i < 10; i++)
            c1.SpeedUp(20);

        // Shut down (which again makes use of the radio).
        c1.CrankTunes(false);
        return 0;
    }
}
```

Figure 3-11 shows the output.

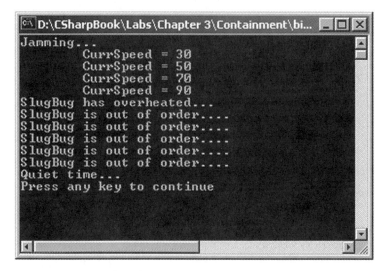

Figure 3-11. Our contained Radio in action

SOURCE CODE *The Containment project is included under the Chapter 3 subdirectory.*

Nested Type Definitions

Before examining the final pillar of OOP, let's explore a programming technique termed *nested classes*. In C#, it is possible to define a type directly within the scope of another type. The syntax is quite straightforward:

```
// C# allows classes, interfaces and structures to nest others.
public class MyClass
{
    // Members of outer class.
    . . .
    public class MyNestedClass
    {
        // Members of inner class.
        . . .
    }
}
```

Although the syntax is clean, understanding *why* you might do this is not readily apparent. Typically, a nested type is regarded only as a helper type of the outer class, and is not intended for use by the outside world. This is slightly along the lines of the "has-a" relationship, however in the case of nested types, you are in greater control of the inner type's visibility. In this light, nested types also help enforce encapsulation services.

To illustrate, you can redesign your current Car application by representing the Radio as a nested type. By doing so, you are assuming the outside world does not need to directly create a Radio. Here is the update:

```
// The Car is nesting the Radio. Everything else is as before.
public class Car : Object
{
. . .
    // A nested, private radio. Cannot be created by the outside world.
    private class Radio
    {
        public Radio(){}
        public void TurnOn(bool on)
```

```
        {
            if(on)
                Console.WriteLine("Jamming. . .");
            else
                Console.WriteLine("Quiet time. . .");
        }
    }

    // The outer class can make instances of nested types.
    private Radio theMusicBox;
...
}
```

Notice that the Car type is able to create object instances of any nested item. Also notice that this class has been declared a *private* type. In C#, nested types may be declared private as well as public. Recall, however, that classes that are directly within a namespace (e.g., nonnested types) cannot be defined as private. As far as the object user is concerned, the Car type works as before. Because of the private, nested nature of the Radio, the following is now illegal:

```
// Can't do it outside the scope of the Car class!
Radio r = new Radio();
```

SOURCE CODE   *The Nested project is included under the Chapter 3 subdirectory.*

The Third Pillar: C#'s Polymorphic Support

Assume the Employee base class has implemented the GiveBonus() method as follows:

```
// Employee defines a new method that gives a bonus to a given employee.
public class Employee
{
...
    public void GiveBonus(float amount)
    {
        currPay += amount;
    }
...
}
```

Because this method has been defined as public, you can now give bonuses to sales persons and managers (Figure 3-12):

```
// Give each child class a bonus.
Manager chucky = new Manager("Chucky", 92, 100000, "333-23-2322", 9000);
chucky.GiveBonus(300);
chucky.DisplayStats();

SalesPerson fran = new SalesPerson("Fran", 93, 3000, "932-32-3232", 31);
fran.GiveBonus(200);
fran.DisplayStats();
```

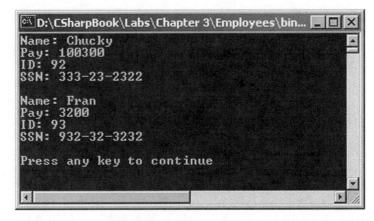

Figure 3-12. The current employee hierarchy does not implement polymorphism

The problem with the current design is that the inherited GiveBonus() method operates identically for each subclass. Ideally, the bonus of a sales person should take into account the number of sales. Perhaps managers should gain additional stock options in conjunction with a monetary bump in salary. Given this, you are suddenly faced with an interesting question: "How can related objects respond differently to the same request?"

Polymorphism is the final pillar of OOP, which provides a way for a subclass to redefine how it responds to a method defined by its base class. To retrofit your current design, you need to understand the use of the C# "virtual" and "override" keywords. When a base class wishes to define a method that may be overridden by a subclass, it must specify the method as virtual:

```
public class Employee
{
    // GiveBonus() has a default implementation, however
    // child classes are free to override this behavior.
    public virtual void GiveBonus(float amount)
```

```
    {
        currPay += amount;
    }
...
}
```

If a subclass wishes to redefine a virtual method, it is required to reimplement the method in question using the override keyword. For example:

```
public class SalesPerson : Employee
{
    // A sales person's bonus is influenced by the number of sales.
    public override void GiveBonus(float amount)
    {
        int salesBonus = 0;

        if(numberOfSales >= 0 && numberOfSales <= 100)
            salesBonus = 10;
        else if(numberOfSales >= 101 && numberOfSales <= 200)
            salesBonus = 15;
        else
            salesBonus = 20;      // Anything greater than 200.

        base.GiveBonus (amount * salesBonus);
    }
...
}
public class Manager : Employee
{
    private Random r = new Random();

    // Managers get some number of new stock options, in addition to raw cash.
    public override void GiveBonus(float amount)
    {
        // Increase salary.
        base.GiveBonus(amount);

        // And give some new stock options. . .
        numberOfOptions += (ulong)r.Next(500);
    }
...
}
```

Notice how each overridden method is free to leverage the default behavior using the base keyword. In this way, you have no need to completely reimplement the logic behind GiveBonus(), but can reuse (and extend) the default behavior of the parent class.

Also assume that Employee.DisplayStats() has been declared virtual, and has been overridden by each subclass to account for displaying the number of sales (for sales folks) and current stock options (for managers). Now that each subclass can interpret what these virtual methods means to itself, each object instance behaves as a more independent entity (see Figure 3-13 for output):

```
// A better bonus system!
Manager chucky = new Manager("Chucky", 92, 100000, "333-23-2322", 9000);
chucky.GiveBonus(300);
chucky.DisplayStats();

SalesPerson fran = new SalesPerson("Fran", 93, 3000, "932-32-3232", 31);
fran.GiveBonus(200);
fran.DisplayStats();
```

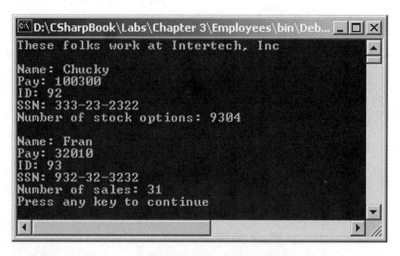

Figure 3-13. A better bonus system (thanks to polymorphism)

Excellent! At this point you are not only able to establish is-a and has-a relationships among related classes, but also have injected polymorphic activity into your employee hierarchy. As you may suspect, the story of polymorphism goes beyond simply overriding base class behavior.

Defining (and Understanding) Abstract Classes

Currently, the Employee base class has been designed to supply protected member variables for its descendents, as well as supply two virtual methods (GiveBonus() and DisplayStats()) that may be overridden by a given descendent. While this is all well and good, there is a rather odd byproduct of the current design: You can directly create instances of the Employee base class:

```
// What exactly does this mean?
Employee X = new Employee();
```

Now think this one through. The only real purpose of the Employee base class is to define default state data and behaviors for any given subclass. In all likelihood, you did not intend anyone to create a direct instance of this class. The Employee type itself is too general of a concept. A far better design is to prevent the ability to directly create a new Employee instance. In C#, this is facilitated by using the "abstract" keyword:

```
// Update the Employee class as abstract to prevent direct instantiation.
abstract public class Employee
{
    // Same public interface and state data as before...
}
```

If you do not attempt to create an instance of the Employee class, you are issued a compile time error.

```
// Error! Can't create an instance of an abstract class.
Employee X = new Employee();
```

Enforcing Polymorphic Activity: Abstract Methods

Once a class has been defined as an abstract base class, it may define any number of *abstract members* (which is analogous to a C++ pure virtual function). Abstract methods can be used whenever you wish to define a method that *does not* supply a default implementation. By doing so, you enforce a polymorphic trait on each descendent, leaving them to contend with the task of providing the details behind your abstract methods.

The first logical question you might have is: "Why would I ever want to do this?" To understand the role of abstract methods, let's return to the shapes hierarchy seen earlier in this chapter (Figure 3-14).

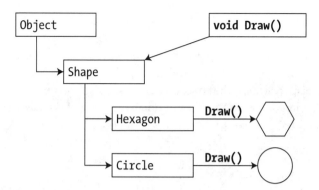

Figure 3-14. Our current shapes hierarchy

Much like the Employee hierarchy, you should be able to tell that you don't want to allow the object user to create an instance of Shape directly. To illustrate, update your initial classes as follows:

```
namespace Shapes
{
public abstract class Shape
{
    // Shapes can be assigned a friendly pet name.
    protected string petName;

    // Constructors.
    public Shape(){petName = "NoName"; }
    public Shape(string s) { petName = s;}

    // Draw() is virtual and may be overridden.
    public virtual void Draw()
    {
        Console.WriteLine("Shape.Draw()");
    }
    public string PetName
    {
        get {return petName;}
        set { petName = value;}
    }
}
```

```
// Circle does NOT override Draw().
public class Circle : Shape
{
    public Circle() {}
    public Circle(string name): base(name) {}
}
```

```
// Hexagon DOES override Draw().
public class Hexagon : Shape
{
    public Hexagon(){}
    public Hexagon(string name): base(name) {}
    public override void Draw()
    {
        Console.WriteLine("Drawing {0} the Hexagon", PetName);
    }
}
}
```

Notice that the Shape class has defined a virtual method named Draw(). As you have just seen, subclasses are free to redefine the behavior of a virtual method using the override keyword (as in the case of the Hexagon class). The point of abstract methods becomes crystal clear when you understand that subclasses are *not required* to override virtual methods (as in the case of Circle). Therefore, if you create an instance of the Hexagon and Circle types, you'd find that the Hexagon understands how to draw itself correctly. The Circle, however, is more than a bit confused (see Figure 3-15 for output):

```
// The Circle object did not override the base class implementation of Draw().
public static int Main(string[] args)
{
    // Make and draw a hex.
    Hexagon hex = new Hexagon("Beth");
    hex.Draw();

    Circle cir = new Circle("Cindy");
    // Humm. Using base class implementation.
    cir.Draw();
. . .
}
```

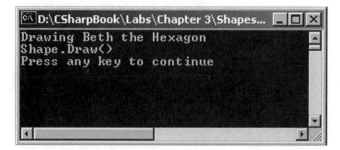

Figure 3-15. Virtual methods do not have to be overridden

Clearly this is not a very intelligent design. To enforce that each child object defines what Draw() means to itself, you can simply establish Draw() as an abstract method of the Shape class, which by definition means you provide no default implementation whatsoever (again, like a C++ pure virtual function):

```
// Force all kids to figure out how to be rendered.
public abstract   class Shape
{
. . .
    // Draw() is now completely abstract (note semicolon).
    public abstract    void Draw();
    public string PetName
    {
        get {return petName;}
        set { petName = value;}
    }
}
```

Given this, we are now obligated to implement Draw() in our Circle class:

```
// If we did not implement the abstract Draw() method, Circle would also be
// considered abstract, and could not be directly created!
public class Circle : Shape
{
    public Circle(){}
    public Circle(string name): base(name) {}

    // Now Each child must decide what Draw() means to itself.
    public override    void Draw()
    {
        Console.WriteLine("Drawing {0} the Circle", PetName);
    }
}
```

With this update, you are now able to find order in your Shapes hierarchy. To illustrate the full story of polymorphism, consider the following code:

```
// Create an array of various Shapes.
public static int Main(string[] args)
{
    // Array of shapes.
    Shape[] s = {new Hexagon(), new Hexagon("Freda"),
                 new Circle(), new Circle("JoJo")};

    // Loop over the array and ask each object to draw itself.
    for(int i = 0; i < s.Length; i++)
        s[i].Draw();
...
}
```

Figure 3-16 shows the output.

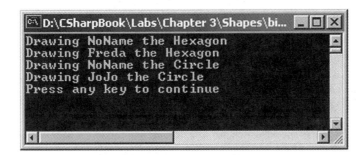

Figure 3-16. Better! Abstract methods must *be overridden*

This illustrates polymorphism at its finest. Recall that when you mark a class as abstract, you are unable to create a *direct instance* of that type. However, you can freely store references to any subclass within an abstract base variable. As you iterate over the array of Shape references, it is at runtime that the correct type is determined. At this point, the correct method is invoked.

Versioning Class Members

C# provides a facility that is the logical opposite of method overriding: method hiding. Assume you are in the process of building a brand new class named Oval. Given that an Oval is-a type of Circle, you may wish to extend the Shapes hierarchy as shown in Figure 3-17.

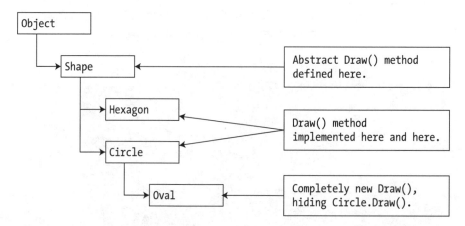

Figure 3-17. Versioning the Draw() method

Now, for the sake of argument, assume that the Oval also defines a method named Draw(). This is good, as we can assure that this class behaves like any other class in the hierarchy. However, what if you wish to *prevent* the Oval class from inheriting any previous drawing logic? Formally, this technique is termed "*versioning*" a class. Syntactically, this can be accomplished using the new keyword on a method-by-method basis. For example:

```
// This class extends Circle, but hides the inherited Draw() method.
public class Oval : Circle
{
    public Oval(){base.PetName = "Joe";}

    // Hide any Draw() implementation above me.
    public new void Draw()
    {
        // Oval specific drawing algorithm.
    }
}
```

Because you used the new keyword in the definition of Draw(), you are guaranteed that if an object user makes an instance of the Oval class and calls Draw(), the most derived implementation is called. In effect, the "new"' method breaks the relationship between the abstract Draw() method defined by the base class and the derived version. Thus:

```
// The Draw() defined by Oval will be called.
Oval o = new Oval();
o.Draw();
```

As an odd caveat, it is possible to trigger the base class implementation of a hidden method using an explicit cast:

```
// The Draw() defined by Circle will be called!
   Oval o = new Oval();
   ((Circle)o).Draw();          // Cast o to base class.
```

At this point, method hiding may seem to be little more than an interesting exercise in class design. However, this technique can be very useful when you are extending types defined within another .NET binary. Imagine that you wish to derive a new class from another class defined in a distinct .NET binary. Now, what if the binary base type defines a Draw() method that is somehow incompatible with your own Draw() method? To prevent object users from triggering a base class implementation, just use "new."

SOURCE CODE   *The Shapes hierarchy can be found under the Chapter 3 subdirectory.*

Casting Between Class Types

At this point we have created a number of class hierarchies in C#. Next, we need to examine the laws of casting between class types. First, recall the Employee hierarchy. The top-most member in our hierarchy is System.Object. Given the terminology of classical inheritance, everything "is-a" object. Furthermore, a part-time sales person "is-a" sales person, and so forth. Therefore, the following cast operations are legal.

```
// A Manager 'is-a' object.
object o = new Manager("Frank Zappa", 9, 40000, "111-11-1111", 5);

// A Manager 'is-a' Employee too.
Employee e = new Manager("MoonUnit Zappa", 2, 20000, "101-11-1321", 1);

// A PT sales person is a sales person.
SalesPerson sp = new PTSalesPerson("Jill", 834, 100000, "111-12-1119", 90);
```

The first law of casting between class types is that when two classes are related by an is-a relationship, it is always safe to reference a derived class using a base class reference. This leads to some powerful programming constructs. For example, if we have a function such as:

```
public class TheMachine
{
    public static void FireThisPerson(Employee e)
    {
        // Remove from database. . .
        // Get key and pencil sharpener from fired employee. . .
    }
}
```

We can effectively pass any descendent from the Employee class into this method. Thus:

```
// Streamline the staff.
TheMachine.FireThisPerson(e);
TheMachine.FireThisPerson(sp);
```

The following logic works as there is an implicit case from the base class type (Employee) to the derived types. Now, what if you also wanted to fire your Manager (currently held in a base class reference)? If you pass the object reference into the FireThisPerson() method as follows:

```
// A Manager 'is-a' object.
object o = new Manager("Frank Zappa", 9, 40000, "111-11-1111", 5);
. . .
TheMachine.FireThisPerson(o);        // Error!
```

you are issued a compiler error! The reason for the error is because of the fact that you cannot automatically receive access from a base type (in this case System.Object) to a derived type (in this case Employee) without first performing an explicit cast. Thus, the previous problem can be avoided as follows:

```
// Error! Must cast when moving from base to derived class!
// FireThisPerson(o);

// Better!
FireThisPerson((Employee)o);
```

Numerical Casts

In addition to making an explicit cast between types, be aware that numerical conversions follow more or less the same rules. If you are attempting to cast a "larger" numerical type to a "smaller" type (such as an integer to a byte) you must also make an explicit cast:

```
int x = 30000;
byte b = (byte)x;          // Loss of information here. . .
```

Excellent! At this point you are able to build custom class hierarchies using C#. Chapters 4 and 5 introduce a number of advanced class construction techniques that extend and complement the information presented thus far. Before moving on however, let's examine two additional aspects of class design: Error handling and memory management.

Exception Handling

Error handling among Windows developers has grown into a confused mishmash of techniques over the years. Many programmers roll their own error handling logic within the context of a given application. For example, a development team may define a set of constants that represent known error conditions, and make use of them as method return values. In addition to these ad hoc techniques, the Window's API defines a number of error codes that come by way of #defines, HRESULTs and far too many variations on the simple Boolean. Many COM developers have made use of a small set of standard COM interfaces (e.g., ISupportErrorInfo, IErrorInfo, ICreateErrorInfo) to return meaningful error information to a COM client.

The obvious problem with these previous techniques is the tremendous lack of symmetry. Each approach is more or less tailored to a given technology, a given language, and perhaps even a given project. In order to put an end to this madness, the .NET platform provides exactly *one* technique to send and trap runtime errors: Structured Exception Handling (SEH).

The beauty of this approach is that developers now have a well-defined approach to error handling, which is common to all languages targeting the .NET universe. Therefore, the way in which a C# programmer handles errors is conceptually identical to that of a VB.NET programmer, a C++ programmer using managed extensions (MC++), and so forth. As an added bonus it is also possible to throw and catch exceptions across binaries, AppDomains (defined in Chapter 6), and machines in a language independent manner.

To begin to understand how to program using exceptions, you must first realize that exceptions are indeed objects. All system- and user-defined exceptions derive from System.Exception (which in turn derives from System.Object). Here is a breakdown of some of the interesting properties defined by the Exception class (Table 3-1).

Table 3-1. Core Members of the System.Exception Type

SYSTEM.EXCEPTION PROPERTY	MEANING IN LIFE
HelpLink	This property returns a URL to a help file describing the error in gory detail.
Message	This read-only property returns the textual description of a given error. The error message itself is set as a constructor parameter.
Source	This property returns the name of the object (or possibly the application) that sent the error.
StackTrace	This read-only property contains a string that identifies the sequence of calls that triggered the error.
InnerException	The InnerException property can be used to preserve the error details between a series of exceptions.

Throwing an Exception

To illustrate the use of System.Exception, let's revisit the Car class defined earlier in this chapter, in particular, the SpeedUp() method. Here is current implementation:

```
// Currently, SpeedUp() reports errors using console IO.
public void SpeedUp(int delta)
{
    // If the car is dead, just say so. . .
    if(dead)
    {
        Console.WriteLine(petName + " is out of order. . ..");
    }
    else    // Not dead, speed up.
    {
        currSpeed += delta;
        if(currSpeed >= maxSpeed)
        {
```

```
            Console.WriteLine(petName + " has overheated...");
            dead = true;
        }
        else
            Console.WriteLine("\tCurrSpeed = " + currSpeed);
    }
}
```

For the sake of illustration, let's retrofit SpeedUp() to throw an exception if the user attempts to speed up the automobile after it has met its maker (dead = = true). First, you want to create and configure a new instance of the Exception class. When you wish to pass the error object back to the calling logic, make use of the C# *throw* keyword. Here is an example:

```
// This time, throw an exception if the user speeds up a trashed automobile.
public void SpeedUp(int delta)
{
    if(dead)
        throw new Exception("This car is already dead");
    else
    {
        . . .
    }
}
```

Before examining how to catch this exception, a few points. First of all, when you are building your custom classes, it is always up to you to decide exactly what constitutes an exception. Here, you are making the assumption that if the program attempts to increase the speed of a car that has expired, an Exception should be thrown to indicate the SpeedUp() method cannot continue.

Alternatively, you could implement SpeedUp() to recover automatically without needing to throw an exception. By and large, exceptions should be thrown only when a more terminal condition has been met. Deciding exactly what constitutes throwing an exception is a design issue you must always contend with. For your current purposes, assume that asking a doomed automobile to increase its speed justified a cause for an exception.

Next, understand that the .NET runtime libraries already define a number of predefined exceptions. For example, the System namespace defines numerous custom exceptions such as ArgumentOutOfRangeException, IndexOutOfRangeException, StackOverflowException, and so forth. Other namespaces define additional exceptions that reflect the behavior of that namespace (e.g., System.Drawing.Printing defines printing exceptions System.IO defines IO based exceptions).

Catching Exceptions

Because the SpeedUp() method is able to throw an exception object, you need to be ready to handle the error should it occur. When you are calling a method that may throw an exception, you need to establish a try/catch block. Here is the simplest form:

```
// Speed up the car safely. . .
public static int Main(string[] args)
{
    // Make a car.
    Car buddha = new Car("Buddha", 100, 20);

    // Try to rev the engine hard!
    try
    {
        for(int i = 0; i < 10; i++)
        {
            buddha.SpeedUp(10);
        }
    }
    catch(Exception e)        // Print message and stack trace.
    {
        Console.WriteLine(e.Message);
        Console.WriteLine(e.StackTrace);
    }

    return 0;
}
```

In essence, a try block is a section of code that is on the lookout for any exception that may be encountered during the flow of execution. If an exception is detected, the flow of program execution is sent to the next available catch block. On the other hand, if the code within a try block does not trigger an exception, the catch block is skipped entirely, and all is right with the world. Figure 3-18 shows a test run of the handled error.

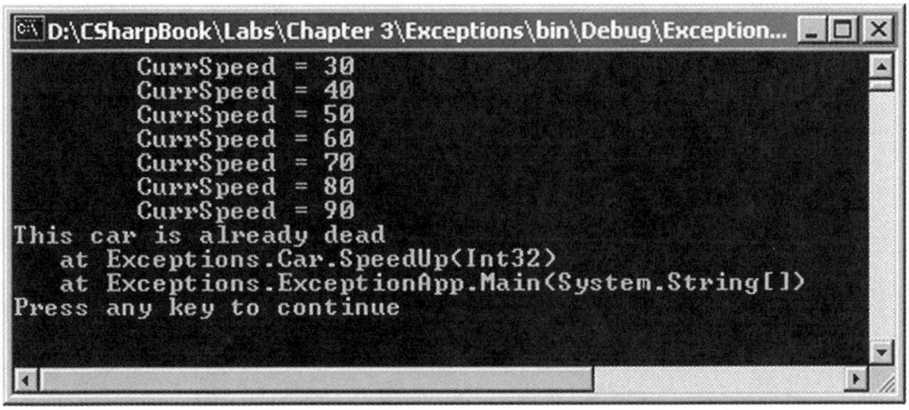

```
CurrSpeed = 30
CurrSpeed = 40
CurrSpeed = 50
CurrSpeed = 60
CurrSpeed = 70
CurrSpeed = 80
CurrSpeed = 90
This car is already dead
   at Exceptions.Car.SpeedUp(Int32)
   at Exceptions.ExceptionApp.Main(System.String[])
Press any key to continue
```

Figure 3-18. Dealing with the error using structured exception handling

Notice how this catch block explicitly specifies the exception it is willing to catch. In C# (as well as numerous other languages targeting the .NET platform) it is also permissible to configure a catch block that does not explicitly define the type of exception. Thus, we could implement the try/catch block as follows:

```
// A generic catch.
catch
{
    Console.WriteLine("Something bad happened. . .");
}
```

Obviously, this is not the most descriptive manner in which to handle runtime exceptions, given that we have no way to obtain meaningful information about the error that occurred. Nevertheless, C# does allow for such a construct.

Building Custom Exceptions, Take One

Although you could simply throw instances of System.Exception to signal a runtime error, it is sometimes advantageous to build a custom class that encapsulates the details of your problem. For example, assume you wish to build a custom exception to represent the error of speeding up a doomed automobile. To begin, create a new class derived from System.Exception (by convention, custom exceptions should end with an "–Exception" suffix). After this point, you are free to include any custom properties, methods or fields that can be used from within the catch block of the calling logic. You are also free to override any virtual member defined by your parent classes:

```
// This custom exception describes the details of the car-is-dead condition.
public class CarIsDeadException : System.Exception
{
    // This custom exception maintains the name of the doomed car.
    private string carName;
    public CarIsDeadException(){}
    public CarIsDeadException(string carName)
    {
        this.carName = carName;
    }

    // Override the Exception.Message property.
    public override string Message
    {
        get
        {
            string msg = base.Message;

            if(carName != null)
                msg += carName + " has bought the farm. . .";

            return msg;
        }
    }
}
```

Here, the CarIsDeadException type maintains a private data member that holds the name of the car that threw the exception. You have also added two constructors to the class, and overrode the Message property in order to include the pet name of the car in the description. Throwing this error from within SpeedUp() should be self-explanatory:

```
// Throw the custom exception.
public void SpeedUp(int delta)
{
    // If the car is dead, just say so. . .
    if(dead)
    {
        // Throw 'Car is dead' exception.
        throw new CarIsDeadException(this.petName);
    }
    else     // Not dead, speed up.
```

```
    {
        currSpeed += delta;
        if(currSpeed >= maxSpeed)
        {
            dead = true;
        }
        else
            Console.WriteLine("\tCurrSpeed = {0}", currSpeed);
    }
}
```

Catching the error is just as easy:

```
try
{
    . . .
}
catch(CarIsDeadException e)
{
    Console.WriteLine(e.Message);
    Console.WriteLine(e.StackTrace);
}
```

Figure 3-19 shows another test run.

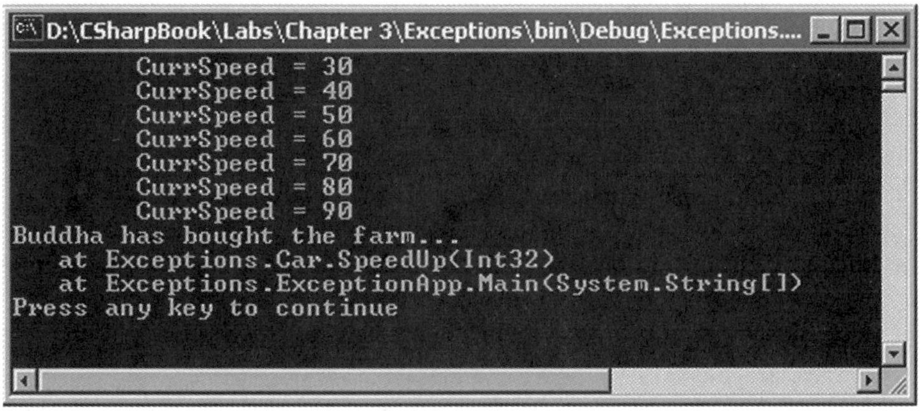

Figure 3-19. Catching the custom exception

In this scenario, you may not necessarily need to build a custom exception class, given that you are free to simply set the Message property at the time of construction. Typically, you only need to create custom exceptions when the error is tightly bound to the class issuing the error (for example, a File class that throws a number of file-related errors). Nevertheless, at this point you should understand the basic process of constructing a custom exception type.

Building Custom Exceptions, Take Two

Our current CarIsDeadException type has overridden the Message property, in order to configure a custom error message. This class also has an overloaded constructor that accepts the pet name of the automobile that has currently met its maker. As you build custom exceptions, you are able to build the type as you see fit. However, the recommended approach is to build a relatively simple type that supplies three named constructors matching the following signature:

```csharp
public class CarIsDeadException : System.Exception
{
    // Constructors for this custom exception.
    public CarIsDeadException(){}

    public CarIsDeadException(string message)
        : base(message){}

    public CarIsDeadException(string message, Exception innerEx)
        : base(message, innerEx){}
}
```

Notice that this time you have *not* provided a private string to hold the pet name, and have *not* overridden the Message property. Rather, you are simply passing all the relevant information to your base class. When you wish to throw an exception of this type, you would send in all necessary information as a constructor argument (the output would be identical):

```csharp
public void SpeedUp(int delta)
{
    . . .

    // If the car is dead, just say so. . .
    if(dead)
    {
        // Pass pet name and message as ctor argument.
        throw new CarIsDeadException(this.petName + " has bought the farm!");
    }
    else    // Not dead, speed up.
```

```
    {
        . . .
    }
}
```

Using this design, our custom exception is little more than a semantically defined name, devoid of any unnecessary member variables (or overrides).

Handling Multiple Exceptions

In its simplest form, a try block has a single corresponding catch block. In reality, you often run into a situation where the code within a try block could trigger numerous exceptions. For example, assume the car's SpeedUp() method not only throws an exception when you attempt to speed up a doomed automobile, but throws another if you send in an invalid parameter (that is, any number less than zero):

```
// Test for bad parameter.
public void SpeedUp(int delta)
{
    // Bad param?  Throw system supplied exception.
    if(delta < 0)
    throw new ArgumentOutOfRangeException("Must be greater than zero");

    // If the car is dead, just say so. . .
    if(dead)
    {
        // Throw 'Car is dead' exception.
        throw new CarIsDeadException(this.petName + " has bought the farm!");
    }

    . . .
}
```

The calling logic would look like this:

```
// Here, we are on the lookout for multiple exceptions.
try
{
    for(int i = 0; i < 10; i++)
        buddha.SpeedUp(10);
}
```

```
catch(CarIsDeadException e)
{
    Console.WriteLine(e.Message);
    Console.WriteLine(e.StackTrace);
}
catch(ArgumentOutOfRangeException e)
{
    Console.WriteLine(e.Message);
    Console.WriteLine(e.StackTrace);
}
```

The "finally" Block

A try/catch block may also be augmented with an optional "finally" block. The idea behind a finally block is to ensure that any acquired resources can be cleaned up, even if an exception interferes with the normal flow of execution. For example, assume you wish to always power down the car's radio before exiting Main(), regardless of any errors:

```
// Provide a manner to clean up.
public static int Main(string[] args)
{
    Car buddha = new Car("Buddha", 100, 20);
    buddha.CrankTunes(true);

    // Try to rev the engine hard!
    try
    {
        // Speed up car. . .
    }
    catch(CarIsDeadException e)
    {
        Console.WriteLine(e.Message);
        Console.WriteLine(e.StackTrace);
    }
    catch(ArgumentOutOfRangeException e)
    {
        Console.WriteLine(e.Message);
        Console.WriteLine(e.StackTrace);
    }
```

```
    finally
    {
        // This will always occur. Error or not.
        buddha.CrankTunes(false);
    }
    return 0;
}
```

If you did include a finally block, the radio would *not* be turned off if an exception is caught (which may or may not be problematic). If you need to clean up any allocated memory, close down a file, detach from a data source (or whatever), you must add that code within a finally block to ensure proper clean up. It is important to realize, that the code contained within a finally block executes *all the time* even if the logic within your try clause does not generate an exception.

SOURCE CODE   *The Exceptions project is included under the Chapter 3 subdirectory.*

Final Thoughts Regarding Exceptions

Unlike ad hoc error-handling techniques, .NET exceptions cannot be ignored. One obvious question that may be on your mind is what would happen if you do not handle an exception thrown your direction? Assume that the logic in Main() that increases the speed of the Car object has no error handling logic. The result of ignoring the generated error would be highly obstructive to the end user of your application, as the following "last chance exception" dialog is displayed (Figure 3-20).

Now that you see the inherent goodness of catching an exception programmatically, you may wonder what to do with the exception once you have trapped it. Again, this is a design issue based on your current project. In your trivial Car example, you simply dumped your custom message and call stack to the console. A more realistic scenario may include freeing up acquired resources or writing to a log file. The exception-handling schema is simply a pattern to follow when sending and receiving errors. What you do with them is largely up to you.

Also, beware that it is permissible to "re-throw" an error. To do so, simply make use of the throw keyword within a catch block. This passes the exception up the chain of calling logic:

```
try
{ // Speed up car logic. . .}
catch(CarIsDeadException e)
```

```
{
    // Do any partial processing of this error and pass the buck.
    // Here, we are re-throwing the CarIsDeadException type.
    // HOWEVER, you are also free to throw a different exception if need be.
    throw e;
}
```

Finally, it is important to keep in mind that exceptions should only be thrown if the underlying problem is truly fatal. In other words, if you are able to recover from a user, logical, or general design error without throwing a system defined or custom exception—do so. In this light, the CarIsDeadException may be of arguable necessity. Chapter 5 revisits the SpeedUp() method, and substitutes the custom exception with a more appropriate custom event.

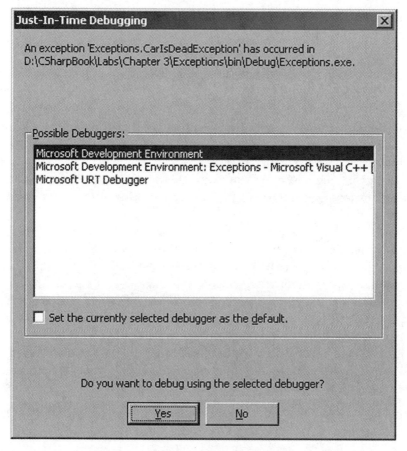

Figure 3-20. Unhandled exceptions can be a real drag. . .

Understanding Object Lifetime

As a C# programmer, the rules of memory management are simple: Use the new keyword to allocate an object onto the managed heap. The .NET runtime destroys the object when it is no longer needed. Next question: How does the runtime determine when an object is no longer needed? The short (i.e., incomplete) answer is that the runtime deallocates memory when there are no longer any outstanding references to an object within the current scope. To illustrate:

```
// Create a local Car variable.
public static int Main(string[] args)
{
    // Place a car onto the managed heap.
    Car c3 = new Car("Viper", 200, 100);
    . . .
    return 0;

} // If c3 is the only reference to the Car object,
    // it can be reclaimed when it drops out of scope.
```

Now, assume that your application has allocated three Car types. As long as there is enough room on the heap, you are returned an active reference to each object in memory. Technically speaking, an active reference to an object on the managed heap is called a *root*. The process can be visualized as illustrated in Figure 3-21.

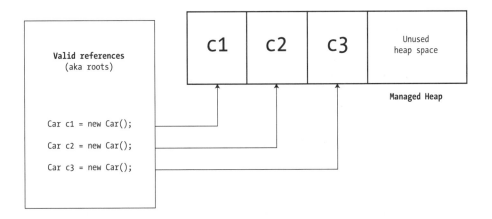

Figure 3-21. Valid (i.e., rooted) references point to a location on the managed heap

As you are busy creating more and more objects, the managed heap may eventually become full. If you attempt to create a new object on a heap plump and full of active object references, an OutOfMemoryException exception is thrown. Therefore, if you want to be extremely defensive in your coding practices (which will seldom need to be the case), you could allocate a new object as follows:

```
// Try to add these cars to the managed heap and check for errors...
public static int Main(string[] args)
{
...
    Car  yetAnotherCar;
    try
    {
        yetAnotherCar = new Car();
    }
    catch(OutOfMemoryException e)
    {
        Console.WriteLine(e.Message);
        Console.WriteLine("Managed heap is FULL! Running GC...");
    }
...
    return 0;
}
```

Regardless of how defensive your object allocation logic may be, understand that when the memory allocated to the managed heap runs dry, the garbage collection algorithm kicks in automatically. At this time, all objects on the managed heap are tested for outstanding object references in your application (i.e., active roots). If the garbage collector determines that a given root is no longer used by a given application (i.e., the object has fallen out of scope or was set to null), the object is marked for termination. Once the entire heap has been searched for "severed roots," the heap is swept clean, and the underlying memory is reclaimed.

Finalizing an Object Reference

As you might have gathered from the previous section, the .NET garbage collection scheme is rather nondeterministic. In other words, you are typically unable to determine exactly when an object will be deallocated from memory. Although this approach to memory management can simplify coding efforts, you are left with the unappealing byproduct of your objects possibly holding onto unmanaged resources (Hwnds, database connections, etc.) longer than necessary. For example, if the Car type was to obtain a connection to a remote machine during its lifetime, you would like to ensure that this resource is guaranteed to be released in a timely manner.

One choice you face as a C# class designer is to determine whether or not your classes should support the System.Object.Finalize() method (the default implementation does nothing). The odd thing is, the C# language does not allow you to directly override the Object.Finalize() method. In fact, it is illegal to call Finalize() directly within a C# application! Rather, when you wish to configure your custom class types to support the Finalize() method, make use of the following (C++ like) destructor syntax to achieve the same effect:

```
// This looks familiar. . .
public class Car : Object
{
    // A C# destructor?
    ~Car()
    {
        // Clean up your resources here!
        // Base.Finalize() called automatically In C#!
    }
...
}
```

If you have a background in C++, this syntax should look quite familiar. In C++, class destructors are class methods marked with a tilde prefixed to the name of the class. These methods are guaranteed to be called whenever the object reference falls out of scope (for stack allocated types) or when the C++ "delete" keyword is used (for free store allocated types).

When you place a C# object onto the managed heap using the new operator, the runtime automatically determines if your object supports the Finalize() method (represented in C# using the destructor syntax). If so, the object reference is marked as "finalizable" and a pointer to this object is stored on an internal queue named (of course) the finalization queue. When the garbage collector determines it is time to free the heap from orphaned references, it explicitly triggers the destructor logic for each object on the finalization queue before deallocating the memory for the object.

Finalization Details

Assume that you have now defined some additional automobile classes (minivans, sports cars, and jeeps). Also assume that minivans and sports cars do not support a C# destructor. Because the Car and Jeep classes have (indirectly) overridden Object.Finalize(), the finalization queue would contain listings for any active Car or Jeep reference. Internally, the process would look something like what you see in Figure 3-22.

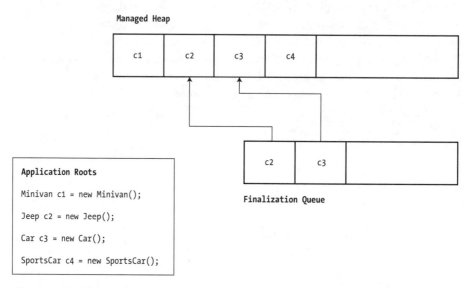

Figure 3-22. Objects that support a C# destructor are placed onto the finalization queue

As you may be able to infer, classes that support destructors take longer to remove from memory. c1 and c4 do not support a destructor, and can therefore be deallocated from memory immediately (if a garbage collection were to occur). c2 and c3 on the other hand, have additional overhead imposed by the call to Finalize(). Nevertheless, when you wish to ensure that your objects are given a chance to release any acquired resources, you should support a C# destructor.

Building an Ad Hoc Destruction Method

Again assume the Car class obtains recourses during its lifetime. If this type supports a C# destructor it will take longer to remove from memory than objects which do not (which may or may not be a problem). Given the fact that resources such as database connections are a precious commodity, you may not want to wait for the .NET garbage collector to trigger your destructor logic at "some time in the future." A logical question at this point is how can we provide a way for the object user to deallocate the resources held by an object as soon as possible?

One alternative is to define a custom ad hoc method that you can assume all objects in your system implement. Let's call this method Dispose(). The assumption is that when object users are finished using your object, they manually call Dispose() before allowing the object reference to drop out of scope. In this way, your objects can perform any amount of cleanup necessary (i.e., release a database connection) without incurring the hit of being placed on the finalization queue and without waiting for the garbage collector to trigger the class' destructor logic:

```
// Equipping our class with an ad hoc destructor.
public Car
{
. . .
    // This is a custom method we expect the object user to call manually.
    public void Dispose()
    {
        // . . . Clean up your Internal resources.
    }
}
```

The IDisposable Interface

In order to provide symmetry among all objects that support an explicit destruction routine, the .NET class libraries define an interface named IDisposable which (surprise, surprise) supports a single member named Dispose():

```
public  interface IDisposable
{
    public  void Dispose();
}
```

Now, rest assured that the concepts behind interface based programming are fully detailed in Chapter 4. Until then, understand that the recommended design pattern to follow is to implement the IDisposable interface for all types that wish to support an explicit form of resource deallocation. Thus, we may update the Car type as follows:

```
// Implementing IDisposable.
public Car : IDisposable
{
. . .
    // This is still  a custom method we expect the object user to call
    // manually.
    public void Dispose()
```

```
    {
        // . . . Clean up your Internal resources.
    }
}
```

Again, using this approach, you provide the object user with a way to manually dispose of acquired resources as soon as possible, and avoid the overhead of being placed on the finalization queue. As you may be guessing, it is possible for a single C# class to support a destructor as well as implement the IDisposable interface. You see this technique in just a moment.

Interacting with the Garbage Collector

Like everything in the .NET universe, you are able to interact with the garbage collector using an object reference. System.GC is the class that enables you to do so. GC is a sealed class, which, as you recall, means it cannot function as a base class to other types. You access the GC's functionality using a small set of static members. Table 3-2 gives a rundown of some of the more interesting items.

Table 3-2. Select Members of the System.GC Type

SYSTEM.GC MEMBER	MEANING IN LIFE
Collect()	Forces the GC to call the Finalize() method for every object on the managed heap. You can also (if you choose) specify the generation to sweep (more on generations soon).
GetGeneration()	Returns the generation to which an object currently belongs.
MaxGeneration	This property returns the maximum of generations supported on the target system.
ReRegisterForFinalize()	Sets a flag indicating that a suppressed object should be reregistered as finalizable. This (of course) assumes the object was marked as nonfinalizable using SuppressFinalize().
SuppressFinalize()	Sets a flag indicating that a given object should not have its Finalize() method called.
GetTotalMemory()	Returns the amount of memory (in bytes) currently being used by all objects in the heap, including objects that are soon to be destroyed.
	This method takes a Boolean parameter, which is used to specify if a garbage collection should occur during the method invocation.

To illustrate programmatic interaction with the .NET garbage collector, let's retrofit our automobile's destruction logic as follows:

```
// Memory clean up.
public class Car : IDisposable
{
. . .
    ~Car()
    {
        // If a garbage collection occurs, call our class' Dispose()
        // Implementation.
        Dispose();
    }

    // Our custom Dispose() method.
    public void Dispose()
    {
        // . . . Clean up any Internal resources.
        // No need to finalize if user called Dispose(),
        // so supress finalization.
        GC.SuppressFinalize(this);
    }

}
```

Notice that this iteration of the Car class supports both a C# style destructor as well as the IDisposable interface. Here, your Dispose() method has been altered to call GC.SuppressFinalize(), which informs the system that it should no longer call the destructor for the specified object, as the end user has called Dispose() manually (and has therefore cleaned up any internal resources of the Car type).

To illustrate the interplay between explicit and implicit object deallocation, assume the following updated Main() method. GC.Collect() is called to force all objects on the finalization queue to have their destructor triggered before this application shuts down. However, given that two of the Car types have been manually disposed by the object user, these types do not have their destructor logic triggered due to the call to GC.SuppressFinalize():

```
// Interacting with the GC.
public class GCApp
{
    public static int Main(string[] args)
```

```
        {
            Console.WriteLine("Heap memory in use: {0}",
                                GC.GetTotalMemory(false).ToString());

            // Add these cars to the managed heap.
            Car c1, c2, c3, c4;

            c1 = new Car("Car one", 40, 10);
            c2 = new Car("Car two", 70, 5);
            c3 = new Car("Car three", 200, 100);
            c4 = new Car("Car four", 140, 80);

            // Manually dispose some objects.
            // This will tell the GC to suppress finalization.
            c1.Dispose();
            c3.Dispose();

            // Call Finalize() for objects remaining on the finalization queue.
            GC.Collect();

            return 0;
        }
    }
```

Garbage Collection Optimizations

The next topic of interest has to do with the notion of "generations." When the .NET garbage collector is about to mark objects for deletion, is does *not* literally walk over each and every object placed on the managed heap looking for orphaned roots. Doing so would involve considerable time, especially in larger (i.e., real-world) applications.

Recall that the GC forces a collection as soon as it determines there is not enough memory to hold a new object instance. If the GC were to search every single object in memory for severed roots, this could easily entail checking hundreds, if not thousands, of objects. In this case, you could easily envision sluggish performance.

To help optimize the collection process, every object on the heap is assigned to a given "generation." The idea behind generations is simple: The longer an object has existed on the heap, the more likely it is to stay there (such as the application level object). Conversely, objects that have been recently placed on the heap are more likely to be unreferenced by the application rather quickly (e.g., a temporary object created in some method scope). Given these assumptions, each object belongs to one of the following generations:

- Generation 0: Identifies a newly allocated object that has never been marked for collection.

- Generation 1: Identifies an object that has survived a garbage collection sweep (i.e., it was marked for collection, but was not removed due to the fact that the heap had enough free space).

- Generation 2: Identifies an object that has survived more than one sweep of the garbage collector.

Now, when a collection occurs, the GC marks and sweeps all generation 0 objects first. If this results in the required amount of memory, the remaining objects are promoted to the next available generation. If all generation 0 objects have been removed from the heap, but more memory is still necessary, generation 1 objects are marked and swept, followed (if necessary) by generation 2 objects. In this way, the newer objects (i.e., local variables) are removed quickly while an older object (i.e., the object defining the Main() method) is assumed to be in use. In a nutshell, the GC is able to quickly free heap space using the generation as a baseline.

Programmatically speaking, you are able to investigate the generation an object currently belongs to using GC.GetGeneration(). Furthermore, GC.Collect() does allow you to specify which generation should be checked for orphaned roots. Consider the following:

```
// Just how old are you?
public static int Main(string[] args)
{
    Console.WriteLine("Heap memory in use: "
                        + GC.GetTotalMemory(false).ToString());

    // Add these cars to the managed heap.
    Car c1, c2, c3, c4;
    c1 = new Car("Car one", 40, 10);
    c2 = new Car("Car two", 70, 5);
    c3 = new Car("Car three", 200, 100);
    c4 = new Car("Car four", 140, 80);

    // Display generations.
    Console.WriteLine("C1 is gen {0}", GC.GetGeneration(c1));
    Console.WriteLine("C2 is gen {0}", GC.GetGeneration(c2));
```

```
Console.WriteLine("C3 is gen {0}", GC.GetGeneration(c3));
Console.WriteLine("C4 is gen {0}", GC.GetGeneration(c4));

// Dispose some cars manually.
c1.Dispose();
c3.Dispose();

// Collect all gen 0 objects?
GC.Collect(0);

// Display generations again (each will be promoted).
Console.WriteLine("C1 is gen {0}", GC.GetGeneration(c1));
Console.WriteLine("C2 is gen {0}", GC.GetGeneration(c2));
Console.WriteLine("C3 is gen {0}", GC.GetGeneration(c3));
Console.WriteLine("C4 is gen {0}", GC.GetGeneration(c4));

// Force memory to be freed for all generations.
GC.Collect();    // Calls destructors for each remaining object on heap.
Console.WriteLine("Heap memory in use: "
                        + GC.GetTotalMemory(false).ToString());
return 0;
}
```

The output is shown in Figure 3-23. Notice that when you request a collection of generation 0, each object is promoted to generation 1, given that these objects did not need to be removed from memory (as the heap was not exhausted).

To close, keep in mind that your interactions with the GC should be slim-to-none. The whole point of having a managed heap is to move the responsibility of memory management from your hands into the hands of the runtime. Do remember however, that when you build classes that support a C# style destructor, your objects will require more time to remove from the managed heap (due to the extra logic of the finalization queue). If you wish to support an implicit means of freeing the resources used by an object, you may implement the IDisposable interface.

SOURCE CODE   *The GC project is located under the Chapter 3 subdirectory.*

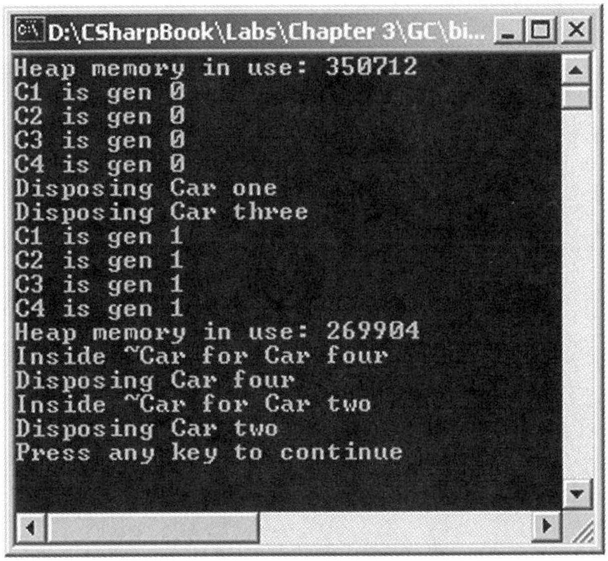

Figure 3-23. Interacting with the garbage collector

Summary

If you already come to the universe of .NET from another object-oriented language, this chapter may have been more of a quick compare and contrast between your current language of choice and C#. On the other hand, those of you who are exploring OOP for the first time may have found many of the concepts presented here a bit confounding. Regardless of your background, rest assured that the information presented here is the foundation for any .NET application.

This chapter began with a review of the pillars of OOP: Encapsulation, inheritance, and polymorphism. As you have seen, C# provides full support for each aspect of object orientation. In addition, the use of structured exception handling was introduced, which is *the* way to report and respond to error information in the .NET platform.

Finally, the chapter wrapped up by examining exactly how the .NET runtime frees you from the need of manually cleaning up the memory you allocate by the virtue of a managed heap. You have also explored the interplay between Object.Finalize(), the IDisposable interface and the C# destructor and examined how to programmatically interact with the garbage collector using the System.GC type.

CHAPTER 4

Interfaces and Collections

THIS CHAPTER BUILDS ON YOUR current understanding of object-oriented development by introducing the topic of interface-based programming. You learn how to use C# to create and implement custom interfaces, and come to understand the benefits of building types that support multiple behaviors. Along the way, a number of related topics are also discussed, such as obtaining interface references, explicit interface implementation, and the construction of interface hierarchies.

The remainder of this chapter is spent examining some of the standard interfaces defined within the .NET base class libraries. As you will see, your custom types are free to implement these predefined interfaces to support a number of advanced behaviors such as object cloning, object enumeration, and object sorting.

To wrap things up, you get a high-level view of the various predefined interfaces that are implemented by various collection classes (ArrayList, Stack, etc.) defined by the System.Collections namespace.

Understanding Interface-Based Programming

COM programmers have lived and died by the notion of interface-based programming for years. In fact, one of the central tenants of COM is that the only way a client can communicate with a COM class is via an interface pointer (not a direct object reference). Although the .NET universe still honors the use of interfaces, they are not the only means by which two binaries can communicate (as the CLR supports true object references). Be aware however, that this does not in any way imply that interfaces are obsolete! These syntactic entities are still the most elegant manner by which you can safely extend the functionality of a custom type without breaking existing code.

First, a formal definition: An interface is nothing more than a collection of semantically related *abstract members*. The exact number of members defined by a given interface always depends on the exact *behavior* you are attempting to model. Yes it's true. An interface expresses a behavior that a given class may wish to support. At a syntactic level, an interface is defined using the following C# syntax:

```
// This interface defines the behavior of 'having points'.
public interface IPointy
{
    byte GetNumberOfPoints();        // Implicitly abstract.
}
```

.NET interfaces are also able to support any number of properties (and events). For example, you could design the IPointy interface with the following read/write property:

```
// The pointy behavior as a read / write property.
public interface IPointy
{
    // Remove 'get' or 'set' to build read/write only property.
    byte Points{get; set;}
}
```

In any case, because an interface is nothing more than a named set of abstract members, any class (or structure) that chooses to implement an interface, is obligated to flesh out the details behind each member. Thus, interface-based programming provides yet another way to inject polymorphic behavior into a system: If multiple classes (or structures) implement the same interface in their unique ways, you have the power to treat each type in the same manner.

Here, IPointy is a simple interface that expresses the behavior of "having points." As you can tell, this behavior might be useful in the Shapes hierarchy developed in Chapter 3. The idea is simple: Some objects in the Shapes application have points (such as the Hexagon and Triangle) while others (such as the Circle) do not. If you configure the Hexagon and Triangle to support the IPointy interface, you can safely assume that each class supports a common behavior.

At this point, you may be wondering why you need the interface keyword in the first place. After all, C# allows you to build base classes containing abstract methods. When a child class derives from an abstract base class, it is also under obligation to flesh out the details of the abstract methods. However, abstract base classes typically do far more than define a group of abstract methods. They are free to define public, private, and protected state data, as well as any number of concrete methods that can be accessed by the subclasses.

Interfaces on the other hand, are pure protocol. Interfaces *never* define data types, and *never* provide a default implementation of the methods. Every member of an interface (whether it is a property or method) is automatically abstract. Furthermore, given that C# (and .NET-aware languages in general) only support single inheritance, the interface-based protocol allows a given type to support numerous behaviors, while avoiding the issues that arise when deriving from multiple base classes.

Implementing an Interface

When a C# class (or structure) chooses to extend its functionality by supporting a given interface, it does so using a comma-delimited list in the class definition. Be aware that the direct base class must be listed *first:*

```
// A given class may implement as many interfaces as necessary, but may have
// exactly 1 base class.
public class Hexagon : Shape, IPointy
{
    public Hexagon(){}
    public Hexagon(string name): base(name){}

    public override void Draw()
    {
        // Recall the Shape class defined the PetName property.
        Console.WriteLine("Drawing {0} the Hexagon", PetName);
    }

    // IPointy Implementation.
    public byte GetNumberOfPoints()
    {
        return 6;
    }
}

public class Triangle : Shape, IPointy
{
    public Triangle() {}
    public Triangle(string name): base(name) {}

    public override void Draw()
    {
        Console.WriteLine("Drawing {0} the Triangle", PetName);
    }

    // IPointy Implementation.
    public byte GetNumberOfPoints()
    {
        return 3;
    }
}
```

Each class now returns the number of points to the outside world when asked to do so. Notice that implementing an interface is an all-or-nothing proposition. The supporting class is not able to selectively choose which methods it will implement. Given that our IPointy interface defines a single method, this is not too much of a burden.

To sum up the story so far, the following diagram illustrates IPointy compatible objects using the popular "COM lollipop" notation. For those coming from a non-Microsoft view of the world, COM objects are graphically represented using a lollipop (aka jack) for each interface supported by a given class. For those who are familiar with the COM lifestyle, notice that the Hexagon and Triangle classes (see Figure 4-1) do *not* implement IUnknown and derive from a common base class (again illustrating the stark differences between COM and .NET):

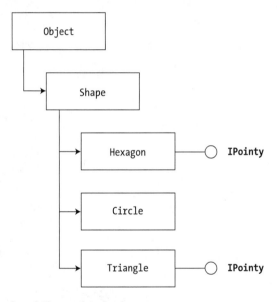

Figure 4-1. The updated Shapes hierarchy

Obtaining Interface References

As far as obtaining an interface reference from a type, C# provides a number of options. First, assume you have created an instance of the Hexagon class, and wish to discover if it supports the pointy behavior. One approach is to make use of an explicit cast:

```
// Grab a reference to the IPointy interface using a dynamic cast.
Hexagon hex = new Hexagon("Bill");
```

```
IPointy itfPt = (IPointy)hex;
Console.WriteLine(itfPt.GetNumberOfPoints());
```

Here, you are asking the Hexagon instance for access to the IPointy interface. If the object does support this interface, you are then able to exercise the behavior accordingly. However, what if you were to create an instance of Circle? Given that the Circle class does not support the IPointy interface, you are issued a runtime error! When you attempt to access an interface not supported by a given class using a direct cast, the system throws an InvalidCastException, as seen in Figure 4-2.

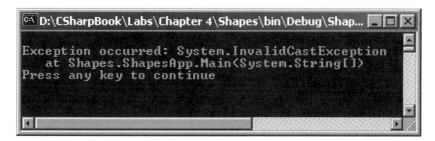

Figure 4-2. Bad cast

To safely recover from this exception you need to catch this exception:

```
// Catch the exception programmatically to recover gracefully. . .
Circle c = new Circle("Lisa");
IPointy itfPt;
try
{
    itfPt = (IPointy)c;
    Console.WriteLine(itfPt.GetNumberOfPoints());
}
catch(InvalidCastException e)
{ Console.WriteLine("OOPS!  Not pointy. . ."); }
```

The second way you can obtain an interface from an object reference using the "as" keyword. For example:

```
// Second way to obtain an interface:
Hexagon hex2 = new Hexagon("Peter");
IPointy itfPt2;
itfPt2 = hex2 as IPointy;
if(itfPt2 != null)
```

```
        Console.WriteLine(itfPt2.GetNumberOfPoints());
else
        Console.WriteLine("OOPS!  Not pointy. . .");
```

The "as" syntax sets the interface variable to null if a given interface is not supported by the object (notice that you check your IPointy reference for null before continuing) rather than throwing an exception. Finally, you may also obtain an interface from an object using the "is" operator. If the object in question is not IPointy-compatible, the condition fails:

```
// Are you pointy?
Triangle t = new Triangle();
if(t is IPointy)
        Console.WriteLine(t.GetNumberOfPoints());
else
        Console.WriteLine("OOPS!  Not pointy. . .");
```

In these examples, you could have avoided checking the outcome of asking for the IPointy reference, given that you knew ahead of time which shapes were IPointy-compatible. However, what if you were to create an array of generic Shape references, each of which has been assigned to a given subclass? You may make use of any of the previous techniques to discover at runtime which items in the array support this behavior:

```
// Let's discover which shapes are pointy at runtime. . .
Shape[] s = {new Hexagon(), new Circle(), new Triangle("Joe"),
new Circle("JoJo")};

for(int i = 0; i < s.Length; i++)
{
    // Recall the Shape base class defines an abstract Draw() member.
    s[i].Draw();

    // Who's pointy?
    if(s[i] is IPointy)
        Console.WriteLine("Points: {0}", ((IPointy)s[i]).GetNumberOfPoints());
    else
        Console.WriteLine(s[i].PetName + "\'s not pointy!");
}
```

The output follows in Figure 4-3.

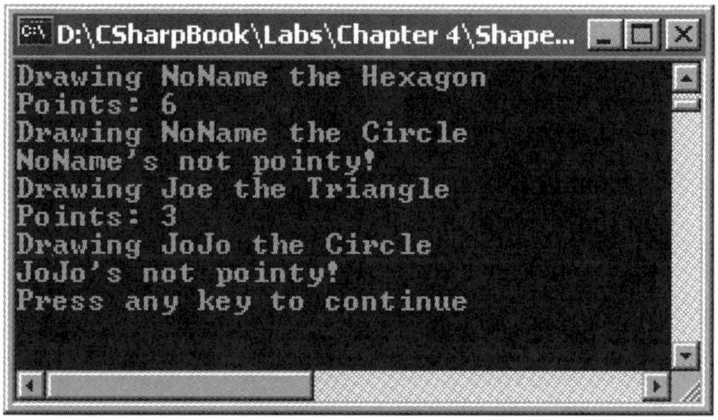

Figure 4-3. Discovering behaviors at runtime

Interfaces as Parameters

Interfaces are strongly typed variables and therefore you may construct methods that take interfaces as parameters as well as return values. To begin, assume you have defined another interface named IDraw3D as follows:

```
// The 3D drawing behavior.
public interface IDraw3D
{
    void Draw3D();
}
```

Next, assume that two of your three shapes (Circle and Hexagon) have been configured to support this new behavior:

```
// Circle supports IDraw3D.
public class Circle : Shape, IDraw3D
{
...
    public void Draw3D()
    {
        Console.WriteLine("Drawing Circle in 3D!");
    }
}
```

```
// If your types support multiple interfaces, simply tack them to the end of the
// class definition.
public class Hexagon : Shape, IPointy, IDraw3D
```

```
{
. . .
    public void Draw3D()
    {
        Console.WriteLine("Drawing Hexagon in 3D!");
    }
}
```

If you now define a method taking an IDraw3D interface as a parameter, you are able to effectively send in *any* object supporting IDraw3D. Consider the following:

```
// Make some shapes. If they can be rendered in 3D, do it!
public class ShapesApp
{
    // I'll draw anyone supporting IDraw3D!
    public static void DrawThisShapeIn3D(IDraw3D itf3d)
    {
        itf3d.Draw3D();
    }

    public static int Main(string[] args)
    {
        Shape[] s = {new Hexagon(), new Circle(),
                    new Triangle(), new Circle("JoJo")};

        for(int i = 0; i < s.Length; i++)
        {
            // Can I draw you in 3D?
            if(s[i] is IDraw3D)
                DrawThisShapeIn3D((IDraw3D)s[i]);
        }
        return 0;
    }
}
```

Notice that the triangle is never drawn, as it is not IDraw3D compatible (Figure 4-4).

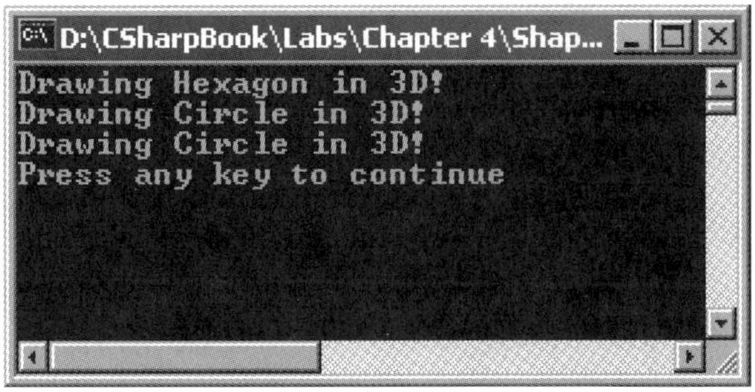

Figure 4-4. Discovering all IDraw3D compatible types

Understanding Explicit Interface Implementation

In our previous definition of IDraw3D, you were forced to name your method
Draw3D() in order to avoid clashing with the abstract Draw() method defined in
the Shapes base class:

```
// The 3D drawing behavior.
public interface IDraw3D
{
    void Draw3D();
}
```

While there is nothing horribly wrong with this interface definition, a more
natural method name would simply be Draw():

```
// The 3D drawing behavior.
public interface IDraw3D
{
    void Draw();
}
```

If you were to create a new class that derives from Shape *and* implements
IDraw3D, you are in for some problematic behavior. Before seeing the problem
firsthand, assume you have defined the following new class named Line:

```
// Problems. . .
public class Line : Shape, IDraw3D          // Both define a Draw() method!
{
    public override void Draw()
```

```
    {
        Console.WriteLine("Drawing a line. . .");
    }
}
```

The Line class compiles without a hitch. But, consider the following object user code:

```
// Calls Line.Draw()
Line myLine = new Line();
myLine.Draw();
```

```
// Also calls Line.Draw().
IDraw3D itfDraw3d= (IDraw3D) myLine;
itfDraw3d.Draw();
```

Given what you already know about the Shapes base class and IDraw3D interface, it looks as if you have inherited *two* abstract methods named Draw(). However, given that the Line class offers a concrete implementation, the compiler is happy to call the same implementation from an interface or object reference. This is problematic in that you would like to have the IDraw3D.Draw() method to render a type in stunning 3D, while the overridden Shape.Draw() method draws in boring 2D.

Now consider a related problem. How can you ensure that the methods defined by a given interface are only accessible from an interface reference? For example, an object user is able to access the members defined by the IPointy interface using either an object reference or an IPointy reference.

The answer to each question comes by way of explicit interface implementation. Using this technique, you are able to ensure that the object user can only access methods defined by a given interface using the correct interface reference, as well as circumvent possible name clashes. To illustrate, here is the updated Line class:

```
// Using explicit method implementation we are able to provide distinct
// Draw() implementations.
public class Line : Shape, IDraw3D
{
    // You can only call this method using an IDraw3D interface reference.
    void IDraw3D.Draw()
    {
        Console.WriteLine("Drawing a 3D line. . .");
    }
```

```
    // You can only call this using a Line (or base class) reference.
    public override void Draw()
    {
        Console.WriteLine("Drawing a line. . .");
    }
}
```

There are a few odds and ends to be aware of when using explicit interface implementation. First and foremost, you cannot make use of an access modifier when using this technique. For example, the following is illegal syntax:

```
// Nope! Illegal.
public class Line : Shape, IDraw3D
{
    public void IDraw3D.Draw()
    {
        Console.WriteLine("Drawing a 3D line. . .");
    }
. . .
}
```

This should make sense. The whole reason to use explicit interface method implementation is to ensure that a given interface method is bound at the interface level. If we were to add the "public" keyword, this would suggest that the method is a member of the public sector of the class, which defeats the point!

Now let's revisit the name clash issue. This technique can be very helpful whenever you are implementing a number of interfaces that happen to contain identical methods. For example, assume you wish to create a class that implements all the following interfaces:

```
// Three interfaces each defining identical methods.
public interface IDraw
{
    void Draw();
}

public interface IDraw3D
{
    void Draw();
}

public interface IDrawToPrinter
```

```
{
    void Draw();
}
```

If you wish to build a shape (using interface-based techniques) that supports basic rendering (IDraw), 3D rendering (IDraw3D), as well as printing services (IDrawToPrinter), the only way to provide unique behaviors for each method is to use explicit interface implementation:

```
// Fine grained control.
public class SuperImage : IDraw, IDrawToPrinter, IDraw3D
{
    void IDraw.Draw()
    {
        // Basic drawing logic.
    }
    void IDrawToPrinter.Draw()
    {
        // Printer logic.
    }
    void IDraw3D.Draw()
    {
        // 3D support.
    }
}
```

SOURCE CODE   *The Shapes project is located under the Chapter 4 subdirectory.*

Building Interface Hierarchies

To wrap up our investigation of building custom interfaces, you must examine the issue of interface hierarchies. Just as a class can serve as a base class to other classes (which can in turn function as base classes to yet another class), it is possible to build derived relationships among interfaces. As you might expect, the top-most interface defines a general behavior, while the most derived interface defines more specific behaviors. Here is a simple interface hierarchy:

```
// The base interface.
interface IDraw
{
    void Draw();
}
```

```
interface IDraw2 : IDraw
{
    void DrawToPrinter();
}


interface IDraw3 : IDraw2
{
    void DrawToMetaFile();
}
```

The relationships between these custom interfaces can be seen in Figure 4-5.

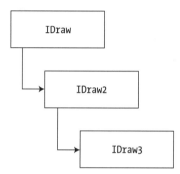

Figure 4-5. Simple interface hierarchy

Now, if a class wished to support each behavior expressed in this interface hierarchy, it would derive from the *nth-most* interface (IDraw3 in this case). Any methods defined by the base interface(s) are automatically carried into the definition. For example:

```
// This class supports IDraw, IDraw2 and IDraw3.
public class SuperImage : IDraw3
{
    // Use explicit interface methods implementation to bind
    // methods to the correct interface.
    void IDraw.Draw()
    {
        // Basic drawing logic
    }


    void IDraw2.DrawToPrinter()
    {
        // Draw to printer.
    }
```

```
        void IDraw3.DrawToMetaFile()
        {
            // Draw to metafile.
        }
}
```

Here is some sample usage (see Figure 4-6 for output):

```
// Exercise the interfaces.
public class TheApp
{
    public static int Main(string[] args)
    {
        SuperImage si = new SuperImage();

        // Get IDraw.
        IDraw itfDraw = (IDraw)si;
        itfDraw.Draw();

        // Now get IDraw3.
        if(itfDraw is IDraw3)
        {
            IDraw3 itfDraw3 = (IDraw3)itfDraw;
            itfDraw3.DrawToMetaFile();
            itfDraw3.DrawToPrinter();
        }

        return 0;
    }
}
```

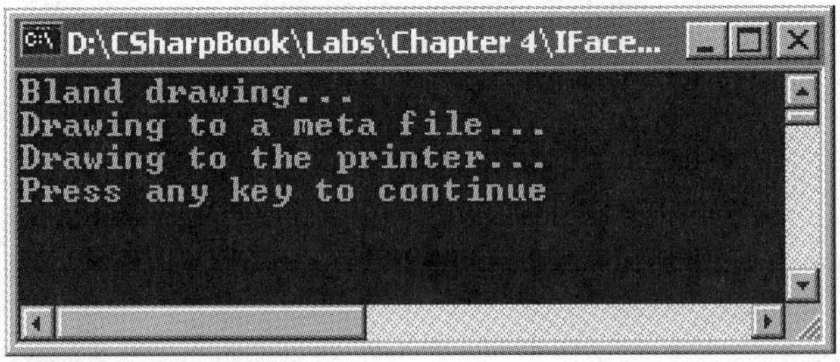

Figure 4-6. Using the SuperImage

Specifying Multiple Base Interfaces

As you build interface hierarchies, be aware that it is completely permissible to create an interface that derives from multiple base interfaces (unlike classic COM). Recall of course, that it is *not* permissible to build a class that derives from multiple base classes. For example assume you are building a new set of interfaces that model automobile behaviors:

```
interface IBasicCar
{
    void Drive();
}
interface IUnderwaterCar
{
    void Dive();
}
// Here we have an interface with TWO base interfaces.
interface IJamesBondCar : IBasicCar, IUnderwaterCar
{
    void TurboBoost();
}
```

If you were to build a class that implements IJamesBondCar, you would now be responsible for implementing TurboBoost(), Dive(), and Drive():

```
public class JBCar : IJamesBondCar
{
    public JBCar(){}

    // Inherited members.
    void IBasicCar.Drive(){Console.WriteLine("Speeding up. . .");}
    void IUnderwaterCar.Dive(){Console.WriteLine("Submerging. . .");}
    void IJamesBondCar.TurboBoost(){Console.WriteLine("Blast off!");}
}
```

This specialized automobile can now be used as you would expect:

```
JBCar j = new JBCar();
if(j is IJamesBondCar)
{
    ((IJamesBondCar)j).Drive();
    ((IJamesBondCar)j).TurboBoost();
    ((IJamesBondCar)j).Dive();
}
```

SOURCE CODE   *The IFaceHierarchy project is located under the Chapter 4 subdirectory.*

Building a Custom Enumerator (IEnumerable and IEnumerator)

Now that you understand how to work with custom interfaces, you can begin to examine some of the standard (i.e., predefined) interfaces defined in the .NET class libraries. As you dig deeper into the .NET universe, you will find that many canned types implement numerous standard interfaces. You are also free to build custom types that support these same interfaces. To illustrate, assume you have developed a class named Cars, which represents a collection of individual Car objects (which we created in Chapter 3). Here is the initial definition:

```
// Cars is a container of Car objects.
public class Cars
{
    private Car[] carArray;

    // Create some Car objects upon start up.
    public Cars()
    {
        carArray = new Car[4];
        carArray[0] = new Car("FeeFee", 200, 0);
        carArray[1] = new Car("Clunker", 90, 0);
        carArray[2] = new Car("Zippy", 30, 0);
        carArray[3] = new Car("Fred", 30, 0);
    }
}
```

Ideally, it would be convenient from the object user's point of view to iterate over the Cars type using the foreach construct, in order to obtain each internal Car:

```
// This seems reasonable. . .
public class CarDriver
{
    public static void Main()
    {
        Cars carLot = new Cars();
```

```
        // Hand over each car in the collection?
        foreach (Car c in carLot)
        {
            Console.WriteLine("Name: {0}", c.PetName);
            Console.WriteLine("Max speed: {0}", c.MaxSpeed);
        }
    }
}
```

Sadly, if you attempt to execute this code, the compiler would complain that the Cars class does not implement the GetEnumerator() method. This method is defined by the IEnumerable interface, which is found in the System.Collections namespace. To rectify the problem, you may update the Cars definition as follows:

```
// The foreach syntax demands that your class support the IEnumerable interface.
public class Cars : IEnumerable
{
. . .
    // IEnumerable defines this method (and only this method).
    public IEnumerator GetEnumerator()
    {
        // OK, now what?
    }
. . .
}
```

So far so good, however as you can see, GetEnumerator() returns yet another interface named IEnumerator. IEnumerator can be obtained from an object to traverse over an internal collection of types. IEnumerator is also defined in the System.Collections namespace and defines the following three methods:

```
// GetEnumerator() returns one of these guys.
public interface IEnumerator
{
    bool MoveNext ();          // Advance the internal position of the cursor.
    object Current {get;}      // Get the current item (read only property).
    void Reset ();             // Reset the cursor to the beginning of the list.
}
```

Now, given that IEnumerable.GetEnumerator() returns an IEnumerator interface, you may update the Cars type as follows:

```
// Getting closer. . .
public class Cars : IEnumerable, IEnumerator
{
. . .
    // Implementation of IEnumerable.
    public IEnumerator GetEnumerator()
    {
        return (IEnumerator)this;
    }
. . .
}
```

The final detail is to flesh out the implementation of MoveNext(), Current, and Reset(). Here then, is the final update of the Cars class:

```
// An enumerable car collection!
public class Cars : IEnumerator, IEnumerable
{
    private Car[] carArray;

    // Current position in array.
    int pos = -1;

    public Cars()
    { // Make some cars and add them to the array. . . }

    // IEnumerator implementation.
    public bool MoveNext()
    {
        if(pos < carArray.Length)
        {
            pos++;
            return true;
        }
        else
            return false;
    }

    public void Reset() { pos = 0; }

    public object Current
```

```
    {
        get { return carArray[pos]; }
    }

    // IEnumerable implementation.
    public IEnumerator GetEnumerator()
    {
        return (IEnumerator)this;
    }
}
```

So then, what have you gained by equipping your class to support the IEnumerator and IEnumerable interfaces? First, your custom type can now be traversed using the foreach syntax.

```
// No problem!
foreach (Car c in carLot)
{
    Console.WriteLine("Name: {0}", c.PetName);
    Console.WriteLine("Max speed: {0}", c.MaxSpeed);
}
```

In addition, this provides an alternative means for an object user to access the underlying automobiles maintained by the Cars type (which as you may be able to tell, looks a lot like manipulating the raw COM IEnumXXXX interface):

```
// Access Car types using IEnumerator.
IEnumerator itfEnum;
itfEnum = (IEnumerator)carLot;

// Reset the cursor to the beginning.
itfEnum.Reset();

// Advance internal cursor by 1.
itfEnum.MoveNext();

// Grab current Car and crank some tunes.
object curCar = itfEnum.Current;
((Car)curCar).CrankTunes(true);
```

SOURCE CODE   *The ObjEnum project is located under the Chapter 4 subdirectory.*

Building Cloneable Objects (ICloneable)

As you recall from Chapter 2, System.Object defines a member named Member-wiseClone(). This method is used to make a *shallow copy* of an object instance. Object users do not call this method directly, however whenever the assignment operator is used to set one object reference equal to another, Memberwise-Clone() is called automatically. First, assume you have a class named Point:

```
// The classic Point example. . .
public class Point
{
    // Field data.
    public int x, y;

    // Ctors.
    public Point(){}
    public Point(int x, int y){this.x = x; this.y = y;}

    // Override Object.ToString().
    public override string ToString()
    { return "X: " + x + " Y: " + y; }
}
```

Given what you already know about reference types and value types, you are aware that if you set one object reference to another reference, you have two pointers to the same memory location (i.e., a shallow copy).

If you wish to equip your objects to support deep-copy semantics, you may implement the standard ICloneable interface. This interface defines a single method named Clone(). The implementation of the Clone() method varies between objects. However the basic functionality tends to be the same: Copy the values of your member variables into a new object instance, and return it to the user. Let's retrofit Point to support a true deep copy:

```
// The Point class supports deep copy semantics ala ICloneable.
public class Point : ICloneable
{
    // State data.
    public int x, y;

    // Ctors.
    public Point(){}
    public Point(int x, int y) {this.x = x; this.y = y;}
```

```
    // The sole method of ICloneable.
    public object Clone()
    {
        return new Point(this.x, this.y);
    }

    public override string ToString()
    { return "X: " + x + " Y: " + y; }
}
```

In this way, you can create exact standalone copies of the Point type, as illustrated by the following code:

```
// Notice Clone() returns a generic object type.
// You must perform an explicit cast to obtain the derived type.
Point p3 = new Point(100, 100);
Point p4 = (Point)p3.Clone();

// Change p4.x (which will not change p3.x).
p4.x = 0;


// Print each object.
Console.WriteLine("Deep copying using Clone()");
Console.WriteLine(p3);
Console.WriteLine(p4);
```

If this code looks vaguely familiar to you, it should. In Chapter 2 you spent some time coming to understand the distinction between value and reference types. As you recall, value types (such as a C# structure) always make use of bit-copy semantics. When you wish to configure a reference type (i.e., a C# class) to produce deep copies, you must implement ICloneable. If you do not, your custom classes will make use of the default shallow copy provided by Object.MemberwiseClone(). Be aware that numerous .NET types support this behavior. Look up ICloneable from online Help for the complete list of cloneable classes supported by the runtime.

SOURCE CODE *The ObjClone project is located under the Chapter 4 subdirectory.*

Building Comparable Objects (IComparable)

The IComparable interface (defined in the System namespace) specifies a behavior that allows an object to be sorted based on some internal key. Here is the formal definition:

```
// This interface allows an object to specify its
// relationship between other like objects.
interface IComparable
{
    int CompareTo(object o);
}
```

Let's assume you have updated the Car class to maintain an internal ID, as well as an owner supplied pet name. Object users might create an array of Car types as follows:

```
// Make an array of Car types.
Car[] myAutos = new Car[5];
myAutos[0] = new Car(123, "Rusty");
myAutos[1] = new Car(6, "Mary");
myAutos[2] = new Car(83, "Viper");
myAutos[3] = new Car(13, "NoName");
myAutos[4] = new Car(9873, "Chucky");
```

As you recall, the System.Array class defines a static method named Sort(). When you invoke this method on an array of intrinsic types (e.g., int, short) you are able to sort the items in the array from lowest to highest. However, what if you were to send an array of Car types into the Sort() method:

```
// Sort my cars?
Array.Sort(myAutos);            // Nope, not yet...sorry!
```

If you run this test, you would find that an ArgumentException exception is thrown by the runtime, with the following message: "At least one object must implement IComparable." Therefore, when you build custom types, you can implement IComparable to allow arrays of your types to be sorted. When you flesh out the details of CompareTo(), it will be up to you to decide what the baseline of the ordering operation will be. For the Car type, the internal ID seems to be the most logical candidate:

```
// The iteration of the Car can be ordered
// based on the CarID.
public class Car : IComparable
{

...

    // IComparable implementation.
    int IComparable.CompareTo(object o)
    {
        Car temp = (Car)o;
        if(this.CarID > temp.CarID)
            return 1;
        if(this.CarID < temp.CarID)
            return -1;
        else
            return 0;
    }
}
```

As you can see, the logic behind CompareTo() is to test the incoming type against the current instance. The return value of CompareTo() is used to discover if this type is less than, greater than, or equal to the object it is being compared with (Table 4-1).

Table 4-1. CompareTo() Return Values

COMPARETO() RETURN VALUE	MEANING IN LIFE
Any number less than zero	This instance is less than object.
Zero	This instance is equal to object.
Any number greater than zero	This instance is greater than object.

Now that your Car type understands how to compare itself to like objects, you can write the following user code:

```
// Exercise the IComparable interface.
public class CarApp
{
    public static int Main(string[] args)
    {
        // Make an array of Car types.
        Car[] myAutos = new Car[5];
        myAutos[0] = new Car(123, "Rusty");
        myAutos[1] = new Car(6, "Mary");
        myAutos[2] = new Car(83, "Viper");
```

```
myAutos[3] = new Car(13, "NoName");
myAutos[4] = new Car(9873, "Chucky");

// Dump current array.
Console.WriteLine("Here is the unordered set of cars:");
foreach(Car c in myAutos)
    Console.WriteLine(c.ID + "   " + c.PetName);

// Now, sort them using IComparable!
Array.Sort(myAutos);

// Dump sorted array.
Console.WriteLine("Here is the ordered set of cars:");
foreach(Car c in myAutos)
    Console.WriteLine(c.ID + "   " + c.PetName);

            return 0;
    }
}
```

Figure 4-7 illustrates a test run.

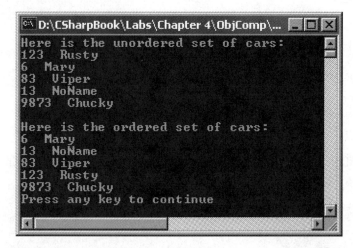

Figure 4-7. Sorting Car types by numerical ID

As a side note, if multiple items in the Car array have the same value assigned to the ID member variable, the sort simply lists them according to their occurrence in the sort (notice in Figure 4-8 we have three cars with the ID of 6).

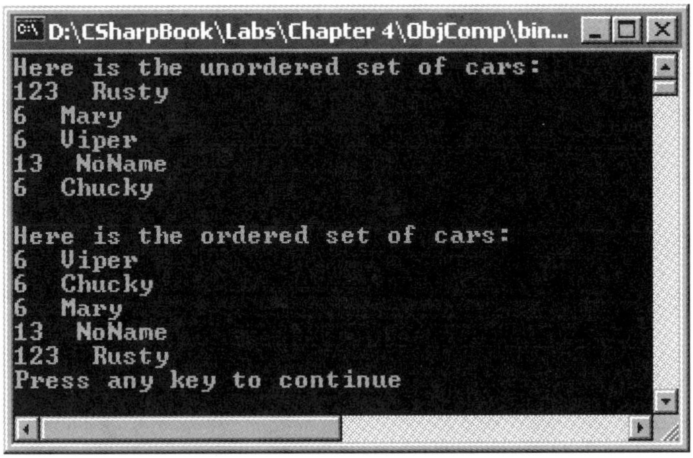

Figure 4-8. Duplicate numerical IDs are listed by order of occurrence

Specifying Multiple Sort Orders (IComparer)

In this version of the Car type, you made use of the underlying ID to function
as the baseline of the sort order. Another design might have used the pet name
of the car as the basis of the sorting algorithm (to list cars alphabetically). Now,
what if you wanted to build a Car that could be sorted by ID *as well as* by pet
name? If this is the behavior you are interested in, you need to make friends with
another standard interface named IComparer, defined within the System.Collec-
tions namespace as follows:

```
// A generic way to compare two objects.
interface IComparer
{
    int Compare(object o1, object o2);
}
```

Unlike the IComparable interface, IComparer is typically *not* implemented
on the type you are trying to sort (i.e., the Car). Rather, you implement this interface on any number of helper objects, one for each sort order (pet name, ID, etc).
Currently, our Car type already knows how to compare itself against other cars
based on the internal car ID. Therefore, to allow the object user to sort an array of
Car types by pet name will require an additional helper class that implements
IComparer. Here's the code:

```
// This helper class is used to sort an array of Cars by pet name.
using System.Collections;
public class SortByPetName : IComparer
```

```
{
    public SortByPetName(){}

    // Test the pet name of each object.
    int IComparer.Compare(object o1, object o2)
    {
        Car t1 = (Car)o1;
        Car t2 = (Car)o2;
        return String.Compare(t1.PetName, t2.PetName);
    }
}
```

The object user code is able to make use of this helper class. System.Array has a number of overloaded Sort() methods, one that just happens to take an object implementing IComparer (Figure 4-9):

```
// Now sort by pet name.
Array.Sort(myAutos, new SortByPetName());

// Dump sorted array.
Console.WriteLine("Ordering by pet name:");
foreach(Car c in myAutos)
    Console.WriteLine(c.ID + "   " + c.PetName);
```

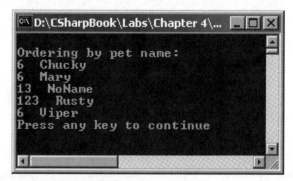

Figure 4-9. Sorting alphabetically by pet name

Custom Properties, Custom Sort Types

It is worth pointing out that you can make use of a custom static property in order to help the object user along when sorting your Car types by pet name.

Assume the Car class has added a static read-only property named SortByPetName() that returns the correct IComparer interface:

```
// We now support a custom property to return the correct IComparer interface.
public class Car : IComparable
{
    . . .
    // Property to return the SortByPetName comparer.
    public static IComparer SortByPetName
    { get { return (IComparer)new SortByPetName(); } }


    . . .
}
```

The object user code can now be modified as follows:

```
// This was a bit cumbersome.
// Array.Sort(myAutos, new SortByPetName());

// Cleaner!  Just ask the car for the correct sort object.
Array.Sort(myAutos, Car.SortByPetName);
```

SOURCE CODE   *The ObjComp project is located under the Chapter 4 sub-directory.*

Exploring the System.Collections Namespace

The most primitive C# collection construct is System.Array. As you have already seen in Chapter 2, this class does provide quite a number of member functions that encapsulate a number of interesting services (e.g., reversing, sorting, cloning, and enumerating). In a similar vein, this chapter has also shown you how to build custom types with many of the same services using standard interfaces. To round out your appreciation of the various .NET collection constructs, the final order of business is to review the numerous types defined within the System.Collections namespace.

First, System.Collections defines a number of standard interfaces (many of which you have already implemented during the course of this chapter). Most of the classes defined within the System.Collections namespace implement these interfaces to provide access to their contents. Table 4-2 gives a breakdown of the core collection-centric interfaces:

Table 4-2. Interfaces of System.Collections

SYSTEM.COLLECTIONS INTERFACE	MEANING IN LIFE
ICollection	Defines generic characteristics (e.g., read-only, thread safe, etc.) for a collection class.
IComparer	Allows two objects to be compared.
IDictionary	Allows an object to represent its contents using name/value pairs.
IDictionaryEnumerator	Used to enumerate the contents of an object supporting IDictionary.
IEnumerable	Returns the IEnumerator interface for a given object.
IEnumerator	Generally used to support foreach style iteration of subtypes.
IHashCodeProvider	Returns the hash code for the implementing type using a customized hash algorithm.
IList	Provides behavior to add, remove, and index items in a list of objects.

As you may suspect, many of these interfaces are related by an interface hierarchy, while others are standalone entities. Figure 4-10 illustrates the relationship between each type (recall that it is permissible for a single interface derive from multiple interfaces).

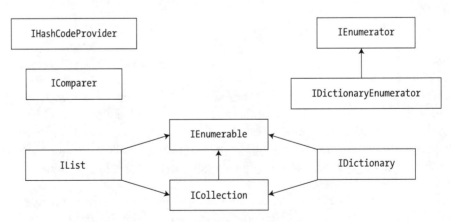

Figure 4-10. The System.Collections interface hierarchy

Now that you understand the basic functionality provided by each interface, Table 4-3 provides a rundown of the core collection classes.

Table 4-3. Classes of System.Collections

SYSTEM.COLLECTIONS CLASS	MEANING IN LIFE	KEY IMPLEMENTED INTERFACES
ArrayList	A dynamically sized array of objects.	IList, ICollection, IEnumerable and ICloneable.
Hashtable	Represents a collection of associated keys and values that are organized based on the hash code of the key.	Types stored in a Hashtable should always override system.Object.GetHashCode(). IDictionary, ICollection, IEnumerable and ICloneable.
Queue	Represents a standard first-in-first-out (FIFO) queue.	ICollection, ICloneable and IEnumerable.
SortedList	Like a dictionary, however the elements can also be accessed by ordinal position (e.g., index).	IDictionary, ICollection, IEnumerable and ICloneable.
Stack	A last-in-first-out (LIFO) queue providing push, pop (and peek) functionality.	ICollection and IEnumerable.

System.Collections.Specialized Namespace

In addition to the types defined within the System.Collections namespace, you should also be aware that the System.Collections.Specialized namespace provides another set of types that are more (pardon the redundancy) specialized. For example, the StringDictionary and ListDictionary types each provide a stylized implementation of the IDictionary interface. Now the focus is on the generic types defined within System.Collections; see online Help for additional details.

Retrofitting the Cars Type

As you begin to experiment with the System.Collections types, you will find they all tend to share common functionality (that's the point of interface-based programming). Thus, rather than listing out the members of each and every collection class, the final task of this chapter is to illustrate how to build a custom collection that makes use of a specific .NET collection class: ArrayList. Once you understand this type's functionality, gaining an understanding of the remaining collection classes should naturally follow.

Previously in this chapter, you created the Cars type that was responsible for holding a number of Car objects. Internally, the set of Car objects was represented with an instance of System.Array, and because of this fact, you needed to write a good deal of extra code to allow the outside world to interact with our subobjects. Furthermore, the Car array is defined with a fixed upper limit.

A more intelligent design would be to represent the internal set of Car objects as an instance of System.Collections.ArrayList. Given that this class already has a number of methods to insert, remove, and enumerate its contents, the only duty of the Cars type is to supply a set of public functions that delegate to the inner ArrayList (in other words, the Cars type "has-a" ArrayList). As with any containment/delegation scenario, it is up to you to decide how much functionality of the inner object to expose to the object user. Here then, is one possible implementation of the updated Cars type:

```csharp
// Notice we no longer need to implement IEnumerator, given that
// ArrayList already does so.
public class Cars : IEnumerable      // ,IEnumerator . . . Don't need this anymore!
{
    // This class maintains an array of cars.
    private ArrayList carList;

    // Make the ArrayList.
    public Cars() {carList = new ArrayList ();}

    /* Expose select methods of the ArrayList to the outside world. */

    // Insert a car.
    public void AddCar(Car c)
    { carList.Add(c);}

    // Remove a car.
    public void RemoveCar(int carToRemove)
    { carList.RemoveAt(carToRemove);}

    // Return number of cars.
    public int CarCount
    { get{ return carList.Count;} }

    // Kill all cars.
    public void ClearAllCars()
    { carList.Clear(); }
```

```
// Determine if the incoming car is already in the list.
public bool CarIsPresent(Car c)
{ return carList.Contains(c); }

// Note we simply return the IEnumerator of the ArrayList.
public IEnumerator GetEnumerator()
{ return carList.GetEnumerator();}
}
```

This new implementation also makes using the Cars type a bit less of a burden for the object user:

```
// Use the new Cars container class.
public static void Main()
{
    Cars carLot = new Cars();

    // Add some cars.
    carLot.AddCar( new Car("Jasper", 200, 80));
    carLot.AddCar( new Car("Mandy", 140, 0));
    carLot.AddCar( new Car("Porker", 90, 90));
    carLot.AddCar( new Car("Jimbo", 40, 4));

    // Get each one and print out some stats.
    Console.WriteLine("You have {0} in the lot:\n", carLot.CarCount);
    foreach (Car c in carLot)
    {
        Console.WriteLine("Name: {0}", c.PetName);
        Console.WriteLine("Max speed: {0}\n", c.MaxSpeed);
    }

    // Kill the third car.
    carLot.RemoveCar(3);
    Console.WriteLine("You have {0} in the lot.\n", carLot.CarCount);

    // Add another car and verify it is in the collection.
    Car temp = new Car("Zippy", 90, 90);
    carLot.AddCar(temp);

    if(carLot.CarIsPresent(temp))
        Console.WriteLine(temp.PetName + " is already in the lot.");
```

```
    // Kill 'em all.
    carLot.ClearAllCars();
    Console.WriteLine("You have {0} in the lot.\n", carLot.CarCount);
}
```

The output is shown in Figure 4-11.

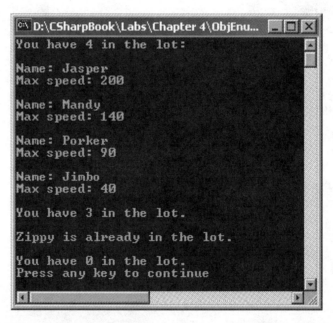

Figure 4-11. The updated Cars container

You may be wondering why you bothered to make the custom Cars type at all, given that the object user could create an ArrayList type directly. The reason is that ArrayList can contain *any* object reference. If you did not create a custom wrapper class such as Cars, the ArrayList instance could contain Cars, Boats, Airplanes, strings, or any other type!

```
ArrayList ar = new ArrayList();
ar.Add(carLot);
ar.Add("Hello");
ar.Add(new JamesBondCar());
ar.Add(23);
```

Using the containment/delegation model, you are able to leverage the functionality of the ArrayList type, while maintaining control over what can be inserted into the container.

SOURCE CODE *This updated Cars collection (ObjectEnumWithCollection) can be found under the Chapter 4 subdirectory.*

Summary

If you are a COM programmer by trade, this chapter must have given you warm fuzzies. The interface is a collection of abstract members that may be implemented by a given class. Because an interface does not supply any implementation details, it is common to regard an interface as a behavior that may be supported by a given type. When two or more classes implement the same interface, you are able to treat each type the same way (aka interface-based polymorphism). C# provides the interface keyword to allow you to define a new interface. As you have seen, a type can support as many interfaces as necessary using a comma-delimited list. Furthermore, it is permissible to build interfaces that derive from multiple base interfaces.

In addition to building your custom interfaces, the .NET libraries define a number of standard (i.e., framework-supplied) interfaces. This chapter focused on the interfaces defined within the System.Collections namespace. As you have seen, you are free to build custom types that implement these predefined interfaces to gain a number of desirable traits such as cloning, sorting, and enumerating.

Finally, you spent some time investigating the stock collection classes defined within the System.Collections namespace and examined the flexibility that can be obtained when combining the has-a relationship with an existing container class.

CHAPTER 5

Advanced C# Class Construction Techniques

This chapter rounds out your introduction to the core aspects of the C# language by examining a number of advanced (but extremely useful) syntactic constructs. To begin, you learn how to construct and use an *indexer method*. This C# mechanism enables you to build custom types, which exposes internal subtypes using the familiar bracket operator (i.e., []). If you have a C++ background, you will find that creating a C# indexer method is analogous to overloading the [] operator on a C++ class. Once you learn how to build an indexer, you then examine how to overload various operators (+, -, <, > and so forth) for a custom C# type.

This chapter then examines three techniques that enable the objects in your system to engage in bidirectional communications. First, you learn about the C# "delegate" keyword, which is little more than a type-safe function pointer. Once you learn how to create and manipulate delegates, you are in a perfect position to investigate the .NET event protocol, which is based on the delegation model. Finally, you discover how the use of custom interfaces can also enable bidirectional communications (which should ring a bell for those coming from a COM background).

I wrap up by examining how you can document your types using XML attributes, and how the Visual Studio.NET IDE automatically generates Web-based documentation for your projects. Although this might not qualify as a truly "advanced" technique, it is a high note on which to end the chapter.

Building a Custom Indexer

At this point, you should feel confident building C# types using traditional OOP (refer to Chapter 3) as well as interface-based programming techniques (refer to Chapter 4). In this chapter, I take some time to examine some additional aspects of C# that you may not be readily familiar with, beginning with the concept of an *indexer*.

Most programmers (such as yourself) are very familiar with the process of accessing discrete items held within a standard array using the index (aka *bracket*) operator:

```
// Declare an array of integers.
int[] myInts = {10, 9, 100, 432, 9874};

// Use the [] operator to access each element.
for(int j = 0; j < myInts.Length; j++)
    Console.WriteLine("Index {0} = {1}", j,  myInts[j]);
```

The C# language supports the capability to build custom classes that may be indexed just like an array of intrinsic types. It should be no big surprise that the method that provides the capability to access items in this manner is termed an "indexer."

Before exploring how to create such a construct, let's begin by seeing one in action. Assume you have added support for an indexer method to the Cars container developed in the previous chapter. Observe the following usage:

```
// Indexers allow you to access items in an array-like fashion.
public class CarApp
{
    public static void Main()
    {
        // Assume the Cars type has an indexer method.
        Cars carLot = new Cars();

        // Make some cars and add them to the car lot.
        carLot[0] = new Car("FeeFee", 200, 0);
        carLot[1] = new Car("Clunker", 90, 0);
        carLot[2] = new Car("Zippy", 30, 0);

        // Now obtain and display each item.
        for(int i = 0; i < 3; i++)
        {
            Console.WriteLine("Car number {0}:", i);
            Console.WriteLine("Name: {0}", carLot[i].PetName);
            Console.WriteLine("Max speed: {0}", carLot[i].MaxSpeed);
        }
    }
}
```

A test run would look something like Figure 5-1.

As you can see, indexers behave much like a custom collection supporting the IEnumerator and IEnumerable interfaces. The only major difference is that rather than accessing the contents using interface references, you are able to manipulate the internal collection of automobiles just like a standard array.

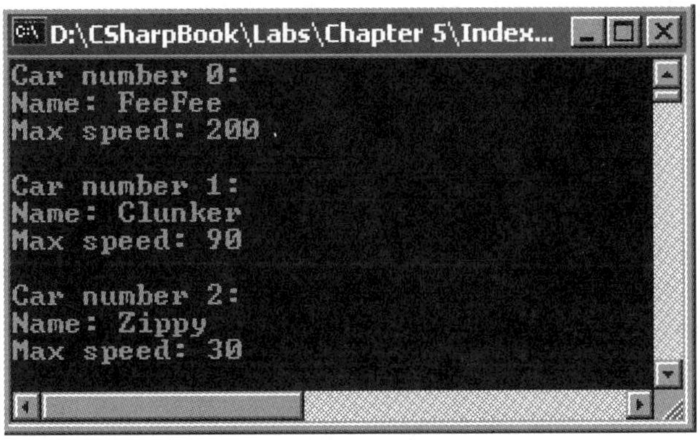

Figure 5-1. Accessing cars using an indexer

Now for the big question: How do you configure the Cars class (or any class) to do so? The indexer itself is represented as a slightly mangled C# property. In its simplest form, an indexer is created using the this[] syntax:

```
// Add the indexer to the existing class definition.
public class Cars : IEnumerator, IEnumerable
{
...
    // Let's rollback to the basics and simply make use of a standard array
    // to contain the cars.  You are free to use an ArrayList if you desire...
    private Car[] carArray;

    public Cars()
    {
        carArray = new Car[10];
    }

    // The indexer returns a Car based on a numerical index.
    public Car this[int pos]
    {
        // Accessor returns an item in the array.
        get
        {
            if(pos < 0 || pos > 10)
                throw new IndexOutOfRangeException("Out of range!");
            else
                return (carArray[pos]);
        }
```

```
        // Mutator populates the array.
        set { carArray[pos] = value;}
    }
}
```

Beyond the use of the "this" keyword, the indexer looks just like any other C# property declaration. Do be aware that indexers do not provide any array-like functionality beyond the use of the subscript operator. In other words, the object user cannot write code such as:

```
// Use System.Array.Length? Nope!
Console.WriteLine("Cars in stock: {0}", carLot.Length);
```

To support this functionality, you would need to add your own Length property to the Cars type, and delegate accordingly:

```
public class Cars
{
    . . .
    // Containment / delegation in action once again.
    public int Length() { /* figure out number of non-null entries in array. */}
}
```

However, if you are in need of this functionality, you will find your task will be much easier if you make direct use of one of the System.Collections types to hold your internal items, rather than a simple array.

SOURCE CODE   *The Indexer project is located under the Chapter 5 subdirectory.*

Overloading Operators

C#, like any programming language, has a canned set of tokens that are used to perform basic operations on intrinsic types. For example, everyone knows that the + operator can be applied to two integers in order to yield a new integer:

```
// The + operator in action.
int a = 100;
int b = 240;
int c = a + b; // c = = 340
```

This is no major news flash, but have you ever stopped and noticed how the same + operator can be applied to any intrinsic C# data type? For example:

```
// + operator with strings.
string s1 = "Hello";
string s2 = " world!";
string s3 = s1 + s2;  // s3 = = Hello world!
```

In essence, the + operator has been overloaded to function correctly on various individual data types. When the + operator is applied to numerical types, the result is the summation of the operands. However, when applied to string types, the result is string concatenation. The C# language (like C++ and unlike Java) provides the capability for you to build custom classes and structures that also respond uniquely to the same set of basic tokens (such as the + operator). Thus, if you equip a type to do so, it is possible to apply various operators to a custom class.

To keep your wits about you, assume the following simple Point class:

```
// You can't get much lamer than this!
public class Point
{
    private int x, y;
    public Point(){}
    public Point(int xPos, int yPos)
    {
        x = xPos;
        y = yPos;
    }
    public override string ToString()
    {
        return "X pos: " + this.x + " Y pos: " + this.y;
    }
}
```

Now, logically speaking it makes sense to add Points together. On a related note, it would be helpful to subtract one Point from another. For example, if you created two Point objects with some initial startup values, you would *like* to do something like this:

```
// Adding and subtracting two Points.
public static int Main(string[] args)
{
    // Make two points
    Point ptOne = new Point(100, 100);
    Point ptTwo = new Point(40, 40);
```

```
// Add the points to make a new point.
Point bigPoint = ptOne + ptTwo;
Console.WriteLine("Here is the big point: {0}", bigPoint.ToString());

// Subtract the points to make a new point.
Point minorPoint = bigPoint - ptOne;
Console.WriteLine("Just a minor point: {0}", minorPoint.ToString());

    return 0;
}
```

Clearly, your goal is to somehow make your Point class react uniquely to the + and – operators. To allow a custom type to respond to these intrinsic tokens, C# provides the "operator" keyword, which can only be used in conjunction with *static* methods. To illustrate:

```
// A more intelligent Point class.
public class Point
{
    private int x, y;
    public Point(){}
    public Point(int xPos, int yPos){ x = xPos; y = yPos; }

    // The Point class can be added. . .
    public static Point operator + (Point p1, Point p2)
    {
        Point newPoint = new Point(p1.x + p2.x, p1.y + p2.y);
        return newPoint;
    }

    // . . .and subtracted.
    public static Point operator - (Point p1, Point p2)
    {
        // Figure new X (assume [0,0] base).
        int newX = p1.x - p2.x;
        if(newX < 0)
            throw new ArgumentOutOfRangeException();

        // Figure new Y (also assume [0,0] base).
        int newY = p1.y - p2.y;
        if(newY < 0)
            throw new ArgumentOutOfRangeException();
```

```
        return new Point(newX, newY);
    }

    public override string ToString()
    {
        return "X pos: " + this.x + " Y pos: " + this.y;
    }
}
```

Notice that the class now contains two strange looking methods called *operator* + and *operator* –. The logic behind operator + is simply to return a brand new Point based on the summation of the incoming Point objects. Thus, when you write pt1 + pt2, under the hood you can envision the following hidden call to the static operator + method:

```
// p3 = Point.operator + (p1, p2)
p3 = p1 + p2;
```

Likewise, p1 – p2 maps to:

```
// p3 = Point.operator - (p1, p2)
p3 = p1 - p2;
```

If you were to take your class out for a test run, you would see something like Figure 5-2.

Figure 5-2. Overloaded operators at work

The capability to overload operators is useful in that it enables the object user to work with your types (more or less) like any intrinsic data item. Other languages (such as Java) do not support this capability. Also understand that the capability to overload operators is *not a requirement* of the Common Language Specification; thus, not all .NET-aware languages support types containing overloaded operators. However, you can achieve the same functionality using public methods. For example, you could write the Point class as so:

```
// Making use of methods rather than overloaded ops.
public class Point
{
...
    // Operator + as AddPoints()
    public static Point AddPoints (Point p1, Point p2)
    {
        return new Point(p1.x + p2.x, p1.y + p2.y);
    }

    // Operator - as SubtractPoints()
    public static Point SubtractPoints (Point p1, Point p2)
    {
        // Figure new X.
        int newX = p1.x - p2.x;
        if(newX < 0)
            throw new ArgumentOutOfRangeException();

        // Figure new Y.
        int newY = p1.y - p2.y;
        if(newY < 0)
            throw new ArgumentOutOfRangeException();

        return new Point(newX, newY);
    }
}
```

You could then add Points as follows:

```
// As member f(x)'s
Point finalPt = Point.AddPoints(ptOne, ptTwo);
Console.WriteLine("My final point: {0}", finalPt.ToString());
```

Seen in this light, overloaded operators are always an optional construct you may choose to support for a given class. Remember however, that they are little more than a friendly variation on a traditional public method, and are not CLS-compliant. When you are building production level classes that support overloaded operators, you should always support member function equivalents. To maximize your coding efforts, simply have the overloaded operator call the member function alternative (or vice versa). For example:

```
public class Point
{
. . .
    // For overload operator aware languages.
    public static Point operator + (Point p1, Point p2)
    {
        return AddPoints(p1, p2);
    }

    // For overloaded challenged languages.
    public static Point AddPoints (Point p1, Point p2)
    {
        return new Point(p1.x + p2.x, p1.y + p2.y);
    }
}
```

Overloading the Equality Operators

As you recall, System.Object.Equals() can be overridden in order to perform value-based (rather than referenced-based) comparisons between objects. In addition to overriding Equals() and GetHashCode(), an object may choose to override the equality operators (= = and !=).To illustrate, here is the updated Point class:

```
// This incarnation of Point also overloads the = = and != operators.
public class Point
{
    public int x, y;
    public Point(){}
    public Point(int xPos, int yPos){x = xPos; y = yPos;}
. . .
    public override bool Equals(object o)
    {
        if( ((Point)o).x = = this.x &&
            ((Point)o).y = = this.y)
                return true;
        else
                return false;
    }

    public override int GetHashCode()
    { return this.ToString().GetHashCode(); }
```

```
        // Now let's overload the = = and != operators.
        public static bool operator = =(Point p1, Point p2)
        {
                return p1.Equals(p2);
        }

        public static bool operator !=(Point p1, Point p2)
        {
                return !p1.Equals(p2);
        }
}
```

Notice how the implementation of operator = = and operator != simply makes a call to the overridden Equals() method to get the bulk of the work done. Given this, you can now exercise your Point class as so:

```
// Make use of the overloaded equality operators.
public static int Main(string[] args)
{
. . .
    if(ptOne = = ptTwo)              // Are they the same?
        Console.WriteLine("Same values!");
    else
        Console.WriteLine("Nope, different values.");

    if(ptOne != ptTwo)              // Are they different?
        Console.WriteLine("These are not equal.");
    else
        Console.WriteLine("Same values!");
}
```

As you can see, it is quite intuitive to compare two objects using the well-known = = and != operators rather than making a call to Object.Equals(). As a rule of thumb, classes that override Object.Equals() should always overload the = = and !+ operators.

If you do overload the equality operators for a given class, keep in mind that C# demands that if you override operator = =, you *must* also override operator !=, just as when you override Equals() you will need to override GetHashCode(). This ensures that an object behaves in a uniform manner during comparisons and functions correctly if placed into a hash table (if you forget, the compiler will let you know).

SOURCE CODE *The OverLoadOps project is located under the Chapter 5 sub-directory.*

Overriding the Comparison Operators

In the previous chapter, you learned how to implement the IComparable interface, in order to compare the relative relationship between two like objects. Additionally, you may also overload the comparison operators (<, >, <= and >=) for the same class. Like the equality operators, C# demands that < and > are overloaded as a set. The same holds true for the <= and >= operators. If the Car type you developed in Chapter 4 overloaded these comparison operators, the object user could now compare types as so:

```
// Exercise the overloaded < operator for the Car class.
public class CarApp
{
    public static int Main(string[] args)
    {
        // Make an array of Car types.
        Car[] myAutos = new Car[5];

        myAutos[0] = new Car(123, "Rusty");
        myAutos[1] = new Car(6, "Mary");
        myAutos[2] = new Car(6, "Viper");
        myAutos[3] = new Car(13, "NoName");
        myAutos[4] = new Car(6, "Chucky");

        // Is Rusty less than Chucky?
        if(myAutos[0] < myAutos[4])
            Console.WriteLine("Rusty is less than Chucky!");
        else
            Console.WriteLine("Chucky is less than Rusty!");
        return 0;
    }
}
```

Because the Car type already implements IComparable (see Chapter 4), overloading the comparison operators is trivial. Here is the updated class definition:

```
// This class is also comparable using the comparison operators.
public class Car : IComparable
```

```
{
...
    public int CompareTo(object o)
    {
        Car temp = (Car)o;
        if(this.CarID > temp.CarID)
            return 1;
        if(this.CarID < temp.CarID)
            return -1;
        else
            return 0;
    }
    public static bool operator < (Car c1, Car c2)
    {
        IComparable itfComp = (IComparable)c1;
        return (itfComp.CompareTo(c2) < 0);
    }
    public static bool operator > (Car c1, Car c2)
    {
        IComparable itfComp = (IComparable)c1;
        return (itfComp.CompareTo(c2) > 0);
    }
    public static bool operator <= (Car c1, Car c2)
    {
        IComparable itfComp = (IComparable)c1;
        return (itfComp.CompareTo(c2) <= 0);
    }
    public static bool operator >= (Car c1, Car c2)
    {
        IComparable itfComp = (IComparable)c1;
        return (itfComp.CompareTo(c2) >= 0);
    }
}
```

SOURCE CODE   *The ObjCompWithOps project is located under the Chapter 5 subdirectory.*

Final Thoughts Regarding Operator Overloading

As you have just seen, C# provides the capability to build types that can respond uniquely to various intrinsic, well-known operators. Now, before you go and retrofit all your classes to support such behavior, you must be sure that the operator(s) you are about to overload make some sort of logical sense in the world at large.

For example, let's say you overloaded the multiplication operator for the Engine class. What exactly would it mean to multiply two Engine objects? Not much. Overloading operators is generally only useful when building utility types. Strings, points, rectangles, fractions, and hexagons make good candidates for operator overloading. People, managers, cars, headphones, and baseball hats do not. Use this feature wisely.

Also, always remember that not all languages targeting the .NET platform will support overloaded operators for custom types! Therefore, always test your types against any language that may make use of a class defining overloaded operators. If you want to be completely sure that your types will work in any .NET-aware language, supply the same functionality using custom methods in addition to your operator set (as illustrated earlier in this chapter).

Finally, be aware that you cannot overload each and every intrinsic C# operator. Table 5-1 outlines the "overloadability" of each item:

Table 5-1. Valid Overloadable Operators

C# OPERATOR	MEANING IN LIFE (CAN THIS OPERATOR BE OVERLOADED?)
+, -, !, ~, ++, --, true, false	This set of unary operators can be overloaded.
+, -, *, /, %, &, |, ^, <<, >>	These binary operators can be overloaded.
= =, !=, <, >, <=, >=	The comparison operators can be overloaded. Recall, however, the C# will demand that "like" operators (i.e., < and >, <= and >=, = =, and !=) are overloaded together.
[]	The [] operator cannot technically be overloaded. As you have seen earlier in this chapter, however, the indexer construct provides the same functionality.

Understanding (and Using) Delegates

Up until this point, every sample application you have developed added various bits of code to Main(), which (in some way or another) sent messages *to* a given object. However, you have not yet examined how these objects can *talk back* to the object that created them in the first place. In the "real world" it is quite common for the objects in a system to engage in a two-way conversation. Thus, let's examine a number of ways in which objects can be programmed to do this very thing.

As you may know, the Windows API makes frequent use of function pointers to create entities termed "callback functions" or simply "callbacks." Using callbacks, programmers are able to configure one function to report back to (call back) another function in the application. The problem with standard C(++)callback functions is that they represent nothing more than a simple memory address. Ideally, C(++) callbacks could be configured to include additional type-safe information such as the number of (and types of) parameters, return value, and calling convention. Sadly, this is not the case in traditional C(++)/Win32 callback functions.

In C#, the callback technique is accomplished in a much safer and more object-oriented manner using the "delegate" keyword. When you wish to create a delegate in C#, you not only specify the name of the method, but the set of parameters (if any) and return type as well. Under the hood, the "delegate" keyword represents an instance of a class deriving from System.MulticastDelegate. Thus, when you write:

```
public delegate void PlayAcidHouse(object PaulOakenfold, int volume);
```

the C# compiler produces a new class, which looks something like the following:

```
public class PlayAcidHouse : System.MulticastDelegate
{
    PlayAcidHouse(object target, int ptr);

    // The synchronous Invoke() method.
    public void virtual Invoke(object PaulOakenfold, int volume);

    // You also receive an asynchronous version of the same callback.
    public virtual IAsyncResult BeginInvoke(object PaulOakenfold, int volume,
                                    AsyncCallback cb, object o);
    public virtual void EndInvoke(IAsyncResult result);
}
```

Notice that the class that is created on your behalf contains two public methods that enable you to synchronously or asynchronously work with the delegate (Invoke() and BeginInvoke() respectively). To keep things simple, I will focus only on the synchronous behavior of the MulticastDelegate type.

Building an Example Delegate

To illustrate the use of delegates, let's begin by updating the Car class to include two new Boolean member variables. The first is used to determine if your automobile is due for a wash (isDirty); the other represents if the car in question is in need of a tire rotation (shouldRotate). To enable the object user to interact with this new state data, Car also defines some additional properties and an updated constructor. Here is the story so far:

```
// Another updated Car class.
public class Car
{
. . .
    // NEW!  Are we in need of a wash? Need to rotate tires?
    private bool isDirty;
    private bool shouldRotate;

    // Extra params to set bools.
    public Car(string name, int max, int curr, bool dirty, bool rotate)
    {
        . . .
        isDirty = dirty;
        shouldRotate = rotate;
    }
    public bool Dirty        // Get and set isDirty.
    {
        get{ return isDirty; }
        set{ isDirty = value; }
    }
    public bool Rotate       // Get and set shouldRotate.
    {
        get{ return shouldRotate; }
        set{ shouldRotate = value; }
    }
}
```

Now, assume you have declared the following delegate (which again, is nothing more than an object-oriented wrapper around a function pointer) within your current namespace:

```
// This delegate is actually a class encapsulating a function pointer
// to 'some method' taking a Car as a parameter and returning void.
public delegate void CarDelegate(Car c);
```

Here, you have created a delegate named CarDelegate. The CarDelegate type represents "some" function taking a Car as a parameter and returning void. If you were to examine the internal representation of this type using ILDasm.exe, you would see something like Figure 5-3 (notice the "extends" informational node).

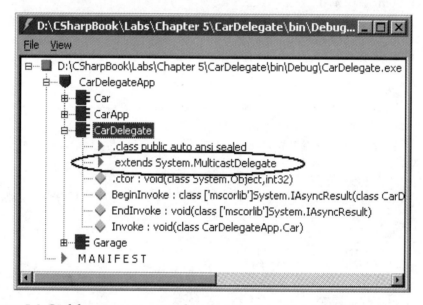

Figure 5-3. C# delegates represent a class deriving from MulticastDelegate.

Delegates as Nested Types

Currently, your delegate is decoupled from its logically related Car type (given that you have simply declared the CarDelegate type within the defining namespace). While there is nothing horribly wrong with the approach, a more enlightened alternative would be to define the CarDelegate directly within the Car class:

```
// This time, define the delegate as part of the class definition.
public class Car : Object
```

```
{
    // This is represented as Car$CarDelegate (i.e., a nested type).
    public delegate void CarDelegate(Car c);
...
}
```

Given that the "delegate" keyword produces a new class deriving from System.MulticastDelegate, the CarDelegate is in fact a nested type definition! If you check ILDasm.exe (see Figure 5-4), you will see the truth of the matter.

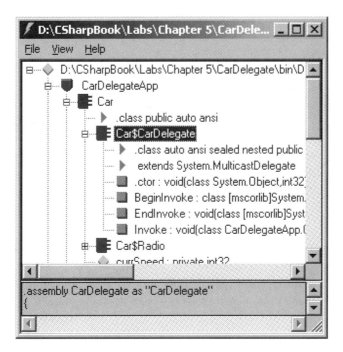

Figure 5-4. Nesting the delegate

Members of System.MulticastDelegate

So to review thus far, when you create delegates, you indirectly build a type that derives from System.MulticastDelegate (which by the way, derives from the System.Delegate base class). Table 5-2 illustrates some interesting inherited members to be aware of.

Table 5-2. Select Inherited Members

INHERITED MEMBER	MEANING IN LIFE
Method	This property returns the name of the method pointed to.
Target	If the method pointed to is a member of a class, this member returns the name of the class. If the value returned from Target equals null, the method pointed to is static.
Combine()	This static method is used to build a delegate that points to a number of different functions.
GetInvocationList()	Returns an array of Delegate types, each representing an entry in the list of function pointers.
Remove()	This static method removes a delegate from the list of function pointers.

Multicast delegates are capable of pointing to any number of functions, because this class has the capability to hold multiple function pointers using an internal linked list. The function pointers themselves can be added to the linked list using the Combine() method or the overloaded + operator. To remove a function from the internal list, call Remove().

Using the CarDelegate

Now that you have a pointer to "some" function, you can create other functions that take this delegate as a parameter. To illustrate, assume you have a new class named Garage. This type maintains a collection of Car types contained in an ArrayList. Upon creation, the ArrayList is filled with some initial Car types.

More importantly, the Garage class defines a public ProcessCars() method, which takes a single argument of type Car.CarDelegate. In the implementation of ProcessCars(), you pass each Car in your collection as a parameter to the "function pointed to" by the delegate.

To help understand the inner workings of the delegation model, let's also make use of two members defined by the System.MulticastDelegate class (Target and Method) to determine exactly which function the delegate is currently pointing to. Here, then, is the complete definition of the Garage class:

```
// The Garage class has a method that makes use of the CarDelegate.
public class Garage
{
    // A list of all cars in the garage.
    ArrayList theCars = new ArrayList();
```

```
// Create the cars in the garage.
public Garage()
{
    // Recall, we updated the ctor to set isDirty and shouldRotate.
    theCars.Add(new Car("Viper", 100, 0, true, false));
    theCars.Add(new Car("Fred", 100, 0, false, false));
    theCars.Add(new Car("BillyBob", 100, 0, false, true));
    theCars.Add(new Car("Bart", 100, 0, true, true));
    theCars.Add(new Car("Stan", 100, 0, false, true));
}

// This method takes a Car.CarDelegate as a parameter.
// Therefore!  'proc' is nothing more than a function pointer!
public void ProcessCars(Car.CarDelegate proc)
{
    // Diagnostics: Where are we forwarding the call?
    Console.WriteLine("***** Calling: {0} *****",
                        d.Method.ToString());

    // Diagnostics: Are we calling an instance method or a static method?
    if(proc.Target != null)
        Console.WriteLine("->Target: {0}", proc.Target.ToString());
    else
        Console.WriteLine("->Target is a static method");

    // Real Work: Now call the method, passing in each car.
    foreach(Car c in theCars)
        proc(c);
}
}
```

When the object user calls ProcessCars(), it will send in the name of the method that should handle this request. For the sake of argument, assume these are static members named WashCar() and RotateTires(). Consider the following usage:

```
// The garage delegates all work orders to these static functions
// (finding a good mechanic is always a problem. . .)
public class CarApp
```

```
{
    // A target for the delegate.
    public static void WashCar(Car c)
    {
        if(c.Dirty)
            Console.WriteLine("Cleaning a car");
        else
            Console.WriteLine("This car is already clean...");
    }

    // Another target for the delegate.
    public static void RotateTires(Car c)
    {
        if(c.Rotate)
            Console.WriteLine("Tires have been rotated");
        else
            Console.WriteLine("Don't need to be rotated...");

    }

    public static int Main(string[] args)
    {
        // Make the garage.
        Garage g = new Garage();

        // Wash all dirty cars.
        g.ProcessCars(new Car.CarDelegate(WashCar));

        // Rotate the tires.
        g.ProcessCars(new Car.CarDelegate(RotateTires));

        return 0;
    }
}
```

Notice (of course) that the two static methods are an exact match to the delegate type (void return value and a single Car argument). Also, recall that when you pass in the name of your function as a constructor parameter, you are adding this item to the internal linked list maintained by System.MulticastDelegate. Figure 5-5 shows the output of this test run. (Notice the output messages supplied by Target and Method properties.)

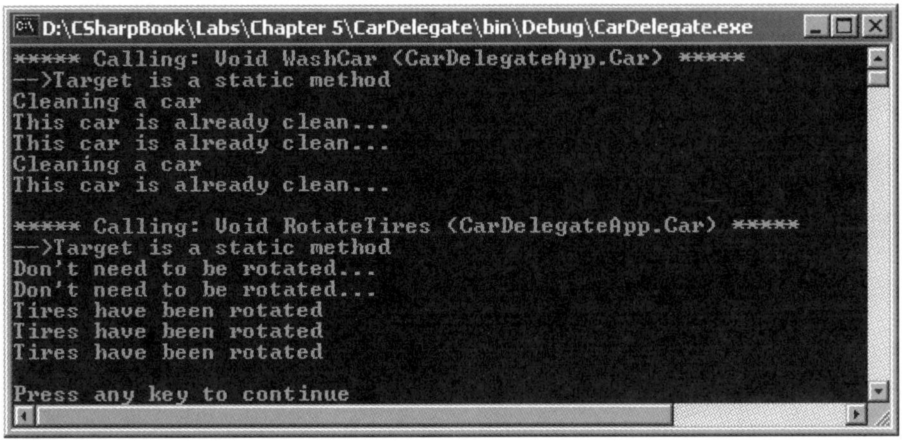

Figure 5-5. Delegate output, take one

Analyzing the Delegation Code

As you can see, the Main() method begins by creating an instance of the Garage type. This class has been configured to delegate all work to other named static functions. Now, when you write the following:

```
// Wash all dirty cars.
g.ProcessCars(new Car.CarDelegate(WashCar));
```

what you are effectively saying is "Add a pointer to the WashCar() function to the CarDelegate type, and pass this delegate to Garage.ProcessCars()." Like most real-world garages, the real work is delegated to another part of the system (which explains why a 30-minute oil change takes 2 hours). Given this, you can assume that ProcessCars() *actually* looks like the following under the hood:

```
// CarDelegate points to the WashCar function:
public void ProcessCars(Car.CarDelegate proc)
{
...
    foreach(Car c in theCars)
        proc(c);            // proc(c) => CarApp.WashCar(c)
...
}
```

Likewise, if you say:

```
// Rotate the tires.
g.ProcessCars(new Car.CarDelegate(RotateTires));
```

ProcessCars() can be understood as:

```
// CarDelegate points to the RotateTires function:
public void ProcessCars(Car.CarDelegate proc)
{
    foreach(Car c in theCars)
        proc(c);            // proc(c) => CarApp.RotateTires(c)
...
}
```

Also notice that when you are calling ProcessCars(), you must create a new instance of the custom delegate:

```
// Wash all dirty cars.
g.ProcessCars(new Car.CarDelegate(WashCar));
// Rotate the tires.
g.ProcessCars(new Car.CarDelegate(RotateTires));
```

This might seem odd at first, given that a delegate represents a function pointer. However, remember that this function pointer is represented by an instance of type System.MulticastDelegate, and therefore must be "new-ed."

Multicasting

Recall that a multicast delegate is an object that is capable of calling any number of functions. In the current example, you did not make use of this feature. Rather, you made two calls to Garage.ProcessCars(), sending in a new instance of the CarDelegate each time. To illustrate multicasting, assume you have updated Main() to look like the following:

```
// Add two function pointers to the internal linked list.
public static int Main(string[] args)
{
    // Make the garage.
    Garage g = new Garage();

    // Create two new delegates.
    Car.CarDelegate wash = new Car.CarDelegate(WashCar);
    Car.CarDelegate rotate = new Car.CarDelegate(RotateTires);
```

```
    // The overloaded + operator can be applied to multicast delegates.
    // The result is a new delegate that maintains pointers to
    // both functions.
    g.ProcessCars(wash + rotate);
    return 0;
}
```

Here, you begin by creating two new CarDelegate objects, each of which points to a given function. When you call ProcessCars(), you are actually passing in a new delegate, which holds each function pointer within the internal linked list (crazy huh?). Do note that the + operator is simply a shorthand for calling the static Delegate.Combine() method. Thus, you could write the following equivalent (but uglier) code:

```
// The + operator has the same effect as calling the Combine() method.
g.ProcessCars((Car.CarDelegate)Delegate.Combine(wash, rotate));
```

Furthermore, if you wish to hang on to the new delegate for later use, you could write the following instead:

```
// Create two new delegates.
Car.CarDelegate wash = new Car.CarDelegate(WashCar);
Car.CarDelegate rotate = new Car.CarDelegate(RotateTires);

// Store the new delegate for later use.
MulticastDelegate d = wash + rotate;

// Send the new delegate into the ProcessCars() method.
g.ProcessCars((Car.CarDelegate)d);
```

Regardless of how you configure a multicast delegate, understand that when you call Combine() (or use the overloaded + operator) you are adding a new function pointer to the internal list. If you wish to remove an item from this internal linked list, you can call the static Remove() method. The first parameter marks the delegate you wish to manipulate, while the second parameter marks the item to remove:

```
// The static Remove() method returns a Delegate type.
Delegate washOnly = MulticastDelegate.Remove(d, rotate);
g.ProcessCars((Car.CarDelegate)washOnly);
```

Before you view the output of this program, let's also update ProcessCars() to print out each function pointer stored in the linked list using

Delegate.GetInvocationList(). This method returns an array of Delegate objects, which you iterate over using foreach:

```
// Now print out each member in the linked list.
public void ProcessCarsCar.(CarDelegate proc)
{
    // Where are we passing the call?
    foreach(Delegate d in proc.GetInvocationList())
    {
        Console.WriteLine("***** Calling: " +
                        d.Method.ToString() + " *****");
    }
...
}
```

The output is shown in Figure 5-6.

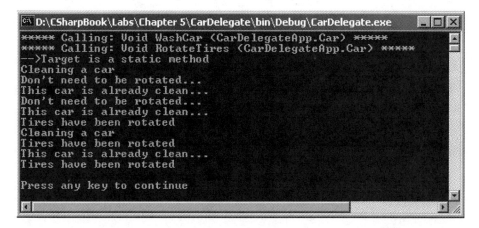

Figure 5-6. Delegate output, take two

Instance Methods as Callbacks

Currently, the CarDelegate type is storing pointers to *static functions*. This is not a requirement of the delegate protocol. It is also possible to delegate a call to a method defined on any *object instance*. To illustrate, assume that the WashCar() and RotateTires() methods have now been moved into a new class named ServiceDept:

```
// We have now moved the static functions into a helper class.
public class ServiceDept
```

```
{
    // Not static!
    public void WashCar(Car c)
    {
        if(c.Dirty)
            Console.WriteLine("Cleaning a car");
        else
            Console.WriteLine("This car is already clean...");
    }

    // Still not static!
    public void RotateTires(Car c)
    {
        if(c.Rotate)
            Console.WriteLine("Tires have been rotated");
        else
            Console.WriteLine("Don't need to be rotated...");

    }
}
```

You could now update Main() as so:

```
// Delegate to instance methods of the ServiceDept type.
public static int Main(string[] args)
{
    // Make the garage.
    Garage g = new Garage();

    // Make the service department.
    ServiceDept sd = new ServiceDept();

    // The garage delegates the work to the service department.
    Car.CarDelegate wash = new Car.CarDelegate(sd.WashCar);
    Car.CarDelegate rotate = new Car.CarDelegate(sd.RotateTires);
    MulticastDelegate d = wash + rotate;

    // Tell the garage to do some work.
    g.ProcessCars((Car.CarDelegate)d);

    return 0;
}
```

Now notice the output in Figure 5-7 (check out the name of the target).

```
D:\CSharpBook\Labs\Chapter 5\CarDelegate\bin\Debug\CarDelegate.exe      _ □ X
***** Calling: Void WashCar (CarDelegateApp.Car) *****
***** Calling: Void RotateTires (CarDelegateApp.Car) *****
-->Target: CarDelegateApp.ServiceDept
Cleaning a car
Don't need to be rotated...
This car is already clean...
Don't need to be rotated...
This car is already clean...
Tires have been rotated
Cleaning a car
Tires have been rotated
This car is already clean...
Tires have been rotated

Press any key to continue
```

Figure 5-7. Delegating to instance methods

SOURCE CODE   *The CarDelegate project is located under the Chapter 5 sub-directory.*

Understanding (and Using) Events

Delegates are fairly interesting constructs because you can resolve the name of a function to call at runtime, rather than compile time. Admittedly, this syntactic orchestration can take a bit of getting used to. However, because the ability for one object to call back to another object is such a helpful construct, C# provides the "event" keyword to lessen the burden of using delegates in the raw.

The most prevalent use of the event keyword would be found in GUI-based applications, in which Button, TextBox, and Calendar widgets all report back to the containing Form when a given action (such as clicking a Button) has occurred. However, events are not limited to GUI-based applications. Indeed, they can be quite helpful when creating "non-GUI" based projects (as you will now see).

Recall that the current implementation of Car.SpeedUp() (see Chapter 3) throws an exception if the user attempts to increase the speed of an automobile that has already been destroyed. This is a rather brute force way to deal with the problem, given that the exception has the potential to halt the program's execution if the error is not handled in an elegant manner. A better design would be to simply inform the object user when the car has died using a custom event, and allow the caller to act accordingly.

Let's reconfigure the Car to send two events to those who happen to be listening. The first event (AboutToBlow) will be sent when the current speed is 10 miles below the maximum speed. The second event (Exploded) will be sent when the user attempts to speed up a car that is already dead. Establishing an event is a two-step process. First, you need to define a delegate, which as you recall represents a pointer to the method(s) to call when the event is sent. Next, you define the events themselves using the "event" keyword. Here is the updated Car class:

```
// This car can 'talk back' to the user.
public class Car
{
. . .
    // Is the car alive or dead?
    private bool dead;

    // Holds the function(s) to call when the event occurs.
    public delegate void EngineHandler(string msg);

    // This car can send these events.
    public static event EngineHandler Exploded;
    public static event EngineHandler AboutToBlow;
 . . .
}
```

Firing an event (i.e., sending the event to those who happen to be listening) is as simple as specifying the event by name and sending out any specified parameters as defined by the related delegate. To illustrate, update the previous implementation of SpeedUp() to send each event accordingly (and remove the previous exception logic):

```
// Fire the correct event based on our current state of affairs.
public void SpeedUp(int delta)
{
    // If the car is dead, send exploded event.
    if(dead)
    {
        if(Exploded != null)
            Exploded("Sorry, this car is dead. . .");
    }
    else
    {
        currSpeed += delta;
```

```
        // Almost dead?  Send about to blow event.
        if(10 = = maxSpeed - currSpeed)
            if(AboutToBlow != null)
                AboutToBlow("Careful, approaching terminal speed!");

        // Still OK!  Proceed as usual.
        if(currSpeed >= maxSpeed)
            dead = true;
        else
            Console.WriteLine("\tCurrSpeed = {0}", currSpeed);
    }
}
```

With this, you have configured the car to send two custom events (under the correct conditions). You will see the usage of this new automobile in just a moment, but first, let's check the event architecture in a bit more detail.

Events Under the Hood

A given event actually expands into two hidden public functions, one having an "add_" prefix, the other having a "remove_" prefix. For example, the Exploded event expands to the following methods:

```
// The following event expands to:
// add_Exploded()
// remove_Exploded()
//
public static event EngineHandler Exploded;
```

In addition to defining hidden add_XXX() and remove_XXX() methods, each event also actually maps to a private static class, which associates the corresponding delegate to a given event. In this way, when an event is raised, each method maintained by the delegate will be called. This is a convenient way to allow an object to broadcast the event to multiple "event sinks."

To illustrate, check out Figure 5-8, a screenshot of the Car type as seen through the eyes of ILDasm.exe.

As you can see, each event (Exploded and AboutToBlow) is internally represented as the following members:

- A private static class

- An add_XXX() method

- A remove_XXX() method

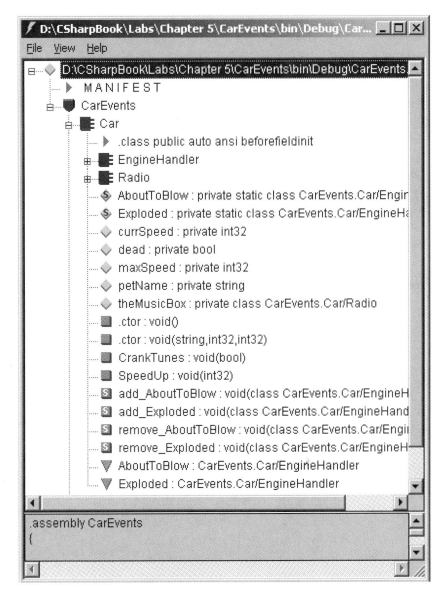

Figure 5-8. Events under the hood

If you were to check out the IL instructions behind add_AboutToBlow(), you would find the following (note the call to Delegate.Combine() is handled on your behalf):

```
.method public hidebysig specialname static
void  add_AboutToBlow(class CarEvents.Car/EngineHandler 'value') cil managed
synchronized
```

```
{
  // Code size       22 (0x16)
  .maxstack  8
  IL_0000:  ldsfld     class CarEvents.Car/EngineHandler
CarEvents.Car::AboutToBlow
  IL_0005:  ldarg.0
  IL_0006:  call       class [mscorlib]System.Delegate
[mscorlib]System.Delegate::Combine(class [mscorlib]System.Delegate,
  class [mscorlib]System.Delegate)
  IL_000b:  castclass  CarEvents.Car/EngineHandler
  IL_0010:  stsfld     class CarEvents.Car/EngineHandler
CarEvents.Car::AboutToBlow
  IL_0015:  ret
} // end of method Car::add_AboutToBlow
```

As you would expect, remove_AboutToBlow() will make the call to Delegate.Remove() automatically:

```
.method public hidebysig specialname static
    void  remove_AboutToBlow(class CarEvents.Car/EngineHandler 'value')
                                                    cil managed synchronized
{
  // Code size       22 (0x16)
  .maxstack  8
  IL_0000:  ldsfld     class CarEvents.Car/EngineHandler
CarEvents.Car::AboutToBlow
  IL_0005:  ldarg.0
  IL_0006:  call       class [mscorlib]System.Delegate
[mscorlib]System.Delegate::Remove(class [mscorlib]System.Delegate,
                                  class [mscorlib]System.Delegate)
  IL_000b:  castclass  CarEvents.Car/EngineHandler
  IL_0010:  stsfld     class CarEvents.Car/EngineHandler
CarEvents.Car::AboutToBlow
  IL_0015:  ret
} // end of method Car::remove_AboutToBlow
```

The IL instructions for the event itself make use of the [.addon] and [.removeon] tags to establish the correct add_XXX and remove_XXX methods (also note the static private class is mentioned by name):

```
.event CarEvents.Car/EngineHandler AboutToBlow
{
  .addon void CarEvents.Car::add_AboutToBlow(class CarEvents.Car/EngineHandler)
```

```
.removeon
        void CarEvents.Car::remove_AboutToBlow(class
CarEvents.Car/EngineHandler)
} // end of event Car::AboutToBlow
```

So, now that you understand how to build a class that can send events, the next big question is how you can configure an object to receive these events.

Listening to Incoming Events

Assume you have now created an instance of the Car class and wish to listen to the events it is capable of sending. The goal is to create a method that represents the "event sink" (i.e., the method called by the delegate). To do so, you need to call the correct add_XXX() method to ensure that your method is added to the list of function pointers maintained by your delegate. However, you do not call add_XXX() and remove_XXX() directly, but rather use the overloaded += and -= operators. Basically, when you wish to listen to an event, follow the pattern shown here:

```
// I'm listening. . .
// ObjectVariable.EventName += new ObjectVariable.DelegateName(functionToCall);
//
Car.Exploded += new Car.EngineHandler(OnBlowUp);
```

When you wish to detach from a source of events, use the -= operator:

```
// Shut up already!
// ObjectVariable.EventName -= new ObjectVariable.DelegateName(functionToCall);
//
Car.Exploded -= new Car.EngineHandler(OnBlowUp);
```

Here is a complete example (output is shown in Figure 5-9):

```
// Make a car and listen to the events.
public class CarApp
{
    public static int Main(string[] args)
    {
        Car c1 = new Car("SlugBug", 100, 10);

        // Hook into events.
        Car.Exploded += new Car.EngineHandler(OnBlowUp);
        Car.AboutToBlow += new Car.EngineHandler(OnAboutToBlow);
```

```
        // Speed up (this will generate the events.)
        for(int i = 0; i < 10; i++) c1.SpeedUp(20);

        // Detach from events.
        Car.Exploded -= new Car.EngineHandler(OnBlowUp);
        Car.Exploded -= new Car.EngineHandler(OnAboutToBlow);

        // No response!
        for(int i = 0; i < 10; i++) c1.SpeedUp(20);
        return 0;
    }


    // OnBlowUp event sink.
    public static void OnBlowUp(string s)
    {
        Console.WriteLine("Message from car: {0}", s);
    }
    // OnAboutToBlow event sink.
    public static void OnAboutToBlow(string s)
    {
        Console.WriteLine("Message from car: {0}", s);
    }
}
```

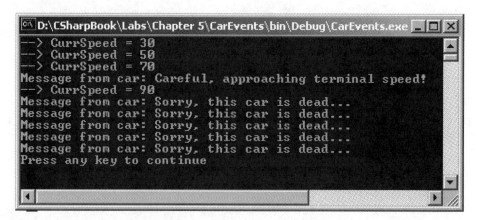

Figure 5-9. Handling your Car's event set

If you wish to have multiple event sinks called by a given event, simply repeat the process:

```
// Multiple event sinks.
public class CarApp
```

```
{
    public static int Main(string[] args)
    {
        // Make a car as usual.
        Car c1 = new Car("SlugBug", 100, 10);

        // Hook into events.
        Car.Exploded += new Car.EngineHandler(OnBlowUp);
        Car.Exploded += new Car.EngineHandler(OnBlowUp2);
        Car.AboutToBlow += new Car.EngineHandler(OnAboutToBlow);

        // Speed up (this will generate the events.)
        for(int i = 0; i < 10; i++)
            c1.SpeedUp(20);

        // Detach from events.
        Car.Exploded -= new Car.EngineHandler(OnBlowUp);
        Car.Exploded -= new Car.EngineHandler(OnBlowUp2);
        Car.Exploded -= new Car.EngineHandler(OnAboutToBlow);

        . . .
    }


    // OnBlowUp event sink A.
    public static void OnBlowUp(string s)
    {
        Console.WriteLine("Message from car: {0}", s);
    }


    // OnBlowUp event sink B.
    public static void OnBlowUp2(string s)
    {
        Console.WriteLine("->AGAIN I say: {0}", s);
    }


    // OnAboutToBlow event sink.
    public static void OnAboutToBlow(string s)
    {
            Console.WriteLine("Message from car: {0}", s);
    }
}
```

Now, when the Exploded event is sent, the associated delegate calls OnBlowUp() as well as OnBlowUp2(), as shown in Figure 5-10.

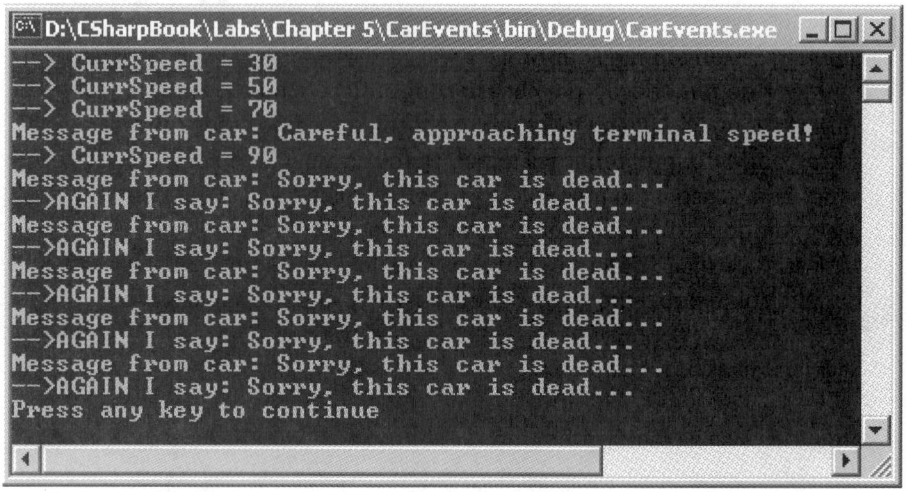

Figure 5-10. Working with multiple event handlers

Objects as Event Sinks

At this point, you have the background to build objects that can participate in a two-way conversation. However, understand that you are free to build a helper object to respond to an object's event set, much in the same way that you created a helper class to be called by all delegates. For example, let's move your event sink methods out of the CarApp class and into a new class named CarEventSink:

```csharp
// Car event sink
public class CarEventSink
{
    // OnBlowUp event handler.
    public void OnBlowUp(string s)
    {
        Console.WriteLine("Message from car: {0}", s);
    }

    // OnBlowUp event handler version 2.
    public void OnBlowUp2(string s)
    {
        Console.WriteLine("->AGAIN I say: {0}", s);
    }
```

```
    // OnAboutToBlow handler.
    public void OnAboutToBlow(string s)
    {
        Console.WriteLine("Message from car: {0}", s);
    }
}
```

The CarApp class is then a bit more self-contained, as the event sink methods have been pulled out of the CarApp definition and into their own custom type. Here is the update:

```
// Note the creation and use of the CarEventSink.
public class CarApp
{
    public static int Main(string[] args)
    {
        Car c1 = new Car("SlugBug", 100, 10);

        // Make the sink object.
        CarEventSink sink = new CarEventSink();

        // Hook into events using sink object.
        Car.Exploded += new Car.EngineHandler(sink.OnBlowUp);
        Car.Exploded += new Car.EngineHandler(sink.OnBlowUp2);
        Car.AboutToBlow += new Car.EngineHandler(sink.OnAboutToBlow);

        for(int i = 0; i < 10; i++)
            c1.SpeedUp(20);

        // Detach from events using sink object.
        Car.Exploded -= new Car.EngineHandler(sink.OnBlowUp);
        Car.Exploded -= new Car.EngineHandler(sink.OnBlowUp2);
        Car.Exploded -= new Car.EngineHandler(sink.OnAboutToBlow);

        return 0;
    }
}
```

The output is (of course) identical.

SOURCE CODE *The CarEvents project is located under the Chapter 5 subdirectory.*

Designing an Event Interface

COM programmers may be familiar with the notion of defining and implementing "callback interfaces." This technique allows a COM client to receive events from a coclass using a custom COM interface, and is often used to bypass the overhead imposed by the official COM connection point architecture. For an illustration of using the interface as a callback, let's examine how callback interfaces can be created using C# (and .NET in general). Consider this last topic a bonus section, which proves the point that there is always more than one way to solve a problem.

First, let's keep the same assumption that the Car type wishes to inform the outside world when it is about to blow (current speed is 10 miles below the maximum speed) and has exploded. However, this time you will *not* be using the "delegate" or "event" keywords, but rather the following custom interface:

```
// The engine event interface.
public interface IEngineEvents
{
    void AboutToBlow(string msg);
    void Exploded(string msg);
}
```

This interface will be implemented by a sink object, on which the Car will make calls. Here is a sample implementation:

```
// Car event sink.
public class CarEventSink : IEngineEvents
{
    public void AboutToBlow(string msg)
    {
        Console.WriteLine(msg);
    }

    public void Exploded(string msg)
    {
        Console.WriteLine(msg);
    }
}
```

Now that you have an object that implements the event interface, your next task is to pass a reference to this sink into the Car. The Car holds onto the reference, and makes calls back on the sink when appropriate. In order to allow the Car to obtain a reference to the sink, you can assume some method has been added to the default public interface.

In keeping with the COM paradigm, let's call this method Advise(). When the object user wishes to detach from the event source, he may call another method (Unadvise() in COM-speak). In order to allow the object user to register multiple event sinks, let's assume that the Car maintains an ArrayList to represent each outstanding connection (analogous to the array of IUnknown* types used with classic COM connection points). Here is the story so far:

```
// This Car does not make any use of C# delegates or events.
public class Car
{
    // The set of connected sinks.
    ArrayList itfConnections = new ArrayList();

    // Attach or disconnect from the source of events.
    public void Advise(IEngineEvents itfClientImpl)
    {
        itfConnections.Add(itfClientImpl);
    }

    public void Unadvise(IEngineEvents itfClientImpl)
    {
        itfConnections.Remove(itfClientImpl);
    }
...
}
```

Now, Car.SpeedUp() can be retrofitted to iterate over the list of connections and fire the correct notification when appropriate (i.e., call the correct method on the sink):

```
// Interface based event protocol!
//
class Car
{
...
    public void SpeedUp(int delta)
    {
        // If the car is dead, send exploded event to each sink.
        if(dead)
        {
            foreach(IEngineEvents e in itfConnections)
                e.Exploded("Sorry, this car is dead. . .");
        }
        else
```

```
        {
            currSpeed += delta;

            // Dude, you're almost dead!  Proceed with caution!
            if(10 = = maxSpeed - currSpeed)
            {
                foreach(IEngineEvents e in itfConnections)
                    e.AboutToBlow("Careful buddy!  Gonna blow!");
            }

            // Still OK!
            if(currSpeed >= maxSpeed)
                dead = true;
            else
                Console.WriteLine("\tCurrSpeed = {0}", currSpeed);
        }
    }
```

The following is some client-side code, now making use of a callback interface to listen to the Car events:

```
// Make a car and listen to the events.
public class CarApp
{
    public static int Main(string[] args)
    {
        Car c1 = new Car("SlugBug", 100, 10);

        // Make sink object.
        CarEventSink sink = new CarEventSink();

        // Pass the Car a reference to the sink.
        // (The lab solution registers multiple sinks. . .).
        c1.Advise(sink);

        // Speed up (this will generate the events.)
        for(int i = 0; i < 10; i++)
            c1.SpeedUp(20);

        // Detach from events.
        c1.Unadvise(sink);
        return 0;
    }
}
```

The output should look very familiar (see Figure 5-11).

```
D:\CSharpBook\Labs\Chapter 5\EventInterface\bin\Debug\...    _ □ X
->CurrSpeed = 30
->CurrSpeed = 50
->CurrSpeed = 70
First sink reporting: Careful buddy!  Gonna blow!
Other sink reporting: Careful buddy!  Gonna blow!
->CurrSpeed = 90
First sink reporting: Sorry, this car is dead...
Other sink reporting: Sorry, this car is dead...
First sink reporting: Sorry, this car is dead...
Other sink reporting: Sorry, this car is dead...
```

Figure 5-11. Interfaces as an event protocol

SOURCE CODE   *The EventInterface project is located under the Chapter 5 subdirectory.*

XML-Based Documentation

This final topic of this chapter is by no means as mentally challenging as the .NET delegation protocol, and is not necessarily an "advanced" technique. Nevertheless, your next goal is to examine a technique provided by C#, which enables you to turn your source code documentation into a corresponding XML file. If you have a background in Java, you are most likely familiar with the javadoc utility. Using javadoc, you are able to turn Java source code into an HTML representation. The C# documentation model is slightly different, in that the "source code to XML formatting" process is the job of the C# compiler (csc.exe) rather than a standalone utility.

So, why use XML to represent your type definitions rather than HTML? The primary reason is that XML is a very enabling technology. Given that XML separates raw data from the presentation of that data, you (as a programmer) can apply any number of XML transformations to the raw XML. As well, you could programmatically read the XML file using types defined in the .NET base class library.

When you wish to document your types in XML, your first step is to make use of a special comment syntax, the triple forward slash (///) rather than the C++ style double slash (//) or C-based (/*. . . */) syntax. After the triple slash, you are free to use any well-formed XML tags, including the following predefined set (see Table 5-3).

Table 5-3. Stock XML Tags

PREDEFINED XML DOCUMENTATION TAG	MEANING IN LIFE
<c>	Indicates that text within a description should be marked as code
<code>	Indicates multiple lines should be marked as code
<example>	Used to mock up a code example for the item you are describing
<exception>	Used to document which exceptions a given class may throw
<list>	Used to insert a list into the documentation file
<param>	Describes a given parameter
<paramref>	Associates a given XML tag with a specific parameter
<permission>	Used to document access permissions for a member
<remarks>	Used to build a description for a given member
<returns>	Documents the return value of the member
<see>	Used to cross-reference related items
<seealso>	Used to build an "also see" section within a description
<summary>	Documents the "executive summary" for a given item
<value>	Documents a given property

The following is a very streamlined Car type with some XML-based comments. In particular, note the use of the <summary> and <param> tags:

```
/// <summary>
///    This is a simple Car that illustrates
///    working with XML style documentation.
/// </summary>
public class Car
{
    /// <summary>
    /// Do you have a sunroof?
    /// </summary>
    private bool hasSunroof = false;

    /// <summary>
    /// The ctor lets you set the sunroofedness.
    /// </summary>
    /// <param name="hasSunroof"> </param>
    public Car(bool hasSunroof)
    {
        this.hasSunroof = hasSunroof;
    }
}
```

```
/// <summary>
/// This method allows you to open your sunroof.
/// </summary>
/// <param name="state"> </param>
public void OpenSunroof(bool state)
{
    if(state = = true && hasSunroof = = true)
    {
        Console.WriteLine("Put sunscreen on that bald head!");
    }
    else
    {
        Console.WriteLine("Sorry. . .you don't have a sunroof.");
    }
}
/// <summary>
/// Entry point to application.
/// </summary>
public static void Main()
{
    SimpleCar c = new SimpleCar(true);
    c.OpenSunroof(true);
}
}
```

Once you have your XML documentation in place, you can specify the /doc flag as input to the C# compiler. Note that you must specify the name of the XML output file as well as the C# input file:

```
csc /doc:simplecar.xml simplecar.cs
```

As you would hope, the Visual Studio.NET IDE enables you to specify the name of an XML file to describe your types. To do so, click the Properties button from the Solution Explorer window (see Figure 5-12).

Once you've activated the Project Properties dialog, select the Build option from the Configuration Properties folder. Here you will find an edit box (XML Documentation File) that enables you to specify the name of the file that will contain XML definitions for the types in your project (which is automatically regenerated as you rebuild your project).

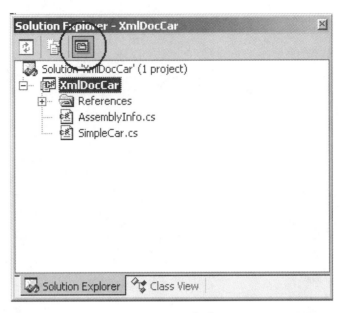

Figure 5-12. Activating the Project Properties dialog

Viewing the Generated XML File

If you were now to open the simplecar.xml file from within the Visual Studio.NET
IDE, you would find the display shown in Figure 5-13.

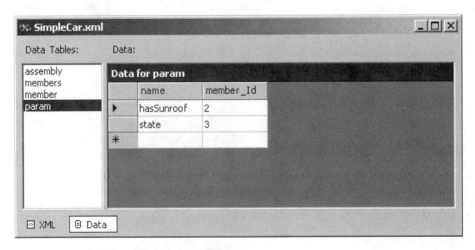

Figure 5-13. The Visual Studio.NET XML viewer

If you were to select the XML button from the XML editor window, you would
find the raw XML format. Be aware that assembly members are denoted with the

<member> tag, fields are marked with an F prefix, types with T, and members with M. Table 5-4 provides some additional XML format characters.

Table 5-4. XML Format Characters

FORMAT CHARACTER	MEANING IN LIFE
N	Denotes a namespace
T	Represents a type (i.e., class, interface, struct, enum, delegate)
F	Represents a field
P	Represents type properties (including indexers)
M	Represents method (including such constructors and overloaded operators)
E	Denotes an event
!	Represents an error string that provides information about the error. The C# compiler generates error information for links that cannot be resolved.

At this point, you have a raw XML file that can be rendered into HTML using an XSL style sheet or programmatically manipulated using .NET types. Although this approach gives you the biggest bang for the buck when it comes to customizing the look and feel of your source code comments, there is another alternative.

Visual Studio.NET Documentation Support

If the thought of ending up with a raw XML file is a bit anticlimactic, be aware that VS.NET does offer another comment-formatting option. Using the same XML tags you have just examined, you may make use of the "Tools | Build Comment Web Pages. . ." menu option. When you select this item, you will be asked if you wish to build the entire solution or a specific project within the solution set, as shown in Figure 5-14.

The Build Comment Web Pages option will respond by creating a new folder in your project directory that holds a number of images and HTML files built based on your XML documentation. You can now open the main HTML file and view your commented project. For example, check out Figure 5-15.

SOURCE CODE   *The XmlDocCar project is located under the Chapter 5 subdirectory.*

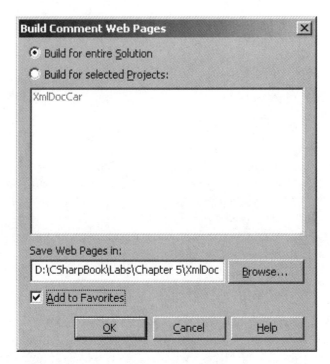

Figure 5-14. Configuration of your HTML-based documentation

Figure 5-15. The generated XmlCarDoc online documentation

Summary

The purpose of this chapter was to round out your understanding of the key features of the C# language. You are now well-equipped to build sophisticated object models that function well within the .NET universe. The chapter began by examining how to build a custom indexer method, which allows the object user to access discrete sub-items using array-like notation. Next, the chapter examined how the C# language enables you to overload various operators in order to let your custom types behave a bit more intuitively to the object users of the world.

You have also seen three ways in which multiple objects can partake in a bidirectional conversation. The first two approaches (delegates and events) are official, well-supported constructs in the .NET universe. The third approach (event interfaces) is more of a design pattern than a language protocol; however, it does allow two entities to communicate in a type-safe manner.

I wrapped up this chapter by examining how to comment your types using XML comment tags, and you learned how the Visual Studio.NET IDE can make use of these tags to generate online documentation for your current project. Using these techniques, you enable your peers to fully understand the fruit of your .NET labors.

CHAPTER 6

Assemblies, Threads, and AppDomains

Each of the applications developed during the first five chapters are along the lines of traditional "stand alone" applications, given that all programming logic was contained within a single (EXE) binary. One aspect of the .NET lifestyle is the notion of binary reuse. Like COM, .NET provides the ability to access types between binaries in a language-independent manner. However, the .NET platform provides far greater language integration than classic COM. For example, the .NET platform supports cross-language inheritance (imagine a Visual Basic.NET class *deriving* from a C# class). To understand how this is achieved requires a deeper understanding of assemblies.

Once you understand the logical and physical layout of an assembly (and the related manifest), you then learn to distinguish between "private" and "shared" assemblies. You also examine exactly how the .NET runtime resolves the location of an assembly and come to understand the role of the Global Assembly Cache (GAC). Closely related to location resolution is the notion of application configuration files. As you will see, the .NET runtime can read the XML-based data contained within this file to bind to a specific version of a shared assembly (among other things).

This chapter wraps up with an examination of building multithreaded assemblies, using the types defined within the System.Threading namespace. If you are coming from a Win32 background, you will be pleased to see how nicely thread manipulation has cleaned up under the .NET framework.

Problems with Classic COM Binaries

Binary reuse (i.e., portable code libraries) is not a new idea. To date, the most popular way in which a programmer can share types between binaries (and in some respects, across languages) is to build what can now be regarded as "classic COM servers." Although the construction and use of COM binaries is a well-established industry standard, these little blobs have caused each of us a fair share of headaches. Beyond the fact that COM demands a good deal of complex infrastructure (IDL, class factories, scripting support, and so forth), I am sure you have also pondered the following related questions:

- Why is it so difficult to version my COM binary?

- Why is it so complex to distribute my COM binary?

The .NET framework greatly improves on the current state of affairs and addresses the versioning and deployment problems head-on using a new binary format termed an *assembly*. However, before you come to understand how the assembly offers a clean solution to these issues, let's spend some time recapping the problems in a bit more detail.

Problem: COM Versioning

In COM, you build entities named *coclasses* that are little more than a custom UDT (user defined type) implementing any number of COM interfaces (including the mandatory IUnknown). The coclasses are then packaged into a binary home, which is physically represented as a DLL or EXE file. Once all the (known) bugs have been squashed out of the code, the COM binary eventually ends up on some user's computer, ready to be accessed by other programs.

The versioning problem in COM revolves around the fact that the COM runtime offers no intrinsic support to enforce that the correct version of a binary server is loaded for the calling client. It is true that a COM programmer can modify the version of the type library, update the registry to reflect these changes, and even reengineer the client's code base to reference a particular library. But, the fact remains that these are tasks delegated to *the programmer* and typically require rebuilding the code base. As many of you have learned the hard way, this is far from ideal.

Assume that you have jumped through the necessary hoops to try to ensure the COM client activates the correct version of a COM binary. Your worries are far from over given that some other application may be installed on the target machine that overrides your carefully configured registry entries (and maybe even replaces a COM server or two with an earlier version during the process). Mysteriously, your client application may now fail to operate.

For example, if you have 10 applications that all require the use of MyCOMServer.dll version 1.4, and another application installs MyCOMServer.dll version 2.0, all 10 applications are at risk of breaking. This is because we cannot be assured of complete backward compatibility. In a perfect world, all versions of a given COM binary are fully compatible with previous versions. In practice however, keeping COM servers (and software in general) completely backward compatible is extremely difficult.

The lump sum of each of these versioning issues is lovingly referred to as "DLL Hell" (which, by the way, is not limited to COM DLLs; traditional C DLLs suffer the same hellish existence). As you'll see during the course of this chapter, the .NET framework solves this nightmare by using a number of techniques including side-by-side execution and a very robust (yet very simple) versioning scheme.

In a nutshell, .NET allows multiple versions of the same binary to be installed on the same target machine. Therefore, under .NET, if client A requires MyDotNETServer.dll version 1.4 and client B demands MyDotNETServer.dll version 2.0, the correct version is loaded for the respective client automatically. You are also able to bind to a specific version using an application configuration file.

Problem: COM Deployment

The COM runtime is a rather temperamental service. When a COM client wishes to make use of a coclass, the first step is to load the COM libraries for use by a given thread by calling CoInitialize(). At this point, the client makes additional calls to the COM runtime (e.g., CoCreateInstance(), CoGetClassObject() and so forth) to load a given binary into memory. The end result is that the COM client receives an interface reference that is then used to manipulate the contained coclass.

In order for the COM runtime to locate and load a binary, the COM server must be configured correctly on the target machine. From a high level, registering a COM server sounds so simple: Build an installation program (or make use of a system supplied registration tool) to trigger the correct logic in the COM binary (DllRegisterServer() for DLLs or WinMain() for EXEs) and call it a day. However, as you may know, a COM server requires a vast number of registration entries to be made. Typically, every COM class (CLSID), interface (IID), library (LIBID), and application (AppID) must be inserted into the system registry.

The key point to keep in mind is that the relationship between the binary image and the correct registry entries is extremely loose, and therefore extremely fragile. In COM, the location of the binary image (e.g., MyServer.dll) is entirely separate from the massive number of registry entries that completely describe the component. Therefore, if the end user were to relocate (or rename) a COM server, the entire system breaks, as the registration entries are now out of sync.

The fact that classic COM servers require a number of external registration details also introduces another deployment difficulty: The same entries must be made on *every machine referencing the server.* Thus, if you have installed your COM binary on a remote machine, and if you have 100 client machines accessing this COM server, this means 101 machines must be configured correctly. To say the least, this is a massive pain in the neck.

The .NET platform makes the process of deploying an application extremely simple given the fact that .NET binaries (i.e., assemblies) are not registered in the system registry at all. Plain and simple. Instead, assemblies are completely self-describing entities. Deploying a .NET application can be (and most often is) as simple as copying the files that compose the application to some location on the machine, and running your program.. In short, be prepared to bid a fond farewell to HKEY_CLASSES_ROOT.

An Overview of .NET Assemblies

Now that you understand the problem, let's check out the solution. .NET applications are constructed by piecing together any number of assemblies. Simply put, an assembly is nothing more than a versioned, self-describing binary (DLL or EXE) containing some collection of types (classes, interfaces, structures, etc.) and optional recourses (images, string tables and whatnot). One thing to be painfully aware of right now, is that the internal organization of a .NET assembly is nothing like the internal organization of a classic COM server (regardless of the shared file extensions).

For example, an in-process COM server exports four functions (DllCanUnloadNow(), DllGetClassObject(), DllRegisterServer() and DllUnregisterServer()), in order to allow the COM runtime to access its contents. .NET DLLs on the other hand require only one function export, DllMain().

Local COM servers define WinMain() as the sole entry point into the EXE, which is implemented to test for various command line parameters to perform the same duties as a COM DLL. Not so under the .NET protocol. Although .NET EXE binaries do provide a WinMain() entry point (or main() for console applications), the behind-the-scenes logic is entirely different.

The physical format of a .NET binary is actually more similar to a traditional portable executable (PE) and COFF (Common Object File Format) file formats. The true difference is that a traditional PE / COFF files contains instructions that target a specific platform and specific CPU. In contrast, .NET binaries contain code constructed using Microsoft Intermediate Language (MSIL or simply IL), which is platform- and CPU-agnostic. At runtime, the internal IL is compiled on the fly (using a just-in-time compiler) to platform and CPU specific instructions. This is a powerful extension of classic COM in that .NET assemblies are poised to be platform neutral entities that are not necessarily tied to the Windows operating system.

In addition to raw IL, recall that an assembly also contains metadata that completely describes each type living in the assembly, as well as the full set of members supported by each type. For example, if you created a class named JoyStick using some .NET aware language, the corresponding compiler emits metadata describing all the fields, methods, properties, and events defined by this custom type. The .NET runtime uses this metadata to resolve the location of types (and their members) within the binary, create object instances, as well as to facilitate remote method invocations.

Unlike traditional file formats or classic COM server, an assembly must contain an associated *manifest* (also referred to as "assembly metadata"). The manifest documents each module within the assembly, establishes the version of the assembly, and also documents any *external* assemblies referenced by the current assembly (unlike a classic COM type library that does not document required external dependencies). Given this, a .NET assembly is completely self-describing.

Single File and Multifile Assemblies

Under the hood, a given assembly can be composed of multiple *modules*. A module is really nothing more than a generic name for a valid file. In this light, an assembly can be viewed as a unit of deployment (often termed a "logical DLL"). In many situations, an assembly is in fact composed of a single module. In this case, there is a one-to-one correspondence between the (logical) assembly and the underlying (physical) binary, as shown in Figure 6-1.

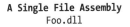

A Single File Assembly
Foo.dll

Manifest
Type Metadata
MSIL Code
(Optional) Resources

Figure 6-1. A single file assembly

When you create an assembly that is composed of multiple files, you gain efficient code download. For example, assume you have a remote client that is referencing a multifile assembly composed of three modules. If the remote application references only one of these modules, the .NET runtime only downloads the currently referenced file. If each module is 1 MB in size, I'm sure you can see the benefits.

Understand that multifile assemblies are not literally linked together into a new (larger) file. Rather, multifile assemblies are logically related by information contained in the corresponding manifest. On a related note, multifile assemblies contain a single manifest that may be placed in a standalone file, but is more typically bundled into one of the related modules. The big picture is seen in Figure 6-2.

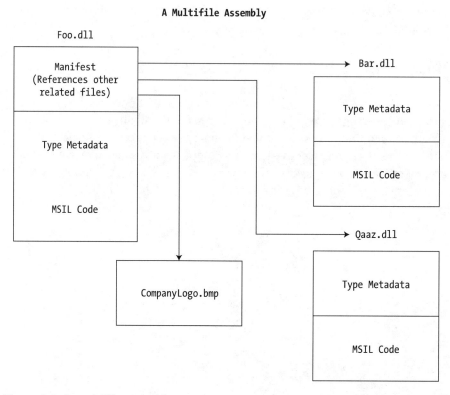

Figure 6-2. A multifile assembly

This text is not concerned with the construction of multifile assemblies. However, be aware that online Help does document the process (which boils down to little more than passing the /addmodule flag to the C# compiler).

Two Views of an Assembly: Physical and Logical

As you begin to work with .NET binaries, it can be helpful to regard an assembly (both single file and multifile) as having two conceptual views. When you build an assembly, you are interested in the *physical* view. In this case, the assembly can be realized as some number of files that contain your custom types and resources (Figure 6-3).

As an assembly consumer, you are interested in a *logical* view of the assembly (Figure 6-4). In this case, you can understand an assembly as a versioned collection of public types that you can use in your current application (recall that "internal" types can only be referenced by the assembly in which they are defined):

Physical View of an Assembly

| Foo.dll | Resource files |
| Bar.dll | Manifest |

Figure 6-3. Physically, an assembly is a collection of modules

Logical View of an Assembly

| Classes | Enumerations | Delegates |
| Interfaces | Resources | Structures |

Figure 6-4. Logically, an assembly is a collection of types

For example, the kind folks in Redmond who developed System.Drawing.dll created a physical assembly for you to consume in your applications. However, although System.Drawing.dll can be physically viewed as a binary DLL, you logically regard this assembly as a collection of related types. Of course, ILDasm.exe is the tool of choice when you are interested in discovering the logical layout of a given assembly (Figure 6-5).

The chances are good that you will play the role of both an assembly builder and assembly consumer, as is the case throughout this book. However, before digging into the code, let's briefly examine some of the core benefits of this new file format.

Assemblies Promote Code Reuse

Assemblies contain code that is executed by the .NET runtime. As you might imagine, the types and resources contained within an assembly can be shared and reused by multiple applications, much like a traditional COM binary. Unlike COM, it is possible to configure "private" assemblies as well (in fact, this is the default behavior). Private assemblies are intended to be used only by a single application on a given machine. As you will see, private assemblies greatly simplify the deployment and versioning of your applications.

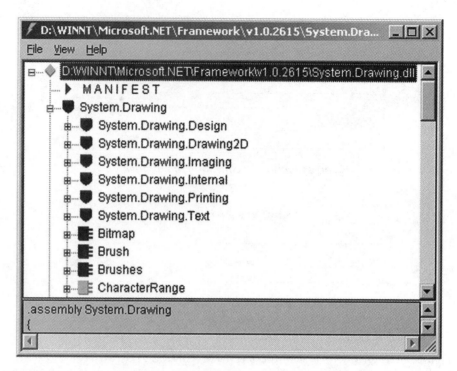

Figure 6-5. Logical view of the physical System.Drawing.dll assembly

Like COM, binary reuse under the .NET platform honors the ideal of language independence. C# is one of numerous languages capable of building managed code, with even more languages to come. When a .NET-aware language adheres to the rules of the Common Language Specification (CLS), your choice of language becomes little more than a personal preference.

Therefore, it is not only possible to reuse types between languages, but to extend types across languages as well. In classic COM, developers were unable to derive COM object A from COM object B (even if both types were developed in the same language). In short, classic COM did not support classical inheritance (the "is-a" relationship). Later in this chapter you see an example of cross-language inheritance.

Assemblies Establish a Type Boundary

Assemblies are used to define a boundary for the types (and resources) they contain. In .NET, the identity of a given type is defined (in part) by the assembly in which it resides. Therefore, if two assemblies each define an identically named type (class, structure, or whatnot) they are considered independent entities in the .NET universe.

Assemblies Are Versionable and Self-Describing Entities

As mentioned, in the world of COM, the developer is in charge of correctly versioning a binary. For example, to ensure binary compatibility between MyComServer.dll version 1.0 and MyComServer.dll version 2.4, the programmer must use basic common sense to ensure interface definitions remained unaltered or run the risk of breaking client code. While a healthy dose of versioning common sense also comes in handy under the .NET universe, the problem with the COM versioning scheme is that these programmer-defined techniques are *not* enforced by the runtime.

Another major headache with current versioning practices is that COM does not provide a way for a binary server to explicitly list the set of other binaries that must be present for it to function correctly. If an end user mistakenly moves, renames, or deletes a dependency, the solution fails. Under .NET, an assembly's manifest is the entity in charge of explicitly listing all internal and external contingencies.

Each assembly has a version identifier that applies to all types and all resources contained within each module of the assembly. Using a version identifier the runtime is able to ensure that the correct assembly is loaded on behalf of the calling client, using a well defined versioning policy (detailed later). An assembly's version identifier is composed of two basic pieces: A friendly text string (termed the *informational* version) and a numerical identifier (termed the *compatibility* version).

For example, assume you have created a new assembly with an informational string of "MyInterestingTypes." This same assembly would also define a compatibility number, such as 1.0.70.3. The compatibility version number always takes the same general format (four numbers separated by periods). The first and second numbers identify the major and minor version of the assembly (1.0 in this case). The third value (70) marks the build number, followed by the current revision number (3).

As you discover later in this chapter, the .NET runtime makes use of an assembly's version to ensure the correct binary is loaded on behalf of the client (provided that the assembly is shared). Because the manifest explicitly lists all external dependencies, the runtime is able to determine the "last known good" configuration (i.e., the set of versioned assemblies that are known to function correctly).

Assemblies Define a Security Context

An assembly may also contain security information. Under the architecture of the .NET runtime, security measures are scoped at the assembly level. For example, if AssemblyA wishes to use a class contained within AssemblyB, AssemblyB is the entity that chooses to provide access (or not). The security constraints defined by an assembly are explicitly listed within its manifest. While a treatment of .NET security measures is outside the mission of this text, simply be aware that access to an assembly's contents is verified using assembly metadata.

Assemblies Enable Side-by-Side Execution

Perhaps the biggest advantage of the .NET assembly is the ability of multiple versions of the same assembly to be loaded (and understood) by the runtime. Thus, it is possible to install and load multiple versions of the same assembly on a single machine. In this way, clients are isolated from other incompatible versions of the same assembly.

Furthermore, it is possible to control which version of a (shared) assembly should be loaded using application configuration files. These files are little more than a simple text file describing (via XML syntax) the version, and specific location, of the assembly to be loaded on behalf of the calling application. You learn how to author application configuration files later in this chapter.

Building a Single File Test Assembly

Now that you have a better understanding of .NET assemblies, let's build a minimal and complete code library using C#. Physically, this will be a single file assembly named CarLibrary. To build a code library using the Visual Studio.NET IDE, you would select a new Class Library project workspace (Figure 6-6).

The design of our automobile library begins with an abstract base class named Car that defines a number of protected data members exposed through custom properties. This class has a single abstract method named TurboBoost() and makes use of a single enumeration (EngineState). Here is the initial definition of the CarLibrary namespace:

```
// Our first code library (CarLibrary.dll)
namespace CarLibrary
{
using System;

public enum EngineState        // Holds the state of the engine.
{
    engineAlive,
    engineDead
}
```

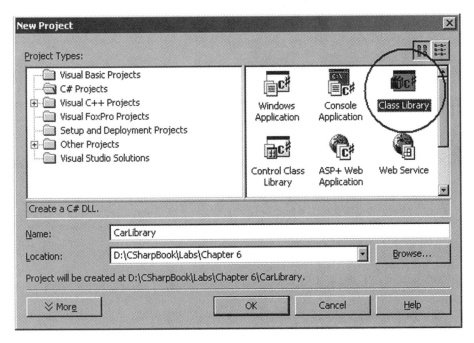

Figure 6-6. Selecting a Class Library project workspace

```csharp
public abstract class Car     // The abstract base class in the hierarchy.
{
    // Protected state data.
    protected string petName;
    protected short currSpeed;
    protected short maxSpeed;
    protected EngineState egnState;

    public Car(){egnState = EngineState.engineAlive;}
    public Car(string name, short max, short curr)
    {
        egnState = EngineState.engineAlive;
        petName = name; maxSpeed = max; currSpeed = curr;
    }

    public string PetName
    {
        get { return petName; }
        set { petName = value; }
    }
    public short CurrSpeed
```

```
        {
            get { return currSpeed; }
            set { currSpeed = value; }
        }

        public short MaxSpeed
        { get { return maxSpeed; } }

        public EngineState EngineState
        { get { return egnState; } }

        public abstract void TurboBoost();
    }
}
```

Now assume that you have two direct descendents of the Car type named MiniVan and SportsCar. Each implements the abstract TurboBoost() method in an appropriate manner:

```
namespace CarLibrary
{
using System;
using System.Windows.Forms;        // Needed for MessageBox definition.

// The SportsCar
public class SportsCar : Car
{
    // Ctors.
    public SportsCar(){}
    public SportsCar(string name, short max, short curr)
        : base (name, max, curr){}

    // TurboBoost impl.
    public override void TurboBoost()
    {
        MessageBox.Show("Ramming speed!", "Faster is better...");
    }
}

// The MiniVan
public class MiniVan : Car
```

```
{
    // Ctors.
    public MiniVan(){}
    public MiniVan(string name, short max, short curr)
        : base (name, max, curr){}

    // TurboBoost impl.
    public override void TurboBoost()
    {
        // Minivans have poor turbo capabilities!
        egnState = EngineState.engineDead;
        MessageBox.Show("Time to call AAA", "Your car is dead");
    }
}
}
```

Notice how each subclass implements TurboBoost() using the MessageBox class, which is defined in the System.Windows.Forms.dll assembly. In order for your assembly to make use of the types defined within this assembly, the Car-Library project must include a reference to this binary using the "Project | Add Reference" menu selection (Figure 6-7).

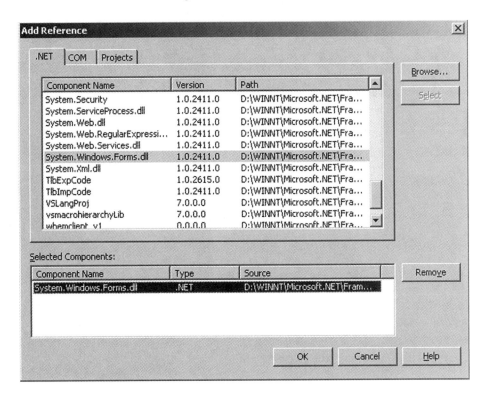

Figure 6-7. Referencing external assemblies

In Chapter 8, the System.Windows.Forms namespace is described in detail. As you can tell by the name of the namespace, this assembly contains numerous types to help you build GUI applications. For now, the MessageBox class is all you need to concern yourself with. If you are following along, go ahead and compile your new code library.

A C# Client Application

Because each of our automobiles has been declared "public," other binaries are able to use our custom classes. In a moment, you learn how to make use of these types from other .NET aware languages such as Visual Basic. Until then, let's create a C# client. Begin by creating a new C# Console Application project (CSharp-CarClient). Next, set a reference to your CarLibrary.dll, using the Browse button to navigate to the location of your custom assembly (again using the Add Reference dialog).

Once you add a reference to your CarLibrary assembly, the Visual Studio.NET IDE responds by making a full copy of the referenced assembly and placing it into your Debug folder (assuming, of course, you have configured a debug build) (Figure 6-8).

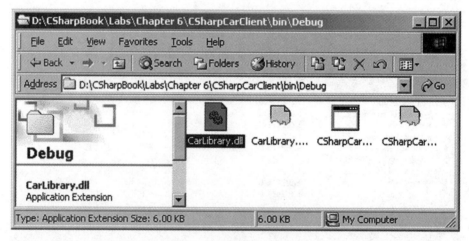

Figure 6-8. Local copies of referenced assemblies are placed in your Debug folder

Obviously this is a huge change from classic COM, where the resolution of the binary is achieved using the system registry.

Now that our client application has been configured to reference the CarLibrary assembly, you are free to create a class that makes use of these types. Here is a test drive (pun intended):

```
// Our first taste of binary reuse.
namespace CSharpCarClient
{
using System;

// Make use of the CarLib types!
using CarLibrary;

public class CarClient
{
    public static int Main(string[] args)
    {
        // Make a sports car.
        SportsCar viper = new SportsCar("Viper", 240, 40);
        viper.TurboBoost();

        // Make a minivan.
        MiniVan mv = new MiniVan();
        mv.TurboBoost();

        return 0;
    }
}
}
```

This code looks just like the other applications developed thus far. The only point of interest is that the C# client application is now making use of types defined within a unique assembly. Go ahead and run your program. As you would expect, the execution of this program results in the display of two message boxes.

A Visual Basic.NET Client Application

When you install Visual Studio.NET, you receive four languages that are capable of building managed code: JScript.NET, C++ with managed extensions (MC++), C# and Visual Basic.NET. A nice feature of Visual Studio.NET is that all languages share the same IDE. Therefore, Visual Basic.NET, ATL, C#, and MFC programmers all make use of a common development environment. Given this fact, the process of building a Visual Basic.NET application making use of the CarLibrary is simple. Assume a new VB.NET Windows Application project workspace named VBCarClient (Figure 6-9) has been created.

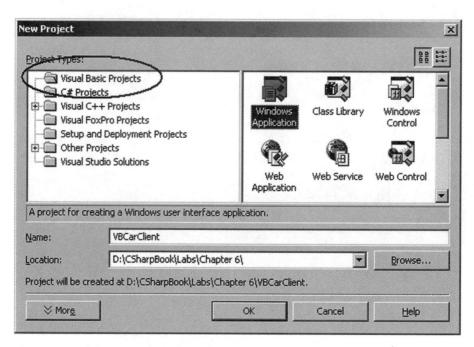

Figure 6-9. Selecting a VB.NET Windows Application project

Similar to Visual Basic 6.0, this project workspace provides a design time template used to build the GUI of the main window. However, VB.NET is a completely different animal. The template you are looking at is actually a subclass of the Form type, which is quite different from a VB 6.0 Form object (more details in Chaper 8).

Now, set a reference to the C# CarLibrary, again using the Add Reference dialog. Like C#, VB.NET requires you to list each namespace used within your project. However, VB.NET makes use of the "imports" keyword rather than the C# "using" directive. Thus, open the code window for your Form and add the following:

```
' Like C#, VB.NET needs to 'see' the namespaces used by a given class.
Imports System
Imports System.Collections
...
Imports CarLibrary
```

Using the design time template, construct a minimal and complete user interface to exercise your automobile types (Figure 6-10). Two buttons should fit the bill (simply select the Button widget from the Toolbox and draw it on the Form object).

Figure 6-10. A painfully simply UI

The next step is to add event handlers to capture the Click event of each Button object. To do so, simply double-click each button on the Form. The IDE responds by writing stub code that will be called when a button is clicked. Here is some sample code:

```
' A little bit of VB.NET!
Protected Sub btnMiniVan_Click(ByVal sender As Object,
                    ByVal e As System.EventArgs) Handles btnMiniVan.Click

        Dim sc As New MiniVan()
        sc.TurboBoost()
End Sub


Protected Sub btnCar_Click(ByVal sender As Object,
                    ByVal e As System.EventArgs) Handles btnCar.Click

        Dim sc As New SportsCar()
        sc.TurboBoost()
End Sub
```

Although the goal of this book is not to turn you into a powerhouse VB.NET developer, here is one point of interest. Notice how each Car subclass is created using the New keyword. Unlike VB 6.0 however, classes now have true constructors! Therefore, the empty parentheses suffixed on the class name do indeed invoke a given constructor on the class. As you would expect, when you run the program, each automobile responds appropriately.

Cross-Language Inheritance

A very sexy aspect of .NET development is the notion of cross-language inheritance. To illustrate, let's create a new VB.NET class that derives from CarLibrary.SportsCar. Impossible you say? Well, if you were using Visual Basic 6.0 this would be the case. However with the advent of VB.NET, programmers are able to use the same object-oriented features found in C#, Java and C++, including classical inheritance (i.e., the "is-a" relationship).

To illustrate, add a new class named PerformanceCar to your current VB.NET client application (using the "Project | Add Class" menu selection). In the code that follows, notice you are deriving from the C# Car type using the VB.NET "Inherits" keyword. As you recall, the Car class defined an abstract TurboBoost() method, which we implement using the VB.NET "Overrides" keyword:

```
' Yes, VB.NET supports each pillar of OOP!
Imports CarLibrary
Imports System.Windows.Forms


' This VB type is deriving from the C# SportsCar!
Public Class PerformanceCar
        Inherits CarLibrary.SportsCar

            ' Implementation of abstract Car method.
            Overrides Sub TurboBoost()
                MessageBox.Show("Blistering speed", "VB PerformanceCar says")
            End Sub
End Class
```

If we update our existing Form to include an additional Button to exercise the performance car, we could write the following test code:

```
Protected Sub btnPreCar_Click(ByVal sender As Object,
                    ByVal e As System.EventArgs) Handles btnPerfCar.Click

            Dim pc As New PerformanceCar()
            pc.PetName = "Hank"      ' Inherited property.

            ' Display base class.
MessageBox.Show(pc.GetType().BaseType.ToString(),
            "Base class of Perf car")

            ' Custom Implementation of Car.TurboBoost()
            pc.TurboBoost()
End Sub
```

Notice that we are able to identify our base class programmatically (Figure 6-11).

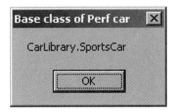

Figure 6-11. Cross language inheritance

Excellent! At this point you have begun the process of breaking your applications into discrete binary building blocks. Given the language-independent nature of .NET, any language targeting the runtime is able to create (and extend) the types described within a given assembly.

SOURCE CODE   *The CarLibrary, CSharpCarClient and VBCarClient projects are each included under the Chapter 6 subdirectory.*

Exploring the CarLibrary's Manifest

At this point, you have successfully created a single file assembly and two client applications. Your next order of business is to gain a deeper understanding of how .NET assemblies are constructed under the hood. To begin, recall that every assembly contains an associated manifest, which can be regarded as the Rosetta stone of .NET. A manifest contains metadata that specifies the name and version of the assembly, as well as a listing of all internal and external modules that compose the assembly as a whole. Additionally, a manifest may contain culture information (used for internalization), a corresponding "strong name" (required by shared assemblies) and optional security and resource information (we will examine the .NET resource format in Chapter 10).

.NET aware compilers (such as csc.exe) automatically create a manifest at compile time. As you see in Chapter 7, it is possible to augment the compiler-generated manifest using attribute-based programming techniques. For now, go ahead and load the CarLibrary assembly into ILDasm.exe. As you can see, this tool has read the metadata to display relevant information for each type (Figure 6-12).

Now, open the manifest by double clicking on the MANIFEST icon (Figure 6-13).

The first code block contained in a manifest is used to specify all external assemblies that are required by the current assembly to function correctly. As you recall, CarLibrary.dll made use of mscorlib.dll and System.Windows.Forms.dll, each of which are marked in the manifest using the [.assembly extern] tag:

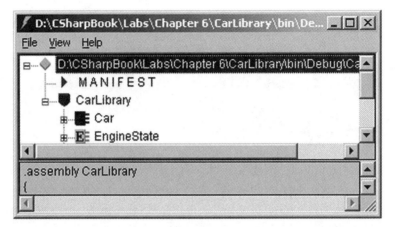

Figure 6-12. Your car library

```
MANIFEST                                                _ □ ×
.assembly extern mscorlib
{
  .publickeytoken = (B7 7A 5C 56 19 34 E0 89 )
  .ver 1:0:2411:0
}
.assembly extern System.Windows.Forms
{
  .publickeytoken = (B7 7A 5C 56 19 34 E0 89 )
  .ver 1:0:2411:0
}
.assembly CarLibrary
{
  .custom instance void [mscorlib]System.Reflection.Asse
  .custom instance void [mscorlib]System.Reflection.Asse
  .custom instance void [mscorlib]System.Reflection.Asse
  .custom instance void [mscorlib]System.Reflection.Asse
  .custom instance void [mscorlib]System.Reflection.Asse
  .custom instance void [mscorlib]System.Reflection.Asse
  .custom instance void [mscorlib]System.Reflection.Asse
  .custom instance void [mscorlib]System.Reflection.Asse
  .custom instance void [mscorlib]System.Reflection.Asse
  .custom instance void [mscorlib]System.Reflection.Asse
  // --- The following custom attribute is added automat
  //   .custom instance void [mscorlib]System.Diagnostics
  //
  .hash algorithm 0x00008004
  .ver 1:0:454:30104
}
.module CarLibrary.dll
```

Figure 6-13. The CarLibrary manifest

```
.assembly extern mscorlib
{
  .publickeytoken = (B7 7A 5C 56 19 34 E0 89 )                    // .z\V.4
  .ver 1:0:2411:0
}
```

```
.assembly extern System.Windows.Forms
{
  .publickeytoken = (B7 7A 5C 56 19 34 E0 89 )                    // .z\V.4..
  .ver 1:0:2411:0
}
```

Here, each [.assembly extern] block is colored by the [.publickeytoken] and [.ver] directives. The [.publickeytoken] instruction is only present if the assembly has been configured as a shared assembly and is used to reference the "strong name" of the shared assembly (more details later). [.ver] is (of course) the numerical version identifier.

After enumerating each of the external references, the manifest then enumerates each module contained in the assembly. Given that the CarLibrary is a single file assembly, you will find exactly one [.module] tag. This manifest also lists a number of attributes (marked with the [.custom] tag) such as company name, trademark and so forth, all of which are currently empty (more information on these attributes in Chapter 7):

```
.assembly CarLibrary
{
  .custom instance void [mscorlib]
System.Reflection.AssemblyKeyNameAttribute::.ctor(string) = ( 01 00 00 00 00 )
  .custom instance void [mscorlib]
System.Reflection.AssemblyKeyFileAttribute::.ctor(string) = ( 01 00 00 00 00 )
  .custom instance void [mscorlib]
System.Reflection.AssemblyDelaySignAttribute::.ctor(bool) = ( 01 00 00 00 00 )
  .custom instance void [mscorlib]
System.Reflection.AssemblyTrademarkAttribute::.ctor(string) = ( 01 00 00 00 00 )
  .custom instance void [mscorlib]
System.Reflection.AssemblyCopyrightAttribute::.ctor(string) = ( 01 00 00 00 00 )
  .custom instance void [mscorlib]
System.Reflection.AssemblyProductAttribute::.ctor(string) = ( 01 00 00 00 00 )
  .custom instance void [mscorlib]
System.Reflection.AssemblyCompanyAttribute::.ctor(string) = ( 01 00 00 00 00 )
  .custom instance void [mscorlib]
System.Reflection.AssemblyConfigurationAttribute::.ctor(string)=( 01 00 00 00 00
)
```

```
  .custom instance void [mscorlib]
System.Reflection.AssemblyDescriptionAttribute::.ctor(string) = ( 01 00 00 00 00
)
  .custom instance void [mscorlib]
System.Reflection.AssemblyTitleAttribute::.ctor(string) = ( 01 00 00 00 00 )

  .hash algorithm 0x00008004
  .ver 1:0:454:30104
}
.module CarLibrary.dll
```

Here, you can see that the [.assembly] tag is used to mark the friendly name of your custom assembly (CarLibrary). Like external declarations, the [.ver] tag defines the compatibility version number for this assembly, where [.hash] marks the file's generated hash code. Do note that the CarLibrary assembly does *not* define an [.publickeytoken] tag, given that CarLibrary has not been configured as a shared assembly.

To summarize the tags that dwell in the assembly manifest, ponder Table 6-1.

Table 6-1. Manifest IL Tags

MANIFEST DECLARATION TAG	MEANING IN LIFE
.assembly	Marks the assembly declaration, indicating that the file is an assembly.
.file	Marks extra files in the same assembly.
.class extern	Classes exported by the assembly but declared in another module.
.exeloc	Indicates the location of the executable for the assembly.
.manifestres	Indicates the manifest resources (if any). You see this tag in action in Chapter 9 (GDI+).
.module	Module declaration, indicating that the file is a module (i.e., a .NET binary with no manifest) and not an assembly.
.module extern	Modules of this assembly contain items referenced in this module.
Assembly extern	The assembly reference indicates another assembly containing items referenced by this module.
.publickey	Contains the actual bytes of the public key.
.publickeytoken	Contains a token of the actual public key.

Exploring the CarLibrary's Types

Recall that an assembly does not contain platform specific instructions, but rather platform agnostic intermediate language (IL). When the .NET runtime loads an assembly into memory, the underlying IL is compiled (using the JIT compiler) into instructions that can be understood by the target platform. Also recall that in addition to raw IL and the assembly manifest, an assembly contains metadata that describes and members of each type contained within a given module.

For example, if you were to double click the TurboBoost() method of the SportsCar class, ILDasm.exe would open a new window showing the raw IL instructions. Notice in the following screen shot, that the [.method] tag is used to identify (of course) a method defined by the SportsCar type (Figure 6-14).

```
SportsCar::TurboBoost : void()                        _ |□| X|
.method public hidebysig virtual instance void
        TurboBoost() cil managed
{
  // Code size        17 (0x11)
  .maxstack  8
  IL_0000:  ldstr      "Ramming speed!"
  IL_0005:  ldstr      "Faster is better..."
  IL_000a:  call       valuetype [System.Windows.F

  IL_000f:  pop
  IL_0010:  ret
} // end of method SportsCar::TurboBoost
```

Figure 6-14. IL for the TurboBoost() method

As you might expect, public data defined by a type is marked with the [.field] tag (Figure 6-15). Recall that the Car class defined a set of protected data, such as currSpeed (note that the "family" tag signifies protected data).

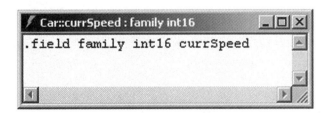

```
Car::currSpeed : family int16              _ |□| X|
.field family int16 currSpeed
```

Figure 6-15. IL for the currSpeed field

Properties are also marked with the [.property] tag (Figure 6-16). The figure shows the IL describing the public property that provides access to the underlying currSpeed data point (note the read/write nature of the CurrSpeed property is marked by .get and .set tags):

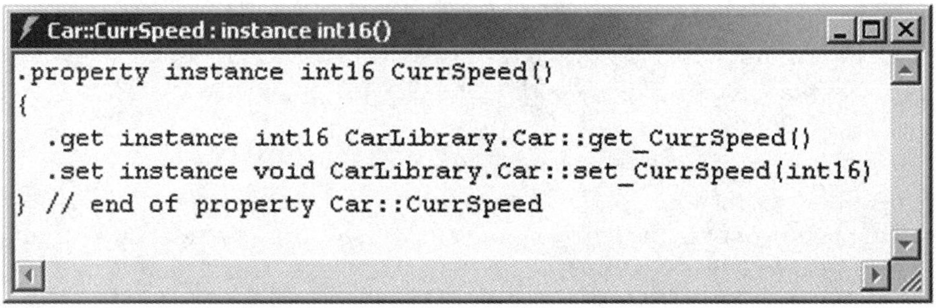

```
Car::CurrSpeed : instance int16()                                    _ □ ×
.property instance int16 CurrSpeed()
{
  .get instance int16 CarLibrary.Car::get_CurrSpeed()
  .set instance void CarLibrary.Car::set_CurrSpeed(int16)
} // end of property Car::CurrSpeed
```

Figure 6-16. IL for the CurrSpeed property

If you now select the "Ctrl + M" keystroke, ILDasm.exe would display the metadata for each type (Figure 6-17).

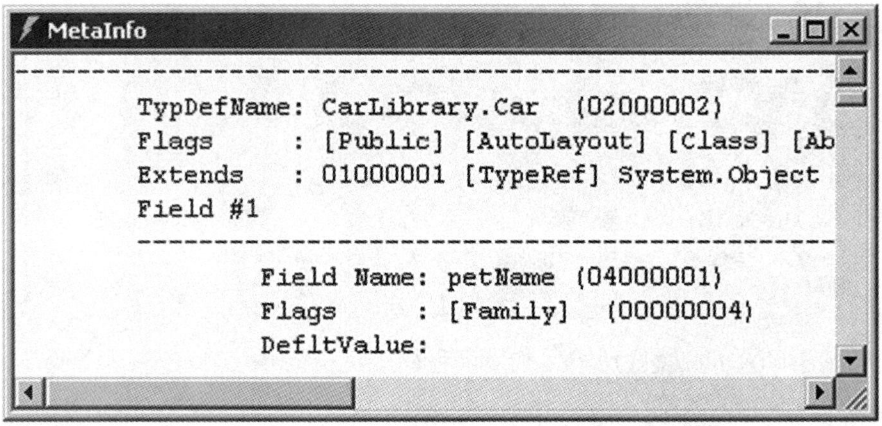

```
MetaInfo                                                             _ □ ×
------------------------------------------------------------------------
      TypDefName: CarLibrary.Car   (02000002)
      Flags     : [Public] [AutoLayout] [Class] [Ab
      Extends   : 01000001 [TypeRef] System.Object
      Field #1
      ----------------------------------------------------------
              Field Name: petName (04000001)
              Flags     : [Family]   (00000004)
              DefltValue:
```

Figure 6-17. Type metadata

Using this metadata, the .NET runtime is able to locate and construct object instances, and invoke methods. Various tools (such as Visual Studio.NET) make use of metadata at design time in order to validate the number of (and type of) parameters during compilation. To summarize the story so far, make sure the following points are clear in your mind:

• An assembly is a versioned, self-describing set of modules. Each module contains some number of types and optional resources.

- Every assembly contains metadata that describes all types within a given module. The .NET runtime (as well as numerous design time tools) read the metadata to locate and create objects, validate method calls, activate IntelliSense, and so on.

- Every assembly contains a manifest that enumerates the set of all internal and external files required by the binary, version information as well as other assembly-centric details.

Next you need to distinguish between private and shared assemblies. If you are coming into the .NET paradigm from a classic COM perspective, be prepared for some significant changes.

Understanding Private Assemblies

Formally speaking, an assembly is either "private" or "shared." The good news is each variation has the same underlying structure (i.e., some number of modules and an associated manifest). Furthermore, each flavor of assembly provides the same kind of services (for example, access to some number of public types). The real differences between a private and shared assembly boils down to naming conventions, versioning policies, and deployment issues. Let's begin by examining the traits of a private assembly, which is far and away the most common of the two options.

Private assemblies are a collection of types that are only used by the application with which it has been deployed. For example, CarLibrary.dll is a private assembly used by the CSharpCarClient and VBCarClient applications. When you create a private assembly, the assumption is that the collection of types are only used by the "owning" application, and *not* shared with other applications on the system.

Private assemblies are required to be located within the main directory of the owning application (termed the *application directory*) or a subdirectory thereof. For example, recall that when you set a reference to the CarLibrary assembly (as we did in the CSharpCarClient and VBCarClient applications), the Visual Studio.NET IDE responded by making a full copy of the assembly that was placed it in your project's application directory. This is the default behavior, as private assemblies are assumed to be deployment option of choice.

Note the painfully stark contrast to classic COM. There is no need to register any items under HKEY_CLASSES_ROOT and no need to enter a hard-coded path to the binary using an InprocServer32 or LocalServer32 listing. The resolution and loading of the private CarLibrary happens by virtue of the fact that the assembly is placed in the application directory. In fact, if you moved CSharpCarClient.exe and CarLibrary.dll to a new directory, the application would still run. To illustrate this point, copy these two files to your desktop and run the client (Figure 6-18).

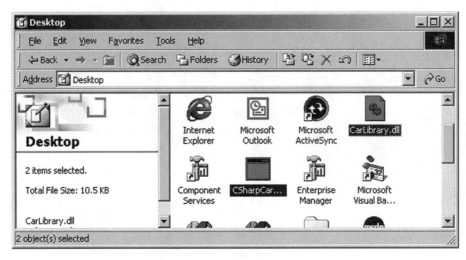

Figure 6-18. Can you say "XCopy installation?"

Uninstalling (or replicating) an application that makes exclusive use of private assemblies is a no-brainer. Delete (or copy) the application folder. Unlike classic COM, you do not need to worry about dozens of orphaned registry settings. More important, you do not need to worry that the removal of private assemblies will break any other applications on the machine!

Probing Basics

Later in this chapter, you are exposed to a number of gory details regarding location resolution of an assembly. Until then, the following overview should help prime the pump. Formally speaking, the .NET runtime resolves the location of a private assembly using a technique termed *probing*, which is much less invasive than it sounds. Probing is the process of mapping an external assembly reference (i.e., [.assembly extern]) to the correct corresponding binary file. For example, when the runtime reads the following line from the VBCarClient's manifest:

```
.assembly extern CarLibrary
{
. . .
}
```

a search is made in the application directory for a file named CarLibrary.DLL. If a DLL binary cannot be located, an attempt is made to locate an EXE version (CarLibrary.EXE). If neither of these files can be found, a further examination ensues for a shared assembly (examined in just a bit).

The Identity of a Private Assembly

The identity of a private assembly consists of a friendly string name and numerical version, both of which are recorded in the assembly manifest. The friendly name is created based on the name of the binary module that contains the assembly's manifest. For example, if you examine the manifest of the CarLibrary.dll assembly, you find the following (the exact version may vary):

```
.assembly CarLibrary as "CarLibrary"
{
. . .
   .ver 1:0:454:30104
}
```

However, given the nature of a private assembly, it should make sense that the .NET runtime does *not* bother to apply any version policies when loading the assembly. The assumption is that private assemblies do not need to have any elaborate version checking, given that the client application is the only entity that "knows" of its existence. As an interesting corollary you should understand that it is (very) possible for a single machine to have multiple copies of the same private assembly in various application directories.

Private Assemblies and XML Configuration Files

When the .NET runtime is instructed to bind to an assembly, the first step is to determine the presence of an application configuration file. These optional files contain XML tags that control the binding behavior of the launching application. By law, configuration files must have the same name as the launching application and take a *.config file extension.

As mentioned, configuration files can be used to specify any optional subdirectories to be searched during the process of binding to private assemblies. As you have seen earlier in this chapter, a componentized .NET application can be deployed simply by placing all assemblies into the same directory as the launching application. Often, however, you may wish to deploy an application such that the application directory contains a number of related subdirectories, in order to give some meaningful structure to the application as a whole.

You see this all the time in commercial software. For example, assume our main directory is called MyRadApplication, which contains a number of subdirectories (\Images, \Bin, \SavedGames, \OtherCoolStuff). Using application configuration files, you can instruct the runtime where it should probe while attempting to locate the set of private assemblies used by the launching application.

To illustrate, let's create a simple configuration file for the previous CSharp-CarClient application. Our goal is to move the referenced assembly (CarLibrary) from the Debug folder into a new subdirectory named Foo \ Bar. Go ahead and move this file now (Figure 6-19).

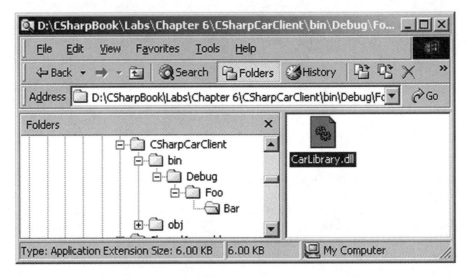

Figure 6-19. Relocating your assembly

Now, create a new configuration file named CSharpCarClient.exe.config (notepad will do just fine) and save it into the *same* folder containing the CSharp-CarClient.exe application. The beginning of an application configuration file is marked with the <Configuration> tag. Before the closing </Configuration> tag, specify an assemblyBinding row, which is used to specify alternative locations to search for a given assembly, using the privatePath attribute (FYI, multiple subdirectories can be specified using a semicolon delimited list):

```
<configuration>
     <runtime>
          <assemblyBinding xmlns="urn:schemas-microsoft-com:asm.v1">
                    <probing privatePath="foo\bar"/>
          </assemblyBinding>
     </runtime>
</configuration>
```

Once you are done, save the file and launch the client. You will find that the CSharpCarClient application runs without a hitch. As a final test, change the name of your configuration file and attempt to run the program once again (Figure 6-20).

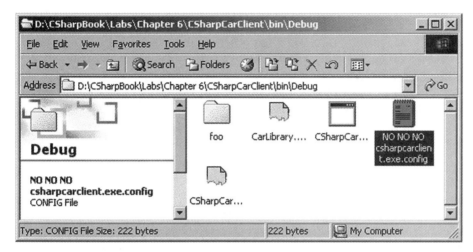

*Figure 6-20. *.config files must have the same name as the launching application*

The client application silently fails. Recall that configuration files must have the same name as the launching application. Because you have renamed this file, the .NET runtime assumes you do not have a configuration file, and thus attempts to probe for the referenced assembly in the application directory (which it cannot locate).

Specifics of Binding to a Private Assembly

To wrap up the current discussion, let's formalize the specific steps involved in binding to a private assembly at runtime. First, a request to load an assembly may be either *explicit* or *implicit*. An implicit load request occurs whenever the manifest makes a direct reference to some external assembly. As you recall, external references are marked with the [.assembly extern] instruction:

```
// An implicit load request. . .
.assembly extern CarLibrary
{
    . . .
}
```

An explicit load request occurs programmatically using System.Reflection.Assembly.Load().The Assembly class is examined in Chapter 7, but be aware that the Load() method allows you to specify the name, version, strong name, and culture information syntactically (note you are not required to specify each characteristic):

```
// An explicit load request. . .
Assembly asm = Assembly.Load("CarLibrary");
```

Collectively, the name, version, strong name, and culture information is termed an *assembly reference* (or simply AsmRef). The entity in charge of locating the correct assembly based on an AsmRef is termed the *assembly resolver,* which is a facility of the CLR.

As mentioned earlier, an application directory is nothing more than a folder on your hard drive (for example, C:\MyApp) that contains all the files for a given application. If necessary, an application directory may specify additional subdirectories (e.g., C:\MyApp\Bin, C:\MyApp\Tools, and so on) to establish a more stringent file hierarchy.

When a binding request is made, the runtime passes an AsmRef to the assembly resolver. If the resolver determines the AsmRef refers to a private assembly (meaning there is no strong name recorded in the manifest), the following steps are followed:

1. First, the assembly resolver attempts to locate a configuration file in the application directory. As you will see, this file can specify additional subdirectories to include in the search, as well as establish a version policy to use for the current bind.

2. If there is no configuration file, the runtime attempts to discover the correct assembly by examining the current application directory. If a configuration file does exist, any specified subdirectories are searched.

3. If the assembly cannot be found within the application directory (or a specified subdirectory) the search stops here and a TypeLoadException exception is raised, as private assemblies are always located within the application directory (or a specified subdirectory).

To solidify this sequence of events, Figure 6-21 illustrates the process outlined above.

Again, as you can see, the location of a private assembly is fairly simply to resolve. If the application directory does not contain a configuration file, the assembly resolver simply looks for a binary that matches the correct string name. If the application directory does contain a configuration file, any specified subdirectories are also searched.

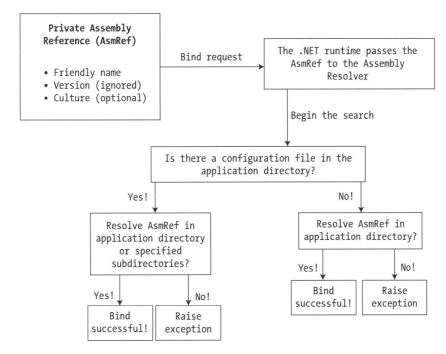

Figure 6-21. Searching for a private assembly

Understanding Shared Assemblies

Like a private assembly, a "shared" assembly is a collection of types and (optional) resources contained within some number of modules. The most obvious difference between shared and private assemblies is the fact that shared assemblies can be used by several clients on a single machine. Clearly, if you wish to create a machine-wide class library, a shared assembly is the way to go.

A shared assembly is typically not deployed within the same directory as the application making use of it. Rather, shared assemblies are installed into a machine-wide Global Assembly Cache, which lends itself to yet another colorful acronym in the programming universe: the GAC. The GAC itself is located under the <drive>: \ WinNT \ Assembly subdirectory (Figure 6-22).

This is yet another major difference between the COM and .NET architectures. In COM, shared applications can reside anywhere on a given machine, provided they are properly registered. Under .NET, shared assemblies are typically placed into a centralized well-known location (the GAC).

Unlike private assemblies, a shared assembly requires additional version information beyond the friendly text string. As you may have guessed, the .NET runtime *does* enforce version checking for a shared assembly before it is loaded on behalf of the calling application. In addition, a shared assembly must be assigned a "shared name" (also known as a "strong name").

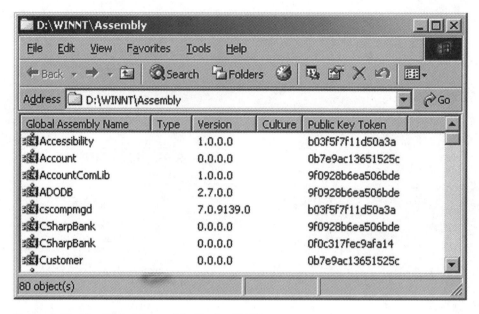

Figure 6-22. The Global Assembly Cache (GAC)

Problems with Your GAC?

By way of a quick side note, as of Beta2 (on which this text is based) I have noticed that some of my development machines are unable to display the GAC correctly. The problem is that the GAC is a shell extension that requires the registration of a COM server named shfusion.dll. During installation, this server may fail to register correctly. If you are having problems opening the GAC on your machine, simply register this COM server using regsvr32.exe and you should be just fine.

Understanding Shared (Strong) Names

When you wish to create an assembly that can be used by numerous applications on a given machine, your first step is to create a unique shared name for the assembly. A shared name contains the following information:

- A friendly string name and optional culture information (just like a private assembly).

- A version identifier.

- A public/private key pair.

- A digital signature.

The composition of a shared name is based on standard public key cryptography. When you create a shared assembly, you must generate a public/private key pair (that you do momentarily). The key pair is included in the build cycle using a .NET aware compiler, which in turn lists a token of the public key in the assembly's manifest (via the [.publickeytoken] tag). The private key is not listed in the manifest, but rather, is signed with the public key. The resulting signature is stored in the assembly itself (in the case of a multifile assembly, the private key is stored with the file defining the manifest).

Now, assume some client has referenced this shared assembly (which is no different than referencing a private assembly). When the compiler generates the client binary, the public key is recorded in its manifest. At runtime, the .NET runtime ensures that both the client and the shared assembly are making using of the same key pair. If these keys are identical, the client application can rest assured that the correct assembly as been loaded. Figure 6-23 presents the basic picture.

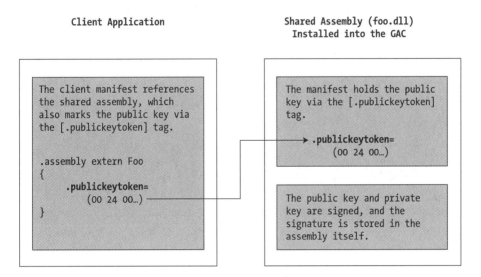

Figure 6-23. Key matching

As you might guess, there are additional details regarding key pairs. We really don't need more details for now, so check out online Help if you so choose.

Building a Shared Assembly

To generate a strong name for your assembly, you need to make use of the sn.exe (strong name) utility. Although this tool has numerous command line options, all we need to concern ourselves with is the "-k" argument, which instructs the tool to generate a new strong name key that will be saved to a specified file (Figure 6-24).

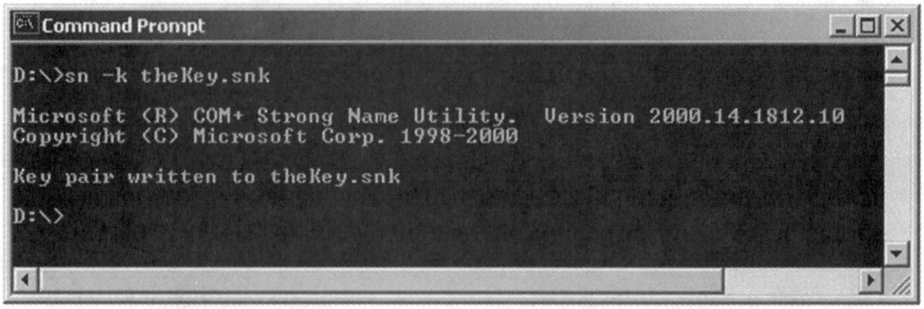

*Figure 6-24. Creating a *.snk file*

If you examine the contents of this new file (theKey.snk) you see the binary markings of the key pair (Figure 6-25).

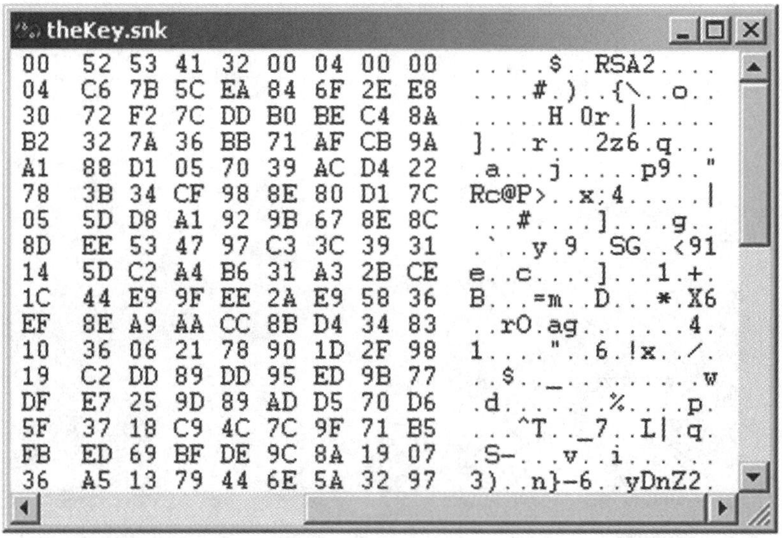

*Figure 6-25. The *.snk file, up close and personal*

To continue with the example, assume you have created a new C# Class Library called (of course) SharedAssembly, which contains the following class definition:

```csharp
using System;
using System.Windows.Forms;

namespace SharedAssembly
{
public class VWMiniVan
```

```
{
    public VWMiniVan(){}

    public void Play60sTunes()
    {
        MessageBox.Show("What a loooong, strange trip it's been...");
    }

    private bool isBustedByTheFuzz = false;
    public bool Busted
    {
        get { return isBustedByTheFuzz; }
        set { isBustedByTheFuzz = value; }
    }
}
}
```

The next step is to record the public key in the assembly manifest. The easiest way to do so is to leverage the use of an attribute named AssemblyKeyFile. When you create a new C# project workspace, you will notice that one of your initial project files is named "AssemblyInfo.cs" (Figure 6-26).

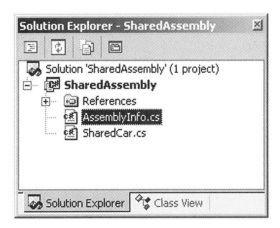

Figure 6-26. The AssemblyInfo.cs file

This file contains a number of (initially empty) attributes that are consumed by a .NET aware compiler. If you examine this file, you find one such attribute named AssemblyKeyFile. To specify the strong name for a shared assembly, simply update the initial empty value with a string specifying the location of your *.snk file:

```
[assembly: AssemblyKeyFile(@"D:\SharedAssembly\theKey.snk")]
```

Using this assembly level attribute, the C# compiler now merges the necessary information into the corresponding manifest, as can be seen using ILDasm.exe (note the [.publickey] tag in Figure 6-27).

```
/ MANIFEST                                          _ |□| X|
.publickey = 00 24 00 00 04 80 00 00 94 00 00 00 06 02 00
             00 24 00 00 52 53 41 31 00 04 00 00 01 00 01
             23 A0 29 04 C6 7B 5C EA 84 6F 2E E8 B2 B7 7F
             9D 48 0C 30 72 F2 7C DD B0 BE C4 8A 5D 14 8D
             72 8A 11 B2 32 7A 36 BB 71 AF CB 9A D9 61 9B
             B1 6A 8E A1 88 D1 05 70 39 AC D4 22 52 63 40
             3E 12 19 78 3B 34 CF 98 8E 80 D1 7C E6 00 89
             97 AF E4 05 5D D8 A1 92 9B 67 8E 8C 93 60 A1
             79 11 39 8D EE 53 47 97 C3 3C 39 31 65 BA 8E
             9F 2E A0 14 5D C2 A4 B6 31 A3 2B CE 42 9F 8B
  .hash algorithm 0x00008004
  .ver 1:0:455:41284
}
.module SharedAssembly.dll
// MVID: {A0E6E31A-6A84-4DCB-8FE6-93DE718BEAD2}
```

Figure 6-27. The markings of a shared assembly

SOURCE CODE *The SharedAssembly project is located under the Chapter 6 subdirectory.*

Installing Assemblies into the GAC

Once you have established a strong name for your shared assembly, the final step is to install it into the GAC. The simplest approach to install a private assembly into the GAC is to drag and drop the file(s) onto the active window (you are also free to make use of the gacutil.exe command line utility). SeeFigure 6-28.

Do be aware that you must have Administrative rights on the computer to install assemblies into the GAC. This is a good thing, in that it prevents the casual user from accidentally breaking existing applications.

The end result is that your assembly has now been placed into the GAC, and may be shared by multiple applications on the target machine. On a related note, when you wish to remove an assembly from the GAC, you may do so with a simple right-click (just select Delete from the Context menu).

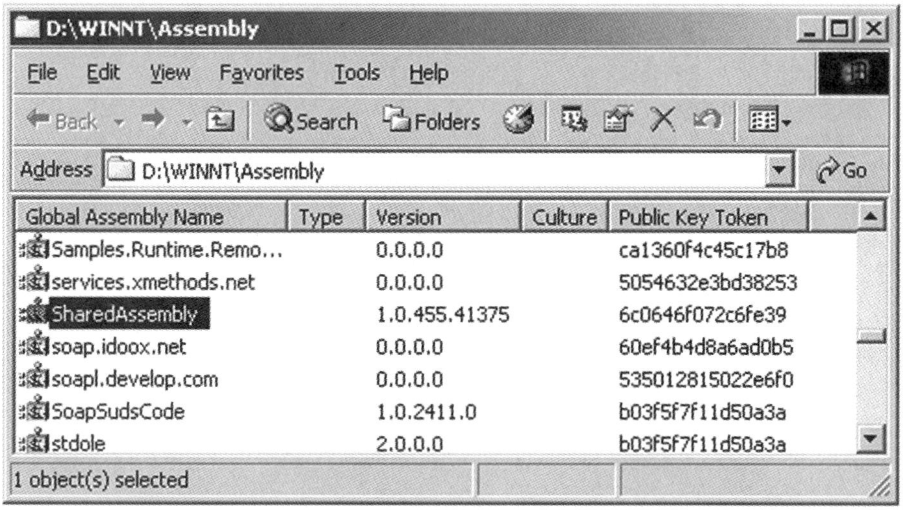

Figure 6-28. Installing your assembly into the GAC

Using a Shared Assembly

Now to prove the point, assume you have created a new C# Console application
(called SharedAssemblyUser), set a reference to the SharedAssembly binary, and
created the following class definition:

```
namespace SharedLibUser
{
using System;
using SharedAssembly;

public class SharedAsmUser
{
    public static int Main(string[] args)
    {
        try
        {
            VWMiniVan v = new VWMiniVan();
            v.Play60sTunes();
        }
        catch(TypeLoadException e)
        {
            // Can't find assembly!
            Console.WriteLine(e.Message);
        }
```

```
        return 0;
    }
}
}
```

Recall, that when you reference a shared assembly, IDE automatically creates a local copy of the assembly for use by the client application. However, when you reference an assembly that contains a public key (as is the case with the SharedAssembly.dll), you do not receive a local copy. The assumption is that assemblies containing a public key are designed to be shared (and are therefore placed in the GAC).

Do be aware that the VS.NET IDE allows you to explicitly control the copying of a given assembly using the Properties window. For example, if you have set a reference to the external binary, select this assembly using the Solution Explorer and set Copy Local to false. This will delete the local copy (Figure 6-29).

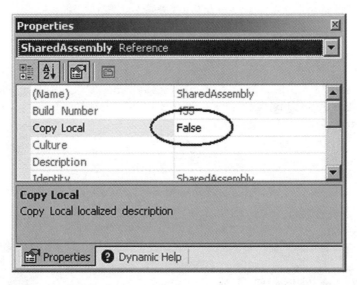

Figure 6-29. Manipulating the local copy

Now run the client application once again. If all is well, everything should still function correctly, as the .NET runtime consulted the GAC during its quest to resolve the location of the requested assembly (Figure 6-30).

SOURCE CODE *The SharedLibUser application can be found under the Chapter 6 subdirectory. Before you run this application, be sure to install SharedAssembly.dll into the GAC!*

Figure 6-30. Strange indeed

Understanding .NET Version Policies

As you have already learned, the .NET runtime does not bother to perform version checks for private assemblies. The versioning story changes significantly when a request is made to load a shared assembly. Given that the version of a shared assembly is of prime importance, let's review the composition of version numbers. As you recall, a version number is marked by four discrete parts (for example 2.0.2.11). Logically however, the .NET runtime is able to extract three meaningful bits of information regarding version compatibility, as illustrated in Figure 6-31.

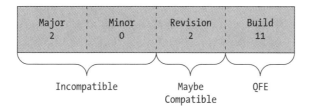

Figure 6-31. Anatomy of an assembly version number

Whenever two assemblies differ by either the major or minor version number (e.g., 2.0 vs. 2.5) they are considered to be *completely incompatible* with each other as far as the .NET runtime is concerned. When assemblies differ by major or minor numerical markings, you can assume significant changes have occurred (e.g., method name changes, types have been added or removed, parameters have changed, and so forth). Therefore, if a client is requesting a bind to version 2.0 but the GAC only contains version 2.5, the bind request fails (unless overridden by an application configuration file).

If two assemblies have identical major and minor version numbers, but have different revision numbers (e.g., 2.5.0.0 vs. 2.5.1.0) the .NET runtime assumes they *might be* compatible with each other (in other words, backward compatibility is assumed, but not guaranteed). By way of a concrete example, a Service Pack release typically involves modifying the revision number of an assembly.

Finally, you have the Quick Fix Engineering (QFE) number. When two assemblies differ only by their QFE value, the .NET runtime assumes they are fully compatible. QFEs are typically modified with the release of a software patch. The idea here is that all calling conventions (e.g., method names, parameters, supported interfaces, and so forth) are identical to previous versions.

Recording Version Information

One question you might be asking yourself at this point is *where* was this version number specified? Recall that every C# project defines a file named Assembly-Info.cs. If you examine this file, you will see an attribute named AssemblyVersion, which is initially set to a string reading "1.0.*":

```
[assembly: AssemblyVersion("1.0.*")]
```

Every new C# projects begins life versioned at 1.0. As you build new versions of a shared assembly, part of your task is to update the four-part version number for your shared assembly. Do be aware that the IDE automatically increments the build and revision numbers (as marked by the '*' tag). If you wish to enforce an application-specific value for the assembly's build and/or revision, simply update accordingly:

```
[assembly: AssemblyVersion("1.0.0.0")]
```

Freezing the Current SharedAssembly

To really understand .NET versioning policies, we need to have a concrete example. The current goal is to update your previous SharedAssembly.dll to support additional functionality, update the version number, and then place the new version into the GAC. At this point, you are able to experiment with the use of application configuration files to specify various version policies, as well as side-by-side execution.

To begin, let's update the constructor of the VWMiniVan class to display a message verifying the *current* version:

```
public VWMiniVan()
{
    MessageBox.Show("Using version 1.0.0.0!", "Shared Car");
}
```

Next, update the AssemblyVersion attribute to be fully qualified to version 1.0.0.0 (as seen in the previous section). Go ahead and recompile the project.

The next thing you need to do is ensure that our original SharedAssembly.dll is removed from the GAC (go ahead and delete this assembly now). Next, move your existing 1.0.0.0 assembly into a new folder (I called mine Version1) to ensure you freeze this version (Figure 6-32).

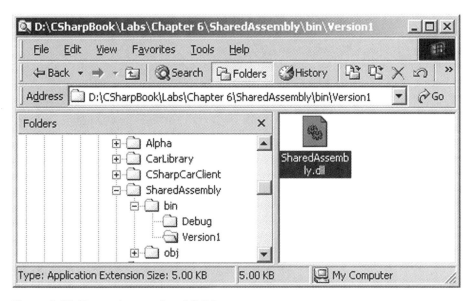

Figure 6-32. Preserving version 1.0.0.0

Now (once again!) place this assembly back into the GAC. Notice that the version of this assembly is <1.0.0.0> (Figure 6-33).

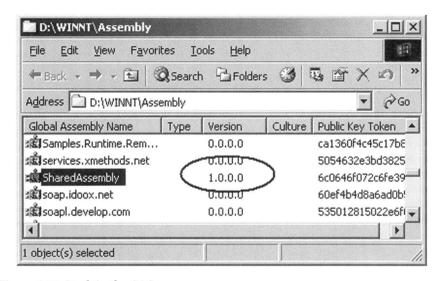

Figure 6-33. Back in the GAC

Once version 1.0.0.0 of the SharedAssembly has been inserted into the GAC, right-click this assembly and select Properties from the context-sensitive pop-up menu. Verify that the path to this binary maps to the Version1 subdirectory. Finally, rebuild and run the current SharedAssemblyUser application. Things should continue to work just fine.

Building SharedAssembly Version 2.0

To illustrate the .NET version policy, let's modify the current SharedAssembly project. Update your VWMiniVan class with a new member (which makes use of a custom enumeration) to allow the user to play some more modern musical selections. Also be sure to update the message displayed from within the constructor logic.

```
// Which band do you want?
public enum BandName
{
    TonesOnTail, SkinnyPuppy, deftones, PTP
}

public class VWMiniVan
{
    public VWMiniVan()
    { MessageBox.Show("Using version 2.0.0.0!", "Shared Car"); }
...
    public void CrankGoodTunes(BandName band)
    {
        switch(band)
        {
            case BandName.deftones:
                MessageBox.Show("So forget about me...");
                break;
            case BandName.PTP:
                MessageBox.Show("Tick tick tock...");
                break;
            case  BandName.SkinnyPuppy:
                MessageBox.Show("Water vapor, to air...");
                break;
            case  BandName.TonesOnTail:
                MessageBox.Show("Oooooh the rain. Oh the rain.");
                break;
```

```
            default:
                break;
        }
    }
}
```

Before you compile, let's upgrade this version of this assembly to 2.0.0.0:

```
// Update your assemblyinfo.cs file as so. . .
[assembly: AssemblyVersion("2.0.0.0")]
```

If you look in your project's debug folder, you see that you have a new version of this assembly (2.0) while the previous version is safe in storage under the Version1 directory. Finally, let's install this new assembly into the GAC. Notice that you now have *two* versions of the same assembly (Figure 6-34).

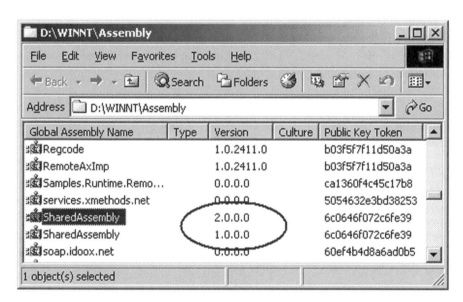

Figure 6-34. Side-by-side execution

Now that you have a distinctly versioned assembly recorded in the GAC, you can begin to work with application configuration files to control how a client binds to a given version. But first, a few words about the default binding policy.

Understanding the Default Version Policy

As mentioned earlier in the chapter, if a client is referencing a shared assembly, the major and minor versions must be identical if the bind is to succeed. However, the .NET runtime binds to a given assembly if the assembly reference differs by the revision or build numbers. This behavior is termed the default version policy and is used to ensure that a client always gets the latest and greatest service release (i.e., bug fix) of a given assembly. Thus, if the client's manifest explicitly requests version 1.0.0.0, but the GAC has a newer version by specifying a QFE (such as 1.0.2.2), the client automatically receives the most recent fix. In this way, a client application is guaranteed that the assembly that it is referencing is backward compatible, in addition to being as bug-free as possible.

Specifying Custom Version Policies

When you wish to dynamically control how an application binds to an assembly (such as disabling QFEs), you need to author an application configuration file. As you have already seen during the discussion of private assemblies, configuration files are blocks of XML that are used to customize the binding process. Recall that these files must have the same name as the owning application (with a *.config extension) and be placed directly in the application directory. In addition to the privatePath tag (used to specify where to probe for private assemblies), a configuration file may specify information for shared assemblies.

The first point of interest is using an application configuration file to specify a specific assembly version that is to be loaded, regardless of what may be listed in the corresponding manifest. When you wish to redirect a client to bind to an alternate shared assembly, you make use of the <dependentAssembly> and <bindingRedirect> attributes. For example, the following configuration file forces version 2.0.0.0:

```
<configuration>
    <runtime>
        <assemblyBinding xmlns="urn:schemas-microsoft-com:asm.v1">
            <dependentAssembly>
                <assemblyIdentity name="sharedassembly"
                        publicKeyToken="6c0646f072c6fe39"
                        culture=""/>

                <bindingRedirect oldVersion= "1.0.0.0"
                                 newVersion= "2.0.0.0"/>

            </dependentAssembly>
        </assemblyBinding>
    </runtime>
</configuration>
```

Here, the oldVersion tag is used to specify the version that you wish to override. The newVersion tag marks a specific version to load.

To test this out yourself, create the previous configuration file and save it into the directory of the SharedAssemblyUser application (be sure you name this configuration file correctly). Now, run the program. You should see the message that appears in Figure 6-35.

Figure 6-35. Activating version 2.0.0.0

If you update the newVersion attribute to 1.0.0.0, you now see the message that appears in Figure 6-36.

Figure 6-36 Activating version 1.0.0.0

Way cool. What you have just observed is the notion of side-by-side execution mentioned earlier in the chapter. Because the .NET framework allows you to place multiple versions of the same assembly into the GAC, you can easily configure custom version policies as you (or a system administrator) see fit.

As you have seen, the .NET framework does indeed take the version of a shared assembly seriously. Through the use of application configuration files, you are able to control a number of details regarding which version of a given assembly should be loaded by an owning application. As you may expect, there are additional attributes that may be listed in an application's configuration file.

Investigate these details as you wish. However, there is one final aspect to consider. . .

The Administrator Configuration File

The configuration files you have been examining in this chapter each have a common theme. They only apply to a specific application (that is why they had the same name as the owning application). The .NET framework does allow an additional type of configuration file called the *administrator configuration file.* Each .NET-aware machine has a file named "machine.config" that contains listings used to override any application-specific configuration files. As you might guess, reading this file is a great way to learn more *.config centric tags.

Now that you have an intimate understanding of .NET assemblies, let's switch gears completely and examine the related topics of application domains and multithreaded assemblies. Although this may seem like a drastic change of content, you will see that assemblies, application domains, and threads are interrelated.

Review of Traditional Win32 Thread Programming

Depending on your programming background, you may be extremely interested in building multithreaded binaries, could care less about building multithreaded binaries, or are a little unsure what multithreading means in the first place. In order to level the playing field, let's take the time to quickly review the basics of multithreading. Once you have reviewed multithreading from a traditional Win32 perspective, you will then come to understand how things have changed under the .NET platform.

To begin, recall that under traditional Win32, each application is hosted by a process. Understand that *process* is a generic term used to describe the set of external resources (such as a COM server) as well as the necessary memory allocations used by a given application. For each EXE loaded into memory, the operating system creates a separate and isolated memory partition (i.e., process) for use during its lifetime.

Every running process has at least one main "thread" that serves as the entry point for the application. Formally speaking, the first thread created in a given process is termed the *primary thread*. Simply put, a thread is a specific path of execution within the Win32 process. A traditional Windows applications defines the WinMain() method to function as the application's entry point. On the other hand, Console application provides the main() method for the same purpose.

Applications that contain only a single thread of execution are automatically "thread-safe" given the fact that there is only one thread that can access the data in the application at a given time. On the downside, a single-threaded application can appear a bit unresponsive to the end user if this single thread is performing a complex operation (such as printing out a lengthy text file, performing an exotic calculation, or connecting to a remote server).

Under Win32, it is possible for the primary thread to spawn additional secondary threads in the background, using a handful of Win32 API functions such as CreateThread(). Each thread (primary or secondary) becomes a unique path of execution in the process and has concurrent access to all data in that process. As you may have guessed, developers typically create additional threads to help improve the program's overall responsiveness.

Multithreaded applications provide the illusion that numerous activities are happening at more or less the same time. For example, you could spawn a background worker thread to perform a labor-intensive unit of work (again, such as printing a large text file). As this secondary thread is churning away, the main thread is still responsive to user input, which gives the entire process the potential of delivering greater performance. However, this is only a possibility. Too many threads in a single process can actually degrade performance, as the CPU must switch between the active threads in the process (which takes time).

In reality, multithreading is often a simple illusion provided by the operating system. Machines that host a single CPU do not have the ability to literally handle multiple threads at the same exact time. Rather, a single CPU will execute one thread for a unit of time (called a *time-slice*) based on the thread's priority level. When a thread's time-slice is up, the existing thread is suspended to allow the other thread to perform its business. In order for a thread to remember what was happening before it was kicked out of the way, each thread is given the ability to write to Thread Local Storage (TLS) and is provided a separate call stack, as illustrated in Figure 6-37.

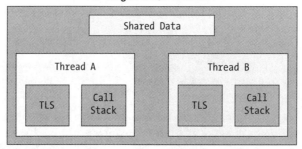

Figure 6-37. A traditional Win32 process

Problem of Concurrency and Thread Synchronization

Beyond taking time, the process of switching between threads can cause additional problems. For example, assume a given thread is accessing a shared point of data, and in the process begins to modify it. Now assume that the first thread is told to wait, to allow another thread to access the same point of data. If the first thread was not finished with its task, the second thread may be modifying data that is in an unstable state.

To protect the application's data from possible corruption, the Win32 developer must make use of any number of Win32 threading primitives such as critical sections, mutexes or semaphores to synchronize access to shared data. Given this, multithreaded applications are much more volatile, as numerous threads can operate on the application's data at the same time. Unless the developer has accounted for this possibility using threading primitives (such as a critical section) the program may end up with a good amount of data corruption.

Although the .NET platform cannot make the difficulties of building robust multithreaded applications completely disappear, the process has been simplified considerably. Using types defined within the System.Threading namespace, you are able to spawn additional threads with minimal fuss and bother. Likewise, when it comes time to lock down shared points of data, you will find additional types that provide the same functionality as the Win32 threading primitives.

Understanding System.AppDomain

Before we examine the full details of the System.Threading namespace, we need to examine the concept of application domains. As you know, .NET applications are created by piecing together any number of related assemblies. However, unlike a traditional (non-.NET) Win32 EXE application, .NET applications are hosted by an entity termed an "application domain" (aka AppDomain). Be very aware that the term AppDomain is *not* a synonym for a Win32 process.

In reality, a single process can host any number of AppDomains, each of which is fully and completely isolated from other AppDomains within this process (or any other process). Applications that run in different AppDomains are unable to share any information of any kind (global variables or static fields) unless they make use of the .NET remoting protocol. The big picture is shown in Figure 6-38.

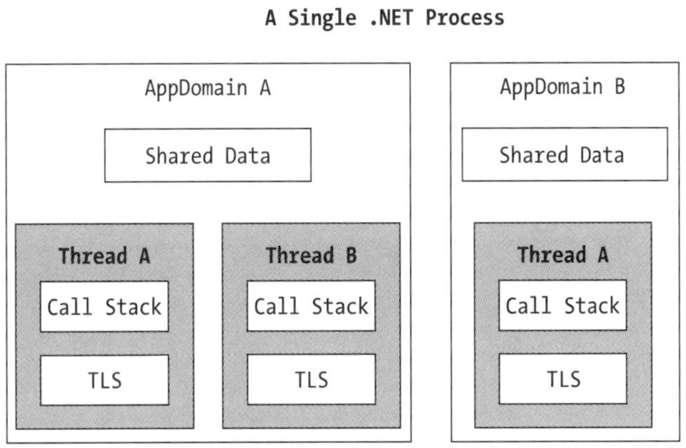

Figure 6-38. A process can contain one or more AppDomains. Each AppDomain can contain one or more threads

Notice the stark difference from a traditional Win32 process. Under .NET, a single process may contain multiple AppDomains. Each AppDomain may contain multiple threads. In some respects, this layout is reminiscent of the "apartment" architecture of classic COM. Of course, .NET AppDomains are managed types whereas the COM apartment architecture is built on an unmanaged (and much more complex) architecture.

AppDomains are programmatically represented by the System.AppDomain type. Some core members to be aware of are shown in Table 6-2.

Table 6-2. Select Members of AppDomain

APPDOMAIN MEMBER	MEANING IN LIFE
CreateDomain()	This static method creates a new AppDomain in the current process.
GetCurrentThreadId()	This static method returns the ID of the current thread.
Unload()	Another static method that unloads the specified AppDomain.
BaseDirectory	This property returns the base directory that the assembly resolver used to probe for assemblies.
CreateInstance()	Creates an instance of a specified type defined in a specified assembly file.
ExecuteAssembly()	Executes the assembly given its file name.
GetAssemblies()	Gets the assemblies that have been loaded into this application domain.
Load()	Loads an assembly into this application domain.

Fun with AppDomains

As you can see, the members of AppDomain provide numerous process-like behaviors, with a .NET flair. To illustrate some of this flair, consider the following namespace definition:

```
namespace MyAppDomain
{
    using System;
    using System.Windows.Forms;

    // Need this namespace to work with the Assembly type.
    using System.Reflection;

    public class MyAppDomain
    {
        public static void PrintAllAssemblies()
        {
            // Ask the current AppDomain for a list of all
            // loaded assemblies.
            AppDomain ad = AppDomain.CurrentDomain;
            Assembly[] loadedAssemblies = ad.GetAssemblies();
```

```
        Console.WriteLine("Here are the assemblies loaded in " +
                           "this appdomain\n");

        // Now print the fully qualified name of each one.
        foreach(Assembly a in loadedAssemblies)
        {
            Console.WriteLine(a.FullName);
        }
    }
    public static int Main(string[] args)
    {
        // Force the loading of the Windows Forms assembly.
        MessageBox.Show("Loaded System.Windows.Forms.dll");
        PrintAllAssemblies();
        return 0;
    }
  }
}
```

First of all, notice that you are making use of a new namespace, System.Reflection. Full details of this namespace are seen in Chapter 7. For the time being, just understand that this namespace defines the Assembly type, which we need access to given the role of the PrintAllAssemblies() method.

This static member obtains a reference to the hosting AppDomain, and enumerates over the list of loaded assemblies. To make it more interesting, notice that the Main() method launches a message box in order to force the assembly resolver to load the System.Windows.Forms.dll assembly (which in turn loads other referenced assemblies). Figure 6-39 shows the output.

SOURCE CODE *The MyAppDomain application is included under the Chapter 6 subdirectory.*

```
D:\CSharpBook\Labs\Chapter 6\MyAppDomain\bin\Debug\MyAppDoma... _ □ ×
Here are the assemblies loaded in this appdomain

mscorlib, Version=1.0.2411.0, Culture=neutral, PublicKeyTok
MyAppDomain, Version=1.0.456.842, Culture=neutral, PublicKe
System.Windows.Forms, Version=1.0.2411.0, Culture=neutral,
561934e089
System, Version=1.0.2411.0, Culture=neutral, PublicKeyToken
Press any key to continue
```

Figure 6-39. Investigating loaded assemblies

System.Threading Namespace

The System.Threading namespace provides a number of types that enable multi-threaded programming. In addition to providing types that represent a specific thread, this namespace also defines types that can manage a collection of threads (ThreadPool), a simple (non-GUI based) Timer class and numerous types to provide synchronized access to shared data. Table 6-3 lists some (but not all) of the core items.

Table 6-3. Select Types of the System.Treading Namespace

SYSTEM.THREADING TYPE	MEANING IN LIFE
Interlocked	The Interlocked class is used to provide synchronized access to shared data.
Monitor	Provides the synchronization of threading objects using locks and wait/signals.
Mutex	Synchronization primitive that can be used for inter process synchronization.
Thread	Represents a thread that executes within the CLR. Using this type, you are able to spawn additional threads in the owning AppDomain.
ThreadPool	This type manages related threads in a given process.
Timer	Specifies a delegate to be called at a specified time. The wait operation is performed by a thread in the thread pool.
WaitHandle	Represents all synchronization objects (that allow multiple wait) in the runtime.
ThreadStart	The ThreadStart class is a delegate that points to the method that should be executed first when a thread is started.
TimerCallback	Delegate for the Timers.
WaitCallback	This class is a Delegate that defines the callback method for ThreadPool user work items.

Examining the Thread Class

The most primitive of all types in the System.Threading namespace is Thread. This class represents an object-oriented wrapper around a given path of execution within a particular AppDomain. This type defines a number of methods (both static and shared) that allow you to create new threads from a current thread, as well as suspend, stop, and destroy a given thread. First, consider the list of core static members given in Table 6-4.

Table 6-4. Static Members of the Thread Type

THREAD STATIC MEMBER	MEANING IN LIFE
CurrentThread	This (read-only) property returns a reference to the currently running thread.
GetData() SetData()	Retrieves the value from the specified slot on the current thread, for that thread's current domain.
GetDomain() GetDomainID()	Returns a reference to the current AppDomain (or the ID of this domain) in which the current thread is running.
Sleep()	Suspends the current thread for a specified time.

Thread also supports the object level members shown in Table 6-5.

Table 6-5. Object Methods of the Thread Type

THREAD INSTANCE LEVEL MEMBER	MEANING IN LIFE
IsAlive	This property returns a boolean that indicates if this thread has been started.
IsBackground	Gets or sets a value indicating whether or not this thread is a background thread.
Name	This property allows you to establish a friendly textual name of the thread.
Priority	Gets or Sets the priority of a thread, which may be assigned a value from the ThreadPriority enumeration.
ThreadState	Gets the state of this thread, which may be assigned a value from the ThreadState enumeration.
Interrupt()	Interrupts the current thread.
Join()	Instructs the thread to wait for a given thread.
Resume()	Resumes a thread that has been suspended.
Start()	Begins execution of the thread that is specified by the ThreadStart delegate.
Suspend()	Suspends the thread. If the thread is already suspended, a call to Suspend() has no effect.

Spawning Secondary Threads

When you wish to create additional threads to carry on some unit of work, you need to interact with the Thread class as well as a special threading-related delegate named ThreadStart. The general process is quite simple. To begin, you need to create a function to perform the background work. To keep things well focused, let's build a simple helper class that simply prints out a series of numbers by way of the DoSomeWork() member function:

```
internal class WorkerClass
{
    public void DoSomeWork()
    {
        // Get some information about this worker thread.
        Console.WriteLine("ID of worker thread is: {0}",
                            Thread.CurrentThread.GetHashCode());

        // Do the work.
        Console.Write("Worker says: ");
        for(int i = 0; i < 10; i++)
        {
            Console.Write(i + ", ");
        }
        Console.WriteLine();
    }
}
```

Now assume you have another class (MainClass) that creates a new instance of WorkerClass. In order for the MainClass to continue processing its workflow, it creates and starts a new Thread that is used by the worker. In the code below, notice the Thread type requests a new ThreadStart delegate type:

```
public class MainClass
{
    public static int Main(string[] args)
    {
        // Get some information about the current thread.
        Console.WriteLine("ID of primary thread is: {0}",
                            Thread.CurrentThread.GetHashCode());

        // Make worker class.
        WorkerClass w = new WorkerClass();
```

```
        // Now make (and start) the background thread.
        Thread backgroundThread =
                new Thread(new ThreadStart(w.DoSomeWork));

        backgroundThread.Start();

        return 0;
    }
}
```

If you run the application (Figure 6-40) you would find each thread has a unique ID (which is a good thing, as you should have two separate threads at this point).

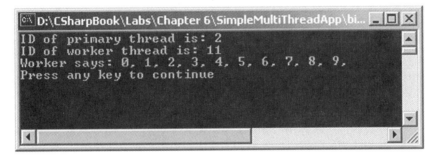

Figure 6-40. Thread hash codes

Naming Threads

One interesting aspect of the Thread class is that it provides the ability to assign a friendly string name to the underlying path of execution. To do so, make use of the Name property. For example, you could update the MainClass as follows:

```
public class MainClass
{
    public static int Main(string[] args)
    {
        // Name the current thread.
        Thread primaryThread = Thread.CurrentThread;
        primaryThread.Name = "Boss man";

        Console.WriteLine("ID of {0} is {1}", primaryThread.Name,
                                        primaryThread.GetHashCode());
```

```
    // same code as before. . .
}
}
```

The output is now as shown in Figure 6-41.

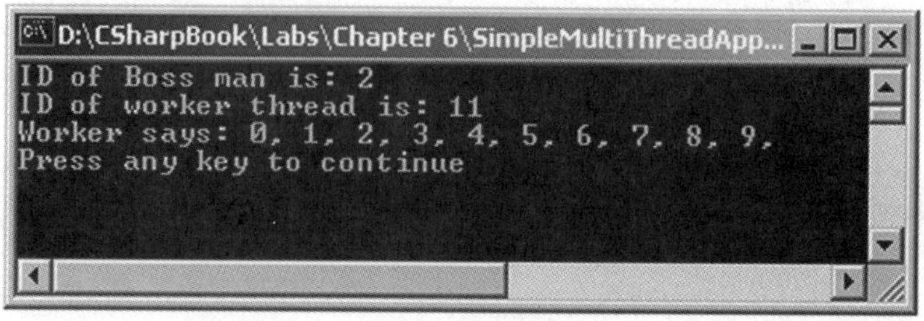

```
C:\  D:\CSharpBook\Labs\Chapter 6\SimpleMultiThreadApp...  _ □ X
ID of Boss man is: 2
ID of worker thread is: 11
Worker says: 0, 1, 2, 3, 4, 5, 6, 7, 8, 9,
Press any key to continue
```

Figure 6-41. Named threads

As you may be thinking, this property provides a more user-friendly way to identify the threads in your system.

Clogging Up the Primary Thread

The current application creates a secondary thread to perform a unit of work. The problem is the fact that printing 10 numbers takes no time at all, and therefore we are not really able to appreciate the fact that the primary thread is free to continue processing. Let's update the application in order to illustrate this very fact. First, let's update the WorkerClass to print out 30,000 numbers (using WriteLine() rather than Write() so you can see the print out) rather than a mere 10:

```
internal class WorkerClass
{
    public void DoSomeWork()
    {
        . . .
        // Do a lot of work.
        Console.Write("Worker says: ");
        for(int i = 0; i < 30000; i++)
        {
            Console.WriteLine(i + ", ");
        }
        Console.WriteLine();
    }
}
```

Next, let's update the MainClass such that it launches a message box directly after it creates the background worker thread:

```csharp
public class MainClass
{
    public static int Main(string[] args)
    {
        // Name the current thread.
        . . .

        // Make worker class.
        . . .

        // Now make the thread.
        . . .

        // Now while background thread is working,
        // do some additional work.
        MessageBox.Show("I'm busy");

        return 0;
    }
}
```

If you were to now run the application, you would see that the message box is displayed and can be moved around the desktop, while the background worker thread is busy pumping numbers to the console (Figure 6-42).

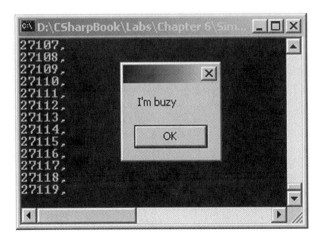

Figure 6-42. Two active threads

Now, contrast this behavior with what you might find if you had a single-threaded application. Assume the Main() method has been updated with logic that allows the user to enter the number of threads used within the AppDomain:

```
public static int Main(string[] args)
{
    Console.Write("Do you want [1] or [2] threads? ");
    string threadCount = Console.ReadLine();

    // Name the current thread.
    . . .

    // Make worker class.
    WorkerClass w = new WorkerClass();

    // Only make a new thread if the user said so.
    if(threadCount = = "2")
    {
        // Now make the thread.
        Thread backgroundThread =
            new Thread(new ThreadStart(w.DoSomeWork));
        backgroundThread.Start();
    }
    else
        w.DoSomeWork();

    // Do some additional work.
    MessageBox.Show("I'm busy");

    return 0;
}
```

As you can guess, if the user enters the value "1" he or she must wait for all 30,000 numbers to be printed before seeing the message box appear, given that there is only a single thread in the AppDomain. However, if the user enters "2" he or she is able to interact with the message box while the secondary thread spins right along.

Putting a Thread to Sleep

The static Thread.Sleep() method can be used to currently suspend the current thread for a specified amount of time (specified in milliseconds). To illustrate,

let's update the WorkerClass once again. This time around, the DoSomeWork()
method does not print out 30,000 lines to the console, but 5 lines. The trick is,
between each call to Console.WriteLine(), this background is put to sleep for
approximately 5 seconds.

```
internal class WorkerClass
{
    public void DoSomeWork()
    {
        // Get some information about the worker thread.
        Console.WriteLine("ID of worker thread is: {0}",
                        Thread.CurrentThread.GetHashCode());

        // Do the work (and take a nap).
        Console.Write("Worker says: ");
        for(int i = 0; i < 5; i++)
        {
            Console.WriteLine(i + ", ");
            Thread.Sleep(5000);
        }
        Console.WriteLine();
    }
}
```

The output is shown in Figure 6-43.

SOURCE CODE *The SimpleMultiThreadApp project is included under the Chapter 6 subdirectory.*

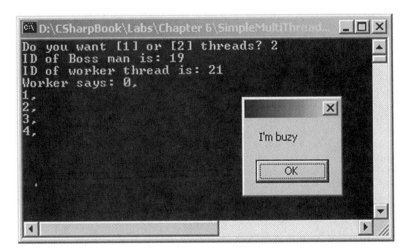

Figure 6-43. Two active threads (one sleeping on the job)

341

Concurrency Revisited

Given this previous example, you might be thinking that threads are the magic bullet you have been looking for. Simply create threads for each part of your application and the end result will be increased application performance. You already know this is a loaded question, as the previous statement is false. If not used carefully and thoughtfully, too many threads can actually degrade an application's performance.

Even more important is the fact that each and every thread in a given App-Domain has direct access to the shared data of the application. In the current example, this is not a problem. However, imagine what might happen if the primary and secondary threads were both modifying a shared point of data. As you know, the thread scheduler will force threads to suspend their work at random. Since this is the case, what if thread A is kicked out of the way before it has fully completed its work? The answer is thread B is now reading unstable data.

To illustrate, let's build a new multithreaded C# Console Application named MultiThreadSharedData. This application also has a class named WorkerClass, which is functionally similar to the previous type of the same name:

```
internal class WorkerClass
{
    public void DoSomeWork()
    {
        // Do the work.
        for(int i = 0; i < 5; i++)
        {
            Console.WriteLine("Worker says: {0},", i);
        }
    }
}
```

You also have a type named MainClass. In this application, MainClass is responsible for creating three distinct secondary threads. The problem is that each of these threads is making calls to the shared instance of the WorkerClass type:

```
public class MainClass
{
    public static int Main(string[] args)
    {
        // Make the single worker object.
        WorkerClass w = new WorkerClass();
```

```
// Create three secondary threads,
// each of which makes calls to the same shared object.
Thread workerThreadA =
        new Thread(new ThreadStart(w.DoSomeWork));
Thread workerThreadB =
        new Thread(new ThreadStart(w.DoSomeWork));
Thread workerThreadC =
        new Thread(new ThreadStart(w.DoSomeWork));

// Now start each one.
workerThreadA.Start();
workerThreadB.Start();
workerThreadC.Start();

        return 0;
    }
}
```

Now before you see some test runs, let's recap the problem. The primary thread of this AppDomain begins life by spawning three secondary worker threads. Each worker thread is told to make calls on the shared WorkerClass object instance. Given that we have taken no precautions to lock down this shared resource, the chances are very good that a given thread will be kicked out of the way before the WorkerClass is able to print out the results for the current thread. Because you don't know when this might happen, you are bound to get a number of strange results. For example, check out Figure 6-44.

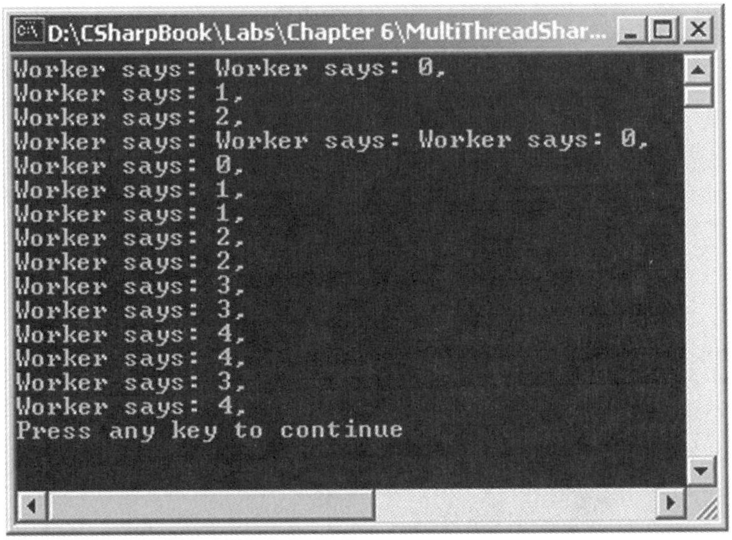

Figure 6-44. Bad output. . .dueling threads

Figure 6-45 shows another run.

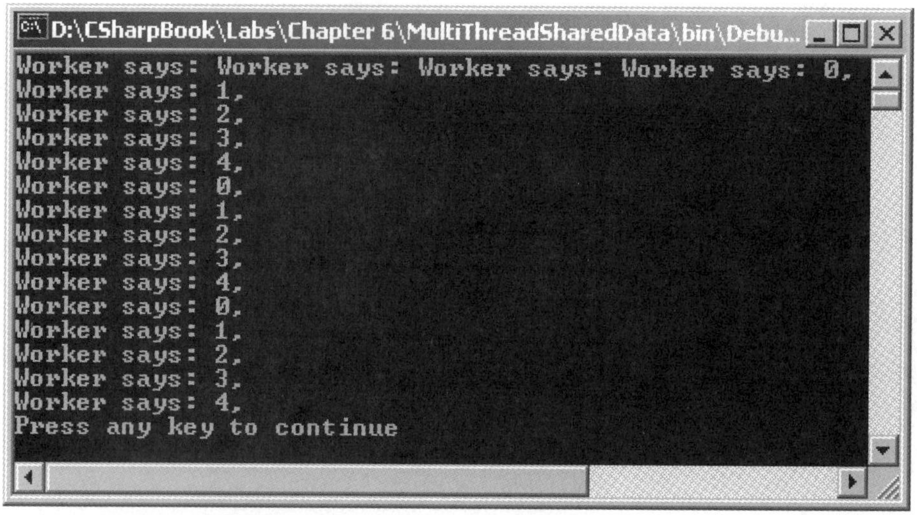

```
Worker says: Worker says: Worker says: Worker says: 0,
Worker says: 1,
Worker says: 2,
Worker says: 3,
Worker says: 4,
Worker says: 0,
Worker says: 1,
Worker says: 2,
Worker says: 3,
Worker says: 4,
Worker says: 0,
Worker says: 1,
Worker says: 2,
Worker says: 3,
Worker says: 4,
Press any key to continue
```

Figure 6-45. More bad output. . .dueling threads

And one more, just for good measure, appears in Figure 6-46.

```
Worker says: Worker says: 0,
Worker says: 1,
Worker says: 2,
Worker says: 3,
Worker says: 4,
Worker says: Worker says: 0,
Worker says: 1,
Worker says: 2,
Worker says: 3,
Worker says: 4,
Worker says: Worker says: 0,
Worker says: 1,
Worker says: 2,
Worker says: 3,
Worker says: 4,
Press any key to continue
```

Figure 6-46. Even more bad output. . .dueling threads

Humm. There are clearly some problems. Given that each thread is telling the WorkerClass to "do some work" in a random way, the output is mangled (to say the least). What we need is a way to programmatically enforce synchronized access to the shared type. Like the Win32 API, the .NET base class libraries provide a number of synchronization techniques. Let's examine one possible approach.

C# "lock" Keyword

The first approach to providing synchronized access to our DoSomeWork() method is to make use of the C# lock statement. This intrinsic keyword allows you to lock down a block of code so that incoming threads must wait in line for the current thread to finish up its work. Using the lock statement is trivial:

```
internal class WorkerClass
{
    public void DoSomeWork()
    {
        // Only 1 thread at a time can tell the worker to get busy!
        lock(this)
        {
            // Do the work.
            for(int i = 0; i < 5; i++)
            {
                Console.WriteLine("Worker says: {0},", i);
            }
        }
    }
}
```

If you rerun the application, you can see that the threads are instructed to politely wait in line for the current thread to finish its business Figure 6-47.

As you might guess, working with the C# lock statement is semantically equivalent to working with a raw Win32 CRITICAL_SECTION and related API function calls.

SOURCE CODE *The MultiThreadSharedData application is included under the Chapter 6 subdirectory.*

Using System.Threading.Monitor

The C# lock statement is really just a shorthand notation for working with the System.Threading.Monitor class type. Thus, if you were able to see what lock() actually resolves to under the hood, you would find the following:

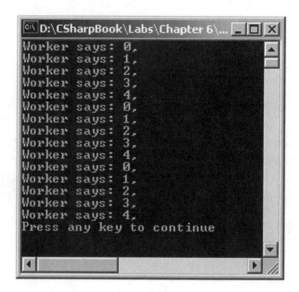

Figure 6-47. Harmonious threads

```csharp
internal class WorkerClass
{
    public void DoSomeWork()
    {
        // Define the item to monitor for synchronization.
        Monitor.Enter(this);
        try
        {
            // Do the work.
            for(int i = 0; i < 5; i++)
            {
                Console.WriteLine("Worker says: {0},", i);
            }
        }
        finally
        {
            // Error or not, you must exit the monitor.
            Monitor.Exit(this);
        }
    }
}
```

If you run the modified application, you would see no changes in the output (which is good). Here, we are making use of the static Enter() and Exit() members of the Monitor type, to enter (and leave) a locked block of code.

Using System.Threading.Interlocked

On a related note, the System.Threading namespace also provides a type that allows you to increment or decrement a variable by 1 in a thread-safe manner. To illustrate, assume that you have a class type (named IHaveNoIdea) which maintains an internal reference counter. One method of the class is responsible for incrementing this number by 1, while the other is responsible for decrementing this number by 1 (look familiar?):

```
public class IHaveNoIdea
{
    private long refCount = 0;

    public void AddRef()
    { ++refCount; }

    public void Release()
    {
        if(--refCount = = 0)
        {
            GC.Collect();
        }
    }
}
```

If we have numerous threads of execution in the current AppDomain that are all making calls to AddRef() and Release(), the possibility exists that the internal refCount member variable could in fact have a value less that zero before the collection request can be posted to the garbage collector. Imagine threadA calls Release(), and is bumped out of the way by the thread scheduler just after the point at which it decremented the refCount. The next thread calling Release() would decrement the count again, at which point refCount is at currently at –1!

To prevent this behavior, you can make use of System.Threading.Interlocked, which atomically increments or decrements a given variable. Notice that a reference to the variable that is being modified is sent in, and thus you need to make use of the C# "ref" keyword:

```
public class IHaveNoIdea
{
    private long refCount = 0;

    public void AddRef()
```

```
    {
        Interlocked.Increment(ref refCount);
    }

    public void Release()
    {
        if(Interlocked.Decrement(ref refCount) = = 0)
        {
            GC.Collect();
        }
    }
}
```

At this point you have just enough information to become dangerous in the world of multithreaded assemblies. While this chapter does not dig into each and every aspect of the System.Threading namespace, you should be equipped to investigate additional details as you see fit.

Summary

This chapter drilled into the details behind the innocent looking .NET DLLs and EXEs located on your development machine. You began the journey by examining the core concepts of the assembly: metadata, manifests, and MSIL. Next, you contrasted shared and private assemblies, and investigated the steps taken by the assembly resolver to locate a given binary using application configuration files.

Assemblies are the building blocks of a .NET application. In essence, assemblies can be understood as binary units that contain some number of types that can be used by another application. As you have seen, assemblies may be private or shared. In stark contrast to classic COM, private assemblies are the default. When you wish to configure a shared assembly, you are making an explicit choice, and need to generate a corresponding strong name.

As you have also learned, the .NET framework defines the concept of an AppDomain. In many ways, AppDomains can be viewed as a lightweight process. Within a single AppDomain can exist any number of threads. Using the types defined within the System.Threading namespace, you are able to build thread-safe types that (as you have seen) can provide the end user with a more responsive application.

CHAPTER 7

Type Reflection and Attribute-Based Programming

As detailed in the previous chapter, assemblies are the basic unit of deployment in the .NET universe. Tools such as Visual Studio.NET have integrated Object Browsers that allow you to examine the internal types of referenced assemblies. Furthermore, external tools such as ILDasm.exe allow us to peek into the underlying IL code, type metadata, and assembly manifest. In addition to the design-time investigation of .NET assemblies, you are also able to *programmatically* obtain this same information using the types defined within the System.Reflection namespace.

Once you understand how to manipulate this namespace to examine an assembly at runtime, the remainder of the chapter examines a number of closely related topics. For example, you will explore the types defined within the System.Reflection.Emit namespace, and learn the basics of building a dynamic assembly on the fly. Furthermore, this chapter illustrates how a .NET client may employ "late binding" to a given type. As you will see later in this book, late binding is an important aspect of .NET/COM interoperability.

The chapter wraps up with an investigation of how to insert custom metadata into your .NET assemblies through the use of system supplied and custom attributes. If you have a background in classic COM, you will be happy to discover that the spirit of IDL attributes has been included (and extended) in the .NET architecture.

Understanding Reflection

In the .NET universe, *reflection* is the process of runtime type discovery. Using reflection services, you are able to load an assembly at runtime and discover the same sort of information as ILDasm.exe. For example, you can obtain a list of all types contained within a given module, including the methods, fields, properties, and events defined by a given type. You can also dynamically discover the set of interfaces supported by a given class (or structure), the parameters of a method as well as other related details (base class, namespace information, and so forth).

In order to understand reflection services, you need to come to terms with the Type class (defined in the System namespace) as well as a new namespace, System.Reflection. As you will see, the System.Type class contains a number of methods that allow you to extract valuable information about the current type you happen to be observing. The System.Reflection namespace contains numerous related types to facilitate late binding and dynamic loading of assemblies. To begin, let's investigate System.Type in some detail.

The Type Class

Many of the items defined within the System.Reflection namespace make use of the abstract System.Type class. This class provides a number of methods that can be used to discover the details behind a given item. The complete set of members is quite expansive, however Table 7-1 offers a partial snapshot of the members supported by Type.

Obtaining a Type Object

There are numerous ways in which you can obtain an instance of the Type class. However, the one thing you cannot do is directly create a Type object using the "new" keyword, as Type is an abstract class. First, as you recall, System.Object defines a method named GetType() that returns an instance of the Type class:

```
// Extract Type using a valid Foo instance.
Foo theFoo = new Foo();
Type t = theFoo.GetType();
```

In addition to the previous technique, you may also obtain a Type using (of all things) the Type class itself. To do so, call the static GetType() member and specify the textual name of the item you are interested in examining:

```
// Get a Type using the static Type.GetType() method.
Type t = null;
t = Type.GetType("Foo");
```

Finally, you can also obtain an instance of Type using the typeof() keyword:

```
// Get the Type using typeof.
Type t = typeof(Foo);
```

Table 7-1. Members of the Type Class

TYPE MEMBER	MEANING IN LIFE
IsAbstract IsArray IsClass IsCOMObject IsEnum IsInterface IsPrimitive IsNestedPublic IsNestedPrivate IsSealed IsValueType	These properties (among others) allow you to discover a number of basic traits about the Type you are referring to (e.g., if it is an abstract method, an array, a nested class, and so forth).
GetConstructors() GetEvents() GetFields() GetInterfaces() GetMethods() GetMembers() GetNestedTypes() GetProperties()	These methods (among others) allow you to obtain an array representing the items (interface, method, property, etc.) you are interested in. Each method returns a related array (e.g., GetFields() returns a FieldInfo array, GetMethods() returns a MethodInfo array, etc.). Be aware that each of these methods has a singular form (e.g., GetMethod(), GetProperty()) that allows you to retrieve a specific item by name, rather than an array of all related items.
FindMembers()	Returns an array of MemberInfo types, based on search criteria.
GetType()	This method returns a Type instance given a string name.
InvokeMember()	This method allows late binding to a given item.

Notice that Type.GetType() and typeof() are helpful in that you do not need to first create an object instance in order to extract type information. Now that you have a Type reference, let's examine how we can exercise it.

Fun with the Type Class

To illustrate the usefulness of System.Type, assume you have a class named Foo that has been defined as follows (the implementation of the various methods are irrelevant for this example):

```
// These are the items we will discover at runtime.
namespace TheType
{
// Two interfaces.
public interface IFaceOne
{ void MethodA(); }

public interface IFaceTwo
{ void MethodB(); }

// Foo supports these 2 interfaces.
public class Foo: IFaceOne, IFaceTwo
{
    // Fields.
    public int myIntField;
    public string myStringField;

    // A method.
    public void myMethod(int p1, string p2){...}

    // A property.
    public int MyProp
    {
        get { return myIntField; }
        set { myIntField = value; }
    }

    // IFaceOne and IFaceTwo methods.
    public void MethodA() {...}
    public void MethodB() {...}
}
}
```

Now, let's create a program that is able to discover the methods, properties, supported interfaces, and fields for a given Foo object (in addition to some other points of interest). The FooReader class defines a number of static methods that look more or less identical. First you have ListMethods(), which extracts each method from Foo using a Type object. Notice how Type.GetMethods() returns an array of MethodInfo types:

```csharp
// Suck out all method names from Foo.
public static void ListMethods(Foo f)
{
    Console.WriteLine("***** Methods of Foo *****");

    Type t = f.GetType();
    MethodInfo[] mi = t.GetMethods();
    foreach(MethodInfo m in mi)
        Console.WriteLine("Method: {0}", m.Name);

    Console.WriteLine("************************\n");
}
```

The implementation of ListFields() is similar. The only notable difference is the call to Type.GetFields() and the resulting FieldInfo array:

```csharp
// Suck out all fields from Foo.
public static void ListFields(Foo f)
{
    Console.WriteLine("***** Fields of Foo *****");

    Type t = f.GetType();
    FieldInfo[] fi = t.GetFields();
    foreach(FieldInfo field in fi)
        Console.WriteLine("Field: {0}", field.Name);

    Console.WriteLine("************************\n");
}
```

The ListVariousStats(), ListProps(), and ListInterfaces() methods should be self-explanatory at this point:

```csharp
// Suck out some interesting statistics about Foo.
public static void ListVariousStats(Foo f)
{
    Console.WriteLine("***** Various stats about Foo *****");
    Type t = f.GetType();

    Console.WriteLine("Full name is: {0}", t.FullName);
    Console.WriteLine("Base is: {0}", t.BaseType);
    Console.WriteLine("Is it abstract? {0}", t.IsAbstract);
```

```
        Console.WriteLine("Is it a COM object? {0}", t.IsCOMObject);
        Console.WriteLine("Is it sealed? {0}", t.IsSealed);
        Console.WriteLine("Is it a class? {0}", t.IsClass);

        Console.WriteLine("**********************************\n");
}

// Gather all properties.
public static void ListProps(Foo f)
{
        Console.WriteLine("***** Properties of Foo *****");

        Type t = f.GetType();
        PropertyInfo[] pi = t.GetProperties();
        foreach(PropertyInfo prop in pi)
                Console.WriteLine("Prop: {0}", prop.Name);

        Console.WriteLine("****************************\n");
}

// Dump all interfaces supported by Foo.
public static void ListInterfaces(Foo f)
{
        Console.WriteLine("***** Interfaces of Foo *****");

        Type t = f.GetType();
        Type[] ifaces = t.GetInterfaces();
        foreach(Type i in ifaces)
                Console.WriteLine("Interface: {0}", i.Name);

        Console.WriteLine("*****************************\n");
}
```

The Main() method of FooReader() simply calls each static method:

```
// Put Foo under the magnifying glass.
namespace TheType
{
using System;

// Needed to gain definitions of MethodInfo, FieldInfo, etc.
using System.Reflection;
```

```
public class FooReader
{
    // ...Static methods seen previously...

    public static int Main(string[] args)
    {
        // Make a new Foo object.
        Foo theFoo = new Foo();

        // Now examine everything.
        ListVariousStats(theFoo);
        ListMethods(theFoo);
        ListFields(theFoo);
        ListProps(theFoo);
        ListInterfaces(theFoo);
        return 0;
    }
}
}
```

Figure 7-1 shows a test run.

Interesting stuff, huh? Here, I made use of Object.GetType() to gather information about a class (Foo) defined in our current namespace. While the Type class can be very helpful on its own, reflection becomes even more powerful when you make use of the Assembly class defined within the System.Reflection namespace.

SOURCE CODE *The TheType project can be found under the Chapter 7 subdirectory.*

Investigating the System.Reflection Namespace

Like any namespace, System.Reflection contains a number of related types. Like any namespace, some types are of more immediate interest than others. Table 7-2 lists some of the core items you should be familiar with, many of which you have already seen in the previous Foo example.

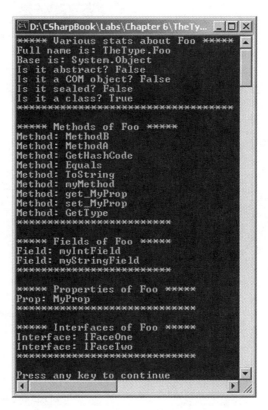

Figure 7-1. Reflecting on Foo

Loading an Assembly

The real workhorse of System.Reflection is the Assembly class. Using this type, you are able to dynamically load an assembly, invoke class members at runtime (late binding), as well as discover numerous properties about the assembly itself.

The first step to investigate the contents of a .NET binary is to load the assembly in memory. Assume you have a new console project named CarReflector, which has set a reference to the CarLibrary assembly created in Chapter 6. The static Assembly.Load() method can now be called by passing in the friendly string name:

```
// Investigate the CarLibrary assembly.
namespace CarReflector
{
using System;
using System.Reflection;
using System.IO;            // Needed for FileNotFoundException definition.
```

```
public class CarReflector
{
    public static int Main(string[] args)
    {
        // Use Assembly class to load the CarLibrary.
        Assembly a = null;
        try
        {
            a = Assembly.Load("CarLibrary");
        }
        catch(FileNotFoundException e)
        {Console.WriteLine(e.Message);}

        return 0;
    }
}
}
```

Table 7-2. Select Members of System.Reflection

SYSTEM.REFLECTION TYPE	MEANING IN LIFE
Assembly	This class (in addition to numerous related types) contains a number of methods that allow you to load, investigate, and manipulate an assembly.
AssemblyName	This class allows you to discover numerous details behind an assembly's identity (version information, culture information, and so forth).
EventInfo	Holds information for a given event.
FieldInfo	Holds information for a given field.
MemberInfo	This is the abstract base class that defines common behaviors for the EventInfo, FieldInfo, MethodInfo, and PropertyInfo types.
MethodInfo	Contains information for a given method.
Module	Allows you to access a given module within a multifile assembly.
ParameterInfo	Holds information for a given parameter.
PropertyInfo	Holds information for a given property.

Notice that the static Assembly.Load() method has been passed in the friendly name of the assembly we are interested in loading into memory. As you may suspect, this method has been overloaded a number of times, in order to provide a number of ways in which you can bind to an assembly. One variation to be aware of is that the textual information sent into Assembly.Load() may contain additional string segments beyond the friendly name. Specifically, you may choose to specify a version number, public key value, locale, and strong name.

Collectively speaking, the set of items identifying an assembly is termed the "display name." The format of a display name is a comma-delimited string that begins with the friendly name, followed by optional qualifiers (that may appear in any order). Here is the template to follow (optional items have been placed in parentheses):

```
Name (,Loc = CultureInfo) (,Ver = Major.Minor.Revision.Build) (,SN = StrongName)
```

When supplying a display name, the convention SN=null, indicates that binding and matching against a simply named assembly is required. Additionally, the convention Loc= "" (double quote representing empty string) indicates matching against the default culture. To illustrate:

```
// A fully specified AssemblyName for simply named assembly with default locale:
a = Assembly.Load(@"CarLibrary, Ver=1.0.454.30104, SN=null, Loc=""");
```

Also be aware that the System.Reflection namespace supplies the AssemblyName type, which allows you to represent the above string information in a handy object instance. Typically, this class is used in conjunction with System.Version, which is an OO wrapper round the assembly's version. Once you have established the display name, it can then be passed into the overloaded Assembly.Load() method:

```
// Our OO-Aware display name.
AssemblyName asmName;
asmName = new AssemblyName();
asmName.Name = "CarLibrary";

Version v = new Version("1.0.454.30104");
asmName.Version = v;

a = Assembly.Load(asmName);
```

Enumerating Types in a Referenced Assembly

Now that you have a reference to the CarLibrary assembly, you can discover the name of each type it contains using Assembly.GetTypes(). Here is a helper method named ListAllTypes() that does this very thing:

```
public class CarReflector
{
    public static int Main(string[] args)
    {
        Assembly a = null;
        try
        {
            a = Assembly.Load("CarLibrary");
        }
        catch(FileNotFoundException e)
        {Console.WriteLine(e.Message);}

        ListAllTypes(a);
        return 0;
    }

    // List all members of the within the assembly.
    private static void ListAllTypes(Assembly a)
    {
        Console.WriteLine("Listing all types in {0}", a.FullName);
        Type[] types = a.GetTypes();
        foreach(Type t in types)
            Console.WriteLine("Type: {0}", t);
    }
}
```

Enumerating Class Members

Let's now assume you are interested in discovering the full set of members supported by one of our automobiles. To do so, you can make use of the GetMembers() method defined by the Type class. As you recall, the Type class also defined a number of related methods (GetInterfaces(), GetProperties(), GetMethods(), and so forth) that allow you to specify a specific kind of member. GetMembers() returns an array of MemberInfo types. Here is an example that lists the type and signature of each method defined by the MiniVan (output in Figure 7-2):

```
// Another static method of the CarReflector class.
private static void ListAllMembers(Assembly a)
{
    Type miniVan = a.GetType("CarLibrary.MiniVan");
    MemberInfo[] mi = miniVan.GetMembers();
```

```
        foreach(MemberInfo m in mi)
            Console.WriteLine("Type {0}: {1} ", m.MemberType.ToString(), m);
}
```

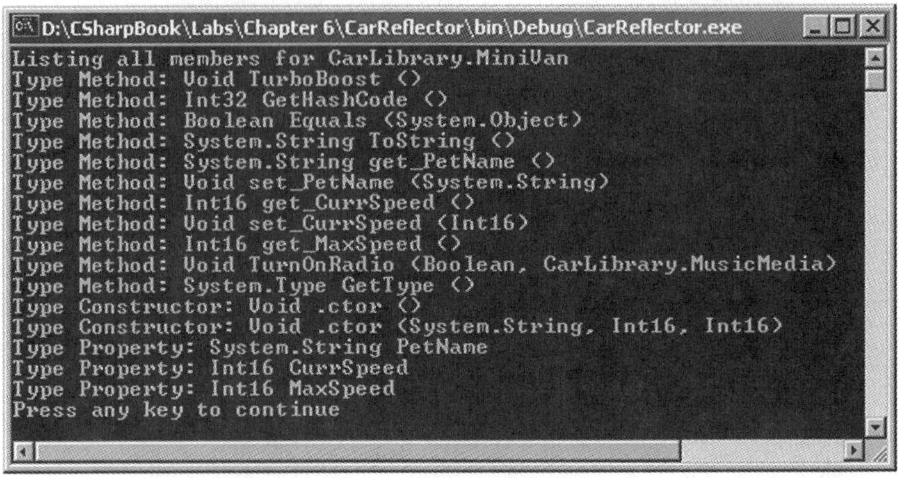

```
D:\CSharpBook\Labs\Chapter 6\CarReflector\bin\Debug\CarReflector.exe
Listing all members for CarLibrary.MiniVan
Type Method: Void TurboBoost ()
Type Method: Int32 GetHashCode ()
Type Method: Boolean Equals (System.Object)
Type Method: System.String ToString ()
Type Method: System.String get_PetName ()
Type Method: Void set_PetName (System.String)
Type Method: Int16 get_CurrSpeed ()
Type Method: Void set_CurrSpeed (Int16)
Type Method: Int16 get_MaxSpeed ()
Type Method: Void TurnOnRadio (Boolean, CarLibrary.MusicMedia)
Type Method: System.Type GetType ()
Type Constructor: Void .ctor ()
Type Constructor: Void .ctor (System.String, Int16, Int16)
Type Property: System.String PetName
Type Property: Int16 CurrSpeed
Type Property: Int16 MaxSpeed
Press any key to continue
```

Figure 7-2. The MiniVan type under the microscope

Enumerating Method Parameters

Not only can you use reflection to gather information for the members of a type, you can also obtain information about the parameters of a given member. To illustrate, let's assume that the Car class has defined the following additional method:

```
// A new member of the Car class.
public void TurnOnRadio(bool state, MusicMedia mm)
{
    if(state)
        MessageBox.Show("Jamming with {0}", mm.ToString());
    else
        MessageBox.Show("Quiet time. . .");
}
```

TurnOnRadio() takes two parameters, the second of which is a custom enumeration:

```
// Holds source of music.
public enum MusicMedia
```

```
{
    musicCD,
    musicTape,
    musicRadio
}
```

Extracting information for the parameters of TurnOnRadio() requires the use of MethodInfo.GetParameters(). This method returns a ParameterInfo array. Each item in this array contains numerous properties for a given parameter. Here is another static method of the CarReflector class, GetParams(), which displays various details for each parameter of the TurnOnRadio() method. Check it out:

```
// Get parameter information for the TurnOnRadio() method.
private static void GetParams(Assembly a)
{
    // Get a MethodInfo type.
    Type miniVan = a.GetType("CarLibrary.MiniVan");
    MethodInfo mi = miniVan.GetMethod("TurnOnRadio");

    // Show number of params.
    Console.WriteLine("Here are the params for {0}", mi.Name);
    ParameterInfo[] myParams = mi.GetParameters();
    Console.WriteLine("Method has " + myParams.Length + " params");

    // Show some info for param.
    foreach(ParameterInfo pi in myParams)
    {
        Console.WriteLine("Param name: {0}", pi.Name);
        Console.WriteLine("Position in method: {0}", pi.Position);
        Console.WriteLine("Param type: {0}", pi.ParameterType);
    }
}
```

Figure 7-3 displays the output.

SOURCE CODE   *The CarReflector project is included in the Chapter 7 subdirectory.*

At this point you understand how to use some of the core items defined within the System.Reflection namespace to discover a wealth of information at runtime. And, maybe you are already envisioning the code behind ILDasm.exe. Our examples have dumped information to a console window. ILDasm.exe

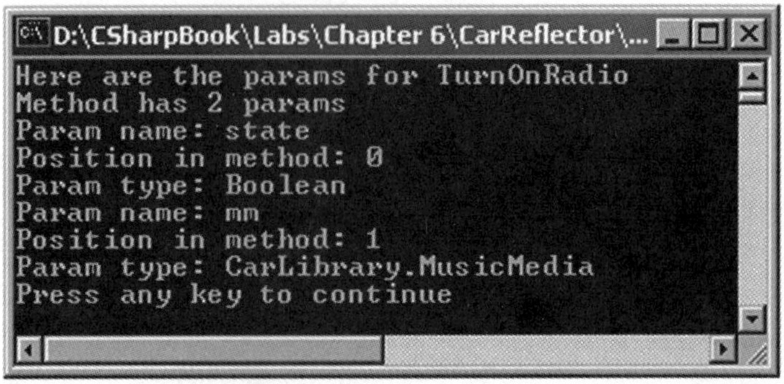

Figure 7-3. Parameter information

obtains the same information, and places it within the various nodes of a tree view control.

Understanding Dynamic Invocation (Late Binding)

The System.Reflection namespace provides additional functionality beyond run-time type discovery. Reflection also provides the ability to exercise late binding to a type. Late binding is a technique, in which you are able to resolve the existence of (and name of) a given type and its members at runtime (rather than compile time). Once the presence of a type has been determined, you are then able to dynamically invoke methods, access properties, and manipulate the fields of a given entity.

The value of late binding may not be immediately understood. It is true that if you can bind early to a type (e.g., use the new keyword) you should opt to do so. Early binding allows you to determine errors at compile time, rather than run-time. Late binding does have a place among tool builders, as well as COM/.NET interoperability. For example, using late binding, a .NET programmer is able to obtain a COM object's IDispatch reference. You examine interoperability issues later in the book. For the time being, let's examine how to dynamically invoke a method on the MiniVan class.

The Activator Class

The System.Activator class is the key to late binding. Beyond the methods inherited from Object, Activator only defines a small set of members. Activator.CreateInstance() is one core method that creates an instance of a type at runtime. This method has been overloaded numerous times in order to provide a good deal of flexibility. One variation of the CreateInstance() member takes a valid Type object:

```
// Create a type dynamically.
public class LateBind
{
    public static int Main(string[] args)
    {
        // Use Assembly class to load the CarLibrary.
        Assembly a = null;
        try
        {
            a = Assembly.Load("CarLibrary");
        }
        catch(FileNotFoundException e)
        {Console.WriteLine(e.Message);}

        // Get the Minivan type.
        Type miniVan = a.GetType("CarLibrary.MiniVan");

        // Create the Minivan on the fly.
        object obj = Activator.CreateInstance(miniVan);
    }
}
```

At this point, the "obj" variable is pointing to a MiniVan instance in memory that has been created indirectly using the Activator class. Now assume you wish to invoke the TurboBoost() method of the MiniVan. As you recall, this will set the state of the engine to "dead" and display an informational message box.

The first step is to obtain a MethodInfo type for the TurboBoost() method using Type.GetMethod(). From a MethodInfo type, you are then able to call the method using Invoke(). MethodInfo.Invoke() requires you to send in all parameters that are to be given to the method represented by MethodInfo. These parameters are represented by an array of Objects. Given that TurboBoost() does not require any parameters, you can simply pass "null" (meaning "this method has no parameters"):

```
public static int Main(string[] args)
{
    // Use Assembly class to load the CarLibrary.
    . . .

    // Get the Minivan type.
    Type miniVan = a.GetType("CarLibrary.MiniVan");

    // Create the Minivan on the fly.
    object obj = Activator.CreateInstance(miniVan);
```

```
    // Get info for TurboBoost.
    MethodInfo mi = miniVan.GetMethod("TurboBoost");

    // Invoke method ('null' for no parameters).
    mi.Invoke(obj, null);
    return 0;
}
```

At this point you are happy to see Figure 7-4.

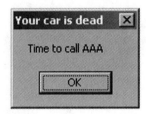

Figure 7-4. Late binding

Now assume you wish to call the following new method defined by MiniVan using late binding:

```
// Quiet down the troops. . .
public void TellChildToBeQuiet(string kidName, int shameIntensity)
{
    for(int i = 0 ; i < numb; i++)
        MessageBox.Show("Be quiet {0}!!", kidName);
}
```

TellChildToBeQuiet() takes two parameters. In this case, the array of parameters must be fleshed out as follows:

```
// Now a method with params.
object[] paramArray = new object[2];
paramArray[0] = "Fred";              // Child name.
paramArray[1] = 4;                   // Shame Intensity.
mi = miniVan.GetMethod("TellChildToBeQuiet");
mi.Invoke(obj, paramArray);
```

If you run this program, you will see four message boxes popping up, shaming young Fredrick (Figure 7-5).

Figure 7-5. Late binding with parameters

SOURCE CODE   *The LateBinding project is included in the Chapter 7 sub-directory.*

Understanding (and Building) Dynamic Assemblies

The next point of interest is the distinction between static and dynamic assemblies. Static assemblies are what I have been (and for the most part, will be) referring to in this book. Simply put, static assemblies are loaded from disk storage, meaning they are located somewhere on your hard drive in a physical file (or possibly numerous files for a multifile assembly).

A dynamic assembly is created in memory on the fly using the functionality provided by the System.Reflection.Emit namespace. This namespace makes is possible to create an assembly, its modules, and any associated types at *runtime*. Once you have done so, you are then free to dynamically save your new types (again at runtime) to disk. This of course, results in a new static assembly! Furthermore, using the System.Reflection.Emit namespace, it is possible to dynamically add new types and members to the runtime representation of an existing assembly.

Understanding the System.Reflection.Emit Namespace

The types defined within the System.Reflection.Emit namespace is of greatest use to individuals who are in the tool building or language development business. For example, imagine that you have been assigned the rather exotic task of creating a version of QuickBasic that targets the .NET runtime (does anyone use QuickBasic anymore?)

Using System.Reflection.Emit, you could take the raw BASIC code and emit corresponding .NET intermediate language (IL) that is then stored in a dynamically created assembly. While this task might seem unlikely, .NET aware Web languages (such as JScript.NET) employ this very same technique. First, Table 7-3 gives a rundown of some (but not all) of the types defined within the System.Reflection.Emit namespace.

Table 7-3. Select Members of System.Reflection.Emit

SYSTEM.REFLECTION.EMIT TYPE	MEANING IN LIFE
AssemblyBuilder	Used to create an assembly at runtime. This type may be used to create both a DLL or EXE binary assembly. EXEs must call the ModuleBuilder.SetEntryPoint() method must set the method that is the entry point to the module. If no entry point is specified, a DLL will be generated.
ModuleBuilder	Used to create a module within an assembly at runtime.
EnumBuilder TypeBuilder	Creates a type (e.g., class, interface, etc) within a module at runtime.
MethodBuilder EventBuilder LocalBuilder PropertyBuilder FieldBuilder ConstructorBuilder CustomAttributeBuilder	These (and other) items are used to create a given member of a type (methods, local variables, properties, constructors, attributes) at runtime.
ILGenerator	Used to create the underlying intermediate language (IL) of a member at runtime.

Emitting a Dynamic Assembly

As you might guess, if you were to build anything other than a trivial dynamic assembly, you would suddenly need to be very comfortable with the intricacies of raw IL code. Although full coverage of raw IL is beyond the scope of this book, you can most certainly take the System.Reflection.Emit namespace out for a test drive (if you desire additional information, check out the official IL documentation in the Tool Developers Guide section of the .NET SDK).

The goal in this section is to create a single file assembly (thus the name of the module is the same as the assembly itself). Within this module, is a class named (of course) HelloWorld. The HelloWorld type supports a custom constructor (taking a string parameter) that is used to assign the value of a private member variable (Msg) of type string. In addition, let's support a public method named SayHello(), which prints a greeting to the standard IO stream, and another method named GetMsg() which returns the internal private string. In effect, you are going to programmatically build the following class:

```
// This class will be build at runtime using System.Reflection.Emit.
public class HelloWorld
```

```
{
    private string Msg;

    // Public interface to class.
    HelloWorld(string s) { Msg = s;}
    public string GetMsg() { return Msg;}
    public void SayHello() { System.Console.WriteLine("Hello there!");
}
```

Assume you have created a new Console Application project workspace named DynAsmBuilder. The first class within the project (MyAsmBuilder) has a single method (CreateMyAsm) that is in charge of building the dynamic assembly, establishing the HelloClass, and saving the binary to disk. Here is the complete code, with analysis to follow:

```
// The caller sends in an AppDomain type.
public int CreateMyAsm(AppDomain curAppDomain)
{
    // Create a name for the assembly.
    AssemblyName assemblyName = new AssemblyName();
    assemblyName.Name = "MyAssembly";
    assemblyName.Version = new Version("1.0.0.0");

    // Create the assembly in memory.
    AssemblyBuilder assembly =
        curAppDomain.DefineDynamicAssembly(assemblyName,
                                        AssemblyBuilderAccess.Save);

    // Here, we are building a single file
    // assembly, so the name of the module is the same as the assembly.
    ModuleBuilder module =
        assembly.DefineDynamicModule("MyAssembly", "MyAssembly.dll");

    // Define a public class named "HelloWorld".
    TypeBuilder helloWorldClass = module.DefineType("MyAssembly.HelloWorld",
                                        TypeAttributes.Public);

    // Define a private String member variable named "Msg":
    // private string msg;
    FieldBuilder msgField =
        helloWorldClass.DefineField("Msg", Type.GetType("System.String"),
                                FieldAttributes.Private);
```

```
// Create the constructor:
// HelloWorld(String s).
Type[] constructorArgs = new Type[1];
constructorArgs[0] = Type.GetType("System.String");
ConstructorBuilder constructor =
    helloWorldClass.DefineConstructor(MethodAttributes.Public,
                                CallingConventions.Standard,
                                constructorArgs);

ILGenerator constructorIL = constructor.GetILGenerator();
constructorIL.Emit(OpCodes.Ldarg_0);
Type objectClass = Type.GetType("System.Object");
ConstructorInfo superConstructor = objectClass.GetConstructor(new Type[0]);
constructorIL.Emit(OpCodes.Call, superConstructor);
constructorIL.Emit(OpCodes.Ldarg_0);
constructorIL.Emit(OpCodes.Ldarg_1);
constructorIL.Emit(OpCodes.Stfld, msgField);
constructorIL.Emit(OpCodes.Ret);

// Now created the GetMsg method:
// public string GetMsg().
MethodBuilder getMsgMethod =
    helloWorldClass.DefineMethod("GetMsg", MethodAttributes.Public,
                            Type.GetType("System.String"), null);

ILGenerator methodIL = getMsgMethod.GetILGenerator();
methodIL.Emit(OpCodes.Ldarg_0);
methodIL.Emit(OpCodes.Ldfld, msgField);
methodIL.Emit(OpCodes.Ret);

// Create the SayHello method:
// public void SayHello().
MethodBuilder sayHiMethod =
    helloWorldClass.DefineMethod("SayHello",
                            MethodAttributes.Public, null, null);
methodIL = sayHiMethod.GetILGenerator();
methodIL.EmitWriteLine("Hello there!");
methodIL.Emit(OpCodes.Ret);

// 'Bake' the class HelloWorld. (Baking is a cute way to say, "make it
//so!").
helloWorldClass.CreateType();
```

```
    // Save the assembly to file.
    assembly.Save("MyAssembly.dll");
    return 0;
}
```

The method body begins by establishing a minimal set of characteristics about your assembly, using the AssemblyName class. Next, create the assembly in memory using the AppDomain type, which was described in Chapter 6 (do note that the CreateMyAsm() helper function takes an incoming AppDomain variable).

```
// Create the assembly in memory.
AssemblyBuilder assembly
    = curAppDomain.DefineDynamicAssembly(assemblyName,
                                        AssemblyBuilderAccess.Save);
```

When calling AppDomain.DefineDynamicAssembly(), you must specify the access mode, which can be any of the following values shown in Table 7-4.

Table 7-4. Values of the AssemblyBuilderAccess Enumeration

ASSEMBLYBUILDERACCESS VALUE	MEANING IN LIFE
Run	Represents that a dynamic assembly can be executed but not saved.
RunAndSave	Represents that a dynamic assembly can be executed and saved.
Save	Represents that a dynamic assembly can be saved but not executed (which may not be the most helpful of all values. . .)

The next task is to insert the module into the assembly. Recall that your assembly is a single file unit. If you were to build a multifile assembly using the DefineDynamicModule() method, you can specify an optional second parameter, which represents the name of a given module (e.g., myMod.dll). When you wish to make a single file assembly, the name of the module (and the binary file) will be identical to the name of the assembly itself:

```
// Our single file assembly.
ModuleBuilder module =
        assembly.DefineDynamicModule("MyAssembly", "MyAssembly.dll");
```

Now for the real fun. Making use of the ModuleBuilder.DefineType() method, you are able to insert a class, structure, or interface into the module, and receive back a TypeBuilder reference that represents the new item (in this case, a class named HelloWorld). At this point, you can insert the private string data member, as shown in the following:

```
// Define a public class named "HelloWorld".
TypeBuilder helloWorldClass = module.DefineType("MyAssembly.HelloWorld",
                                            TypeAttributes.Public);


// Define a private String member variable named "Msg".
FieldBuilder msgField =
    helloWorldClass.DefineField("Msg",
                                Type.GetType("System.String"),
                                FieldAttributes.Private);
```

When it comes to creating the constructor of this class, you need to inject raw IL code into the constructor body, which is responsible for assigning the incoming parameter to the internal private string (among other things). The Emit() method of the ILGenerator class is the entity in charge of placing IL into a member implementation. Emit() itself makes frequent use of the OpCodes enumeration, which is used to specify a ton of features regarding the IL to be inserted. For example, OpCodes.Ret signals the return of a method call. OpCodes.Stfld makes an assignment to a member variable. This said, ponder the following constructor logic:

```
// Create the constructor.
Type[] constructorArgs = new Type[1];
constructorArgs[0] = Type.GetType("System.String");

ConstructorBuilder constructor =
        helloWorldClass.DefineConstructor(MethodAttributes.Public,
                                        CallingConventions.Standard,
                                        constructorArgs);

ILGenerator constructorIL = constructor.GetILGenerator();
constructorIL.Emit(OpCodes.Ldarg_0);
Type objectClass = Type.GetType("System.Object");

ConstructorInfo superConstructor = objectClass.GetConstructor(new Type[0]);

constructorIL.Emit(OpCodes.Call, superConstructor);     // Call base class ctor.

// Load the object's 'this' pointer on the stack.
constructorIL.Emit(OpCodes.Ldarg_0);
```

```
// load a constant 4-byte value of 0 onto the virtual stack.
constructorIL.Emit(OpCodes.Ldarg_1);
constructorIL.Emit(OpCodes.Stfld, msgField);          // Assign msgField.
constructorIL.Emit(OpCodes.Ret);                      // Return.
```

Now let's examine the SayHello() method:

```
// Create the SayHello method.
MethodBuilder sayHiMethod =
    helloWorldClass.DefineMethod("SayHello",
                                 MethodAttributes.Public, null, null);
methodIL = sayHiMethod.GetILGenerator();

// Write a line to the Console.
methodIL.EmitWriteLine("Hello there!");
methodIL.Emit(OpCodes.Ret);
```

Here, you have established a public method (MethodAttributes.Public) that takes no parameters and returns nothing (note the null entries contained in the DefineMethod() call. Also note the EmitWriteLine() call. This member of the ILGenerator class automatically writes a line to the standard output with minimal fuss and bother. I will leave it as an exercise to you to examine the remaining underlying IL in whatever detail you desire.

Using the Dynamically Generated Assembly

Now that we have the logic in place to create and save our assembly, all that's needed is a class to trigger the logic. To come full circle, assume your project defines a second class named AsmReader. The logic in Main() creates an AppDomain to send into the CreateMyAsm() method. Once this call returns, you will exercise some late binding to load this assembly into memory, and call each method of the HelloWorld class. In the code that follows, notice how you are able to programmatically call your overloaded constructor with a specified argument, as well as capture the return value of GetMsg():

```
namespace DynAsmBuilder
{
using System;
using System.Reflection.Emit;
using System.Reflection;
using System.Threading;
```

```
public class AsmReader
{
    public static int Main(string[] args)
    {
        // Get the current application domain.
        AppDomain curAppDomain = Thread.GetDomain();

        // Create the dynamic assembly!
        MyAsmBuilder asmBuilder = new MyAsmBuilder();
        asmBuilder.CreateMyAsm(curAppDomain);

        // Now load it.
        a = Assembly.Load("MyAssembly");

        // Get the HelloWorld type.
        Type hello = a.GetType("MyAssembly.HelloWorld");

        // Create HelloWorld object and call the correct ctor.
        object[] ctorArgs = new object[1];
        ctorArgs[0] = "My amazing message...";
        object obj = Activator.CreateInstance(hello, ctorArgs);

        // Call SayHello and show returned string.
        MethodInfo mi = hello.GetMethod("SayHello");
        mi.Invoke(obj, null);

        // Trigger GetMsg().  Note!  Invoke() returns a Type that
        // holds the method's return value.
        mi = hello.GetMethod("GetMsg");
        Console.WriteLine(mi.Invoke(obj, null));

        return 0;
    }
}
}
```

Figure 7-6 shows the output.

But wait! It gets even better, given the fact that you can locate the new assembly in your project's directory. If you open your assembly using ILDasm.exe you will be extremely pleased to see what appears in Figure 7-7.

SOURCE CODE   *The DynAsmBuilder application is included under the Chapter 7 subdirectory.*

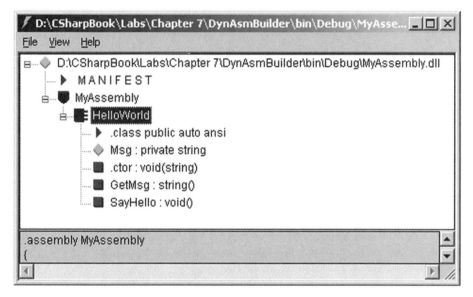

Figure 7-6: Calling members of the dynamically created assembly

Figure 7-7. Hello dynamic assembly

Understanding Attributed Programming

The official meta language of the Component Object Model (COM) is IDL (Interface Definition Language). As you may know, IDL is used to describe the set of types defined within a given classic COM server. In order to describe these types in completely unambiguous terms, IDL makes use of "attributes," which are simply IDL keywords placed within square brackets. A given attribute block always applies to the very next thing. For example, when a COM programmer describes an interface, he or she is required to make use of the [uuid] and [object] attributes (at minimum). Parameters can be specified using the [in], [out], [in, out] and [out, retval] attributes. Here is an example of a classic COM interface, making use of various IDL attributes:

```
[object, uuid(4CB8B79A-E991-4AA4-8DB8-DD5D8751407D), oleautomation]
interface IRememberCOM : IUnknown
```

```
{
    [helpstring("If you send me a string, I will change it...")]
    HRESULT TextManipulation([in] BSTR myStr, [out, retval] BSTR* newStr);
};
```

Notice how the TextManipulation() method has been assigned a [helpstring] attribute, which is used to document how a given item is to be used. Once a COM type has been assigned various attributes, it can be discovered at runtime programmatically, or at design time using various tools. For example, if you examine this COM method using the Visual Basic 6.0 Object Browser utility, you will see the custom [helpstring] is automatically extracted and displayed (Figure 7-8).

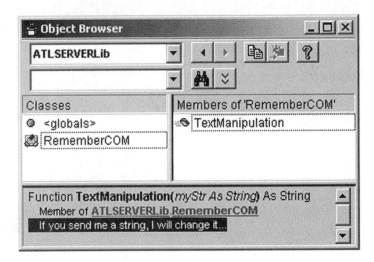

Figure 7-8. COM IDL as seen in Visual Basic 6.0

IDL attributes have proven to be so helpful, that C# (as well as other .NET aware languages) has integrated them as official aspects of the language. Using attributes, you are able to extend the metadata generated by a given compiler with your custom information.

As you explore the .NET namespaces, you will find that there are many predefined attributes that you are able to make use of in your applications. Furthermore, you are free to build custom attributes to further qualify the behavior of your types. Keep in mind that .NET attributes (predefined or custom) are actually *objects* all of that extend System.Attribute (contrast this to IDL, in which attributes are nothing more than simple keywords).

Working with Existing Attributes

Like IDL, C# attributes are nothing more that annotations that can be applied to a given type (class, interface, structure, etc.), member (property, method, etc.) assembly, or module. As mentioned, the .NET library defines a number of predefined attributes in various namespaces. Many of the predefined attributes are most useful in the context of COM and .NET interoperability, debugging and other "exotic" aspects of building managed code. Table 7-5 gives a snapshot of some (but by absolutely no means all) predefined attributes.

Table 7-5. A Tiny Sampling of Predefined Attributes

PREDEFINED .NET ATTRIBUTE	MEANING IN LIFE
CLSCompliant	Enforces that all types in the assembly to conform to the Common Language Specification (CLS). This is the .NET equivalent of the IDL [oleautomation] attribute.
DllImport	Used to make calls to the native OS.
StructLayout	Used to configure the underlying representation of a structure.
Dispid	Specifies the DISPID for a member in a COM dispinterface.
Serializable	Marks a class or structure as being serializable.
NonSerialized	Specifies that a given field in a class or structure is not serializable.

As an example, assume that you wish to assign the [Serializable] attribute to a given item. The Motorcycle class that follows has assigned an attribute to the class itself, as well as a field named temp. As you can see, C# attributes look very much like IDL attributes, in that they are enclosed within square brackets:

```
// This class can be saved to disk.
[Serializable]
public class Motorcycle
{
    bool hasRadioSystem;
    bool hasHeadSet;
    bool hasSissyBar;

    // But when you do, don't bother with this field.
    [NonSerialized]
    float weightOfCurrentPassengers;
}
```

Using ILDasm.exe (Figure 7-9), you can see that these attributes are now specified within the type definition.

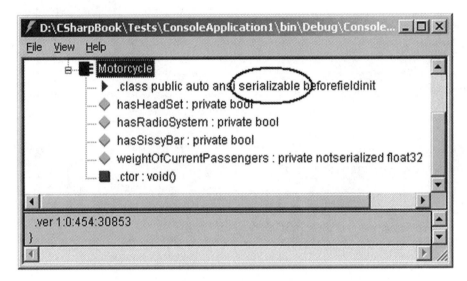

Figure 7-9. Attributes are represented by metadata

Be aware that if you wish to apply more than one attribute to a single type, simply separate each using a comma-delimited list or make use of multiple bracketed attributes stacked on top of one another. Now at this point, don't concern yourself with who or what is on the lookout for the presence of these attributes. Just understand that attributed programming allows you to extend an assembly's metadata with various annotations.

Building Custom Attributes

C# (as well as other .NET aware languages) allows you to build custom attributes. Recall that attributes are in fact instances of a class derived from System.Attribute. Thus, when we applied the [Serializable] attribute to the Motorcycle class, we in fact applied an instance of the System.Serializable type. From a design point of view, an attribute is a class instance that can be applied to some other type. In the world of OOP, this approach is termed *aspect-oriented programming*.

The first step to building your own custom attribute is to create a new class deriving from System.Attribute. The naming convention you should follow is to suffix "-Attribute" to the new type. Here is a basic custom attribute named VehicleDescriptionAttribute that allows a programmer to inject a string into the type metadata describing a particular automobile:

```
// A custom attribute.
public class VehicleDescriptionAttribute : System.Attribute
{
    private string description;
    public string Desc
    {
        get { return description; }
        set { description = value; }
    }

    public VehicleDescriptionAttribute(string desc)
    { description = desc;}
    public VehicleDescriptionAttribute(){}
}
```

As you can see, VehicleDescriptionAttribute maintains a private internal string (description) that can be manipulated using a custom constructor and a named property. Now assume you wish to apply this attribute to a new class named Winnebago. Notice how the constructor signature determines the exact syntax of the attribute:

```
// This class using a custom attributes.
[VehicleDescriptionAttribute("A very long, slow but feature rich auto")]
public class Winnebago
{
    public Winnebago(){}

    // Various methods. . .
}
```

Now, let's see your new type in action. The VehicleDescriptionAttribute attribute (or any attribute) makes use of parentheses to pass arguments to the constructor of the associated System.Attribute-derived class. As you have already seen, one of the constructors does indeed take a string parameter. Now, using ILDasm.exe, you find your string message has been injected into the assembly's metadata (Figure 7-10).

If you look at the IL itself (Figure 7-11), you notice that custom attributes are marked using the IL instruction ".custom."

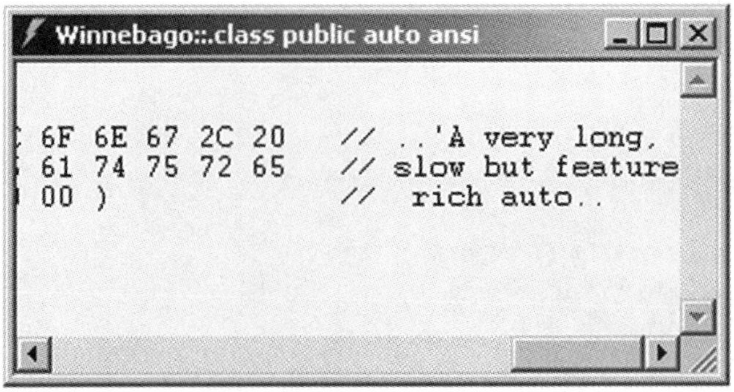

Figure 7-10. Your custom message

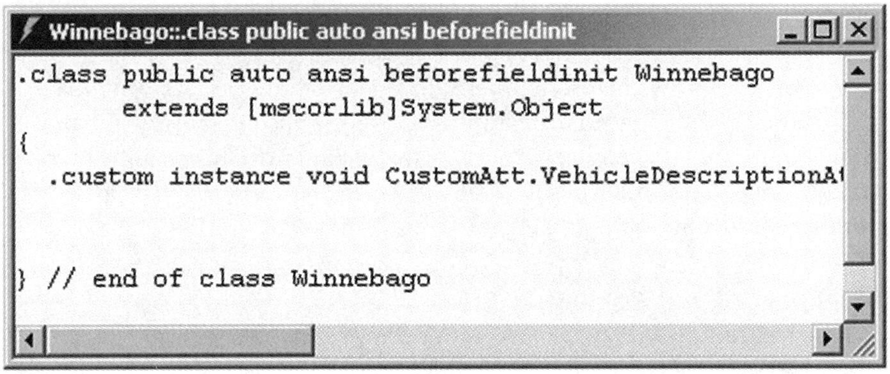

Figure 7-11. The internal representation of our custom attribute

The C# language does offer a shorthand notation for assigning an attribute to a given item. If the name of your custom attribute class does indeed have a "-Attribute" suffix, you are allowed to omit this same suffix in the code base:

```
// This short cut only works if the class is named VehicleDescriptionAttribute.
[VehicleDescription("A very long, slow but feature rich auto")]
public class Winnebago
{
    public Winnebago(){}

    // Various methods. . .
}
```

Be aware that this is a courtesy provided by C#. Not all .NET-enabled languages support this feature.

Restricting Attribute Usage

Currently, our custom attribute has no mechanism to prevent a developer from making illogical aspect specifications. For example, the following is syntactically correct, but semantically out of whack:

```
// OK, but an odd use of this custom attribute. . .
public class Winnebago
{
    [VehicleDescriptionAttribute]      // Calls default ctor of attribute class.
    public void TurnOnRadio()
    {
    }
}
```

Ideally, it would be nice to enforce the fact that this particular custom attribute should only be allowed to modify a class (and perhaps a structure) but nothing else. If you wish to constrain your attributes in this way, you need to make use of the AttributeTargets enumeration:

```
// This enumeration is used to control how a custom attribute can be applied.
public  enum AttributeTargets
{
    All,
    Assembly,
    Class,
    Constructor,
    Delegate,
    Enum,
    Event,
    Field,
    Interface,
    Method,
    Module,
    Parameter,
    Property,
    ReturnValue,
    Struct,
}
```

These values are passed as a parameter to the AttributeUsage attribute. This predefined attribute is used by the C# compiler to enforce the correct application of a custom attribute. The first parameter is an OR-ing together of members from the AttributeTarget enumeration. The second (optional) parameter is typically a named argument (AllowMultiple), which specifies if the custom attribute can be used more than once on the same type. The final (optional) boolean parameter determines if the attribute should be inherited by derived classes.

Thus, we can now configure the VehicleDescriptionAttribute to only apply to classes or structures as follows:

```
// This time, we are use the predefined AttributeUsage attribute
// to modify our custom attribute!
[AttributeUsage(AttributeTargets.Class | AttributeTargets.Struct)]
public class VehicleDescriptionAttribute : System.Attribute
{
    private string description;
    public string Desc
    {
        get { return description; }
        set { description = value; }
    }


    public VehicleDescriptionAttribute() {}
    public VehicleDescriptionAttribute(string desc)
    { description = desc;}
}
```

If we were to recompile our project, the error shown in Figure 7-12 now occurs (thankfully).

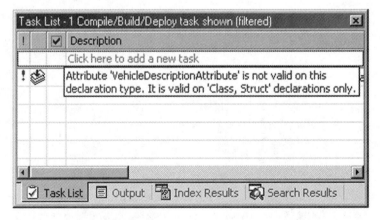

Figure 7-12. Restricted attribute usage

Assembly (and Module) Level Attributes

It is also possible to apply attributes on all types within a given module, or all modules within a given assembly. Doing so requires the use of any number of predefined attribute specifiers, the most useful being [assembly:] and [module:].

For example, assume you wish to ensure that every type defined within your assembly is compliant with the Common Language Specification.

```
// Enforce CLS compliance!
using System;
[assembly:System.CLSCompliantAttribute(true)]

namespace MyAttributes
{
[VehicleDescriptionAttribute("A very long, slow but feature rich auto")]
public class Winnebago
{
    public Winnebago(){}
}
}
```

If we were to now add a bit of code that falls outside the CLS specification:

```
// Ulong types don't jive with the CLS.
public class Winnebago
{
    public Winnebago(){}

    public ulong notCompliant;
}
```

the compiler issues the error shown in Figure 7-13.

The .NET [CLSCompliant] attribute is the rough equivalent of the IDL [oleautomation] attribute. Recall, this IDL attribute ensures all interface members are VARIANT compliant, and can thus be recognized by a COM aware language.

Notice that the [assembly:] syntax is used to inform the compiler that the CLSCompliant attribute must be applied to the assembly level, and not (for example) a single type within the assembly. One fact to be aware of is that the [assembly:] and [module:] modifiers must be placed *outside* of a namespace definition.

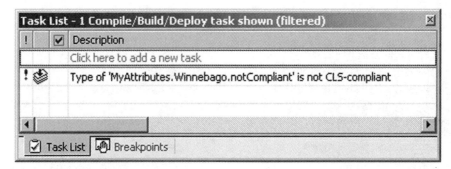

Figure 7-13. Non-CLS compliant types result in compiler errors when you set the CLSCompilant attribute

Visual Studio.NET AssemblyInfo.cs File

Visual Studio.NET projects define a file called AssemblyInfo.cs. This file is a handy place to place attributes that are to be applied at the assembly level. Table 7-6 lists some assembly level attributes to be aware of.

Discovering Attributes at Runtime

And now the final topic! As you have seen, it is possible to obtain attributes at runtime using the Type class. The logic behind doing so should be no surprise at this point:

```
// Reflecting on the custom attributes. . .
public class AttReader
{
    public static int Main(string[] args)
    {
        // Get the Type of Winnebago.
        Type t = typeof(Winnebago);

        // Get all attributes in the assembly.
        object[] customAtts = t.GetCustomAttributes(false);

        // List all info.
        foreach(VehicleDescriptionAttribute v in customAtts)
            Console.WriteLine(v.Desc);
```

```
        return 0;
    }
}
```

Table 7-6. Select Assembly -Level Attributes

ASSEMBLY-LEVEL ATTRIBUTE	MEANING IN LIFE
AssemblyCompanyAttribute	Holds basic company information.
AssemblyConfigurationAttribute	Build information, such as "retail" or "debug."
AssemblyCopyrightAttribute	Holds any copyright information for the product or assembly.
AssemblyDescriptionAttribute	A friendly description of the product or modules that make up the assembly
AssemblyInformationalVersionAttribute	Additional or supporting version information, such as a commercial product version number
AssemblyProductAttribute	Product information.
AssemblyTrademarkAttribute	Trademark information.
AssemblyCultureAttribute	Information on what cultures or languages the assembly supports.
AssemblyKeyFileAttribute	Specifies the name of the file containing the key pair used to sign the assembly (i.e., establish a shared name)
AssemblyKeyNameAttribute	Specifies the name of the key container. Instead of placing a key pair in a file, you can store it in a key container in the CSP. If you choose this option, this attribute will contain the name of the key container
AssemblyOperatingSystemAttribute	Information on which operating system the assembly was built to support.
AssemblyProcessorAttribute	Information on which processors the assembly was built to support.
AssemblyVersionAttribute	Specifies the assembly's version information, in the format major.minor.build.rev

Figure 7-14 shows the output.

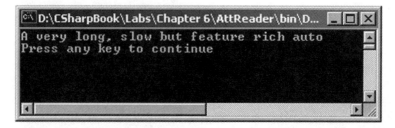

Figure 7-14. Reflecting on your custom attribute

As the name implies, Type.GetCustomAttributes() returns an array (of object types) that represent all the attributes applied to the member represented by the Type. From this array you are able to determine a specific attribute on the fly. What you do with this information is (of course) up to you.

SOURCE CODE *The CustomAtt and AttReader applications are included under the Chapter 7 subdirectory.*

Summary

Reflection is a very interesting aspect of a robust OO environment. In the world of .NET, the keys to reflection services revolve around the System.Type class and the System.Reflection namespace. As you have seen, reflection is the process of placing a type under the magnifying glass at runtime, in order to understand the "who, what, where, why, and how" of a given item.

On a related note, you explored the System.Reflection.Emit namespace, and gained a taste of creating an assembly (and the raw IL) on the fly. Assemblies that are constructed dynamically in memory (and possibly saved to file) are termed "dynamic assemblies."

I closed this chapter with an examination of attribute based programming. When you adorn your type with attributes, the end result is the augmentation of the underlying metadata. While you may never find yourself in the position of *absolutely* having to build custom attributes, you are bound to find the predefined attributes invaluable, especially when building a bridge between your classic COM servers and .NET assemblies.

CHAPTER 8

Building a Better Window (Introducing Windows Forms)

If you have read through the previous seven chapters, you should have a solid handle on the C# programming language as well as the core aspects of the .NET architecture. While you could take your newfound knowledge and begin building the next generation of Console applications (boring!) you are more likely to be interested in building an attractive graphical user interface (GUI) to allow the outside world to interact with your system.

This chapter introduces you to the System.Windows.Forms namespace. Here, you learn how to build a highly stylized main window (e.g., a custom Form-derived object). In the process, you learn about a number of window-related classes, including MenuItem, ToolBar, StatusBar, and Application. This chapter also introduces how to capture and respond to user input (i.e., handling mouse and keyboard events) within the context of a GUI environment.

The chapter wraps up with a final Windows Forms example, which stores user preferences in the system registry, as well as sends application-specific information to the Windows 2000 Event Log. The information presented in this chapter prepares you for the materials presented in Chapters 9 and 10 (GDI+ and control programming). Once you have completed the next three chapters, you will be in a perfect position to build sophisticated user interfaces using the .NET framework.

A Tale of Two GUI Namespaces

The .NET universe supplies two GUI toolkits, known as "Windows Forms" and "WebForms." The System.Windows.Forms namespace contains a number of types that allow you to build traditional desktop applications, as well as a feature rich presentation layers (for example, "fat clients") in a distributed enterprise application. As you would expect, Windows Forms hides raw Win32 primitives from view, allowing you to focus on the functionality of your application using the familiar .NET type system.

WebForms on the other hand, is a GUI toolkit used during ASP.NET development. The bulk of the WebForm types are contained in the System.Web.UI and System.Web.UI.WebControls namespaces. Using these types, you are able to build browser-independent front ends based on various industry standards (HTML, HTTP, and so forth). You examine ASP.NET (as well as the related topic of Web services) in Chapters 14 and 15.

This chapter focuses on building traditional Win32 applications using the Windows Forms namespace. It is worth pointing out that while Windows Forms and WebForms contain a number of similarly named types (e.g., Button, Check-Box, etc.) with similar members, they do not share a common implementation and cannot be treated identically. Nevertheless, as you become comfortable with the Windows Forms namespace, you should find the process of learning Web-Forms far more palatable.

Overview of the Windows Forms Namespace

The System.Windows.Forms namespace contains a large number of types to aid in the process of building rich user interfaces. Like any namespace, System.Windows.Forms is composed of a number of classes, structures, delegates, interfaces, and enumerations. Over the next couple of chapters, you drill into the specifics of a good number of these types. While it is redundant to list every member of the Windows Forms family (as they are all documented in online Help) the Table 8-1 lists some (but by no means all) of the core classes found within System.Windows.Forms.

Interacting with the Windows Forms Types

When you are building a Windows Forms application, you may choose to write all the relevant code by hand (using Notepad perhaps) and send the resulting *.cs file into the C# compiler using the /target:winexe flag. Taking time to build some Windows Forms applications by hand is not only a great learning experience, but also helps you understand the code generated by various GUI wizards.

Another option is to build Windows Forms projects using the Visual Studio.NET IDE. To be sure, the IDE does supply a number of great wizards, starter templates, and configuration tools that make working with Windows Forms extremely simple.

The other (middle-of-the-road) approach to building a Windows Forms application is to make use of a tool shipped with the .NET SDK, named WinDes.exe (Windows Forms Designer). This tool is a lightweight version of the full-blown Visual Studio IDE, that allows you to build applications using C# as well as Visual Basic.NET (there is even an option to save your source code as

Table 8-1. Core Windows Form Types

WINDOWS FORMS CLASS	MEANING IN LIFE
Application	This class represents the guts of a Windows Forms application. Using the methods of Application, you are able to process Windows messages, start and terminate a Windows Forms application, and so forth.
ButtonBase, Button, CheckBox, ComboBox, DataGrid, GroupBox, ListBox, LinkLabel, PictureBox	These classes (in addition to many others) represent types that correspond to various GUI widgets. You examine many of these items in detail in Chapter 10.
Form	This type represents a main window (or dialog box) of a Windows Forms application.
ColorDialog, FileDialog, FontDialog, PrintPreviewDialog	As you might expect, Windows Forms defines a number of canned dialog boxes. If these don't fit the bill, you are free to build custom dialogs.
Menu, MainMenu, MenuItem, ContextMenu	These types are used to build top-most and context-sensitive (pop-up) menu systems.
Clipboard, Help, Timer, Screen, ToolTip, Cursors	Various utility types to facilitate interactive GUIs.
StatusBar, Splitter, ToolBar, ScrollBar	Various types used to adorn a Form with common child controls.

XML). By default, this tool will be installed in \Bin subdirectory of your .NET SDK folder and looks something like what appears in Figure 8-1.

The problem with CASE tools of course, is that if you do not understand what the generated code is doing on your behalf, you cannot gain a true mastery of the underlying technology. Given this fact, we will begin by creating our initial Windows Forms examples in the raw (complete with menus, status bars, and toolbars) and illustrate the use of the wizards supplied by the Visual Studio.NET where appropriate (I'll let you check out WinDes.exe on your own).

Prepping the Project Workspace

To begin understanding Windows Forms programming, let's build a simple main window by hand. Our first order of business is to create a new *empty* C# project workspace named "MyRawWindow" using the VS.NET IDE. Next, insert a new C# class definition (resist the temptation to insert a new Windows Form class!) from the "Project | Add Class. . ." menu option (see Figure 8-2). Let's name this class MainWindow.

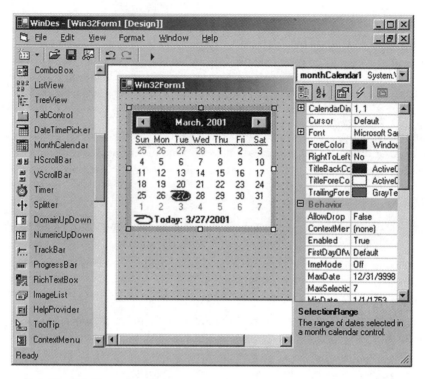

Figure 8-1. The WinDes.exe utility

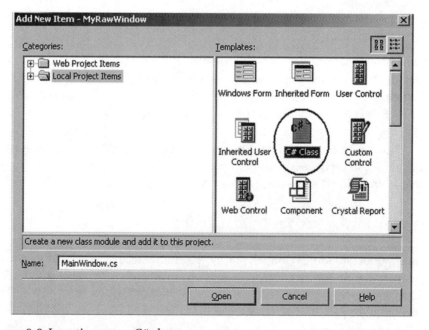

Figure 8-2. Inserting a new C# class

When you build a main window by hand, you need to use the Form and Application types (at minimum), both of which are contained in the System.Windows.Forms.dll assembly. A Windows Forms application is also needed to reference System.dll given that some types in the Windows Forms assembly make use of types in the System.dll assembly. Add references to these assemblies now (Figure 8-3).

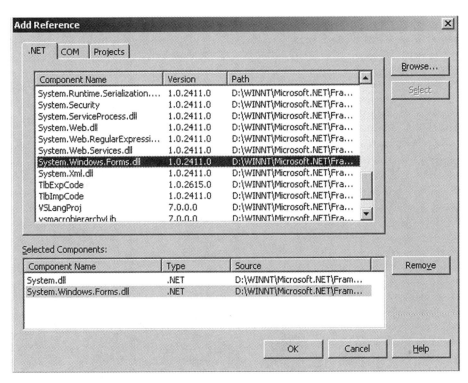

Figure 8-3. You must reference the System.Windows.Forms.dll assembly

Building a Main Window (By Hand)

In the world of Windows Forms, the Form object is used to represent any window in your application. This includes a top-most main window in an SDI (Single Document Interface) application, modeless and modal dialogs as well as the parent and child windows of an MDI (Multiple Document Interface) application. When you are interested in creating a new main window, you have two mandatory steps:

- Derive a new custom class from System.Windows.Forms.Form.

- Configure the application's Main() method to call Application.Run(), passing an instance of your new Form derived class as an argument.

With these steps in mind, you are able to update your initial class definition as follows:

```csharp
namespace MyRawWindow
{
using System;
using System.Windows.Forms;

public class MainWindow : Form
{
    public MainWindow(){}

    // Run this application.
    public static int Main(string[] args)
    {
        Application.Run(new MainWindow());
        return 0;
    }
}
}
```

Figure 8-4 shows a test run.

Figure 8-4. A basic Form

If you notice how your MyRawWindow application has been launched, you should notice an annoying command window looming in the background. This is because we have not yet configured the build settings to generate a Windows EXE application. To supply the /t:winexe flag from within the IDE, open the Project properties window (just right-click the project icon from the Solution Explorer) and expand the "Common Properties | General" node. Finally, configure the "Output Type" property as "Windows Application". When you recompile, the annoying command window will be gone.

So, at this point there is a minimizable, maximizable, resizable, and closable main window (with a default system-supplied icon to boot!) To be sure, it is a great boon to the Win32 programmers of the world to forgo the need to manually configure a WndProc function, establish a WinMain() entry point, and twiddle the bits of a WNDCLASSEX structure. Granted, our MainWindow does not do too much at this point. You enhance its functionality as you move through the chapter.

SOURCE CODE   *The MyRawWindow application can be found under the Chapter 8 subdirectory.*

Building a Visual Studio.NET Windows Forms Project Workspace

The benefit of building Windows Forms applications using Visual Studio.NET is that the integrated CASE tools can take care of a number of mundane coding details by delegating them to a number of wizards, configuration windows, and so forth. To illustrate how to make use of such assistance, close your current workspace. Now, select a new C# Windows Application project type (see Figure 8-5).

When you click OK, you will find that you are automatically given a new class derived from System.Windows.Forms.Form (with a properly configured Main() method) and have references set to each required assembly (as well as some additional assemblies).

You will also see that you are given a design time template that can be used to assemble the user interface of your Form (Figure 8-6). Understand that as you update this design-time template, you are indirectly adding code to the associated Form-derived class (named Form1.cs by default).

Using the Solution Explorer window, you are able to alternate between this design-time template and the underlying C# code. To view the code that represents your current design, simply right-click the *.cs file and select "View Code" (Figure 8-7).

You can also open the code window by double-clicking anywhere on the design-time Form, however this has the (possibly undesirable) effect of writing an event handler for the Form's Load event (more on event processing later in

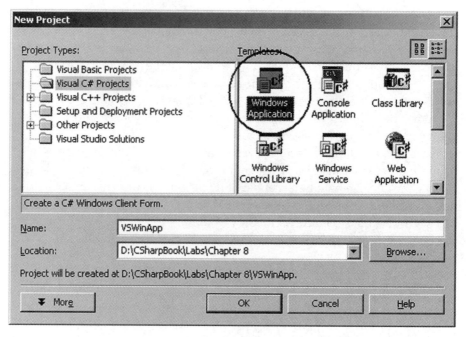

Figure 8-5. Selecting a Windows Application workspace

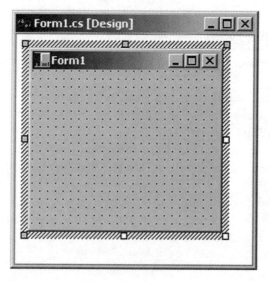

Figure 8-6. The design-time template

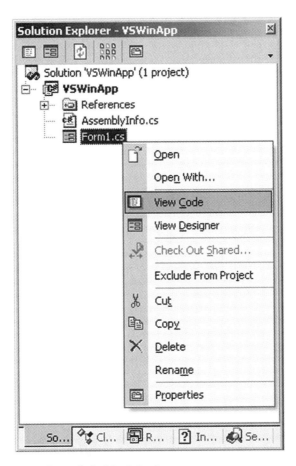

Figure 8-7. Activating the code behind the form

this chapter). Nevertheless, once you open the code window, you will see a class looking very much like the following (XML style comments removed for clarity):

```csharp
namespace VSWinApp
{
...

    public class Form1 : System.Windows.Forms.Form
    {
        private System.ComponentModel.Container components;

        public Form1()
        {
            InitializeComponent();
        }
```

```
            public override void Dispose()
            {
                base.Dispose();
                if(components != null)
                    components.Dispose();
            }

            #region Windows Form Designer generated code
            private void InitializeComponent()
            {
                this.components = new System.ComponentModel.Container();
                this.Size = new System.Drawing.Size(300,300);
                this.Text = "Form1";
            }
            #endregion

            [STAThread]
            static void Main()
            {
                Application.Run(new Form1());
            }
        }
    }
```

As you can see, this class listing is essentially the same code as the previous raw Windows Forms example. Your type still derives from System.Windows.Forms.Form, and the Main() method still calls Application.Run().

The major change is a new method named InitializeComponent(), which is wrapped by a pair of preprocessor directives (#region and #endregion). When a code block is wrapped using the #region directives, it may be collapsed and replaced by a comment block (in this case "Windows Form Designer generated code"):

```
#region Windows Form Designer generated code
private void InitializeComponent()
{
    this.components = new System.ComponentModel.Container();
    this.Size = new System.Drawing.Size(300,300);
    this.Text = "Form1";
}
#endregion
```

The InitializeComponent() method is updated automatically by the form designer to reflect the modifications you make to the Form and its controls using the Visual Studio.NET IDE. For example, if you were to use the Properties window (Figure 8-8) to modify the Form's Text and BackColor properties as follows,

Figure 8-8. The VS.NET IDE Property window

you would find that InitializeComponent() has been modified accordingly:

```
#region Windows Form Designer generated code
private void InitializeComponent()
{
    this.AutoScaleBaseSize = new System.Drawing.Size(5, 13);
    this.BackColor = System.Drawing.Color.FromArgb(255, 128, 0);
    this.ClientSize = new System.Drawing.Size(292, 273);
    this.Text = "My Rad Form";
}
#endregion
```

The Form derived class calls InitializeComponent() within the scope of the default constructor:

```
public Form1()
{
    // Required for Windows Form Designer support
    InitializeComponent();
}
```

The final point of interest is the overridden Dispose() method. This method is called automatically when your Form is about to be destroyed, and is a safe place to destroy any allocated resources. You revisit this method in just a bit, but here is the relevant code blurb:

```
public override void Dispose()
{
    base.Dispose();
    if(components != null)
        components.Dispose();
}
```

Now that you have seen how to build an initial Form using two approaches, you need to spend a bit of time looking deeper into the functionality of the Application class.

The System.Windows.Forms.Application Class

The Application class is a low-level class that defines members that allow you to control behaviors of a Windows Forms application. Additionally, the Application class defines a set of events that allow you to respond to application-level events such as application shutdown and idle processing. For the most part, you do not need to directly interact with this type; however let's check out some of its behavior.

To begin, ponder the following core methods (all of which are static) listed in Table 8-2.

The Application class also defines a number of static properties, many of which are read-only. As you examine the following table, realize that each property represents some "application level" trait such as company name, version number, and so forth. In fact, given what you already know about .NET attributes (see Chapter 7), many of these properties should look vaguely familiar (Table 8-3).

Table 8-2. Core Methods of the Application Type

METHOD OF THE APPLICATION CLASS	MEANING IN LIFE
AddMessageFilter() RemoveMessageFilter()	These methods allow your application to intercept messages for any necessary preprocessing. When you add a message filter, you must specify a class that implements the IMessageFilter interface (as you will do shortly).
DoEvents()	Provides the ability for an application to process messages currently in the message queue, during a lengthy operation (such as a looping construct). Think of DoEvents() as a quick and dirty way to simulate multithreaded behaviors.
Exit()	Terminates the application.
ExitThread()	Exits the message loop on the current thread and closes all windows owned by current thread.
OLERequired()	Initializes the OLE libraries. Consider this the .NET equivalent of manually calling OleInitialize().
Run()	Begins running a standard application message loop on the current thread.

Table 8-3. Core Properties of the Application Type

PROPERTIES OF APPLICATION CLASS	MEANING IN LIFE
CommonAppDataRegistry	Retrieves the registry key for the application data that is shared among all users.
CompanyName	Retrieves the company name associated with the current application.
CurrentCulture	Gets or sets the locale information for the current thread.
CurrentInputLanguage	Gets or sets the current input language for the current thread.
ProductName	Retrieves the product name associated with this application.
ProductVersion	Retrieves the product version associated with this application.
StartupPath	Retrieves the path for the executable file that started the application.

Notice that some properties such as CompanyName and ProductName, provide a handy way to retrieve assembly level metadata. As you recall from Chapter 7, an assembly may be extended using a number of attributes. Thus, if you specify the [assembly:AssemblyCompany("")] attribute, you may obtain this information using Application.CompanyName, without the need to make direct use of the types defined within System.Reflection.

Finally, the Application class defines the following events shown in Table 8-4.

Table 8-4. Events of the Application Type

APPLICATION EVENT	MEANING IN LIFE
ApplicationExit	Occurs when the application is just about to shut down.
Idle	Occurs when the application's message loop has finished processing and is about to enter an idle state (meaning there are no messages to process at the current time).
ThreadExit	Occurs when a thread in the application is about to terminate. If the main thread for an application is about to be shut down, this event will be raised before the ApplicationExit event.

Fun with the Application Class

To illustrate some of the functionality of the Application class (as well as preview Windows Forms event handling), let's enhance our current raw MainWindow to perform the following tasks:

- Display some basic information about this application on startup.

- Respond to the ApplicationExit event.

- Perform some preprocessing of the WM_LBUTTONDOWN message.

To begin, assume that you have extended your manifest using a number of attributes that mark the name of this fine application and the company that created it (this process was defined in Chapter 7, so take a peek if you need a refresher):

```
// Some attributes regarding this assembly.
[assembly:AssemblyCompany("Intertech, Inc.")]
[assembly:AssemblyProduct("A Better Window")]
```

The constructor of our Form-derived class can obtain this information using properties of the Application, which are displayed using the Show() method of the MessageBox type:

```
namespace AppClassExample
{
using System;
using System.Windows.Forms;
using System.Reflection;
public class MainForm : Form
{
    ...
    public MainForm()
    {
        GetStats();
    }

    private void GetStats()
    {
        MessageBox.Show(Application.CompanyName, "Company:");
        MessageBox.Show(Application.ProductName, "App Name:");
        MessageBox.Show(Application.StartupPath, "I live here:");
    }
}
}
```

As you can assume, when you run this application, you see various message boxes that display the relevant information (as shown in Figure 8-9).

Figure 8-9. Extracting information using the Application type

Responding to the ApplicationExit Event

Next, let's configure this Form to respond to the ApplicationExit event. When you wish to respond to events from within a Windows Forms application, you will be happy to find that the same event logic detailed in Chapter 5 is used to handle GUI-based events. Therefore, if you wish to intercept the ApplicationExit event, you simply register a custom method with the delegate using the += operator:

```
public class MainForm : Form
{
    . . .
    public MainForm()
    {
        . . .
        // Intercept the ApplicationExit event.
        Application.ApplicationExit += new EventHandler(Form_OnExit);
    }

    // Event handler.
    private void Form_OnExit(object sender, EventArgs evArgs)
    {
        MessageBox.Show("See ya!", "This app is dead. . .");
    }
}
```

Notice that the signature of the ApplicationExit event handler must conform to a delegate of type System.EventHandler:

```
// Many GUI based events make use of this delegate (EventHandler)
// which requires two parameters:
public delegate void EventHandler(object sender, EventArgs e);
```

The first parameter of the delegate is of type System.Object, which represents the object sending the event. The EventArgs parameter (or a descendent thereof) contains relevant information for the current event. For example, if you have an event handler that responds to a mouse event, the MouseEventArgs parameter will contain mouse related details such as the (*x, y*) position of the cursor. If you run the application, you will be able to respond to the termination of this application.

Preprocessing Messages with the Application Class

The final step of our example is to perform some preprocessing logic of the WM_LBUTTONDOWN message. As you know, this standard Windows message is sent when the left mouse button has been clicked within the client area of a given Form (or any GUI widget that is equipped to respond to this event). Now, be very aware that you will find a much simpler way to intercept standard mouse events a bit later in this chapter. This step of the current project is simply to illustrate how to perform any preprocessing logic before the event is fully dispatched.

When you wish to filter messages in the .NET framework, your first task is to create a new class that implements the IMessageFilter interface. This is extremely

simple, given that IMessageFilter defines only one method, PreFilterMessage().
Return "true" to filter the message and prevent it from being dispatched or "false"
to allow the message to continue on its way.

Within the scope of your implementation, you may examine the incoming
Message.Msg field to extract the numerical value of the Windows message (in our
case, WM_LBUTTONDOWN which is the value 513). For example:

```
using Microsoft.Win32;      // Must reference this namespace!

// Create a message filter.
public class MyMessageFilter : IMessageFilter
{
    public bool PreFilterMessage(ref Message m)
    {
        // Intercept the left mouse button down message.
        if (m.Msg == 513)        // WM_LBUTTONDOWN = 513.
        {
            MessageBox.Show("WM_LBUTTONDOWN is: " + m.Msg);
            return true;
        }
        return false;     // All other messages are ignored. . .
    }
}
```

Once you have created the class that will be filtering the incoming messages,
you must register a new instance of this type using the static AddMessageFilter()
method. Here is the update to our existing MainForm class:

```
public class MainForm : Form
{
    private MyMessageFilter msgFilter = new MyMessageFilter();
    . . .
    public MainForm()
    {
        . . .
        // Add message filter.
        Application.AddMessageFilter(msgFilter);
    }

    // Event handler
    private void Form_OnExit(object sender, EventArgs evArgs)
    {
        MessageBox.Show("See ya!", "This app is dead. . .");
```

```
        // Remove message filter.
        Application.RemoveMessageFilter(msgFilter);
    }
}
```

Of course, when you run this application, you see the message that appears in Figure 8-10 when you click the left mouse button anywhere within the application. As you can tell, filtering messages is not a task you need to perform all that often. Nevertheless, it is nice to know that you are able to drop down to this level of detail if you so choose.

Figure 8-10. Filtering messages

SOURCE CODE   *The AppClassExample project can be found under the Chapter 8 subdirectory.*

The Anatomy of a Form

Now that you understand the role of the Application object, our next task is to examine the functionality of the Form class itself. As you have seen, when you create a new window (or dialog) you need to define a new class deriving from System.Windows.Forms.Form. This class gains a great deal of functionality from the types in its inheritance chain. Figure 8-11 illustrates the big picture.

Detailing each and every member of each class in the Form's inheritance chain would require a small book in itself. However, it is important to understand the core behavior supplied by each base class. I assume that you will spend time examining the full details behind each class at your leisure.

Basic Form Functionality

Before we get to the real meat of the Form's inheritance chain, understand that like any type in the .NET universe, Form ultimately derives from System.Object

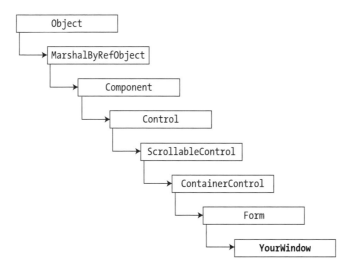

Figure 8-11. The derivation of the Form type

(which should be no surprise to you at this point). MarshalByRefObject defines the behavior to remote this type by reference, rather than by value. Thus, if you remotely instantiate a Form across the wire, you are manipulating a reference to the Form on the remote machine (not manipulating a local copy of the Form).

The Component Class

The first base class of immediate interest is Component. The Component type provides a canned implementation of the IComponent interface. This predefined interface defines a property named Site, which returns (surprise, surprise) an ISite interface. Furthermore, IComponent inherits a single event from the IDisposable interface named Disposed:

```
public interface IComponent : IDisposable
{
    // The Site property.
    public ISite Site { virtual get; virtual set; }

    // The Disposed event.
    public  event EventHandler Disposed;
}
```

The ISite interface defines a number of methods that allow a Control to interact with the hosting container (for example, a Form hosting a Button widget):

```
public interface ISite : IServiceProvider
{
    // Properties of the ISite interface.
    public IComponent Component {  virtual  get; }
    public IContainer Container {  virtual  get; }
    public  bool DesignMode {  virtual  get; }
    public  string Name {  virtual  get;  virtual  set; }
}
```

By and large, the properties defined by the ISite interface are only of interest to you if you are attempting to build a widget that can be manipulated at design time (such as a custom control).

In addition to the Site property, Component also provides an implementation of the Dispose() method (as seen earlier in this chapter). Recall that the Dispose() method is called when a component is no longer required. For example, when a Form has been closed, the Dispose() method is called automatically for the Form and for all widgets contained within that form.

Remember, you are free to override Dispose() in your Form-derived class to free large resources in a timely manner and to remove references to other objects so that they can be garbage collected:

```
public override void Dispose()
{
    base.Dispose();
    // Do your work. . .
}
```

The Control Class

The next base class of interest is System.Windows.Forms.Control, which establishes the common behaviors required by any GUI-centric type. The core members of System.Windows.Forms.Control allow you to configure the size and position of a control, extract the underlying HWND, as well as capture keyboard and mouse input. Table 8-5 defines some of the properties to be aware of.

Table 8-5. Core Properties of the Control Type

CONTROL PROPERTY	MEANING IN LIFE
Top, Left, Bottom, Right, Bounds, ClientRectangle, Height, Width	Each of these properties specifies various attributes about the current dimensions of the Control-derived object. Bounds returns a Rectangle that specifies the size of the control. ClientRectangle returns a Rectangle that corresponds to the size of the client area of the control.
Created, Disposed, Enabled, Focused, Visible	These properties each return a Boolean that specifies the state of the current Control.
Handle	Returns a numerical value (integer) which represents the HWND of this Control.
ModifierKeys	This static property checks the current state of the modifier keys (shift, control, and alt) and returns the state in a Keys type.
MouseButtons	This static property checks the current state of the mouse buttons (left, right, and middle mouse buttons) and returns this state in a MouseButtons type.
Parent	Returns a Control object that represents the parent of the current Control.
TabIndex, TabStop	These properties are used to configure the tab order of the Control.
Text	The current text associated with this Control.

The Control base class also defines a number of methods that allow you to interact with any Control-derived type. A partial list of some of the more common members appears in Table 8-6.

Setting a Form's Styles

Let's examine two interesting methods of the Control type: GetStyle() and Set-Style(). Win32 programmers are no doubt familiar with the WNDCLASSEX structure, and the dozens of oddball styles that can be used to fill the various fields. While Windows Forms hides this Windows 'goo' from view, you are able to modify the default styles of your Form if need be. First, check out the related Control-Styles enumeration:

Table 8-6. Core Methods of the Control Type

CONTROL METHOD	MEANING IN LIFE
GetStyle() SetStyle()	These methods are used to manipulate the style flags of the current Control using the ControlStyles enumeration.
Hide(), Show()	These methods indirectly set the state of the Visible property.
Invalidate()	Forces the Control to redraw itself by forcing a paint message into the message queue. This method is overloaded to allow you to specify a specific Rectangle to refresh, rather than the entire client area.
OnXXXX()	The Control class defines numerous methods that can be overridden by a subclass to respond to various events (e.g., OnMouseMove(), OnKeyDown(), OnResize(), and so forth). As you will see later in this chapter, when you wish to intercept a GUI-based event, you have two approaches. One approach is to simply override one of the existing event handlers. Another is to add a custom event handler to a given delegate.
Refresh()	Forces the Control to invalidate and immediately repaint itself and any children.
SetBounds(), SetLocation(), SetClientArea()	Each of these methods is used to establish the dimensions of the Control derived object.

```
public  enum ControlStyles
{
    AllPaintingInWmPaint,
    CacheText,
    ContainerControl,
    EnableNotifyMessage,
    FixedHeight,
    FixedWidth,
    Opaque,
    ResizeRedraw,
    Selectable,
    StandardClick,
    StandardDoubleClick,
    SupportsTransparentBackColor,
    UserMouse,
    UserPaint,
}
```

The values of the ControlStyle enumeration may OR-ed together if you wish to specify multiple styles and as you would expect, a Form has a default style set (I'll assume you will check out online Help for full details of each value).

Assume you have a Form containing a single Button type. In the Click event handler of this Button, you can check if the Form supports a given style using GetStyle():

```
// Shows false!
private void btnGetStyles_Click(object sender, System.EventArgs e)
{
    MessageBox.Show(GetStyle(ControlStyles.ResizeRedraw).ToString(),
                "Do you have ResizeRedraw?");
}
```

To set the bit of a given style (by specifying true or false) you could write:

```
public StyleForm()
{
    . . .
    SetStyle(ControlStyles.ResizeRedraw, true);
}
```

The ResizeRedraw is one value you typically want to add to a given Form. By default this style is not active and thus, a Form will not automatically redraw itself when resized. This means, if you have intercepted a Paint event (which you will do a bit later) and resize the Form, your drawing logic is not refreshed! If you wish to ensure that the Paint event fires whenever the user resizes the Form, be sure to specify the ResizeRedraw style using SetStyle(). Another (equally valid) alternative is to intercept the Form's Resize event and call Invalidate() directly:

```
private void StyleForm_Resize(object sender, System.EventArgs e)
{
    Invalidate();           // This forces a repaint (more details later...)
}
```

Typically, you would want to intercept the Resize() event when you have *additional* work to do beyond triggering a paint session.

You tackle the topics of GDI+, paint sessions and GUI widgets in the chapters to come. However to illustrate the effect of setting Form styles, assume you have some GDI+ rendering logic that draws a dashed black line around the client area rectangle. If the ResizeRedraw bit is set to false, you find the ugliness shown in Figure 8-12 as you resize the Form.

Figure 8-12. ResizeRedraw is a bit off

If you set it to "true" you have correct rendering (Figure 8-13).

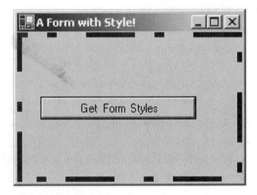

Figure 8-13. ResizeRedraw is correct

SOURCE CODE   *The FormStyles project is under the Chapter 8 subdirectory.*

Control Events

The Control class also defines a number of events that can logically be grouped into two major categories: Mouse events and keyboard events (Table 8-7).

Fun with the Control Class

To be sure, the Control class does define additional properties, methods, and events beyond the subset you have just examined. However, to illustrate some of

Table 8-7. Core Events of the Control Type

CONTROL EVENT	MEANING IN LIFE
Click, DoubleClick, MouseEnter, MouseLeave, MouseDown, MouseUp, MouseMove, MouseHover, MouseWheel	The Control class defines numerous events triggered in response to mouse input.
KeyPress, KeyUp, KeyDown,	The Control class also defines numerous events triggered in response to keyboard input.

these core members, let's build a new Form type (also called MainForm) that provides the following functionality:

- Set the initial size of the Form to some arbitrary dimensions.

- Override the Dispose() method.

- Respond to the MouseMove and MouseUp events (using two approaches).

- Capture and process keyboard input.

To begin, assume you have a new C# class derived from Form. First, update the default constructor to set the top, left, bottom, and right coordinates of the Form using various properties of the Control class. To confirm these changes, make use of Bounds property, and display the string version of the current dimensions. Do be aware that Bounds returns a Rectangle type that is defined in the System.Drawing namespace. Therefore be sure to set an assembly reference (to System.Drawing.dll) if you are building this Form by hand (Visual Studio.NET Windows Forms projects do so automatically):

```
// Need this for Rectangle definition.
using System.Drawing;
. . .

public class MainForm : Form
{
    public static int Main(string[] args)
    {
        Application.Run(new MainForm());
        return 0;
    }
```

```
public MainForm()
{
    Top = 100;
    Left = 75;
    Height = 100;
    Width = 500;
    MessageBox.Show(Bounds.ToString(), "Current rect");
}

}
```

When you run this application, you are able to confirm the coordinates of your Form (Figure 8-14).

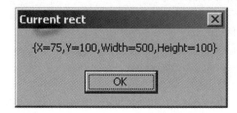

Figure 8-14. The Bounds property

Once you dismiss the message box, you are presented with a rather elongated main window (Figure 8-15).

Figure 8-15. The Top, Left, Height, and Width properties

Now, let's retrofit your class to override the inherited Component.Dispose() method. As you recall from earlier in this chapter, the Application object defines an event named ApplicationExit. If you configure your Form to intercept this event, you are effectively informed of the destruction of the application. As a (much) simpler alternative, you can achieve the same effect by simply overriding the abstract Dispose() method. Do note that you should call your base class' Dispose() method beforehand:

```
public class MainForm : Form
{
...
// Visual Studio.NET Windows Forms projects automatically support this method.
    public override void Dispose()
    {
        base.Dispose();
        MessageBox.Show("Disposing this form...");
    }
}
```

Responding to Mouse Events: Take One

Next, you need to intercept the MouseUp event. The goal is to display the (*x, y*) position at which the MouseUp event occurred. When you wish to respond to events from within a Windows Forms application, you have two general approaches. The first approach should be familiar to you at this point in the game: Use delegates. The second approach is to override the appropriate base class method. Let's examine each technique, beginning with standard delegation. Here is the updated MainForm:

```
public class MainForm : Form
{
    public static int Main(string[] args)
    {
        Application.Run(new MainForm());
        return 0;
    }

    public MainForm()
    {
        Top = 100;
        Left = 75;
        Height = 100;
        Width = 500;
        MessageBox.Show(Bounds.ToString(), "Current rect");

        // Listen for the MouseUp event...
        this.MouseUp += new MouseEventHandler(OnMouseUp);
    }
```

```
// Method called in response to the MouseUp event.
public void OnMouseUp(object sender, MouseEventArgs e)
{
    this.Text = "Clicked at: (" + e.X + ", " + e.Y + ")";
}
...
}
```

Now, recall that GUI-based delegates take an EventArgs (or derivative thereof) as the second parameter. When you process mouse events, the second parameter is of type MouseEventArgs. This type (defined in the System.Windows.Forms namespace) defines a number of interesting properties that may be used to gather various statistics regarding the state of the mouse, as seen in Table 8-8.

Table 8-8. Properties of the MouseEventArgs type

MOUSEEVENTARGS PROPERTY	MEANING IN LIFE
Button	Gets which mouse button was pressed, as defined by the MouseButtons enumeration.
Clicks	Gets the number of times the mouse button was pressed and released.
Delta	Gets a signed count of the number of detents the mouse wheel has rotated.
X	Gets the x-coordinate of a mouse click.
Y	Gets the y-coordinate of a mouse click.

The implementation of the OnMouseUp() method simply extracts the (x, y) position of the cursor and displays this information in the Form's caption via the inherited Text property. Figure 8-16 shows a possible test run.

Figure 8-16. Capturing MouseUp events

To make things even more interesting, we could also capture a MouseMove event, and display the same (x, y) position data in the caption of the Form. In this way, the current location of the cursor is tracked whenever the mouse cursor is moved within the client area:

```
public class MainForm : Form
{
. . .
    public MainForm()
    {
        . . .
        // Track mouse movement and MouseUp event.
        this.MouseUp += new MouseEventHandler(OnMouseUp);
        this.MouseMove += new MouseEventHandler(OnMouseMove);
    }

    public void OnMouseUp(object sender, MouseEventArgs e)
    {
        MessageBox.Show("Stop clicking me!");
    }

    public void OnMouseMove(object sender, MouseEventArgs e)
    {
        this.Text = "Current Pos: (" + e.X + ", " + e.Y + ")";
    }
. . .
}
```

Determining Which Mouse Button Was Clicked

One thing to be aware of is that the MouseUp (or MouseDown) event is sent whenever *any* mouse button is clicked. If you wish to determine exactly which button was clicked (left, right, or middle) you need to examine the Button property of the MouseEventArgs class. The value of Button is constrained by the MouseButtons enumeration. For example:

```
public void OnMouseUp(object sender, MouseEventArgs e)
{
    // Which mouse button was clicked?
    if(e.Button = = MouseButtons.Left)
        MessageBox.Show("Left click!");

    else if(e.Button = = MouseButtons.Right)
        MessageBox.Show("Right click!");
```

```
    else // MouseButtons.Middle
        MessageBox.Show("Middle click!");
}
```

Thus, if you click the middle button you would see what's shown in Figure 8-17.

Figure 8-17. Which mouse button was clicked

Responding to Mouse Events: Take Two

The other approach to capture events in a Control-derived type is to override the correct base class method, which in your case would be OnMouseUp() and OnMouseMove(). The Control type defines a number of protected virtual methods that will be called automatically when the corresponding event is triggered. If you were to update your Form using this technique, you have no need to manually specify a custom event handler:

```
public class MainForm : Form
{
    . . .
    public MainForm()
    {
        . . .
        // No need to do this when overriding!
        // this.MouseUp += new MouseEventHandler(OnMouseUp);
        // this.MouseMove+= new MouseEventHandler(OnMouseMove);

    }

    protected override void OnMouseUp(/*object sender,*/ MouseEventArgs e)
    {
        // Which mouse button was clicked?
        if(e.Button == MouseButtons.Left)
            MessageBox.Show("Left click!");
```

```
                else if(e.Button == MouseButtons.Right)
                    MessageBox.Show("Right click!");
                else if(e.Button == MouseButtons.Middle)
                    MessageBox.Show("Middle click!");
        }

        protected override void OnMouseMove(/*object sender,*/ MouseEventArgs e)
        {
            this.Text = "Current Pos: (" + e.X + ", " + e.Y + ")";
        }
...
}
```

Notice how the signatures of each method takes a single parameter of type MouseEventArg, rather than two parameters that conform to the MouseEventHandler delegate. If you run the program again, you see no change whatsoever (which is good). Typically you only need to override an "OnXXXX()" method if you have additional work to perform before the event is fired. The preferred approach (and the one used by Visual Studio.NET) is to handle the event directly as you did in the first mouse example.

Responding to Keyboard Events

Processing keyboard input is almost identical to responding to mouse activity. The following code captures the KeyUp event and displays the textual name of the character that was pressed in a message box. Here, you capture this event using the delegation technique (there is a method named OnKeyUp() that can be overridden as an alternative):

```
public class MainForm : Form

{
...
    public MainForm()
    {
        Top = 100;
        Left = 75;
        Height = 100;
        Width = 500;
        MessageBox.Show(Bounds.ToString(), "Current rect");
```

```
    . . .
    // Listen to KeyUp Event.
    this.KeyUp += new KeyEventHandler(OnKeyUp);
}

public void OnKeyUp(object sender, KeyEventArgs e)
{
    MessageBox.Show(e.KeyCode.ToString(), "Key Pressed!");
}
. . .
}
```

As you can see, the KeyEventArgs type maintains an enumeration named KeyCode that holds the ID of the key press. In addition, the KeyEventArgs type, defines the useful properties listed in Table 8-9.

Table 8-9. Properties of the KeyEventArgs Type

KEYEVENTARGS PROPERTY	MEANING IN LIFE
Alt	Gets a value indicating whether the ALT key was pressed.
Control	Gets a value indicating whether the CTRL key was pressed.
Handled	Gets or sets a value indicating whether the event was handled.
KeyCode	Gets the keyboard code for a System.Windows.Forms.Control.KeyDown or System.Windows.Forms.Control.KeyUp event.
KeyData	Gets the key data for a System.Windows.Forms.Control.KeyDown or System.Windows.Forms.Control.KeyUp event.
Modifiers	Indicates which modifier keys (CTRL, SHIFT, and/or ALT) were pressed.
Shift	Gets a value indicating whether the SHIFT key was pressed.

Figure 8-18 shows a possible key press.

Figure 8-18. Which key was pressed?

SOURCE CODE *The ControlBehaviors project is included under the Chapter 8 subdirectory.*

The Control Class Revisited

The Control class defines further behaviors to configure background and foreground colors, background images, font characteristics, drag-and-drop functionality and support for context menus. This class provides docking and anchoring behaviors for the derived types (which you examine in Chapter 10). Perhaps the most important duty of the Control class is to establish a mechanism to render images, text, and various geometric patterns onto the client area via the OnPaint() method. To begin, observe these additional properties of the Control class, as seen in Table 8-10:

Table 8-10. Additional Control Properties

CONTROL PROPERTY	MEANING IN LIFE
AllowDrop	If AllowDrop is set to true then this control allows drag-and-drop operations and events to be used.
Anchor	The anchor property determines which edges of the control are anchored to the container's edges.
BackColor, BackgroundImage, Font, ForeColor, Cursor	These properties configure how the client area should be displayed.
ContextMenu	Specifies which context menu (e.g., pop-up menu) will be shown when the user right clicks the control.
Dock	The dock property controls to which edge of the container this control is docked to. For example, when docked to the top of the container, the control is displayed flush at the top of the container, extending the length of the container.
Opacity	Determines the opacity of the control, in percentages (0.0 is completely transparent, 1.0 is completely opaque).
Region	This property configures a Region object that specifies the outline/silhouette/boundary of the control.
RightToLeft	This is used for international applications where the language is written from right to left.

The Control class also defines a number of additional methods and events used to configure how the Control should respond to drag-and-drop operations and respond to painting operations (Table 8-11):

Table 8-11. Additional Control Methods

CONTROL METHOD/EVENT	MEANING IN LIFE
DoDragDrop() OnDragDrop() OnDragEnter() OnDragLeave() OnDragOver()	These methods are used to monitor drag-and-drop operations for a given Control descendent.
ResetFont() ResetCursor() ResetForeColor() ResetBackColor()	These methods reset various UI attributes of a child control to the corresponding value of the parent.
OnPaint()	Inheriting classes should override this method to handle the Paint event.
DragEnter DragLeave DragDrop DragOver	These events are sent in response to drag-and-drop operations.
Paint	This event is sent whenever the Control has become "dirty" and needs to be repainted.

More Fun with the Control Class

To illustrate some of these additional Control members, the following class sets the background color of the Form object to "Tomato" (you just have to love the names of these colors), the opacity to 50 percent, and configures the mouse cursor to display an hourglass icon. More important, let's handle the Paint event in order to render a text string into the Form's client area. Here is the update:

```
using System;
using System.Windows.Forms;
using System.Drawing;     // Needed for Color, Brush, and Font types.

public class MainForm : Form
{
    ...
    public MainForm()
```

```
    {
        // Set some properties that we have inherited from Control.
        BackColor = Color.Tomato;
        Opacity = 0.5d;
        this.Cursor = Cursors.WaitCursor;

        // Handle the Paint event.
        this.Paint += new PaintEventHandler(Form1_Paint);
    }

    private void Form1_Paint(object sender, PaintEventArgs e)
    {
        Graphics g = e.Graphics;
        g.DrawString("What a head trip...",
            new Font("Times New Roman", 20),
            new SolidBrush(Color.Black), 40, 10);
    }
}
```

If you run this application (Figure 8-19) you will see that the Form is indeed transparent! In fact, my screen shot illustrates this point quite clearly (note the code in the background).

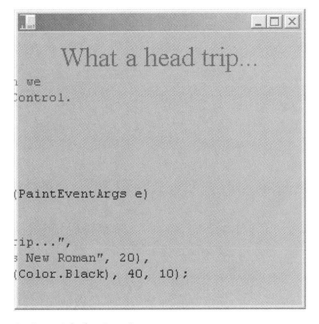

Figure 8-19. Painting with the Opacity property

Painting Basics

The most important aspect of this application is the handling of the Paint event. Notice that the delegate defines a method that takes a parameter of type PaintEventArgs. This type defines two properties to help you configure the current paint session for the Control as seen in Table 8-12.

Table 8-12. Additional Control Properties

PAINTEVENTARGS PROPERTY	MEANING IN LIFE
ClipRectangle	Gets the rectangle in which to paint.
Graphics	Gets the Graphics object used during a paint session.

The critical property of PaintEventArgs is Graphics, which is called to retrieve a Graphics object to use during the painting session. You examine this class (and GDI+ in general) in greater detail in Chapter 9. For now, do understand that the Graphics class defines a number of members that allow you to render text, geometric shapes and images onto a Control-derived type.

Finally, in this example you also configured the Cursor property to display an hourglass symbol whenever the mouse cursor is within the bounding rectangle of this Control. The Cursors type can be assigned to any member of the Cursors enumeration (e.g., Arrow, Cross, UpArrow, Help, and so forth):

```
public MainForm()
{
    . . .
    this.Cursor = Cursors.WaitCursor;
}
```

SOURCE CODE   *The MoreControlBehaviors project is included under the Chapter 8 subdirectory.*

The ScrollableControl Class

ScrollableControl is used to define a small number of members that allow your widget to support vertical and horizontal scrollbars. The most intriguing members of the ScrollableControl type would have to be the AutoScroll property and the related AutoScrollMinSize property. For example, assume you wish to ensure that if the end user resizes your Form, horizontal and vertical scrollbars are automatically inserted if the size of the client area is less than or equal to 300 * 300 pixels. Programmatically, your task is simple:

```
// This could be set in the class constructor or InitializeComponent().
// Note that you need to reference the System.Drawing namespace
// to gain access to the Size type.
this.AutoScroll = true;
this.AutoScrollMinSize = new System.Drawing.Size (300, 300);
```

The ScrollableControl class takes care of the rest. For example, if you had a Form that contained a number of child objects (buttons, labels, or whatnot), you would find that the scrolling logic ensures the entire Form real estate is viewable. For the current example, simply render a large block of text onto the form's client area (see Figure 8-20).

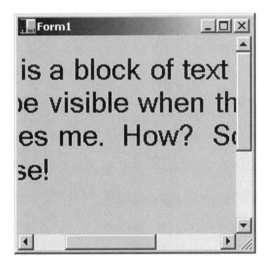

Figure 8-20. Auto scrolling

The ScrollableControl class does define a number of additional members beyond AutoScroll and AutoScrollMinSize, but not many. Also be aware that when you wish to take greater control over the scrolling process, you are able to create and manipulate individual ScrollBar types (such as HScrollBar and VScrollBar). I'll leave it to you to check out the remaining members using online Help.

SOURCE CODE *The ScrollForm project is included under the Chapter 8 sub-directory.*

ContainerControl Class

ContainerControl defines support to manage the focus of a given GUI item. In practice, the behavior defined by System.Windows.Forms.ContainerControl is much more useful when you are building a Form that contains a number of child controls, and wish to allow the user to use the Tab key to alternate focus. Using a small set of members, you can programmatically obtain the currently selected control, force another to receive focus and so forth. Table 8-13 gives a rundown of some of the more interesting members.

Table 8-13. Members of the ContainerControl Type

CONTAINERCONTROL MEMBER	MEANING IN LIFE
ActiveControl ParentForm	These properties allow you to obtain and set the active control, as well as retrieve a reference to the Form that is hosting the item.
ProcessTabKey()	This method allows you to programmatically activate the Tab key to set focus to the next available control.

On a related note, recall that all descendents of System.Windows.Forms.Control inherit the TabStop and TabIndex properties. As you might be able to guess, these items are used to set the tab order of controls maintained by a parent container, and are used in conjunction with the members supplied by the ContainerControl class. You revisit the issue of tab order during the discussion of programming controls (Chapter 10).

The Form Class

This brings us to the Form class itself, which is typically the direct base class for your custom Form types. In addition to the large set of members inherited from the Control, ScrollableControl and ContainerControl classes the Form type adds even greater functionality. Let's start with the core properties (Table 8-14).

The truth of the matter is that the Form class does not define a great deal of additional methods. The bulk of a Form's functionality comes from the base classes you have already examined. However, Table 8-15 gives a partial list of some additional methods to be aware of.

Finally, the Form class does define a number of Events that you should be aware of. Table 8-16 gives a sampling.

Table 8-14. Properties of the Form Type

FORM PROPERTY	MEANING IN LIFE
AcceptButton	Gets or sets the button on the form that is clicked when the user presses the ENTER key.
ActiveMDIChild IsMDIChild IsMDIContainer	Each of these properties is used within the context of an MDI application.
AutoScale	Gets or sets a value indicating whether the form will adjust its size to fit the height of the font used on the form and scale its controls.
BorderStyle	Gets or sets the border style of the form. Used in conjunction with the FormBorderStyle enumeration.
CancelButton	Gets or sets the button control that is to be clicked when the user presses the ESC key.
ControlBox	Gets or sets a value indicating whether the form has a control box.
Menu MergedMenu	Gets or sets the (merged) menu for the Form.
MaximizeBox MinimizedBox	Used to determine if this Form enables the maximize and minimize boxes.
ShowInTaskbar	Should this Form be seen on the Windows taskbar?
StartPosition	Gets or sets the starting position of the form at run time, as specified by the FormStartPosition enumeration.
WindowState	Configures how the Form is to be displayed on startup. Used in conjunction with the FormWindowState enumeration.

Table 8-15. Methods of the Form Type

FORM METHOD	MEANING IN LIFE
Activate()	Activate a given Form and give it focus.
Close()	Closes a Form.
CenterToScreen()	Places the Form dead center on the screen.
LayoutMDI()	Arranges each child Form (as specified by the LayoutMDI enumeration) within the parent Form.
OnResize()	May be overridden to respond to Resize events.
ShowDialog()	Displays a Form as a Modal dialog. More on dialog box programming at a later time.

Table 8-16. Select Events of the Form Type

FORM EVENT	MEANING IN LIFE
Activate	Sent when a form is brought to the front of the active application.
Closed, Closing	These events are used to determine when the Form is about to close, or has closed.
MDIChildActive	Sent when a child window is activated.

Fun with the Form Class

At this point, you should feel quite comfortable with the functionality provided by the Form class and each of its parent classes. Here is a main window (Main-Form) that makes use of various members in the inheritance chain:

```
public class MainForm: Form

{

    . . .
    public MainForm ()
    {
        // Configure the initial look and feel of this form.
        BackColor = Color.LemonChiffon;     // Background color.
        Text = "My Fantastic Form";         // Form's caption.
        Size = new Size(200, 200);          // 200 * 200.
        CenterToScreen();                   // Center Form to the screen.

        // Handle events.
        this.Resize += new EventHandler(this.Form1_Resize);
        this.Paint += new PaintEventHandler(this.Form1_Paint);
    }

    private void MainForm_Resize(object sender, System.EventArgs e)
    {
        // Must invalidate when resizing, as Paint renders a string
        // into the current display rectangle!
        // (could also set the correct ControlStyle bit)
        Invalidate();
    }

    // Reference System.Drawing to render this string.
    private void MainForm_Paint(object sender, PaintEventArgs e)
```

```
        {
            Graphics g = e.Graphics;
            g.DrawString("Windows Forms is for building GUIs!",
                    new Font("Times New Roman", 20),
                    new SolidBrush(Color.Black),
                    this.DisplayRectangle);         // Display in client rect.
        }
}
```

Here, a Form object that begins life centered on the screen has been created. In addition, the Resize event has been handled. Simply call Invalidate() to force the client area to be refreshed. In this way, the text string rendered on the client area always fits within the bounding rectangle Form's client area (note the use of the DisplayRectangle property).

SOURCE CODE   *The SimpleFormApp can be found under the Chapter 8 sub-directory.*

Building Menus with Windows Forms

Now that you understand the composition of the Form class, the next task is to learn how to establish a menu system to provide some degree of user interaction. The System.Windows.Forms namespace provides a number of types that facilitate the building of main menus (i.e., menus mounted at the top of a Form), as well as context-sensitive pop-up menus (e.g., "right-click" menus). To begin, let's examine what it would take to build a top-most menu that allows the end user to exit the application using a standard "File | Exit" menu command (Figure 8-21).

Figure 8-21. A simple menu system

The first class to be aware of is System.Windows.Forms.Menu, which functions as the base class for all other menu-related classes (MainMenu, MenuItem, and ContextMenu). Be aware that System.Windows.Forms.Menu is an abstract class, and therefore you cannot create a direct instance of this type. Rather, you create instances of one (or more) of the derived types. The Menu class defines basic menu-centric behaviors such as providing access to an individual menu item, cloning menus, merging menus (for MDI applications), and so forth. Figure 8-22 shows the relationship between these core types.

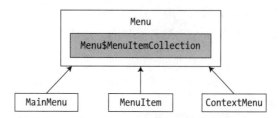

Figure 8-22. The Windows.Form's menu hierarchy

Note that the Menu class defines a nested class named MenuItemCollection, which is inherited by the MainMenu, MenuItem, and ContextMenu subclasses. As you would expect, this collection holds onto a set of related menu items, which is accessed using the Menu.MenuItems property (more details in a moment). The Menu base class defines the core members shown in Table 8-17.

Table 8-17. Members of the Menu Type

MENU MEMBER	MEANING IN LIFE
Handle	This property provides access to the HMENU handle that represents this Menu.
IsParent	This property specifies whether this menu contains any items, or is the top-most item.
MdiListItem	This property returns the MenuItem that contains the list of MDI child windows.
MenuItems	Another property. Returns an instance of the nested Menu.MenuItemCollection type, which represents the submenus owned by the Menu derived class.
GetMainMenu()	Returns the MainMenu item that contains this menu.
MergeMenu()	Merges another menu's items with this one's as specified by their mergeType and mergeOrder properties. Used to merge an MDI container's menu with that of its active MDI child.
CloneMenu()	Sets this menu to be an identical (deep) copy of another menu.

Menu$MenuItemCollection Type

Perhaps the most immediately important member of the Menu class is the MenuItems property, which returns an instance of the nested

Menu$MenuItemCollection type. Recall that nested classes can be helpful when you wish to establish a logical relationship between related types. Here, the Menu$MenuItemCollection type represents the set of all submenus owned by a Menu derived object.

For example, if you created a MainMenu to represent the top-most "File" menu, you would add MenuItems (for example, Open, Save, Close, Save As) into the collection. As you would expect, Menu$MenuItemCollection defines members to add and remove MenuItem types, obtain the current count of MenuItems, as well access a particular member in the collection. Table 8-18 lists some (but not all) of the core members.

Table 8-18. The Nested MenuItemCollection Type

MENU$MENUITEMCOLLECTION

MEMBER	MEANING IN LIFE
Count	Returns the number of MenuItems in the collection.
Add() AddRange() Remove()	Inserts (or removes) a new MenuItem into the collection. Be aware that the Add() method has been overloaded numerous times to allow you to specify shortcut keys, delegates, and whatnot. AddRange() is helpful in that it allows you to add an array of MenuItems in a single call.
Clear()	Removes all items from the collection.
Contains()	Used to determine if a given MenuItem is inside the collection.

Building Your Menu System

Now that you understand the functionality of the abstract Menu class (and the nested MenuItemCollection type), you can build your simple File menu. The process begins by creating a MainMenu object. The MainMenu class represents the collection of top-most menu items (e.g., File, Edit, View, Tools, Help, and so forth). Thus:

```
public class MainForm : Form
{
    // The Form's main menu.
    private MainMenu mainMenu;

    public MainForm()
```

```
        {
            // Create the main menu.
            mainMenu = new MainMenu();
        }
    ...
}
```

Once you have created a MainMenu object, you are able to make use of Menu$MenuItemCollection.Add() to insert the top-most item (the "File" menu). Menu$MenuItemCollection.Add() returns a new MenuItem class that represents the newly inserted File menu.

To insert the subitems (e.g., Exit), you insert additional MenuItems into the Menu$MenuItemCollection maintained by the File MenuItem. Finally, when you are finished constructing your menu system, attach it to the owning Form using (of course) the Menu property:

```
public class MainForm : Form
{
    // The Form's main menu.
    private MainMenu mainMenu;

    public MainForm()
    {
        // Create the main menu.
        mainMenu = new MainMenu();

        // Create the 'File' Menu and add it to the MenuItemCollection.
        MenuItem miFile = mainMenu.MenuItems.Add("&File");

        // Now make the Exit submenu and add it to the File Menu.
        // This version of Add() takes:
        // 1) A new MenuItem.
        // 2) A new delegate (EventHandler).
        // 3) An optional shortcut key.
        miFile.MenuItems.Add(new MenuItem("E&xit",
                            new EventHandler(this.FileExit_Clicked),
                            Shortcut.CtrlX));

        // Attach main menu to the Form object.
        this.Menu = mainMenu;

    }
    ...
}
```

Notice that if you embed an ampersand within the string name of a menu item, this marks which letter should be underlined to designate the ALT key access combination. Thus, when you specify "&File", you allow the end user to activate the File menu by selecting "ALT+F."

When you added the Exit submenu item, you specified an optional shortcut flag. The System.Windows.Forms.Shortcut enumeration is fully detailed in online Help. As you might guess, this enumeration provides fields that specify traditional shortcut keys (CTRL+C, CTRL+V, F1, F2, INS) as well as more exotic combinations.

Here then, is the current code behind the simple menu application. Just for kicks, notice how you are able to set the BackColor property of the Form using the MainMenu.GetForm() member:

```
// The Simple Menu Application.
public class MainForm : Form
{
    // The Form's main menu.
    private MainMenu mainMenu;

    // Run the application.
    [STAThread]
    public static void Main(string[] args)
    {
        Application.Run(new MainForm());
    }

    // Construct the form.
    public MainForm()
    {
        // Configure the initial look and feel of this form.
        Text = "Simple Menu";
        CenterToScreen();

        // First make the main menu object.
        mainMenu = new MainMenu();

        // Create the 'File | Exit' Menu.
        MenuItem miFile = mainMenu.MenuItems.Add("&File");
        miFile.MenuItems.Add(new MenuItem("&Exit",
                             new EventHandler(this.FileExit_Clicked),
                             Shortcut.CtrlX));

        // Attach main menu to the Form object.
        this.Menu = mainMenu;
```

```
        // MainMenu.GetForm() returns a reference to the owning Form.
        // To illustrate. . .
        mainMenu.GetForm().BackColor = Color.Black;
    }


    // File | Exit Menu item handler
    private void FileExit_Clicked(object sender, EventArgs e)
    {
        this.Close();      // Just close the application. . .
    }
}
```

Adding Another Top-Most Menu Item

Now, what if you wish to add another top-most menu named "Help" which contains a single subitem named "About" (Figure 8-23)?

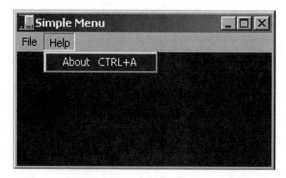

Figure 8-23. Extending our menu system

The code models the "File | Exit" menu logic almost exactly: Begin by adding a new MenuItem to the MainMenu object ("Help"). From here, add a new subitem ("About"):

```
public class MainForm : Form
{
    private MainMenu mainMenu;
. . .
    public MainForm()
```

```
    {
        // Create the 'File | Exit' Menu.
        MenuItem miFile = mainMenu.MenuItems.Add("&File");
        miFile.MenuItems.Add(new MenuItem("E&xit",
            new EventHandler(this.FileExit_Clicked),
            Shortcut.CtrlX));

        // Now create a 'Help | About' menu.
        MenuItem miHelp = mainMenu.MenuItems.Add("Help");
        miHelp.MenuItems.Add(new MenuItem("&About",
            new EventHandler(this.HelpAbout_Clicked),
            Shortcut.CtrlA));
        . . .
    }
    // Help | About Menu handler
    private void HelpAbout_Clicked(object sender, EventArgs e)
    {
        MessageBox.Show("The amazing menu app. . .");
    }
}
```

SOURCE CODE   *The SimpleMenu application is located under the Chapter 8 sub-directory.*

Creating a Pop-Up Menu

Let's now examine the process of building a context-sensitive pop-up (i.e., right-click) menu. The ContextMenu class represents the pop-up menu itself. Like the process of building a MainMenu, your goal is to add individual MenuItems to the MenuItemCollection to represent the possible selectable subitems. The following class makes use of a pop-up menu to allow the user to configure the font size of a string rendered to the client area:

```
namespace MainForm
{
    // Helper struct for font size.
    internal struct TheFontSize
    {
        public static int Huge = 30;
        public static int Normal = 20;
        public static int Tiny = 8;
    }
```

```csharp
public class MainForm : Form
{
    // Current size of font.
    private int currFontSize = TheFontSize.Normal;

    // The Form's popup menu.
    private ContextMenu popUpMenu;

    public static void Main(string[] args)
    {
        Application.Run(new MainForm());
    }

    private void MainForm_Resize(object sender, System.EventArgs e)
    {
        Invalidate();
    }


    public MainForm()
    {
        // First make the context menu.
        popUpMenu = new ContextMenu();

        // Now add the subitems & attach context menu.
        popUpMenu.MenuItems.Add("Huge",
            new EventHandler(PopUp_Clicked));
        popUpMenu.MenuItems.Add("Normal",
            new EventHandler(PopUp_Clicked));
        popUpMenu.MenuItems.Add("Tiny",
            new EventHandler(PopUp_Clicked));

        this.ContextMenu = popUpMenu;

        // Handle events.
        this.Resize += new System.EventHandler(this.MainForm_Resize);
        this.Paint += new PaintEventHandler(this.MainForm_Paint);
    }

    // PopUp_Clicked | X Menu item handler
    private void PopUp_Clicked(object sender, EventArgs e)
```

```
        {
                // Figure out the string name of the selected item.
                MenuItem miClicked = (MenuItem)sender;
                string item = miClicked.Text;

                if(item = = "Huge")
                        currFontSize = TheFontSize.Huge;
                if(item = = "Normal")
                        currFontSize = TheFontSize.Normal;
                if(item = = "Tiny")
                        currFontSize = TheFontSize.Tiny;
                Invalidate();
        }

        private void MainForm_Paint(object sender, PaintEventArgs e)
        {
                Graphics g = e.Graphics;
                g.DrawString("Please click on me. . .",
                        new Font("Times New Roman", (float)currFontSize),
                        new SolidBrush(Color.Black),
                        this.DisplayRectangle);
        }
    }
}
```

Notice that as you add the subitems to the ContextMenu, you have assigned the *same* event handler to each. When a given item is clicked, the flow of logic brings us to the PopUp_Clicked() method. Using the "sender" argument, you are able to determine the name of the MenuItem (i.e., the text string it has been assigned) and take an appropriate course of action (which works just fine, assuming you are not interested in localizing the application):

```
// PopUp_Clicked | X Menu item handler
private void PopUp_Clicked(object sender, EventArgs e)
{
        // Figure out the string name of the selected item.
        MenuItem miClicked = (MenuItem)sender;
        string item = miClicked.Text;

        if(item = = "Huge")
                currFontSize = TheFontSize.Huge;
        if(item = = "Normal")
                currFontSize = TheFontSize.Normal;
```

```
        if(item = = "Tiny")
            currFontSize = TheFontSize.Tiny;

        // Now redraw the client area with the new font size. . .
        Invalidate();
    }
```

Also notice that once you have created a ContextMenu, you associate it to the Form using the Control.ContextMenu property. Be aware that *any* control can be assigned a context menu. For example, you could create a Button object on a dialog box that responds to a particular context menu. In this way, the menu would only be displayed if the mouse button were clicked while within the bounding rectangle of the button.

Adorning Your Menu System

The MenuItem class also defines a number of members that allow you to check, enable, and hide a given menu item. Table 8-19 gives a rundown of some of the interesting properties of MenuItem.

Table 8-19. More Details of the MenuItem Type

MENUITEM MEMBER	MEANING IN LIFE
Checked	Gets or sets a value indicating whether a check mark appears beside the text of the menu item.
DefaultItem	Gets or sets a value indicating whether the menu item is the default.
Enabled	Gets or sets a value indicating whether the menu item is enabled.
Index	Gets or sets the menu item's position in its parent menu.
MergeOrder	Gets or sets the relative position of the menu item when its menu is merged with another.
MergeType	Gets or sets a value that indicates the behavior of this menu item when its menu is merged with another.
OwnerDraw	Gets or sets a value indicating whether code that you provide draws the menu item or Windows draws the menu item.
RadioCheck	Gets or sets a value that indicates whether the menu item, if checked, displays a radio-button mark instead of a check mark.
Shortcut	Gets or sets the shortcut key associated with the menu item.
ShowShortcut	Gets or sets a value that indicates whether the shortcut key that is associated with the menu item is displayed next to the menu item caption.
Text	Gets or sets the text of the menu item.

To illustrate, let's extend the previous pop-up menu to display a check mark next to the currently selected menu item. Setting a check mark on a given menu item is not at all difficult (just set the Checked property to true). However, tracking which menu item should be checked does require some additional logic. One possible approach is to define distinct MenuItem objects to track each submenu item and an additional MenuItem that represents the currently selected item:

```
public class MainForm : Form
{
    // Current size of font.
    private int currFontSize = TheFontSize.Normal;

    // The Form's popup menu.
    private ContextMenu popUpMenu;

    // Used to keep track of the current checked item.
    private MenuItem currentCheckedItem;      // Marks the item checked.
    private MenuItem checkedHuge;
    private MenuItem checkedNormal;
    private MenuItem checkedTiny;
...
}
```

The next step is to associate each of these MenuItems to the correct submenu. Thus, you would update the constructor as follows:

```
// Construct the form.
public MainForm()
{
    // Configure the initial look and feel of this form.
    Text = "PopUp Menu";
    CenterToScreen();

    // First make the context menu.
    popUpMenu = new ContextMenu();

    // Now add the subitems.
    popUpMenu.MenuItems.Add("Huge", new EventHandler(PopUp_Clicked));
    popUpMenu.MenuItems.Add("Normal", new EventHandler(PopUp_Clicked));
    popUpMenu.MenuItems.Add("Tiny", new EventHandler(PopUp_Clicked));

    this.ContextMenu = popUpMenu;
```

```
// Set each MenuItem to the correct submenu.
checkedHuge = this.ContextMenu.MenuItems[0];
checkedNormal = this.ContextMenu.MenuItems[1];
checkedTiny = this.ContextMenu.MenuItems[2];

// Now check the 'Normal' menu item.
currentCheckedItem = checkedNormal;
currentCheckedItem.Checked = true;
}
```

At this point, you have a way to programmatically identify each subitem, as well as the currently checked item (which has been initially set to checkedNormal). The last step is to update the PopUp_Clicked() event handler, in order to check the correct MenuItem in response to the user selection (see Figure 8-24 for a test run):

```
private void PopUp_Clicked(object sender, EventArgs e)
{
    // Uncheck the currently checked item.
    currentCheckedItem.Checked = false;

    // Figure out the string name of the selected item.
    MenuItem miClicked = (MenuItem)sender;
    string item = miClicked.Text;

    // Based on selection, establish the current checked menu item.
    if(item = = "Huge")
    {
        currFontSize = TheFontSize.Huge;
        currentCheckedItem = checkedHuge;
    }
    if(item = = "Normal")
    {
        currFontSize = TheFontSize.Normal;
        currentCheckedItem = checkedNormal;
    }
    if(item = = "Tiny")
    {
        currFontSize = TheFontSize.Tiny;
        currentCheckedItem = checkedTiny;
    }

    // Now check it.
    currentCheckedItem.Checked = true;
    Invalidate();
}
```

Figure 8-24. Checking menu items

SOURCE CODE   *The PopUpMenu project is contained under the Chapter 8 sub-directory.*

Building a Menu Using Visual Studio.NET

Indeed, knowledge is power. On the other hand, now that you understand how you can write raw C# code to create and configure a menu system, let's examine how Visual Studio.NET can offer some design-time assistance. To begin, assume that you have created a new C# Windows Application project workspace. Using the Toolbox window, double-click the MainMenu icon (Figure 8-25).

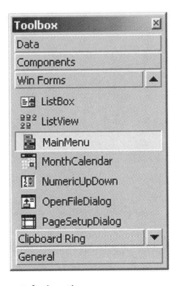

Figure 8-25. Adding menus at design time

Once you do, you see a new icon appear at the icon tray of the design-time template. Furthermore, you see a design-time representation of your menu attached to the top of your Form. To add new menu items, simply double-click a slot and type away! Consider Figure 8-26.

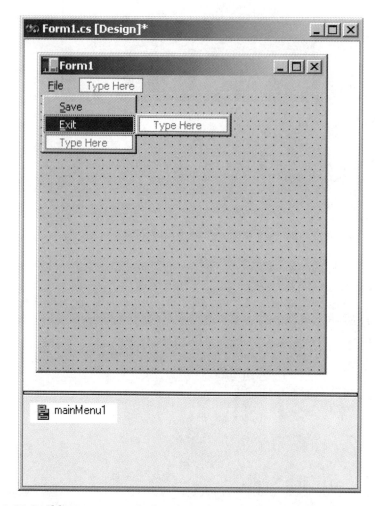

Figure 8-26. Building menus at design time

As far as handling events for a given item (as well as configuring a number of other properties), make use of the Visual Studio.NET Properties window (Figure 8-27).

Once you enter the name of our event handler, the Visual Studio.NET IDE automatically generates stub code for the event handler:

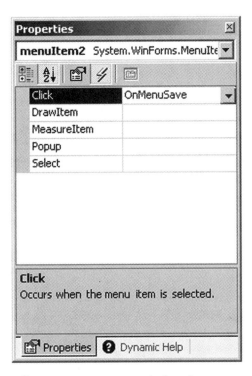

Figure 8-27. Responding to menu events at design time

```
protected void OnMenuSave (object sender, System.EventArgs e)
{
    // Respond to Save selection. . .
}
```

Be aware, that as you modify your menus at design time, the IDE is updating the InitializeComponent() helper function, as well as adding member variables to represent the types you are manipulating at design time. If you examine the code, things (I hope) look very familiar.

Understanding Status Bars

In addition to a menu system, many Forms also maintain a status bar. Status bars may be divided into any number of "panes". Panes hold some textual (or graphical) information such as menu help strings, or other application specific information. The StatusBar type derives directly from System.Windows.Forms.Control. In addition to the inherited members, StatusBar defines the core properties shown in Table 8-20.

Table 8-20. Select StatusBar Properties

STATUSBAR PROPERTY	MEANING IN LIFE
BackgroundImage	Gets or sets the image rendered on the background of the StatusBar control.
Font	Gets or sets the font the StatusBar control will use to display information.
ForeColor	Gets or sets the foreground color of the control.
Panels	Returns a nested StatusBarPanelCollection type that contains each Panel maintained by the StatusBar (much like the menu pattern).
ShowPanels	Gets or sets a value indicating whether panels should be shown.
SizingGrip	Gets or sets a value indicating whether a sizing grip will be rendered on the corner of the StatusBar control.

Once you create a StatusBar, your next task is to add any number of panels (represented by the StatusBarPanel class) into the nested StatusBar$StatusBarPanelCollection. Be aware that the constructor of StatusBarPanel automatically configures the new panel with a default look and feel (therefore, if you are happy with this initial configuration, your programming task is made even simpler). Table 8-21 lists of the core members of the StatusBarPanel type (and default values).

Table 8-21. Properties of the StatusBarPanel Type

STATUSBARPANEL PROPERTY	MEANING IN LIFE
Alignment	Determines the alignment of text in the pane. The default value is HorizontalAlignment.Left
AutoSize	Determines if this pane should automatically resize (and how). Default value is StatusBarPanelAutoSize.None
BorderStyle	Configures border style. Default value is StatusBarPanelBorderStyle.Sunken
Icon	Is there an icon in the pane? A null reference is the default (e.g., no icon).
MinWidth	Default is 10.
Style	What does this pane contain? Default is StatusBarPanelStyle.Text, but there may be other types as specified by the StatusBarPanelStyle enumeration.
Text	Caption of pane. The default is an empty string.
ToolTipText	Any tool-tip? An empty string is the default.
Width	Default is 100.

Building a Status Bar

To illustrate, let's construct a StatusBar object that will be divided into two panes. The first pane will be used to show helpful prompts describing the functionality of each menu selection. The second pane will display the current system time. And let's place a small icon on the extreme left-hand side of the first pane (just to keep things interesting). Check out Figure 8-28.

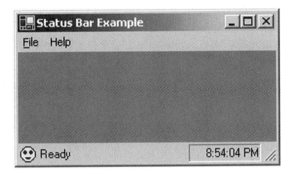

Figure 8-28. Your simple status bar

Assume you have updated the SimpleMenu application created earlier in this chapter, to support this status bar. Like any Control derived type, the StatusBar needs to be added to the Form's Controls collection (more on this collection in Chapter 10). As you might guess, this collection contains an entry for any GUI widget mounted on the client area, including StatusBars types. Here is the status bar logic:

```
public class MainForm : Form
{
    // Member data for the status bar, and each pane.
    private StatusBar statusBar = new StatusBar();
    private StatusBarPanel sbPnlPrompt = new StatusBarPanel();
    private StatusBarPanel sbPnlTime = new StatusBarPanel();

    public MainForm ()
    {
        . . .
        BuildStatBar();        // Do all the status bar stuff...
    }
```

```csharp
private void BuildStatBar()
{
    // Configure the status bar.
    statusBar.ShowPanels = true;
    statusBar.Size = new System.Drawing.Size(212, 20);
    statusBar.Location = new System.Drawing.Point(0, 216);

    // AddRange() allows you to add a set of panes at once.
    statusBar.Panels.AddRange(new StatusBarPanel[]
        {sbPnlPrompt, sbPnlTime});

    // Configure prompt panel.
    sbPnlPrompt.BorderStyle = StatusBarPanelBorderStyle.None;
    sbPnlPrompt.AutoSize = StatusBarPanelAutoSize.Spring;
    sbPnlPrompt.Width = 62;
    sbPnlPrompt.Text = "Ready";

    // Configure time pane.
    sbPnlTime.Alignment = HorizontalAlignment.Right;
    sbPnlTime.Width = 76;

    // Add an icon (more details in Chapter 9).
    try
    {   // This icon must be in the same app directory.
        // Chapter 9 will illustrate how to embed
        // resources into your assembly!
        Icon i = new Icon("status.ico");
        sbPnlPrompt.Icon = i;
    }
    catch(Exception e)
    {
        MessageBox.Show(e.Message);
    }

    // Now add this new status bar to the Form's Controls collection.
    this.Controls.Add(statusBar);
}
}
```

Working with the Timer Type

Recall that the second pane should display the current time. The first step to take to achieve this design goal is to add a Timer member variable to the Form. If you have a Visual Basic background, you should understand this object quite well. C++ programmers also understand the notion of timers given the WM_TIMER message. Regardless of your background, a Windows Forms Timer object is simply a type that calls some method (specified by the Tick event) at a given interval (specified by the Interval property). Table 8-22 lists some core members.

Table 8-22. The Timer Type

TIMER MEMBER	MEANING IN LIFE
Enabled	This property enables or disables the Timer's ability to fire the Tick event. You may also use Start() and Stop() to achieve the same effect.
Interval	Sets the number of milliseconds between ticks.
Start() Stop()	Like the Enabled property, these methods control the firing of the Tick event.
OnTick()	This member may be overridden in a custom class deriving from Timer.
Tick	The Tick event adds a new event handler to the underlying MulticastDelegate.

Thus, you can update our class as follows:

```
public class MainForm : Form
{
. . .
    private Timer timer1 = new Timer();

    public MainForm ()
    {
        // Configure the timer.
        timer1.Interval = 1000;
        timer1.Enabled = true;
        timer1.Tick += new EventHandler(timer1_Tick);

        . . .
    }
```

```
// This method will be called (roughly) every second.
private void timer1_Tick(object sender, EventArgs e)
{
    DateTime t = DateTime.Now;
    string s = t.ToLongTimeString();

    // Change text of pane to current time.
    sbPnlTime.Text = s ;
}
}
```

Notice that the Timer event handler makes use of the DateTime type. Here, you simply find the current system time using the Now property, and use it to set the Text property of the correct StatusBarPanel object.

Displaying Menu Selection Prompts

Finally, you must configure the first pane to hold menu help strings. As you know, most applications send a small bit of text information to the first pane of a status bar whenever the end user selects a menu item (e.g., "This terminates the application").

Assume the menu system for this application is identical to the Simple Menu application. This time however, you need to respond to the Select event of each subitem. When the user selects "File | Exit" or "Help | About" you tell the first StatusBarPanel object to display a given text message. You also handle the MenuComplete event, to ensure that when the user has finished manipulating the menu, place a default message in the first pane of the status bar. Here is the update:

```
public class MainForm: Form
{
    . . .
    public MainForm ()
    {
        . . .
        // The MenuComplete event is sent when the user clicks off
        // the menu. We want to capture this event in order to
        // set the text of the first pane to "Ready". If we did not,
        // the StatusBarPanel text would always be based on the last menu
        // selected!
        this.MenuComplete += new EventHandler(StatusForm_MenuDone);
        BuildMenuSystem();
    }
```

```csharp
private void FileExit_Selected(object sender, EventArgs e)
{
    sbPnlPrompt.Text = "Terminates this app";
}


private void HelpAbout_Selected(object sender, EventArgs e)
{
    sbPnlPrompt.Text = "Displays app info";
}


private void StatusForm_MenuDone(object sender, EventArgs e)
{
    sbPnlPrompt.Text = "Ready";            // See big comment in ctor...
}


// Helper functions.
private void BuildMenuSystem()
{
    // First make the main menu.
    mainMenu = new MainMenu();

    // Create the 'File' Menu.
    MenuItem miFile = mainMenu.MenuItems.Add("&File");
    miFile.MenuItems.Add(new MenuItem("E&xit",
                        new EventHandler(this.FileExit_Clicked),
                        Shortcut.CtrlX));

    // Handle the Select event for the Exit menu item.
    miFile.MenuItems[0].Select += new EventHandler(FileExit_Selected);

    // Now create a 'Help | About' menu.
    MenuItem miHelp = mainMenu.MenuItems.Add("Help");
    miHelp.MenuItems.Add(new MenuItem("&About",
                        new EventHandler(this.HelpAbout_Clicked),
                        Shortcut.CtrlA));

    // Handle the Select event for the About menu item.
    miHelp.MenuItems[0].Select +=
            new EventHandler(HelpAbout_Selected);

    // Attach main menu to the Form object.
    this.Menu = mainMenu;
}
...
}
```

Excellent! As you may guess, the Visual Studio IDE also provides some design-time assistance to facilitate the building of status bar objects. In just a bit, you examine how to build a toolbar using tools provided by the IDE. Once you understand this process, you should have no problems designing status bars using the design-time tools.

SOURCE CODE   *The StatusBar project is included under the Chapter 8 sub-directory.*

Building a Tool Bar

The final Form level GUI item to examine in this chapter is the ToolBar type. As you know, tool bars typically provide an alternate means to activate a given menu item. Thus, if the user would rather click a Save button, this has the same effect as selecting "File | Save." In the Windows Forms namespace, a handful of types are defined to allow you to build such a beast. Let's start with the ToolBar class itself. Note the core properties as seen in Table 8-23.

Table 8-23. Properties of the ToolBar Type

TOOLBAR PROPERTY	MEANING IN LIFE
BorderStyle	The kind of border around this control, as specified by the BorderStyle enumeration.
Buttons	The collection of buttons belonging to the toolbar (e.g., ToolBar$ToolBarButtonCollection).
ButtonSize	Determines the size of a button in the ToolBar.
ImageList	Returns the ImageList control that maintains the images for this ToolBar.
ImageSize	The method to return the size of the images within the toolbar's image list.
ShowToolTips	Indicates whether or not the ToolBar will show tool tips for each button.
Wrappable	ToolBar buttons can optionally "wrap" to the next line when the ToolBar becomes too narrow to include all buttons on the same line.

When a Form maintains a ToolBar (or two), the goal is to create some number of individual ToolBarButton objects and add them to the ToolBar$ToolBarButtonCollection type. Each button may contain text, images, or both. To keep things simple, let's build a toolbar containing two buttons displaying text prompts only. Table 8-24 presents some important members of the ToolBarButton .

Table 8-24. Properties of the ToolBarButton Type

TOOLBARBUTTON PROPERTY	MEANING IN LIFE
DropDownMenu	ToolBarButtons can optionally specify a pop-up menu that is shown whenever the drop-down button is pressed. This property lets you control just which menu is shown. Note that this is only shown if the Style property is set to DropDownButton.
ImageIndex	Returns the index of the image that this ToolBarButton is using. The index comes from the parent ToolBar's ImageList
Style	Returns the style of the ToolBar button. This will form the ToolBarButtonStyle enumeration.
Text	The caption that will be displayed in this ToolBar button.
ToolTipText	If the parent ToolBar has the ShowToolTips property turned on, then this property describes the text that will be displayed for this button
Visible	Indicates whether the button is visible or not. If the button is not visible, it will not be shown and will be unable to receive user input

Your custom toolbar will contain two buttons, echoing the behavior supplied by the Save and Exit menu items. Here is the code update:

```
public class MainForm: Form
{
    // State data for the toolbar and two buttons.
    private ToolBarButton tbSaveButton = new ToolBarButton();
    private ToolBarButton tbExitButton = new ToolBarButton();
    private ToolBar toolBar = new ToolBar();

    public MainForm()
    {
        . . .
        BuildToolBar();      // Helper function.
    }

    . . .
```

```
        private void BuildToolBar()
        {
            // Configure each button.
            tbSaveButton.Text = "Save";
            tbSaveButton.ToolTipText = "Save";
            tbExitButton.Text = "Exit";
            tbExitButton.ToolTipText = "Exit";

            // Configure ToolBar and add buttons.
            toolBar.BorderStyle = System.Windows.Forms.BorderStyle.Fixed3D;
            toolBar.ShowToolTips = true;
            toolBar.Buttons.AddRange( new ToolBarButton[]
                                {tbSaveButton, tbExitButton});
            toolBar.ButtonClick += new
                ToolBarButtonClickEventHandler(ToolBar_Clicked));

            // Add the new bar to the Controls collection.
            this.Controls.Add(toolBar);
        }


        // Button click handler.
        private void ToolBar_Clicked(object sender, ToolBarButtonClickEventArgs e)
        {
            MessageBox.Show(e.Button.ToolTipText);
        }
    }
```

Figure 8-29 shows a test run.

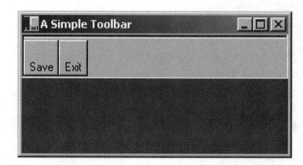

Figure 8-29. A very simple ToolBar

Bland, huh? We will add some images in just a moment, but first let's analyze some code. The BuildToolBar() helper function begins by configuring some basic properties for each ToolBarButton. Next, add them to the ToolBar collection using the AddRange() method (rather than calling Add() multiple times). To handle the click events for a given button, you must handle the ButtonClick event.

```
toolBar.ButtonClick += new ToolBarButtonClickEventHandler(ToolBar_Clicked);
```

The name of the new ToolBarButtonClickEventHandler delegate must have a signature such that the second parameter is of type ToolBarButtonClickEventArgs. This type may be examined to determine which button sent the event, using the Button property:

```
private void ToolBar_Clicked(object sender, ToolBarButtonClickEventArgs e)
{
    // Just show the corresponding tool bar text.
    MessageBox.Show(e.Button.ToolTipText);
}
```

Adding Images to Your Toolbar Buttons

Real Toolbar buttons contain images. When you wish to configure your buttons to do so, the first step is to have the Form create an ImageList type. This class represents a set of images that are consumed by some other type (like a ToolBar). If you have ever created a toolbar using Visual Basic 6.0, you should feel right at home with this aspect of Windows Forms. Let's update your existing ToolBarForm to make use of two icons for display purposes, in addition to simple text strings. Here is the relevant update:

```
public class MainForm: Form
{
    // Contains the images used by the toolbar.
    private ImageList toolBarIcons = new ImageList();
    ...
    private void BuildToolBar()
    {
        // Configure save button.
        tbSaveButton.ImageIndex = 0;
        tbSaveButton.ToolTipText = "Save";

        // Configure exit button.
        tbExitButton.ImageIndex = 1;
        tbExitButton.ToolTipText = "Exit";
```

```
                    // Create ToolBar and add buttons.
                    toolBar.ImageList = toolBarIcons;
                    . . .
                    // Load images (again, the icons need to be in the app dir).
                    toolBarIcons.ImageSize = new System.Drawing.Size(32, 32);
                    toolBarIcons.Images.Add(new Icon("filesave.ico"));
                    toolBarIcons.Images.Add(new Icon("fileexit.ico"));
                    toolBarIcons.ColorDepth = ColorDepth.Depth16Bit;
                    toolBarIcons.TransparentColor = System.Drawing.Color.Transparent;

                    . . .
              }
        }
```

Notice the following points:

- We must tell each ToolBarButton which image to use, via the ImageIndex property.

- We add new images to the ImageList class using the Images.Add() method.

- The ToolBar itself must be told which ImageList it is associated to using the ImageList property.

If you were to now run the application (Figure 8-30), you would see a much more pleasing end result (if you wish these buttons to look more standard, simply adjust the size to 16 x 16):

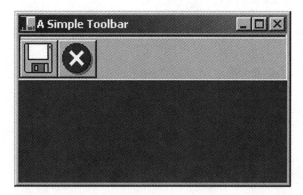

Figure 8-30. A more interesting ToolBar

SOURCE CODE   *The SimpleToolBar project is included under the Chapter 8 subdirectory.*

Building ToolBars at Design Time

Design-time configuration of the ToolBar is accomplished using the Properties Window. For example, if you wish to add buttons to the ToolBar type, double-click the Buttons property (Figure 8-31).

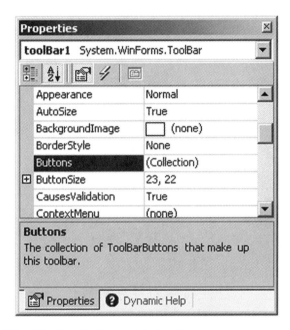

Figure 8-31. Adding ToolBar buttons at design time

This opens a dialog that allows you to add, remove, and configure the individual ToolBarButton items (Figure 8-32).

Adding an ImageList at Design Time

Notice how this same dialog also allows you to assign an iconic image to each button using the ImageIndex property. However, this property is useless until you add an ImageList type to your current project. To add an ImageList member to a Form at design time, return to the Toolbox window and select the icon (see Figure 8-33).

At this point, you can use the Properties window to add the individual images using the Images property (Figure 8-34).

Once you have added each image file to the ImageList, inform the ToolBar which ImageList it is to make use of using the Properties window (Figure 8-35).

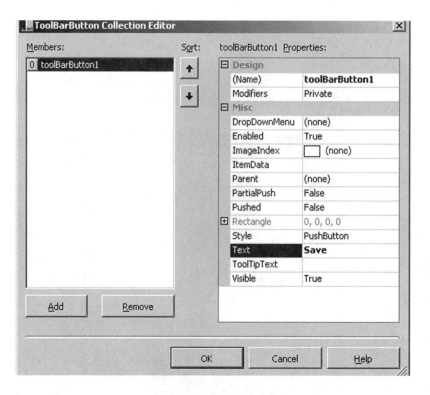

Figure 8-32. Configuring Button types at design time

Figure 8-33. Adding an ImageList

Figure 8-34. Adding Images to your ImageList

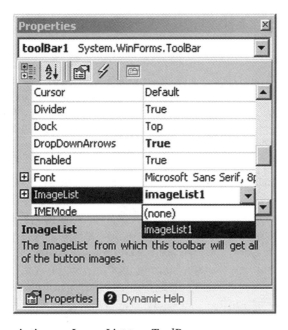

Figure 8-35. Associating an ImageList to a ToolBar

At this point, let's return to the ToolBar button editor and map a given image in the ImageList to each button (Figure 8-36).

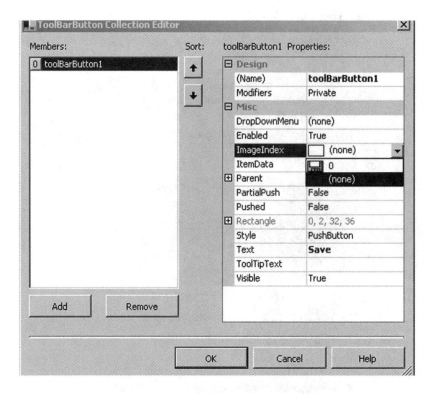

Figure 8-36. Mapping images to buttons

Cool! Now that you understand how to make use of the Visual Studio.NET IDE to configure a ToolBar type, I assume you will continue to explore similar design-time configurations. For example, using (more or less) the same process, you can design a fully functional status bar with minimal coding on your part.

A Minimal and Complete Windows Forms Application

At this point you can build a Form that hosts a main menu, a pop-up menu, a status bar and toolbar. This chapter wraps up by rounding out your current understanding of Windows Forms basics by building a final application that pulls together the information you have learned thus far.

Let's extend the functionality of the StatusBar application created previously. In addition to the existing logic, let's add code to read and write our application data to (and from) the system registry as well as to illustrate how to interact with the Windows 2000 event log.

First, let's create a new top-most menu item ("Background Color") that allows the user to select the background color of the client area from a set of possible choices. Each color submenu has an associated help string to be displayed in the first pane of the StatusBar object. The Clicked event for each Color subitem is handled by the *same* event handler (ColorItem_Clicked). Likewise, the Selected event for each subitem is handled by a method named ColorItem_Selected. Here is the code update:

```
private void BuildMenuSystem()
{
. . .
    // Create the 'Background Color' menu.
    MenuItem miColor = mainMenu.MenuItems.Add("&Background Color");
    miColor.MenuItems.Add("&DarkGoldenrod",
                new EventHandler(ColorItem_Clicked));
    miColor.MenuItems.Add("&GreenYellow",
                new EventHandler(ColorItem_Clicked));
    miColor.MenuItems.Add("&MistyRose",
                new EventHandler(ColorItem_Clicked));
    miColor.MenuItems.Add("&Crimson",
                new EventHandler(ColorItem_Clicked));
    miColor.MenuItems.Add("&LemonChiffon",
                new EventHandler(ColorItem_Clicked));
    miColor.MenuItems.Add("&OldLace",
                new EventHandler(ColorItem_Clicked));

    // All color menu items have the same Selected event handler.
    for(int i = 0; i < miColor.MenuItems.Count; i++)
        miColor.MenuItems[i].Select +=
            new EventHandler(ColorMenuItem_Selected);
. . .
}
```

When the end user selects a given subitem from the Background Color menu, the Select event occurs. In the event handler, your task is to extract the text name of the selected menu item (e.g., OldLace, GreenYellow, etc.) and display it on your status bar. Here is the code:

```
private void ColorMenuItem_Selected(object sender, EventArgs e)
{
    // Figure out the string name of the selected item and strip '&'.
    MenuItem miClicked = (MenuItem)sender;
    string item = miClicked.Text.Remove(0,1);

    // Assume a new data point: StatusBarPanel sbPnlPrompt.
    sbPnlPrompt.Text = "Select " + item;
}
```

When the user clicks a given color menu item, you simply set the Form's BackColor based on the MenuItem's Text property. Notice that we are "remembering" this color by storing the value in a string member variable named currColor:

```
// Color | X Menu item handler.
private void ColorItem_Clicked(object sender, EventArgs e)
{
        // Figure out the string name of the color menu item.
        MenuItem miClicked = (MenuItem)sender;

        // Remove the '&' from the text in the menu item.
        string color = miClicked.Text.Remove(0,1);

        // Now set the color.
        this.BackColor = Color.FromName(color);
        currColor = BackColor;
}
```

So far so good. As you can tell, this is just basic menu logic. Next, let's save the user preferences in the system registry!

Interacting with the System Registry

If you are a COM programmer by trade, there is no escaping the (pain of the) Window's registry. When living in the world of .NET, your reliance on the system registry dwindles away to little more than a convenient place to store user preferences. The Microsoft.Win32 namespace defines a handful of types that make reading from (and writing to) the system registry a piece of cake (Table 8-25).

Table 8-25. Registry Manipulation Types

MICROSOFT.WIN32 TYPE	MEANING IN LIFE
Registry	A high-level abstraction of the registry itself, and all associated hives.
RegistryKey	This is the core type, which allows you to insert, remove and update information stored in the registry.
RegistryHive	A simple enumeration of each hive in the registry.

The goal of the current application is to allow end users to save their preferences (e.g., font size and background color) to the registry for later use. To do so, you must make use of the RegistryKey class, which provides the core members shown in Table 8-26.

Table 8-26. Properties of the RegistryKey Type

REGISTRYKEY MEMBERS	MEANING IN LIFE
Name	This property retrieves the name of the key.
SubKeyCount	This property retrieves the count of subkeys.
ValueCount	This property retrieves the count of values in the key.
Close()	Closes this key and flushes it to disk if the contents have been modified.
CreateSubKey()	Creates a new subkey or opens an existing subkey. The string subKey is not case sensitive.
DeleteSubKey()	Deletes the specified subkey. To delete child subkeys, use DeleteSubKeyTree. The string subKey is not case sensitive.
DeleteSubKeyTree()	Recursively deletes a subkey and any child subkeys. The string subKey is not case sensitive.
GetSubKeyNames()	Retrieves an array of strings containing all the subkey names.
GetValue()	Overloaded. Retrieves the specified value.
GetValueNames()	Retrieves an array of strings containing all the value names.
OpenRemoteBaseKey()	Opens a new RegistryKey that represents the requested key on a foreign machine.
OpenSubKey()	Overloaded. Retrieves a subkey.
SetValue()	Sets the specified value. The string SubKey is not case sensitive.

Assume you have added a new "File | Save" menu item. When this is selected you will create a RegistryKey object and insert the current background color and font size under HKEY_CURRENT_USER\Software\Intertech\Chapter8App. Also assume your Form has two member variables (currFontSize and currColor) to hold the current font size as well as the current background color. Here is the relevant code (note the use of RegistryKey.SetValue()):

```
// Assume the following state data.
// Color currColor = Color.MistyRose;
// private int currFontSize = TheFontSize.Normal;

private void FileSave_Clicked(object sender, EventArgs e)
{
    // Save user preferences to registry.
    RegistryKey regKey = Registry.CurrentUser;
    regKey = regKey.CreateSubKey("Software\\Intertech\\Chapter8App");
```

```
regKey.SetValue("CurrSize", currFontSize);
regKey.SetValue("CurrColor", currColor.Name);
}
```

If the user were now to set the current color to LemonChiffon and the current font size to 30 (and save these settings), you would find the following information inserted into the system registry (Figure 8-37).

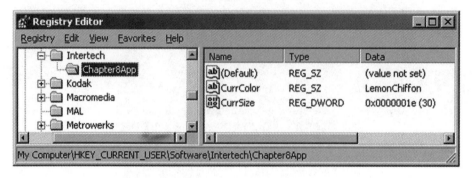

Figure 8-37. Saving application data to HKCU

Reading this information from the registry also makes use of the RegistryKey type. Let's retrofit the constructor of your Form-derived class to read the background color and font size from the registry, to assign the corresponding member data to the correct values. In this way, the application starts up having the same look and feel as the previous session (note the use of RegistryKey.GetValue()):

```
public MainForm()
{
    // Open a subkey.
    RegistryKey regKey = Registry.CurrentUser;
    regKey = regKey.CreateSubKey("Software\\Intertech\\Chapter8App");

    // Read values and assign state data.
    currFontSize = (int)regKey.GetValue("CurrSize", currFontSize);
    string c = (string)regKey.GetValue("CurrColor", currColor.Name);
    currColor = Color.FromName(c);
    BackColor = currColor;

    . . .

}
```

One question that might pop into mind is "What if there are currently no entries for these data points in the registry?" For example, assume the user launched the application for the very first time and has not yet saved any settings. In this case, when the constructor logic is hit, the RegistryKey object is not able to locate the correct data!

The good news is, the GetValue() method may take an optional second parameter (as seen in the previous code). This parameter specifies the value to use in place of an empty registry entry. Notice that you have sent in currFontSize and currColor member variables. Given that the Form sets these variables to an initial value, these will be used in place of any absent registry entries:

```
public class MainForm : Form
{
    Color currColor = Color.MistyRose;
    private int currFontSize = TheFontSize.Normal;
...
}
```

The final touch is to update the BuildMenuSystem() helper function to check the correct subitem on the pop-up menu based on the information read in from the registry. In the previous PopUpMenu application, you specified that the currently selected item was TheFontSize.Normal. This may not be the case anymore, given that the user can save preferences to the registry. Here is the update:

```
private void BuildMenuSystem()
{
...
    // Current size?
    if(currFontSize = = TheFontSize.Huge)
        currentCheckedItem = checkedHuge;

    else if(currFontSize = = TheFontSize.Normal)
        currentCheckedItem = checkedNormal;

    else
        currentCheckedItem = checkedTiny;

    currentCheckedItem.Checked = true;
}
```

Interacting with the Event Viewer

The Windows 2000 operating system supplies an MMC (Microsoft Management Console) snap-in called the "Event Viewer." The Event Viewer maintains three separate logs (Application, Security, and System) that provide a way for you to gather information about hardware, software, and system problems, and to monitor various security events (Figure 8-38).

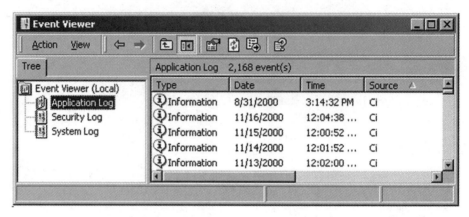

Figure 8-38. The Win2000 Event Viewer

When you wish to programmatically manipulate the Event Viewer, you will want to make use of various types defined within the System.Diagnostics namespace. Table 8-27 gives a rundown of the core items you must be aware of.

Table 8-27. Types of the System.Diagnostics Namespace

SYSTEM.DIAGNOSTICS TYPE	MEANING IN LIFE
EventLog	This class is your entry point to manipulate the Windows 2000 Event Viewer.
EventLog.EventLogEntryCollection	Holds individual EventLogEntry types that represent an entry in a given event log.
EventLogEntry	The EventLogEntry type represents a single record in the event log.
EventLogNames	This sealed type provides fields to define the log you wish to manipulate (Application, Security, or System).

Using the EventLog class, you can read from existing logs (Application, Security, and System), write entries to logs, delete logs, and react to entries your log receives. If you so desire, you can even create new custom logs when creating an event source. Table 8-28 lists some core members.

Table 8-28. Members of the EventLog Type

EVENTLOG MEMBER	MEANING IN LIFE
Entries	Gets the contents of the event log, held in an EventLog.EventLogEntryCollection type. As you would expect, this collection contains individual EventLogEntry items.
Log	Gets or sets the name of the log to read from and write to. This can be "Application," "System," "Security," an application-specific log or a custom log name.
MachineName	Gets or sets the name of the computer on which to read or write events. If you do not specify the MachineName, the local computer (".") is assumed.
Source	Gets or sets the application name (source name) to register and use when writing to the event log.
Clear()	Clears all entries from an event log.
Close()	Closes a log and releases read and write handles.
CreateEventSource()	Establishes an application as an event source.
GetEventLogs()	Creates an array containing the event logs.
WriteEntry()	Inserts an entry in the event log.

As mentioned, your application will write an entry to the Application log when the application is terminated. As a simple example, you might write the following logic in our FileExit_Clicked() event handler:

```
// File | Exit Menu item handler
private void FileExit_Clicked(object sender, EventArgs e)
{
    // Just for kicks, let's log this event to the Application Log...
    EventLog log = new EventLog();
    log.Log = "Application";
    log.Source = Text;
    log.WriteEntry("Hey dude, this app shut down...");    // Insightful, huh?
    log.Close();

    // Now shut down the app.
    this.Close();
}
```

If you were now to examine the Application log, you would find the entry displayed in Figure 8-39 has been inserted.

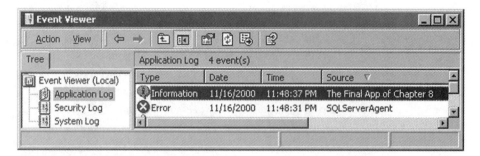

Figure 8-39. Our custom application log

To examine our very helpful message entry (e.g., "Hey dude, this app shut down. . ."), double-click the log entry (Figure 8-40).

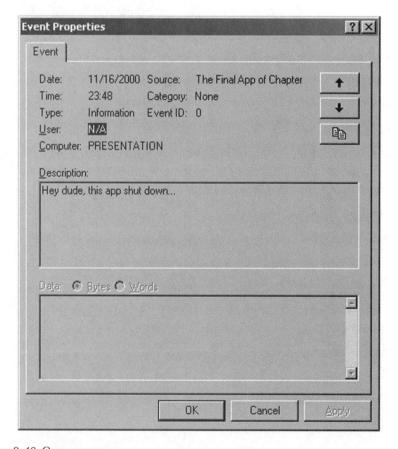

Figure 8-40. Our message

Reading from the Event Log

Now assume you wish to read some information from a given log. This too is quite simple. Recall that the EventLog class defines a property named Entries. This item returns an instance of EventLog.EventLogEntryCollection. This collection contains some number of indexable EventLogEntry types, each of which represents an entry in a given log (Table 8-29).

Table 8-29. The EventLogEntry Type

EVENTLOGENTRY MEMBER	MEANING IN LIFE
Category	Gets the text associated with the CategoryNumber for this entry.
CategoryNumber	Gets the application-specific category number for this entry.
Data	Gets the binary data associated with the entry.
EntryType	Gets the type of this entry.
EventID	Gets the application-specific event identifier of this entry.
MachineName	Gets the name of the computer on which this entry was generated.
Message	Gets the localized message corresponding to this event entry.
Source	Gets the name of the application that generated this event.
TimeGenerated	Gets the time at which this event was generated.
TimeWritten	Gets the time at which this event was written to the log, in local time.
UserName	Gets the name of the user responsible for this event.

If you then update the FileExit_Clicked() method as follows:

```
private void FileExit_Clicked(object sender, EventArgs e)
{
    . . .
    // Display the first 5 entries in the Application log.
    for(int i = 0; i < 5; i++)
    {
        try
        {
        MessageBox.Show("Message: " + log.Entries[i].Message + "\n" +
                        "Box name: " + log.Entries[i].MachineName + "\n" +
                        "App: " + log.Entries[i].Source + "\n" +
```

```
                              "Time entered: " + log.Entries[i].TimeWritten,
                              "Application Log entry:");
                }catch{}
        }
}
```

you would see five messages pop up (what they will be depends on exactly what is in your event log). Here then is your complete Windows Forms application in action (Figure 8-41).

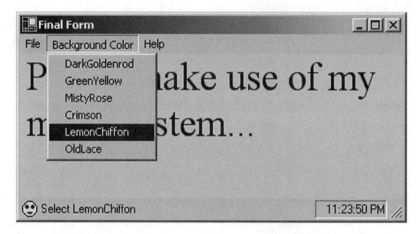

Figure 8-41. The final product

SOURCE CODE   *The FinalFormsApp project is included under the Chapter 8 sub-directory.*

Summary

This chapter introduced the fine art of building a user interface with the types contained in the System.Windows.Forms namespace. It began by examining the basic steps you must take to build a custom Form. This entailed a discussion of the Application object, and its various members. As you have seen, the Form type gains a majority of its functionality from a rather long chain of base types.

During the course of this chapter, you learned how to build top-most menus (and pop-up menus) and how to respond to a number of menu events. You also came to understand how to further enhance your Form objects using toolbars and status bars. Finally, this chapter provided some bonus information, illustrating how to interact with the system registry as well as the Windows 2000 Event Viewer.

CHAPTER 9

A Better Painting Framework (GDI+)

The previous chapter introduced you to the fine art of building a traditional main window using various types contained within the System.Windows.Forms namespace. Now that you can assemble a Form to represent the shell of your GUI-based applications, the next logical task is to understand the details of rendering geometric images (including text and bitmaps) onto the Form's client area.

We begin by taking a high-level overview of the numerous drawing-related namespaces, and examine the process of responding to (and initiating) paint sessions. As well, you will discover various ways of obtaining (and configuring) a Graphics object. Once you understand the general layout of the GDI+ landscape, the remainder of this chapter covers how to manipulate colors, fonts, geometric shapes, and bitmap images. This entails understanding a number of related types such as Brush, Pen, Color, Point, and Rectangle (among others). This chapter also explores a number of GDI+ centric programming techniques such as nonrectangular hit testing and GUI drag-and-drop logic.

The chapter concludes by exploring the new .NET resource format, and you learn how to embed your application's external resources into a .NET assembly. During the process, you explore the System.Resources namespace and learn how to perform read/write operations on the underlying *.resx file by hand, as well as pull resources from an assembly at runtime using the ResourceManager type.

Survey of the GDI+ Namespaces

The .NET framework provides a number of namespaces devoted to two-dimensional graphical rendering. In addition to the basic functionality you would expect to find in a graphics package (color, font, pen, brush, and image manipulation), you also find types that enable geometric transformations, antialiasing, palette blending, and document printing support. Collectively speaking, these namespaces make up the .NET facility we call GDI+. Table 9-1 gives a high-level view of each major player.

Table 9-1. The Core GDI+ Namespaces

GDI+NAMESPACE	MEANING IN LIFE
System.Drawing	This is the core GDI+ namespace, which defines numerous types for basic rendering (fonts, pens, basic brushes, etc) as well as the almighty Graphics type.
System.Drawing.Drawing2D	This namespace offers types used for more advanced two-dimensional graphics functionality (e.g., gradient brushes, geometric transforms, etc).
System.Drawing.Imaging	This namespace defines types that allow you to directly manipulate graphical images (e.g., change the palette, extract image metadata, manipulate metafiles, and so forth).
System.Drawing.Printing	This namespace defines types that allow you to render images to the printed page, interact with the printer itself, and format the appearance of a given print job.
System.Drawing.Text	This namespace allows you to manipulate collections of fonts. For example, as you see in this chapter, the FontCollection type allows you to dynamically discover the set of installed fonts on the target machine.

Configuring a GDI+ Project Workspace

When you wish to make use of GDI+, you must set a reference to the System.Drawing.dll assembly. This single binary contains types for each of the core GDI+ namespaces. Be aware that if you select a new Windows Application Project Workspace using VS.NET, this reference is set on your behalf automatically. Once you have set this reference, just make use of the C# "using" keyword and you are ready to render. To begin the journey, let's examine the functionality defined by the System.Drawing namespace.

Overview of the System.Drawing Namespace

A vast majority of the types used when programming GDI+ applications are found within the System.Drawing namespace. As you would expect, there are classes that represent images, brushes, pens, and fonts. Furthermore, System.Drawing defines a number of related types such as Color, Point, and Rectangle. Table 9-2 lists some (but not all) of the core types.

Table 9-2. Core Members of the System.Drawing Namespace

SYSTEM.DRAWING TYPE	MEANING IN LIFE
Bitmap	Encapsulates a given image file and defines a number of methods to manipulate the underlying graphical data.
Brush Brushes SolidBrush SystemBrushes TextureBrush	Brush objects are used to fill the interiors of graphical shapes such as rectangles, ellipses, and polygons. These types represent a number of brush variations, with Brush functioning as the abstract base class to the remaining types. Additional Brush types are defined in the System.Drawing.Drawing2D namespace.
Color SystemColors ColorTranslator	As you have already seen in the previous chapter, the Color structure defines a number of static fields that can be used to configure the color of fonts, brushes, and pens. The ColorTranslator type allows you to build a new .NET Color type from other color representations (Win32, the OLE_COLOR type, HTML color constants, etc.).
Font FontFamily	The Font type encapsulates the characteristics of a given font (i.e., type name, bold, italic, point size, and so forth). FontFamily provides an abstraction for a group of fonts having a similar generic design but having certain variations in styles.
Graphics	This core class represents a valid drawing surface, as well as a number of methods to render text, images, and geometric patterns. Consider this type the .NET equivalent of a Win32 HDC.
Icon SystemIcons	These classes represent custom icons, as well as the set of standard system supplied icons.
Image ImageAnimator	Image is an abstract base class that provides functionality for the Bitmap, Icon, and Cursor types. ImageAnimator provides a way to iterate over a number of Image-derived types at some specified interval.
Pen Pens SystemPens	Pens are objects used to draw lines and curves. The Pens type defines a number of static properties that return a new Pen of a given color.
Point PointF	These structures represent an (x, y) coordinate mapping to an underlying integer or float (respectively).
Rectangle RectangleF	These structures represent a rectangular dimension (again mapping to an underlying integer or float).
Size SizeF	These structures represent a given height/width (again mapping to an underlying integer or float).

Table 9-2. Continued

SYSTEM.DRAWING TYPE	MEANING IN LIFE
StringFormat	This type is used to encapsulate various features of textual layout (i.e., alignment, line spacing, etc).
Region	Describes the interior of a geometric image composed of rectangles and paths.

Many of these core types make substantial use of a number of related enumerations, most of which are also defined within the System.Drawing namespace. As you can guess, these enumerations are used to configure the look and feel of brushes and pens. For example, ponder the types listed in Table 9-3.

Table 9-3. Enumerations in the System.Drawing Namespace

SYSTEM.DRAWING ENUMERATION	MEANING IN LIFE
ContentAlignment	Specifies how to align content on a drawing surface (center, left, right, and so forth).
FontStyle	Specifies style information applied to text (bold, italic, etc).
GraphicsUnit	Specifies the unit of measure for the given item (much like the Win32 mapping mode constants).
KnownColor	Specifies friendly names for the known system colors.
StringAlignment	Specifies the alignment of a text string relative to its layout rectangle.
StringFormatFlags	Specifies the display and layout information for text strings (e.g. NoWrap, LineLimit, and so on).
StringTrimming	Specifies how to trim characters from a string that does not completely fit into a layout shape.
StringUnit	Specifies the units of measure for a text string.

If you currently have a background using graphics toolkits found in other frameworks (especially Java) you should feel right at home with the functionality provided by the System.Drawing namespace. Next up, let's examine the set of basic utility types that are commonly used in GDI+ programming.

Examining the System.Drawing Utility Types

Many of the drawing methods defined by the Graphics object require you to specify the position or area in which you wish to render a given item. For example, the DrawString() method requires you to specify the location to render the text string on the Control-derived type. Given that DrawString() has been overloaded a number of times, this positional parameter may be specified using an (x, y) coordinate or the location of a "box" to draw within. Other GDI+ type methods may require you to specify the width and height of a given item, or the internal bounds of a geometric image.

To specify such information, the System.Drawing namespace defines the Point, Rectangle, Region, and Size types. Obviously, a Point represents some (x, y) coordinate. Rectangle types capture a pair of points representing the upper left and bottom right bounds of a rectangular region. Size types are similar to Rectangles, however these structures represent a given dimension using a given length and width. Regions provide a way to represent and manipulate nonrectangular drawing surfaces.

The member variables used by the Point, Rectangle, and Size types are internally represented as an integer data type. However, if you need a finer level of granularity, you are free to make use of the corresponding PointF, RectangleF, and SizeF types, which (as you might guess) map to an underlying float. Regardless of the underlying data representation, each type has an identical set of members, including a number of overloaded operators. A quick run-through follows.

Point(F) Type

The first utility type you should be aware of is System.Drawing.Point(F). As you recall, you created a custom Point class in Chapter 5, which in many ways was a slimmed down version of the official GDI+ Point type. A breakdown of each member is shown in Table 9-4.

Table 9-4. Members of the Point(F) Types

POINT AND POINTF MEMBER	MEANING IN LIFE
+ - == !=	Allows you to manipulate the underlying (x, y) point using common overloaded operators.
X Y	These properties allow you to get and set the underlying (x, y) values.
IsEmpty	This property returns true if X and Y are both set to zero.
Offset()	This method translates a given Point type by a given amount.

Although this type is most commonly used when working with GDI+ and user interface applications, do be aware that you may make use of any utility type from any application. To illustrate, here is a console application that makes use of the System.Drawing.Point type (see Figure 9-1 for output).

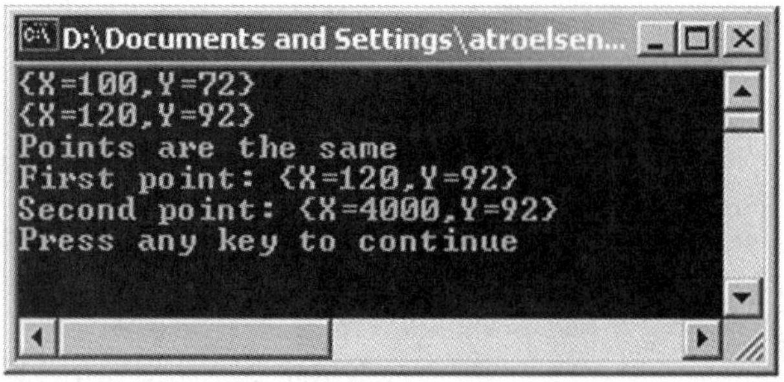

Figure 9-1. Working with basic utility types

```
namespace DrawingUtilTypes
{
using System;
using System.Drawing;      // Need this namespace to access GDI+ types!

public class UtilTypes
{
    public static int Main(string[] args)
    {
        // Create and offset a point.
        Point pt = new Point(100, 72);

        System.Console.WriteLine(pt);
        pt.Offset(20, 20);
        System.Console.WriteLine(pt);

        // Overloaded Point operators.
        Point pt2 = pt;

        if(pt = = pt2)
            Console.WriteLine("Points are the same");
        else
            Console.WriteLine("Different points");

        // Change pt2's X value.
        pt2.X = 4000;

        // Now show each X:
        Console.WriteLine("First point: {0}", pt.ToString());
        Console.WriteLine("Second point: {0}", pt2.ToString());
```

```
        return 0;
    }
}
}
```

Rectangle(F) Type

Rectangles, like Points are useful in any application (GUI-based or otherwise). Some core members to be aware of are listed in Table 9-5.

Table 9-5. Members of the Rectangle(F) Types

RECTANGLE AND RECTANGLEF MEMBER	MEANING IN LIFE
== !=	Allows you to test if two rectangles have identical values (or not).
Inflate() Intersect() Union()	These static methods allow you to expand a rectangle, as well as create new rectangles that are a result of an intersection or union operation.
Top Left Bottom Right	These properties set the dimensions of a new Rectangle type.
Height Width	Configures the height and width of a given Rectangle.
Contains()	This method can be used to determine if a given Point (or Rectangle) is within the bounds of the current Rectangle. Great for hit testing a point within a rectangle.
X Y	These properties return the x or y coordinate of the Rectangle's upper left corner.

One of the most useful methods of the Rectangle type is Contains(). This method allows you to determine if a given Point or Rectangle is within the current bounds of another Rectangle object. Later in this chapter, you see how to make use of this method to reform hit testing of GDI+ images. Until then, here is a simple example:

```
public static int Main(string[] args)
{
    . . .
    Rectangle r1 = new Rectangle(0, 0, 100, 100);
    Point pt3 = new Point(101, 101);
```

```
    if(r1.Contains(pt3))
        Console.WriteLine("Point is within the rect!");
    else
        Console.WriteLine("Point is not within the rect!");

    // Now place point in rectangle's area.
    pt3.X = 50;
    pt3.Y = 30;

    if(r1.Contains(pt3))
        Console.WriteLine("Point is within the rect!");
    else
        Console.WriteLine("Point is not within the rect!");

    return 0;
}
```

Size(F) and Region Types

The Size and SizeF types are quite simple to manipulate, and require little comment. Beyond the inherited members, these types each define Height and Width properties and a handful of overloaded operators (Table 9-6).

Table 9-6. Members of the Size(F) Types

SIZE AND SIZEF MEMBER	MEANING IN LIFE
+ - == !=	Operators to manipulate Size types.
Height Width	These properties are used to manipulate the current dimension of a Size type.

The Region Class

Finally we have the Region class. This type represents the interior of a geometric shape. Given this last statement, it should make sense that the constructors of the Region class require you to send an instance of some existing geometric pattern. For example, assume you have created a rectangle 100 * 100 pixels. If you wish to gain access to the rectangle's interior region, you could write the following:

```
// Get the interior of this rectangle.
Rectangle r = new Rectangle(0, 0, 100, 100);
Region rgn = new Region(r);
```

Once you do have the interior detentions of a given shape, you may manipulate it using the core members shown in Table 9-7.

Table 9-7. Members of the Region Class

REGION MEMBER	MEANING IN LIFE
Complement()	Updates this Region to the portion of the specified graphics object that does not intersect with this Region.
Exclude()	Updates this Region to the portion of its interior that does not intersect with the specified graphics object.
GetBounds()	Returns a RectangleF that represents a rectangular region that bounds this Region.
Intersect()	Overloaded. Updates this Region to the intersection of itself with the specified graphics object.
IsEmpty() MakeEmpty()	Tests whether this Region has an empty interior on the specified drawing surface (or sets the current Region empty).
IsInfinite() MakeInfinite()	Tests whether this Region has an infinite interior on the specified drawing surface (or sets the current Region infinite).
Transform()	Transforms this Region by the specified Matrix.
Translate()	Offsets the coordinates of this Region by the specified amount.
Union()	Updates this Region to the union of itself and the specified graphics object.
Xor()	Updates this Region to the union minus the intersection of itself with the specified graphics object.

I'm sure you get the general idea behind these coordinate primitives. You will have a chance to work with each of them during the course of this chapter (and any time you program against GDI+). Now then, on to some more interesting material!

SOURCE CODE *The UtilTypes project is included under the Chapter 9 subdirectory.*

Understanding Paint Sessions

As you have seen in the previous chapter, the Control class defines a virtual method named OnPaint(). When a Form (or any descendent of Control) wishes to render graphical information, you may override this method and extract a Graphics object from the incoming PaintEventArgs parameter:

```
public class MainForm : Form
{
    public MainForm()
    {
        CenterToScreen();
        this.Text = "Basic Paint Form";
    }

    public static void Main(string[] args)
    {
        Application.Run(new MainForm());
    }

    protected override void OnPaint(PaintEventArgs e)
    {
        Graphics g = e.Graphics;

        g.DrawString("Hello GDI+", new Font("Times New Roman", 20),
                    new SolidBrush(Color.Black), 0, 0);
    }
}
```

Recall that when responding to GUI events, you actually have two options at your disposal. In this last example, you overrode the OnPaint() method directly. The other (preferred) approach is to directly handle the raw Paint event. Thus, you can retrofit the previous class definition as follows:

```
public class MainForm : Form
{
    public MainForm()
    {
        . . .
        // Add a new handler.
        this.Paint += new
            System.Windows.Forms.PaintEventHandler(MainForm_Paint);
    }
```

```
// Note the signature of the event handler...
public void MainForm_Paint(object sender, PaintEventArgs e)
{
    Graphics g = e.Graphics;
    . . .
}

public static void Main(string[] args)
{
    Application.Run(new MainForm());
}
}
```

Regardless of how you respond to the Paint event, be aware that whenever a window becomes "dirty" a paint message is placed into the application's message queue. As you are most likely aware, a window is "dirty" whenever it is resized, covered by another window (partially or completely) or is minimized and then restored. Eventually, the flow of logic is routed to the method that handles repainting the window. In these cases, the .NET framework ensures that when your Form needs to be redrawn, the Paint handler is called automatically.

Invalidating Your Client Area

You may need to explicitly inform a window that it needs to redraw itself (in other words, you need to place a paint message into the queue programmatically). For example, you may have a program that allows the end user to select from a number of bitmap images using a custom dialog. Once the dialog is dismissed, you need to draw the newly selected image onto the client area. Obviously, if you waited for the window to become "naturally dirty," the user would not see the change take place until it was resized or covered by another window. When you need to force a window to repaint itself programmatically, call Invalidate(). For example:

```
public class MainForm: Form
{
. . .
    private void MainForm_Paint(object sender, PaintEventArgs e)
    {
        Graphics g = e.Graphics;
        . . .
        // Logic to render a bitmap...
    }
```

```
        private void GetNewBitmap()
        {
            // Show dialog and get new image. . .

            // Now repaint the client area.
            Invalidate();
        }

    }
```

Do be aware that the Invalidate() method has been overloaded a number of times to allow you to specify a specific rectangular region to repaint, rather than the entire client area (which is the default). If you only wish to update the extreme upper left rectangle of the client area, you could write:

```
// Repaint a given rectangular area of the Form.
private void UpdateUpperArea()
{
    Rectangle myRect = new Rectangle(0, 0, 75, 150);
    Invalidate(myRect);
}
```

Rendering GDI+ Objects Outside Paint Handlers

On a related note, you may find yourself in the position of needing to render some image *outside* the scope of a standard Paint event handler. For example, assume you wish to draw a small circle at the (*x*, *y*) position where the mouse has been clicked. The first step (of course) is to obtain a valid Graphics object, which can be obtained using the static Graphics.FromHwnd() method. Notice that you are passing your current Handle as the sole parameter (recall that the Handle property is inherited from the Control class):

```
private void MainForm_MouseDown(object sender, MouseEventArgs e)
{
    // Grab a Graphics object.
    Graphics g = Graphics.FromHwnd(this.Handle);

    // Now draw a 10*10 circle at mouse click.
    g.DrawEllipse(new Pen(Color.Green), e.X, e.Y, 10, 10);
}
```

Now, while this logic renders a circle outside an OnPaint() event handler, it is very important to understand that if form is invalidated (and thus redrawn), each of the circles is erased! This should make sense, given that this rendering only happens within the context of a mouse click.

A better approach is to have the MouseUp logic add a new point to an internal collection (such as an ArrayList) of Point objects, followed by a call to Invalidate(). At this point, the OnPaint() method can simply iterate over the collection and draw each item:

```csharp
public class MainForm : System.Windows.Forms.Form
{
    // Used to hold all the points.
    private ArrayList myPts = new ArrayList();
    ...

    private void MainForm_MouseDown(object sender, MouseEventArgs e)
    {
        // Grab a new Graphics object.
        Graphics g = Graphics.FromHwnd(this.Handle);

        // Now draw a 10*10 circle at mouse click.
        // g.DrawEllipse(new Pen(Color.Green), e.X, e.Y, 10, 10);

        // Add to points collection.
        myPts.Add(new Point(e.X, e.Y));
        Invalidate();
    }

    private void MainForm_Paint(object sender, PaintEventArgs e)
    {
        Graphics g = e.Graphics;
        g.DrawString("Hello GDI+", new Font("Times New Roman", 20),
                    new SolidBrush(Color.Black), 0, 0);

        // Draw all points.
        foreach(Point p in myPts)
            g.DrawEllipse(new Pen(Color.Green), p.X, p.Y, 10, 10);
    }
}
```

In any case, realize that the Graphics.FromHwnd() method provides a handy way to obtain a Graphics object outside of a registered paint handler. Figure 9-2 shows a test run of this initial GDI+ application.

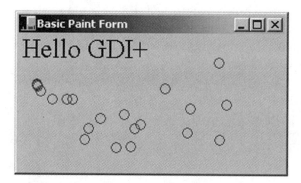

Figure 9-2. A basic GDI+ application

SOURCE CODE   *The BasicPaintForm project is included under the Chapter 9 sub-directory.*

Understanding the Graphics Class

Now that you understand how to obtain a Graphics object, you need to understand exactly how to manipulate it. The System.Drawing.Graphics object is your gateway to GDI+ rendering functionality. This class represents a valid device context (e.g., HDC) coupled together with a slew of methods that allow you to render text, images (icons, bitmaps, and so on), as well as numerous geometric patterns. Table 9-8 gives a partial list of intriguing members.

Table 9-8. Members of the Graphics Class

GRAPHICS METHODS	MEANING IN LIFE
FromHdc() FromHwnd() FromImage()	These static methods provide a way to obtain a valid Graphics object from a given image (e.g., icon, bitmap, etc.) or GUI widget.
Clear()	Fills a Graphics object with a specified color, erasing the current drawing surface in the process.
DrawArc() DrawBezier() DrawBeziers() DrawCurve() DrawEllipse() DrawIcon() DrawLine() DrawLines() DrawPie() DrawPath() DrawRectangle() DrawRectangles() DrawString()	These methods (among others) are used to render a given image or geometric pattern.
FillEllipse() FillPath() FillPie() FillPolygon() FillRectangle()	These methods (among others) are used to fill the interior of a given geometric shape.
MeasureString()	Returns a Size structure that represents the bounds of a given block of text.

As well as providing a number of rendering methods, the Graphics class defines additional members that encapsulate details regarding how the current rendering operation will look and feel. In more concrete terms, the Graphics type allows you to configure the state of the Graphics object using the property set in Table 9-9.

Table 9-9. Stateful Properties of the Graphics Class

GRAPHICS PROPERTY	MEANING IN LIFE
Clip ClipBounds VisibleClipBounds IsClipEmpty IsVisibleClipEmpty	These properties allow you to set the clipping options used with the current Graphics object.
Transform	Allows you to transform "world coordinates" (more later).
PageUnit PageScale DpiX DpiY	These properties allow you to configure the point of origin for your rendering operations, as well as configure the unit of measurement.
SmoothingMode PixelOffsetMode TextRenderingHint	These properties allow you to configure the smoothness of geometric objects and text. These are set with corresponding enumerations defined in the System.Drawing and System.Drawing.Drawing2D namespaces.
CompositingMode CompositingQuality	The CompositingMode property determines whether drawing overwrites the background or is blended with the background. The value is set with the corresponding CompositingMode enumeration defined in the System.Drawing.Drawing2D namespace. The CompositingQuality property specifies the complexity of the blending process. Makes use of the CompositingQuality enumeration, also in System.Drawing.Drawing2D.
InterpolationMode	Specifies how data is interpolated between endpoints, using a related enumeration.

During the course of this chapter you configure a number of these state properties.

Default GDI+ Coordinate System

Before learning about the ins and outs of rendering GDI+ objects, you need a bit of background regarding the underlying coordinate system. Like the raw Win32 API, GDI+ allows you to choose from a variety of coordinate systems. The default unit of measurement is pixel-based and places the origin in the upper left corner with the *x*-axis increasing to the right and the *y*-axis increasing downward (Figure 9-3).

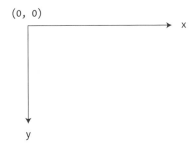

Figure 9-3. The default coordinate system

For example, if you render a Rectangle as follows (Figure 9-4):

```
private void MainForm_Paint(object sender, PaintEventArgs e)
{
    // Draw a rectangle using the default coordinate system.
    e.Graphics.DrawRectangle(new Pen(Color.Red, 5), 10, 10, 100, 100);
}
```

you would see a square rendered 10 pixels down and in from the top left client edge, which spans 90 pixels in both directions.

Figure 9-4. Pixel-based rendering

The default GDI+ coordinate system will most likely be your mapping mode of choice. However, like most things in the .NET framework, you are able to configure the GDI+ mapping mode to your liking.

Specifying an Alternative Unit of Measurement

As just described, the default graphics unit is the pixel. However, you are able to change this default setting by setting the PageUnit property of the Graphics object. The PageUnit property can be assigned any member of the GraphicsUnit enumeration (Table 9-10).

Table 9-10. The GraphicsUnit enumeration

GRAPHICSUNIT ENUMERATION VALUE	DESCRIPTION
Display	Specifies 1/75 inch as the unit of measure.
Document	Specifies the document unit (1/300 inch) as the unit of measure.
Inch	Specifies the inch as the unit of measure.
Millimeter	Specifies the millimeter as the unit of measure.
Pixel	Specifies a device pixel as the unit of measure.
Point	Specifies a printer's point (1/72 inch) as the unit of measure.

For example, if you update your previous rendering code as follows:

```
private void MainForm_Paint(object sender, PaintEventArgs e)
{
    // Draw a rectangle in inches. . .not pixels.
    e.Graphics.PageUnit = GraphicsUnit.Inch;
    e.Graphics.DrawRectangle(new Pen(Color.Red, 5), 0, 0, 100, 100);
}
```

you would find a *radically* different rectangle (Figure 9-5).

The reason that 85% (or so) of the Form's client area is now filled in is due to the fact that you have configured a Pen with a five inch nib! The rectangle itself is 100 * 100 *inches* in size! In fact, the small gray box you see located in the lower right corner is the upper left interior of the rectangle.

Specifying an Alternative Point of Origin

Recall, that when you make use of the default mapping mode, point (0, 0) is at the extreme upper left of the client area. Again, this is typically what you desire. However, what if you wish to alter the location where rendering begins? For

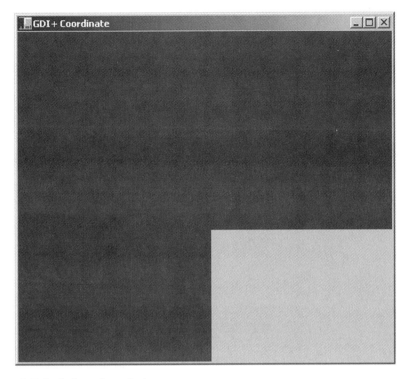

Figure 9-5. Inch-based rendering

example, let's assume that your application always needs to reserve a 100-pixel boundary around the Form's client area (for whatever reason). You need to ensure that all GDI+ operations take place somewhere within this internal region.

One approach you could take is to offset all your rendering code manually. This of course is a huge bother. It would be far better (and simpler) if you could set a property that says in effect "Although *I* might say render a rectangle with a point of origin at (0, 0), make sure *you* begin at point (100, 100). This would simplify your life a great deal, as you can continue to specify your plotting points without modification.

In GDI+, you can adjust the point of origin by setting the transformation value using the TranslateTransform() method of the Graphics class. For example, the following code allows you to keep your logical mapping at (0, 0) while modifying the device view to begin at (100, 100):

```
private void MainForm_Paint(object sender, PaintEventArgs e)
{
    // Configure graphics unit.
    e.Graphics.PageUnit = GraphicsUnit.Point;
```

```
    // Configure device origin to (100, 100).
    e.Graphics.TranslateTransform(100, 100);

    // World origin is still (0, 0).
    e.Graphics.DrawRectangle(new Pen(Color.Red, 1), 0, 0, 100, 100);
}
```

To help you experiment with some of the ways to alter the default GDI+ coordinate system, the companion code contains a sample application named (of course) CoorSystem. Using two top-most menu items, you are able to alter the point of origin as well as the unit of measurement. For an example, check out Figure 9-6.

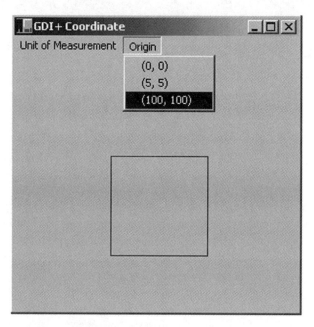

Figure 9-6. The coordinate test application

You configure other state properties of the Graphics object later in this chapter. For now, the next order of business is to examine more details of GDI+ color manipulation.

Establishing an Active Color

Many of the rendering methods defined by the Graphics class require you to specify the color that should be used during the drawing process. The Color structure represents an alpha-red-green-blue (ARGB) color constant. Most of the

Color type's functionality comes by way of a number of static properties, which return a new (correctly configured), Color type:

```
// One of many predefined colors. . .
Color c = Color.PapayaWhip;
```

As shown in Table 9-11, there are other ways you can create a Color type. Regardless of the method you use, you are then able to extract relevant information using any of the members listed in Table 9-11.

Table 9-11. Members of the Color Type

COLOR MEMBER	MEANING IN LIFE
FromArgb()	Returns a new Color object based on numerical red, green, and blue values.
FromKnownColor()	Returns a new Color object based on a member of the KnownColor enumeration.
FromName()	Returns a new Color object based on a string name (e.g., "Red").
A, R, G, B	These properties return the value assigned to the alpha, red, green, and blue aspect of a Color object.
IsNamedColor() Name	These members can be applied to a Color object to determine if the current ARGB values have a predefined name (e.g., "Red") and if so, retrieve it via the Name property.
GetBrightness() GetHue() GetSaturation()	GDI+ Color types have an associated Hue-Saturation-Brightness (HSB) value. These methods retrieve the specifics.
ToArgb() ToKnownColor()	Returns the ARGB value of the Color type, or the KnownColor enumeration value based on a valid Color object.

Examining the ColorDialog Class

On a related note, the System.Windows.Forms namespace provides a predefined dialog box class (ColorDialog) that can be used to prompt the end user for his or her color selection (Figure 9-7). Note that the RGB and HSB values can be adjusted using a slider control or directly via a given edit field.

Working with this dialog is simple. From a valid instance of the ColorDialog type, call ShowDialog() to display the dialog modally. Once the user has closed the dialog, you can extract the corresponding Color object using the ColorDialog.Color property.

For example, assume you wish to allow the user to configure the background color of the client area using the ColorDialog. To keep things simple, let's assume

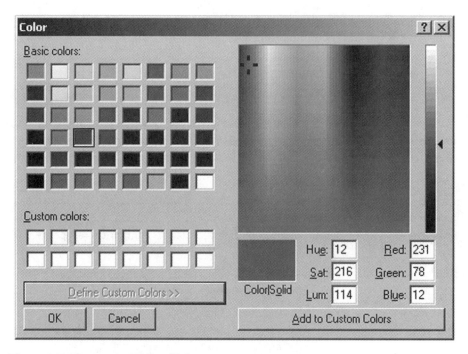

Figure 9-7. The canned Color dialog

that when the user clicks anywhere on the client area, you show the ColorDialog object and act accordingly. Here is the code:

```
public class ColorDlgForm : System.Windows.Forms.Form
{
    // Our ColorDialog.
    private System.Windows.Forms.ColorDialog colorDlg;
    public ColorDlgForm()
    {
        colorDlg = new System.Windows.Forms.ColorDialog();
        Text = "Click on me to change the color";
        this.MouseUp +=
            new MouseEventHandler(this. ColorDlgForm _MouseUp);
    }
...
    private void ColorDlgForm_MouseUp(object sender, MouseEventArgs e)
    {
        if (colorDlg.ShowDialog() != DialogResult.Cancel)
        {
            currColor = colorDlg.Color;
            this.BackColor = currColor;
```

```
        // Show current color.
        string strARGB = colorDlg.Color.ToString();
        MessageBox.Show(strARGB, "Color is:");
      }
    }
}
```

Figure 9-8 shows a test run.

Figure 9-8. Reading ARGB values

Although there has not yet been a formal discussion of how to manipulate dialog boxes, the previous code should not raise too many eyebrows. Notice that you are able to determine which button has been clicked (OK or Cancel) by testing the return value of ShowDialog() against the DialogResult enumeration. You will see additional stock dialog boxes used in this chapter. Later, in Chapter 10, you learn how to build custom dialogs to gather (and validate) user input.

SOURCE CODE   *The ColorDlg application is included under the Chapter 9 sub-directory.*

Manipulating Fonts

Although you have been rendering text since Chapter 8, you have yet to examine the specifics of the Font class (and related types). The System.Drawing.Font type represents a given font installed on the user's machine. While the Font class defines a number of overloaded constructors, here are some common options:

```
// Create a Font of a given type name and size.
Font f = new Font("Times New Roman", 12);
```

```
// Create a Font with a given name, size, and style set.
Font f2 = new Font("WingDings", 50, FontStyle.Bold | FontStyle.Underline);
```

Here, f2 has been created using a set of FontStyle flags. The members of this enumeration allow you to configure a number of properties of the Font object such as bold or italic (if you require more than one FontStyle, simply OR each item together). Table 9-12 lists your choices.

Table 9-12. The FontStyle Enumeration

FONTSTYLE ENUMERATION MEMBER	MEANING IN LIFE
Bold	Bold text
Italic	Italic text
Regular	Normal text
Strikeout	Text with a line through the middle
Underline	Underlined text

Once you have configured the look and feel of your Font object, the next obvious task is to pass it as a parameter to the Graphics.DrawString() method. Although DrawString() has also been overloaded a number of times, each variation typically requires the same basic information: A string to draw, the font to draw it in, a brush used for rendering, and a location to place it. For example:

```
// public void DrawString(String, Font, Brush, Point);
g.DrawString("My string", new Font("Pop", 25),
          new SolidBrush(Color.Black), new Point(0,0));
```

```
// public void DrawString(String, Font, Brush, float, float);
g.DrawString("Another string", new Font("Times New Roman", 16),
          new SolidBrush(Color.Red), 40, 40);
```

In each of these examples, you have made use of a SolidBrush type (of a particular color). It is possible to configure a number of brush types. For the time being, a solid brush fits the bill; you see more exotic brush types a bit later in this chapter.

Once you have created a valid Font type, you are able to extract its current settings using a number of properties (e.g., Bold, Italic, Unit, Height, Size, FontFamily, and so forth).

Working with Font Families

The System.Drawing namespace also defines the FontFamily type, which abstracts a group of typefaces having a similar basic design but having certain style variations (such as point size). A family of fonts, like Verdana, can include several fonts that differ in style and size. For example, Verdana 12-point bold and Verdana 24-point italic are different fonts in the Verdana font family.

The constructor of the FontFamily type takes a string representing the name of the font family you are attempting to capture. Once you create the generic family, you are then able to create a more specific Font object:

```
// Make a family of fonts.
FontFamily myFamily = new FontFamily("Verdana");

// Pass family into ctor of Font.
Font myFont = new Font(myFamily, 12);
e.Graphics.DrawString("Hello?", myFont, Brushes.Blue, 10, 10);
```

Of greater interest is the ability to gather various statistics regarding a given family of fonts. For example, let's say you were building text-processing application and wish to determine the average width of a character in a particular FontFamily. What if you wish to understand the ascending and descending values for a given character? To answer such questions, the FontFamily type defines the members shown in Table 9-13. Note that each requires you to specify the font style using the FontStyle enumeration (Table 9-13).

Table 9-13. Members of the FontFamily Type

FONTFAMILY MEMBER	MEANING IN LIFE
GetCellAscent()	Returns the ascender metric for the members in this family.
GetCellDescent()	Returns the descender metric for members in this family.
GetEmHeight()	Gets the size of the em square for the specified style.
GetLineSpacing()	Returns the distance between two consecutive lines of text for this FontFamily with the specified FontStyle.
GetName()	Returns the name of this FontFamily in the specified language.
IsStyleAvailable()	Indicates whether the specified FontStyle is available.

To illustrate, here is a Paint handler that prints a number of characteristics of the Verdana font family:

```
private void MainForm_Paint(object sender, PaintEventArgs e)
{
    Graphics g = e.Graphics;

    FontFamily myFamily = new FontFamily("Verdana");
    Font myFont = new Font(myFamily, 12);

    int y = 0;                              // Y offset.
    int fontHeight = myFont.Height;         // Get pixel height of font.

    // Show units of measurement for FontFamily members.
    this.Text = "Measurements are in GraphicsUnit." + myFont.Unit.ToString();

    g.DrawString("The Verdana family.", myFont, Brushes.Blue, 10, y);
    y += 20;

    // Print our family ties. . .
    g.DrawString("Ascent for bold Verdana: " +
                myFamily.GetCellAscent(FontStyle.Bold),
                myFont, Brushes.Black, 10, y + fontHeight);
    y += 20;

    g.DrawString("Descent for bold Verdana: " +
                myFamily.GetCellDescent(FontStyle.Bold),
                myFont, Brushes.Black, 10, y + fontHeight);
    y += 20;

    g.DrawString("Line spacing for bold Verdana: " +
                myFamily.GetLineSpacing(FontStyle.Bold),
                myFont, Brushes.Black, 10, y + fontHeight);
    y += 20;

    g.DrawString("Height for bold Verdana: " +
                myFamily.GetEmHeight(FontStyle.Bold),
                myFont, Brushes.Black, 10, y + fontHeight);
    y += 20;
}
```

Figure 9-9 shows the result. Note that these members of the FontFamily type return values using GraphicsUnit.Point (not Pixel) as the unit of measurement, which corresponds to 1/72 inch. You are free to transform these values to other units of measurement as you see fit.

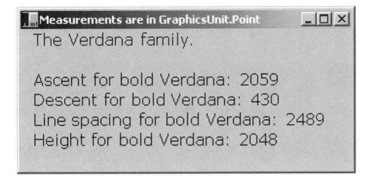

Figure 9-9. Font matrix

SOURCE CODE   *The FontFamily application is included under the Chapter 9 subdirectory.*

Understanding Font Metrics

If you have not worked with Fonts using this level of detail before, here are a few words regarding character measurements. The dimensions of a given Font are all based on the baseline value, which is the imaginary line on which each character "sits." Some characters (such as "j," "y," or "g") have a portion that drops below this baseline. This is called the *descending value*. The *ascending value* represents the amount a given character rises above the baseline. The *leading value* represents the difference between the height and ascent, where height is the total distance between the leading and descending values.

To keep all these items fixed in your mind, ponder Figure 9-10 (the baseline is identified by the thicker line toward the bottom).

Figure 9-10. The anatomy of a Font

Building a Font Application

Now, let's build a more complex application that allows the end user to manipulate a Font object. The application will allow the user to select the current font face using the "Configure | Font Face" menu selection. Figure 9-11 shows the layout.

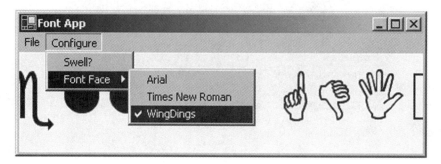

Figure 9-11. The menu system of the Font App

Let's allow the user to indirectly control the size of the Font object using a Windows Forms Timer object. If the user activates the Timer using the "Configure | Swell?" menu item, the size of the Font object increases at a regular interval (checking for a maximum upper limit). In this way, the text appears to swell and thus provides a simple animation cycle of "breathing" text.

To begin, you need to derive a new class from System.Windows.Forms.Form. Next, you need some data members to represent your Timer object, the current font face, and an integer (swellValue) to hold the amount to adjust the font size:

```
public class FontForm : System.Windows.Forms.Form
{
    private Timer timer;
    private int swellValue;
    private string fontFace = " WingDings";     // Default font face.

    public FontForm()
    {
        // The menu system has been designed using the IDE...
        InitializeComponent();

        timer = new Timer();
        Text = "Font App";
        Width = 425;
```

```
        Height = 150;
        BackColor = Color.Honeydew;
        CenterToScreen();

        // Configure the Timer.
        timer.Enabled = true;
        timer.Interval = 100;
        timer.Tick += new EventHandler(FontForm_OnTimer);
    }
}
```

Notice that the constructor calls InitializeComponent() to create and attach the main menu system. The code behind this method is standard menu logic (as described in Chapter 8), and I assume you will examine the companion code for complete details.

Of greater importance is the manipulation of the Timer object. You also saw the use of this type in Chapter 8.

In the Tick event handler, increase the value of the swellValue data member, and refresh your client area. Recall, the swellValue value is added to the current font size to provide a simple animation (notice the swellValue has a maximum upper limit of 50). In order to help reduce the flicker that can occur when redrawing the entire client area, you only refresh the minimum dirty rectangular region:

```
private void FontForm_OnTimer(object sender, EventArgs e)
{
    // Increase current swellValue by 5.
    swellValue += 5;

    // If this value is greater than or equal to 50, reset to zero.
    if(swellValue >= 50)
        swellValue = 0;

    // Just invalidate the 'minimal dirty rectangle' to help reduce flicker.
    Invalidate(new Rectangle(0, 0, ClientRectangle.Width, 100));
}
```

Now that the upper 100 pixels of your client area are refreshed with each tick of the Timer, you better have something to render! In the Form's Paint handler, create a Font object based on the user-defined font face (as selected from the appropriate menu item) and current swellValue (as dictated by the timer). Once you have your Font object fully configured, render a message into the center of the dirty rectangle:

```
private void FontForm_Paint(object sender, PaintEventArgs e)
{
    Graphics g = e.Graphics;

    // The font size can be between 12 and 62,
    // based on the current swellValue.
    Font theFont = new Font(fontFace, 12 + swellValue);

    string message = "Hello GDI+";

    // Display message in the center of the rect.
    float windowCenter = this.DisplayRectangle.Width/2;
    SizeF stringSize = g.MeasureString(message, theFont);
    float startPos = windowCenter - (stringSize.Width/2);

    g.DrawString(message, theFont, new SolidBrush(Color.Blue), startPos, 10);
}
```

The remaining logic of the FontForm class that deserves comment is the menu handler for the Swell menu item. If the user wishes to stop or start the swelling of the text (i.e., enable or disable the animation), you must configure the Clicked handler to enable or disable the Timer as follows:

```
private void ConfigSwell_Clicked(object sender, EventArgs e)
{
    timer.Enabled = !timer.Enabled;
    mainMenu.MenuItems[1].MenuItems[0].Checked = timer.Enabled;
}
```

Enumerating Installed Fonts (System.Drawing.Text)

Next, let's expand the FontApp to programmatically discover the set of installed fonts on the target machine. Doing so gives you a chance to explore another namespace of GDI+, System.Drawing.Text. This namespace contains a (small) handful of useful types that can be used to discover and manipulate the set of fonts installed on the target machine. The highlights are shown in Table 9-14.

To illustrate, assume your current application has an additional menu item named "List Installed Fonts" (Figure 9-12).

When the user selects this menu item, the corresponding Clicked handler creates an instance of the InstalledFontCollection class. This class maintains an array named FontFamily, which represents the set of all fonts on the target machine, and may be obtained using the InstalledFontCollection.Families

Table 9-14. The Text Type

SYSTEM.DRAWING.TEXT TYPE	MEANING IN LIFE
InstalledFontCollection	Represents the set of all fonts installed on the target system.
PrivateFontCollection	Encapsulates a collection of specific Font types.
LineSpacing	This enumeration specifies the spacing between lines of text in a text string that spans more than a single line.
TextRenderingHint	Another enumeration that allows you to specify the quality of the current text rendering operation. For example, the Text value represents a fast (but low quality) rendering. AntiAliased marks better quality but a slower rendering cycle.

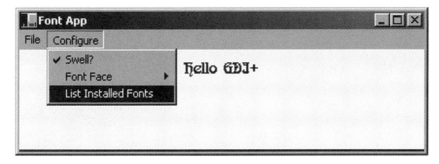

Figure 9-12. Enumerating all installed fonts

property. Using the FontFamily.Name property, you are able to extract the font face (e.g., Times New Roman, Arial, etc.) for each font.

Here, you have added a private string data member named installedFonts to hold each font face. The logic in the "List Installed Fonts" menu handler creates an instance of the InstalledFontCollection type, reads the name of each string, and adds the new font face to the private installedFonts data member:

```
public class FontForm : System.Windows.Forms.Form
{
    // Holds the list of fonts.
    private string installedFonts;

    // Menu handler to get the list of installed fonts.
    private void mnuConfigShowFonts_Clicked(object sender, EventArgs e)
```

```
    {
        InstalledFontCollection fonts = new InstalledFontCollection();

        for(int i = 0; i < fonts.Families.Length; i++)
        {
            installedFonts += fonts.Families[i].Name + "  ";
        }

        // This time, we need to invalidate the entire client area,
        // as we will paint the installedFonts string on the lower half
        // of the client rectangle.
        Invalidate();
    }
    . . .
}
```

The final task is to render the installedFonts string to the client area, directly below the screen real estate that is used for your swelling text:

```
private void FontForm_Paint(object sender, PaintEventArgs e)
{
    Graphics g = e.Graphics;
    Font theFont = new Font(fontFace, 12 + swellValue);
    string message = "Hello GDI+";

    // Display message in the center of the window!
    float windowCenter = this.DisplayRectangle.Width/2;
    SizeF stringSize = e.Graphics.MeasureString(message, theFont);
    float startPos = windowCenter - (stringSize.Width/2);
    g.DrawString(message, theFont, new SolidBrush(Color.Blue), startPos, 10);

    // Show installed fonts in the rectangle below the swell area.
    Rectangle myRect = new Rectangle(0, 100,
        ClientRectangle.Width, ClientRectangle.Height);

    // Paint this area of the Form black.
    g.FillRectangle(new SolidBrush(Color.Black), myRect);
    g.DrawString(installedFonts, new Font("Arial", 12),
                new SolidBrush(Color.White), myRect);
}
```

Recall that the size of the "dirty rectangle" has been mapped to the upper 100 pixels of the client rectangle. Because your Tick handler only invalidates a portion of the Form, the remaining area is not redrawn when the Tick event has been sent (to help optimize the rendering of the client area).

As a final touch, to ensure proper redrawing let's handle the Resize event to insure that if the user resizes the Form, the lower part of client rectangle is redrawn correctly:

```
private void FontForm_Resize(object sender, System.EventArgs e)
{
    Rectangle myRect = new Rectangle(0, 100,
        ClientRectangle.Width, ClientRectangle.Height);
    Invalidate(myRect);
}
```

With that, Figure 9-13 shows the final result.

Figure 9-13. Displaying all installed fonts

SOURCE CODE   *The FontApp application is included under the Chapter 9 sub-directory.*

The FontDialog Class

As you might assume, there is a default font dialog box (FontDialog). Figure 9-14 shows what it looks like.

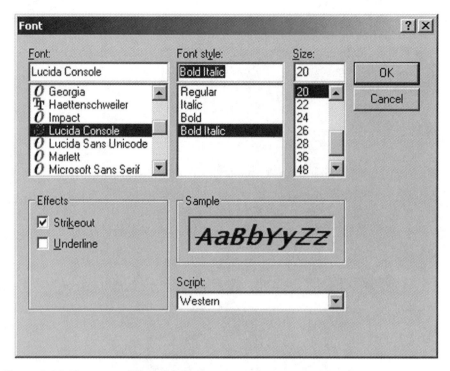

Figure 9-14. The canned Font Dialog

Like the ColorDialog type examined earlier in this chapter, when you wish to work with the FontDialog, simply call the ShowDialog() method. Using the Font property, you may extract the characteristics of the current selection for use in the application. To illustrate, here is a new Form that mimics the logic of the previous ColorDlgForm (i.e., click on the form to launch the File dialog). The output can be seen in Figure 9-15.

```
public class FontDlgForm : System.Windows.Forms.Form
{
    private System.Windows.Forms.FontDialog fontDlg;
    private Font currFont;
    // Event handler for Paint event.
    private void FontDlgForm_Paint(object sender, PaintEventArgs e)
    {
        Graphics g = e.Graphics;
        g.DrawString("Testing. . .", currFont,
            new SolidBrush(Color.Black), 0, 0);
    }
    public FontDlgForm()
```

```
    {
        CenterToScreen();
        fontDlg = new System.Windows.Forms.FontDialog();
        fontDlg.ShowHelp = true;
        Text = "Click on me to change the font";
        currFont = new Font("Times New Roman", 12);
        . . .
    }


    // Event handler for MouseUp event.
    private void FontDlgForm_MouseUp(object sender, MouseEventArgs e)
    {
        if (fontDlg.ShowDialog() != DialogResult.Cancel)
        {
            currFont = fontDlg.Font;
            Invalidate();
        }
    }
}
```

Figure 9-15. Extracting data from the Font dialog

SOURCE CODE   *The FontDlgForm application is included under the Chapter 9 subdirectory.*

Survey of the System.Drawing.Drawing2D Namespace

Your next task is to examine how to manipulate Pen and Brush objects to render geometric patterns. While you could do so making use of nothing more than the types found in the System.Drawing namespace, you should be aware that many of the more "sexy" pen and brush configurations (for example, gradient brushes) require types defined within the System.Drawing.Drawing2D namespace.

This additional GDI+ namespace (which is substantially smaller than System.Drawing) provides a number of classes that allow you to modify the line cap (triangle, diamond, etc) used for a given pen, build textured brushes, as well as work with vector graphic manipulations. Some core types to be aware of, grouped by related functionality are shown in Table 9-15.

Table 9-15. The Classes of System.Drawing.Drawing2D

SYSTEM.DRAWING.DRAWING2D CLASS	MEANING IN LIFE
AdjustableArrowCap CustomLineCap	Pen caps are used to paint the beginning and end points of a given line. These types represent an adjustable arrow-shaped and user-defined cap.
Blend ColorBlend	Used to define a blend pattern (and colors) used in conjunction with a LinearGradientBrush.
GraphicsPath GraphicsPathIterator PathData	A GraphicsPath object represents a series of connected lines and curves. This class allows you to insert just about any type of geometrical pattern (arcs, rectangles, lines, strings, polygons, etc) into the path. PathData holds the graphical data that makes up a path.
HatchBrush LinearGradientBrush PathGradientBrush	Exotic brush types.

Also be aware that the System.Drawing.Drawing2D namespace defines another set of enumerations that are used in conjunction with these core types. Table 9-16 gives a quick rundown.

Establishing the Rendering Quality

Notice that some of the enumerations defined in the System.Drawing.Drawing2D namespace (such as QualityMode and SmoothingMode) allow you to configure the overall quality of the current rendering operation. When you obtain a Graphics object, it has a default rendering mode, which is a middle of the road combination of speed and overall quality. Let's examine one way to tweak a Graphics object to override these default values.

The SmoothingMode enumeration (Table 9-17) is typically used to control how the GDI+ objects being rendered with the current Graphics object are antialiased (or not).

Table 9-16. The Enumerations of System.Drawing.Drawing2D

SYSTEM.DRAWING.DRAWING2D ENUMERATION	MEANING IN LIFE
DashStyle	Specifies the style of dashed lines drawn with a Pen.
FillMode	Specifies how the interior of a closed path is filled.
HatchStyle	Specifies the different patterns available for HatchBrush objects.
LinearGradientMode	Specifies the direction to apply a linear gradient.
LineCap	Specifies the current cap styles used by a Pen.
PenAlignment	Specifies the alignment of a Pen in relation to the line being drawn.
PenType	Specifies the type of fill a Pen uses to fill lines.
QualityMode SmoothingMode RenderingHint	Specifies the overall quality used to render a graphic image.

Table 9-17. Possible Smoothing Values

SMOOTHINGMODE VALUE	MEANING IN LIFE
AntiAlias	Specifies antialiased rendering. The AntiAlias mode uses shades of gray or color to smooth the edges of lines and curves, and is effective on CRT screens as well as LCD screens.
HighQuality	Specifies high quality, lower performance rendering. The high-quality mode uses more sophisticated techniques that take advantage of the subpixel resolution of LCD screens. A single pixel on an LCD screen is divided into three stripes that are set to various shades in order to produce the line or curve that appears the most smooth to the human eye.
HighSpeed	Specifies low quality, high performance rendering. The high-speed mode does no smoothing of the item being rendered; pixels are either on or off.

When you wish to override the default rendering quality for a current GDI+ rendering operation, make use of the SmoothingMode property of the Graphics object:

```
private void MainForm_Paint(object sender, PaintEventArgs e)
{
    Graphics g = e.Graphics;

    // Set quality of GDI+ object rendering.
    g.SmoothingMode = SmoothingMode.AntiAlias;


    . . .
}
```

Be aware that the SmoothingMode property is only used to control the quality of rendering GDI+ objects, not textual information. If you wish to modify the rendering quality for Font types, you need to set the TextRenderingHint property using the related System.Drawing.TextRenderingHint enumeration.

Working with Pens

GDI+ Pen objects are used to draw lines (not too much of a stretch there!). However, a pen in and of itself is of little value. When you need to render a geometric shape onto a Control-derived type, you send a pass valid Pen type to any number of render methods defined by the Graphics class. In general, the DrawXXXX() methods are used to render some set of lines to a graphics surface, and are typically used with Pen objects. The Graphics class also defines a number of FillXXXX() methods that render an image using some sort of Brush-derived type (more on those in just a minute).

Although you have seen many drawing members earlier in the chapter, here they are again (Table 9-18) in a bit more detail (be aware that each of these methods have been overloaded a number of times).

Now that you better understand the core methods used to render geometric images, you can examine the Pen class itself. This class defines a small set of constructors that allow you to determine the initial color and width of the pen nib (you can also construct a new Pen based on an existing Brush object . . . more later). Most of a Pen's functionality comes by way of its supported properties. Table 9-19 gives a partial list.

Table 9-18. Drawing Members of the Graphics Class

DRAWING METHOD OF GRAPHICS CLASS	MEANING IN LIFE
DrawArc()	This method renders an arc given a pen and ellipse on which to base the angle of the arc.
DrawBezier() DrawBeziers()	Given four points, this method draws a cubic Bezier curve (or a number of Beziers).
DrawCurve()	Draws a curve defined by an array of points.
DrawEllipse()	Draws the outline of an ellipse within the scope of a bounding rectangle.
DrawLine() DrawLines()	Given a Point (or an array of Point types), these methods connect the dots (if you will).
DrawPath()	Using the GraphicsPath type defined in the System.Drawing.Drawing2D namespace, this method renders a collection of lines/curves as specified by the path.
DrawPie()	Draws the outline of a pie section defined by an ellipse and two radial lines.
DrawPolygon()	Draws the outline of a polygon defined by an array of Point types.
DrawRectangle() DrawRectangles()	Renders a box, or a whole bunch of boxes, based on top-left-bottom-right coordinates. This can be specified using Rectangle types, integers, or floating point numbers.

Table 9-19. Pen Properties

PEN PROPERTY	MEANING IN LIFE
Brush	Determines the Brush used by this Pen.
Color	Determines the Color type used by this Pen.
CompoundArray	Gets or sets an array of custom dashes and spaces.
CustomStartCap CustomEndCap	Gets or sets a custom cap style to use at the beginning or end of lines drawn with this Pen. Cap styles are simply the term used to describe how the initial and final stroke of the pen should look and feel. These properties allow you to build custom caps for your Pen types.
DashCap	Gets or sets the cap style used at the beginning or end of dashed lines drawn with this Pen.
DashOffset	Gets or sets the distance from the start of a line to the beginning of a dash pattern.

Table 9-19. Continued

PEN PROPERTY	MEANING IN LIFE
DashPattern	Gets or sets an array of custom dashes and spaces. The dashes are made up of line segments.
DashStyle	Gets or sets the style used for dashed lines drawn with this Pen.
LineJoin	Gets or sets the join style for the ends of two overlapping lines drawn with this Pen.
PenType	Gets the style of lines drawn with this Pen.
StartCap EndCap	Gets or sets the predefined cap style used at the beginning or end of lines drawn with this Pen. Set the cap of your Pen using the LineCap enumeration defined in the System.Drawing.Drawing2D namespace.
Width	Gets or sets the width of this Pen.

Remember that in addition to the Pen type, GDI+ also provides a Pens collection. Using a number of static properties, you are able to retrieve a Pen (or a given color) on the fly, rather than creating a custom Pen by hand. Be aware however, that the Pen types returned will always have a Width of 1. If you require a more exotic pen, you will need to build a Pen type by hand.

First, let's render some geometric images using simple Pen types. Assume we have a main Form object, which is capable of responding to paint requests. The implementation is as follows:

```csharp
private void MainForm_Paint(object sender, PaintEventArgs e)
{
    Graphics g = e.Graphics;

    // Make a big blue pen.
    Pen bluePen = new Pen(Color.Blue, 20);

    // Get a stock pen from the Pens type.
    Pen pen2 = Pens.Firebrick;
    pen2.Width = 5;

    // Render some shapes with the pens.
    g.DrawEllipse(bluePen, 10, 10, 100, 100);
    g.DrawLine(pen2, 10, 130, 110, 130);
    g.DrawPie(Pens.Black, 150, 10, 120, 150, 90, 80);
```

```
// Draw a purple dashed polygon as well...
Pen pen3 = new Pen(Color.Purple, 5);
pen3.DashStyle = DashStyle.DashDotDot;

g.DrawPolygon(pen3, new Point[]{      new Point(30, 140),
                                      new Point(265, 200),
                                      new Point(100, 225),
                                      new Point(190, 190),
                                      new Point(50, 330),
                                      new Point(20, 180)} );

// And a rectangle containing some text...
Rectangle r = new Rectangle(150, 10, 130, 60);
g.DrawRectangle(Pens.Blue, r);
g.DrawString("Hello out there...How are ya?",
             new Font("Arial", 12), Brushes.Black, r);
}
```

The output (Figure 9-16), while not earth shattering, should drive the point home.

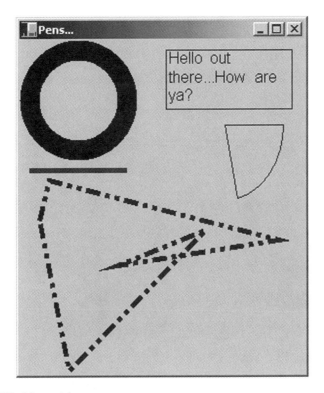

Figure 9-16. Working with pen types

Notice that the Pen that is used to render your polygon makes use of the DashStyle enumeration (defined in System.Drawing.Drawing2D). This is the .NET equivalent of the raw Win32 pen style flags (e.g., PS_SOLID). Table 9-20 lists your choices.

Table 9-20. Dash Styles

DASHSTYLE VALUE	MEANING IN LIFE
Custom	Specifies a user-defined custom dash style.
Dash	Specifies a line comprised of dashes.
DashDot	Specifies a line comprised of an alternating pattern of dash-dot-dash-dot.
DashDotDot	Specifies a line comprised of an alternating pattern of dash-dot-dot-dash-dot-dot.
Dot	Specifies a line comprised of dots.
Solid	Specifies a solid line.

In addition to the preconfigured DashStyles, you are also able to define custom dash types using the DashPattern property of the Pen type (Figure 9-17).

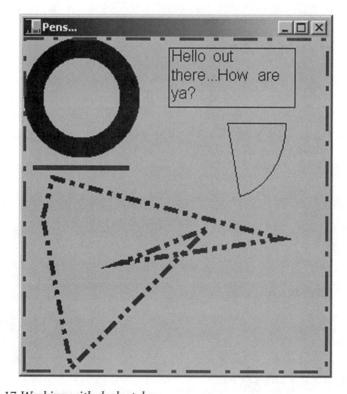

Figure 9-17. Working with dash styles

```
// Draw custom dash pattern all around the boarder of the form.
Pen customDashPen = new Pen(Color.BlueViolet, 5);
float[] myDashes = {5.0f, 2.0f, 1.0f, 3.0f};

customDashPen.DashPattern = myDashes;
g.DrawRectangle(customDashPen, ClientRectangle);
```

SOURCE CODE   *The PenApp project is included under the Chapter 9 subdirectory.*

Working with Pen Caps

If you examine the output of the previous pen example, you should have noticed that the beginning and end of each line was rendered using a standard pen protocol (an end cap composed of 90 degree angles). Using the LineCap enumeration however, you are able to build Pens that exhibit a bit more flair. The core values of this enumeration are seen in Table 9-21.

Table 9-21. LineCap Values

LINECAP VALUES	MEANING IN LIFE
ArrowAnchor	Specifies an arrow-shaped cap.
DiamondAnchor	Specifies a diamond anchor cap.
Flat	Specifies a flat line cap.
Round	Specifies a round line cap.
RoundAnchor	Specifies a round anchor cap.
Square	Specifies a square line cap.
SquareAnchor	Specifies no line cap.
Triangle	Specifies a triangular line cap.

To illustrate, the following Pens application draws a series of lines using each of the LineCap styles. First, the end result can be seen in Figure 9-18.

The code simply loops through each member of the LineCap enumeration, and prints out the name of the item (i.e., ArrowAnchor) and then configures and draws a line with the current cap:

```
private void MainForm_Paint(object sender, PaintEventArgs e)
{
    Graphics g = e.Graphics;
    Pen thePen = new Pen(Color.Black, 10);
    int yOffSet = 10;
```

```
// Get all members of the LineCap enum.
Array obj = Enum.GetValues(typeof(LineCap));

// Draw a line with a LineCap member.
for(int x = 0; x < obj.Length; x++)
{
    // Get next cap and configure pen.
    LineCap temp = (LineCap)obj.GetValue(x);
    thePen.StartCap = temp;
    thePen.EndCap = temp;
```

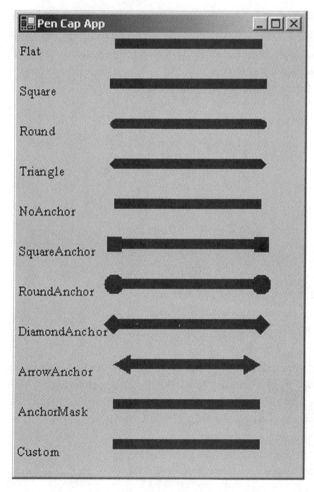

Figure 9-18. Pen caps

```
// Print name of LineCap enum.
g.DrawString(temp.ToString(), new Font("Times New Roman", 10),
        new SolidBrush(Color.Black), 0, yOffSet);
```

```
        // Draw a line with the correct cap.
        g.DrawLine(thePen, 100, yOffSet, Width - 50, yOffSet);

        yOffSet += 40;
    }
}
```

SOURCE CODE   *The PenCapApp project is included under the Chapter 9 sub-directory.*

Working with Solid Brushes

So much for drawing lines. GDI+ Brush-derived types are used to fill the space between the lines, with a given color, pattern or image. Recall that the Brush class is an abstract type, and cannot be directly created. Rather, this type serves as a base class to the other related brush types (for example, SolidBrush, HatchBrush, LinearGradientBrush and so forth). In addition to the aforementioned Brush-derived types, the System.Drawing namespace also defines two types that return a configured brush using a number of static properties: Brushes and SystemBrushes. Using a properly configured brush, you are able to call any number of methods (such as DrawString()), as well as the following set of FillXXXX() methods (Table 9-22).

Table 9-22. Fill Methods of the Graphics Type

FILL METHOD OF GRAPHICS CLASS	MEANING IN LIFE
FillClosedCurve()	Fills the interior of a closed curve defined by an array of points.
FillEllipse()	Fills the interior of an ellipse defined by a bounding rectangle.
FillPath()	Fills the interior of a path.
FillPie()	Fills the interior of a pie section.
FillPolygon()	Fills the interior of a polygon defined by an array of points.
FillRectangle() FillRectangles()	Fills the interior of a rectangle (or a number of rectangles) with a Brush.
FillRegion()	Fills the interior of a Region.

Also recall, that you are able to build a custom Pen type by making use of a given brush. In this way, you are able to build some brush of interest (for example, a brush that paints a bitmap image) and render geometric patterns with config-ured Pen.

To illustrate, here is a small sample program that makes use of the SolidBrush and Brushes types [the output of this program (Figure 9-19) should look familiar. . .]

Figure 9-19. Working with Brush types

If you can't tell, this application is little more than the original Pens application, making use of the FillXXXX() methods and SolidBrush types, rather than pens and the related DrawXXXX() methods. Here is the implementation of the paint handler:

```
private void MainForm_Paint(object sender, PaintEventArgs e)
{
    Graphics g = e.Graphics;

    // Make a blue SolidBrush.
    SolidBrush blueBrush = new SolidBrush(Color.Blue);

    // Get a stock brush from the Brushes type.
    SolidBrush pen2 = (SolidBrush)Brushes.Firebrick;
```

```
// Render some shapes with the brushes.
g.FillEllipse(blueBrush, 10, 10, 100, 100);
g.FillPie(Brushes.Black, 150, 10, 120, 150, 90, 80);

// Draw a purple polygon as well. . .
SolidBrush brush3= new SolidBrush(Color.Purple);

g.FillPolygon(brush3, new Point[]{     new Point(30, 140),
                                       new Point(265, 200),
                                       new Point(100, 225),
                                       new Point(190, 190),
                                       new Point(50, 330),
                                       new Point(20, 180)} );

// And a rectangle with some text. . .
Rectangle r = new Rectangle(150, 10, 130, 60);
g.FillRectangle(Brushes.Blue, r);
g.DrawString("Hello out there. . .How are ya?",
          new Font("Arial", 12), Brushes.White, r);
}
```

SOURCE CODE   *The SolidBrushApp project is included under the Chapter 9 subdirectory.*

Working with Hatch Style Brushes

The System.Drawing.Drawing2D namespace defines another Brush-derived type named HatchBrush. This type allows you to fill a region using a (very large) number of predefined patterns, represented by the HatchStyle enumeration. Here are some (but not all) of the hatch values (Table 9-23).

In addition, when constructing a HatchBrush, you need to specify the foreground and background colors to use during the fill operation. To illustrate, let's rework the logic seen previously from the PenCapApp example. The output renders a filled oval for the first 10 hatch values (Figure 9-20).

Here is the code behind the Form:

```
private void MainForm_Paint(object sender, PaintEventArgs e)
{
    Graphics g = e.Graphics;
    int yOffSet = 10;

    // Get all members of the HatchStyle enum.
    Array obj = Enum.GetValues(typeof(HatchStyle));
```

Table 9-23. Hatch Styles

HATCHSTYLE ENUMERATION VALUE	MEANING IN LIFE
BackwardDiagonal	Creates a brush consisting of backwards diagonal lines.
Cross	Creates a brush consisting of horizontal and vertical crossing lines.
DiagonalCross	Creates a brush consisting of diagonal crossing lines.
ForwardDiagonal	Creates a brush consisting of forward diagonal lines.
Hollow	Configures a "Hollow" brush that doesn't paint anything.
Horizontal	Creates a brush consisting of horizontal lines.
Pattern	Creates a Brush with a pattern consisting of a custom bitmap.
Solid	Creates a solid colored brush (as an alternative to using the SolidBrush type directly).
Vertical	A brush consisting of vertical lines.

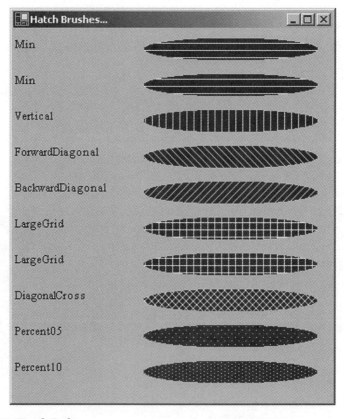

Figure 9-20. Hatch Styles

```
// Draw an oval with a HatchStyle member 1-10.
for(int x = 0; x < 10; x++)
{
    // Configure Brush.
    HatchStyle temp = (HatchStyle)obj.GetValue(x);
    HatchBrush theBrush = new HatchBrush(temp,
                             Color.White, Color.Black

    // Print name of HatchStyle enum.
    g.DrawString(temp.ToString(), new Font("Times New Roman", 10),
             new SolidBrush(Color.Black), 0, yOffSet);

    // Fill a rectangle with the correct brush.
    g. FillEllipse(theBrush, 150, yOffSet, 200, 25);
    yOffSet += 40;
}
}
```

SOURCE CODE *The BrushStyles application is included under the Chapter 9 sub-directory.*

Working with Textured Brushes

Next, we have the TextureBrush type. This type allows you to attach a bitmap image to a brush, which can then be used in conjunction with a fill operation. In just a few pages, you will learn about the details of the GDI+ Image class. For the time being, understand that a TextureBrush is assigned an Image reference for use during its lifetime. The image itself is typically found stored in some local file (*.bmp, *.gif, *.jpg) or embedded into a .NET assembly.

Let's build a sample application that makes use of the TextureBrush type. One brush is used to paint the entire client area with the image found in a file named "clouds.bmp," while the other brush is used to paint text with the image found within "soap bubbles.bmp" (yes, you can use TextureBrush types to render text as well!). The output is shown in Figure 9-21.

The code is very simple. To begin, your Form-derived class maintains two abstract Brush types, which are assigned to a new TextureBrush in the constructor. Notice that the constructor of the TextureBrush type requires an Image object reference:

Figure 9-21. Bitmap brushes

```
public class MainForm : System.Windows.Forms.Form
{

    // Data for the image brush.
    private Brush texturedTextBrush;
    private Brush texturedBGroundBrush;

    public MainForm()
    {
        . . .
        // Load image for background brush.
        Image bGroundBrushImage = new Bitmap("Clouds.bmp");
        texturedBGroundBrush = new TextureBrush(bGroundBrushImage);

        // Now load image for text brush.
        Image textBrushImage = new Bitmap("Soap Bubbles.bmp");
        texturedTextBrush = new TextureBrush(textBrushImage);
    }
. . .
}
```

Now that you have two TextureBrush types to render with, the paint handler should be a no-brainer:

```
private void MainForm_Paint(object sender, PaintEventArgs e)
{
    Graphics g = e.Graphics;
    Rectangle r = ClientRectangle;

    // Paint the clouds on the client area.
    g.FillRectangle(texturedBGroundBrush, r);

    // Some big bold text with a textured brush.
    g.DrawString("Bitmaps as brushes!  Way cool...",
                new Font("Arial", 60,
                FontStyle.Bold | FontStyle.Italic),
                texturedTextBrush,
                r);
}
```

Not bad at all huh? For those of you who have spent time achieving the same effects using the raw Win32 API (or even MFC for that matter), you should be quite pleased with the minimal amount of work required to achieve rather complex end results. Now, before moving on to a discussion of image manipulation, there is one final brush type to consider.

SOURCE CODE   *The TexturedBrushes application is included under the Chapter 9 subdirectory.*

Working with Gradient Brushes

Last but not least, there is the LinearGradientBrush type, which can be used whenever you want to blend two colors together in a gradient pattern. Working with this type is just as simple as working with the other brush types. The only point of interest is that when building a LinearGradientBrush, you need to specify the direction of the blend, using a value from the LinearGradientMode enumeration (Table 9-24).

Table 9-24. LinearGradientMode Enumeration

LINEARGRADIENTMODE VALUE	MEANING IN LIFE
BackwardDiagonal	Specifies a gradient from upper-right to lower-left.
ForwardDiagonal	Specifies a gradient from upper-left to lower-right.
Horizontal	Specifies a gradient from left to right.
Vertical	Specifies a gradient from top to bottom.

To test each type, let's make use of the System.Enum class yet again, and draw a series of rectangles using a LinearGradientBrush (I selected Color.Red and Color.Blue). First, the output as shown in Figure 9-22.

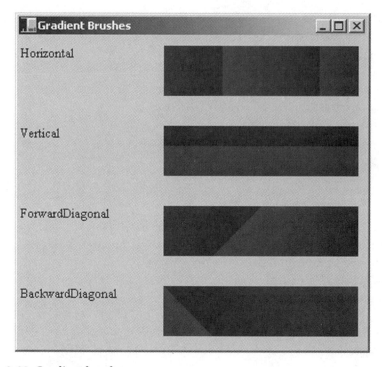

Figure 9-22. Gradient brushes

Now the code, which I assume requires little comment at this point:

```
private void MainForm_Paint(object sender, PaintEventArgs e)
{
    Graphics g = e.Graphics;
    Rectangle r = new Rectangle(10, 10, 100, 100);

    // A gradient brush.
    LinearGradientBrush theBrush = null;
    int yOffSet = 10;

    // Get all members of the LinearGradientMode enum.
    Array obj = Enum.GetValues(typeof(LinearGradientMode));
```

```
// Draw an oval with a LinearGradientMode member.
for(int x = 0; x < obj.Length; x++)
{
    // Configure Brush.
    LinearGradientMode temp = (LinearGradientMode)obj.GetValue(x);
    theBrush = new LinearGradientBrush(r, Color.Red,
                                       Color.Blue, temp);

    // Print name of LinearGradientMode enum.
    g.DrawString(temp.ToString(), new Font("Times New Roman", 10),
                 new SolidBrush(Color.Black), 0, yOffSet);

    // Fill a rectangle with the correct brush.
    g. FillRectangle(theBrush, 150, yOffSet, 200, 50);
    yOffSet += 80;
}
}
```

SOURCE CODE   *The GradientBrush application is included under the Chapter 9 subdirectory.*

Rendering Images

At this point you have examined how to manipulate three of the four major GDI+ types (fonts, pens, and brushes) the final type you examine in this chapter is the Image class, and related subtypes. System.Drawing.Image defines a number of methods and properties that hold various bits of information regarding the underlying pixel set it represents. For example, the Image class supplies the Width, Height, and Size properties to retrieve the dimensions of the image. Other properties allow you to gain access to the underlying palette.

In addition, a number of types defined within the System.Drawing.Imaging namespace define a whole slew of types that facilitate a number of advanced image transformations. The truth of the matter is that a separate book could be written on the topic of GDI+ image manipulation. This is not that book. The goal here is to provide you with a number of imaging techniques you are likely to use on a day-to-day basis (plus some extra eye-candy for good measure). If you require additional information, check out online Help.

With that disclaimer out of the way, the Image class defines the following core members (Table 9-25) many of which are abstract (some of which are static).

Table 9-25. Members of the Image Type

IMAGE MEMBER NAME	MEANING IN LIFE
FromFile()	This static method creates an Image from the specified file.
FromHbitmap()	Creates a Bitmap from a Windows handle (also static).
FromStream()	Creates an Image from the specified data stream (also static).
Height Width Size PhysicalDimensions HorizontalResolution VerticalResolution	These properties return information regarding the dimensions of this Image.
Palette	This property returns a ColorPalette data type that represents the underlying palette used for this Image.
GetBounds()	Returns a Rectangle that represents the current size of this Image.
Save()	Saves an Image to file.

Given that the abstract Image class cannot be directly created, you typically assign objects of type Image to a new instance of the Bitmap class (or simply make a direct instance of the Bitmap type). For example, assume you have some Form-derived class that renders three bitmaps into the client area. To begin, you may create three private Image data members, each of which is assigned to a given Bitmap on startup:

```csharp
public class MainForm : System.Windows.Forms.Form
{

    // The images.
    private Image bMapImageA;
    private Image bMapImageB;
    private Image bMapImageC;

    public MainForm()
    {
        . . .

        // Fill the images with bitmaps.
        bMapImageA = new Bitmap("imageA.bmp");
        bMapImageB = new Bitmap("imageB.bmp");
        bMapImageC = new Bitmap("imageC.bmp");
    }
```

```
. . .
}
```

Rendering these items from within the context of a paint handler is easy as could be, given that the Graphics class has a member named (appropriately enough) DrawImage(). This method has been overloaded numerous times, to provide various ways to place the image onto the drawing surface. For example, you may specify optional ImageAttributes and GraphicsUnit enumerations. For your purposes, all you need to do is specify the location at which to render each image (which may be defined using Point, Rectangles, integers, or floats):

```
protected void OnPaint (object sender, System.Windows.Forms.PaintEventArgs e)
{
    Graphics g = e.Graphics;

    // Render all three images.
    g.DrawImage(bMapImageA, 10, 10, 90, 90);
    g.DrawImage(bMapImageB, 10, 110, 90, 90);
    g.DrawImage(bMapImageC, 10, 210, 90, 90);
}
```

The end result can be seen in Figure 9-23.

Figure 9-23. Rendering images

Also be aware that regardless of the name given to the Bitmap type, you are able to load in images stored in any number of file formats. For example:

```
// The Bitmap type can hold work with any number of file formats!
Bitmap myBMP = new Bitmap("CoffeeCup.bmp");
Bitmap myGIF = new Bitmap("Candy.gif");
Bitmap myJPEG = new Bitmap("Clock.jpg");
Bitmap myPNG = new Bitmap("Speakers.png");
Bitmap myTIFF = new Bitmap("FooFighters.tif");

// Now render each onto the Graphics context.
g.DrawImage(myBMP, 10, 10);
g.DrawImage(myGIF, 220, 10);
g.DrawImage(myJPEG, 280, 10);
g.DrawImage(myPNG, 150, 200);
g.DrawImage(myTIFF, 300, 200);
```

SOURCE CODE   *The Images application is included under the Chapter 9 subdirectory.*

Dragging, Hit Testing, and the PictureBox Control

While you are free to render Bitmap images directly onto a Control-derived type, you will find that you gain far greater control and functionality if you instead choose to create a PictureBox type to hold your image on your behalf. There are numerous reasons to do so. First of all, because the PictureBox type derives from Control, you inherit a great deal of functionality, such as the ability to capture a number of events for a particular image, assign a tool tip or context menu and numerous other details. While you could achieve similar behaviors using a raw Bitmap, you would be required to add a fair amount of boilerplate code.

To illustrate the usefulness of the PictureBox type, let's create an application that illustrates the ability to capture MouseUp, MouseDown, and MouseMove events from a graphical image contained in a PictureBox.

If the user clicks the mouse down somewhere within the bounds of the image, they are in "dragging" mode and can move the image around the Form. To make things more interesting, let's monitor where they release the image. If it is within the bounds of a GDI+-rendered rectangle, we take some additional course of action (seen shortly). As you may know, the process of testing for mouse click events within the context of a region of the screen is termed "hit testing."

When it comes to the functionality provided by the PictureBox type, there is little to say, as all of the necessary functionality comes from the Control base class. Given that you have already explored a number of the members for these types, you can quickly turn your attention to the process of assigning an image to the PictureBox member variable:

```
public class MainForm : System.Windows.Forms.Form
{
    // This holds an image of a smiley face.
    private PictureBox happyBox;

    public MainForm()
    {
        // Configure the PictureBox.
        happyBox = new PictureBox();
        happyBox.SizeMode = PictureBoxSizeMode.StretchImage;
        happyBox.Location = new System.Drawing.Point(64, 32);
        happyBox.Size = new System.Drawing.Size(50, 50);
        happyBox.Cursor = Cursors.Hand;

        happyBox.Image = new Bitmap("happy.bmp");

        // Now add to the Form's Controls collection.
        Controls.Add(happyBox);

    }
    . . .
}
```

The only point of interest is the SizeMode property, which makes use of the PictureBoxSizeMode enumeration. This type is used to control how the associated image should be rendered within the bounding rectangle of the PictureBox. Here, you assigned StretchImage, indicating that you wish to skew the image over the entire client area. Other possible values appear in Table 9-26.

Table 9-26. The PictureBoxSizeMode Enumeration

PICTUREBOXSIZEMODE MEMBER NAME	MEANING IN LIFE
AutoSize	The PictureBox is sized equal to the size of the image that it contains.
CenterImage	The image is displayed in the center if the PictureBox is larger than the image. If the image is larger than the PictureBox, the picture is placed in the center of the PictureBox and the outside edges are clipped.
Normal	The image is located in the upper-left corner of the PictureBox. If the PictureBox is smaller than the image, it will be clipped.

Now that you have configured the initial look and feel of the PictureBox, you need to hook up some handlers for the MouseMove, MouseUp, and MouseDown events. This is simple, as PictureBox "is-a" Control. Thus, you can update your constructor logic as follows:

```
// Add handlers for the following events.
happyBox.MouseDown += new MouseEventHandler(happyBox_MouseDown);
happyBox.MouseUp += new MouseEventHandler(happyBox_MouseUp);
happyBox.MouseMove += new MouseEventHandler(happyBox_MouseMove);
```

The logic behind MouseDown stores the incoming (*x*, *y*) location of the mouse click for later use, and sets a boolean member variable (isDragging) to true, to indicate that a drag operation is in process.

```
// Mouse event handler to initiate dragging the pictureBox around.
private void happyBox_MouseDown(object sender, MouseEventArgs e)
{
    isDragging = true;

    // Save the (x, y) of the mouse down click,
    // because we need it as an offset when dragging the image.
    oldX = e.X;
    oldY = e.Y;
}
```

The MouseMove handler simply relocates the position of the PictureBox (using the Top and Left properties) by offsetting the current cursor location with the (*x*, *y*) position captured at when the mouse went down.

```
// If the user clicks on the image and moves the mouse,
// redraw the image at the new location.
private void happyBox_MouseMove(object sender, MouseEventArgs e)
{
    if (isDragging)
    {
        // Need to figure new Y value based on where the mouse
        // down click happened.
        happyBox.Top = happyBox.Top + (e.Y - oldY);

        // Same deal for X (use oldX as a base line).
        happyBox.Left = happyBox.Left + (e.X - oldX);
    }
}
```

Finally, MouseUp sets the isDragging boolean to false, to signal the end of the drag operation. Recall however, that this application has one extra point of logic. If the MouseUp event occurs when the PictureBox is contained within a GDI+ Rectangle object, you can assume the user has won the game (albeit a rather lame game. . .). That said, here is the remainder of the Form's logic:

```
// When the mouse goes up, they are done dragging.
// See if they dropped the image in the rectangle. . .
private void happyBox_MouseUp(object sender, MouseEventArgs e)
{
    isDragging = false;

    // Is the mouse within the area of the drop rect?
    if(dropRect.Contains(happyBox.Bounds))
    {
        MessageBox.Show("You win!", "What an amazing test of skill. . .");
    }
}
// Assume we have a private Rectangle configured as follows:
// Rectangle dropRect = new Rectangle(100, 100, 150, 150);
private void MainForm_Paint(object sender, PaintEventArgs e)
{
    // Draw the drop box.
    Graphics g = e.Graphics;
    g.FillRectangle(Brushes.AntiqueWhite, dropRect);

    // Display instructions.
    g.DrawString("Drag the happy guy in here. . .",
                new Font("Times New Roman", 25), Brushes.Red, dropRect);
}
```

As a reminder, it is worth pointing out that the Rectangle type defines the Contains() method that has been overloaded to test for a contained Rectangle, Point, or two integer values. This member can be quite helpful when calculating if a mouse click has occurred within a given rectangular region (as seen in the MouseUp event handler). When you run the application, you are presented with what appears in Figure 9-24.

If you have what it takes to win the game, you are rewarded with the kudos shown in Figure 9-25.

SOURCE CODE *The DraggingImages application is included under the Chapter 9 subdirectory.*

Figure 9-24. Dragging, dropping, and hit-testing images

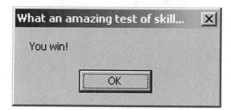

Figure 9-25. A true test of skill

More Hit Testing Details

Validating a hit test against a Control derived type (such as a button) is very simple, as each can respond to mouse events directly. However, what if you wish to perform a hit test on a geometric shape such as a region rendered on the screen using a GDI+ pen? To illustrate, let's revisit the previous Images application, and add some additional functionality.

The goal is to determine when the user clicks on a given image (which as you recall was *not* rendered within a PictureBox control). Once you discover which image was clicked, adjust the Text property of the Form, and highlight the image with a red outline. For example check out Figure 9-26.

Figure 9-26. Highlighting images

The first step is to intercept the MouseDown event for the Form itself. When the event occurs, you need to programmatically figure out if the incoming (x, y) coordinate is somewhere within the bounds of the Rectangles used to represent the dimension of each Image. If the user does click on a given image, you set a private boolean member variable (isImageClicked) to true, and set indicate which image was selected via another member variable (of type integer):

```
public class MainForm : System.Windows.Forms.Form
{
. . .
    // Did they click on an image?
    private bool isImageClicked = false;
    private int imageClicked;
```

```
    protected void OnMouseDown (object sender, MouseEventArgs e)
    {
        // Get (x, y) of mouse click.
        Point mousePt = new Point(e.X, e.Y);

        // See if the mouse is anywhere in the 3 regions. . .
        if(rectA.Contains(mousePt))
        {
            isImageClicked = true;
            imageClicked = 0;
            this.Text = "You clicked image A";
        }
        else if(rectB.Contains(mousePt))
        {
            isImageClicked = true;
            imageClicked = 1;
            this.Text = "You clicked image B";
        }
        else if(rectC.Contains(mousePt))
        {
            isImageClicked = true;
            imageClicked = 2;
            this.Text = "You clicked image C";
        }
        else     // Not in any shape, set defaults.
        {
            isImageClicked = false;
            this.Text = "Images";
        }

        // Redraw the client area.
        Invalidate();
    }
...
}
```

Notice that the final conditional check sets the isImageClicked member variable to false, indicating that the user did not click one of your three images. This is important, as you want to erase the red outline of the previously selected image. Once all items have then been checked, invalidate the client area. Here is the updated Paint handler:

```
private void MainForm_Paint(object sender, PaintEventArgs e)
{
    Graphics g = e.Graphics;

    // Render all three images.
    . . .

    // Draw outline (if clicked. . .)
    if(isImageClicked = = true)
    {
        Pen outline = new Pen(Color.Red, 5);

        switch(imageClicked)
        {
            case 0:
                g.DrawRectangle(outline, rectA);
                break;
            case 1:
                g.DrawRectangle(outline, rectB);
                break;
            case 2:
                g.DrawRectangle(outline, rectC);
                break;
            default:
                break;
        }
    }
}
```

Hit Testing Nonrectangular Images

Now, what if you wish to perform a hit test in a nonrectangular region, rather
than a simple square? Assume you updated your application to render an oddball
geometric shape that will also sport a red outline when clicked (Figure 9-27).

This geometric image was rendered on the Form using the FillPath()
method of the Graphics type. This method takes an instance of a GraphicsPath
object, which was mentioned earlier during your examination of the
System.Drawing.Drawing2D namespace. The GraphicsPath object encapsulates a
series of connected lines, curves, and (interestingly enough) strings. Adding new
items to a GraphicsPath instance is achieved using a number of related "add"
methods (Table 9-27).

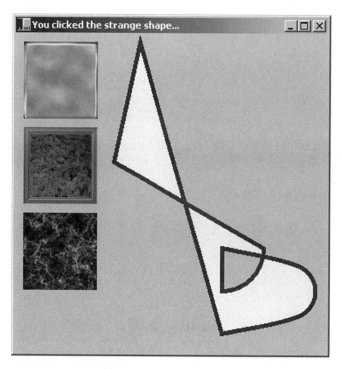

Figure 9-27. Highlighting oddball shapes

Table 9-27. Add-Centric Methods of the GraphicsPath Class

GRAPHICSPATH "ADD" METHOD	MEANING IN LIFE
AddArc()	Appends an elliptical arc to the current figure.
AddBezier() AddBeziers()	Adds a cubic Bezier curve (or set of Bezier curves) to the current figure.
AddClosedCurve()	Adds a closed curve to the current figure.
AddCurve()	Adds a curve to the current figure.
AddEllipse()	Adds an ellipse to the current figure.
AddLine() AddLines()	Appends a line segment to the current figure.
AddPath()	Appends the specified GraphicsPath to the current figure.
AddPie()	Adds the outline of a pie shape to the current figure.
AddPolygon()	Adds a polygon to the current figure.
AddRectangle() AddRectangles()	Adds one (or more) rectangle to the current figure.
AddString()	Adds a text string to the current figure.

Assume that you have added a private GraphicsPath member variable to your current Images application. In the Form's constructor, build the set of items that represent your path as follows:

```
public MainForm : System.Windows.Forms.Form
{
    // A polygon region.
    GraphicsPath myPath = new GraphicsPath();

    public MainForm()
    {
        // Create an interesting region.
        myPath.StartFigure();
            myPath.AddLine(new Point(150, 10), new Point(120, 150));
            myPath.AddArc(200, 200, 100, 100, 0, 90);
            Point point1 = new Point(250, 250);
            Point point2 = new Point(350, 275);
            Point point3 = new Point(350, 325);
            Point point4 = new Point(250, 350);
            Point[] points = {point1, point2, point3, point4};
            myPath.AddCurve(points);
        myPath.CloseFigure();
    . . .
    }
}
```

Notice the calls to StartFigure() and CloseFigure(). When you call StartFigure(), you are able to insert a new item into the current path you are building. A call to CloseFigure() closes the current figure and begins a new figure (if you require one). If the figure contains a sequence of connected lines and curves (as in the case of the myPath instance), the loop is closed by connecting a line from the endpoint to the starting point.

There are more members for System.Drawing.Drawing2D.GraphicsPath, but let's keep focused on the hit-testing logic. The next step would be to update your existing MouseDown event handler to test for the presence of the cursor's (*x*, *y*) position within the bounds of the GraphicsPath. Like a Region type, this can be discovered using the IsVisible() member:

```
protected void OnMouseDown (object sender, MouseEventArgs e)
{
    // Get (x, y) of mouse click.
    Point mousePt = new Point(e.X, e.Y);
```

```
        . . .
    else if(myPath.IsVisible(mousePt))
    {
        isImageClicked = true;
        imageClicked = 3;
        this.Text = "You clicked the strange shape. . .";
    }
. . .
}
```

Finally, you can update the Paint handler as follows:

```
private void MainForm_Paint(object sender, PaintEventArgs e)
{
    Graphics g = e.Graphics;
    . . .

    // Draw the graphics path.
    g.FillPath(Brushes.AliceBlue, myPath);

    // Draw outline (if clicked. . .)
    if(isImageClicked == true)
    {
        Pen outline = new Pen(Color.Red, 5);

        switch(imageClicked)
        {
            . . .
            case 3:
                g.DrawPath(outline, myPath);
                break;
            default:
                break;
        }
    }
}
```

SOURCE CODE   *The Images project is included under the Chapter 9 subdirectory.*

Understanding the .NET Resource Format

Up to this point, each application that made use of external resources (such as bitmaps) assumed that they were located in a separate standalone file. For example, the previous Images application rendered three bitmap images, which as you recall were loaded directly from file:

```
// Fill the images with bitmaps.
bMapImageA = new Bitmap("imageA.bmp");
bMapImageB = new Bitmap("imageB.bmp");
bMapImageC = new Bitmap("imageC.bmp");
```

This logic of course demands that the application directory does indeed contain three files named "imageA.bmp," "imageB.bmp," and "imageC.bmp" (see Figure 9-28).

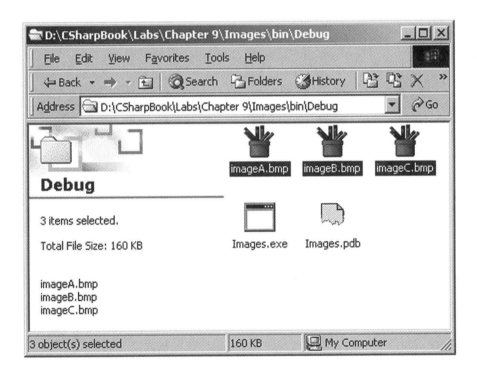

Figure 9-28. Standalone external resources

If any of these files are deleted, renamed, or relocated outside of the application directory, the program fails to execute (give it a try just for verification's sake). Now, as you recall from Chapter 6, an assembly is a collection of types and *optional resources*. The time has now come to learn how to bundle external resources (such as image files and strings) into the assembly itself. In this way, your .NET binary is truly self-contained. In a nutshell, bundling external resources into a .NET assembly involves the following steps:

- Create an *.resx file which establishes name/value pairs for each resource in your application using XML syntax.

- Use the resgen.exe utility to convert your XML-based *.resx file into a binary equivalent (a *.resources file).

- Using the /resource flag (or the shorthand /res flag) of the C# compiler, embed the binary *.resources file into your assembly.

As you might suspect, all these steps are followed automatically when using the Visual Studio.NET IDE. You examine how the IDE will assist you in just a bit. For now, take the time to work with the .NET resource format in the raw.

System.Resources Namespace

The key to understanding the .NET resource format is to know the types defined within the System.Resources namespace. This set of types provides the programmatic means to manipulate both *.resx (XML) and *.resources (binary) files. Table 9-28 provides a rundown of the core types.

Table 9-28. Members of the System.Resources Namespace

SYSTEM.RESOURCES TYPE	MEANING IN LIFE
IResourceReader IResourceWriter	These interfaces are implemented by types that understand how to read and write .NET resources (in various formats). You do not need to implement these interfaces yourself unless you are interested in building a custom resource reader/writer.
ResourceReader ResourceWriter	These classes provide an implementation of the IResourceReader and IResourceWriter interfaces. Using the ResourceReader and ResourceWriter types, you are able to read from and write to binary *.resources files.
ResXResourceReader ResXResourceWriter	These classes also provide an implementation of the IResourceReader and IResourceWriter interfaces. Using the ResXResourceReader and ResXResourceWriter types, you are able to read from and write to XML *.resx files. This file may be turned into a binary equivalent (the *.resources file) using the resgen.exe utility.
ResourceManager	Provides easy access to culture-specific resources (BLOBs and string resources) at runtime.

Programmatically Creating an *.resx File

As mentioned, an *.resx file is a block of XML data that assigns name/value pairs for each resource in your application. The ResXResourceWriter class provides a set of members that allow you to create the *resx file, add binary and string-based resources, and commit them to storage. To illustrate, assume you have a simple application whose job in life is to build an *.resx file containing an entry for the happy.bmp image seen earlier in this chapter, and a single string resource. The GUI is as simple as possible (Figure 9-29).

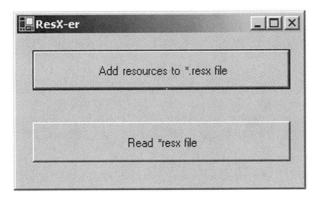

Figure 9-29. The simple UI

The Click event handler for the "Add resources" button does the grunt work of adding the happy.bmp and string resource to the *.resx file. Here is the code:

```
protected void btnMakeResxFile_Click (object sender, System.EventArgs e)
{
    // Make a resx writer & specify the file to write to.
    ResXResourceWriter w =
        new ResXResourceWriter("ResXForm.resx");

    // Add happy dude.
    Image i = new Bitmap("happy.bmp");
    w.AddResource("happyDude", i);

    // Add a string.
    w.AddResource("welcomeString", "Hello new resource format!");

    // Commit it.
    w.Generate();
    w.Close();
}
```

The member of interest is ResXResourceWriter.AddResource(). This method has been overloaded a few times to allow you to insert binary BLOB data (as you did with the happy.bmp image), as well as textual data (as you have done for your test string). Notice that each version takes two parameters: the name of a given resources in the *resx file and the data itself. The Generate() method commits the information to file.

Understand that you are not the one in charge of writing the raw XML that describes your resources. Rather, the logic within the ResXResourceWriter class is responsible for building the XML description of the inserted items. To prove the point, load the new *.resx file using Visual Studio.NET and peek inside the contents (Figure 9-30). To do so, simply access the "Project | Add Existing Item" menu command and navigate to the *resx data file (which of course will not be present until you click the correct button!).

Figure 9-30. The XML representation of your external resources

Here, you can see the raw XML that describes your resources. If you look carefully, you should be able to identify happyDude and welcomeString by name. The XML syntax which is used to represent your name/value pairs follows (note the binary representation of the happy dude bitmap. . .):

```
< data name="happyDude" mimetype="text/microsoft-urt/binary-serialized/base64" >
<value>AAEAAAD/////AQAAAAAAAAMAgAAADxTeXNOZWOuRHJhd2luZywgVmVyPTEuMC4yMjALjIxLC
BMb2M9IiIsIFNOPTAzNjg5MTE2ZDNhNGFlMzMFAQAAABVTeXNOZWOuRHJhd2luZy5CaXRtYXABAAAAABER
```

hdGEDDVN5c3RlbS5CeXRlW1oCAAAACQMAAAAHAwAAAAABAAAATgEAAACiVBORwOKGgoAAAANSUhEUgAA
ACAAAAAgBAMAAAACBVGfHAAAAAXNSR0IArs4c6QAAAARnQU1BAACxjwv8YQUAAAAgYOhSTQAAeiYAAICEA
AD6AAAAgOgAAHUwAADqYAAAOpgAABdwnLpRPAAAADBQTFRFAAAAgAAAAIAAgIAAAACAgICAwM
DA/wAAAP8A//8AAD//wD/AP//////ex+xxAAAAAlwSFlzAAAOxAAADsQBlSsOGwAAAHtJREFUKM+FkUE
OwCAIBLkaPu+VX3X3Dnc21Bt6A2JfHgAMK6ROewO9KVzUNLPteYVcIvOKVglKzg6VCO4z2RiOMlv4ArOA+A
KQNMcZ9A554cIMs/tZChh7GpYjZW9+eGFlfdidqU74kmOsuPqQgDQB6cWW3Yjdqt3MzOcQEjV+MdZ/YPN
QAAAABJRU5ErkJgggsAAAAAAAAAAAAAAAAAAA= **</value>**
</data>

<data name="welcomeString">
<value>Hello new resource format!**</value>**
</data>

Programmatically Reading an *.resx File

To illustrate how you can load and investigate an *resx file programmatically let's examine the code behind the "Read *resx" button. This time, make use of a ResXResourceReader type. Once the correct file has been opened, ask the reader for a reference to its IDictionaryEnumerator interface, and loop over each name/value pair:

```
protected void btnReadResxFile_Click (object sender, System.EventArgs e)
{
    // Make a resx reader.
    ResXResourceReader r = new ResXResourceReader("ResXForm.resx");

    // Grab the IDictionaryEnumerator interface and show everything.
    IDictionaryEnumerator en = r.GetEnumerator();

    while (en.MoveNext())
    {
        MessageBox.Show("Value:" + en.Value.ToString(),
                        "Key: " + en.Key.ToString());
    }
    r.Close();
}
```

When you click the button, you see a pair of message boxes pop up, as the ResXResourceReader type loops through the XML file for each named value. For example, Figure 9-31 offers the listing for the happy dude.

Figure 9-31. Extracting the name/value pair

Building the *.resources File

Now that you understand how to build and manipulate an *.resx file, you can make use of the resgen.exe utility to produce the binary equivalent. Again, Visual Studio.net will do so automatically, but just for the love of learning, here is the raw command:

```
resgen resxform.resx resxform.resources
```

Of course, you must open a command prompt in the directory containing the *resx file before running resgen.exe. Once you do however, you are able to open the new *resources file and check out the binary (Figure 9-32).

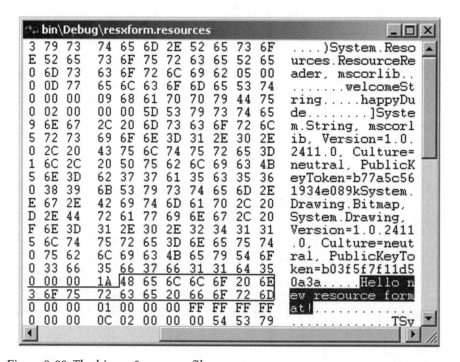

*Figure 9-32. The binary *resources file*

*Binding the *resources File into the Owning Assembly*

Cool! At this point you are able to add this *resources file as a command-line argument to the C# compiler (again using the /res flag). Recall that doing so also requires you to reference each external assembly (i.e., System.Drawing.dll):

```
csc /res:resxform.resources /r:System.Drawing.dll
/r:System.Windows.Forms.dll /r:System.dll resxform.cs
```

If you were to now open your new assembly using ILDasm.exe, you would find the entry shown in Figure 9-33 in the assembly metadata.

```
MANIFEST
    //   .custom instance void [mscorlib]System.Diagnostic
    //
    .hash algorithm 0x00008004
    .ver 0:0:0:0
}
.mresource public MyResXApp.ResXForm.resources
{
}
.module MyResXApp.exe
```

Figure 9-33. The updated manifest

As you can see, the manifest has recorded the name of the binary resources that are now contained in the owning assembly. In just a bit you will see how to programmatically read this information from an assembly to make use of it in your application.

SOURCE CODE   *The ResXWriterReader project is included under the Chapter 9 subdirectory.*

Working with ResourceWriters

The previous example made use of the ResXResourceReader and ResXResourceWriter types to generate an XML file that contains name/value pairs for each application resource. The resulting *.resx file was then run through the resgen.exe utility. Finally the *.resources file was bound into the owning assembly using the /res flag. The truth of the matter is that you do not need to build an *.resx file (although having an XML representation of your resources can come in handy).

If you do not require an *.resx file, you can make use of the ResourceWriter type to automatically create a *.resources file. To illustrate, assume you have created a new C# Console Application named ResourceTest. The Main() method of the ResourceGenerator class uses the ResourceWrite type to directly generate the myResources.resources file:

```csharp
class ResourceGenerator
{
    static void Main(string[] args)
    {
        // Make a new *.resources file.
        ResourceWriter rw;
        rw = new ResourceWriter("myResources.resources");

        // Add 1 image and 1 string.
        rw.AddResource("happyDude", new Bitmap("happy.bmp"));
        rw.AddResource("welcomeString", "Welcome to .NET resources.");
        rw.Generate();
    }
}
```

At this point, compile and run the application to generate the *.resource file. Now, we can bind the contained binary data to the owning assembly as before:

```
csc /res:myresources.resources /r:System.Drawing.dll
/r:System.Windows.Forms.dll /r:System.dll ResourcesGen.cs
```

If you wish to read the raw name/value data from the binary *.resources file, you are free to make use of the ResourceReader class. This is almost identical to working with the ResXResourceWriter type.

Working with ResourceManagers

Rather than working with the ResourceReader class directly, you will most likely use the ResourceManager type. The reason is simple: It is easier to work with! Using the ResourceManager, you are able to extract binary and textual data from an assembly for use in your application.

To illustrate, assume you have added a new class to the current project named MyResourceReader. This type uses a ResourceManager type to pull the happyDude and welcomeString resources from the assembly and dump them into a PictureBox and Label object using the GetObject() and GetString() members. Be very aware however, that the double quoted strings you send into these methods are *case sensitive*. Here is the code:

```
class MyResourceReader
{
    public void ReadMyResources()
    {
        // Open the resources file.
        ResourceManager rm = new ResourceManager("myResources",
                Assembly.GetExecutingAssembly());

        // Load image resource.
        PictureBox p = new PictureBox();
        Bitmap b = (Bitmap)rm.GetObject("happyDude");
        p.Image = (Image)b;
        p.Height = b.Height;
        p.Width = b.Width;
        p.Location = new Point(10, 10);

        // Load string resource.
        Label label1 = new Label();
        label1.Location = new Point(50, 10);
        label1.Font = new Font( label1.Font.FontFamily, 12, FontStyle.Bold);
        label1.AutoSize = true;
        label1.Text = rm.GetString("welcomeString");

        // Build a Form to show the resources.
        Form f = new Form();
        f.Height = 100;
        f.Width = 370;
        f.Text = "These resources are embedded in the assembly!";

        // Add controls and show Form.
        f.Controls.Add(p);
        f.Controls.Add(label1);
        f.ShowDialog();
    }
}
```

Before you run the application, be sure to update Main() to call the ReadMyResources() method:

```
static void Main(string[] args)
{
    . . .
    MyResourceReader r = new MyResourceReader();
    r.ReadMyResources();
}
```

When you run this application, you should find what appears in Figure 9-34.

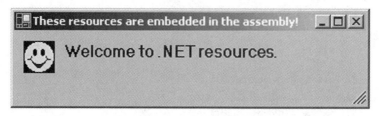

Figure 9-34. Extracting resources with the ResourceManager

SOURCE CODE   *The ResourceTest project is included under the Chapter 9 subdirectory.*

Automatic Resource Configuration a la Visual Studio.NET

To wrap things up, let's look at how the Visual Studio.NET IDE gets you up and running with the correct resource file configuration automatically.

When you create a new Windows Forms project workspace using Visual Studio.NET, the IDE automatically defines an *.resx file for your application. Furthermore, when you insert new resources to the project, the name/value pairs contained in the *.resx file are updated on your behalf. You can view the project's *resx file by selecting the "Show all files" option from the Solution Explorer window (Figure 9-35).

Once you select this file, check out the Properties window. You will see that the build action for this file has been configured as "Embedded Resource" (Figure 9-36).

This option compiles the *.resx file to produce the corresponding *.resources file, which is then embedded into your assembly.

To illustrate this process, create a new C# Windows Application workspace named ResLoader. The Form contains two PictureHolder types, one of which has its Image property set to the happy.bmp file, the other of which is empty. In

*Figure 9-35. Viewing the freebee *resx file*

*Figure 9-36. Configuring the Build Action for the *resx file*

addition, a single button type will be used to dynamically read this happy dude from file, and place it into the empty PictureHolder. The GUI is shown in Figure 9-37.

Figure 9-37. Before loading happy dude

As you insert resources (such as a bitmap) into the project, the IDE responds by creating an instance of the ResourceManager type within the scope of your InitializeComponent() method:

```
private void InitializeComponent()
{
    System.Resources.ResourceManager resources =
        new System.Resources.ResourceManager (typeof(MainForm));
    . . .

    pictureBox1.Image =
        (System.Drawing.Image) resources.GetObject ("pictureBox1.Image");
}
```

Needless to say, you are free to add a private ResourceManager member variable for use throughout your application. To illustrate, here is the code behind the button's Click event:

```
// Be sure to specify 'using System.Resources'
private void btnLoadRes_Click(object sender, System.EventArgs e)
{
    // Make a ResourceManager
    ResourceManager resources = new ResourceManager (typeof(MainForm));

    // Read happy dude from assembly and place it
    // into the second PictureBox object.
    this.pictureBox2.Image =
        ((System.Drawing.Bitmap)(resources.GetObject("pictureBox1.Image")));

    // All done!
    resources.ReleaseAllResources();
}
```

If you were to run the application and click the button, you would find that the image has been extracted from the assembly and placed into the second PictureBox (Figure 9-38):

Figure 9-38. After loading happy dude

SOURCE CODE   *The ResLoader project is included under the Chapter 9 subdirectory.*

Summary

GDI+ is the name given to a number of related .NET namespaces, each of which is used to render graphic images to a Control derived type. The chapter began by examining the core types defined within the System.Drawing namespace (including a number of useful utility types), and learned how to intercept paint events. A key aspect to GDI+ is, of course, the Graphics object.

The bulk of this chapter was spent examining how to work with core GDI+ object types. The Pen and Brush types provide a good deal of specialized functionality, especially when making use of the more exotic types defined in System.Drawing.Drawing2D. Font types require a fair amount of information (a Brush type, Color type, location to render the text, etc), however this does offer a good deal of functionality.

This chapter wrapped up by examining the new .NET resource format. As you have seen, an application does not *need* to bundle its external resources into the containing assembly, however if you do so, your binary image is far more portable. The *.resx file is used to describe (in XML syntax) a set of name/value pairs. This file is fed into the resgen.exe utility, resulting in a binary format (*.resources) that can then be embedded into the owning assembly. The ResourceManager type is your key to programmatically obtaining this information.

CHAPTER 10

Programming with Windows Form Controls

This chapter is concerned with providing a roadmap of the suite of GUI widgets defined in the System.Windows.Forms namespace. If you have been reading this book from the beginning, you have already had a chance to work with some Form-level Control types such as MainMenu, MenuItem, StatusBar, and ToolBar (see Chapter 8). In this chapter, I am interested in examining the types that tend to exist within the boundaries of a Form's client area (e.g., Buttons, TrackBars, TextBoxes, Panels, and the like).

In addition to giving you a formal grounding in the Windows Forms Control set, this chapter also details a number of related topics, such as establishing the tab order for your widgets, as well as configuring the "docking" and "anchoring" behaviors for your family of GUI types.

The chapter wraps up with a discussion of building custom dialog boxes, including techniques for responding to (and validating) user input. Finally, I examine a new facility offered by the .NET Windows Forms architecture: Form inheritance. As you will see, it is now possible to establish "is-a" relationships between related Forms.

Understanding the Windows Forms Control Hierarchy

The System.Windows.Forms namespace contains a number of types that represent common GUI widgets. Using these types, you can respond to user input in a Windows Forms application. Because .NET is a system of types built on standard OO principles, these Controls are arranged in a hierarchy of related types. Figure 10-1 illustrates the big picture. (Note that Control is the common base class for all widgets.)

As you learned in Chapter 8, the Control type is the base class that provides a minimal and complete set of behaviors for all descending widgets. This includes the ability to process mouse and keyboard events, establish the physical dimensions of the widget using various properties (Height, Width, Left, Right, Location, and so on), manipulate background and foreground colors, establish the active font, and so forth.

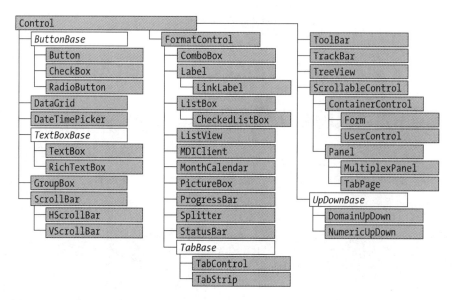

Figure 10-1. The Windows Forms control hierarchy

As you read through this chapter, remember that the Controls I examine gain most of their functionality from the Control base class. Here I focus (more or less) on a given type's unique members. (I assume you will explore the base class functionality on your own.) And now, on to the show!

Adding Controls to Forms (by Hand)

Regardless which type of Control you choose to place on a Form, you follow a similar set of steps. First of all, create any number of private member variables that represent the GUI items maintained by the Form. Next, inside the Form's constructor (or in the InitializeComponent() method), configure the look and feel of each Control using the provided properties, methods, and events. Finally (and most important), once the Control has been set to its initial state, add it to the Form's Controls collection (using the Control property). If you forget this final step, your Control will *not* be visible at runtime! To illustrate the process, consider the MyForm class, shown here:

```
// Don't forget to add a reference to System.Windows.Forms.dll.
using System.Windows.Forms;

class MyForm : Form
{
    // 1) Add the private data member....
    private TextBox firstNameBox = new TextBox();

    MyForm()
    {
        this.Text = "Controls in the raw";

        // 2) Configure new TextBox.
        firstNameBox.Text = "Chucky";
        firstNameBox.Size = new Size(150, 50);
        firstNameBox.Location = new Point(10, 10);

        // 3) Add new Controls to the Form's Controls collection.
        this.Controls.Add(firstNameBox);
    }
    ...
}
```

The Control$ControlCollection Type

While the process of adding a new widget to a Form is quite simple, I'd like to discuss the Controls property in a bit more detail. This property returns a reference to a nested class named ControlCollection defined by the Control class (i.e., Control$ControlCollection). The Control$ControlCollection type maintains an entry for each widget placed on the Form. You can obtain a reference to this collection any time you want to "walk the list" of child widgets, as shown here:

```
// Get access to the Control$ControlCollection type for this Form.
Control.ControlCollection coll = this.Controls;
```

Once you have a reference, you can call any of the members described in table 10-1 (which should look quite familiar, given your work in Chapter 5). Be aware that by default Controls are placed in the ControlCollection type using an $(n + 1)$ insertion policy.

Table 10-1. Nested ControlCollection Properties

CONTROL$CONTROLCOLLECTION

PROPERTY	MEANING IN LIFE
Add() AddRange()	Used to insert a new Control-derived type (or array of types) in the collection
Clear()	Removes all entries in the collection.
Count	Returns the number of items in the collection.
GetChildIndex() SetChildIndex()	Returns (or sets) the index value for a specified item in the collection.
GetEnumerator()	Returns the IEnumerator interface for this collection.
Remove()	Removes a given Control from the collection, given its index .

To illustrate programmatic manipulation of this very important collection, assume you have now added another widget (a Button) to the Form's collection. Also assume you have added an event handler for the Button's Click event. In the implementation of this method, you loop over each item in the Controls collection and print out some relevant information about the current Control, as shown here:

```
class MyForm : Form
{
    private TextBox firstNameBox = new TextBox();
    private Button btnShowControls = new Button();

    MyForm()
    {

        // Configure new TextBox

        . . .

        // Add a new Button.

        btnShowControls.Text = "Examine Controls collection";

        btnShowControls.Size = new Size(90, 90);

        btnShowControls.Location = new Point(10, 70);

        btnShowControls.Click +=
            new EventHandler(btnShowControls_Clicked);
```

```
            this.Controls.Add(btnShowControls);
    }


    protected void btnShowControls_Clicked(object sender, EventArgs e)
    {
        // Display information for each item in the collection.
        Control.ControlCollection coll = this.Controls;
        foreach(Control c in coll)
        {
            // Second parameter of GetChildIndex() enables or disables
            // the throwing of an exception if the item is not present.
            if(c != null)
                MessageBox.Show(c.Text, "Index numb: "
                                    + coll.GetChildIndex(c, false));
        }
    }
    . . .
}
```

Figure 10-2 shows the complete GUI. Notice how the default behavior of the Button.Text property is to wrap text in the display rectangle.

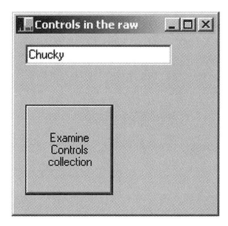

Figure 10-2. Form Controls

Clicking the Button widget results in two messages, which identify the Controls in the internal collection (Figure 10-3).

SOURCE CODE *The ControlsByHand project is included under the Chapter 10 subdirectory.*

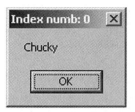

Figure 10-3. Investigating contained Controls

Adding Controls to Forms (the Easy Way)

Although you are always free to write Windows Forms code "in the raw," you will probably choose to use the Visual Studio.NET IDE instead. When you drop a widget on the design time Form, the IDE responds by adding a member variable on your behalf. Of course, you will typically want to change the name of this new variable to represent its overall functionality (e.g., "btnFirstName" rather than the default "button1").

As you design the look and feel of the widget using the IDE's Properties window (Figure 10-4), the underlying code changes are added to the InitializeComponent() member function.

Figure 10-4. Configuring Controls at design time

Be aware that this window allows you to configure not only the property set of a given GUI item, but the set of events as well (Figure 10-5). Simply select the widget from the drop-down list and type in the name of the method to be called for the events you are interested in responding to.

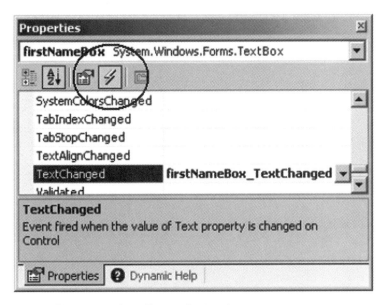

Figure 10-5. Building event handlers at design time

If you examine the code generated in the InitializeComponent() method, you find something like the following (note that the new GUI item is inserted in the Form's Controls collection on your behalf using the AddRange() method):

```
private void InitializeComponent()
{
    this.firstNameBox = new System.Windows.Forms.TextBox();
    this.firstNameBox.Location = new System.Drawing.Point(32, 40);
    this.firstNameBox.TabIndex = 0;
    this.firstNameBox.Text = "Chucky";
    this.firstNameBox.TextChanged += new
        System.EventHandler(this.firstNameBox_TextChanged);
    this.AutoScaleBaseSize = new System.Drawing.Size(5, 13);
    this.ClientSize = new System.Drawing.Size(292, 273);
    this.Controls.AddRange(new System.Windows.Forms.Control[]
                            {this.firstNameBox});
    . . .
}
```

Finally, you are given the following empty code stub to handle the TextChanged event for this TextBox, as shown here:

```
protected void firstNameBox_TextChanged (object sender, System.EventArgs e)
{
    // Do whatever you need to do. . .
}
```

The remainder of this chapter focuses on a number of behaviors offered by numerous GUI widgets by examining the "raw" code behind the scenes. If you decide to use the Visual Studio.NET IDE, be sure to examine the code generated inside the IntializeComponent() method to gain a true understanding of Windows Form programming.

The TextBox Control

The TextBox Control is the first item under investigation. This GUI widget holds some blurb of text or possibly multiple lines of text. A TextBox Control can also be configured as read only and support scroll bars. The immediate base class of TextBox is TextBoxBase, which provides many common behaviors for the TextBox and RichTextBox Controls. Table 10-2 describes some of the core properties provided by the TextBoxBase type.

The TextBoxBase type also defines a number of methods, which allow the derived type to handle clipboard operations (via the Cut(), Copy(), and Paste() methods), undo operations (Undo(), of course), and carry out other related functionality (Clear(), AppendText(), and so on).

As far as the events defined by TextBoxBase, the item of interest is TextChange (the Windows Forms equivalent of the raw EN_CHANGE message). As you may know, this event is fired whenever the content in a TextBoxBase derived type is modified. This can be very helpful when you wish to block the user from entering in certain types of characters (e.g., numerical data only or alphabetic data only).

In addition to the behavior inherited by TextBoxBase, the TextBox type grabs a good deal of functionality from the Control base class. In fact, the properties defined by TextBox alone are quite limited (Table 10-3).

Table 10-2. TextBoxBase Properties

TEXTBOXBASE PROPERTY	MEANING IN LIFE
AcceptsTab	Indicates if pressing the Tab key in a multiline TextBox Control tabs in the Control itself, rather than moving the focus to the next Control in the tab order.
AutoSize	Determines if the size of the Control automatically adjusts when the assigned font is changed.
BackColor ForeColor	Gets or sets the background or foreground color of the Control.
HideSelection	Gets or sets a value indicating whether the selected text in the TextBox Control remains highlighted when the Control loses focus.
MaxLength	Configures the maximum number of characters that can be entered in the TextBox Control.
Modified	Gets or sets a value that indicates that the TextBox Control has been modified by the user since the Control was created or its contents were last set.
Multiline	Specifies if this TextBox can contain multiple lines of text.
ReadOnly	Marks this TextBox as read only.
SelectedText SelectionLength	Contains the currently selected text (or some number of characters) in the Control.
SelectionStart	Gets or sets the starting point of text selected in the TextBox.
WordWrap	Indicates whether a multiline TextBox Control automatically wraps words to the beginning of the next line when necessary.

Table 10-3. TextBox Properties

TEXTBOX PROPERTY	MEANING IN LIFE
AcceptsReturn	Gets or sets a value indicating whether pressing Enter in a multiline TextBox Control creates a new line of text in the Control or activates the default Button for the Form.
CharacterCasing	Gets or sets whether the TextBox Control modifies the case of characters as they are typed.
PasswordChar	Gets or sets the character used to mask characters in a single-line TextBox Control used to enter passwords.
ScrollBars	Gets or sets which scroll bars should appear in a multiline TextBox Control.
TextAlign	Gets or sets how text is aligned in a TextBox Control, using the HorizontalAlignment enumeration.

The HorizontalAlignment enumeration used in conjunction with the TextAlign property offers the values described in Table 10-4.

Table 10-4. HorizontalAlignment Values

HORIZONTALALIGNMENT VALUE	MEANING IN LIFE
Center	The object or text is aligned in the center of the Control element.
Left	The object or text is aligned on the left of the Control element.
Right	The object or text is aligned on the right of the Control element.

Fun with TextBoxes

To illustrate some of the more exotic aspects of the TextBox, build a multiline text area that has been configured to accept Return and Tab keystrokes and supports a vertical scroll bar. Here is the configuration code (assume you have already created a member of type TextBox named multiLineBox):

```
// Your first TextBox.
multiLineBox.Location = new System.Drawing.Point (152, 8);
multiLineBox.Text = "Type some stuff here (and hit the return and tab keys...)";
multiLineBox.Multiline = true;
multiLineBox.AcceptsReturn = true;
multiLineBox.ScrollBars = System.Windows.Forms.ScrollBars.Vertical;
multiLineBox.TabIndex = 0;
multiLineBox.AcceptsTab = true;
```

Notice that the ScrollBars property is assigned a value from the ScrollBars enumeration, which defines the values Vertical, Horizontal, None, and Both.

Now assume you have placed a simple Button on the Form and added an event handler for the Button's Click event. The implementation of this method simply places the TextBox's text in a message box (just to illustrate grabbing values from a TextBox Control). The current UI is shown in Figure 10-6.

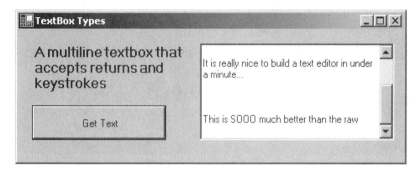

Figure 10-6. Building event handlers at design time

The code behind the Button Click event is simple, as shown here:

```
protected void btnGetMultiLineText_Click (object sender, System.EventArgs e)
{
    MessageBox.Show(multiLineBox.Text, "Here is your text");
}
```

The equally simple response is shown in Figure 10-7.

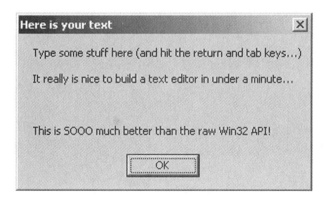

Figure 10-7. Extracting data from the TextBox

Next, add some additional TextBoxes to the Form, this time focusing on the masking capabilities of the widget (Figure 10-8). The second TextBox (capsOnlyBox) forces all keystrokes to be converted to uppercase. The third TextBox (passwordBox) forces all keystrokes to be converted to a password character (which I have chosen to be "$," signifying how your financial life as a .NET developer should pan out).

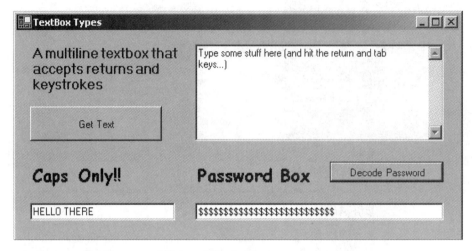

Figure 10-8. Masking capabilities of the TextBox

The additional Button (btnPasswordDecoderRing) supports a Click event handler that extracts the real keystrokes typed in the passwordBox TextBox, as shown here:

```
protected void btnGetMultiLineText_Click (object sender, System.EventArgs e)
{
    MessageBox.Show(multiLineBox.Text, "Here is your text");
}
```

Here is the relevant code that configures these new TextBox types:

```
// The 'Caps Only!' Button.
// Note that CharacterCasing is established by an associated enumeration,
// which can be assigned Upper, Lower, or Normal.
capsOnlyBox.Location = new System.Drawing.Point (14, 176);
capsOnlyBox.CharacterCasing = System.Windows.Forms.CharacterCasing.Upper;
capsOnlyBox.Size = new System.Drawing.Size (120, 20);

// The password TextBox
passwordBox.Location = new System.Drawing.Point (160, 176);
passwordBox.PasswordChar = '$';
```

As mentioned, TextBoxBase has an additional derived type named RichTextBox. This class is a Control that supports the display and manipulation of (highly) formatted text. For example, you can configure multiple font selections in a single widget, URLs, bulleted text, and so forth. I assume interested readers will consult online help for further details.

SOURCE CODE   *The TextBoxes application is included under the Chapter 10 sub-directory.*

The Mighty Button Type (and the ButtonBase Parent Class)

Of all user interface widgets, the Button can be regarded as the simplest, but most well-respected GUI input device. The role of the System.Windows.Forms.Button type is to provide a simple vehicle for user input, typically in response to a mouse click or key press. The Button class immediately derives from an abstract type named ButtonBase, which provides a number of key behaviors for all Button-related types (CheckBox, RadioButton, and Button). Table 10-5 describes some (but by no means all) core ButtonBase properties.

Table 10-5. ButtonBase Properties

BUTTONBASE PROPERTY	MEANING IN LIFE
FlatStyle	Gets or sets the flat style appearance of the Button Control, using members of the FlatStyle enumeration.
Image	Configures which (optional) image is displayed somewhere within the bounds of a ButtonBase derived type. Recall that Control also defines a BackgroundImage property, which is used to render an image over the entire surface area of a widget.
ImageAlign	Sets the alignment of the image on the Button Control, using the ContentAlignment enumeration.
ImageIndex ImageList	Work together to set the image list index value of the image displayed on the Button Control, from the corresponding ImageList Control.
IsDefault	Specifies whether the Button Control is the default Button (i.e., receives focus in response to pressing of the Enter key).
TextAlign	Gets or sets the alignment of the text on the Button Control, using the ContentAlignment enumeration.

The FlatStyle property controls the general appearance of the Button itself and can be assigned any member of the related FlatStyle enumeration (Table 10-6).

Table 10-6. FlatStyle Values

FLATSTYLE ENUMERATION VALUE	MEANING IN LIFE
Flat	The Control appears flat, with no three-dimensional rendering. When the cursor is over the Button, the text color changes to indicate it has the current focus.
Popup	A Control appears flat until the cursor moves over it, at which point it appears three dimensional.
Standard	The Control appears three dimensional, like the familiar standard pushbutton.
System	The appearance of the Control is determined by the user's operating system.

The Button class itself defines almost no additional functionality beyond that inherited by the ButtonBase base class, with the core exception of the DialogResult property. As you will see later in this chapter, a dialog box makes use of this property to return a value representing which Button was clicked (e.g., OK, Cancel, and so on) when the dialog box was terminated.

Configuring the Content Position

Most people assume that the text contained in a Button is always placed on the middle of the Button, equidistant from all sides. While this can be a well-established standard, the TextAlign property of the ButtonBase type makes it extremely simple to position text at just about any location. To set the position of your Button's caption, use the ContentAlignment enumeration (Table 10-7). Be aware that this same enumeration is used to configure the location of any optional Button image (as you will see).

Fun with Buttons

To illustrate working with this most primitive of user input widgets, the following application uses the FlatStyle, ImageAlign, and TextAlign properties. The most interesting aspect of the underlying code is in the Click event handler for the btn-Standard type (which would be the Button in the middle of the Form). This illustration cycles through each member of the ContentAlignment enumeration and changes the Button's caption text and caption location based on the current value.

Table 10-7. ContentAlignment Values

CONTENTALIGNMENT VALUE	MEANING IN LIFE
BottomCenter	Content is vertically aligned at the bottom and horizontally aligned at the center.
BottomLeft	Content is vertically aligned at the bottom and horizontally aligned on the left.
BottomRight	Content is vertically aligned at the bottom and horizontally aligned on the right.
MiddleCenter	Content is vertically aligned in the middle and horizontally aligned at the center.
MiddleLeft	Content is vertically aligned in the middle and horizontally aligned on the left.
MiddleRight	Content is vertically aligned in the middle and horizontally aligned on the right.
TopCenter	Content is vertically aligned at the top and horizontally aligned at the center.
TopLeft	Content is vertically aligned at the top and horizontally aligned on the left.
TopRight	Content is vertically aligned at the top and horizontally aligned on the right.

Also, the fourth Button on the Form (btnImage) supports a background image and a small bull's-eye icon, which is also dynamically relocated based on the current value of the ContentAlignment enumeration. Figure 10-9 shows the program in action.

Here is the relevant code:

```
public class ButtonForm: System.Windows.Forms.Form
{
    // You have 4 Buttons on this Form.
    private System.Windows.Forms.Button btnImage;
    private System.Windows.Forms.Button btnStandard;
    private System.Windows.Forms.Button btnPopup;
    private System.Windows.Forms.Button btnFlat;

    // Hold the current alignment value.
    ContentAlignment currAlignment = ContentAlignment.MiddleCenter;
    int currEnumPos = 0;

    // InitializeComponent() omitted. . .
    protected void btnStandard_Click (object sender, System.EventArgs e)
    {
        // Get all possible values of the ContentAlignment enum.
        Array values = Enum.GetValues(currAlignment.GetType());
```

```
                // Bump the current position in the enum.
                // & check for wraparound.
                currEnumPos++;
                if(currEnumPos >= values.Length)
                    currEnumPos = 0;

                // Change the current enum value.
                currAlignment =
                (ContentAlignment)ContentAlignment.Parse(currAlignment.GetType(),
                values.GetValue(currEnumPos).ToString());

                // Paint enum value name on Button.
                btnStandard.Text = currAlignment.ToString();
                btnStandard.TextAlign = currAlignment;

                // Now assign the location of the ICON on btnImage...

                btnImage.ImageAlign = currAlignment;
        }
        ...
    }
```

Figure 10-9. ContentAlignment in action

SOURCE CODE   *The Buttons application is included under the Chapter 10 sub-directory.*

Working with CheckBoxes

The other two ButtonBase-derived types of interest are CheckBox (which can support up to three possible states) and RadioButton (which can be either selected or not selected). Like the Button, these types also receive most of their functionality from the Control base class. However, each class defines some additional functionality. First, consider the core properties of the CheckBox widget described in Table 10-8.

Table 10-8. CheckBox Properties

CHECKBOX PROPERTY	MEANING IN LIFE
Appearance	Configures the appearance of a CheckBox Control, using the Appearance enumeration.
AutoCheck	Gets or sets a value indicating whether the Checked or CheckState value and the CheckBox's appearance are automatically changed when it is clicked.
CheckAlign	Gets or sets the horizontal and vertical alignment of a CheckBox on a CheckBox Control, using the ContentAlignment enumeration (see the Button type for a full description).
Checked	Returns a Boolean value representing the state of the CheckBox (checked or unchecked). If the ThreeState property is set to true, the Checked property returns true for either checked or indeterminately checked values.
CheckState	Gets or sets a value indicating whether the CheckBox is checked, using a CheckState enumeration, rather than a Boolean value. This is very helpful when working with tristate CheckBoxes.
ThreeState	Configures whether the CheckBox supports three states of selection (as specified by the CheckState enumeration) rather than two.

The ThreeState property is configured using the CheckState enumeration (Table 10-9).

Table 10-9. CheckState Values

CHECKSTATE VALUE	MEANING IN LIFE
Checked	The Control is checked.
Indeterminate	The Control is indeterminate. An indeterminate Control generally has a shaded appearance.
Unchecked	The Control is unchecked.

You have probably seen examples of Controls with these check states. For example, imagine a TreeView Control supporting a main node that expands to 10 checkable subnodes. If the user selects 6 of the 10 subnodes, the main node is in an indeterminate state (as 4 items are left unchecked).

Working with RadioButtons and GroupBoxes

The RadioButton type really requires little comment, given that it is (more or less) just a slightly redesigned CheckBox. In fact, the members of a RadioButton are almost identical to those of the CheckBox type. The only notable difference is the CheckedChanged event, which is fired when the Checked value changes. Also, the RadioButton type does not support the ThreeState property, as a RadioButton must be on or off.

Typically, multiple RadioButton objects are logically and physically grouped together to function as a whole. For example, if you have a set of four RadioButton types representing the color choice of a given automobile, you may wish to ensure that only one of the four types can be checked at a time. Rather than writing code programmatically to do so, use the GroupBox Control. Like the RadioButton, there is little to say about the GroupBox Control, given that it receives all of its functionality from the Control base class.

Fun with RadioButtons (and CheckBoxes)

To illustrate working with the CheckBox, RadioButton, and GroupBox types, create a new Windows Form Application named CarConfig. The main Form allows users to enter in (and confirm) information about a new vehicle they intend to purchase. Figure 10-10 shows the user interface.

Assume you have initialized a number of private member variables representing each GUI widget. First, you have your CheckBox, constructed as shown here:

Figure 10-10. Grouped RadioButtons

```
// Create your CheckBox.
checkFloorMats.Location = new System.Drawing.Point (16, 16);
checkFloorMats.Text = "Extra Floor Mats";
checkFloorMats.Size = new System.Drawing.Size (136, 24);
checkFloorMats.FlatStyle = System.Windows.Forms.FlatStyle.Popup;

// Add to Control collection.
this.Controls.Add (this.checkFloorMats);
```

Programmatically speaking, when you wish to place a widget under the ownership of a related GroupBox, you want to add each item to the GroupBox's Controls collection (in the same way you add widgets to the Form's Controls collection). To make things a bit more interesting, respond to the Enter and Leave events sent by the GroupBox object as shown here:

```
// Yellow RadioButton.
radioYellow.Location = new System.Drawing.Point (96, 24);
radioYellow.Text = "Yellow";
radioYellow.Size = new System.Drawing.Size (64, 23);

// Green, Red and Pink Buttons configured in a similar vein....

// Now build the group of radio items.
groupBox1.Location = new System.Drawing.Point (16, 56);
```

```
groupBox1.Text = "Exterior Color";
groupBox1.Size = new System.Drawing.Size (264, 88);

groupBox1.Leave += new System.EventHandler (groupBox1_Leave);
groupBox1.Enter += new System.EventHandler (groupBox1_Enter);

groupBox1.Controls.Add (this.radioPink);
groupBox1.Controls.Add (this.radioYellow);
groupBox1.Controls.Add (this.radioRed);
groupBox1.Controls.Add (this.radioGreen);
```

Understand that you do not *need* to capture the Enter or Leave events for a GroupBox. However, to illustrate, the event handlers update the caption text of the GroupBox as shown here:

```
// Figure out when the focus is in your group.
protected void groupBox1_Leave (object sender, System.EventArgs e)
{
    groupBox1.Text = "Exterior Color: Thanks for visiting the group. . .";
}

protected void groupBox1_Enter (object sender, System.EventArgs e)
{
    groupBox1.Text = "Exterior Color: You are in the group. . .";
}
```

The final GUI widgets on this Form (the Label and Button types) also need to be configured and inserted in the Form's Controls collection. The Label is used to display the order confirmation, which is formatted in the Click event handler of the order Button, as shown here:

```
protected void btnOrder_Click (object sender, System.EventArgs e)
{
    // Build a string to display information.
    string orderInfo = "";

    if(checkFloorMats.Checked)
        orderInfo += "You want floor mats.\n";

    if(radioRed.Checked)
        orderInfo += "You want a red exterior.\n";

    if(radioYellow.Checked)
```

```
            orderInfo += "You want a yellow exterior.\n";

    if(radioGreen.Checked)
            orderInfo += "You want a green exterior.\n";

    if(radioPink.Checked)
            orderInfo += "Why do you want a PINK exterior?\n";

    // Send this string to the Label.
    infoLabel.Text = orderInfo;
}
```

Notice that both the CheckBox and RadioButton support the Checked property, which allows you to investigate the state of the widget. Recall that if you have configured a tristate CheckBox, you want to check the state of the widget using the CheckState property (and the corresponding CheckState enumeration).

Examining the CheckedListBox Control

Now that I have explored the basic Button-centric widgets, I will move on to the set of list selection-centric types. Specifically, the CheckedListBox, ListBox, and ComboBox types. The CheckedListBox widget allows you to group together related CheckBox options in a scrollable list Control. Assume you have added such a Control to your CarConfig application, which allows the user to configure a number of options for regarding the automobile's sound system (Figure 10-11).

Like the Controls examined thus far, the CheckedListBox type gains most of its functionality from the Control base class type. Also, the CheckedListBox type inherits additional functionality from its direct base class, ListBox (examined later in this chapter).

To insert new items in a CheckedListBox, call Add() for each item or use the AddRange() method and send in an array of objects (strings, to be exact) that represent the full set of checkable items. Here is the configuration code (be sure to check out online help for details about these new properties):

```
// Configure the CheckedListBox.
checkedBoxRadioOptions.Location = new System.Drawing.Point (16, 48);
checkedBoxRadioOptions.Cursor = Cursors.Hand;
checkedBoxRadioOptions.Size = new System.Drawing.Size (256, 64);
checkedBoxRadioOptions.CheckOnClick = true;

// Add items to the CheckedListBox.
checkedBoxRadioOptions.Items.AddRange(new object[6]
                        {"Front Speakers", "8-Track Tape Player",
                        "CD Player", "Cassette Player",
```

```
                          "Rear Speakers", "Ultra Base Thumper"});

// As always, add the new widget to the Controls collection.
this.Controls.Add (this.checkedBoxRadioOptions);
```

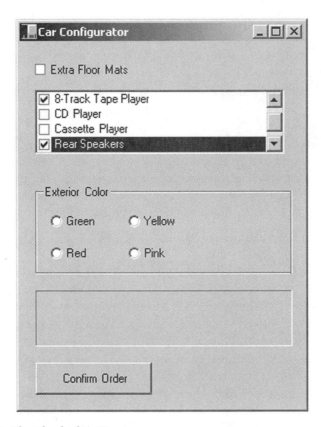

Figure 10-11. The CheckedListBox type

Now update the logic behind the Click event for the Order Button. Ask the CheckedListBox which of its items are currently selected and add them to the orderInfo string. Here is the relevant code:

```
protected void btnOrder_Click (object sender, System.EventArgs e)
{
    // Build a string to display information.
    string orderInfo = "";
```

```
    . . .
    // For each item in the CheckedListBox:
    for(int i = 0; i < checkedBoxRadioOptions.Items.Count; i++)
    {
        // Is the current item checked?
        if(checkedBoxRadioOptions.GetItemChecked(i))
        {
            // Get text of checked item and append to orderinfo string.
            orderInfo += "Radio Item: ";
            orderInfo += checkedBoxRadioOptions.Items[i].ToString();
            orderInfo += "\n";
        }
    }
    . . .
}
```

The final note regarding the CheckedListBox type is that it supports the use of multiple columns through the inherited MultiColumn property. Thus, if you make the following update:

```
checkedBoxRadioOptions.MultiColumn = true;
```

You see the multiline CheckedListBox shown in Figure 10-12.

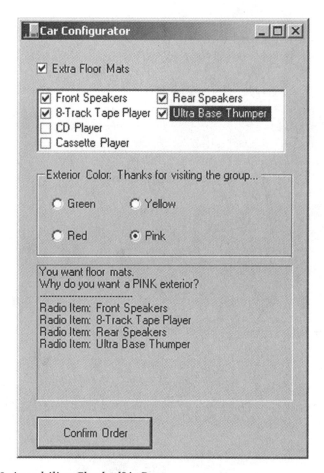

Figure 10-12. A multiline CheckedListBox

ListBoxes and ComboBoxes

As mentioned, the CheckedListBox type inherits most of its functionality from the ListBox type. The same holds true for the ComboBox class. Some core properties provided by System.Windows.Forms.ListBox are described in Table 10-10.

In addition to this property set, the ListBox also defines a number of methods. As most of them echo the functionality in various class properties, I'll leave it to you to check things out on your own.

To illustrate using the ListBox type, add another feature to the current CarConfig application: the ability to select the make (BMW, Yugo, and so on) of the automobile. Figure 10-13 shows the desired UI.

As always, begin by creating a member variable to manipulate your type (in this case a ListBox type). Next, configure the look and feel and insert the new widget in the Form's Controls collection, as shown here:

```
// Configure the list box.
carMakeList.Location = new System.Drawing.Point (168, 48);
carMakeList.Size = new System.Drawing.Size (112, 67);
carMakeList.BorderStyle = System.Windows.Forms.BorderStyle.FixedSingle;
carMakeList.ScrollAlwaysVisible = true;
carMakeList.Sorted = true;

// Populate the listBox using the AddRange() method.
carMakeList.Items.AddRange( new object[9] {"BMW", "Caravan", "Ford",
"Grand Am", "Jeep", "Jetta", "Saab", "Viper", "Yugo"});

// Add new widget to Form's Control collection.
this.Controls.Add (this.carMakeList);
```

Table 10-10. ListBox Properties

LISTBOX PROPERTY	MEANING IN LIFE
ScrollAlwaysVisible	Determines if the associated scroll bar is shown at all times.
SelectedIndex	The index of the currently selected item in the list (if any). The value of –1 indicates "no selection." If the value is 0 or greater, the value is the index of the currently selected item.
SelectedIndices	A collection of the indices of the selected items in the list box. If no selected items are in the list box, the result is an empty collection.
SelectedItem	The value of the currently selected item in the list. If the value is null, there is currently no selection.
SelectedItems	Returns a collection of all selected items (for a multiselection list box).
SelectionMode	Controls how many items at a time can be selected in the list box, using the SelectionMode enumeration.
Sorted	Indicates if the ListBox is sorted (alphabetically) or not.
TopIndex	Returns the index of the first visible item in a list box.

The update to the btnOrder_Click() event handler is also simple, as shown here:

```
protected void btnOrder_Click (object sender, System.EventArgs e)
{
    // Build a string to display information.
    string orderInfo = "";
    ...
    // Get the currently selected item (not index of the item).
    if(carMakeList.SelectedItem != null)
        orderInfo += "Make: " + carMakeList.SelectedItem + "\n";
    ...
}
```

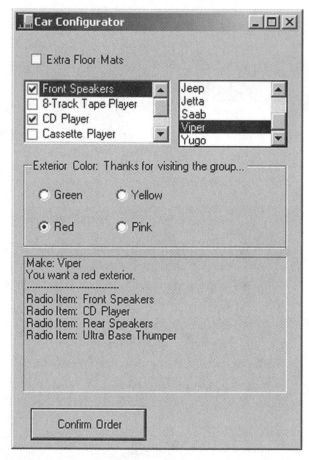

Figure 10-13. The ListBox type

Fun with ComboBoxes

Like a ListBox, a ComboBox allows the user to make a selection from a well-defined set of possibilities. However, the ComboBox type is unique in that the user can also insert additional items. Recall that ComboBox derives from ListBox (which then derives from Control). Beyond this mass of functionality, ComboBox offers the additional properties described in Table 10-11.

Table 10-11. ComboBox Properties

COMBOBOX PROPERTY	MEANING IN LIFE
DroppedDown	Indicates whether the drop-down portion of the combo is dropped down.
MaxDropDownItems	Indicates the maximum number of items to be shown in the drop-down portion of the ComboBox. This number can be from 1 to 100.
MaxLength	Indicates the maximum length of the text the user can type in the edit Control of a combo box.
SelectedIndex	Indicates the zero-based index of the selected item in the combos list. If the value of index is –1, there is no selected item.
SelectedItem	Indicates the handle to the object selected in the combos list.
SelectedText	Indicates the selected text in the edit component of the ComboBox.
SelectionLength	Indicates the length, in characters, of the selection in the edit box portion of the ComboBox.
Style	Indicates the type of combo. The value comes from the ComboBoxStyle enumeration.
Text	Gives access to whatever is in the edit box. The inherited Text property is generally most useful when working with ComboBoxes.

A given ComboBox has an associated style that is specified using the ComboBoxStyle enumeration (Table 10-12).

Table 10-12. ComboBox Styles

COMBOBOX STYLE	MEANING IN LIFE
DropDown	The text portion is editable. The user must click the Arrow Button to display the list portion.
DropDownList	The user cannot directly edit the text portion. The user must click the Arrow Button to display the list portion.
Simple	The text portion is editable. The list portion is always visible.

To illustrate, add yet another GUI widget to the CarConfig application, which allows a user to enter the name of a preferred salesperson. If the salesperson in

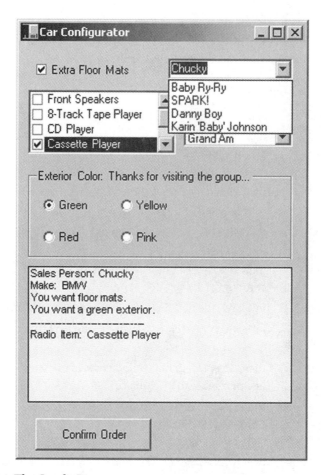

Figure 10-14. The ComboBox type

question is not on the list, the user can enter a custom name. The GUI update is shown in Figure 10-14 (this time with a more attractive output Label).

This modification begins with configuring the ComboBox itself. As you can see here, the logic looks identical to that for the ListBox:

```
// ComboBox configuration.
comboSalesPerson.Location = new System.Drawing.Point (152, 16);
comboSalesPerson.Size = new System.Drawing.Size (128, 21);
comboSalesPerson.Items.AddRange( new object[4] {"Baby Ry-Ry", "SPARK!", "Danny
Boy", "Karin 'Baby' Johnson"});
this.Controls.Add (this.comboSalesPerson);
```

The update to the btnOrder_Click() event handler is again simple, as shown here:

```
protected void btnOrder_Click (object sender, System.EventArgs e)
{
    // Build a string to display information.
    string orderInfo = "";
    . . .

    // Use the Text property to figure out the user's salesperson.
    if(comboSalesPerson.Text != "")
        orderInfo += "Sales Person: " + comboSalesPerson.Text + "\n";
    else
        orderInfo += "You did not select a sales person!" + "\n";
    . . .
}
```

Configuring the Tab Order

To finish up this first attempt at functional user interface, I will address the issue of tab order. As you know, when a Form or dialog box contains multiple GUI widgets, users expect to be able to shift focus using the Tab key. Configuring the tab order for your set of Controls requires that you understand two properties: TabStop and TabIndex.

The TabStop property can be set to true or false, based on whether or not you wish this GUI item to be reachable using the Tab key. Assuming the TabStop property has been set to true for a given widget, the TabOrder property is then set to establish its order of activation in the tabbing sequence. Consider this example:

```
// Configure tabbing properties.
radioRed.TabIndex = 2;
radioRed.TabStop = true;
```

As you would expect, these properties can be set using the Properties window (Figure 10-15).

The Tab Order Wizard

The Visual Studio.NET IDE supplies a Tab Order Wizard, accessed using the View | Tab Order menu selection (Figure 10-16). Once activated, your design time Form displays the current TabIndex value for each widget. To change these values, click each item in the order you choose. (Notice that Controls added to a GroupBox's Control collection function as a collective.)

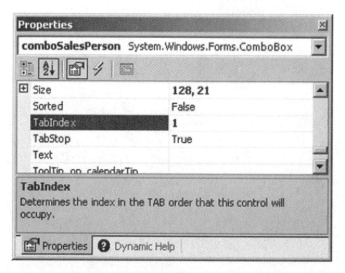

Figure 10-15. Configuring tab properties

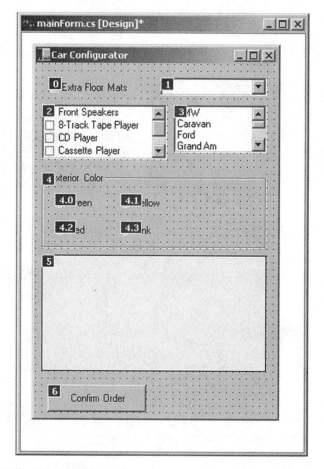

Figure 10-16. The TabOrder Wizard

Excellent! At this point you have learned about some very common GUI types. Now that you have the basics in mind, you can begin to examine some more exotic widgets.

SOURCE CODE   *The CarConfig project is included under the Chapter 10 sub-directory.*

The TrackBar Control

The TrackBar Control allows users to select from a range of values, using a scroll bar–like input mechanism. In many respects a TrackBar is functionally similar to a traditional scroll bar. When working with this type, you need to set the minimum and maximum range, the minimum and maximum change increments, and the starting location of the slider's thumb. Each of these aspects can be set using the properties described in Table 10-13.

Table 10-13. TrackBar Properties

TRACKBAR PROPERTY	MEANING IN LIFE
LargeChange	The number of ticks by which the TrackBar changes when an event considered a large change occurs (e.g., clicking the mouse button while the cursor is on the sliding range and using the Page Up or Page Down key.
Maximum Minimum	Configure the upper and lower bounds of the TrackBar's range.
Orientation	The orientation for this TrackBar. Valid values are from the Orientation enumeration (i.e., horizontally or vertically).
SmallChange	The number of ticks by which the TrackBar changes when an event considered a small change occurs (e.g., using the arrow keys).
TickFrequency	Indicates how many ticks are drawn. For a TrackBar with an upper limit of 200, it is impractical to draw all 200 ticks on a Control 2 inches long. If you set the TickFrequency property to 5, the TrackBar draws 20 total ticks (each tick represents 5 units).
TickStyle	Indicates how the TrackBar Control draws itself. This affects both where the ticks are drawn in relation to the movable thumb and how the thumb itself is drawn (using the TickStyle enumeration).
Value	Gets or sets the current location of the TrackBar. Use this property to obtain the numeric value contained by the TrackBar for use in your application.

Now you can build an application that makes use of three TrackBars. Each widget has an upper range of 255 and a lower range of 0. As the user slides each thumb, the application intercepts the Scroll event and dynamically builds a new Color type based on the value of each slider. In this way, the user is able to view the underlying RGB value (and see the color) for a given selection. (Of course, the System.Windows.Forms namespace already provides a ColorDialog type for this purpose.) Figure 10-17 shows the GUI for this application.

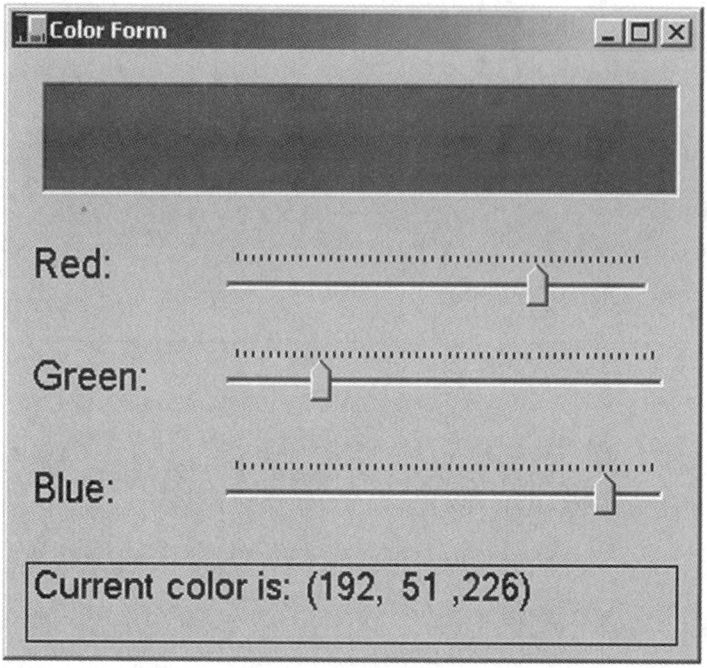

Figure 10-17. TrackBars

First you need to configure each TrackBar. Assume your Form contains three private TrackBar member variables (redTrackBar, greenTrackBar, and blueTrackBar). Here is the relevant code for blueTrackBar (the remaining bars look almost identical, with the exception of the name of the Scroll event handler):

```
// Here is the blue TrackBar.
blueTrackBar.TickFrequency = 5;
blueTrackBar.Location = new System.Drawing.Point (104, 200);
blueTrackBar.TickStyle = System.Windows.Forms.TickStyle.TopLeft;
blueTrackBar.Maximum = 255;
blueTrackBar.Scroll += new System.EventHandler (this.blueTrackBar_Scroll);
```

Note that the default minimum value of the TrackBar is 0 and thus does not need to be explicitly set. In the event handlers for each TrackBar, you make a call to an internal private helper function named UpdateColor(), which does the real grunt work, as shown here:

```
protected void blueTrackBar_Scroll (object sender, System.EventArgs e)
{
    UpdateColor();
}
```

UpdateColor() is responsible for two major tasks. First you read the current value of each TrackBar and send this state data to a new Color variable (using the FromArgb() member). Once you have the newly configured color, you update a Form-level member variable of type PictureBox (named colorBox), which in this case does not hold an actual bitmap image, but simply maintains the current background color. Finally, the UpdateColor() method formats this information in a string placed on the Form's color display label (lblCurrColor), as shown here:

```
private void UpdateColor()
{
    // Get the new color.
    Color c = Color.FromArgb(redTrackBar.Value,
                        greenTrackBar.Value,
                        blueTrackBar.Value);

    // Change the color in the PictureBox.
    colorBox.BackColor = c;

    // Set color label.
    lblCurrColor.Text = "Current color is: " + "(" +
                        redTrackBar.Value + ", " +
                        greenTrackBar.Value + " ," +
                        blueTrackBar.Value + ")";
}
```

The final detail is to set the initial values of each slider when the Form comes to life and render the current color, as shown here:

```
public TrackForm()
{
    InitializeComponent();
    CenterToScreen();
```

```
// Set initial position of each slider.
redTrackBar.Value = 100;
greenTrackBar.Value = 255;
blueTrackBar.Value = 0;
UpdateColor();
}
```

SOURCE CODE   *The Tracker application can be found under the Chapter 10 sub-directory.*

The MonthCalendar Control

The System.Windows.Forms namespace provides an extremely useful widget, which allows the user to select a date (or range of dates) using a friendly user interface: the MonthCalendar Control. To showcase this new Control, update the existing CarConfig application to allow the user to enter in the new vehicle's delivery date. Figure 10-18 shows the updated (and slightly rearranged) Form.

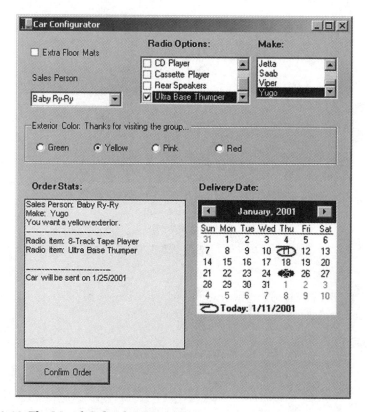

Figure 10-18. The MonthCalendar Control

To begin understanding this new type, examine the core MonthCalendar properties described in Table 10-14.

Table 10-14. MonthCalendar properties

MONTHCALENDAR PROPERTY	MEANING IN LIFE
BoldedDates	The array of DateTime objects that determine dates are shown in bold.
CalendarDimensions	The number of columns and rows of months displayed in the MonthCalendar Control.
FirstDayOfWeek	The first day of the week for the MonthCalendar Control.
MaxDate	The maximum allowable date that can be selected. (The default is no maximum date.)
MaxSelectionCount	The maximum number of days that can be selected in a MonthCalendar Control.
MinDate	The minimum allowable date that can be selected. (The default is no minimum date.)
MonthlyBoldedDates	The array of DateTime objects that determine which monthly days to bold.
SelectionEnd	Indicates the end date of the selected range of dates.
SelectionRange	Retrieves the selection range for a MonthCalendar Control.
SelectionStart	Indicates the start date of the selected range of dates.
ShowToday ShowTodayCircle	Indicates whether the MonthCalendar Control displays the today date at the bottom of the Control, as well as circle the current date.
ShowWeekNumbers	Indicates whether the MonthCalendar Control displays the week numbers (1–52) to the left of each row of days.
TodayDate	The date shown as Today in the MonthCalendar Control. By default, Today is the current date at the time the MonthCalendar Control is created.
TodayDateSet	Indicates whether or not the TodayDate property has been explicitly set by the user. If TodayDateSet is true, TodayDate returns whatever the user has set it to.

Although the MonthCalendar Control offers a fair bit of functionality, it is very simple to programmatically capture the range of dates selected by the user. The default behavior of this type is to always select (and circle) today's date automatically. To obtain the currently selected date programmatically, you can update the Click event handler for the order Button, as shown here:

```
protected void btnOrder_Click (object sender, System.EventArgs e)
{
    // Build a string to display information.
    string orderInfo = "";
    . . .
    // Get ship date.
    DateTime d = monthCalendar.SelectionStart;
    string dateStr = d.Month + " / " + d.Day + " / " + d.Year;
    orderInfo += "Car will be sent: " + dateStr;
    . . .
}
```

Notice that you can ask the MonthCalendar Control for the currently selected date by using the SelectionStart property. This property returns a DateTime reference, which you store in a local variable (d). Using a handful of properties of the DateTime type, you can extract out the information you need in a custom format. (Note that this type returns the clock time as well, which you are not interested in.)

At this point I assume the user will specify exactly one day on which to deliver the new auto. However, what if you want to allow the user to select a range of possible shipping dates? In that case all the user needs to do is drag the cursor across the range of possible shipping dates (Figure 10-19).

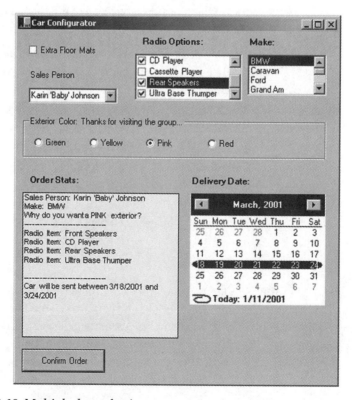

Figure 10-19. Multiple date selection

You already have seen that you can obtain the start of the selection using the SelectionStart property. The end of the selection can be determined using the SelectionEnd property. Here is the code update:

```
protected void btnOrder_Click (object sender, System.EventArgs e)
{
    // Build a string to display information.
    string orderInfo = "";
    . . .

    // Get ship date range....
    DateTime startD = monthCalendar.SelectionStart;
    DateTime endD = monthCalendar.SelectionEnd;

    string dateStartStr = startD.Month + " / " + startD.Day + " / " +
                          startD.Year;
    string dateEndStr = endD.Month + " / " + endD.Day + " / " + endD.Year;

    // The DateTime type supports overloaded operators!
    if(dateStartStr != dateEndStr)
    {
        orderInfo += "Car will be sent between "
+ dateStartStr + " and\n" + dateEndStr;
    }
    else // they picked a single date.
        orderInfo += "Car will be sent on "  + dateStartStr;
    . . .
}
```

More on the DateTime Type

In the current example, you extracted a DateTime type from the MonthCalendar widget using the SelectionStart and SelectionEnd properties, as shown here:

```
// Get a DateTime (or two).
DateTime startD = monthCalendar.SelectionStart;
DateTime endD = monthCalendar.SelectionEnd;
```

After this point, you used the Month, Day, and Year properties to build a custom format string. While this is permissible, it is not optimal, given that the DateTime type has a number of built-in formatting options (Table 10-15).

Table 10-15. DateTime Members

DATETIME MEMBER	MEANING IN LIFE
Date	Retrieves the date of the instance with the time value set to midnight.
Day Month Year	Extract the day, month, and year of the current DateTime type.
DayOfWeek	Retrieves the day of the week represented by this instance.
DayOfYear	Retrieves the day of the year represented by this instance.
Hour Minute Second Millisecond	Extract various time-related details from a DateTime variable.
MaxValue MinValue	Represent the minimum and maximum DateTime value.
Now Today	These *static* members retrieve a DateTime type representing the current date and time (Now) or date (Today).
Ticks	Retrieves the 100-nanosecond tick count for this instance.
ToLongDateString() ToLongTimeString() ToShortDateString() ToShortTimeString()	Convert the current value of the DateTime type to a string representation.

Using these members, you can replace the previous formatting you programmed by hand with the following (you will see no change in the program's output):

```
// Ditch the custom formatting!
// string dateStartStr = startD.Month + " / " + startD.Day + " / " + startD.Year;
// string dateEndStr = endD.Month + " / " + endD.Day + " / " + endD.Year;

string dateStartStr = startD.Date.ToShortDateString();
string dateEndStr = endD.Date.ToShortDateString();
```

The Spin Controls: DomainUpDown and NumericUpDown

Windows Forms provide two widgets that function as "spin controls" (also known as up/down controls). Like the ComboBox and ListBox types, these new items also allow the user to choose an item from a range of possible selections. The difference is that when using a DomainUpDown or NumericUpDown Control, the information is selected using a small pair of up and down arrows. For example, check out Figure 10-20.

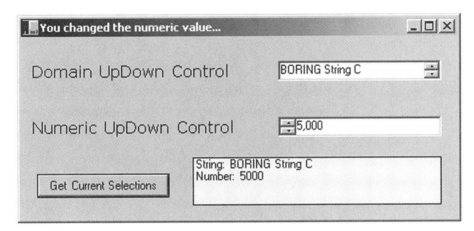

Figure 10-20. Spin Controls

Given your work with previous (and similar) types, you should find working with the UpDown Controls painless. The DomainUpDown widget allows the user to select from a set of string data. NumericUpDown allows selections from a range of numeric data points. Each widget derives from a common direct base class: UpDownBase. Table 10-16 describes some important properties of this class.

Table 10-16. UpDownBase Properties

UPDOWNBASE PROPERTY	MEANING IN LIFE
InterceptArrowKeys	Gets or sets a value indicating whether the user can use the Up Arrow and Down Arrow keys to select values.
ReadOnly	Gets or sets a value indicating whether the text can only be changed by the use of the up or down arrows and not by typing in the Control to locate a given string.
Text	Gets or sets the current text displayed in the spin Control.
TextAlign	Gets or sets the alignment of the text in the spin Control.
UpDownAlign	Gets or sets the alignment of the up and down arrows on the spin Control, using the LeftRightAlignment enumeration.

The DomainUpDown Control adds a small set of properties (Table 10-17), which allow you to configure and manipulate the textual data in the widget.

Table 10-17. DomainUpDown Properties

DOMAINUPDOWN PROPERTY	MEANING IN LIFE
Items	Allows you to gain access to the set of types stored in the widget.
SelectedIndex	Returns the zero-based index of the currently selected item.
SelectedItem	Returns the selected item itself (not its index).
Sorted	Configures whether or not the strings should be alphabetized.
Wrap	Controls if the collection of items continues to the first or last item if the user continues past the end of the list.

The NumericUpDown type is just as simple (Table 10-18).

Table 10-18. NumericUpDown Properties

NUMERICUPDOWN PROPERTY	MEANING IN LIFE
DecimalPlaces ThousandsSeparator Hexadecimal	Used to configure how the numerical data is to be displayed.
Increment	Sets the numerical value to increment the value in the Control when the up or down arrow is clicked. The default is to advance the value by 1.
Minimum Maximum	Sets the upper and lower limits of the value in the Control.
Value	Returns the current value in the Control.

Here is the code behind the sample application. Each Control is configured using a subset of all possible properties:

```
// Configure DomainUpDown widget.
domainUpDown.Sorted = true;
domainUpDown.Wrap = true;
domainUpDown.Items.AddRange( new object[4] {"Another Boring String named B",
"Boring String A", "BORING String C", "Final Boring string (D)"});
domainUpDown.SelectedIndex = 2;


// Configure NumericUpDown widget.
numericUpDown.Maximum = new decimal (5000);
numericUpDown.ThousandsSeparator = true;
numericUpDown.UpDownAlign = LeftRightAlignment.Left;
```

The Click event handler for the Form's Button type simply asks each type for its current value and places it in the appropriate Label as a formatted string, as shown here:

```
protected void btnGetSelections_Click (object sender, System.EventArgs e)
{
    // Get info from updowns.
    lblCurrSel.Text = "String: "
                    + domainUpDown.Text
                    + "\n"
                    + "Number: "
                    + numericUpDown.Value;
}
```

Of course, the DomainUpDown and NumericUpDown types support a number of events. If you ever need to capture when the selection changes, you can use SelectedItemChanged (for DomainUpDown types) or ValueChanged (for NumericUpDown types). Here is an example:

```
// Intercept the SelectedItemChanged event.
domainUpDown.SelectedItemChanged
    += new EventHandler (domainUpDown_SelectedItemChanged);
```

. . .

```
// Handle the event.
protected void domainUpDown_SelectedItemChanged (object sender,
                                            System.EventArgs e)
{
    this.Text = "You changed the string value...";
}
```

SOURCE CODE   *The UpAndDown application is included under the Chapter 10 subdirectory.*

Working with Panel Controls

As you have seen earlier in this chapter, the GroupBox Control can be used to logically bind a number of Controls (such as RadioButtons) to function as a collective. Closely related to the GroupBox is the Panel Control. Panels are also used to group related Controls in a logical unit. One difference is that the Panel type derives from the ScrollableControl class, and thus it can support scroll bars, which is not possible with a GroupBox. Another subtle difference is that a Panel does not support an automatic caption (unlike a GroupBox).

Panels can be used to conserve screen real estate. For example, if you have a group of Controls that take up the entire bottom half of a Form, you can contain them in a Panel that is half the size and set the AutoScroll property to true. In this way, the user can use the scroll bar(s) to view the hidden items. To illustrate, update the previous TrackBar application. This time, each TrackBar is contained in a single Panel. Figure 10-21 shows the update.

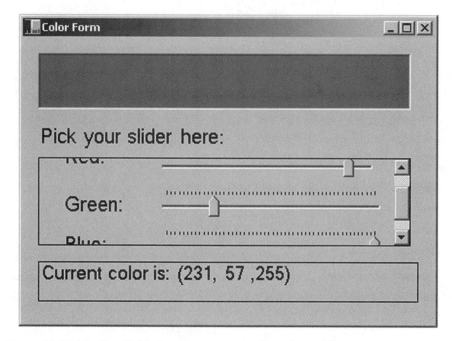

Figure 10-21. The Scrollable Panel type containing other widgets

The underlying code looks almost identical to that of a GroupBox. Begin by declaring a Panel data member (panel1) and add each item using the Controls property, as shown here:

```
// Configure the panel.
panel1.AutoScroll = true;
panel1.Controls.Add (this.label2);
panel1.Controls.Add (this.blueTrackBar);
panel1.Controls.Add (this.label3);
panel1.Controls.Add (this.greenTrackBar);
panel1.Controls.Add (this.redTrackBar);
panel1.Controls.Add (this.label1);
```

Assigning ToolTips to Controls

Most modern user interfaces support tool tips. In the System.Windows.Forms namespace, the ToolTip type represents this functionality. These widgets are simply small floating windows that display a helpful message when the cursor hovers over a given item. Table 10-19 describes the core properties of the ToolTip type.

Table 10-19. ToolTip Properties

TOOLTIP PROPERTY	MEANING IN LIFE
Active	Configures if the tool tip is activated or not. For example, perhaps you have a menu item that disables all tool tips for advanced users. This property allows you to turn off the pop-up text.
AutomaticDelay	Gets or sets the time (in milliseconds) that passes before the ToolTip appears.
AutoPopDelay	The period of time (in milliseconds) that the ToolTip remains visible when the cursor is stationary in the ToolTip region. The default value is 10 times the AutomaticDelay property value.
GetToolTip()	Returns the tool tip text assigned to a specific Control.
InitialDelay	The period of time (in milliseconds) that the cursor must remain stationary in the ToolTip region before the ToolTip text is displayed. The default is equal to the AutomaticDelay property.
ReshowDelay	The length of time (in milliseconds) that it takes subsequent ToolTip instances to appear as the cursor moves from one ToolTip region to another. The default is 1/5 of the AutomaticDelay property value.
SetToolTip()	Associates a tool tip to a specific Control.

To illustrate, add a tool tip to the CarConfig application. Specifically, you want to add the tool tip for the MonthCalendar widget shown in Figure 10-22.

Like with any widget, begin by creating a new member variable, this time of type ToolTip. Next, configure the set of properties for the new item. Notice that you make a call to SetToolTip(), which configures not only the text to be displayed, but also the widget to which it is assigned:

```
// Create and associate a tool tip to the calendar
calendarTip.Active = true;
calendarTip.SetToolTip (monthCalendar,
"Please select the date (or dates)\n when we can deliver your new car!");
```

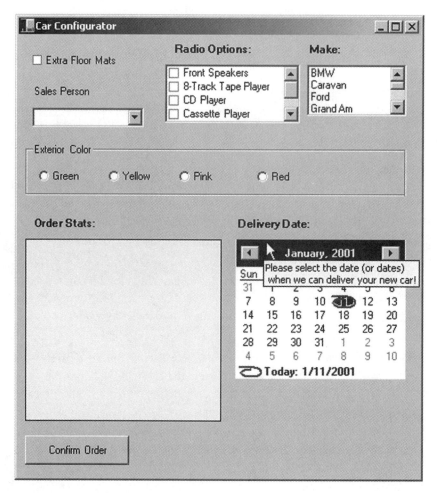

Figure 10-22. Tool tip

Adding ToolTips at Design Time

If you use the Visual Studio.NET IDE to build your tool tips, begin by adding a ToolTip widget to your Form using the Toolbox window (Figure 10-23).

At this point, you can configure the ToolTip using the Properties window. To associate the new tip with a given widget, select the widget that should activate the tip and set the "ToolTip on. . ." property (Figure 10-24).

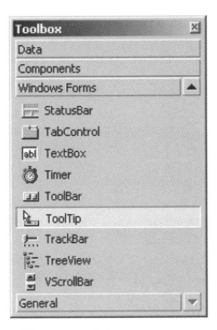

Figure 10-23. Adding ToolTip types at design time

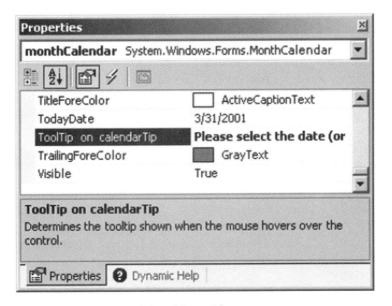

Figure 10-24. Associating a ToolTip with a widget

Working with the ErrorProvider

Your Windows Forms application will need to validate user input. This is especially true when with dialog boxes, as you should inform users if they make a processing error before continuing forward. (I examine dialog box programming later in this chapter.)

The ErrorProvider type can be used to provide a visual cue of user input error. For example, assume you have a Form containing a TextBox and Button widget. If the user enters more than five characters in the TextBox, the error information shown in Figure 10-25 is displayed.

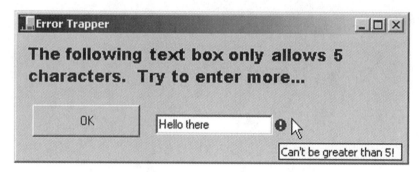

Figure 10-25. The ErrorProvider

Here, you have detected that the user entered more than five characters and responded by placing a small error icon (!) next to the TextBox object. When the user places the cursor over this icon, the descriptive error text appears as a pop-up. Also, this ErrorProvider is configured to blink the icon a number of times to strengthen the visual cue (which of course you can't see without running the application).

If you wish to support this type of input validation, the first step is to understand the properties of the Control class (Table 10-20).

Table 10-20. Control Properties

CONTROL PROPERTY	MEANING IN LIFE
CausesValidation	Indicates whether selecting this Control causes validation on the Controls requiring validation.
Validated	Occurs when the Control is finished performing its validation logic.
Validating	Occurs when the Control is validating user input (e.g., when the Control loses focus).

Every GUI widget can set the CausesValidation property to true or false. (The default is false.) If you set this bit of state data to true, the Control forces the other Controls on the Form to validate themselves when it receives focus (provided the CausesValidation property is also set to true).

Once a validating Control has received focus, the Validating and Validated events are fired for each Control. It is in the scope of the Validating event handler in which you configure a corresponding ErrorProvider. Optionally, the Validated event can be handled to determine when the Control has finished its validation cycle.

To begin, assume you have set the CausesValidation property to true for the Button and TextBox and have added a member variable of type ErrorProvider. Here is the configuration code:

```
// Configure the error provider.
errorProvider1.DataMember = "";
errorProvider1.DataSource = null;
errorProvider1.ContainerControl = null;
errorProvider1.BlinkStyle = System.Windows.Forms.ErrorBlinkStyle.AlwaysBlink;
errorProvider1.BlinkRate = 500;
```

The ErrorProvider type has a small set of members. The most important item for your purposes is the BlinkStyle property, which can be set to any of the values of the ErrorBlinkStyle enumeration described in Table 10-21.

Table 10-21. ErrorBlinkStyle Properties

ERRORBLINKSTYLE PROPERTY	MEANING IN LIFE
AlwaysBlink	Blinks the error icon when the error is first displayed or when a new error description string is set for the Control and the error icon is already displayed.
BlinkIfDifferentError	Blinks only if the error icon is already displayed, but a new error string is set for the Control.
NeverBlink	Never blinks the error icon.

The ErrorProvider also has additional members beyond BlinkStyle and BlinkRate. For example, if you wish to associate a custom icon to the error, you can do so using the Icon property. Nevertheless, once you have configured how the ErrorProvider looks and feels, you bind the error to the TextBox within the scope of its Validating event handler, as shown here:

```
protected void txtInput_Validating (object sender, System.EventArgs e)
{
    // Check if the text length is greater than 5.
    if(txtInput.Text.ToString().Length > 5)
    {
        errorProvider1.SetError( txtInput, "Can't be greater than 5!");
    }
    else // Things are OK, don't show anything.
        errorProvider1.SetError(txtInput, "");
}
```

SOURCE CODE   *The ErrorProvider application is included under the Chapter 10 subdirectory.*

Configuring a Control's Anchoring Behavior

When you are creating a Form containing widgets, you need to decide whether the Form should be resizable. Typically speaking, main windows are resizable, whereas dialog boxes are not. To configure the resizability of your Form, adjust the FormBorderStyle property to any of the values described in Table 10-22.

Table 10-22. FormBorderStyle Properties

FORMBORDERSTYLE PROPERTY	MEANING IN LIFE
Fixed3D	A nonresizable, three-dimensional border.
FixedDialog	A thick, nonresizable dialog box–style border.
FixedSingle	A nonresizable, single-line border.
FixedToolWindow	A tool window border that is not resizable.
None	No border at all.
Sizable	A resizable border.
SizableToolWindow	A resizable tool window border.

Assume that you have configured your Form to be resizable. This brings up some interesting questions regarding the contained Controls. For example, if the user makes the Form smaller than the rectangle needed to display each Control, should the Controls adjust their size (and possibly location) to morph correctly with the Form?

In the Windows Forms worldview, the Anchor property is used to define a relative fixed position in which the Control should always be rendered. Every Control derived type has an Anchor property, which can be set to any of the values from the AnchorStyles enumeration described in Table 10-23.

Table 10-23. AnchorStyles Values

ANCHORSTYLES VALUE	MEANING IN LIFE
Bottom	The Control is anchored to the bottom edge of its container.
Left	The Control is anchored to the left edge of its container.
None	The Control is not anchored to any edges of its container.
Right	The Control is anchored to the right edge of its container.
Top	The Control is anchored to the top edge of its container.

To anchor a widget at the upper left corner, you are free to OR styles together (e.g., AnchorStyles.Top|AnchorStyles.Left). Again, the idea behind the Anchor property is to configure which edges of the Control are anchored to the edges of its container. For example, if you configure a Button with the following Anchor value:

```
// Anchor this widget relative to the right position.
myButton.Anchor = AnchorStyles.Right;
```

you are ensured that as the Form is resized, this Button maintains its position relative to the right side of the Form (which is not very easy to visualize on the printed page).

Configuring a Control's Docking Behavior

Another aspect of Windows Forms programming is establishing the docking behavior of your Controls. If you so choose, you can set a widget's Dock property to configure which side (or sides) of a Form the widget should be attached to. The value you assign to a Control's Dock property is honored, regardless of the Form's current dimensions. Table 10-24 describes possible options.

Table 10-24. DockStyle Values

DOCKSTYLE VALUE	MEANING IN LIFE
Bottom	The Control's bottom edge is docked to the bottom of its containing Control.
Fill	All the Control's edges are docked to all the edges of its containing Control and sized appropriately.
Left	The Control's left edge is docked to the left edge of its containing Control.
None	The Control is not docked.
Right	The Control's right edge is docked to the right edge of its containing Control.
Top	The Control's top edge is docked to the top of its containing Control.

So, for example, if you want to ensure that a given widget is always docked on the left side of a Form, you would write:

```
// This item is always located on the left of the Form, regardless
// of the Form's current size.
myButton.Dock = DockStyle.Left;
```

Figure 10-26 shows the output.

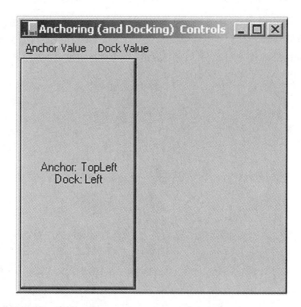

Figure 10-26. Anchoring behaviors

To explore the various anchor and docking styles, check out the AnchoringControls application (under the Chapter 10 subdirectory). Using the topmost menu system, you can select from a set of AnchorStyles and DockStyles values and observe the change in behavior of the Button type (Figure 10-27).

Building Custom Dialog Boxes

Now that you have a solid understanding of the core Controls defined in the System.Windows.Forms namespace, you need to examine the construction of custom dialog boxes. The good news is that everything you have already learned about System.Windows.Forms applies directly to dialog box programming. There is no Dialog base class in the System.Windows.Forms namespace. Rather, a dialog box is nothing more than a stylized Form.

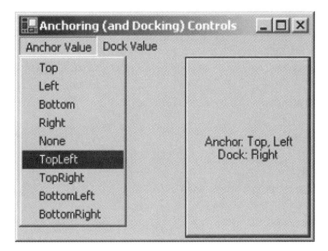

Figure 10-27. Docking and anchoring behaviors

First of all, understand that most dialog boxes are nonsizable. Therefore, you will typically want to set the BorderStyle property to FormBorderStyle.FixedDialog. Also, you will want to set the ControlBox, MinimizeBox, and MaximizeBox properties to false. In this way the dialog box is configured to be a fixed constant.

To launch a Form as a modal dialog box (i.e., the owning Form cannot receive focus until the dialog box is dismissed), call the ShowDialog() method. Assume you have a topmost menu item, which triggers the following logic:

```csharp
// Launch a modal dialog box.
protected void mnuModalBox_Click (object sender, System.EventArgs e)
{
    SomeCustomForm myForm = new SomeCustomForm();

    // Could assign in the ctor of SomeCustomForm as well.
    myForm.BorderStyle = FormBorderStyle.FixedDialog;
    myForm.ControlBox = false;
    myForm.MinimizeBox = false;
    myForm.MaximizeBox = false;

    // Passing in a reference to the parent Form.
    myForm.ShowDialog(this);

    DoSomeMoreWork();
}
```

Notice that directly after the ShowDialog() call, you have a private helper function named DoSomeMoreWork(). Be aware that when you show a modal dialog box, the flow of processing is stopped until the ShowDialog() method returns. (After all, that is what makes it modal!) To show a modeless dialog box (i.e., the launching window and dialog box can alternate focus), substitute the ShowDialog() call with a call to Show(), as shown here:

```
// Launch a modeless dialog box.
protected void menuShowMyDlg_Click (object sender, System.EventArgs e)
{
    SomeCustomForm myForm = new SomeCustomForm();
    myForm.BorderStyle = FormBorderStyle.FixedDialog;
    myForm.ControlBox = false;
    myForm.MinimizeBox = false;
    myForm.MaximizeBox = false;
    myForm.Show();

    DoSomeMoreWork();
}
```

In this case, DoSomeMoreWork() would be hit immediately after the call to Show().

A Dialog Box Example Application

Now you can put some real code behind the previous example. Assume you have a Form named mainForm, which supports a topmost menu, allowing the user to launch a modal dialog box (Figure 10-28).

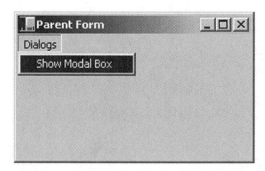

Figure 10-28. Launching your dialog box

When the user selects this option, a simple dialog box is displayed. The goal is to allow the user to type in some text, which is then painted on the parent Form (but only if the OK Button is selected). Figure 10-29 shows the UI of your dialog box.

Figure 10-29. The simple dialog box

When the user clicks the OK Button, the end result is that the string is extracted from the TextBox maintained by the custom dialog box and painted in the parent Form's client area (Figure 10-30).

Figure 10-30. Using dialog box data

Moreover, if the user reactivates the dialog box, the parent Form assigns the previous text message to the dialog box's TextBox (Figure 10-31).

The code representing the custom dialog box should be of no surprise, given that a dialog box is nothing more than a Form with minor modifications. Here is the relevant code:

```
// Your dialog box.
public class SomeCustomForm : System.Windows.Forms.Form
{
    private System.Windows.Forms.Button btnCancel;
    private System.Windows.Forms.Button btnOK;
```

Figure 10-31. Prepping the dialog box

```
private System.Windows.Forms.Label label1;
private System.Windows.Forms.TextBox txtMessage;

public SomeCustomForm()
{
    InitializeComponent();
    this.StartPosition = FormStartPosition.CenterParent;
}
. . .

private void InitializeComponent()
{
    . . .
    // OK Button configuration.
    btnOK.DialogResult = System.Windows.Forms.DialogResult.OK;
    btnOK.Size = new System.Drawing.Size (96, 24);
    btnOK.Text = "OK";

    // Cancel Button configuration.
    btnCancel.DialogResult = System.Windows.Forms.DialogResult.Cancel;
    btnCancel.Size = new System.Drawing.Size (96, 24);
    btnCancel.Text = "Cancel";

    // Form configured to function as dialog box.
    this.Text = "Some Custom Dialog";
    this.MaximizeBox = false;
    this.ControlBox = false;
    this.MinimizeBox = false;

    . . .
    }
}
```

The first point of interest is in the constructor of the Form. Notice that you are setting the StartPosition property on startup. Earlier you directly called CenterToScreen() to ensure that the Form was centered correctly. Using the StartPosition property (and the FormStartPosition enumeration), you can gain a finer level of granularity. Usually you should use FormStartPosition.CenterParent to ensure that the location of the dialog box is centered with regard to the parent (regardless of the parent's location on the screen), as shown here:

```
// Place dialog box centered to parent.
public SomeCustomForm()
{
    InitializeComponent();
    this.StartPosition = FormStartPosition.CenterParent;
}
```

Another important aspect of dialog box programming is to assign the termination Buttons to a value defined by the DialogResult enumeration. As you know, most dialog boxes define an OK Button that says, in effect, "I am happy with my selections. Please use them in the program." Furthermore, most dialog boxes have a Cancel Button that allows the user to back out of a selection. To configure how the dialog box's Button should respond with respect to dialog box processing, use the DialogResult property, as shown here:

```
private void InitializeComponent()
{
    . . .
    // OK Button configuration.
    btnOK.DialogResult = System.Windows.Forms.DialogResult.OK;

    // Cancel Button configuration.
    btnCancel.DialogResult = System.Windows.Forms.DialogResult.Cancel;

    . . .
}
```

What exactly does it mean to assign a Button's DialogResult value? First of all, when a Button has been set to DialogResult.OK or DialogResult.Cancel, the Form *automatically* closes. Also, you can query this property back in the code that launched this dialog box to see which Button the user selected, as shown here:

```
protected void mnuModalBox_Click (object sender, System.EventArgs e)
{
    // Style props set in Form.
    SomeCustomForm myForm = new SomeCustomForm();
```

```
    // Passing in a reference to the launching dialog box is optional.
    myForm.ShowDialog(this);

    if(myForm.DialogResult == DialogResult.OK)
    {
        // User hit OK, do whatever.
    }

    DoSomeMoreWork();
}
```

Table 10-25 describes the possible values of the DialogResult enumeration. (Remember, in the dialog box itself you assign these values to the Button widgets. In the launching code you ask the dialog box itself for the value!)

Table 10-25. DialogResult Values

DIALOGRESULT VALUE	MEANING IN LIFE
Abort	The dialog box's return value is Abort (usually sent from a Button labeled Abort).
Cancel	The dialog box's return value is Cancel (usually sent from a Button labeled Cancel).
Ignore	The dialog box's return value is Ignore (usually sent from a Button labeled Ignore).
No	The dialog box's return value is No (usually sent from a Button labeled No).
None	Nothing is returned from the dialog box. This means that the modal dialog box continues running.
OK	The dialog box's return value is OK (usually sent from a Button labeled OK).
Retry	The dialog box's return value is Retry (usually sent from a Button labeled Retry).
Yes	The dialog box's return value is Yes (usually sent from a Button labeled Yes).

Grabbing Data from a Dialog Box

Now that you can configure, launch, and test for a dialog box's Button click, you need to understand how to obtain the information from the dialog box. Your current dialog box allows the user to enter a custom string, which is used in the parent Form. Thus, the first step you need to take is to add some number of member variables that represent the data the dialog box is responsible for, as shown here:

```
public class SomeCustomForm : System.Windows.Forms.Form
{
    public SomeCustomForm()
    {
        InitializeComponent();
        this.StartPosition = FormStartPosition.CenterParent;
    }

    // The dialog box's state data (and a way to get it).
    private string strMessage;

    public string Message
    {
        get{ return strMessage;}

        // The set function allows the owner to send
        // in a startup string that you place in the
        // TextBox.
        set
        {
            strMessage = value;
            txtMessage.Text = strMessage;
        }
    }
...
}
```

Now, to transfer the value in the TextBox to this private member variable requires that you intercept the Click event for the OK Button. Remember that the DialogResult.OK assignment already ensures that your Form is destroyed when this Button is clicked. This time, however, you need to do some additional work, as shown here:

```
protected void btnOK_Click (object sender, System.EventArgs e)
{
    // OK Button clicked! Configure new message.
    strMessage = txtMessage.Text;
}
```

That's it! Of course, if you had a more elaborate dialog box (such as the CarConfig Form), you would no doubt need a number of custom properties to represent the full set of user selections. To complete your example dialog box application, you can update the code that launched this dialog box to extract the internal message and use it in the program. Here is the complete menu selection logic:

```
protected void mnuModalBox_Click (object sender, System.EventArgs e)
{
    // Style props set in Form.
    SomeCustomForm myForm = new SomeCustomForm();

    // Assume this Form has a string variable named 'dlgMsg'.
    myForm.ShowDialog(this);
    myForm.Message = dlgMsg;

    if(myForm.DialogResult == DialogResult.OK)
    {
        dlgMsg = myForm.Message;
        Invalidate();
    }

    DoSomeMoreWork();
}
```

The extracted string is then painted on the client area using standard GDI+ logic, as shown here:

```
protected void mainForm_Paint (object sender, PaintEventArgs e)
{
    // Paint the message obtained from the dialog box.
    Graphics g = e.Graphics;
    g.DrawString(dlgMsg, new Font("times New Roman", 24),
                Brushes.Blue, this.ClientRectangle);
}
```

SOURCE CODE   *The SimpleDialog application is included under the Chapter 10 subdirectory.*

Form Inheritance

The final topic of this chapter is Form inheritance. As you are aware, inheritance is the pillar of OOP that allows one class to extend the functionality of another class. Typically, when you speak of inheritance, you envision one non-GUI type deriving from another non-GUI type. However, in the world of Windows Forms it is possible for one Form to derive from another Form and bring with it all the previously configured widgets and base class functionality.

For the sake of illustration, assume you have placed your CarConfigForm.cs class in a new C# Code Library application (CarConfigLib) and compiled the binary. Once this is done, create a new Windows Application project workspace. To derive one Form from another, the first step is to set a reference to the external assembly (in this case, the new DLL). Next, specify the base Form using standard C# syntax, as shown here:

```
// The namespace of the base Form.
using CarConfig;

// Your new Form is really a subclass of CarConfigForm!
public class DerivedForm : CarConfig.CarConfigForm
{...};
```

If you now save and reopen the DerivedForm type, you will see that the new class has inherited all the widgets! If you examine the generated code, you will see basic startup code placed in InitializeComponent(). Also be aware that all Controls that have been declared as private may not be repositions. If you update the logic in the CarConfigLib.dll to specify protected members, you can then relocate these items using the design time template. At this point, you are free to extend this Form any way you choose. For test purposes, simply add a new MainMenu that allows the user to exit this application (Figure 10-32).

The Click event handler simply shuts down the application, as shown here:

```
private void mnuFileExit_Click(object sender, System.EventArgs e)
{
    this.Close();
}
```

Finally, it is worth pointing out that the Visual Studio.NET IDE provides an integrated Wizard to create derived forms. To access its functionality, activate the "Project | Add Inherited Form" menu item. Once you provide a name for your new class, you are asked to specify the name of the DLL assembly that contains the base class Form.

SOURCE CODE *The MyDerivedForm and CarConfigLib applications are included under the Chapter 10 subdirectory.*

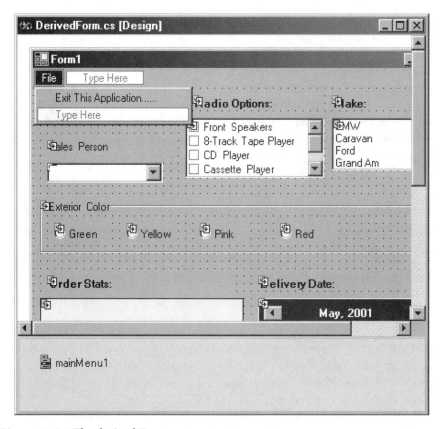

Figure 10-32. The derived Form supports a topmost menu

Summary

This chapter rounded off your current understanding by examining the programming of numerous GUI widgets from the simple (Button) to the exotic (MonthCalendar). Of course, there are some remaining types for you to explore on your own. However, given your current understanding of these core types, you are in the perfect position to do so.

You also explored the various anchoring and docking behaviors that can be used to enforce a specific layout of your GUI types, regardless of the size of the owning Form.

In the later half of this chapter, you learned how to turn a Form into a dialog box (and vice versa) and examined a number of issues related to dialog boxes. Finally you learned how you can now derive a new Form from an existing Form type using Form inheritance.

CHAPTER 11

Input, Output, and Object Serialization

When you are creating full-blown desktop applications, the ability to save information between user sessions is imperative. This chapter examines a number of IO-related topics as seen through the eyes of the .NET framework. The first order of business is to explore the core types defined in the System.IO namespace and come to understand how to programmatically modify a machine's directory and file structure. Once you can do so, the next task is to explore various ways to read to and write from character-based, binary-based, string-based, and memory-based data stores.

The second half of this chapter examines the .NET serialization schema. Serialization is the process of transforming the state of an object (or set of related objects) in a byte pattern (or XML format), which can then be placed in (and later recovered from) a stream. During this discussion, you will learn the role of the [Serializable] and [NonSerialized] attributes. You will also see how to take more control over the serialization process through the implementation of the ISerializable interface.

Finally, to showcase some of these concepts from a real-world point of view, I conclude this chapter with a complete Windows Forms application, which allows the end user to manage a collection of Car types that can be persisted to (and recovered from) a file. As an interesting bonus, the application in question also examines the use of the DataGrid widget (uses extensively during the examination of ADO.NET).

Exploring the System.IO Namespace

In the framework of .NET, the System.IO namespace is the region of the base class libraries devoted to file-based (and memory-based) input and output services. Like any namespace, System.IO defines a set of classes, enumerations, structures, and delegates, all of which are contained in mscorlib.dll. Figure 11-1 shows a partial ILDasm.exe dump.

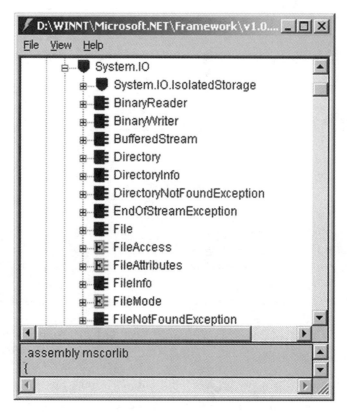

Figure 11-1. The System.IO namespace

As you will see during this chapter, the classes in the System.IO namespace typically focus on the manipulation of physical directories and files. However, additional types provide support to read data from and write data to string buffers as well as raw memory locations. To give you a roadmap of the functionality in System.IO, Table 11-1 outlines the core (nonabstract) classes.

In addition to these creatable types, there are a number of enumerations and abstract classes (Stream, TextReader, TextWriter, and so forth) that define a shared polymorphic interface to all descendents. You will read about many of these types in this chapter.

The Directory(Info) and File(Info) Types

System.IO provides four types that allow you to manipulate individual files, as well as interact with a machine's directory structure. The first two types, Directory and File, expose creation, deletion, and manipulation operations using various static members. The closely related FileInfo and DirectoryInfo types expose

Table 11-1. System.IO Namespace Core Types

CREATABLE IO TYPE	MEANING IN LIFE
BinaryReader BinaryWriter	Allow you to store and retrieve primitive data types (integers, Booleans, strings, and so on) as binary values.
BufferedStream	Provides temporary storage for a stream of bytes, which can be committed to storage later.
Directory DirectoryInfo File FileInfo	Used to manipulate the properties for a given directory or physical file as well as create new files and extend the current directory structure. The Directory and File types expose their functionality primarily as static methods. The DirectoryInfo and FileInfo types expose similar functionality from a valid object instance.
FileStream	Allows for random file access (i.e., seeking capabilities) with data represented as a stream of bytes.
MemoryStream	Allows random access to streamed data, stored in memory, rather than a physical file.
StreamWriter StreamReader	Used to store (and retrieve) textual information to (or from) a file. These types do not support random file access.
StringWriter StringReader	Like the StreamReader/StreamWriter types, these classes also work with textual information. However, the underlying storage is a string buffer rather than a physical file.

similar functionality as instance-level methods. In Figure 11-2, notice that the Directory and File types directly extend System.Object, while DirectoryInfo and FileInfo derive from the abstract FileSystemInfo type.

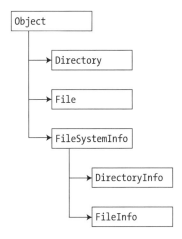

Figure 11-2. The File- and Directory-centric types

The Abstract FileSystemInfo Base Class

The DirectoryInfo and FileInfo types receive many behaviors from the abstract FileSystemInfo type. By and large, the members of the FileSystemInfo class can be used to discover general characteristics (such as time of creation, various attributes, and so forth) about a given file or directory. Table 11-2 lists some core properties of interest.

Table 11-2. FileSystemInfo Properties

FILESYSTEMINFO PROPERTY	MEANING IN LIFE
Attributes	Gets or sets the attributes associated to the current file, which are represented by the FileAttributes enumeration.
CreationTime	Gets or sets the time of creation for the current file or directory.
Exists	Can be used to determine if a given file or directory exists.
Extension	Used to retrieve a file's extension.
FullName	Gets the full path of the directory or file.
LastAccessTime	Gets or sets the time the current file or directory was last accessed.
LastWriteTime	Gets or sets the time when the current file or directory was last written to.
Name	Returns the name of a given file; is a read-only property. For directories, gets the name of the last directory in the hierarchy if possible; otherwise, retrieves the fully qualified name.

The FileSystemInfo type also defines the Delete() method. This is implemented by derived types to delete a given file or directory from the hard drive. As well, Refresh() can be called prior to obtaining attribute information to ensure that the information is not outdated.

Working with the DirectoryInfo Type

The first creatable type you must understand is the DirectoryInfo class. This class contains a set of members used for creating, moving, deleting, and enumerating over directories and subdirectories. In addition to the functionality provided by the FileSystemInfo base class, DirectoryInfo offers the following members (Table 11-3).

You begin working with the DirectoryInfo type by specifying a specific directory path (e.g., "C:\," "D:\WinNT," "\\CompanyServer\\Utils," "A:\," or what have

Table 11-3. Directory Members

DIRECTORYINFO MEMBERS	MEANING IN LIFE
Create() CreateSubdirectory()	Creates a directory (or subdirectories) given a path name.
Delete()	Deletes a directory and all its contents.
GetDirectories()	Returns an array of strings that represent all subdirectories in the current directory.
GetFiles()	Gets the files in the specified directory (as an array of FileInfo types).
MoveTo()	Moves a directory and its contents to a new path.
Parent	Retrieves the parent directory of the specified path.

you) as a constructor parameter. If you want access to the active directory (i.e., the directory of the executing application), use the "." notation. Here are some examples:

```
// Create a new directory bound to the current directory.
DirectoryInfo dir1 = new DirectoryInfo(".");
```

```
// Create a new directory bound to C:\Foo\Bar.
DirectoryInfo dir2 = new DirectoryInfo(@"C:\Foo\Bar");
```

If you attempt to map to a nonexistent directory, you are thrown a System.IO.DirectoryNotFoundException. Assuming that this error has not been thrown, you can investigate the underlying directory contents using any of the properties inherited from FileSystemInfo. To illustrate, the following class creates a new DirectoryInfo type mapped to "D:\WinNT" (adjust your letter drive if need be) and dumps out a number of interesting statistics (see Figure 11-3 for output):

```
class MyDirectory
{
    public static void Main(String[] args)
    {
        // Create a new directory bound to the D drive.
        DirectoryInfo dir = new DirectoryInfo(@"D:\WinNT");

        // Dump directory information.
        Console.WriteLine("***** Directory Info *****");
        Console.WriteLine("FullName: {0}", dir.FullName);
        Console.WriteLine("Name: {0}", dir.Name);
        Console.WriteLine("Parent: {0}", dir.Parent);
```

```
        Console.WriteLine("Creation: {0}", dir.CreationTime);
        Console.WriteLine("Attributes: {0}", dir.Attributes.ToString());
        Console.WriteLine("Root: {0}", dir.Root);
        Console.WriteLine("*************************\n");
    }
}
```

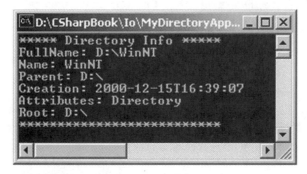

Figure 11-3. D:\WinNT directory information

The FileAttributes Enumeration

As shown in the previous code sample, the Attributes property obtains various traits for the current directory or file, all of which are represented by the FileAttributes enumeration. Table 11-4 describes some core values.

Table 11-4. Select FileAttributes Values

FILEATTRIBUTES ENUMERATION VALUE	MEANING IN LIFE
Archive	The file's archive status. Applications use this attribute to mark files for backup or removal.
Compressed	The file is compressed.
Directory	The file is a directory.
Encrypted	The file is encrypted.
Hidden	The file is hidden and thus is not included in an ordinary directory listing.
Normal	The file is normal and has no other attributes set. This attribute is valid only if used alone.
Offline	The file is offline. The data of the file is not immediately available.
ReadOnly	The file is read only.
System	The file is a system file. The file is part of the operating system or is used exclusively by the operating system.

Enumerating Files with the DirectoryInfo Type

You can extend the current MyDirectory class to use some methods of the DirectoryInfo type. First, use the GetFiles() method to read all *.bmp files located under the "D:\WinNT" directory. This method returns an array of FileInfo types, which you can iterate over using the foreach construct (details of the FileInfo type are explored later in this chapter), as shown here:

```csharp
class MyDirectory
{
    public static void Main(String[] args)
    {
        // Create a new directory object bound to the D drive.
        DirectoryInfo dir = new DirectoryInfo(@"D:\WinNT");
        ...

        // Get all files with a BMP extension.
        FileInfo[] bitmapFiles = dir.GetFiles("*.bmp");

        // How many did you find?
        Console.WriteLine("Found {0} *.bmp files\n", bitmapFiles.Length);

        // Now print out info for each file.
        foreach (FileInfo f in bitmapFiles)
        {
            Console.WriteLine("***************************\n");
            Console.WriteLine("File name: {0}", f.Name);
            Console.WriteLine("File size: {0}", f.Length);
            Console.WriteLine("Creation: {0}", f.CreationTime);
            Console.WriteLine("Attributes: {0}", f.Attributes.ToString());
            Console.WriteLine("***************************\n");
        }
    }
}
```

Once you run the application, you see a listing something like that shown in Figure 11-4. (Your bitmaps may vary!)

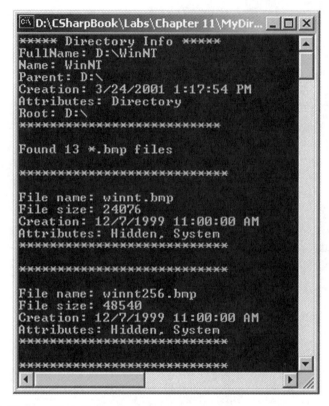

Figure 11-4. Bitmap file information

Creating Subdirectories with the DirectoryInfo Type

You can programmatically extend a directory structure using the CreateSubdirectory() method. This method can create a single subdirectory on the root, as well as multiple nested subdirectories. To illustrate, here is a block of code that extends the directory structure of "D:\WinNT" with some custom sub-directories:

```
class MyDirectory
{
    public static void Main(String[] args)
    {
        DirectoryInfo dir = new DirectoryInfo(@"D:\WinNT");

        ...

        // Now add new directories to D:\WinNT:
        try
        {
            // Create D:\WinNT\MyFoo
```

```
            dir.CreateSubdirectory("MyFoo");

            // Create D:\WinNT\MyBar\MyQaaz
            dir.CreateSubdirectory(@"MyBar\MyQaaz");
        }
        catch(IOException e) { Console.WriteLine(e.Message);}
    }
}
```

If you examine your WinNT folder using Windows Explorer, you will see the new subdirectories there (Figure 11-5).

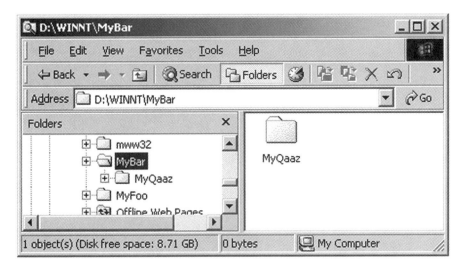

Figure 11-5. Creating subdirectories

Although you are not required to capture the return value of the CreateSubdirectory() method, be aware that a Directory type is passed back on successful execution, as shown here:

```
// CreateSubdirectory() returns a Directory representing the new item.
try
{
    Directory d = dir.CreateSubdirectory("MyFoo");
    Console.WriteLine("Created: {0}", d.FullName);

    d = dir. CreateSubdirectory(@"MyBar\MyQaaz");
    Console.WriteLine("Created: {0}", d.FullName);
}
catch(IOException e) { Console.WriteLine(e.Message); }
```

The Static Members of the Directory Class

Now that you have seen the DirectoryInfo type in action, you can learn about the Directory type. By and large, the members of the Directory mimic the same functionality provided by the instance-level members defined by DirectoryInfo, with a few notable exceptions (GetLogicalDrives() for one). Due to the common public interface of each type, I assume you will consult online help to view each member of the Directory class.

This final iteration of the MyDirectory class lists the names of all drives mapped to the current computer and uses the static Delete() method to remove the \MyFoo and \MyBar\MyQaaz subdirectories previously created:

```
class MyDirectory
{
    public static void Main(String[] args)
    {
        // Create a new directory object bound to the D drive.
        DirectoryInfo dir = new DirectoryInfo(@"D:\WinNT");
        ...

        // Now call some static members of the Directory class.

        // List all drives.
        string[] drives = Directory.GetLogicalDrives();
        Console.WriteLine("Here are your drives:");
        foreach(string s in drives)
        {
            Console.WriteLine("->{0}", s);
        }

        // Delete what you made.
        Console.Write("Going to delete\n->" + dir.FullName +
                    "\\MyBar\\MyQaaz.\nand\n->" + dir.FullName +
                    "\\MyFoo.\n" +"Press a key to continue!");
        Console.Read();

        try
        {
            Directory.Delete(@"D:\WinNT\MyFoo");

            // The optional second parameter specifies if you
            // wish to blow away any internal subdirectories.
            Directory.Delete(@"D:\WinNT\MyBar", true);
        }
```

```
        catch(IOException e)
        {
            Console.WriteLine(e.Message);
        }
    }
}
```

Figure 11-6 shows the final output of the application.

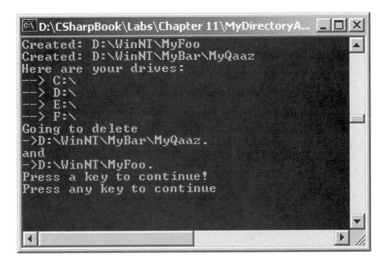

Figure 11-6. Working with the static members of a directory

Great! At this point you have investigated some core behaviors of the Directory and DirectoryInfo types. Next, you need to learn how to create, open, close, and destroy the files that populate a given directory.

SOURCE CODE   *The MyDirectoryApp project is located under the Chapter 11 subdirectory.*

The FileInfo Class

The role of the FileInfo class is to encapsulate a number of details regarding existing files on your hard drive (time created, size, file attributes, and so forth) as well as aid in the creation and destruction of new files. In addition to the set of functionality inherited by FileSystemInfo, Table 11-5 describes some core members unique to the FileInfo class.

Table 11-5. FileInfo Core Members

FILEINFO MEMBER	MEANING IN LIFE
AppendText()	Creates a StreamWriter type (described later) that appends text to a file.
CopyTo()	Copies an existing file to a new file.
Create()	Creates a new file and returns a FileStream type (described later) to interact with the created file.
CreateText()	Creates a StreamWriter type that writes a new text file.
Delete()	Deletes the file to which a FileInfo instance is bound.
Directory	Gets an instance of the parent directory.
DirectoryName	Gets the full path to a file.
Length	Gets the size of the current file or directory.
MoveTo()	Moves a specified file to a new location, providing the option to specify a new file name.
Name	Gets the name of the file.
Open()	Opens a file with various read/write and sharing privileges.
OpenRead()	Creates a read-only FileStream.
OpenText()	Creates a StreamReader type (described later) that reads from an existing text file.
OpenWrite()	Creates a read/write FileStream type.

First, you should be aware that many methods defined by FileInfo return a specific type (FileStream, StreamWriter, StreamReader, and so forth) that allows you to begin reading and writing data to (or from) the associated file in a variety of ways. This chapter examines these new types. Until then, the following class illustrates the most generic (and least flexible) way to create a file programmatically:

```
public class FileManipulator
{
    public static int Main(string[] args)
    {
        // Make a new file on the C: drive.
        FileInfo f = new FileInfo(@"C:\Test.txt");
        FileStream fs = f.Create();

        // Print some basic traits of the test.txt file.
        Console.WriteLine("Creation: {0}", f.CreationTime);
        Console.WriteLine("Full name: {0}", f.FullName);
        Console.WriteLine("Full atts: {0}", f.Attributes.ToString());\
```

```
            Console.Write("Press a key to delete file");
            Console.Read();

            // Close the file stream and delete the file.
            fs.Close();
            f.Delete();

            return 0;
        }
    }
}
```

Notice that the Create() method returns a FileStream type that allows you to close the new file before removing it from the hard drive. (You will see additional uses of FileStream later in the chapter.) When you run this application, you can see your new file at the specified directory (Figure 11-7) given the call to Create().

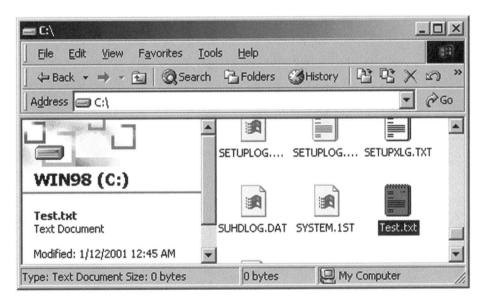

Figure 11-7. Programmatically creating a physical file

Examining the FileInfo.Open() Method

The Open() method of the FileInfo type can be used to open existing files as well as create new files with far more precision than the FileInfo.Create() method. To illustrate, ponder the following logic:

```
// Open (or create) a file with read/write attributes (no sharing),
// and store file handle in a FileStream object.
```

```
FileInfo f2 = new FileInfo(@"C:\HelloThere.ini");
FileStream s = f2.Open(FileMode.OpenOrCreate, FileAccess.ReadWrite,
                       FileShare.None);
s.Close();
f2.Delete();
```

This version of the overloaded Open() method requires three parameters. The first parameter specifies the general flavor of the open request (e.g., make a new file, open an existing file, append to a file, and so on), which is specified using the FileMode enumeration (Table 11-6).

Table 11-6. FileMode Enumeration Values

FILEMODE ENUMERATION VALUE	MEANING IN LIFE
Append	Opens the file if it exists and seeks to the end of the file. If the specified file does not exist, a new file is created. Be aware that FileMode.Append can only be used in conjunction with FileAccess.Write.
Create	Specifies that the operating system should create a new file. Be very aware that if the file already exists, it is overwritten!
CreateNew	Specifies that the operating system should create a new file. If the file already exists, an IOException is thrown.
Open	Specifies that the operating system should open an existing file.
OpenOrCreate	Specifies that the operating system should open a file if it exists; otherwise, a new file should be created.
Truncate	Specifies that the operating system should open an existing file. Once opened, the file should be truncated so that its size is zero bytes.

The second parameter, FileAccess, is used to determine the read/write behavior of the underlying stream (Table 11-7).

Table 11-7. FileAccess Enumeration Values

FILEACCESS ENUMERATION VALUE	MEANING IN LIFE
Read	Specifies read-only access to the file (i.e., data can only be obtained from the file).
ReadWrite	Specifies read and write access to the file (i.e., data can be added to or obtained from the file).
Write	Specifies write access to the file (i.e., data can only be added to the file).

Finally, you have the third parameter (FileShare), which specifies how the currently open file is to be shared among other file handles (Table 11-8).

Table 11-8. FileShare Enumeration Values

FILESHARE ENUMERATION VALUE	MEANING IN LIFE
None	Declines sharing of the current file. Any request to open the file (by this process or another process) fails until the file is closed.
Read	Allows subsequent opening of the file for reading. If this flag is not specified, any request to open the file for reading (by this process or another process) fails until the file is closed.
ReadWrite	Allows subsequent opening of the file for reading or writing. If this flag is not specified, any request to open the file for writing or reading (by this process or another process) fails until the file is closed.
Write	Allows subsequent opening of the file for writing. If this flag is not specified, any request to open the file for writing (by this process or another process) fails until the file is closed.

The FileInfo.OpenRead() and FileInfo.OpenWrite() Members

In addition to the Open() method, the FileInfo class also has members named OpenRead() and OpenWrite(). As you would imagine, these methods return a read-only or write-only FileStream type. Here is an example:

```
// Get a FileStream object with read-only permissions.
FileInfo f3 = new FileInfo(@"C:\boot.ini");
FileStream readOnlyStream = f3.OpenRead();
readOnlyStream.Close();

// Now get a FileStream object with write-only permissions.
FileInfo f4 = new FileInfo(@"C:\config.sys");
FileStream writeOnlyStream = f4.OpenWrite();
writeOnlyStream.Close();
```

SOURCE CODE   *The BasicFileApp project is included under the Chapter 11 sub-directory.*

The FileInfo.OpenText(), FileInfo.CreateText(), and FileInfo.AppendText() Members

Another "open-centric" member of the FileInfo type is OpenText(). Unlike Open(), OpenRead(), and OpenWrite(), the OpenText() method returns an instance of the StreamReader type, rather than a FileStream derived type, as shown here:

```
// Get a StreamReader object.
FileInfo f5 = new FileInfo(@"C:\bootlog.txt");
StreamReader sreader = f5.OpenText();
sreader.Close();
```

The final two methods of interest at this point are CreateText() and AppendText(), both of which return a StreamWriter reference, as shown here:

```
// Get some StreamWriters.
FileInfo f6 = new FileInfo(@"D:\AnotherTest.txt");
f6.Open(FileMode.Create, FileAccess.ReadWrite);
StreamWriter swriter = f6.CreateText();
swriter.Close();

FileInfo f7 = new FileInfo(@"D:\FinalTest.txt");
f7.Open(FileMode.Create, FileAccess.ReadWrite);
StreamWriter swriterAppend = f7.AppendText();
swriterAppend.Close();
```

At this point, you have a good feel for the functionality provided by the FileInfo type. (You will see exactly what to do with the FileStream, StreamReader, and StreamWriter types shortly.) Be aware that the File type provides almost identical functionality using a number of static members. You will see the File type in action where appropriate, but be sure to check out online help for an exhaustive listing of each member.

The Abstract Stream Class

In the world of IO manipulation, a *stream* is an entity that is able to obtain or produce chunks of data. The abstract System.IO.Stream class defines a number of members that provide support for synchronous and asynchronous interactions with the storage medium (e.g., an underlying file or memory location). Figure 11-8 shows the basic stream hierarchy.

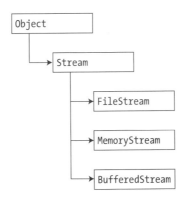

Figure 11-8. Stream-derived types

Stream descendents represent data as a raw stream of bytes (rather than text-based data). Also, Streams-derived types support seeking, which refers to the process of obtaining and adjusting the current position in a stream. To begin understanding the functionality provided by the Stream class, take note of the core members described in Table 11-9.

Table 11-9. Abstract Stream Members

STREAM MEMBER	MEANING IN LIFE
CanRead CanSeek CanWrite	Determines whether the current stream supports reading, seeking, and/or writing.
Close()	Closes the current stream and releases any resources (such as sockets and file handles) associated with the current stream.
Flush()	Updates the underlying data source or repository with the current state of the buffer and then clears the buffer. If a stream does not implement a buffer, this method does nothing.
Length	Returns the length of the stream, in bytes.
Position	Determines the position in the current stream.
Read() ReadByte()	Reads a sequence of bytes (or a single byte) from the current stream and advances the current position in the stream by the number of bytes read.
Seek()	Sets the position in the current stream.
SetLength()	Sets the length of the current stream.
Write() WriteByte()	Writes a sequence of bytes (or a single byte) to the current stream and advances the current position in this stream by the number of bytes written.

Working with FileStreams

The FileStream class provides implementations for the abstract Stream members in a manner appropriate for file-based streaming. Like the DirectoryInfo and FileInfo types, FileStream provides the ability to open existing files as well as create new files. FileStreams are usually created using the FileMode, FileAccess, and FileShare enumerations. For example, the following logic creates a new file (test.dat) in the application directory:

```
// Create a new file in the working directory.
FileStream myFStream = new FileStream("test.dat", FileMode.OpenOrCreate,
                                   FileAccess.ReadWrite);
```

You can experiment with the synchronous read/write capabilities of the FileStream type. To write a stream of bytes to a file, make calls to the inherited WriteByte() or Write() method, both of which advance the internal file pointer automatically. To read the bytes back from a file, simply call Read() or ReadByte(). Here is an example:

```
// Write bytes to the *.dat file.
for(int i = 0; i < 256; i++)
{
    myFStream.WriteByte((byte)i);
}

// Reset internal position.
myFStream.Position = 0;

// Read bytes from the *.dat file.
for(int i = 0; i < 256; i++)
{
    Console.Write(myFStream.ReadByte());
}
myFStream.Close();
```

If you open this new file from the Visual Studio.NET IDE, you can see the underlying byte stream (Figure 11-9).

Working with MemoryStreams

The MemoryStream type works much like FileStream, with the obvious difference that you are now writing to memory rather than a physical file. Given that each of

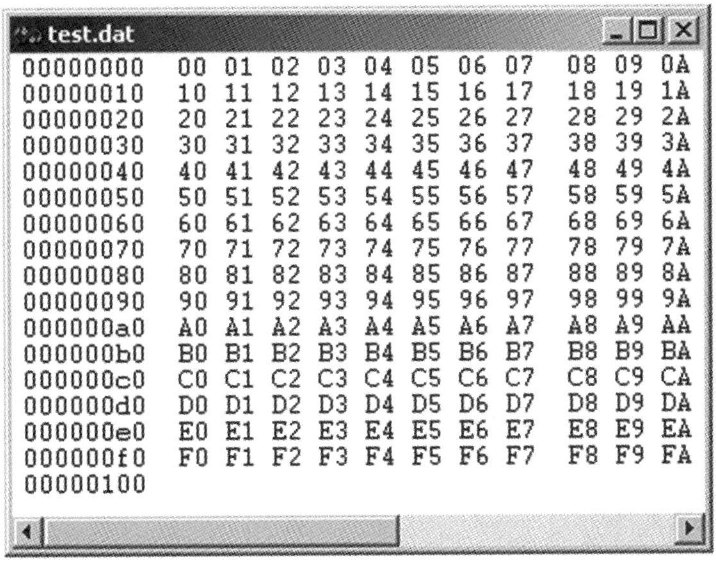

Figure 11-9. The binary dump

these types derives from Stream, you can update the previous FileStream logic as shown here:

```
// Create a memory stream with a fixed capacity.
MemoryStream myMemStream = new MemoryStream();
myMemStream.Capacity = 256;

// Write bytes to stream.
for(int i = 0; i < 256; i++)
{
    myMemStream.WriteByte((byte)i);
}

// Reset internal position.
myMemStream.Position = 0;

// Read bytes from stream.
for(int i = 0; i < 256; i++)
{
    Console.Write(myMemStream.ReadByte());
}
myMemStream.Close();
```

The output of this logic is identical to that of the previous FileStream example. The only difference is where you stream the information (file or memory). In addition to the inherited members, MemoryStream supplies other members. For example, the previous code used the Capacity property to specify how much memory to carve out for the streaming operation. Table 11-10 shows the core MemoryStream type members.

Table 11-10. MemoryStream Core Members

MEMORYSTREAM MEMBER	MEANING IN LIFE
Capacity	Gets or sets the number of bytes allocated for this stream.
GetBuffer()	Returns the array of unsigned bytes from which this stream was created.
ToArray()	Writes the entire stream contents to a byte array, regardless of the Position property.
WriteTo()	Writes the entire contents of this MemoryStream to another stream-derived type (such as a file).

Notice the possible interplay between the MemoryStream and FileStream types. Using the WriteTo() method, you can easily transfer data stored in memory to a file. Furthermore, you can also retrieve the memory stream as a byte array:

```
// Dump memory data to file.

FileStream dumpFile = new FileStream("Dump.dat", FileMode.Create,
                                FileAccess.ReadWrite);
myMemStream.WriteTo(dumpFile);


// Dump memory data to a byte array.
byte[] bytesinMemory = myMemStream.ToArray();
myMemStream.Close();
```

Working with BufferedStreams

The final Stream-derived type to consider is BufferedStream. This type can be used as a temporary location to read or write information, which can later be committed to permanent storage. For example, assume you have opened a data file and need to write out a large series of bytes. While you could stuff each item directly to file using FileStream.Write(), you may wish to help optimize the process by storing the new items in a BufferedStream type and make a final commit when each addition has been accounted for. In this way, you can reduce the number of times you must hit the physical file. Here is an example:

```
// Build a buffer attached' to a valid FileStream.
BufferedStream myFileBuffer = new BufferedStream(dumpFile);

// Add some bytes to the buffer.
byte[] str = {127, 0x77, 0x4, 0x0, 0x0, 0x16};
myFileBuffer.Write(str, 0, str.Length);

// Commit changes to file.
myMemStream.Close();      // Flushes.
```

SOURCE CODE *The Streamer project illustrates working with the FileStream, MemoryStream and BufferedStream types, and is located under the Chapter 11 subdirectory.*

Working with StreamWriters and StreamReaders

The StreamWriter and StreamReader classes are useful whenever you need to read or write character-based data (e.g., strings). Both of these types work by default with Unicode characters; however, this can be changed by supplying a properly configured System.Text.Encoding object reference. To keep things simple, let's assume that the default Unicode encoding fits the bill. (Be sure to check out the System.Text namespace for other possibilities.)

StreamReader derives from an abstract type named TextReader, as does the related StringReader type (discussed later in this chapter). The TextReader base class provides a very limited set of functionality to each of these descendents, specifically the ability to read and peek into a character stream.

The StreamWriter type (as well as StringWriter, also examined later in this chapter) derives from a base class named TextWriter. This class defines members that allow derived types to write textual data to a given character stream. The relationship between each of these new IO-centric types is shown in Figure 11-10.

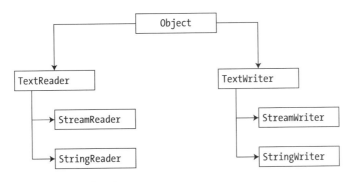

Figure 11-10. Readers and writers

To understand the writing capabilities of the StreamWriter class, you need to examine the base class functionality inherited from the TextWriter type. This abstract class defines the members described in Table 11-11.

Table 11-11. System.IO Namespace Core Types

TEXTWRITER MEMBER NAME	MEANING IN LIFE
Close()	Closes the writer and frees any associated resources. In the process, the buffer is automatically flushed.
Flush()	Clears all buffers for the current writer and causes any buffered data to be written to the underlying device, but does not close the writer.
NewLine	Used to make the new line constant for the derived writer class. The default line terminator is a carriage return followed by a line feed ("\r\n").
Write()	Writes a line to the text stream, without a new line constant.
WriteLine()	Writes a line to the text stream, with a new line constant.

The last two members of the TextWriter class probably look familiar to you. If you recall, the System.Console type has similar members that write textual data to the standard output device. Here, TextWriter moves the information to a specified file.

The derived StreamWriter class provides an appropriate implementation for the Write(), Close(), and Flush() methods, as well as defines the additional AutoFlush property. This property, when set to true, forces StreamWriter to flush all data every time you perform a write operation. Be aware that you can gain better performance by setting AutoFlush to false, provided you always call Close() when you are done writing with a StreamWriter.

Writing to a Text File

Now for an example of working with the StreamWriter type. The following class creates a new file named thoughts.txt using the FileInfo class. Using the CreateText() method, you can obtain a valid StreamWriter. At this point, you add some textual data to the new file, as shown here:

```
public class MyStreamWriterReader
{
    public static int Main(string[] args)
    {
        // Make a file.
        FileInfo f = new FileInfo("Thoughts.txt");
```

```
        // Get a StreamWriter and write some stuff.
        StreamWriter writer = f.CreateText();
        writer.WriteLine("Don't forget Mother's Day this year...");
        writer.WriteLine("Don't forget Father's Day this year...");
        writer.WriteLine("Don't forget these numbers:");

        for(int i = 0; i < 10; i++)
        {
            writer.Write(i + " ");
        }
        writer.Write(writer.NewLine);    // Insert a carriage return.

        // Closing automatically flushes!
        writer.Close();
        Console.WriteLine("Created file and wrote some thoughts...");
    }
}
```

If you locate this new file, you should be able to double-click it to open it a la Notepad. Figure 11-11 shows the content of your new file.

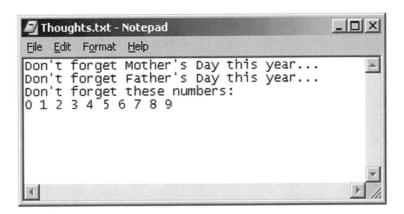

Figure 11-11. The contents of your *.txt file

Cool! As you can see, the StreamWriter has written your data to a file. The Write() and WriteLine() methods have each been overloaded numerous times to provide a number of ways to add textual and numeric data (which defaults to Unicode encoding).

Reading from a Text File

Now you need to understand how to programmatically read data from a file using the corresponding StreamReader type. As you probably recall, this class derives from TextReader, which offers the following functionality described in Table 11-12.

Table 11-12. TextReader Core Members

TEXTREADER MEMBER NAME	MEANING IN LIFE
Peek()	Returns the next available character without actually changing the position of the reader.
Read()	Reads data from an input stream.
ReadBlock()	Reads a maximum of count characters from the current stream and writes the data to a buffer, beginning at index.
ReadLine()	Reads a line of characters from the current stream and returns the data as a string. (A null string indicates EOF.)
ReadToEnd()	Reads all characters from the current position to the end of the TextReader and returns them as one string.

If you now extend the current MyStreamWriterReader class to use a StreamReader, you can read in the textual data from the thoughts.txt file, as shown here:

```
public class MyStreamWriterReader
{
    public static int Main(string[] args)
    {
        // Writing logic as before.

        // Now read it all back in using a StreamReader.
        Console.WriteLine("Here are your thoughts:\n");
        StreamReader sr = File.OpenText("Thoughts.txt");

        string input = null;
        while ((input = sr.ReadLine()) != null)
        {
            Console.WriteLine (input);
        }
        sr.Close();

        return 0;
    }
}
```

Running the program, you would see the output shown in Figure 11-12.

```
D:\CSharpBook\Io\StreamWriterReaderApp\bin\D...  _ □ X
Created file and wrote some thoughts...
Here are your thoughts:

Don't forget Mother's Day this year...
Don't forget Father's Day this year...
Don't forget these numbers:
0 1 2 3 4 5 6 7 8 9
Press any key to continue
```

Figure 11-12. Reading from a file

You obtained a valid StreamReader using the static File.OpenText() method. The read logic makes use of StreamReader.Peek() to ensure that you have an additional character ahead of the reader's current position. If so, you read the next line and pump it to the console. To obtain the contents of the entire file, you could avoid the "peeking" and simply call ReadToEnd(), as shown here:

```
// I want it all!
string allOfTheData = sr.ReadToEnd();
MessageBox.Show(allOfTheData, "Here it is:");
sr.Close();
```

As you can see, the StreamReader and StreamWriter types provide a custom implementation of the abstract members defined by their respective base classes. Just remember that these two types are concerned with moving text-based data to and from a specified file.

SOURCE CODE   *The StreamWriterReaderApp project is included under the Chapter 11 subdirectory.*

Working with StringWriters

Using the StringWriter and StringReader types, you can treat textual information as a stream of in-memory characters. This can prove helpful when you wish to append character-based information to an underlying buffer. To gain access to the underlying buffer from an instance of a StringWriter type, you can call the overridden ToString() method (to receive a System.String type) or the

GetStringBuilder() method, which returns an instance of StringBuilder. Recall from Chapter 2 that the System.Text.StringBuilder type allows you to directly modify a string buffer.

To illustrate, reengineer the previous example to write the character information to a StringWriter instance rather than a generated file. As you should notice, the two programs are nearly identical, given that both StringWriter and StreamWriter inherit the same base class functionality, as shown here:

```
public class MyStringWriterReader
{
    public static int Main(string[] args)
    {
        // Get a StringWriter and write some stuff.
        StringWriter writer = new StringWriter();
        writer.WriteLine("Don't forget Mother's Day this year...");
        writer.WriteLine("Don't forget Father's Day this year...");
        writer.WriteLine("Don't forget these numbers:");

        for(int i = 0; i < 10; i++)
        {
            writer.Write(i + " ");
        }

        writer.Write(writer.NewLine);      // Insert a carriage return.

        // Closing automatically flushes!
        writer.Close();
        Console.WriteLine("Stored thoughts in a StringWriter...");

        // Get a copy of the contents (stored in a string) and pump
        // to console.
        Console.WriteLine("Contents: {0}", writer.ToString());

        return 0;
    }
}
```

Running this program of course dumps out textual data to the console (Figure 11-13).

Figure 11-13. Dumping the StringWriter

Now gain access to the underlying StringBuilder maintained by the StringWriter, and add the following logic:

```csharp
// For StringBuilder type!
using System.Text;

public class MyStringWriterReader
{
    public static int Main(string[] args)
    {
        // Previous logic. . .
        . . .

        // Get the internal StringBuilder.
        StringBuilder str = writer.GetStringBuilder();
        string allOfTheData = str.ToString();
        Console.WriteLine("StringBuilder says:\n{0} ", allOfTheData);

        // Insert item to buffer at position 20.
        str.Insert(20, "INSERTED STUFF");
        allOfTheData = str.ToString();
        Console.WriteLine("New StringBuilder says:\n{0} ", allOfTheData);

        // Remove the inserted string.
        str.Remove(20, "INSERTED STUFF".Length);
        allOfTheData = str.ToString();
        Console.WriteLine("Original says:\n{0}", allOfTheData);

        return 0;
    }
}
```

Here, you can write some character data to a StringWriter type and extract and manipulate a copy of the contents using the GetStringBuilder() member function. Figure 11-14 shows the output.

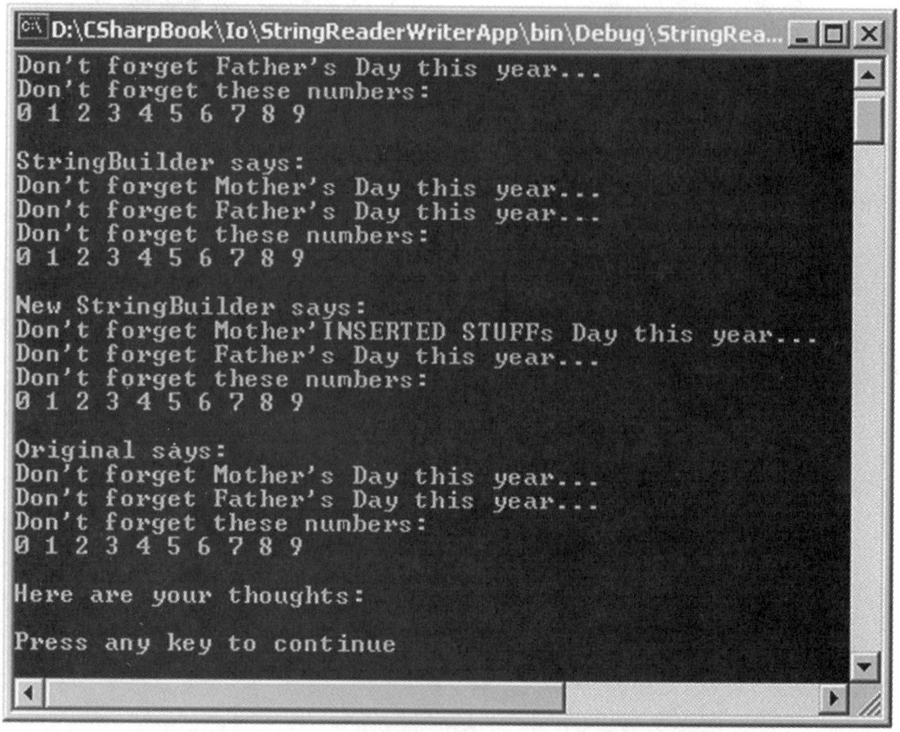

Figure 11-14. Manipulating the StringBuilder

Working with StringReaders

Next is the StringReader type, which (as you would expect) functions identically to the related StreamReader class. In fact, the StringReader class does nothing more than override the inherited members to read from a block of character data, rather than a file, as shown here:

```
// Now dump using a StringReader.

StringReader sr = new StringReader(writer.ToString());

string input = null;
while ((input = sr.ReadLine()) != null)
```

```
{
    Console.WriteLine (input);
}
sr.Close();
```

If you were paying attention to the previous sample applications, you may have noticed one limitation of the TextReader and TextWriter descendents. None of these types has the ability to provide random access to its contents (e.g., seeking). For example, StreamReader has no members that allow you to reset the internal file cursor or jump over some number of characters and begin reading from that point. To gain this sort of functionality, you need to use various descendents of the Stream type.

SOURCE CODE *The StringReaderWriterApp is included under the Chapter 11 subdirectory.*

Working with Binary Data (BinaryReaders and BinaryWriters)

The final two core classes provided by the System.IO namespace are BinaryReader and BinaryWriter, both of which derive directly from Object, as shown in Figure 11-15.

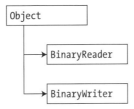

Figure 11-15. Binary readers and writers

These types allow you to read and write discrete data types to an underlying stream. The BinaryWriter class defines a highly overloaded method named (of course) Write() to place a data type in the corresponding stream. The BinaryWriter class also provides some other familiar-looking members (Table 11-13).

Table 11-13. BinaryWriter Core Members

BINARYWRITER MEMBER	MEANING IN LIFE
BaseStream	Represents the underlying stream used with the binary reader.
Close()	Closes the binary stream.
Flush()	Flushes the binary stream.
Seek()	Sets the position in the current stream.
Write()	Writes a value to the current stream.

The BinaryReader class complements the functionality offered by BinaryWriter with the members described in Table 11-14.

Table 11-14. BinaryReader Core Members

BINARYREADER MEMBER	MEANING IN LIFE
BaseStream	Enables access to the underlying stream.
Close()	Closes the binary reader.
PeekChar()	Returns the next available character without actually advancing the position in the stream.
Read()	Reads a given set of bytes or characters and stores them in the incoming array.
ReadXXXX()	The BinaryReader class defines numerous ReadXXXX methods, which grab the next type from the stream (ReadBoolean(), ReadByte(), ReadInt32(), and so forth).

The following class writes a number of character types to a new *.dat file created and opened using the FileStream class. Once you have a valid FileStream, pass this object to the constructor of the BinaryWriter type. Understand that the constructor of BinaryWriter takes any Stream-derived type (for example, FileStream, MemoryStream, or BufferedStream). Once the data has been written, a corresponding BinaryReader reads each byte back, as shown here:

```
public class ByteTweaker
{
    public static int Main(string[] args)
    {
        Console.WriteLine("Creating a file and writing binary data. . .");
        FileStream myFStream
            = new FileStream("temp.dat", FileMode.OpenOrCreate,
                            FileAccess.ReadWrite);
```

```csharp
// Write some binary info.
BinaryWriter binWrit = new BinaryWriter(myFStream);
binWrit.WriteString("Hello as binary info...");
int myInt = 99;
float myFloat = 9984.82343F;
bool myBool = false;
char[] myCharArray = {'H', 'e', 'l', 'l', 'o'};
binWrit.Write(myInt);
binWrit.Write(myFloat);
binWrit.Write(myBool);
binWrit.Write(myCharArray);

// Reset internal position.
binWrit.BaseStream.Position = 0;

// Read the binary info as raw bytes.
Console.WriteLine("Reading binary data...");
BinaryReader binRead = new BinaryReader(myFStream);
int temp = 0;
while(binRead.PeekChar() != -1)
{
    Console.Write(binRead.ReadByte());
    temp = temp + 1;
    if(temp == 5)
    {
        // Add a blank line every 5 bytes.
        temp = 0;
        Console.WriteLine();
    }
}

// Clean things up.
binWrit.Close();
binRead.Close();
myFStream.Close();
    }
}
```

Figure 11-16 shows the output.

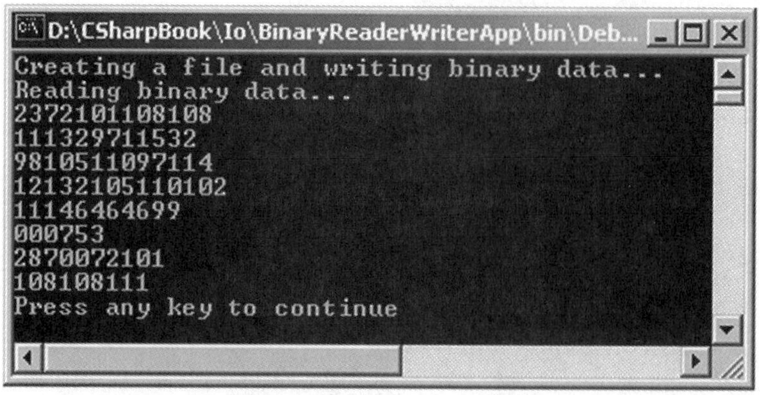

Figure 11-16. A binary read/write session

An Interesting Side Note

Although you may never need to read and write individual bytes to a stream, you should know that other types in the .NET namespaces use these same IO primitives behind the scenes. For example, the System.Windows.Forms.Bitmap type supports a member named Save(), which writes binary data to a new file. It is also possible to construct a new Bitmap type by passing in a Stream-derived type. Given these aspects of the Bitmap type, it is possible to modify the underlying pixel information at runtime. While you could calculate these (*x, y*) coordinates by hand, it is far simpler to use the SetPixel() method, as shown here:

```
// Now open a bitmap in the application directory.
Console.WriteLine("Modifying a bitmap in memory");
myFStream = new FileStream("Paint Splatter.bmp", FileMode.Open,
            FileAccess.ReadWrite);

// Build a Bitmap based on a stream.
Bitmap rawBitmap = new Bitmap(myFStream);
// Draw a white 'X' over the image.
// (This logic assumes the height and width of the image are identical.)
for(int i = 0; i < rawBitmap.Width; i++)
{
    rawBitmap.SetPixel(i, i, Color.White);
    rawBitmap.SetPixel((rawBitmap.Width - i) - 1, i - 1, Color.White);
}

// Now save the modified image to file.
rawBitmap.Save("newImage.bmp");
myFStream.Close();
```

Figure 11-17 shows how the paint splatter.bmp file looks before the pixel modification.

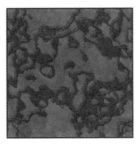

Figure 11-17. The unmodified image

Figure 11-18 shows how the newImage.bmp file looks after new pixels are rendered.

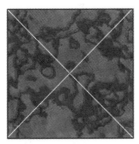

Figure 11-18. The modified image

That wraps up the investigation of the core types in the System.IO namespace. At this point, you are in a position to read and write textual, binary, and intrinsic data types. This chapter concludes with an examination of how the .NET framework supports the serialization of custom types.

SOURCE CODE   *The BinaryReaderWriter application is included under the Chapter 11 subdirectory.*

Object Persistence in the .NET Framework

As you have seen, the System.IO namespace defines a number of types that allow you to send binary and character-based data to some storage device (such as a file or memory location). What has not yet been addressed is how to save instances of custom class types to a stream and how to read instances back from storage.

In the .NET framework, *serialization* is the term describing the process of converting the state of an object to a linear sequence of bytes. This byte stream contains all necessary information to reconstruct (or *deserialize*) the state of the object for use later. The .NET serialization services are quite sophisticated: when an object is serialized to a stream, any additional object references required by the root object are serialized as well. For example, when a derived class is serialized, each object up the chain of inheritance is able to write its own custom state data to the byte stream.

Once a set of objects has been saved to a stream, the byte pattern can be relocated as necessary. For example, imagine you have serialized a stream of objects to a MemoryStream. This stream could be forwarded to a remote computer or the Windows clipboard, burned to a CD, or simply stored in a file. The byte stream itself does not care where it is stored. All that matters is the fact that this stream of 1's and 0's correctly represents the state of the serialized objects.

The Role of Object Graphs

The chain of related objects serialized to a stream is collectively referred to as an *object graph*. Object graphs provide a simple way to document how a set of objects refer to each other and are *not* intended to directly model classic OO relationships (such as the "is-a" or "has-a" relationship). To establish the relations among objects in a graph, each object is assigned a unique numerical value, followed by a graph of all related items. Keep in mind that the numbers assigned to the members in an object graph are arbitrary and have no real meaning to the outside world.

As a simple example, assume you have created a set of classes that model (of course) some automobiles. You have a topmost type named Car, which "has-a" Radio. Another class named JamesBondCar extends the basic Car type. An object graph that models these relationships is shown in Figure 11-19.

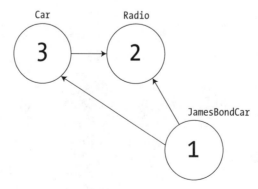

Figure 11-19. A simple object graph

In Figure 11-19 you can see that the Car class refers to the Radio class (given the "has-a" relationship). The JamesBondCar refers to the Car (as it is a subclass) as well as the Radio (as it inherits this protected member). Given that each object reference has been assigned an arbitrary number, you can build the following formula:

```
[Car 3, ref 2], [Radio 2], [JamesBondCar 1, ref 3, ref 2]
```

This formula is the pattern that is serialized to a stream, along with the values for each member variable in the Car, Radio, and JamesBondCar types. You can see that the Car type has a dependency on item 2 (the Radio). Also, the JamesBondCar has a dependency on item 3 (the Car) as well as item 2 (the Radio). If you serialize an instance of JamesBondCar to a stream, the object graph ensures that the Radio and Car types also participate in the process. The beautiful thing about the serialization process is that the graph representing the relationships among your objects is established automatically behind the scenes.

Configuring Objects for Serialization

To make an object available for serialization, you mark each class with the [Serializable] attribute. That's it (really). If you determine that a given class has some member data that should not participate in the serialization scheme, you can mark such fields with the [NonSerialized] attribute. This can be helpful if you have member variables (or properties) in a serializable class that do not need to be "remembered" (e.g., constants, transient data, and so on). For example, here is the Radio class, which has been marked as serializable (except for a single member variable):

```
// The Radio class can participate in the .NET serialization scheme.
[Serializable]
public class Radio
{
    // But you don't care to save this member.
    [NonSerialized]
    private int objectIDNumber = 9;

    public Radio(){}
    public void On(bool state)
    {
        if(state == true)
            MessageBox.Show("Music is on. . .");
        else
            MessageBox.Show("No tunes. . .");
    }
}
```

These attributes are marked in the type's metadata, as seen from ILDasm.exe (Figure 11-20).

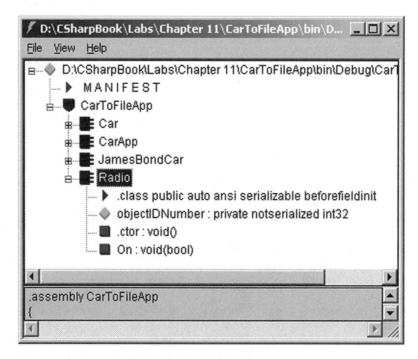

Figure 11-20. The Serializable and NonSerialized attributes

To finish the coding of this car hierarchy, here are the definitions for the Car base class and JamesBondCar subtype, each marked with the [Serializable] attribute:

```
// The Car class is serializable!
[Serializable]
public class Car
{
    protected string petName;
    protected int maxSpeed;
    protected Radio theRadio = new Radio();

    public Car(string petName, int maxSpeed)
    {
        this.petName = petName;
        this.maxSpeed = maxSpeed;
    }
    public Car() {}     // state data set to defaults automatically. . .
```

```
        public String PetName
        {
            get { return petName; }
            set { petName = value; }
        }

        public int MaxSpeed
        {
            get { return maxSpeed; }
            set { maxSpeed = value; }
        }
        public void TurnOnRadio(bool state)
        {
            theRadio.On(state);
        }
}
// The JamesBondCar class is also serializable!
[Serializable]
public class JamesBondCar : Car
{
        protected bool isFlightWorthy;
        protected bool isSeaWorthy;

        public JamesBondCar(){}
        public JamesBondCar(string petName, int maxSpeed,
                            bool canFly, bool canSubmerge)
            : base(petName, maxSpeed)
        {
            this.isFlightWorthy = canFly;
            this.isSeaWorthy = canSubmerge;
        }
        public void Fly()
        {
            if(isFlightWorthy)
                MessageBox.Show("Taking off!");
            else
                MessageBox.Show("Falling off cliff!");
        }
        public void GoUnderWater()
        {
            if(isSeaWorthy)
                MessageBox.Show("Diving....");
```

```
        else
            MessageBox.Show("Drowning!!!");
    }
}
```

Choosing a Formatter

Once you have configured your types to participate in the .NET serialization scheme, your next step is to choose which format to use to persist your object graph. The System.Runtime.Serialization.Formatters namespace contains two additional nested namespaces (*.Binary and *.Soap) that provide two default formatters. As you can guess, the BinaryFormatter type serializes your object graph to a stream using a compact binary format. The SoapFormatter type represents your graph as a SOAP (Simple Object Access Protocol) message (which is expressed in XML format).

The BinaryFormatter type is defined in the mscorlib.dll assembly. Therefore, to serialize your objects to a binary format, all you need to do is specify the following using directive:

```
// Need to send objects to a binary format!
using System.Runtime.Serialization.Formatters.Binary;
```

However, the SoapFormatter type is defined in a separate assembly. To format your object graph as a SOAP message, begin by setting a reference to the System.Runtime.Serialization.Formatters.Soap.dll assembly and make the following using directive:

```
// Need to send objects to a SOAP format!
using System.Runtime.Serialization.Formatters.Soap;
```

The Role of the System.Runtime.Serialization Namespace

If you ever need to build a custom formatter, you will need to use a number of types defined in the System.Runtime.Serialization namespace. Also, if you wish to configure your objects to employ custom serialization, these types will also be of interest. Although building a custom formatter is outside the scope of this book, Table 11-15 describes some (but not all) of the core classes to be aware of.

In addition to these types, there are two core interfaces to be aware of: IFormatter and ISerializable. Later this chapter revisits the ISerializable interface and the issue of custom serialization.

Table 11-15. System.Runtime.Serialization Namespace Core Types

TYPES OF THE SYSTEM.RUNTIME.SERIALIZATION NAMESPACE	MEANING IN LIFE
Formatter	An abstract base class that provides base functionality for runtime serialization formatters.
ObjectIDGenerator	Generates IDs for objects in an object graph.
ObjectManager	Keeps track of objects as they are being deserialized.
SerializationBinder	An abstract base class that provides functionality to serialize a type to a stream.
SerializationInfo	Used by objects that have custom serialization behavior. SerializationInfo holds together all of the data needed to serialize or deserialize an object. In essence, this class is a "property bag" that allows you to establish name/value pairs to represent the state of an object.

Regardless which formatter you choose (including any custom formatter you dream up), the formatter is in charge of transmitting all of the information required to persist the object during the serialization process. The necessary information includes the full type name of the object (e.g., MyProject.MyClasses.Foo), the name of the assembly containing the object (e.g., friendly name, version, and an optional strong name), as well as any stateful information, represented by the SerializationInfo type.

During the deserialization process, the formatter uses this information to build an identical copy of the object, using the information extracted from the underlying stream. The big picture can be visualized as shown in Figure 11-21.

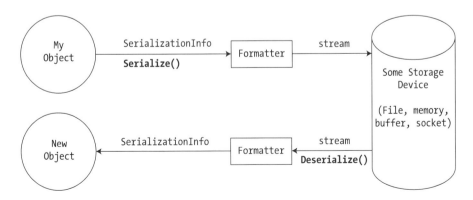

Figure 11-21. The serialization process

Serialization Using a Binary Formatter

Recall that the BinaryFormatter type is a member of the System.Runtime.Serialization.Formatters.Binary namespace, which is located in the mscorlib.dll assembly. BinaryFormatter defines two core methods that read and write an object graph to a stream (Table 11-16).

Table 11-16. BinaryFormatter Members

BINARYFORMATTER MEMBER	MEANING IN LIFE
Deserialize()	Deserializes a stream of bytes to an object graph.
Serialize()	Serialize an object or graph of connected objects to a stream.

In addition, the BinaryFormatter type defines a number of properties that configure specific details regarding the (de)serialization process. By and large, the default configuration of BinaryFormatter is all you need to concern yourself with.

To illustrate, assume you have created an instance of JamesBondCar, modified some state data, and want to persist your spymobile in a *.dat file, as shown here:

```
using System.Runtime.Serialization.Formatters.Binary,

public static void Main()
{
    Make a car and operate vehicle.
    JamesBondCar myAuto = new JamesBondCar("Fred", 50, false, true);
    myAuto.TurnOnRadio(true);
    myAuto.GoUnderWater();

    // Create a file stream.
    FileStream myStream = File.Create("CarData.dat");

    // Move your graph into the stream using a binary format.
    BinaryFormatter myBinaryFormat = new BinaryFormatter();
    myBinaryFormat.Serialize(myStream, myAuto);
    myStream.Close();
    . . .
}
```

As you can see, the BinaryFormatter.Serialize() method is the member responsible for composing the object graph and moving the byte sequence to some Stream-derived type. In this case, the stream happens to be a physical file. However, you could also serialize your object types to any Stream-derived type (such as a memory location, given that MemoryStream is a descendent of the Stream type). If you open the underlying binary file, you can peek inside the byte sequence (Figure 11-22).

```
bin\Debug\CarData.dat                            _ □ ×
FF   FF 01 00 00 00 00 00 00    . . . . . . . . . . . . . .
43   61 72 54 6F 46 69 6C 65    . . . . . .ICarToFile
72   73 69 6F 6E 3D 31 2E 30    App, Version=1.0
33   39 36 2C 20 43 75 6C 74    .462.34396, Cult
74   72 61 6C 2C 20 50 75 62    ure=neutral, Pub
6F   6B 65 6E 3D 6E 75 6C 6C    licKeyToken=null
61   72 54 6F 46 69 6C 65 41    . . . . . .CarToFileA
73   42 6F 6E 64 43 61 72 08    pp.JamesBondCar.
6C   69 67 68 74 57 6F 72 74    . . . .isFlightWort
61   57 6F 72 74 68 79 07 70    hy.isSeaWorthy.p
6D   61 78 53 70 65 65 64 08    etName.maxSpeed.
6F   0B 43 61 72 2B 70 65 74    theRadio.Car+pet
72   2B 6D 61 78 53 70 65 65    Name.Car+maxSpee
68   65 52 61 64 69 6F 02 00    d.Car+theRadio..
00   00 04 46 72 65 64 32 00    . . . . . . . . .Fred2.
09   03 00 00 00 32 00 00 00    . . . . . . . . . . .2. . .
00   00 00 12 43 61 72 54 6F    . . . . . . . . . . .CarTo
2E   52 61 64 69 6F 00 00 00    FileApp.Radio. . .
                                . . . . . .
```

Figure 11-22. JamesBondCar serialized using a BinaryFormatter

Suppose you want to read the persisted JamesBondCar back to an object variable. To do so, use the BinaryWriter.Deserialize() method. Be aware that Deserialize() returns a generic System.Object type, and therefore you need to impose an explicit cast, as shown here:

```
// Read in the Car from the binary stream.
myStream = File.OpenRead("CarData.dat");

JamesBondCar carFromDisk =
    (JamesBondCar)myBinaryFormat.Deserialize(myStream);

Console.WriteLine(carFromDisk.PetName + " is alive!");
carFromDisk.TurnOnRadio(true);
myStream.Close();
```

Notice that when you call Deserialize(), you pass the Stream-derived type that represents the location of the persisted objects (again a file stream in this case). Now if that is not painfully simple, I'm not sure what is. In a nutshell, mark each class you wish to persist to a stream with the [Serializable] attribute. After this point, use the BinaryFormatter type to move your object graph to and from a stream.

Serialization Using a SOAP Formatter

The other available formatter for serializing your types is SoapFormatter. To use this type, you need to set a reference to the containing assembly, System.Runtime.Serialization.Formatters.Soap.dll. The following block of code extends the previous serialization example to persist the JamesBondCar using the SoapFormatter type (Chapter 15 describes SOAP messages in greater detail):

```
using System.Runtime.Serialization.Formatters.Soap;

// Save the same car to XML format.
FileStream myStream = File.Create("CarData.xml");
SoapFormatter myXMLFormat = new SoapFormatter();
myXMLFormat.Serialize(myStream, myAuto);
myStream.Close();

// Read in the Car from the XML file.
myStream = File.OpenRead("CarData.xml");
JamesBondCar carFromXML =
            (JamesBondCar)myXMLFormat.Deserialize(myStream);

Console.WriteLine(carFromXML.PetName + " is alive!");
myStream.Close();
```

As you can see, the SoapFormatter type has the same public interface as the BinaryFormatter. As before, use Serialize() and Deserialize() to move the object graph in and out of the stream. If you open the resulting *.xml file (Figure 11-23), you can locate the XML tags that mark the stateful values of the current JamesBondCar (as well as the relationship maintained by the graph).

SOURCE CODE   *The CarToFile application (demonstrating both binary and SOAP formatting) is located under the Chapter 11 subdirectory.*

```
bin\Debug\CarData.xml                                    _ | □ | X |
    1   <SOAP-ENV:Envelope xmlns:xsi="http://www.w3.org
    2   <SOAP-ENV:Body>
    3   <a1:JamesBondCar id="ref-1">
    4   <isFlightWorthy>false</isFlightWorthy>
    5   <isSeaWorthy>true</isSeaWorthy>
    6   <petName id="ref-3">Fred</petName>
    7   <maxSpeed>50</maxSpeed>
    8   <theRadio href="#ref-4"/>
    9   <Car_0x2b_petName href="#ref-3"/>
   10   <Car_0x2b_maxSpeed>50</Car_0x2b_maxSpeed>
   11   <Car_0x2b_theRadio href="#ref-4"/>
   12   </a1:JamesBondCar>
   13   <a1:Radio id="ref-4">
   14   </a1:Radio>
   15   </SOAP-ENV:Body>
   16   </SOAP-ENV:Envelope>

 □ XML    □ Data
```

Figure 11-23. JamesBondCar serialized using a SoapFormatter

Custom Serialization (and the ISerializable Interface)

The default approach to persist a custom type is simple: Mark a class with the [Serializable] attribute. When a formatter is passed the object graph, all referenced objects are sent to the stream. While this is typically exactly the behavior you desire, the System.Runtime.Serialization namespace provides ways to customize how the serialization process occurs.

When you wish to "get involved" with the serialization process, your first step is to implement the standard ISerializable interface on the class that will use custom serialization, as shown here:

```
// When you wish to tweak the serialization process, implement ISerializable.
public interface ISerializable
{
    public virtual void GetObjectData(SerializationInfo info,
                                      StreamingContext context);
}
```

This interface defines a single method named GetObjectData(), which is called by the formatter during the serialization process. The implementation of this method populates the incoming SerializationInfo parameter with a series of name/value pairs. The SerializationInfo type is essentially a "property bag," which is no doubt familiar to classic COM programmers.

In addition to implementing the ISerializable interface, all objects that are implementing custom serialization must provide a special constructor taking the following signature:

```
// You must supply a custom constructor with this signature
// to allow the runtime engine to set the state of your object.
class SomeClass
{
    private SomeClass (SerializationInfo si, StreamingContext ctx){...}
}
```

Notice that the visibility of this constructor is set as private. This is permissible given that the formatter will have access to this member regardless of its visibility. These special constructors tend to be marked as private to ensure that the casual object user would never create an object in this manner.

As you can see, the first parameter of this constructor is an instance of the SerializationInfo type, which allows you to configure a set of name/value pairs representing the state of your object. The SerializationInfo type defines a member named AddValue(), which has been overloaded numerous times to allow you to specify any type of data (strings, integers, floats, Booleans, and so on). Also, numerous GetXXXX() methods are supplied to extract information from the SerializationInfo type to populate the object's member variables. You will see these in action in just a moment.

The second parameter to this special constructor is a StreamingContext type, which contains information regarding the source or destination of the bits. The most informative member of this type is the State property, which represents a value from the StreamingContextStates enumeration (Table 11-17).

A Simple Example

Let me reiterate that you will typically not need to bypass the default serialization mechanism provided by the .NET runtime. However, to illustrate, here is an updated version of the Car type that has been configured to take part of custom serialization. You are not doing anything special in the implementation of GetObjectState() or the custom constructor. Rather, each method dumps out information regarding the current context and manipulates the incoming SerializationInfo type:

Table 11-17. StreamingContextStates Enumeration Members

STREAMINGCONTEXTSTATES	
MEMBER NAME	**MEANING IN LIFE**
All	Specifies that the serialized data can be transmitted to or received from any of the other contexts.
Clone	Specifies that the object graph is being cloned.
CrossAppDomain	Specifies that the source or destination context is a new AppDomain.
CrossMachine	Specifies that the source or destination context is a different machine.
CrossProcess	Specifies that the source or destination context is a different process on the same machine.
File	Specifies that the source or destination context is a file.
Other	Specifies that the serialization context is unknown.
Persistence	Specifies that the source or destination context is a persisted store. This could include databases, files, or other backing stores. Users should assume that persisted data is more long lived than the process that created the data and not serialize objects in such a way that deserialization requires accessing any data from the current process.
Remoting	Specifies that the source or destination context is remoting to an unknown location. Users cannot make any assumptions as to whether this is on the same machine.

```csharp
public class CustomCarType : ISerializable
{
    public string petName;
    public int maxSpeed;
    public CustomCarType(string s, int i) { petName = s; maxSpeed = i;}

    // Return state info to the formatter.
    public void GetObjectData(SerializationInfo si, StreamingContext ctx)
    {
        // What context is the stream?
        Console.WriteLine("[GetObjectData] Context State: {0}",
                        ctx.State.Format());

        si.AddValue("CapPetName", petName);
        si.AddValue("maxSpeed", maxSpeed);
    }
```

```
// Rehydrate a new object based on incoming SerializationInfo type.
private CustomCarType(SerializationInfo si, StreamingContext ctx)
{
    // What context is the stream?
    Console.WriteLine("[ctor] Context State: {0}", ctx.State.Format());

    petName = si.GetString("CapPetName");
    maxSpeed = si.GetInt32("maxSpeed");
}
}
```

Now that the type has been configured with the correct infrastructure, you will be happy to see that the serialization and deserialization process remains unaltered (see Figure 11-24 for output):

```
public static int Main(string[] args)
{
    CustomCarType myAuto = new CustomCarType("Siddhartha", 50);
    Stream myStream = File.Create("CarData.dat");

    // ISerializable interface obtained!
    BinaryFormatter myBinaryFormat = new BinaryFormatter();
    myBinaryFormat.Serialize(myStream, myAuto);
    myStream.Close();

    myStream = File.OpenRead("CarData.dat");

    // Special constructor called!
    CustomCarType carFromDisk =
        (CustomCarType)myBinaryFormat.Deserialize(myStream);

    Console.WriteLine(carFromDisk.petName + " is alive!");
    return 0;
}
```

Figure 11-24. Custom serialization

SOURCE CODE   *The CustomSerialization project is included under the Chapter 11 subdirectory.*

A Windows Forms Car Logger Application

To wrap up this examination of object serialization, the remainder of this chapter walks you through a minimal and complete Windows Forms application that uses many of the techniques examined thus far. The CarLogApp allows the end user to create an inventory of Car types (contained in an ArrayList), which are displayed in yet another Windows Form control, the DataGrid (Figure 11-25). To keep focused on the serialization logic, this grid is read only.

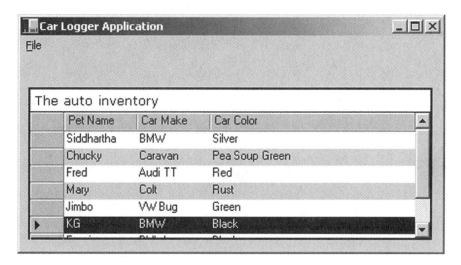

Figure 11-25. *The car logger application*

The topmost File menu provides a number of choices, which operate on the underlying ArrayList. Table 11-18 describes the possible selections.

I will not bother to detail the menu construction logic, as you have already seen these steps during the formal discussion of Windows Forms (see Chapter 8). The first task is to define the Car type itself. This is the class that represents not only a unique row in the DataGrid, but also an item in the serialized object graph.

Table 11-18. The CarLogApp Menu System

FILE SUBMENU ITEM	MEANING IN LIFE
Clear All Cars	Empties the ArrayList and refreshes the DataGrid.
Exit	Duh!
Make New Car	Displays a custom dialog box that allows the user to configure a new Car and refreshes the DataGrid.
Open Car File	Allows the user to open an existing *.car file and refreshes the DataGrid. This file is the result of a BinaryFormatter.
Save Car File	Saves all cars displayed in the DataGrid to a *.car file.

There are numerous iterations of the Car class throughout this book, so this version is brutally bland:

```
[Serializable]
public class Car
{
    // Make public for easy access.
    public string petName, make, color;

    public Car(string petName, string make, string color)
    {
        this.petName = petName;
        this.color = color;
        this.make = make;
    }
}
```

Next, you need to add a few members to the main Form class. The overall UI of the DataGrid type is configured using a small set of properties, all of which have been assigned using the Property window of the Visual Studio.NET IDE. The most important property for this example is the ReadOnly member (set to true), which prevents the user from editing the cells in the DataGrid. The remaining configurations establish the type's color scheme and physical dimensions (which you can explore at your leisure).

In addition, the main Form maintains a private ArrayList type, which holds each of the Car references. The Form's constructor adds a number of default cars to allow the user to view some initial items in the grid. Once these Car types have been added to the collection, you call a helper function named UpdateGrid(), as shown here:

```
public class mainForm : System.Windows.Forms.Form
{
    // List for object serialization.
    private ArrayList arTheCars = null;

    public mainForm()
    {
        InitializeComponent();
        CenterToScreen();

        // Add some cars.
        arTheCars = new ArrayList();
        arTheCars.Add(new Car("Siddhartha", "BMW", "Silver"));
        arTheCars.Add(new Car("Chucky", "Caravan", "Pea Soup Green"));
        arTheCars.Add(new Car("Fred", "Audi TT", "Red"));

        // Display data in grid.
        UpdateGrid();
    }
...
}
```

The UpdateGrid() method is responsible for creating a System.Data.DataTable type that contains a row for each Car in the ArrayList. Once the DataTable has been populated, you then bind it the DataGrid type. Chapter 13 examines the ADO.NET types (such as the DataTable) in much greater detail, so here the focus is on the basics for the time being. Here is the code:

```
private void UpdateGrid()
{
    if(arTheCars != null)
    {
        // Make a DataTable object named Inventory.
        DataTable inventory = new DataTable("Inventory");

        // Create DataColumn objects.
        DataColumn make = new DataColumn("Car Make");
        DataColumn petName = new DataColumn("Pet Name");
        DataColumn color = new DataColumn("Car Color");

        // Add columns to data table.
        inventory.Columns.Add(petName);
        inventory.Columns.Add(make);
        inventory.Columns.Add(color);
```

```
    // Iterate over the array list to make rows.
    foreach(Car c in arTheCars)
    {
        DataRow newRow;
        newRow = inventory.NewRow();
        newRow["Pet Name"] = c.petName;
        newRow["Car Make"] = c.make;
        newRow["Car Color"] = c.color;
        inventory.Rows.Add(newRow);
    }

    // Now bind this data table to the grid.
    carDataGrid.DataSource = inventory;
}
}
```

Begin by creating a new DataTable type named Inventory. In the world of ADO.NET, a DataTable is an in-memory representation of a single table of information. While you might assume that a DataTable would be created as a result of some SQL query, you can also use this type as a stand-alone entity.

Once you have a new DataTable, you need to establish the set of columns that should be listed in the table. The System.Data.DataColumn type represents a single column. Given that this iteration of the Car type has three public fields (make, color, and pet name), create three DataColumns and insert them in the table using the DataTable.Columns property.

Next, you need to add each row to the table. Recall that the main Form maintains an ArrayList that contains some number of Car types. Given that ArrayList implements the IEnumerable interface, you can fetch each Car from the collection, read each public field, and compose and insert a new DataRow in the table. Finally, the new DataTable is bound to the GUI DataGrid widget using the DataSource property.

Now then! If you run the application at this point, you will find that the grid is indeed populated with the default automobiles. This is a good start, but you can do better.

Implementing the Add New Car Logic

The CarLogApp project defines another Form-derived type (AddCarDlg), which functions as a modal dialog box (Figure 11-26). Because you examined the construction of custom dialog boxes in Chapter 10, I'll hold off on the details. However, from a GUI point of view, this type is composed of a TextBox (to hold the pet name) and two ListBox types (to allow the user to select the color and make).

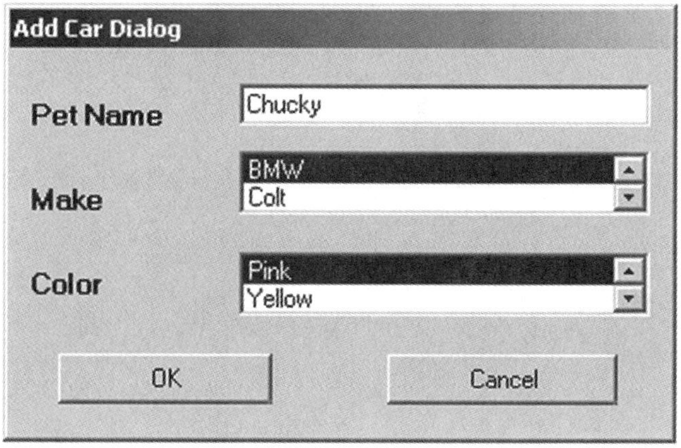

Figure 11-26. The Add a Car dialog box

As far as the code behind the Form, the OK button has been assigned the DialogResult property DialogResult.OK. As you recall from Chapter 10, this value marks a Button type to function as a standard OK button. Also, this Form maintains a public Car type (for easy access), which is configured when the user clicks the OK button. The remainder of the code is nothing more than some GUI control prep work. The relevant logic is as follows:

```
public class AddCarDlg : System.Windows.Forms.Form
{
    // Make public for easy access.
    public Car theCar = null;

    . . .

    protected void btnOK_Click (object sender, System.EventArgs e)
    {
        // Configure a new Car when user clicks OK button.
        theCar = new Car(txtName.Text, listMake.Text, listColor.Text);
    }
}
```

The main Form displays this dialog box when the user selects the Make New Car menu item. Here is the code behind that object's Clicked event:

```
protected void menuItemNewCar_Click (object sender, System.EventArgs e)
{
    // Show the dialog and check for OK click.
    AddCarDlg d = new AddCarDlg();
    if(d.ShowDialog() == DialogResult.OK)
    {
        // Add new car to array list.
        arTheCars.Add(d.theCar);
        UpdateGrid();
    }
}
```

No surprises here. You just show the Form as a modal dialog box, and if the OK button has been clicked, you read the public Car member variable, add it to the ArrayList, and refresh your grid.

The Serialization Logic

The core logic behind the Save Car File and Open Car File Click event handlers should pose no problems at this point. When the user chooses to save the current inventory, you create a new file and use a BinaryFormatter to serialize the object graph. However, just to keep things interesting, the user can establish the name and location of this file using a System.Windows.Forms.SaveFileDialog type. This type is yet another standard dialog box and is illustrated in Figure 11-27.

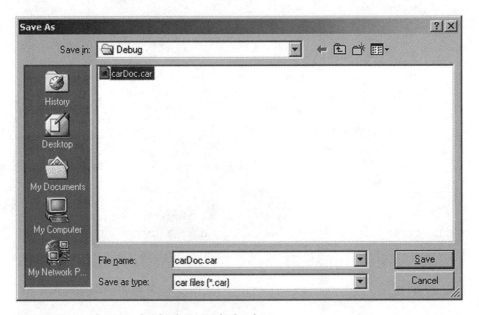

Figure 11-27. The Standard File Save dialog box

Notice that the SaveFileDialog is listing a custom file extension (*.car). While I leave the task of investigating the complete functionality of the SaveFileDialog in your capable hands, it is worth pointing out that this has been assigned using the Filter property. This property takes an OR-delimited string that represents the text to be used in the drop-down "File name" and "Save as type" combo boxes. Here is the full implementation:

```
protected void menuItemSave_Click (object sender, System.EventArgs e)
{
    // Configure look and feel of save dialog box.
    SaveFileDialog mySaveFileDialog = new SaveFileDialog();
    mySaveFileDialog.InitialDirectory = ".";
    mySaveFileDialog.Filter = "car files (*.car)|*.car|All files (*.*)|*.*"  ;
    mySaveFileDialog.FilterIndex = 1 ;
    mySaveFileDialog.RestoreDirectory = true ;
    mySaveFileDialog.FileName = "carDoc";

    // Do you have a file?
    if(mySaveFileDialog.ShowDialog() = = DialogResult.OK)
    {
        Stream myStream = null;
        if((myStream = mySaveFileDialog.OpenFile()) != null)
        {
            // Save the cars!
            BinaryFormatter myBinaryFormat = new BinaryFormatter();
            myBinaryFormat.Serialize(myStream, arTheCars);
            myStream.Close();
        }
    }
}
```

Also note that the OpenFile() member of the SaveFileDialog type returns a Stream that represents the specified file selected by the end user. As seen earlier in this chapter, this is the very thing needed by the BinaryFormatter type.

The logic behind the Open Car File Click event handler looks very similar. This time you create an instance of the System.Windows.Forms OpenFileDialog type, configure accordingly, and obtain a Stream reference based on the selected file. Next you dump the contents of the ArrayList and read in the new object graph using the BinaryFormatter.Deserialize() method, as shown here:

```
protected void menuItemOpen_Click (object sender, System.EventArgs e)
{
    // Configure look and feel of open dialog box.
    OpenFileDialog myOpenFileDialog = new OpenFileDialog();
    myOpenFileDialog.InitialDirectory = ".";
    myOpenFileDialog.Filter = "car files (*.car)|*.car|All files (*.*)|*.*"  ;
    myOpenFileDialog.FilterIndex = 1 ;
    myOpenFileDialog.RestoreDirectory = true ;

    // Do you have a file?
    if(myOpenFileDialog.ShowDialog() = = DialogResult.OK)
    {
        // Clear current array list.
        arTheCars.Clear();

        Stream myStream = null;
        if((myStream = myOpenFileDialog.OpenFile()) != null)
        {
            // Get the cars!
            BinaryFormatter myBinaryFormat = new BinaryFormatter();
            arTheCars = (ArrayList)myBinaryFormat.Deserialize(myStream);
            myStream.Close();
            UpdateGrid();
        }
    }
}
```

Great! At this point, the application can save and load the entire set of Car types held in the ArrayList using a BinaryFormatter. The final menu items are self-explanatory, as shown here:

```
protected void menuItemClear_Click (object sender, System.EventArgs e)
{
    arTheCars.Clear();
    UpdateGrid();
}

protected void menuItemExit_Click (object sender, System.EventArgs e)
{
    Application.Exit();
}
```

SOURCE CODE   *The CarLogApp project is included under the Chapter 11 subdi-rectory.*

Summary

This chapter began by examining the use of the Directory(Info) and File(Info) types. As you have seen, these classes allow you to manipulate a physical file or directory on your hard drive.

The chapter next examined a number of types derived from the abstract Stream class, including FileStream, MemoryStream, and BufferedStream. Given that each of these types has (more or less) the same public interface, you can easily swap them in and out of your code to alter the ultimate location of your byte array. When you are interested in persisting textual data, the StreamReader and StreamWriter types usually fit the bill.

Finally, this chapter concluded by examining how the .NET framework provides the necessary infrastructure needed to persist your objects in a binary or SOAP message format. Although the [Serializable] and [NonSerialized] attributes are typically all you need to concern yourself with, you also saw how to configure a class to support custom serialization (e.g., the ISerializable interface).

CHAPTER 12

Interacting with Unmanaged Code

By now, you have gained a solid foundation of the C# language and the core services provided by the .NET platform. I suspect that when you contrast the object model provided by .NET to previous frameworks and architectures (classic COM, MFC, and so forth), you are no doubt on your way to becoming a .NET head. Sadly, few of us are in a position to completely abandon the ways of COM, ATL, Visual Basic 6.0, and classic Windows DNA. The truth is that hundreds of thousands of person hours have been spent building systems that make substantial use of these technologies. If .NET is to succeed as a platform, it must have a way to interact gracefully with the legacy systems of today.

This chapter begins with an examination of how .NET types can access the raw Win32 API using a service termed *PInvoke* (Platform Invoke). Next it covers the more exciting topic of .NET to COM interoperability and the related Runtime Callable Wrapper (RCW). The later part of this chapter examines the opposite situation: a COM type communicating with a .NET type using a COM Callable Wrapper (CCW). Finally, I examine the process of building managed types that can interact with the services provided by the COM+ runtime layer (e.g., object pooling, object constructor strings, and so on).

Understanding Interoperability Issues

When you build assemblies using a .NET-aware compiler, you are creating "managed code" that can be hosted by the Common Language Runtime (CLR). Managed code offers a number of benefits such as automatic memory management, a unified type system (CTS), self-describing assemblies, and so forth. As you have seen, .NET assemblies have a particular internal composition. In addition to IL instructions and type metadata, assemblies contain a manifest that fully describes the internal types and documents any required external assemblies.

On the other side of the spectrum are classic COM servers (which are of course "unmanaged code"). These binaries bear no relationship to .NET assemblies beyond a shared file extension. First, COM servers contain platform-specific machine code, not platform-agnostic IL instructions. COM servers work with a unique set of data types (BSTRs, VARIANTs, and so forth) that are mapped very differently between COM-aware languages. In addition to the necessary COM-goo required by all COM binaries (e.g., class factories, registry entries, and IDL code) is the fact that COM types demand to be reference counted. Mismanaged reference counting can lead to memory leaks, as coclasses are not allocated on a managed heap.

Given that .NET types and COM types have so little in common, you may wonder how these two architectures can coexist. Unless you are lucky enough to work for a company dedicated to "100% Pure .NET" development, you will most likely need to build .NET solutions that use legacy COM types. Furthermore, you will probably never need to fire up Visual Basic 6.0 or the ATL AppWizard again during your career. The chances are good that you will still need to build a COM server or two that need to communicate with a shiny new .NET assembly.

The bottom line is that for some time to come, COM and .NET must learn how to get along. This chapter examines the issues that arise when managed and unmanaged types attempt to coexist. In general, the .NET framework supports the following types of interoperability:

- .NET types calling raw C DLLs (e.g., the Win32 API or custom DLLs)

- .NET types calling COM types

- COM types calling .NET types

- .NET types using COM+ services

As you will see throughout this chapter, the .NET SDK supplies a number of tools that help bridge the gap between these unique architectures. Also, the .NET base class libraries define a number of types dedicated solely to the issue of interoperability.

The `System.Runtime.InteropServices` Namespace

When you use .NET interoperability services, you directly or indirectly interact with the types defined in the System.Runtime.InteropServices namespace. Table 12-1 offers a high-level overview of some (but not all) core types.

As you may have noticed, all of these types are attributes used to help marshal data between .NET types and COM types. Of course, the System.Runtime.InteropServices namespace also defines a number of interfaces, enumerations, and structures. (Examples are given where appropriate.) The journey begins by examining the use of PInvoke.

Table 12-1. Select Members of the System.Runtime.InteropServices Namespace

SYSTEM.RUNTIME.INTEROPSERVICES TYPE	MEANING IN LIFE
ClassInterfaceAttribute	Used to control how a managed type exposes its public members to COM clients.
ComRegisterFunctionAttribute ComUnregisterFunctionAttribute	May be associated to custom methods to indicate that they should be called when the assembly is registered (or unregistered) for use by COM.
ComSourceInterfacesAttribute	Identifies the list of interfaces that are sources of events for the class (e.g., outbound interfaces).
DispIdAttribute	Custom attribute that specifies the COM DISPID of a method, field, or property.
DllImportAttribute	Used by the platform invoke services (PInvoke) to call unmanaged code.
GuidAttribute	Used to define a specific GUID for a class, interface, or type library.
IDispatchImplAttribute	Indicates which IDispatch implementation the CLR should use when exposing dual interfaces and dispinterfaces.
InterfaceTypeAttribute	Controls how a managed interface is exposed to COM clients (IDispatch derived or IUnknown derived).
OutAttribute InAttribute	Used on a parameter or field to indicate that data should be marshaled out from callee back to caller or from caller to callee.
ProgIdAttribute	Custom attribute that allows the user to specify the prog ID of a .NET type.

Interacting with C DLLs

Platform Invocation Services (PInvoke) provides a way for managed code to call unmanaged functions implemented in a traditional C (non-COM) DLL. Using PInvoke, the .NET developer is shielded from the task of locating and invoking the correct function export. Furthermore, PInvoke takes care of marshaling managed data (e.g., integers, strings, arrays, and structures) to and from their unmanaged counterparts.

The most typical use of PInvoke is to allow .NET components to interact with the Win32 API in the raw. As you know, the .NET base class library exists to hide the low-level API from view. Thus, while you might not ever need to drop down to the raw Win32, PInvoke provides the ability to do so. PInvoke can also be used to access function exports defined in custom DLLs. Therefore, if you have a body of legacy C code wrapped up in a dynamic link library, you will be happy to know that your .NET components can still use them.

To illustrate the use of PInvoke, you can build a C# class that makes a call to the Win32 MessageBox() function. First, the source code, shown here:

```
namespace PInvokeExample
{
using System;

    // Must reference to gain access to the PInvoke types.
    using System.Runtime.InteropServices;

    public class PInvokeClient
    {
        // The Win32 MessageBox() function lives in user32.dll.
        [DllImport("user32")]
        public static extern int MessageBox(int hWnd,
                                        String  pText,
                                        String  pCaption,
                                        int uType);

        public static int Main(string[] args)
        {
            // Send in some managed data.
            String pText = "Hello World!";
            String pCaption = "PInvoke Test";
            MessageBox(0, pText, pCaption, 0);

            return 0;
        }
    }
}
```

The process of calling a C-style DLL begins by declaring the function to call using the static and extern C# keywords. (This step is not optional.) Notice that when you declare the C function prototype, you must list the return type function name and arguments in terms of managed data types. Thus, you do not send in char* or wchar_t* arrays, but the managed System.String type.

Once you have prototyped the method you intend to call, your next step is to adorn this member with the DllImport attribute. At absolute minimum, you need to specify the name of the raw DLL that contains the function you are attempting to call, as shown here:

```
[DllImport("user32")]
public static extern int MessageBox(. . .);
```

The DllImportAttribute type defines a set of public fields, which can be specified to further configure the process of binding to the function export. Table 12-2 describes these fields.

Table 12-2. Fields of the DllImportAttribute Type

DLLIMPORTATTRIBUTE FIELD	MEANING IN LIFE
CallingConvention	Used to establish the calling convention used in passing method arguments.
CharSet	Indicates how string arguments to the method should be marshaled.
EntryPoint	Indicates the name or ordinal of the function to be called.
ExactSpelling	As you will see, PInvoke attempts to match the name of the function you specify with the real name as prototyped. If this field is set to true, you are indicating that the name of the entry point in the unmanaged .dll must exactly match the name you are passing in.
PreserveSig	When set to true (the default setting), unmanaged method signatures *not* transformed into a managed signature that returns an HRESULT and has an additional [out, retval] argument for the return value.
SetLastError	Set to true to indicate that the caller can call the Win32 GetLastError() function to determine if an error occurred while executing the method; the default is false.

To set these values for your current DllImportAttribute object instance, simply specify each as a name/value pair to the class constructor. If you check out the definition of the DllImportAttribute constructor, you can see that it takes a single parameter of type System.String, as shown here:

```
class DllImportAttribute
{
    // Constructor takes a string that holds all field values.
    public DllImportAttribute( string val );
. . .
}
```

It should be clear that it does not matter in which order you specify these values. The DllImport class simply parses the string internally and uses the values to set its internal state data.

Specifying the ExactSpelling Field

The first field of interest is ExactSpelling, which is used to control if the name of the managed function is identical to that of the name of the unmanaged function. For example, as you may know, there is no function named MessageBox in the Win32 API. Rather there are an ANSI version (MessageBoxA) and a Unicode version (MessageBoxW). Given that you specified a method named MessageBox, you can correctly assume that the default value of ExactSpelling is false. However, if you set this value to true, you have the following:

```
[DllImport("user32", ExactSpelling = true)]
public static extern int MessageBox(...);     // Uh-oh!
```

You now receive an EntryPointNotFoundException exception, as there is no function named MessageBox in user32.dll! As you can see, the ExactSpelling field basically allows you to "be lazy" and ignore the details of W or A suffixes. Clearly, however, PInvoke does need to ultimately resolve the exact name of the function you are calling. When you leave ExactSpelling as its default value (false), the letter A is appended to the method name under ANSI environments or the letter W under Unicode environments.

Specifying the Character Set

To explicitly specify the character set used to marshal data between managed code and the raw DLL export, you can set the value of the CharSet field using a value from the related CharSet enumeration (Table 12-3).

Table 12-3. CharSet Values

CHARSET MEMBER NAME	MEANING IN LIFE
Ansi	Specifies that strings should be marshaled as ANSI 1-byte chars.
Auto	Informs PInvoke to marshal string correctly as required by the target platform (Unicode on WinNT/Win2000 and ANSI on Win 9x).
None	Signifies that you didn't specify how to marshal strings (default) and wish the runtime to figure things out automatically.
Unicode	Specifies that strings should be marshaled as Unicode 2-byte chars.

By way of example, to enforce that all strings be marshaled as Unicode (and thus risk not working correctly on Win95, Win98, or WinME platforms), you would write the following:

```
// Demand the exact name, and specify the Unicode character set.
[DllImport("user32", ExactSpelling = true, CharSet=CharSet.Unicode)]
public static extern int MessageBoxW(...);
```

Generally speaking, it is safer to set the CharSet value to CharSet.Auto (or simply accept the default). In this way, textual parameters are marshaled correctly regardless of the target platform, leaving your code base far more portable.

Specifying Calling Conventions and Entry Points

The final fields of interest are CallingConvention and EntryPoint. As you know, Win32 API functions can be adorned with a number of typedefs that specify how parameters should be passed to the function (C declaration, fast call, standard call, and so forth). You can set CallingConvention field using any value from the CallingConvention enumeration. This enumeration specifies values such as Cdecl, Winapi, StdCall, and so forth. The default of this field is StdCall, and thus you can typically ignore explicitly setting this field (since this is the most common Win32 calling convention).

Last but not least is the EntryPoint field. By default, this value is the same as the name of the function you are prototyping. Therefore, in the following declaration, EntryPoint is implicitly set to MessageBoxW:

```
// EntryPoint automatically set to'MessageBoxW'.
[DllImport("user32", ExactSpelling = true, CharSet=CharSet.Unicode)]
public static extern int MessageBoxW(...);
```

To establish an alias for the exported function, you can specify the real name using the EntryPoint field, effectively renaming the function for use in your managed code. Obviously, this is a helpful way to avoid possible name clashes. To illustrate, here is the final iteration of the PInvoke example, which maps MessageBoxW() function to a friendly alias (DisplayMessage):

```
public class PInvokeClient
{
    // Map the MessageBoxW function to DisplayMessage.'
    [DllImport("user32", ExactSpelling = true,
            CharSet=CharSet.Unicode, EntryPoint = "MessageBoxW")]
    public static extern int DisplayMessage(int hWnd, String  pText,
                                        String  pCaption, int uType);
```

```
public static int Main(string[] args)
{
    String pText = "Hello World!";
    String pCaption = "PInvoke Test";

    // This really calls MessageBoxW()....
    DisplayMessage(0, pText, pCaption, 0);
    return 0;
}
}
```

SOURCE CODE   *The PInvokeExample application is included under the Chapter 12 subdirectory.*

Understanding .NET to COM Interoperability

Next is an examination of how managed code can use unmanaged COM types. As you begin to build .NET solutions, your fancy new assemblies will probably like to use the logic in existing COM servers. To do so, there must be some intervening layer that correctly exposes COM types as .NET equivalents. In the best of all possible worlds, the mapping process would be extremely transparent, thus allowing the .NET type to treat the COM type as one of its own.

The black box to which I am referring to is termed the RCW (Runtime Callable Wrapper). The RCW can be understood as a proxy to the real COM class (coclass). Every coclass accessed by a .NET client requires a corresponding RCW. Thus, if you have a single .NET application that uses three COM coclasses, you end up with three distinct RCWs that map .NET calls into COM requests. Figure 12-1 illustrates the big picture.

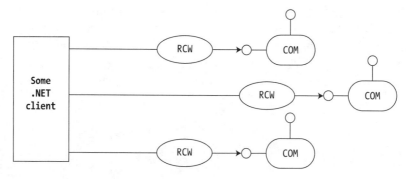

Figure 12-1. RCW functions as proxies to the coclass

Also be aware that there is a single RCW per COM object, regardless how many discrete interfaces the .NET client has obtained from a given COM class. Using this technique, the RCW can maintain the correct COM identity (and reference count) of the COM type.

The good news is that the RCW is generated automatically using a tool named tlbimp.exe (type library importer). The other bit of good news is that legacy COM classes do not require any modifications to be consumed by a .NET-aware language. The intervening RCW takes care of the internal work. I will explain how this is achieved by formalizing the responsibilities of the RCW.

Exposing COM Types as .NET Equivalents

The RCW is in charge of exposing COM data types as their managed equivalents. As a simple example, assume you have a COM interface method defined in IDL, as shown here:

```
// COM IDL method definition.
HRESULT DisplayThisString([in] BSTR msg);
```

The RCW exposes this method to a .NET client as the following:

```
// C# mapping of COM IDL method.
void DisplayThisString(String msg);
```

Most COM data types (including all of the [oleautomation] compatible data types) have a corresponding .NET equivalent. To help you gain your bearings, Table 12-4 documents the mapping between COM (IDL) data types and .NET data types (including the corresponding C# alias).

Also be aware that if you have an IDL pointer definition (e.g., int* rather than int), it will map to the same base class and C# alias (i.e., System.Int32 / int). Later in this chapter, when you build your ATL COM server, you will have a chance to see conversion of more interesting COM types such as SAFEARRAYs and COM enums.

Managing a Coclass's Reference Count

Another important duty of the RCW is to manage the reference count of the underlying coclass. The COM reference-counting scheme is a joint venture between coclass and client and revolves around the proper use of AddRef() and Release() calls. COM classes self-destruct when they detect that they have no outstanding references.

Table 12-4. Mapping Intrinsic COM Types to .NET Types

COM (IDL) DATA TYPE	.NET DATA TYPE	C# ALIAS
char, boolean, small	System.SByte	sbyte
wchar_t, short	System.Int16	short
long, int	System.Int32	int
hyper	System.Int64	long
unsigned char, byte	System.Byte	byte
unsigned short	System.UInt16	ushort
unsigned long, unsigned int	System.UInt32	uint
unsigned hyper	System.UInt64	ulong
single	System.Single	float
double	System.Double	double
VARIANT_BOOL	n/a	bool
HRESULT	System.Int32	int
BSTR	System.String	string
LPSTR or char *	System.String	string
LPWSTR or		
wchar_t *	System.String	string
VARIANT	System.Object	object
DECIMAL	System.Decimal	n/a
DATE	System.DateTime	n/a
GUID	System.Guid	n/a
CURRENCY	System.Decimal	n/a
IUnknown *	System.Object	object
IDispatch *	System.Object	object

However, .NET types do not use the COM reference-counting scheme, and therefore a .NET client should not be forced to call Release() on the COM types it uses. To keep each participant happy, the RCW caches all interface references internally and triggers the final release when the type is no longer used by the .NET client. The bottom line is that .NET clients never explicitly call AddRef(), Release() or QueryInterface().

Hiding Low-Level COM Interfaces

The final role of the RCW is to consume a number of select COM interfaces. Because the RCW tries to do everything it can to fool the .NET client into thinking it is using a .NET type, the RCW must hide various low-level COM interfaces from view. In many respects, the RCW takes the same approach as Visual Basic 6.0.

For example, when you build a COM class that supports IConnectionPointContainer (and maintains a subobject or two supporting

IConnectionPoint), the coclass in question is able to fire events back to the COM client. With C++ COM clients you would have to take a number of steps to establish a connection with the object (e.g., build a sink that implements the [source] interface, obtain an IConnectionPoint reference, call Advise(), and so forth).

Visual Basic 6.0 hides this entire process from view using the WithEvents keyword. In the same vein, the RCW also hides such COM-goo from the .NET client. Because the RCW hides these low-level interfaces, the external .NET client only sees (and interacts with) the set of custom interfaces implemented by the coclass. Table 12-5 outlines some of these hidden COM interfaces.

Table 12-5. Hidden COM Interfaces

HIDDEN COM INTERFACE	MEANING IN LIFE
IClassFactory	Provides a language- and location-neutral way to activate a COM class.
IConnectionPointContainer IConnectionPoint	Enable a coclass to send events back to an interested client.
IDispatch IDispatchEx IProvideClassInfo	Used to facilitate late binding to a coclass.
IEnumVariant	COM classes can expose collections of internal types. This interface facilitates this possibility.
IErrorInfo ISupportErrorInfo ICreateErrorInfo	Enable COM clients and coclasses to send and respond to error objects.
IUnknown	Manages the reference count and allows clients to obtain a discrete interface from the coclass

At this point you have a solid understanding of the role of the Runtime Callable Wrapper. I will now begin examining the programmatic details of .NET to COM communications with a very simple example using Visual Basic 6.0 (to build the COM server) and C# (to build the .NET client). Later in this chapter I will develop a more exotic (and complex) COM server using ATL 3.0.

Building a Painfully Simple Visual Basic COM Server

To wet your feet with the topic of .NET to COM interoperability using VB 6.0 let's build an appropriately named COM server (PainfullySimpleVBCOMServer). Begin by opening up Visual Basic 6.0 and selecting an ActiveX DLL project workspace (Figure 12-2) from the New Project dialog box. (If you are coming from an

ATL background, understand that this workspace type is just another name for an in-process COM server.)

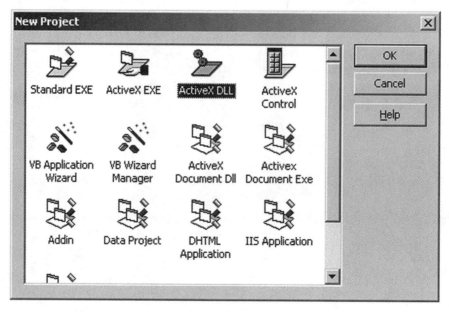

Figure 12-2. Building a VB COM server

Using the Properties Window, you can take the plunge and rename the project to PainfullySimpleVBCOMServer (or perhaps something shorter) and rename your initial class to CoCalc. This information will be used to build the coclass's ProgID using the standard *ServerName.ObjectName* notation.

Next, open the code window for the VB 6.0 CoCalc class and add the following trivial function definition:

```
' Recall! This is really a method of the
' default interface: _CoCalc!
'
Public Function Add(ByVal x As Integer, ByVal y As Integer) As Integer
    Add = x + y
End Function
```

Finally, save your workspace and compile the COM server using the File|Make. . . menu option (which automatically registers the server into the system registry). Figure 12-3 shows the resulting ProgID.

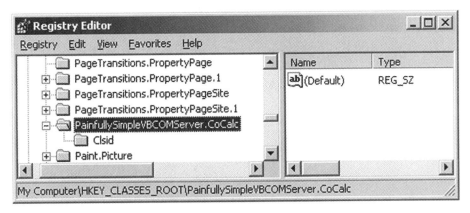

Figure 12-3. The COM type's ProgID

The end result is a new COM server containing a single coclass (CoCalc) that implements a single [default] interface named _CoCalc. (In the world of VB COM, you always receive an initial interface for free.)

Before you shut down this VB project, be sure to select the Project | Properties menu option and set Binary Compatibility for this COM server (Figure 12-4). This informs VB to stop generating new GUIDs with each compile.

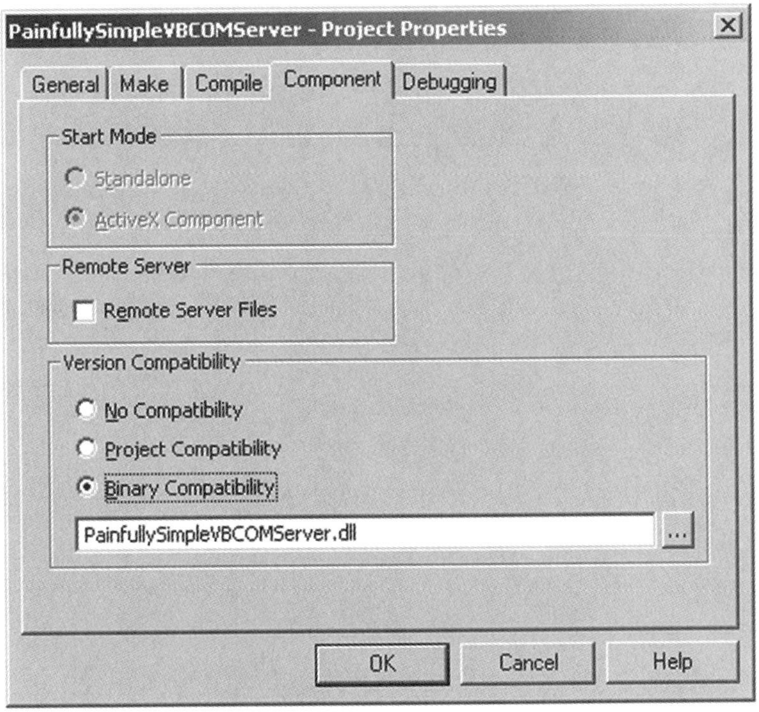

Figure 12-4. Stopping VB GUID generation

SOURCE CODE   *The PainfullySimpleVBCOMServer project is included under the Chapter 12 subdirectory.*

Observing the Generated IDL for Your VB COM Server

Open the OLE/COM Object Viewer and hunt down the ProgID of your VB COM server (Figure 12-5). You should see the name of your default custom interface (CoCalc) as well as a number of other COM interfaces implemented by VB on your behalf.

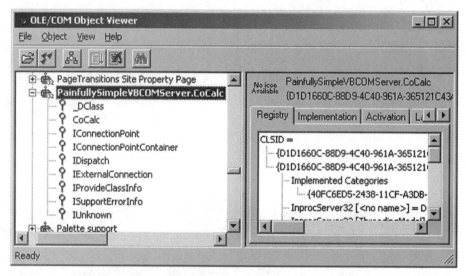

Figure 12-5. Hunting down the coclass using the OLE/COM object viewer

To view the underlying IDL, right-click the coclass and select the View Type Information menu option. If you examine the IDL file's library statement, you can see the relevant code that configures the [default] interface, as shown here:

```
[ odl, uuid(DDA5B80E-8DA4-45DF-B8FF-B6BFFFBCD9E6),
version(1.0), hidden, dual, nonextensible, oleautomation ]
interface _CoCalc : IDispatch
{
        [id(0x60030000)]
        HRESULT Add([in] short x, [in] short y, [out, retval] short* );
};
```

```
[uuid(D1D1660C-88D9-4C40-961A-365121C43AF1), version(1.0)]
coclass CoCalc
{
        [default] interface _CoCalc;
};
```

As you can see, Visual Basic always configures your custom interfaces as [dual] interfaces. This enables your coclass to be manipulated by various scripting languages via the IDispatch interface. With this, the VB COM server is complete! Now that you have a simple COM server, it's time to test it with an equally simple VB COM client.

Building a Painfully Simple COM Client

Open VB once again, but this time select a Standard EXE project workspace. Next, add a reference to the PainfullySimpleVBCOMServer using the Project|References menu selection and find the name of your classic COM server (Figure 12-6).

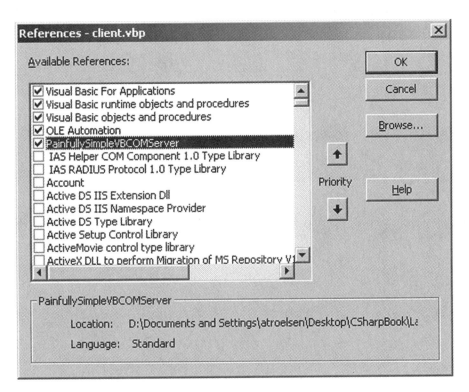

Figure 12-6. Setting a reference to the COM server

As for the GUI front end, keep things simple. Place two TextBox objects, a Button and some descriptive labels, onto the main Form. Figure 12-7 shows one possible design.

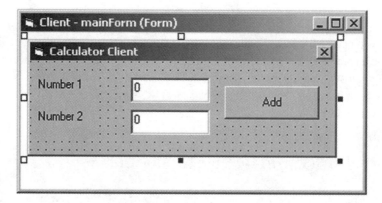

Figure 12-7. The painfully simple GUI

The only code you need to write is in response to the Button's Click event. Create an instance of your coclass and send in the values in each text box to the Add() method. For simplicity, place the result in a VB message box, as shown here:

```
Private Sub btnAdd_Click()
    Dim c As New CoCalc
    MsgBox c.Add(txtNumb1, txtNumb2)
End Sub
```

At this point you have a COM client and COM server chatting in harmony. Now build a C# client that uses this same classic COM binary.

SOURCE CODE *The PainfullySimpleVBCOMClient project is included under the Chapter 12 subdirectory.*

Importing the Type Library

The first step you must take before you can call classic COM servers from managed code is build a proxy class that contains the necessary information used to create the RCW. The tool responsible for building the proxy is named tlbimp.exe (type library importer).

To run this utility at the command line, begin by navigating to the location of the COM binary from a Command Prompt window. Next, specify the name of the

COM server and the name of the resulting RCW assembly (using the /out: flag). Here is the command:

```
tlbimp PainfullySimpleVBCOMServer.dll /out:SimpleAssembly.dll
```

At this point, you can open the generated assembly using ILDasm.exe (Figure 12-8). The details of what the underlying IL actually boils down to are discussed later in this chapter. For the time being, just notice that the [default] _CoCalc interface as well as the CoCalc coclass have each been mapped as .NET equivalents:

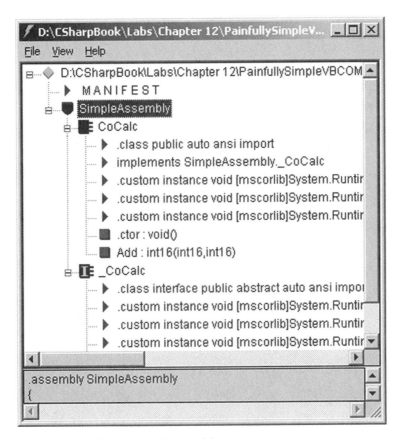

Figure 12-8. Types in the generated assembly

Referencing the Assembly

When a .NET binary makes calls to the generated proxy, the request is forwarded to the associated COM class. To illustrate how simple the process can be on the surface, build a C# COM client (CSharpCalcClient). Begin by creating a new C#

Console Application. Once you have your new project workspace, set a reference to the generated assembly using the Add Reference dialog box. If you examine your Solution Explorer window, you will see that the corresponding reference is now listed as part of your C# project (Figure 12-9).

Figure 12-9. Managed code must reference the generated assembly.

Early Binding to the CoCalc COM Class

Because you have added a direct reference to the generated assembly, you can use early binding. In the following code, notice that as far as the C# client is concerned, CoCalc is nothing more than a .NET type contained in a valid assembly. In reality, the RCW is intercepting calls and forwarding them to the coclass in question:

```
namespace CSharpCalcClient
{
    using System;

    // You need to reference the namespace containing the proxy.
    using SimpleAssembly;

    public class CalcClient
    {
        public static int Main(string[] args)
```

```
        {
            // Make the calc!
            CoCalc c = new CoCalc();

            // Add some numbers!
            Console.WriteLine("30 + 99 is: " + c.Add(30, 99));

            return 0;
        }
    }
}
```

As you can see, the conversion process exposes all members of a coclass's [default] interface directly from an object instance. Should you need to explicitly reference the underlying _CoCalc interface, you could write the following (logically equivalent) code:

```
public class CalcClient
{
    public static int Main(string[] args)
    {
        // Make the calc!
        CoCalc c = new CoCalc();

        // Explicitly obtain the [default] interface.
        _CoCalc icalc = c;
        Console.WriteLine(icalc.Add(9, 80));

        return 0;
    }
}
```

SOURCE CODE   *The CSharpCalcClient project is included under the Chapter 12*
subdirectory.

Early Binding Using Visual Studio.NET

It is worth noting that the VS.NET IDE allows you to select a classic COM server using the COM tab of the Add Reference dialog box (Figure 12-10).

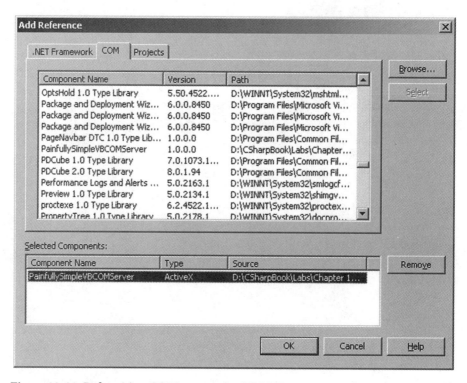

Figure 12-10. Referencing COM types using VS.NET

This automatically invokes the tlbimp.exe utility on your behalf and saves the new assembly under your Debug (or Release) folder. I assume that you will use the Add Reference dialog box during the remainder of this chapter.

Late Binding to the CoCalc Coclass

As you recall from Chapter 7, the System.Reflection namespace provides a way for you to programmatically inspect the types contained in a given assembly at runtime. In COM, the same sort of functionality is supported through the use of a set of standard interfaces (e.g., ITypeLib, ITypeInfo, and so on). When a client binds to a member at runtime (rather than compile time), the client is said to exercise late binding.

By and large, you should always prefer the early binding technique just examined. There are times, however, when you must use late binding to a coclass. For example, some legacy COM servers may have been constructed in such a way that they provide no type information whatsoever. If this is the case, it should be clear that you cannot run the tlbimp.exe utility in the first place! For these rare occurrences, you can access classic COM types using .NET reflection services.

The process of late binding begins with a client obtaining the IDispatch interface from a given coclass. This standard COM interface defines a total of four methods, only two of which need to concern you at the moment. First, you have GetIDsOfNames(). This method allows a late bound client to obtain the numerical value (called the DISPID) used to identify the method it is attempting to invoke.

In COM IDL, a member's DISPID is assigned using the [id] attribute. If you examine the IDL code generated by Visual Basic (using the OLE/COM Object Viewer), you will see that the DISPID of the Add() method has been assigned a DISPID such as the following:

```
[id(0x60030000)] HRESULT Add( [in] short x, [in] short y, [out, retval] short* );
```

This is the value that GetIDsOfNames() returns to the late bound client. Once the client obtains this value, it makes a call to the next method of interest, Invoke(). This method of IDispatch takes a number of arguments, one of which is the DISPID obtained using GetIDsOfNames().

In addition, the Invoke() method takes an array of COM VARIANT types that represent the parameters passed to the function. In the case of the Add() method, this array contains two shorts (of some value). The final argument of Invoke() is another VARIANT that holds the return value of the method invocation (again, a short).

Although a .NET client using late binding does not directly use the IDispatch interface, the same general functionality comes through using the System.Reflection namespace. To illustrate, here is another C# client that uses late binding to trigger the Add() logic. Notice that this application does *not* make reference to the assembly in any way and therefore does not require the use of the tlbimp.exe utility.

```
using System;
using System.Reflection;

public class LateBinder
{
    public static int Main(string[] args)
    {
        // First get IDispatch reference from coclass.
        Type calcObj =
        Type.GetTypeFromProgID("PainfullySimpleVBCOMServer.CoCalc");

        object calcDisp = Activator.CreateInstance(calcObj);

        // Make the array of args.
        object[] addArgs = { 100, 34 };
```

```
        // Invoke the Add() method and obtain summation.
        object sum = null;
        sum = calcObj.InvokeMember("Add", BindingFlags.InvokeMethod,
                                    null, calcDisp, addArgs);

        // Display result.
        Console.WriteLine("Late bound adding:\n100 + 24 is: {0}", sum);
        return 0;
    }
}
```

SOURCE CODE   *The CSharpLateBoundCalcClient application is included under the Chapter 12 subdirectory.*

Examining the Generated Assembly

Now that you understand how to activate a COM type from managed code, take a look at some specific details. To begin, load the assembly into ILDasm.exe and open the manifest. Like in any assembly, you will first notice an external reference to mscorlib.dll (the core .NET class library), followed by the necessary version information.

The real gems of information appear as a number of .NET attributes. When you examine the manifest, you will find references to the GuidAttribute and ImportedFromTypeLibAttribute types. If you look at the value of ImportedFromTypeLibAttribute, you will see the hard-coded path to the classic COM server (Figure 12-11).

```
  MANIFEST                                          _ □ ✕
B 34 30 37     // ..$4d4702a6-3407
2 31 61 39     // -4aa0-a1b0-621a9
               // df477ee..
B 68 61 72 70 42 6F 6F 6B     // ..WD:\CSharpBook
B 61 70 74 65 72 20 31 32     // \Labs\Chapter 12
C 6C 79 53 69 6D 70 6C 65     // \PainfullySimple
2 76 65 72 5C 50 61 69 6E     // VBCOMServer\Pain
D 70 6C 65 56 42 43 4F 4D     // fullySimpleVBCOM
4 6C 6C 00 00 )               // Server.dll..
```

Figure 12-11. The ImportedFromTypeLib attribute marks the path to the COM server.

This illustrates a very important point. If the COM server is relocated (or re-named) on the target machine, you need to regenerate the assembly. Figure 12-12 illustrates what you see if you examine the value assigned to GuidAttribute.

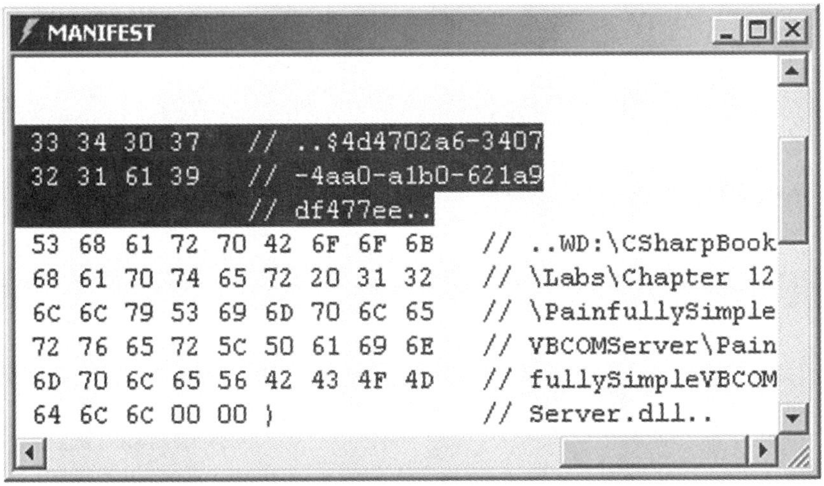

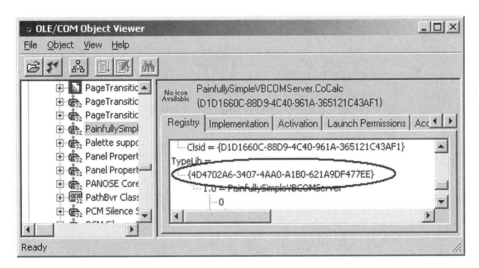

Figure 12-12. GuidAttribute contains the GUID for various COM items.

This value is the GUID Visual Basic assigned to the type library (LIBID). If you open the OLE/COM Object Viewer and check out the assigned LIBID, you will find an exact match (Figure 12-13).

Figure 12-13. Verifying the GUID

Next you have the CoCalc class type itself. In addition to the Add() method, the CoCalc has to be supplied with a default constructor. This should make sense, given that the RCW is attempting to expose the raw coclass as a .NET type, and thus you need a constructor to active it. Also, if you examine the definition of the CoCalc type using ILDasm.exe, you will see various IL instructions marking the CoCalc's base class (System.Object) and implemented interfaces (_CoCalc), as shown here:

```
.class public auto ansi import CoCalc
extends [mscorlib] System.Object
implements SimpleAssembly._CoCalc
{
. . .

} // end of class CoCalc
```

To further explore the COM to .NET type conversion, here is an updated Main() method that interrogates your COM type using members of System.Object and System.Type:

```
public static int Main(string[] args)
{
    // Make the calc!
    CoCalc c = new CoCalc();

    // Your COM type now supports System.Object.ToString().
    Console.WriteLine("-> CoCalc to string: {0}", c.ToString());

    // Extract out some type info.
    Type t = c.GetType();
    Console.WriteLine("-> COM class? : {0}", t.IsCOMObject);
    Console.WriteLine("-> Full name? : {0}", t.FullName);
    Console.WriteLine("-> CLSID? : {0}", t.GUID.ToString());
    Console.WriteLine("-> Is it a interface? : {0}", t.IsInterface);

    return 0;
}
```

Figure 12-14 shows the output.

Great! At this point you looked at a (painfully) simple COM server and examined the basic process used to allow .NET types to make calls to unmanaged coclasses. The next step is to move deeper into this conversion process and come to understand the specific rules used by the tlbimp.exe conversion utility.

```
-> CoCalc to string: PainfullySimpleVBCOMServer.CoCalc
-> COM class? : True
-> Full name? : PainfullySimpleVBCOMServer.CoCalc
-> CLSID? : d1d1660c-88d9-4c40-961a-365121c43af1
-> Is it a interface? : False

Press any key to continue
```

Figure 12-14. Interrogating your COM type

Building an ATL Test Server

So much for our warm up exercise. To *really* understand the conversion process, you will now focus on building an ATL COM server. This will give you a chance to work with IDL in the raw. You will have an intimate view of how COM SAFEARRAYs, BSTRs, enums, coclasses, and interfaces map to corresponding .NET equivalents. Now, understand that this book is not an ATL tutorial. Therefore, the following section walks through the step-by-step process of building an ATL COM server. If you are interested in further information on ATL (or classic COM), I assume you will check out other resources (perhaps even my own offering: Developer's Workshop to COM and ATL 3.0).

To begin, open Visual Studio 6.0 and select a new ATL project workspace named ClassicATLCOMServer. (While you could use ATL 4.0 and Visual Studio.NET, let's stick with ATL 3.0, as it is probably the more familiar of the two versions.) Next, open the ATL Object Wizard (using the Insert menu) and add a new Simple Object name CoCar. Using the Names tab, rename the initial [default] interface to ICar (Figure 12-15).

Before you select OK, access the Attributes tab and select support for ISupportErrorInfo as well as for COM connection points, because the coclass you are building will be able to send COM errors and fire events back to the .NET client (Figure 12-16).

Finally, be sure you select a [dual] interface (rather than the default Custom). All other settings can be left at their default. Go ahead and click OK and perform your first compile.

Populating the [default] COM Interface

Next you need to add some initial members to the [default] ICar interface. Using the Add Method wizard (accessed by right-clicking the COM interface icon from Class View), add two methods. The first method, SpeedUp(), takes a single input parameter of type int (Figure 12-17).

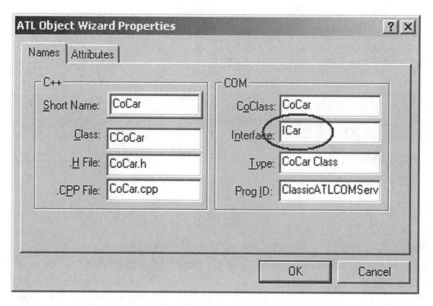

Figure 12-15. Naming your new ATL coclass

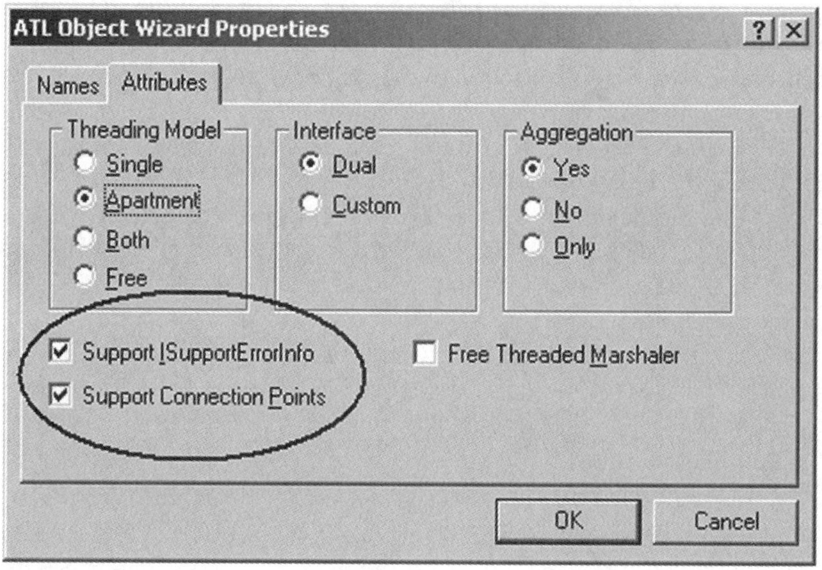

Figure 12-16. Adding support for COM errors and COM events

The second method, named GetCurSpeed(), returns an int pointer by way of an [out, retval] parameter. Once you have added each member, your initial IDL interface definition should look like this:

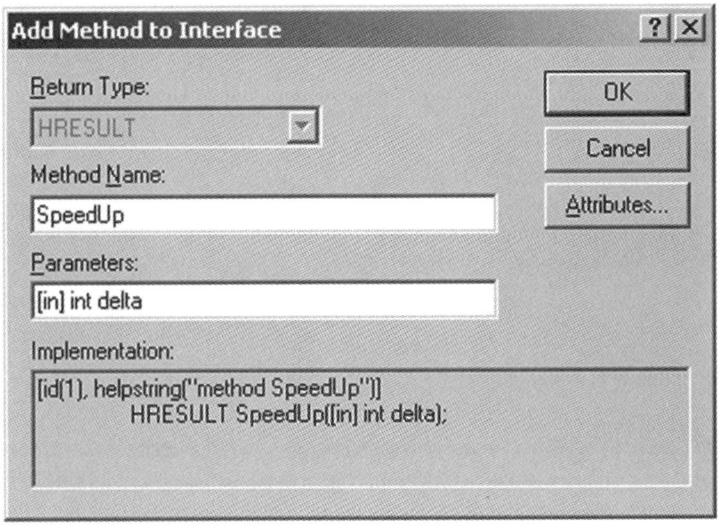

Figure 12-17. Defining parameters using IDL attributes

```
[ object, uuid(A8E01A32-0300-402A-B1EC-ADCD2DC526B4), dual,
   helpstring("ICar Interface"), pointer_default(unique) ]
interface ICar : IDispatch
{
    [id(1), helpstring("method SpeedUp")]
    HRESULT SpeedUp([in] int delta);

    [id(2), helpstring("method GetCurSpeed")]
    HRESULT GetCurSpeed([out, retval] int* currSp);
};
```

Implementing this logic in the supporting coclass is simple. First, add a private int data type (named curSpeed) to your new CoCar class, initialize it to 0 in the constructor, and implement each method as shown here:

```
STDMETHODIMP CCoCar::SpeedUp(int delta)
{
    // Add delta to current speed.
    curSpeed += delta;
    return S_OK;
}
```

```
STDMETHODIMP CCoCar::GetCurSpeed(int *currSp)
{
    // Return current speed.
    *currSp = curSpeed;
    return S_OK;
}
```

Just to be sure you have not injected any bugs, go ahead and recompile your server.

Firing a COM Event

Now, you will equip your CoCar coclass to raise a COM event. The first step is to add a method to your outbound interface that represents the methods the coclass will call on the client sink (recall that outbound interfaces are defined by the COM server but implemented by the client). In ATL, the outbound interface is listed at the top of Class View and is marked with a "_" prefix and "Events" suffix. Right-click this interface and access the New Method Wizard. Add a single event named Exploded, which sends the client a BSTR parameter (Figure 12-18).

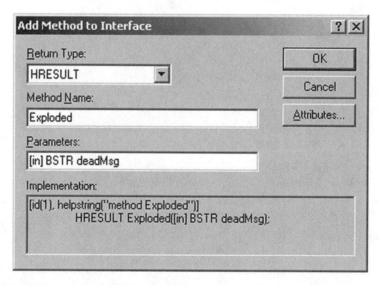

Figure 12-18. Populating the [source] interface

Here is the resulting IDL code:

```
[uuid(E88DA278-AD04-407F-9BBB-D8C00AFE7984),
helpstring("_ICarEvents Interface") ]
dispinterface _ICarEvents
```

```
{
    properties:
    methods:
    [id(1), helpstring("method Exploded")]
    HRESULT Exploded([in] BSTR deadMsg );
}
```

Once you have added this event to your outbound interface, recompile the project to refresh the COM type information. Next you need to build an event proxy, which is used by the ATL framework to fire the Exploded event to any connected client. To do so, right-click the CoCar type from the Class View window and select Implement Connection Point. In the resulting dialog box, check the name of your event interface (_CarEvents) and click OK.

This tool responds by updating your CoCar in a number of ways. First, you will find that the CONNECTION_MAP (listed in the header file of your CoCar) has been updated with a new entry. It does not really matter what that entry is doing, but you need to be aware that this tool has a bug that can cause this map to be updated incorrectly. At times, the parameter to the CONNECTION_POINT_ENTRY macro is generated without the required D prefix. Here is the repaired connection map (if you did not get the bug, don't worry about it; just keep coding):

```
BEGIN_CONNECTION_POINT_MAP(CCoCar)
    // Oops! Wizard forgot D prefix!
    // CONNECTION_POINT_ENTRY(IID__ICarEvents)    // Bad...
    CONNECTION_POINT_ENTRY(DIID__ICarEvents)      // Good...
END_CONNECTION_POINT_MAP()
```

The second major update this tool performs is adding a new class in your CoCar class's inheritance chain (CProxy_ICarEvents). This class implements a method named Fire_Exploded() that hides the work of calling the list of currently connected clients.

To fire the Exploded event, add two new member variables named maxSpeed and dead. (Don't forget to assign initial values in the constructor.) The first (integer) data type is used to represent the maximum speed of the COM car. The second (Boolean) data type is used to represent whether the car has already exploded. Once these members have been added to your header file, update SpeedUp() with the following logic:

```
STDMETHODIMP CCoCar::SpeedUp(int delta)
{
    // Add delta and check for event condition.
    curSpeed += delta;
```

```
    // If I am not currently dead, and I went above the max speed. . .
    if(curSpeed >= maxSpeed && !dead)
    {
        // Fire event and set the'dead' Boolean.
        CComBSTR msg("You are toast. . .");

        Fire_Exploded(msg.Detach());
        curSpeed = maxSpeed;
        dead = true;
    }
    return S_OK;
}
```

Throwing a COM Error

Recall that when you created your ATL CoCar, you added support for the COM error protocol. For your current purposes, you do not need to examine the low-level details of COM error objects. All you need to know is that when you wish to report an error using the ATL framework, you call the inherited Error() method. To illustrate, update the implementation of GetCurSpeed() to return a COM error object if the user attempts to obtain the current speed on a car that is already dead:

```
STDMETHODIMP CCoCar::GetCurSpeed(int *currSp)
{
    // Send error if dead.
    if(!dead)
    {
        *currSp = curSpeed;
        return S_OK;
    }
    else
    {
        *currSp = 0;
        Error("Sorry, this car has met it's maker");
        return E_FAIL;
    }
}
```

At this point you have created a COM class that supports a single [default] interface. Also, this coclass can send out COM error information and errors to the connected clients. Go ahead and compile once again to ensure that you have no typos.

Exposing an Internal Subobject
(and Using SAFEARRAYs)

You will add two final bits of functionality to your ATL COM server. The first is exposing an internal subobject from the CoCar type named CoEngine. To begin, insert a new ATL Simple Object using the ATL Object Wizard, change the name of the [default] interface to IEngine, and set the interface type to be [dual] from the Attributes tab.

Next, use the Add Method Wizard to add a single method to the IEngine interface named GetCylinders(). This method returns a COM SAFEARRAY of BSTRs that represents the pet names of each cylinder placed inside the engine. (OK, I admit most of us don't give pet names to our cylinders, but this illustrates returning an array of strings to a .NET-aware client.) Here is the IDL:

```
// The inner engine interface.
[object, uuid(23DT GetCyl2BB87-A8F8-4301-BED5-9D0CA77AE403), dual,
helpstring("IEngine Interface"), pointer_default(unique) ]
interface IEngine : IDispatch
{
    [id(1), helpstring("method GetCylinders")]
    HRESUL GetCylinders([out, retval] VARIANT* arCylinders);
};
```

And here is the implementation for an engine supporting four cylinders:

```
STDMETHODIMP CCoEngine::GetCylinders(VARIANT *arCylinders)
{
    // Init and set the type of variant.
    VariantInit(arCylinders);
    arCylinders->vt = VT_ARRAY | VT_BSTR;     // An array of strings.

    // Create the array.
    SAFEARRAY *pSA;
    SAFEARRAYBOUND bounds = {4, 0};
    pSA = SafeArrayCreate(VT_BSTR, 1, &bounds);

    // Fill the array.
    BSTR *theStrings;
    SafeArrayAccessData(pSA, (void**)&theStrings);
        theStrings[0] = SysAllocString(L"Grinder");
        theStrings[1] = SysAllocString(L"Oily");
        theStrings[2] = SysAllocString(L"Thumper");
        theStrings[3] = SysAllocString(L"Crusher");
    SafeArrayUnaccessData(pSA);
```

```
// Return the array.
arCylinders->parray = pSA;

return S_OK;
}
```

Now, if you have never worked with COM SAFEARRAYs in raw C++ before, you are most likely horrified by the previous code block (yet another case for using System.Array). The basic idea of a SAFEARRAY is that it is a self-describing array of [oleautomation] compatible types and maintains the upper and lower bounds of the items it contains. SAFEARRAY types are created, filled, and manipulated using a set of COM library functions (as shown in the previous code). Again, you have no need to deal with these details here. All that matters at this point is that the GetCylinders() method allows the outside world to obtain an array of COM strings (BSTRs).

The next step is to allow the COM client to obtain a valid IEngine interface reference from a CoCar type. To do so, you use standard COM containment. The outer CoCar provides access to the inner CoEngine using the following addition method of the ICar interface:

```
// Recall! Returning an interface pointer requires double indirection.
// Also be sure the definition of IEngine is placed above the ICar definition
// so the MIDL complier can 'see' the interface definition.
interface ICar : IDispatch
{
    . . .
    [id(3), helpstring("method GetEngine")]
    HRESULT GetEngine([out, retval] IEngine** pEngine);
};
```

The implementation of GetEngine() uses some ATL types, so if you are not familiar with these items, just understand that the static CComObject<>::CreateInstance() method is what creates the CoEngine. After this point, query for the IEngine interface and return it to the client, as shown here:

```
STDMETHODIMP CCoCar::GetEngine(IEngine **pEngine)
{
    // Create a CoEngine and then return the IEngine interface to the client.
    CComObject<CCoEngine> *pEng;
    CComObject<CCoEngine>::CreateInstance(&pEng);
    pEng->QueryInterface(IID_IEngine, (void**)pEngine);

    return S_OK;
}
```

If you really want to address the finer details of this contained type, you can add the noncreatable attribute to the CoEngine IDL definition. This attribute is used by numerous languages (such as Visual Basic 6.0) to prevent the end user from New-ing the item (if this is attempted, a compiler error is issued):

```
[ uuid(32C07E17-F966-4EFD-B301-9729FE2D60B5),
helpstring("CoEngine Class"), noncreatable ]
coclass CoEngine
{
    [default] interface IEngine;
};
```

Also, update the ATL OBJECT_MAP to mark CoEngine as a noncreatable type, which prevents its direct creation by an external client, as shown here:

```
BEGIN_OBJECT_MAP(ObjectMap)
    OBJECT_ENTRY(CLSID_CoCar, CCoCar)
    OBJECT_ENTRY_NON_CREATEABLE(CCoEngine)
END_OBJECT_MAP()
```

The Final Step: Configuring an IDL Enumeration

There is one final step before you can create a proxy for this COM server. Open your project's IDL file and define a single COM enumeration named CarType directly after the import statements at the top of the file, as shown here:

```
// This COM enum is used to ID the car type.
typedef enum CarType {Jetta, BMW, Ford, Colt} CarType;
```

To allow the outside world to obtain a CarType enum, add one final method to the ICar interface named GetCarType(), as shown here:

```
interface ICar : IDispatch
{
    [id(1), helpstring("method SpeedUp")]
    HRESULT SpeedUp([in] int delta);

    [id(2), helpstring("method GetCurSpeed")]
    HRESULT GetCurSpeed([out, retval] int* currSp);

    [id(3), helpstring("method GetEngine")]
    HRESULT GetEngine([out, retval] IEngine** pEngine);
```

```
        [id(4), helpstring("method GetCarType")]
        HRESULT GetCarType([out, retval] CarType* ct);
};
```

The implementation of GetCarType() creates and sets the value of the [out, retval] CarType enumeration for use by the COM client, as shown here:

```
STDMETHODIMP CCoCar::GetCarType(CarType *ct)
{
    *ct = Colt;      // Pick your favorite car....
    return S_OK;
}
```

I bet you did not intend to learn about ATL in the course of a C# book! In my defense, the topic of this chapter *is* all about COM and .NET interoperability. The reason you took the time to build a more complex server is because that programming is complex! The sorts of COM servers you will want to use from a .NET client are bound to do far more than add some numbers together. Here you have a COM server that supports error objects, connection points, COM containment, enumerations, and some core COM data types such as SAFEARRAY and BSTR.

Now that you have fully created your ATL COM server, you can build a proxy and check out exactly how these exotic COM types are mapped to .NET. Before doing that, however, look at the CoCar in action from the viewpoint of a Visual Basic 6.0 COM client.

SOURCE CODE *The ClassicATLCOMServer project is included under the Chapter 12 subdirectory.*

Examining a Visual Basic 6.0 Test Client

Before we build a managed client, let's create a classic COM client using VB. I will just cover the highlights here. First of all, Figure 12-19 shows the client application in action.

When the Form is loaded, create a new instance of the Car type (declared using the WithEvents keyword to respond to the incoming Exploded event). The Exploded event handler does little more than display the message sent by the doomed automobile, as shown here:

```
Private Sub myCar_Exploded(ByVal deadMsg As String)
      MsgBox deadMsg, , "Message from CoCar!"
End Sub
```

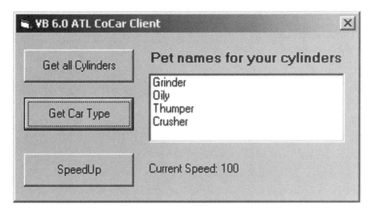

Figure 12-19. The VB 6.0 COM client

The Speed Up button does just that. Recall that when you max out the speed of the car, the Exploded event is sent by the CoCar. Also recall that when the user attempts to speed up a previously exploded car, you are sent a COM error object (which is caught in VB using the On Error Goto construct), as shown here:

```
Private Sub btnSpeedUp_Click()
On Error GoTo OOPS

    myCar.SpeedUp 50
    Label2.Caption = "Current Speed: " & myCar.GetCurSpeed

Exit Sub

OOPS:
    MsgBox Err.Description, , "Error from car!"
Resume Next
End Sub
```

Finally, the Get all Cylinders button obtains the IEngine interface from the CoCar, and calls GetCylinders(), as shown here:

```
Private Sub btnGetCylinders_Click()

    ' First we need to get the engine.
    Dim q As CoEngine
    Set q = myCar.GetEngine

    ' Now get cylinders.
    Dim strs As Variant
    strs = q.GetCylinders
```

```
' Now get each name from SAFEARRAY and place in list box.
Dim upper As Integer
Dim i As Integer
upper = UBound(strs)
For i = 0 To upper
        lstCylinderList.AddItem strs(i)
Next i

End Sub
```

SOURCE CODE   *The VB6ATL project is included under the Chapter 12 subdirectory.*

Building the Assembly (and Examining the Conversion Process)

Open a command prompt window and run the tlbimp.exe utility to create the new assembly representing the ClassicATLCOMServer.dll, as shown here:

tlbimp classicatlcomserver.dll /out:AtlServerAssembly.dll

Now, load this assembly into ILDasm.exe and check out the generated types (Figure 12-20). As you can see, the CarType, CoCar, and CoEngine COM types have all been mapped to .NET equivalents. (The generated event helpers will be examined soon.)

I will discuss the details of this conversion, beginning with the COM type library.

Type Library Conversion

As you have already seen, every COM type (enum, coclass, or custom interface) listed in a COM server's library statement is used to populate the generated .NET namespace.

One additional point of interest is that the [version] attribute of the type library is used to designate the version of the assembly. Thus, if you update your IDL version attribute as shown here:

```
[ uuid(69D8B2E2-4CC1-4414-9757-49C53620FF0C), version(9.7),
    helpstring("ClassicATLCOMServer 1.0 Type Library") ]
library CLASSICATLCOMSERVERLib
{
    // All your stuff...
}
```

Figure 12-20. The managed ATL CoCar

you find the following listing in the manifest:

```
.assembly AtlServerAssembly
{
...
    .ver 9:7:0:0
}
```

COM Interface Conversion

When a COM interface is represented as a .NET type, it is qualified using various attributes from the System.Runtime.InteropServices namespace. First is the GuidAttribute type, which is used in this case to document the interface's IID, as specified by the [uuid] attribute in the IDL file.

Next is the InterfaceTypeAttribute type, which is used to catalog how the interface was originally defined in IDL syntax (custom, dual, or dispinterface). This attribute can be assigned any value from the ComInterfaceType enumeration (Table 12-6).

Table 12-6. COM Interface Types

COMINTERFACETYPE MEMBER NAME	MEANING IN LIFE
InterfaceIsDual	Indicates that the interface should be exposed to COM as a dual interface.
InterfaceIsIDispatch	Indicates that an interface should be exposed as a dispinterface.
InterfaceIsIUnknown	Indicates that an interface should be exposed as an IUnknown-derived interface, as opposed to a dispinterface or a dual interface.

Oddly enough, if the proxy is representing a dual interface (as in this case), this attribute is omitted. Instead, dual interfaces are marked using the TypeLibTypeAttribute, which is used to document various aspects of the [dual] interface (e.g., licensed, hidden, appobject, and so on).

IDL Parameter Attribute Conversion

In classic COM, parameters are configured using a set of IDL attributes. These attributes are used to clearly mark the direction of travel of a given argument and to determine proper memory management. Your ATL coclasses used the [in] and [out, retval] IDL attributes. Additionally, a COM method parameter can be marked with the [out] or [in, out] attribute. To illustrate each possibility, assume you have defined the following IParams interface in IDL:

```
interface IParams : IDispatch
{
    // [in] params are allocated by the caller and sent to the method.
    [id(1)] HRESULT OnlyInParams([in] int x, [in] int y);

    // [out] params are filled by the callee.
    [id(2)] HRESULT OnlyOutParams([out] int* x, [out] int* y);

    // [retval] types map an output param to the physical return value
    // of the function (for example, VB would call this as"ans = Retval()").
    [id(3)] HRESULT Retval([out, retval] int* answer);

    // [in, out] params are passed into the callee and can be changed
    // during the process of the method invocation.
    [id(4)] HRESULT InAndOut([in, out] int* byRefParam);
};
```

Once you run this interface definition through the tlbimp.exe utility, you would find that these items are mapped to the familiar C# out and ref keywords. (See chapter 2.) Figure 12-21 shows how your IParams interface is seen using the VS.NET Object Browser.

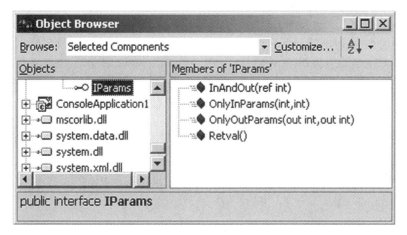

Figure 12-21. The managed IParams interface

Consider the following IDL to C# parameter conversions (Table 12-7).

Table 12-7. Mapping IDL Parameter Attributes to C# Keywords

IDL PARAMETER ATTRIBUTE	C# PARAMETER KEYWORD	MEANING IN LIFE
[in]	No keyword. This is the assumed direction of travel.	Called function receives a copy of the data.
[out]	out	Value is assigned in the called function and returned to the caller.
[in, out]	ref	Value is assigned by the caller, but can be reallocated by the called function.
[out, retval]	n/a	These types become the physically returned value of the function. If no [out, retval] is formally declared, it is converted to a void return type.

Interface Hierarchy Conversion

Although you did not define a COM interface hierarchy in your ATL project, assume for the sake of argument that you decided to derive a new interface from IEngine named ITurboEngine. Here is the IDL:

```
interface ITurboEngine : IEngine
{
    HRESULT PowerBoost();
};
```

In terms of the conversion process, a derived interface is represented as a union of all methods defined in the chain of inheritance (Figure 12-22). Thus, if you examine ITurboEngine using ILDasm.exe, you find that you support not just PowerBoost(), but GetCylinders() as well. (Also notice that the [implements] tag specifies the name of the base interface.)

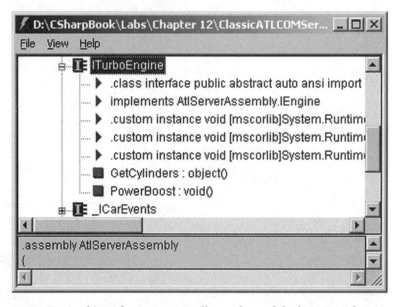

Figure 12-22. Derived interfaces support all members of the base interface(s).

Coclass (and COM Properties) Conversions

As illustrated by the previous VB COM server example, when the assembly is generated using the tlbimp.exe utility, you receive .NET types for each standalone interface as well as the coclass itself. Thus, you can exercise a new CoCar type using two approaches. First, you can create a direct instance of the coclass that provides access to each interface member, as shown here:

```
// Here, you are really working with the [default] ICar interface.
CoCar viper = new CoCar();
viper.SpeedUp(30);
```

As an alternative, you can explicitly ask for the [default] interface, as shown here:

```
// Get ICar explicitly.
CoCar viper = new CoCar();
ICar ic = (ICar)viper;
ic.SpeedUp(30);
```

In the current ATL example, the CoCar and CoEngine types each implement a single [default] interface. However, assume you define the following additional interface, which supports a single COM property (of type BSTR):

```
interface IDriverInfo : IDispatch
{
    [id(1), propget, helpstring("property DriverName")]
    HRESULT DriverName([out, retval] BSTR *pVal);

    [id(1), propput, helpstring("property DriverName")]
    HRESULT DriverName([in] BSTR newVal);
};
```

Also assume that the CoCar now implements this new interface (the implementation simply gets or sets a private BSTR), as shown here:

```
coclass CoCar
{
    [default] interface ICar;
    interface IDriverInfo;
    [default, source] dispinterface _ICarEvents;
};
```

Given that CoCar now supports two custom interfaces, you might wonder exactly how this is represented in terms of managed code. As you might suspect, the managed class supports each member defined by the supported interfaces. In other words, if you now create an instance of CoCar, you can call SpeedUp(),

GetCurrentSpeed(), GetEngine(), and GetCarType() as well as manipulate the
DriverName property, as shown here:

```
// Notice we can get access to the property defined by IDriverInfo
// directly from the supporting coclass.
CoCar viper = new CoCar();
viper.DriverName = "Fred";
Console.WriteLine(viper.DriverName);
```

If you would rather, you can also explicitly access the IDriverInfo interface, as
shown here:

```
// Get and set the property using IDriverInfo.
IDriverInfo idi = (IDriverInfo)viper;
idi.DriverName = "Fred";
Console.WriteLine("Name of driver is: " + idi.DriverName);
```

Oddly enough, if you check out the CoCar type using ILDasm.exe, you might
be surprised to find that the CoCar type does not directly define these members
(Figure 12-23).

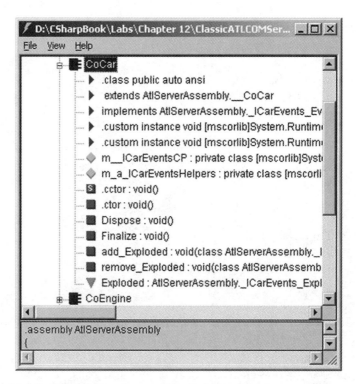

Figure 12-23. Managed classes do not directly define interface members

If you examine the situation a bit more closely, however, you will notice that CoCar derives from a generated type named __CoCar. This intermediate class type defines the members of the ICar and IDriverInfo interfaces (Figure 12-24).

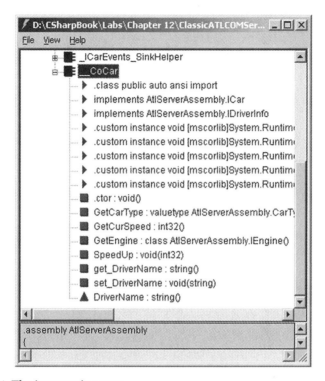

Figure 12-24. The intervening type

When you check out the type metadata, you will find the following derivation of __CoCar (in addition to a small set of attributes):

```
.class public auto ansi import __CoCar
    extends [mscorlib]System.Object
    implements      CLASSICATLCOMSERVERLib.ICar,
                    CLASSICATLCOMSERVERLib.IDriverInfo
{
    // TypeLibTypeAttribute attribute...
    // ComSourceInterfacesAttribute attribute...
    // GuidAttribute attribute...
    // HasDefaultInterfaceAttribute attribute...


} // end of class __CoCar
```

COM Enumeration Conversions

COM enumerations are mapped to managed types deriving from System.Enum. Therefore, you can use any of the (very helpful) supported members. Here is an example:

```
public static int Main(string[] args)
{
    // Begin by making a car.
    CoCar viper = new CoCar();

    // Now get car type.
    CarType t = viper.GetCarType();
    Console.WriteLine("Car type: {0}", t.ToString());

    return 0;
}
```

Working with the COM SAFEARRAY

Next, examine how the COM SAFEARRAY is represented as managed code. As you recall, the IEngine interface supports a single method named GetCylinders(), which returns an array of BSTRs. The outside world accesses the IEngine interface by calling the GetEngine() method of an existing CoCar. So, to begin you could write the following:

```
// First make the CoCar.
CoCar viper = new CoCar();

// Get engine reference.
IEngine e = viper.GetEngine();

// Ask engine for cylinder SAFEARRAY.
object o = e.GetCylinders();
```

Recall that the SAFEARRAY was declared as an array of VARIANTs, using the VT_ARRAY and VT_BSTR variant type flags, as shown here:

```
STDMETHODIMP CCoEngine::GetCylinders(VARIANT *arCylinders)
{
    // Init and set the type of variant.
    VariantInit(arCylinders);
    arCylinders->vt = VT_ARRAY | VT_BSTR;

    // Ugly COM goo removed for sanity.

    // Set return value.
    arCylinders->parray = pSA;

    return S_OK;
}
```

In the eyes of .NET, a VARIANT type is represented as an instance of System.Object. However, given that you set the vt field of the VARIANT structure using the VT_ARRAY and VT_BSTR flags, you will find System.String[] printed to the console:

```
// Who does 'o' think he is anyway?
IEngine e = viper.GetEngine();
object o = e.GetCylinders();
// o is of type System.String[]

Console.WriteLine("o is really this type: {0}", o);
```

To print the pet names for each cylinder, you could write the following (see Figure 12-25 for output):

```
// Get array of strings.
String[] cylinders = (string[])o;

// Print each item.
Console.WriteLine("Your cylinders are:");
foreach(string s in cylinders)
{
    Console.WriteLine("->" + s);
}
```

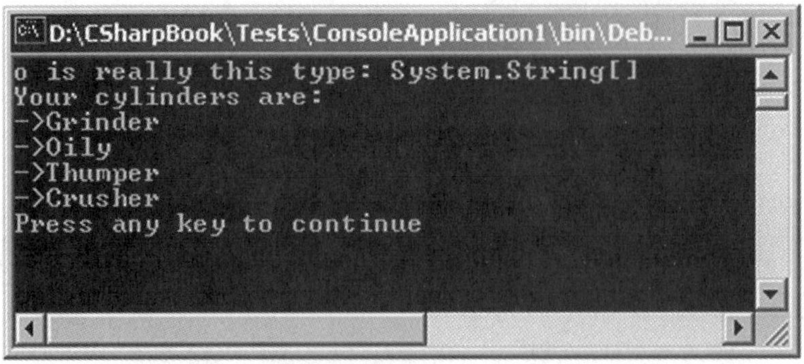

Figure 12-25. Iterating over your SAFEARRAY

Slick, isn't it? The next point of interest is to check out the process of hooking into the CoCar's Exploded event.

Intercepting COM Events

In Chapter 5 you learned about the .NET event model. Recall that this architecture is based on delegating the flow of logic from one part of the application to another. The entity in charge of forwarding a request is a type deriving from System.MulticastDelegate. The client is able to add a target to or remove a target from the internal list using the overloaded += and -= operators.

When the tlbimp.exe utility encounters a [source] interface in the COM server's type library, it responds by creating a number of managed types that wrap the low-level COM connection point architecture. Using these types, you can pretend to add a member to a System.MulticastDelegate's internal linked list. Under the hood, of course, the proxy is mapping the incoming COM event to their managed equivalents. Recall that your unmanaged CoCar defined the following outbound interface:

```
dispinterface _ICarEvents
{
    properties:
    methods:
    [id(1), helpstring("method Exploded")]
    HRESULT Exploded([in] BSTR deadMsg );
};
```

Tlbimp.exe responded by creating a set of types used to help map the COM connection point architecture into the .NET delegate event system. Table 12-8 briefly describes these types.

Table 12-8. COM Event Helper Types

GENERATED TYPE (BASED ON _CAREVENTS [SOURCE] INTERFACE)	MEANING IN LIFE
_ICarEvents	This is the managed definition for the outbound interface (and is generally not directly used).
_ICarEvents_Event	This is a managed interface that defines the add and remove members used to add (or remove) a method to (or from) the System.MulticastDelegate's linked list. This type is also not generally used directly.
_ICarEvents_ExplodedEventHandler	This is the managed delegate (which derives from System.MulticastDelegate). The return type of a given managed event handler must return an int. The parameters will map to the original COM event.
_ICarEvents_SinkHelper	This generated class implements the outbound interface in a .NET-aware sink object. This class assigns the cookie generated by the COM type to the m_dwCookie member variable. Also, this class maintains an internal member variable (m_ExplodedDelegate) representing the outbound interface (_ICarEvents_ExplodedEventHandler).

In addition to these generated types, the coclass that defined the outbound interface (CoCar) has been updated as well. First (and most importantly) you have a new event named Exploded in your public sector, as shown here:

```
.class public auto ansi CoCar
        extends AtlServerAssembly._CoCar
        implements AtlServerAssembly._ICarEvents_Event
{
        . . .
} // end of class CoCar
```

Your managed CoCar will also have two private members that maintain the connection to the COM event source (add_X and remove_X), as shown in Figure 12-26.

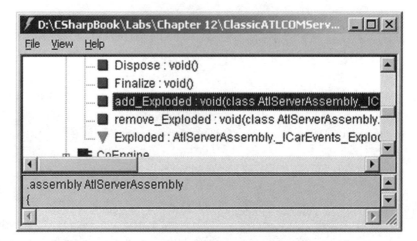

Figure 12-26. COM events mapped to a pair of functions

If you check out the underlying IL instruction set for add_Exploded(), you will find that a new _ICarEvents_SinkHelper type created on your behalf. After this point, the assembly proxy obtains the correct IConnectionPoint interface from the ATL CoCar, calls Advise(), and caches the returned cookie. For completion, here are the generated IL instructions (but remember, you can always choose to remain blissfully unaware of these low-level details):

```
.method public virtual instance void  add_Exploded(class
AtlServerAssembly._ICarEvents_ExplodedEventHandler A_1) cil managed
{
. . .
// Make Sink helper object.
  IL_0000:  newobj     instance void
AtlServerAssembly._ICarEvents_SinkHelper::.ctor()
  IL_0005:  stloc.0
  IL_0006:  ldc.i4.0
  IL_0007:  stloc.1
  IL_0008:  ldarg      0
  IL_000c:  ldfld      class

// Get IConnectionPoint interface.
[mscorlib]System.Runtime.InteropServices.UCOMIConnectionPoint
AtlServerAssembly.CoCar::m__ICarEventsCP
  IL_0011:  ldloc.0
  IL_0012:  castclass  [mscorlib]System.Object
  IL_0017:  ldloca.s   V_1
  IL_0019:  callvirt   instance void
```

```
// Call IConnectionPoint::Advise().
[mscorlib]System.Runtime.InteropServices.UCOMIConnectionPoint::Advise(object,
                                                        int32&)

  IL_001e:  ldloc.0
  IL_001f:  ldloc.1
```

```
// Store Cookie returned from Advise().
  IL_0020:  stfld      int32 AtlServerAssembly._ICarEvents_SinkHelper::m_dwCookie
  IL_0025:  ldloc.0
  IL_0026:  ldarg      A_1
```

```
// Add SinkHelper to delegate.
  IL_002a:  stfld      class AtlServerAssembly._ICarEvents_ExplodedEventHandler
AtlServerAssembly._ICarEvents_SinkHelper::m_ExplodedDelegate
  IL_002f:  ldarg      0
  IL_0033:  ldfld      class [mscorlib]System.Collections.ArrayList
AtlServerAssembly.CoCar::m_a_ICarEventsHelpers
  IL_0038:  ldloc.0
  IL_0039:  castclass  [mscorlib]System.Object
  IL_003e:  callvirt   instance int32
[mscorlib]System.Collections.ArrayList::Add(object)
  IL_0043:  pop
  IL_0044:  ret
} // end of method CoCar::add_Exploded
```

Hooking into the COM Event

Now that you have a better feeling for how COM events are handled, you can learn how easy it is to hook into a COM event from managed code. As you can see here, this looks identical to the process of working with .NET delegates:

```
public class CoCarClient
{
    // The method that will be called when the car sends the event.
    // The delegation target must return an int!
    public static int ExplodedHandler(String msg)
    {
        Console.WriteLine("\nCar says: (COM Events)\n->"
                            + msg + "\n");
        return 0;
    }
```

```
public static int Main(string[] args)
{
    CoCar viper = new CoCar();

    // Rig into event.
    viper.Exploded +=
        new _ICarEvents_ExplodedEventHandler(ExplodedHandler);

    // Do something to trigger the event.
    for(int i = 0; i < 5; i++)
    {
        try
        {
            viper.SpeedUp(50);
            Console.WriteLine("->Curr speed is: "
                            + viper.GetCurSpeed());
        }
        catch(Exception ex)
        {
            Console.WriteLine("->COM error! " + ex.Message + "\n");
        }
    }
}
```

All you need to do to be done is establish a delegate with the Exploded event, as shown here:

```
// Rig into event.
viper.Exploded += new _ICarEvents_ExplodedEventHandler(ExplodedHandler);
```

When the CoCar fires the Exploded event (when the speed is over the maximum limit), your event handler (ExplodedHandler) is called automatically.

Handling the COM Error

Last but not least, also notice that you wrapped the speedup logic in a try/catch block. If the end user attempts to speed up a car that has exploded, the coclass returns a COM error object, which is mapped into a .NET exception.

The Complete C# Client

Now that you have seen how each COM atom is expressed in the terms of .NET, here is the complete C# client code that uses the generated proxy:

```
using System;
using AtlServerAssembly;       // The assembly containing the proxy.
using System.Reflection;

public class CoCarClient
{
    public static int ExplodedHandler(String msg)
    {
        Console.WriteLine("\nCar says: (COM Events)\n->" + msg + "\n");
        return 0;
    }

    public static int Main(string[] args)
    {
        // Begin by making a car.
        CoCar viper = new CoCar();

        // Rig into event.
        viper.Exploded += new
            _ICarEvents_ExplodedEventHandler(ExplodedHandler);

        // Set (and get) the driver name.
        viper.DriverName = "Fred";
        Console.WriteLine("Driver is named: (COM property)\n->" +
                        viper.DriverName + "\n");

        // List type of car.
        CarType t = viper.GetCarType();
        Console.WriteLine("Car type is: (COM enum)\n->" + t.ToString() + "\n");

        // Get engine & cylinders.
        IEngine e = viper.GetEngine();
        object o = e.GetCylinders();

        // Unbox object ref into array of strings.
        String[] cylinders = (string[])o;
```

```
                    // Print each item.
            Console.WriteLine("Your cylinders are: ");
            foreach(string s in cylinders)
            {
                    Console.WriteLine("->" + s);
            }
// Now speed up the car to trigger event.
            for(int i = 0; i < 5; i++)
            {
                try
                {
                    viper.SpeedUp(50);
                    Console.WriteLine("->Curr speed is: "
                                    + viper.GetCurSpeed());
                }
                catch(Exception ex)      // Catch COM error!
                {
                    Console.WriteLine("->COM error! " + ex.Message + "\n");
                }
            }

        return 0;
        }
}
```

Figure 12-27 shows the final output.

Understanding COM to .NET Interoperability

The next topic of this chapter is the logically opposite interoperability scenario of
what we have just examined: a COM class calling a .NET type. As you might imagine, this situation is less likely to occur than .NET to COM communications, but it
is still worth examining.

For a COM class to use a .NET type, you need to fool the coclass into believ-
ing that the managed type is in fact *unmanaged*. In essence, you need to allow
the coclass to interact with the type using the functionality provided by the COM
architecture. For example, the COM type should be able to obtain new interfaces
through QueryInterface() calls, simulate unmanaged memory management
using AddRef() and Release(), make use of the COM connection point protocol,
and so on.

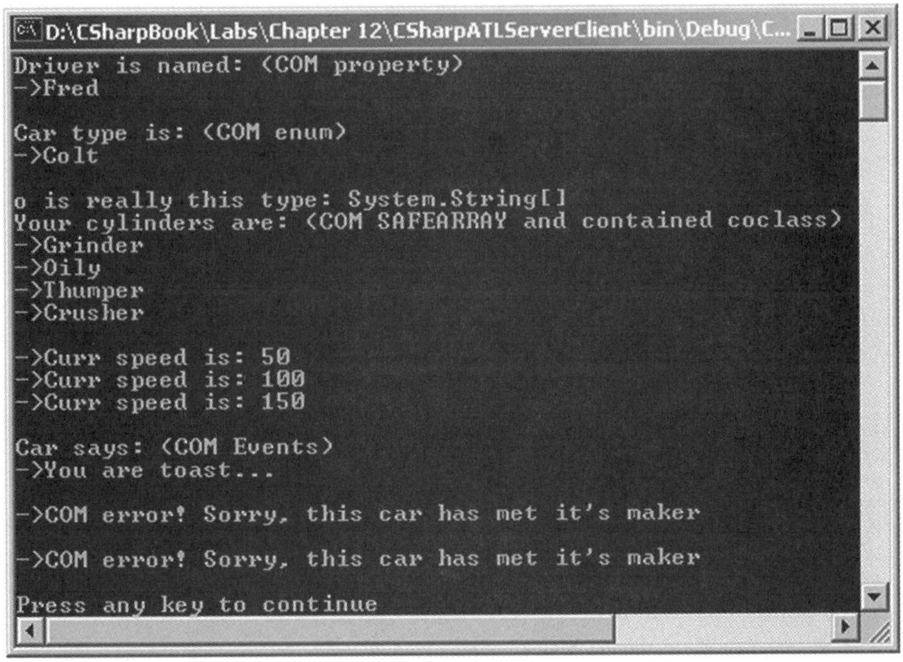

Figure 12-27. C# code interacting with ATL code

Beyond fooling the COM client, COM to .NET interoperability also involves fooling the COM runtime. As you know, a classic COM server is activated using the Service Control Manager (SCM). For this to happen, the SCM must look up numerous bits of information in the system registry (ProgIDs, CLSIDs, IIDs, and so forth). The problem of course is that .NET assemblies are not registered (at all).

In a nutshell, to make your .NET assemblies available to classic COM clients, you must take the following steps:

- Register your .NET assembly into the system registry to allow the COM SCM to locate it.

- Generate a COM type library (*.tlb) file (based on the .NET metadata) to allow the COM client to interact with the exposed types.

- Deploy the assembly in the same directory as the COM client or install the assembly into the GAC.

You will examine the tool that automates these steps in just a moment. For now, check out exactly how COM clients interact with .NET types using a CCW.

The Role of the CCW

When the COM client accesses a .NET type, the CLR uses a proxy termed the *COM Callable Wrapper* (*CCW*) to negotiate the COM to .NET conversion (Figure 12-28).

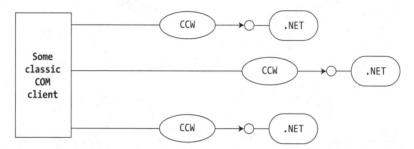

Figure 12-28. COM types talk to .NET types using a CCW.

Understand that the CCW is a reference-counted entity. This should make sense, given that the COM client is assuming that the CCW is a real COM type and thus must abide by the rules of AddRef() and Release(). When the COM client has issued the final release, the CCW releases its reference to the real .NET type, at which point it is ready to be garbage collected.

The CCW implements a number of COM interfaces automatically to further the illusion that the proxy represents a genuine coclass. In addition to the set of custom interfaces defined by the .NET type (including an entity named the class interface that you will examine in just a moment), the CCW provides support for the standard COM behaviors described in Table 12-9.

Understanding the Class Interface

In classic COM, the only way a COM client can communicate with a COM object is using an interface reference. However, some COM-aware languages (such as Visual Basic 6.0) attempt to hide this fact from the programmer to facilitate the VB is easy mindset. The fact remains that Visual Basic generates a [default] interface for each coclass in the COM binary. Any member declared as Public is placed in the [default] interface. In this way, VB clients can pretend to work with an object reference, when in fact they are working with an interface reference, as shown here:

```
' Recall that VB hides the [default] interface.
' Dim o as New MyComClass          ' Query for [default] _MyComClass
o.Hello                            ' Really calls _MyComClass->Hello()
```

Table 12-9. The CCW supports numerous core COM interfaces.

CCW IMPLEMENTED INTERFACE	MEANING IN LIFE
IConnectionPointContainer IConnectionPoint	If the .NET type supports any events, they are represented as COM connection points.
IEnumVariant	If the .NET type supports the IEnumerable interface, it appears to the COM client as a standard COM enumerator.
ISupportErrorInfo IErrorInfo	These interfaces allow coclasses to send COM error objects.
ITypeInfo IProvideClassInfo	These interfaces allow the COM client to pretend to manipulate an assembly's COM type information. In reality, the COM client is interacting with .NET metadata.
IUnknown IDispatch IDispatchEx	These core COM interfaces provide support for early and late binding to the .NET type. IDispatchEx can be supported by the CCW if the .NET type implements the IExpando interface.

In contrast, .NET types do not need to support any interfaces. It is possible to build a complete solution using nothing but object references. However, given that classic COM clients cannot work with object references, another responsibility of the CCW is to support a class interface to represent each property, method, field, and event defined by the type's public sector. As you can see, the CCW is taking the same approach as Visual Basic 6.0.

Defining a Class Interface

The ClassInterface attribute is an optional but very important type. By default, any method defined on a .NET class is exposed to COM as a raw dispinterface (i.e., a given implementation of IDispatch). Thus, all COM clients that want to use class-level methods must exercise late binding to manipulate your .NET types! To alter this default behavior, use the ClassInterfaceAttribute type, which can be assigned any value of the ClassInterfaceType enumeration (Table 12-10).

Table 12-10. Values of the ClassInterfaceType Enumeration

CLASSINTERFACETYPE MEMBER NAME	MEANING IN LIFE
AutoDispatch	Indicates that a dispatch-only interface be generated for the class.
AutoDual	Indicates that a dual interface be generated for the class.
None	Indicates that no interface be generated for the class.

In the next example, you will specify ClassInterfaceType.AutoDual as the class interface designation. In this way, late binding clients such as VBScript can access the Add() and Subtract() methods using IDispatch, while early bound clients (such as VB proper and C++) can use the class interface (named _CSharpCalc). Like in Visual Basic 6.0, the name of your class interface is always based on your type name and prefixed with an underbar.

Building Your .NET Type

To illustrate a COM type communicating with managed code, assume you have created a simple C# Class Library that defines a single class named CSharpCalc, which supports two methods named Add() and Subtract(). Also, assume you have defined (and implemented) another interface named IAdvancedMath to allow multiplication and division. The logic behind the class is simple; however, notice the use of the ClassInterface attribute, as shown here:

```
namespace DotNetClassLib
{
    using System;
    using System.Runtime.InteropServices;

    public interface IAdvancedMath
    {
        int Multiple(int x, int y);
        int Divide(int x, int y);
    }

    [ClassInterface(ClassInterfaceType.AutoDual)]
    public class CSharpCalc: IAdvancedMath
    {
        public CSharpCalc(){}
        public int Add(int x, int y) {return x + y;}
        public int Subtract(int x, int y) {return x - y;}

        int IAdvancedMath.Multiple(int x, int y) {return x * y; }

        int IAdvancedMath.Divide(int x, int y)
        {
            if(y = = 0)
                // Intercepted as COM error object.
```

```
                throw new DivideByZeroException();
            return x / y;
        }
    }
}
```

Generating the Type Library and Registering the .NET Types

Once you compile the project, you have two approaches you can take to generate the type information and register the assembly in the system registry. Your first approach is to use the regasm.exe utility shipped with the .NET SDK. The default functionality of this tool is to enter the necessary COM registration goo into the system, to allow the COM SCM to locate and load the assembly on behalf of the COM client. However, if you specify the /tlb flag, this tool also generates the required type library, as shown here:

```
regasm DotNetClassLib.dll /tlb:simpledotnetserver.tlb
```

As an alternative, you can use regasm.exe to register the correct information in the system registry and generate the type information using a separate tool named tlbexp.exe. (See online help for command-line options.) In either case, the end result is that your .NET assembly has been configured in the system registry, and you have a COM type library that describes its contents.

SOURCE CODE *The DotNetClassLib application is included under the Chapter 12 subdirectory.*

Examining the Exported Type Information

Now that you have generated the corresponding COM type library, you can view its contents using the OLE/COM Object Viewer by simply loading the *tlb file. From there, you will find the following IDL definition for the CSharpCalc class interface (_CSharpCalc):

```
[uuid(AA165958-53F3-3129-83AE-7AE174FE923F), hidden,
dual, nonextensible,
custom({0F21F359-AB84-41E8-9A78-36D110E6D2F9}, "DotNetClassLib.CSharpCalc")]
```

```
interface _CSharpCalc : IDispatch
{
    // System.Object methods!
    [id(00000000), propget] BSTR ToString();
    [id(0x60020001)] VARIANT_BOOL Equals([in] VARIANT obj);
    [id(0x60020002)] long GetHashCode();
    [id(0x60020003)] _Type* GetType();

    // Methods of class interface.
    [id(0x60020000)]
    HRESULT Add( [in] long x,  [in] long y,  [out, retval] long* pRetVal);
    [id(0x60020001)]
    HRESULT Subtract( [in] long x, [in] long y,  [out, retval] long* pRetVal);
};
```

As specified by the ClassInterface attribute, the [default] has been configured as a [dual]. (Notice that the members have been assigned automatic DISPIDs.) As you can see, the class interface also has explicit listings for the members of System.Object. (More on this in just a bit.)

One point of interest is the fact that the class interface does *not* support the members of IAdvancedMath. The reason has to do with the fact that this interface is implemented using explicit interface implementation. (See Chapter 4.) Thus, the generated type library also contains an IDL definition of this custom interface, as shown here:

```
interface IAdvancedMath : IDispatch
{
    [id(0x60020000)] HRESULT Multiple( [in] long x,  [in] long y,
                                       [out, retval] long* pRetVal);

    [id(0x60020001)] HRESULT Divide( [in] long x, [in] long y,
                                     [out, retval] long* pRetVal);
};
```

If you had not used explicit interface inheritance, you would still have a standalone definition for IAdvancedMath. However, you would also find that the default class interface would be populated with the Multiply() and Divide() members.

The _Object Interface

The generated IDL contains an interface named _Object. This interface is the unmanaged representation of System.Object. Thus, COM types that consume

.NET types can use the core members of this supreme base class. Here is the definition:

```
[ uuid(98417C7D-32E8-3FA0-A54B-0F0B2EFBE91F), hidden, dual,
  nonextensible, custom({0F21F359-AB84-41E8-9A78-36D110E6D2F9},
 "System.Object")]
dispinterface _Object
{
    properties:
    methods:
    [id(00000000), propget] BSTR ToString();
    [id(0x60020001)] VARIANT_BOOL Equals([in] VARIANT obj);
    [id(0x60020002)] long GetHashCode();
    [id(0x60020003)] _Type* GetType();
};
```

The IDL coclass definition automatically adds support for this interface type, as shown here:

```
coclass CSharpCalc {
    interface IManagedObject;
    [default] interface _CSharpCalc;
    interface _Object;
    interface IAdvancedMath;
};
```

You will see the _Object interface in action in just a bit.

The Generated Library Statement

The final point of interest regarding the generated type information is the configuration of the library statement. In classic COM, the library statement is used to represent every IDL type that should be placed in the binary *.tlb file. This file is nothing more than a binary equivalent of the underlying IDL and is the key to COM's language independence (and plays a major role in marshaling types between boundaries). The rules used by tlbexp.exe are simple. .NET namespaces are populated based on the COM library statement.

You have already seen the definitions of the .NET types (class interface, IAdvancedMath, coclass, and so on). However, it is interesting to note that in addition to the import of the standard OLE type information, your library statement also imports type information that describes mscorlib.dll (the core .NET base class library assembly) and the runtime execution engine (mscoree.dll), as shown here:

```
[ uuid(5C202075-222E-30A4-BF50-4EFC20DDCD27), version(1.0) ]
library DotNetClassLib            // Based on namespace name.
{
    // TLib: {BED7F4EA-1A96-11D2-8F08-00A0C9A6186D}
    importlib("mscorlib.tlb");

    . . .

    importlib("mscoree.tlb");

    . . .
}
```

Viewing the Type Using the OLE/COM Object Viewer

COM supports the idea of component categories. Ultimately, a COM category is a
GUID (termed a CATID) that identifies a collection of related coclasses. The
OLE/COM Object Viewer allows you to browse the registered CATIDs on your
machine from a friendly GUI Tree View control. One new category that has been
added given the advent of the CLR is the .NET Category (Figure 12-29).

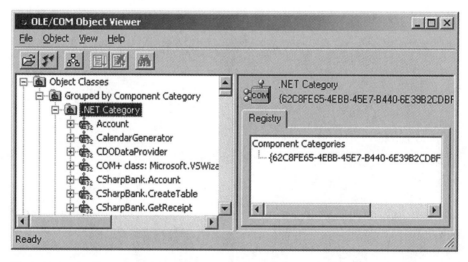

Figure 12-29. All registered assemblies gain membership to the .NET category.

If you search for the ProgID of your DotNetServerLib assembly, you will
notice that when you try to expand the related node, you are issued an error. This
is a deployment issue. Recall that when a COM client is attempting to use a .NET
assembly, the assembly must be in the same folder as the launching application
(or installed into the GAC).

To rectify the problem, simply copy the assembly into the folder where the
OLE/COM Object Viewer utility is located (or install the assembly into the GAC).

Once you have done this, you will be able to examine the interfaces supported by the proxy (Figure 12-30).

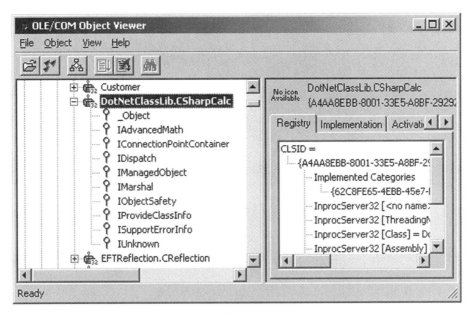

Figure 12-30. Interfaces implemented by the CCW

Examining the Registration Entries

The final details to examine before you can make use of your assembly from a COM client are the registration entries installed by the regasm.exe utility. First and foremost, you will receive the mandatory ProgID for each coclass defined in the assembly (Figure 12-31).

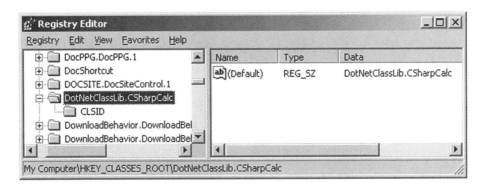

Figure 12-31. The registered ProgID

From the ProgID, you can navigate to the next item of interest, the CLSID (Figure 12-32).

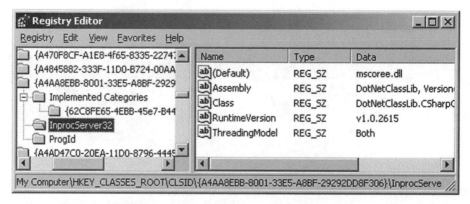

Figure 12-32. The registered CLSID

When a COM client makes an activation request to the SCM, it responds by consulting HKCR\CLSID to resolve the location of the registered server. The most important subdirectory for our current purposes is InprocServer32, which holds the path to the binary SCM will load for the client. However, you will not find a listing for the DotNetClassLib.dll (due to the fact that it is not a COM server!). Rather, you will find the path points to the CLR execution engine (Figure 12-33).

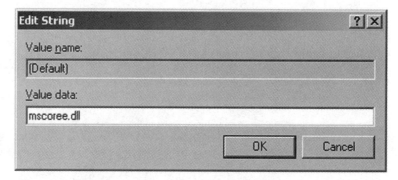

Figure 12-33. InprocServer32 points to the .NET execution engine

Also listed under the InprocServer32 subdirectory is a new entry named Assembly. This value holds the fully quantified name of the assembly (Figure 12-34).

Of course, there are other entries made by regasm.exe. For example, given that .NET types always come through as IDispatch-based interfaces, each interface is configured to use oleaut32.dll. The type information itself is registered under HKCR\TypeLib. The end result is that as far as the COM SCM is concerned,

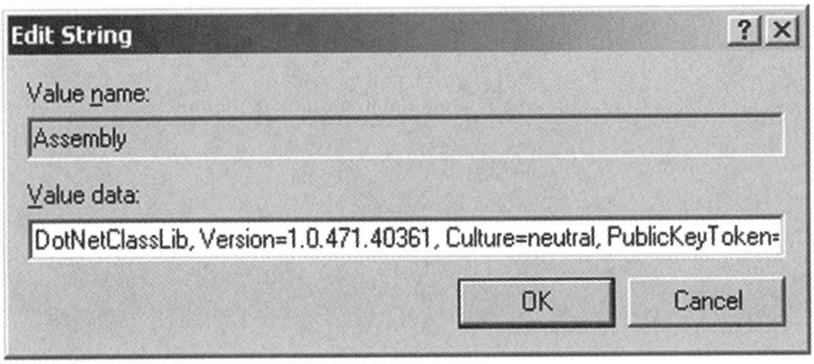

Figure 12-34. The value of the assembly entry

it can load and manipulate the contents of the .NET assembly. Under the hood, the CLR execution engine loads the assembly, builds the CCW, and takes over the show.

Building a Visual Basic 6.0 Test Client

Now that the .NET assembly has been properly configured to interact with the COM runtime, you can build some COM clients. You can create a simple VB 6.0 Standard EXE project type and set a reference to the new generated type library. Before you add any code, save the entire project to an easy-to-remember location on your hard drive. Next, make a copy of the C# assembly and place it in the same folder as the calling client (or install the assembly into the GAC).

As for the GUI front end, keep things really simple. A single Button object will be used to manipulate the .NET type. However, recall that when you created your C# calculator, you configured the Divide() method of the IAdvancedMath interface to send out a DivideByZeroException under the correct circumstances. Thus, you can trap this .NET exception as a classic COM error object. Here is the code (notice that you are also using some inherited methods defined by the _Object interface):

```
Private Sub btnDoEverything_Click()
On Error GoTo OOPS:

    ' Make .NET type and add some numbers.
    Dim o As New CSharpCalc
    MsgBox o.Add(30, 30), , "Adding"

    ' Call some members of _Object.
    MsgBox o.ToString, , "To String"
    MsgBox o.GetHashCode, , "Hash code"
```

```
        Dim t As Object
        Set t = o.GetType()
        MsgBox t, , "Type"

        ' Get new interface (and trigger exception).
        Dim i As IAdvancedMath
        Set i = o

        MsgBox i.Multiple(4, 22), , "Multiply"
        MsgBox i.Divide(20, 2), , "Divide"
        MsgBox i.Divide(20, 0)  ' Throw error.
OOPS:
MsgBox Err.Description, , "Error!"        ' Print out exception.
End Sub
```

Notice that Visual Basic 6.0 does not allow you to gain access to the _Type interface returned from _Object.GetType(), as it has been marked as a [hidden] interface. The best you can do is hold it in a generic object variable (which makes things far less exciting).

SOURCE CODE   *The VBDotNetClient application is included under the Chapter 12 subdirectory.*

.NET to COM Mapping Issues

Always keep in mind the fact that the Common Type System (CTS) defines a number of constructs that simply cannot be represented in classic COM. For example, C# class types can support any number of constructors, overloaded operators, and overloaded methods and can derive from each other using classical inheritance. None of these programming atoms can be understood by classic COM. Therefore, as you might imagine, some under-the-hood voodoo needs to occur when tlbexp.exe builds the COM type library.

To understand these issues, you need a test case. Assume a C# code library that contains one base and one derived class. The base class defines some public field data, a constructor set, and a single virtual method, as shown here:

```
[ClassInterface(ClassInterfaceType.AutoDual)]
public class BaseClass
{
    // State data.
    private int memberVar;
    public string fieldOne;
```

```
// Constructors.
public BaseClass(){}
public BaseClass(int m, string f)
{ memberVar = m; fieldOne = f;}

// Virtual method.
public virtual void VirMethod()
{ Console.WriteLine("Base VirMethod impl");}
}
```

The derived type overrides the virtual member and declares an overloaded method, as shown here:

```
[ClassInterface(ClassInterfaceType.AutoDual)]
public class DerivedClass : BaseClass
{
    // State data.
    public float fieldTwo;

    // Constructor.
    DerivedClass(int m, string f) :base(m, f) {}

    // Overridden method.
    public override void VirMethod()
    {
        Console.WriteLine("Derived VirMethod impl");
        base.VirMethod();
    }

    // Overloaded member.
    public void SomeMethod(){}
    public void SomeMethod(int x){}
    public void SomeMethod(int x, object o){}
    public void SomeMethod(int x, float f){}
}
```

Obviously you don't really care what these methods are doing. At this point, you are only interested in how the tlbexp.exe utility will map these .NET-centric types to COM primitives.

Examining the BaseClass Type Information

First, examine the coclass definition for the managed BaseClass type (load your
*tlb file into the OLE/COM Object Viewer to check things out firsthand), shown
here:

```
coclass BaseClass {
    interface IManagedObject;
    [default] interface _BaseClass;
    interface _Object;
};
```

Not too much to say here, as you already understand the concept of a class
interface and the role of the _Object interface definition. The real meat is contained in the definition of the class interface itself, as shown here:

```
interface _BaseClass : IDispatch
{
    // _Object methods. . .

    [id(0x60020004)] HRESULT VirMethod();
    [id(0x60020005), propget] HRESULT fieldOne([out, retval] BSTR* pRetVal);
    [id(0x60020005), propput] HRESULT fieldOne([in] BSTR pRetVal);
};
```

Notice that public field data is represented as a COM property. This should
make sense, given that the COM client never has an object-level reference and is
forced to work with a type on an interface-by-interface level. Now take a look at
the derived class.

Examining the DerivedClass Type Information

Because classic COM does not support classical inheritance between types, it
should be clear that tlbexp.exe is unable to model the is-a relationship between
the base and derived type. However, you get the next best thing: interface implementation, as shown here:

```
coclass DerivedClass {
    interface IManagedObject;
    [default] interface _DerivedClass;
    interface _BaseClass;
    interface _Object;
};
```

Notice that the derived type implements the class interface of its parent. In this way, the derived type can remain functionally equivalent to the base class type. The class interface of the DerivedClass is also of interest. Recall that the managed implementation of this type supported a single overloaded member. Given that COM does not support this syntactical construct, the tlbexp.exe tool hacked out the following solution:

```
interface _DerivedClass : IDispatch
{
    // _Object methods...

    // 'Inherited' methods of base type.
    [id(0x60020004)] HRESULT VirMethod();
    [id(0x60020005), propget] HRESULT fieldOne([out, retval] BSTR* pRetVal);
    [id(0x60020005), propput] HRESULT fieldOne([in] BSTR pRetVal);

    // 'Overloaded' method.
    [id(0x60020007)] HRESULT SomeMethod();
    [id(0x60020008)] HRESULT SomeMethod_2([in] long x);
    [id(0x60020009)] HRESULT SomeMethod_3([in] long x, [in] VARIANT o);
    [id(0x6002000a)] HRESULT SomeMethod_4([in] long x,  [in] single f);

    // Field data.
    [id(0x6002000b), propget] HRESULT fieldTwo([out, retval] single* pRetVal);
    [id(0x6002000b), propput] HRESULT fieldTwo([in] single pRetVal);
};
```

Here, you can see that a simple numerical suffix is used to signify overloaded methods. Although some hacking takes place when converting .NET types into COM types, the process is not all that offensive to our eyes. Other possible mappings that you may encounter include nested namespaces, abstract base classes, value types (enums and structs), and so forth. I assume you will take matters into your own hands at this point and convert some C# code into a COM type library. (One very enlightening task is to send the CarLibrary.dll assembly you developed in Chapter 6 to the tlbexp.exe utility . . . hint, hint.)

SOURCE CODE *The NetToComIssuesServer project is included under the Chapter 12 subdirectory.*

Controlling the Generated IDL (or Influencing TlbExp.exe)

As you have seen, when you use the tlbimp.exe utility to create a proxy, the generated metadata is automatically adorned with various attributes. When you build .NET types that you expect to be used by classic COM clients, you can also make direct use of these attributes (such as the ClassInterfaceAttribute type) in your managed code. Typically, this would be done only to override the default mappings produced by the tlbexp.exe utility.

To illustrate the process of gaining some control over the generated COM type information, here is a new namespace (AttribDotNetObjects) that defines a single interface (IBasicMath) as well as a single class type (Calc). Notice that you are using various attributes to control the generated GUID of the types as well as the underlying definition of the IBasicMath interface and Add() method. Also notice here that the Calc class defines two static functions that are also adorned with specific attributes (which I'll mention shortly):

```
namespace AttribDotNetObjects
{
    using System;
    using System.Runtime.InteropServices;
    using System.Windows.Forms;

    // This .NET interface has been adorned with various attributes
    // that will be used by the tlbimp.exe utility.
    [GuidAttribute("47430E06-718D-42c6-9E45-78A99673C43C"),
    InterfaceTypeAttribute(ComInterfaceType.InterfaceIsDual)]
    public interface IBasicMath
    {
        [DispId(777)] int Add(int x, int y);
    }

    [GuidAttribute("C08F4261-C0C0-46ac-87F3-EDE306984ACC")]
    public class DotNetCalc : IBasicMath
    {
        public DotNetCalc(){}

        public int Add(int x, int y) { return x + y;}

        // This attribute configures this method
        // to be called during the registration of the assembly.
        [ComRegisterFunctionAttribute]
        public static void AddExtraRegLogic(string regLoc)
```

```
        {
            // Do any extra logic when registration occurs.
            MessageBox.Show("Inside AddExtraRegLogic f(x)",
                            ".NET assembly says:");
        }


        // This attribute configures this method
        // to be called during the unregistration of the assembly.
        [ComUnregisterFunctionAttribute]
        public static void RemoveExtraRegLogic(string regLoc)
        {
            // Do any extra logic when unregistration occurs.
            MessageBox.Show("Inside RemoveExtraRegLogic f(x)",
                            ".NET assembly says:");
        }
    }
}
```

SOURCE CODE   *The AttribDotNetObjects is included under the Chapter 12 subdirectory.*

Examining the Generated COM Type Information

If you run this assembly through the tlbexp.exe utility, you will find that the IID and CLSID are the same values as listed here and also that your IBasicMath interface has been configured as a [dual]. Here is the IDL for the IBasicMath interface:

```
// In the assembly you wrote the following attributes:
// [GuidAttribute("47430E06-718D-42c6-9E45-78A99673C43C"),
// InterfaceTypeAttribute(ComInterfaceType.InterfaceIsDual)]
```

```
// Generated IDL.
[ odl, uuid(47430E06-718D-42C6-9E45-78A99673C43C), dual, oleautomation,
custom({0F21F359-AB84-41E8-9A78-36D110E6D2F9},
"AttribDotNetObjects.IBasicMath")]
interface IBasicMath : IDispatch
{
    [id(0x00000309)]      // We wrote: [DispId(777)]
    HRESULT Add( [in] long x, [in] long y, [out, retval] long* pRetVal);
};
```

If you go back to the .NET representation of the IBasicMath interface and update the InterfaceTypeAttribute() constructor logic as shown here:

```
// Make it a custom (not dual) interface.
[GuidAttribute("47430E06-718D-42c6-9E45-78A99673C43C"),
 InterfaceTypeAttribute(ComInterfaceType.InterfaceIsIUnknown)]
public interface IBasicMath
{
    int Add(int x, int y);
}
```

you will find the following IDL definition once you rerun the tlbexp.exe utility:

```
// No longer [dual]!
[
  odl,
  uuid(47430E06-718D-42C6-9E45-78A99673C43C),
  oleautomation,
  custom({0F21F359-AB84-41E8-9A78-36D110E6D2F9},
         "AttribDotNetObjects.IBasicMath")
]
interface IBasicMath : IUnknown
{
    // No dispid!
    HRESULT _stdcall Add([in] long x, [in] long y, [out, retval] long* pRetVal);
};
```

Interacting with Assembly Registration

Next, you need to examine the use of the ComRegisterFunctionAttribute and ComUnregisterFunctionAttribute types. As you know, classic COM servers export two functions (DllRegisterServer and DllUnregisterServer), which are called by various registration utilities to insert (or remove) the required COM registration information. .NET binaries do not export such functions; however, by declaring static methods with these attributes, you can simulate the same behavior. To illustrate, if you now register the .NET assembly using regasm.exe, you will see the message box shown in Figure 12-35.

I am sure you can think of more useful logic to write in the method taking the ComRegisterFunctionAttribute attribute, but I think you get the general idea. A few final points on these two registration attributes. First, the name of the method makes no difference whatsoever. However, it must take a single string

Figure 12-35. Interacting with COM registration

argument that holds the current location of the registry being updated. Also, if you configure a static method that takes the ComRegisterFunctionAttribute, you should also configure a method that takes the ComUnregisterFunctionAttribute. In this way, you can simulate a self-registering COM server.

Interacting with COM+ Services

The final topic of this chapter is an examination of how the base class libraries make it possible to build .NET types that can be configured to take advantage of the COM+ runtime layer. Before illustrating the general process, I'll begin with a high-level overview regarding the role of COM+. Again, if you require additional information, I assume you will check out an appropriate resource.

You may be aware of a product named Microsoft Transaction Server (MTS). MTS is an application server that provides the ability to host classic COM DLLs in a manner fitting for an enterprise-level, *n*-tier environment. For example, assume you have created a classic COM binary that is in charge of connecting to a data source (perhaps using ADO) to update a number of related tables. Once this COM server has been installed under MTS, it inherits a number of core traits, such as support for declarative transactions, JIT activation, and ASAP deactivation (to increase scalability) as well as a very nice role-based security model. The end result is that you can configure how the MTS-aware type should behave in a declarative manner, rather than with hard-coded logic.

Every MTS-aware COM class has an associated context object used to hold a number of specific traits about how the MTS object is being used. For example, the context may contain information about the security credentials of the caller, about this object's transactional outcome (i.e., the happy bit), and whether the object is ready to be reclaimed from memory (i.e., the done bit).

By and large, MTS COM types are created to be stateless entities. This simply refers to the fact that the object can be created and destroyed by the MTS runtime (to reclaim system resources) without affecting the connected base client (i.e., the entity making calls to the MTS runtime layer). Thus, MTS types are GUI-less and play the role of traditional business objects that perform a unit of work for the base client and quietly pass away. If the base client makes a call on the object it *thinks* it still has a reference to, the MTS runtime simply creates a new copy.

While MTS opened the door to building highly scalable and very reliable distributed systems, it had an ugly side. Specifically, the MTS and COM runtimes were not very well integrated. For example, each architecture wrote to unique parts of the registry, which could prevent the COM DLL from functioning as a typical in-proc server. Also, the object creation mechanism used by COM was not the same model used by MTS. When objects are installed under MTS, they must create other MTS-hosted COM types using a specific method supported by their associated context.

COM+ is in many respects a cleaned up version of MTS proper. Under COM+, classic COM and classic MTS have been unified into a single system to take care of the registration and object creation inconsistencies. COM+ applications still inherit the same core MTS traits (declarative transactions, role-based security, and so on) and some additional traits. Here is a quick rundown of some of these COM+ specific behaviors:

- Support for object pooling. The COM+ runtime layer can maintain a collection of active coclasses that can be quickly handed off to the base client. This trait can help decrease the time the base client needs to wait to be returned an interface reference from the COM+ type. However, this places additional memory demands on COM+ server machine(s).

- A new event model termed Loosely Coupled Events (LCE). The LCE event model of COM+ allows clients and COM+ types to communicate in a disconnected manner. This means that a given COM+ class can send out an event, without any foreknowledge of who (if anyone) is listening. Also, a COM+ client can receive events without needing to be connected to the sender.

- Support for object construction strings. Given that classic COM does not allow the client to trigger constructor logic, COM+ introduced a standard interface (IObjectConstruct) that gives the coclass the ability to be sent any startup parameters in the form of a BSTR (which may be parsed internally by the type).

- The ability to control the queuing behavior of a COM+ type in a declarative manner.Microsoft Message Queue (MSMQ) is an enterprise-level messaging service that entails lots of boilerplate grunge. COM+ introduces Queued Components (QC), which hide much of this grunge from view.

As you can see, the services provided by COM+ can greatly simplify the development of distributed applications. The only problem is that these traits were originally intended to be used by classic COM objects. To allow .NET developers to obtain these same benefits, the base class libraries provided numerous .NET equivalents defined in the System.EnterpriseServices namespace.

Understanding the System.EnterpriseServices Namespace

To build managed types that can be configured to function under the COM+ runtime, you need to equip your .NET entities with numerous attributes defined in the System.EnterpriseServices namespace. If you already have a background in classic MTS and/or COM+, you will find most of these items very familiar. Table 12-11 offers a brief rundown.

Building COM+ Aware Types

To create a .NET assembly that can be hosted by the COM+ runtime, you need to follow a cookbook approach to build the exposed types. To begin, each .NET class type will derive from System.ServicedComponent. This base class provides default implementations of the classic MTS interface, IObjectControl (Activate(), Deactivate(), and CanBePooled()). If you wish to override these default implementations, you are free to do so.

Once you add any number of additional COM+ centric attributes to your .NET types, you need to compile the assembly. However, to place this assembly under control of the COM+ runtime, you need to use a new .NET utility, regsvcs.exe. As you will see in just a bit, this tool is responsible for a number of steps beyond installing your type in the COM+ catalog.

Finally, and perhaps most importantly, you should install your assembly into the GAC (see Chapter 6). The reason is simple. Given that the dllhost.exe (the COM+ surrogate) needs to locate your assembly to host it in a given activity, it must be able to locate this binary. As I am sure you would agree, installing your assemblies in the GAC is the most logical choice for this situation.

Once you have performed each of these steps, you can build any number of base clients. Now for a complete example.

Building a COM+ Aware C# Type

To illustrate how to build a .NET type that can use the COM+ runtime, build a new managed code library named DotNetCOMPlusServer. (Remember, the

Table 12-11. Select Types of the System.EnterpriseServices Namespace

SYSTEM.ENTERPRISESERVICES TYPE	MEANING IN LIFE
ApplicationActivationAttribute	Allows you to specify if the components contained in the assembly run in the creator's process (library application) or in a system process (server application).
ApplicationIDAttribute	Specifies the assembly's application ID (as a GUID).
ApplicationQueuingAttribute InterfaceQueuingAttribute	Used to enable QC (Queued Component) support.
AutoCompleteAttribute	Marks the attributed method as AutoComplete. If the function terminates properly, SetComplete() is called automatically. If an exception is thrown during the course of the method, SetAbort() is called automatically.
ComponentAccessControlAttribute	Enables security checking on calls to a given component.
ConstructionEnabledAttribute	Enables COM+ object construction support.
ContextUtil	Is the preferred method for obtaining information about the COM+ 1.0 object context. This type defines a number of static members that allow you to obtain COM+ centric contextual information.
DescriptionAttribute	Set this description on an assembly (application), component, method, or interface.
EventClassAttribute EventTrackingEnabledAttribute	Used to interact with the COM+ LCE event model.
JustInTimeActivationAttribute	Turns JIT activation on or off.
SecurityCallContext SecurityCallers SecurityIdentifier SecurityIdentity SecurityRoleAttribute	Used to allow your .NET types to interact with the role-based security model used by MTS/COM+.
SharedPropertyGroupManager SharedPropertyGroup SharedProperty	Provide access to the MTS/COM+ shared property manager (SPM).
TransactionAttribute	Specifies the type of transaction that should be available to this object. Permissible values are members of the TransactionOption enumeration.

COM+ runtime can only host types contained in DLLs.) Configure the single class (ComPlusType) with the following COM+ properties:

- The class supports an object constructor string.

- The class is poolable, with an upper pool limit of 100 and an initial pool size of 5.

- The class supports a single method, which may succeed or fail. To inform the runtime about its current state of affairs, this method supports the AutoComplete attribute.

Here then, is the complete listing:

```
// Need to set a reference to System.EnterpriseServices.dll!
using System.EnterpriseServices;
using System.Windows.Forms;
. . .

// This object is poolable and supports a ctor string.
[ObjectPooling(true, 5, 100)]
[ConstructionEnabledAttribute(true)]
[ClassInterface(ClassInterfaceType.AutoDual)]
public class ComPlusType : ServicedComponent,
                           IObjectConstruct
{
    // Impl of IObjectConstruct.
    public void Construct(object o)
    {
        // Get IOCS interface.
        IObjectConstructString ics = (IObjectConstructString)o;
        MessageBox.Show(ics.ConstructString, "Ctor string is");
    }

    // Impl of inherited abstract members.
    public override void Activate()
    { MessageBox.Show("In activate!"); }

    public override void Deactivate()
    { MessageBox.Show("In deactivate!"); }

    public override bool CanBePooled()
    { return true; }
```

```
    public ComPlusType(){}

    // The sole method of the COM+ aware .NET type.
    public void DeleteCar(int id)
    {
        MessageBox.Show("Deleting car number " + id.ToString(),
                        "Delete car");
    }
}
```

Of course, this object is rather simplistic, since it really does not perform any enterprise-level functionality (such as deleting a car from a data store). This is just fine for your purpose, given that you are currently only studying the basics of .NET/COM+ interaction.

You must take one additional step before installing this assembly in a new COM+ application. Given that this binary will eventually end up in the GAC, you need to build a strong name for the assembly. As you recall from Chapter 6, the sn.exe utility is used for this purpose. Once you generate the resulting *.snk file, update the following assembly-level attribute in your AssemblyInfo.cs file (using your path of course!), as shown here:

```
[assembly: AssemblyKeyFile(@"D:\DotNetComPlusServer\bin\Debug\thekey.snk")]
```

Also, you may wish to freeze the auto-generated build and revision numbers, as shown here:

```
[assembly: AssemblyVersion("1.0.0.0")]
```

At this point you can compile the project.

Adding COM+ Centric Assembly-Level Attributes

At this point your .NET assembly is ready to be installed into the COM+ Catalog. As you will see, the regsvcs.exe utility generates an AppID and application name automatically. However, if you wish to specify certain aspects of the containing COM+ application, you can add the following assembly-level attributes (simply place them in your AssemblyInfo.cs file):

```
[ assembly: ApplicationActivation(ActivationOption.Server)]
[ assembly: ApplicationID("4fb2d46f-efc8-4643-bcd0-6e5bfa6a174c")]
[ assembly: ApplicationName("DotNetComPlusServer")]
[ assembly: Description("This app really kicks.")]
```

The ApplicationID attribute should be self-explanatory. This is the GUID of the resulting COM+ application. ApplicationName and Description should also make sense. The one attribute of special interest is ApplicationActivation. Recall that MTS and COM+ applications can be hosted as a library (e.g., activated in the caller's process) or server (e.g., in a new instance of dllhost.exe). Given that the default setting is to configure your COM+ application as a library, you will typically want to explicitly specify ActivationOption.Server.

Configuring the Assembly in the COM+ Catalog

To configure a .NET assembly into the COM+ catalog, you still need to generate a COM type library (tlbexp.exe) and register the type in the system registry (regasm.exe). You also need to enter the correct information into the COM+ catalog (RegDB). Rather than using these utility tools individually, the .NET SDK ships with an additional tool, regsvcs.exe. This utility simplifies the process by taking care of each necessary detail in a single step. Specifically, the following operations are performed:

- The assembly is loaded into memory.

- The assembly is registered correctly (e.g., as with regasm.exe).

- A type library is generated and registered (e.g., as with tblexp.exe).

- The type library is installed in a specified COM+ application.

- The components are configured according to the attributes specified in the type definitions.

While this tool provides a number of optional arguments, the simplest syntax is as follows:

```
regsvcs /fc DotNetComPlusServer.dll
```

Here, you are specifying the /fc (find or create) flag to instruct the regsvcs.exe tool to build a new COM+ application if one does not currently exist. Optionally, you can specify the name of the COM+ application as a command-line parameter. If you omit this item (as shown here), the name is based on the name of the binary assembly. Finally, place the assembly into the GAC (Figure 12-36).

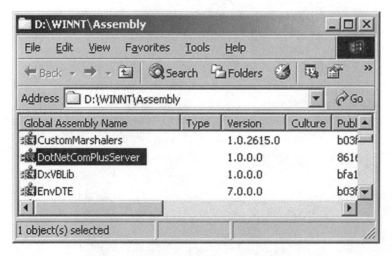

Figure 12-36. Install COM+ aware assemblies in the GAC

Examining the Component Services Explorer

Once you execute the command, you can open up with Windows 2000 Component Services Explorer and find that your .NET assembly is now recognized as a valid COM+ type (Figure 12-37).

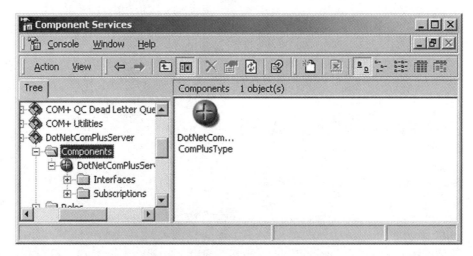

Figure 12-37. The famed COM+ aspirin icon

If you explore the various property windows for your new type, you will notice that the various attributes you specified in the C# class have been used to configure your type correctly in the COM+ catalog. For example, right-click the installed component and check out the Activation tab (Figure 12-38).

COMPlusAssembly.MyCOMPlusType Properties   ? X

General | Transactions | Security | Activation | Concurrency | Advanced

☑ Enable object pooling

Object pooling

Minimum pool size: 5

Maximum pool size: 100

Creation timeout (ms): 60000

☑ Enable object construction

Object construction

Constructor string:

☐ Enable Just In Time Activation

☐ Component supports events and statistics

☐ Must be activated in caller's context

OK   Cancel

Figure 12-38. The configured component

These settings have been configured based on the following class-level attribute set:

```
// This object is poolable and supports a ctor string.
[ObjectPooling(5, 100),
 ConstructionEnabledAttribute(true)]
public class MyCOMPlusType : ServicedComponent,
                             IObjectConstruct
{...}
```

SOURCE CODE   *The DotNetComPlusServer project is included under the Chapter 12 subdirectory.*

Summary

.NET is a wonderful thing. Nevertheless, it will be the case that managed and unmanaged code must learn to work together for some time to come. Given this fact, the .NET platform provides various techniques that allow you to blend the best of both worlds. This chapter began by examining the role of PInvoke, which allows managed code to make low-level Win32 API calls.

A major section of this chapter focused on the details of .NET types using legacy COM components. As you have seen, the process begins by generating an assembly proxy for your COM types. The RCW forwards calls to the underlying COM binary and takes care of the details of mapping COM types to their .NET equivalents.

The chapter concluded by examining how COM types can call on the services of newer .NET types. As you have seen, this requires that the creatable types in the .NET assembly are registered to point to the CLR execution engine. The final task of this chapter was to introduce you to the types defined in System.EnterpriseServices. Using this namespace, you can build types that can take advantage of the COM+ runtime layer.

CHAPTER 13

Data Access
with ADO.NET

Unless you are a video game developer by trade, you are probably interested in database manipulation. As you would expect, the .NET platform defines a number of types (in a handful of related namespaces) that allow you to interact with local and remote data stores. Collectively speaking, these namespaces are known as ADO.NET, which as you will see is a major overhaul of the classic ADO object model.

This chapter begins by examining some core types defined in the System.Data namespace—specifically DataColumn, DataRow, and DataTable. These classes allow you to define and manipulate a local in-memory table of data. Next, you spend a good deal of time learning about the centerpiece of ADO.NET, the DataSet. As you will see, the DataSet is an in-memory representation of a *collection* of interrelated tables. During this discussion, you will learn how to programmatically model table relationships, create custom views from a given table, and submit queries against your in-memory DataSet.

After discussing how to manipulate a DataSet in memory, the remainder of this chapter illustrates how to obtain a populated DataSet from a Database Management System (DBMS) such as MS SQL Server, Oracle, or MS Access. This entails an examination of .NET "managed providers" and the OleDbDataAdapter and SqlDataAdapter types.

The Need for ADO.NET

The very first thing you must understand when learning ADO.NET is that it is *not* simply the latest and greatest version of classic ADO. While it is true that there is some symmetry between the two systems (e.g., each has the concept of "connection" and "command" objects), some familiar types (e.g., the Recordset) no longer exist. Furthermore, there are a number of new ADO.NET types that have no direct equivalent under classic ADO (e.g., the DataSet).

In a nutshell, ADO.NET is a new database access technology specifically geared at facilitating the development of disconnected systems using the .NET platform. *N*-tier applications (especially Web-based applications) are fast becoming the norm, rather than the exception, for most new development efforts.

Unlike classic ADO, which was primarily designed for tightly coupled client/server systems, ADO.NET greatly extends the notion of the primitive ADO disconnected recordset with a new creature named the DataSet. This type represents a *local* copy of any number of related tables. Using the DataSet, the client is able to manipulate and update its contents while disconnected from the data source and submit the modified data back for processing using a related "data adapter."

Another major difference between classic ADO and ADO.NET is that ADO.NET has full support for XML data representation. In fact, the data obtained from a data store is internally represented, and transmitted, as XML. Given that XML is transported between layers using standard HTTP, ADO.NET is not limited by firewall constraints.

As you might be aware, classic ADO makes use of the COM marshaling protocol to move data between tiers. While this was appropriate in some situations, COM marshaling poses a number of limitations. Specifically, most firewalls are configured to reject COM RPC packets, which makes moving data between machines tricky.

Perhaps the most fundamental difference between classic ADO and ADO.NET is that ADO.NET is a managed library of code and therefore plays by all the same rules as any managed library. The types that comprise ADO.NET use the CLR memory management protocol, adhere to the same programming model, and work with many languages. Therefore, the types (and their members) are accessed in the same exact manner, regardless of which .NET-aware language you use.

ADO.NET: The Big Picture

The types that compose ADO.NET work together for a common goal: populate a DataSet, disconnect from the data store, and return the DataSet to the caller. A DataSet is a very interesting data type, given that it represents a local collection of tables (as well as the relationships between these tables) used by the client application. In some respects, this may remind you of the classic ADO disconnected recordset. The key difference is that a disconnected recordset represents a single table of data, whereas ADO.NET DataSets can model a collection of related tables. In fact, it is completely possible to have a client-side DataSet that represents the *entire* remote database.

Once you have obtained a DataSet, you can perform queries against the local tables to obtain specific subsets of information as well as navigate between related tables programmatically. As you would expect, you can add new rows to a given table in the DataSet as well as remove, filter, or update existing records. Once the modifications have been made, the client then submits the modified DataSet back to the data store for processing.

An obvious question at this point is "How do I get the DataSet?" Under the ADO.NET model, DataSets are populated through the use of a managed provider, which is a collection of classes that implement a set of core interfaces defined in the System.Data namespace; specifically IDbCommand, IDbDataAdapter, IDbConnection, and IDataReader (see Figure 13-1).

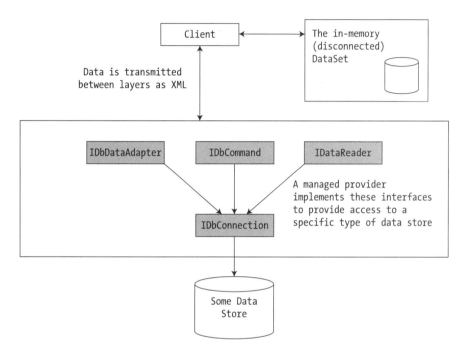

Figure 13-1. Clients interacting with managed providers

ADO.NET ships with two managed providers out of the box. First is the SQL provider, which provides highly optimized interactions with data stored in MS SQL Server (7.0 or higher). If the data you desire is not in an SQL Server data file, you can use the OleDb provider, which allows access to any data store that supports the OLE DB protocol. Be aware, however, that the OleDb provider uses native OLE DB (and therefore requires COM Interop) to enable data access.

As you might suspect, this is always a slower process than talking to a data store in its native tongue. Other vendors will soon begin shipping custom-managed providers for their proprietary data stores. Until then, the OleDb provider does the trick.

Understanding ADO.NET Namespaces

Like other aspects of the .NET universe, ADO.NET is defined in a handful of related namespaces. Table 13-1 gives a quick rundown of each.

Table 13-1. ADO.NET Namespaces

ADO.NET NAMESPACE	MEANING IN LIFE
System.Data	This is the core namespace of ADO.NET. It defines types that represent tables, rows, columns, constraints, and DataSets. This namespace does not define types to connect to a data source. Rather, it defines the types that represent the data itself.
System.Data.Common	This namespace contains the types shared between managed providers. Many of these types function as base classes to the concrete types defined by the OleDb and SqlClient managed providers.
System.Data.OleDb	This namespace defines the types that allow you to connect to an OLE DB–compliant data source, submit SQL queries, and fill DataSets. The types in this namespace have a look and feel similar (but not identical) to that of classic ADO.
System.Data.SqlClient	This namespace defines the types that constitute the SQL-managed provider. Using these types, you can talk directly to Microsoft SQL Server and avoid the level of indirection associated with the OleDb equivalents.
System.Data.SqlTypes	These types represent native data types used in Microsoft SQL Server. Although you are always free to use the corresponding CLR data types, the SqlTypes are optimized to work with SQL Server.

All of these ADO.NET namespaces are in a single assembly named System.Data.dll (Figure 13-2). Thus, like in any project referencing external assemblies, you must be sure to set a reference to this .NET binary.

Of all the ADO.NET namespaces, System.Data is the lowest common denominator. You simply cannot build ADO.NET applications without specifying this namespace in your data access applications. In addition, to establish a connection with a data store, you also need to specify a using directive for the System.Data.OleDb or System.Data.SqlClient namespaces. The exact reasons for this are discussed soon. For now, get to know some of the core types defined in System.Data.

The Types of System.Data

As mentioned, this namespace contains types that represent the data you obtain from a data store, but not the types that make the literal connection. In addition to a number of database-centric exceptions (NoNullAllowedException,

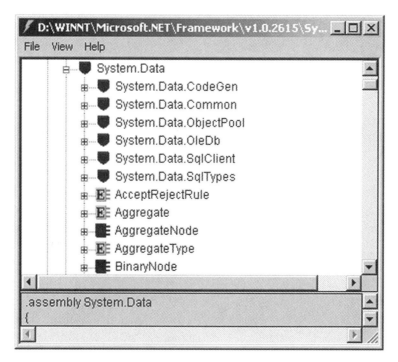

Figure 13-2. The System.Data.dll assembly

RowNotInTableException, MissingPrimaryKeyException, and the like), these types are little more than OO representations of common database primitives (tables, rows, columns, constraints, and so on). Table 13-2 lists some of the core types, grouped by related functionality.

To get the ball rolling, the first half of this chapter discusses how to manipulate these items in a disconnected mode by hand. Once you understand how to build a DataSet in the raw, you should have no problem manipulating a DataSet populated by a managed provider.

Examining the DataColumn Type

The DataColumn type represents a single column maintained by a DataTable. Collectively speaking, the set of all DataColumn types bound to a given DataTable represents the table's schema. For example, assume you have a table named Employees with three columns (EmpID, FirstName, and LastName). Programmatically, you would use three ADO.NET DataColumn objects to represent them in memory. As you will see in just a moment, the DataTable type maintains an internal collection (which is accessed using the Columns property) to maintain its DataColumn types.

Table 13-2. Types of the System.Data Namespace

SYSTEM.DATA TYPE	MEANING IN LIFE
DataColumnCollection DataColumn	DataColumnCollection is used to represent all of the columns used by a given DataTable. DataColumn represents a specific column in a DataTable.
ConstraintCollection Constraint	ConstraintCollection represents all constraints (foreign key constraints, unique constraints) assigned to a given DataTable. Constraint represents an OO wrapper around a single constraint assigned to one or more DataColumns.
DataRowCollection DataRow	These types represent a collection of rows for a DataTable (DataRowCollection) and a specific row of data in a DataTable (DataRow).
DataRowView DataView	DataRowView allows you to carve out a predefined view from an existing row. DataView represents a customized view of a DataTable that can be used for sorting, filtering, searching, editing, and navigating.
DataSet	Represents an in-memory cache of data, which may consist of multiple related DataTables.
ForeignKeyConstraint UniqueConstraint	ForeignKeyConstraint represents an action restriction enforced on a set of columns in a primary key/foreign key relationship. The UniqueConstraint type represents a restriction on a set of columns in which all values must be unique.
DataRelationCollection DataRelation	This collection represents all relationships (i.e., DataRelation types) between the tables in a DataSet.
DataTableCollection DataTable	DataTableCollection represents all the tables (i.e., DataTable types) for a particular DataSet.

If you have a background in relational database theory, you know that a given column in a data table can be assigned a set of constraints (e.g., configured as a primary key, assigned a default value, configured to contain read-only information, and so on). Also, every column in a table must map to an underlying data type (int, varchar, and so forth). For example, the Employees table's schema may demand that the EmpID column maps to an integer, while FirstName and LastName map to an array of characters. The DataColumn class has numerous properties that allow you to configure these very things. Table 13-3 provides a rundown of some core properties.

Table 13-3. Properties of the DataColumn

DATACOLUMN PROPERTY	MEANING IN LIFE
AllowDBNull	Used to indicate if a row can specify null values in this column. The default value is true.
AutoIncrement AutoIncrementSeed AutoIncrementStep	These properties are used to configure the autoincrement behavior for a given column. This can be helpful when you wish to ensure unique values in a given DataColumn (such as a primary key). By default, a DataColumn does not support autoincrementation.
Caption	Gets or sets the caption to be displayed for this column (for example, what the end user sees in a DataGrid).
ColumnMapping	This property determines how a DataColumn is represented when a DataSet is saved as an XML document using the DataSet.WriteXml() method.
ColumnName	Gets or sets the name of the column in the Columns collection (meaning how it is represented internally by the DataTable). If you do not set the ColumnName explicitly, the default values are Column with ($n+1$) numerical suffixes (i.e., Column1, Column2, Column3, and so forth).
DataType	Defines the data type (boolean, string, float, and so on) stored in the column.
DefaultValue	Gets or sets the default value assigned to this column when inserting new rows. This is used if not otherwise specified.
Expression	Gets or sets the expression used to filter rows, calculate a column's value, or create an aggregate column.
Ordinal	Gets the numerical position of the column in the Columns collection maintained by the DataTable.
ReadOnly	Determined if this column can be modified once a row has been added to the table. The default is false.
Table	Gets the DataTable that contains this DataColumn.
Unique	Gets or sets a value indicating whether the values in each row of the column must be unique or if repeating values are permissible. If a column is assigned a primary key constraint, the Unique property should be set to true.

Building a DataColumn

To illustrate the basic use of the DataColumn, assume you need to model a column named FirstName, which internally maps to an array of characters.

Furthermore, assume this column (for whatever reason) must be read only. Programmatically, you can write the following logic:

```
protected void btnColumn_Click (object sender, System.EventArgs e)
{
    // Build the FirstName column.
    DataColumn colFName = new DataColumn();

    // Set a bunch of values.
    colFName.DataType = Type.GetType("System.String");
    colFName.ReadOnly = true;
    colFName.Caption = "First Name";
    colFName.ColumnName = "FirstName";

    // Get a bunch of values.
    string temp =    "Column type: " + colFName.DataType + "\n" +
                     "Read only? " + colFName.ReadOnly + "\n" +
                     "Caption: " + colFName.Caption + "\n" +
                     "Column Name: " + colFName.ColumnName + "\n" +
                     "Nulls allowed? " + colFName.AllowDBNull;

    MessageBox.Show(temp, "Column properties");
}
```

This gives the result shown in Figure 13-3.

Figure 13-3. Select properties of the DataColumn

Given that the DataColumn provides several overloaded constructors, you can specify a number of properties directly at the time of creation, as shown here:

```
// Build the FirstName column (take two).
DataColumn colFName = new DataColumn("FirstName",
                                     Type.GetType("System.String"));
colFName.ReadOnly = true;
colFName.Caption = "First Name";
```

In addition to the properties already examined, the DataColumn does have a small set of methods, which I assume you will check out on your own.

Adding a DataColumn to a DataTable

The DataColumn type does not typically exist as a stand-alone entity, but is instead inserted in a DataTable. To do so, begin by creating a new DataTable type (fully detailed later in the chapter). Next insert each DataColumn in the DataTable.DataColumnCollection type using the Columns property. Here is an example:

```
// Build the FirstName column.
DataColumn myColumn = new DataColumn();

// Create a new DataTable.
DataTable myTable = new DataTable("MyTable");

// The Columns property returns a DataColumnCollection type.
// Use the Add() method to insert the column in the table.
myTable.Columns.Add(myColumn);
```

Configuring a DataColumn to Function as a Primary Key

One common rule of database development is that a table should have at least one column that functions as the primary key. A primary key constraint is used to uniquely identify a record (row) in a given table. In keeping with the current Employees example, assume you now wish to build a new DataColumn type to represent the EmpID field. This column will be the primary key of the table and thus should have the AllowDBNull and Unique properties configured as shown here:

```
// This column is functioning as a primary key.
DataColumn colEmpID = new DataColumn(EmpID, Type.GetType("System.Int32"));
colEmpID.Caption = "Employee ID";
colEmpID.AllowDBNull = false;
colEmpID.Unique = true;
```

Once the DataColumn has been correctly set up to function as a primary key, the next step is to assign this DataColumn to the DataTable's PrimaryKey property. You will see how to do in just a bit during the discussion of the DataTable, so put this on the back burner for the time being.

Enabling Autoincrementing Fields

One aspect of the DataColumn you may choose to configure is its ability to autoincrement. Simply put, autoincrementing columns are used to ensure that when a new row is added to a given table, the value of this column is assigned automatically, based on the current step of the incrementation. This can be helpful when you wish to ensure that a column has no repeating values (such as a primary key). This behavior is controlled using the AutoIncrement, AutoIncrementSeed, and AutoIncrementStep properties.

To illustrate, build a DataColumn that supports autoincrementation. The seed value is used to mark the starting value of the column, where the step value identifies the number to add to the seed when incrementing, as shown here:

```
// Create a data column.
DataColumn myColumn = new DataColumn();
myColumn.ColumnName = "Foo";
myColumn.DataType = System.Type.GetType("System.Int32");

// Set the autoincrement behavior.
myColumn.AutoIncrement = true;
myColumn.AutoIncrementSeed = 500;
myColumn.AutoIncrementStep = 12;
```

Here, the Foo column has been configured to ensure that as rows are added to the respective table, the value in this field is incremented by 12. Because the seed has been set at 500, the first five values should be 500, 512, 524, 536, and 548.

To prove the point, insert this DataColumn in a DataTable. Then add a number of new rows to the table, which of course automatically bumps the value in the Foo column, as shown here:

```
protected void btnAutoCol_Click (object sender, System.EventArgs e)
{
    // Make a data column that maps to an int.
    DataColumn myColumn = new DataColumn();
    myColumn.ColumnName = "Foo";
    myColumn.DataType = System.Type.GetType("System.Int32");
```

```
// Set the autoincrement behavior.
myColumn.AutoIncrement = true;
myColumn.AutoIncrementSeed = 500;
myColumn.AutoIncrementStep = 12;

// Add this column to a new DataTable.
DataTable myTable = new DataTable("MyTable");
myTable.Columns.Add(myColumn);

// Add 20 new rows.
DataRow r;
for(int i =0; i < 20; i++)
{
    r = myTable.NewRow();
    myTable.Rows.Add(r);
}

// Now list the value in each row.
string temp = "";
DataRowCollection rows = myTable.Rows;
for(int i = 0;i < myTable.Rows.Count; i++)
{
    DataRow currRow = rows[i];
    temp += currRow["Foo"] + " ";
}
MessageBox.Show(temp, "These values brought ala auto-increment");
}
```

If you run the application (and click the corresponding Button), we see the message shown in Figure 13-4.

Figure 13-4. An autoincremented column

Configuring a Column's XML Representation

While many of the remaining DataColumn properties are rather self-explanatory (provided you are comfortable with database terminology), I would like to discuss the ColumnMapping property. The DataColumn.ColumnMapping property is used to configure how this column should be represented in XML, if the owning DataSet dumps its contents using the WriteXml() method. The value of the ColumnMapping property is configured using the MappingType enumeration (Table 13-4).

Table 13-4. Values of the MappingType enumeration

MAPPINGTYPE ENUMERATION VALUE	MEANING IN LIFE
Attribute	The column is mapped to an XML attribute.
Element	The column is mapped to an XML element (the default).
Hidden	The column is mapped to an internal structure.
TableElement	The column is mapped to a table value.
Text	The column is mapped to text.

The default value of the ColumnMapping property is MappingType.Element. Assume that you have instructed the owning DataSet to write its contents to a new file stream as XML. Using this default setting, the EmpID column would appear as shown here:

```
<Employee>
      <EmpID>500</EmpID>
</Employee>
```

However, if the DataColumn's ColumnMapping property is set to MappingType.Attribute, you see the following XML representation:

```
<Employee EmpID = "500"/>
```

This chapter examines the ADO.NET/XML integration in greater detail when discussing the DataSet. Nevertheless, at this point, you understand how to create a stand-alone DataColumn type. Now for an examination of the basic behavior of the DataRow.

SOURCE CODE   *The DataColumn application is included under the Chapter 13 subdirectory.*

Examining the DataRow Type

As you have seen, a collection of DataColumn objects represents the schema of a table. A DataTable maintains its columns using the internal DataColumnCollection type. In contrast, a collection of DataRow types represents the actual data in the table. Thus, if you have 20 listings in a table named Employees, you can represent these entries using 20 DataRow types. Using the members of the DataRow class, you are able to insert, remove, evaluate, and manipulate the values in the table.

Working with a DataRow is a bit different from working with a DataColumn, because you do not create a direct instance of this type, but rather obtain a reference from a given DataTable. For example, assume you wish to insert a new row in the Employees table. The DataTable.NewRow() method allows you to obtain the next slot in the table, at which point you can fill each column with new data, as shown here:

```
// Build a new Table.
DataTable empTable = new DataTable("Employees");

// ...Add EmpID, FirstName and LastName columns to table...

// Build a new Employee record.
DataRow row = empTable.NewRow();
row["EmpID"] = 102;
row["FirstName"] = "Joe";
row["LastName"] = "Blow";

// Add it to the Table's DataRowCollection.
empTable.Rows.Add(row);
```

Notice how the DataRow class defines an indexer that can be used to gain access to a given DataColumn by numerical position as well as column name. Also notice that the DataTable maintains another internal collection (DataRowCollection) to hold each row of data. The DataRow type defines the following core members, grouped by related functionality in Table 13-5.

Understanding the DataRow.RowState Property

Most of the methods of the DataRow class only make sense in the context of an owning DataTable. You will see the process of inserting, removing, and updating rows in just a moment; first, however, you should get to know the RowState property. This property is useful when you need to programmatically identify the set of all rows in a table that have changed, have been newly inserted, and so forth. This property may be assigned any value from the DataRowState enumeration (Table 13-6).

Table 13-5. *Members of the DataRow*

DATAROW MEMBER	MEANING IN LIFE
AcceptChanges() RejectChanges()	Commits or rejects all the changes made to this row since the last time AcceptChanges was called.
BeginEdit() EndEdit() CancelEdit()	Begins, ends, or cancels an edit operation on a DataRow object.
Delete()	Marks a row to be removed when the AcceptChanges() method is called.
HasErrors GetColumnsInError() GetColumnError() ClearErrors() RowError	The HasErrors property returns a boolean value indicating if there are errors in a column's collection. If so, the GetColumnsInError() method can be used to obtain the offending members, GetColumnError() can be used to obtain the error description, while the ClearErrors() method removes each error listing for the row. The RowError property allows you to configure a textual description of the error for a given row.
IsNull()	Gets a value indicating whether the specified column contains a null value.
ItemArray	Gets or sets all of the values for this row using an array of objects.
RowState	Used to pinpoint the current state of the DataRow using values of the RowState enumeration.
Table	Use this property to obtain a reference to the DataTable containing this DataRow.

Table 13-6. *Values of the DataRowState Enumeration*

DATAROWSTATE ENUMERATION VALUE	MEANING IN LIFE
Deleted	The row was deleted using the Delete method of the DataRow.
Detached	The row has been created but is not part of any DataRowCollection. A DataRow is in this state immediately after it has been created and before it is added to a collection, or if it has been removed from a collection.
Modified	The row has been modified, and AcceptChanges() has not been called.
New	The row has been added to a DataRowCollection, and AcceptChanges() has not been called.
Unchanged	The row has not changed since AcceptChanges() was last called.

To illustrate the various states a DataRow may have, the following class documents the changes to the RowState property as a new DataRow is created, inserted in, and removed from a DataTable:

```
public class DRState
{
    public static void Main()
    {
        // Build a single-column DataTable.
        DataTable myTable = new DataTable("Employees");
        DataColumn colID = new DataColumn("EmpID",
                            Type.GetType("System.Int32"));
        myTable.Columns.Add(colID);

        // The DataRow.
        DataRow myRow;

        // Create a new (detached) DataRow.
        myRow = myTable.NewRow();
        Console.WriteLine(myRow.RowState.ToString());

        // Now add it to table.
        myTable.Rows.Add(myRow);
        Console.WriteLine(myRow.RowState.ToString());

        // Trigger an 'accept.
        myTable.AcceptChanges();
        Console.WriteLinemyRow.RowState.ToString());

        // Modify it.
        myRow["EmpID"] = 100;
        Console.WriteLine(myRow.RowState.ToString());

        // Now delete it.
        myRow.Delete();
        Console.WriteLine(myRow.RowState.ToString());
        myRow.AcceptChanges();
    }
}
```

The output should be clear (Figure 13-5).

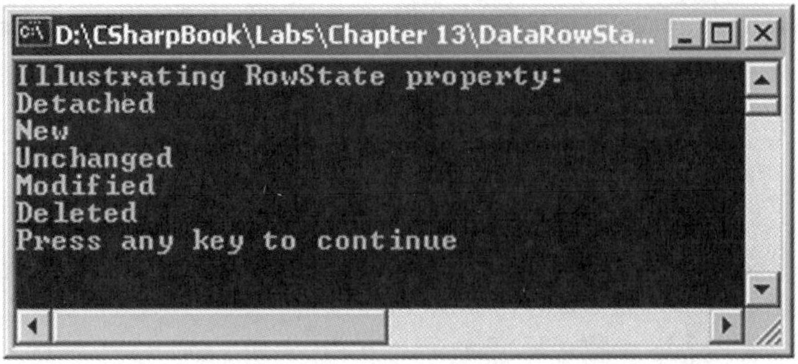

Figure 13-5. Changes in row states

As you can see, the ADO.NET DataRow is smart enough to remember its current state of affairs. Given this, the owning DataTable is able to identify which rows have been modified. This is a key feature of the DataSet, given that when it comes time to send updated information to the data store, only the modified values are submitted. Clearly this behavior helps optimize trips between the layers of your system.

The ItemArray Property

Another helpful member of the DataRow is the ItemArray property. This method returns a complete snapshot of the current row as an array of System.Object types. Also, you can insert a new row using the ItemArray property, rather than listing each DataColumn explicitly. Assume the current table now has two DataColumns (EmpID and FirstName). The following logic adds some new rows by assigning an array of objects to the ItemArray property and then promptly prints the results (see Figure 13-6):

```
// Declare the array variable.
object [] myVals = new object[2];
DataRow dr;

// Create some new rows and add to DataRowCollection.
for(int i = 0; i < 5; i++)
{
    myVals[0] = i;
    myVals[1]= "Name " + i;
    dr = myTable.NewRow();
    dr.ItemArray = myVals;
    myTable.Rows.Add(dr);
}
```

```
// Now print each value.
foreach(DataRow r in myTable.Rows)
{
    foreach(DataColumn c in myTable.Columns)
    {
        Console.WriteLine(r[c]);
    }
}
```

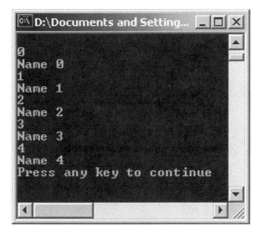

Figure 13-6. Using the ItemArray property

SOURCE CODE   *The DataRowState is included under the Chapter 13 subdirectory.*

Details of the DataTable

The DataTable is an in-memory representation of a tabular block of data. While you can manually compose a DataTable programmatically, you will more commonly obtain a DataTable dynamically using a DataSet and the types defined in the System.Data.OleDb or System.Data.SqlClient namespaces. Table 13-7 describes some core properties of the DataTable.

To help visualize the key components of a DataTable, consider Figure 13-7. Be aware that this is *not* a traditional class hierarchy that illustrates the is-a relations between these types (e.g., the DataRow *does not* derive from DataRowCollection). Rather, this diagram points out the logical has-a relationships between the DataTable's core items (e.g., the DataRowCollection has a number of DataRow types).

Table 13-7. Properties of the DataTable

DATATABLE PROPERTY	MEANING IN LIFE
CaseSensitive	Indicates whether string comparisons in the table are case sensitive (or not). The default value is false.
ChildRelations	Returns the collection of child relations (DataRelationCollection) for this DataTable (if any).
Columns	Returns the collection of columns that belong to this table.
Constraints	Gets the collection of constraints maintained by the table (ConstraintCollection).
DataSet	Gets the DataSet that contains this table (if any).
DefaultView	Gets a customized view of the table that may include a filtered view or a cursor position.
MinimumCapacity	Gets or sets the initial number of rows in this table. (The default is 25.)
ParentRelations	Gets the collection of parent relations for this DataTable.
PrimaryKey	Gets or sets an array of columns that function as primary keys for the data table.
Rows	Returns the collection of rows that belong to this table.
TableName	Gets or sets the name of the table. This same property may also be specified as a constructor parameter.

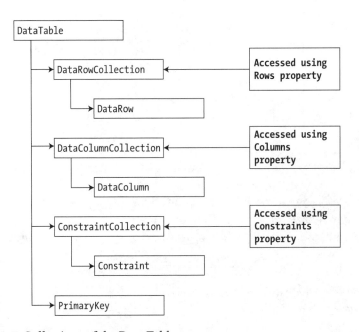

Figure 13-7. Collections of the DataTable

Building a Complete DataTable

Now that you have been exposed to the basics, let's see a complete example of creating and manipulating an in-memory data table. Assume you are interested in building a DataTable representing the current inventory in a database named Cars. The Inventory table will contain four columns: CarID, Make, Color, and PetName. Also, the CarID column will function as the table's primary key (PK) and support autoincrementation. The PetName column will allow null values. (Sadly, not everyone loves their automobiles as much as we might!) Figure 13-8 shows the overall schema.

CarID (PK)	Make	Color	PetName
0	BMW	Green	Chucky
1	Yugo	White	Tiny
2	Jeep	Tan	(null)
3	Caravan	Pink	Pain Inducer

Figure 13-8. The Inventory DataTable

The process begins by creating a new DataTable type. When you do so, you specify the friendly name of the table as a constructor parameter. This friendly name can be used to reference this table from the containing DataSet, as shown here:

```
// Create a new DataTable.
DataTable inventoryTable = new DataTable("Inventory");
```

The next step is to programmatically insert each column using the Add() method of the DataColumnCollection (accessed using the DataTable.Columns property). The following logic adds the CarID, Make, Color, and PetName columns to the current DataTable (recall that the underlying data type of each column is set using the DataType property):

```
// DataColumn var.
DataColumn myDataColumn;

// Create CarID column and add to table.
myDataColumn = new DataColumn();
myDataColumn.DataType = Type.GetType("System.Int32");
myDataColumn.ColumnName = "CarID";
myDataColumn.ReadOnly = true;
myDataColumn.AllowDBNull = false;
myDataColumn.Unique = true;
```

```
// Set the autoincrement behavior.
myDataColumn.AutoIncrement = true;
myDataColumn.AutoIncrementSeed = 1000;
myDataColumn.AutoIncrementStep = 10;
inventoryTable.Columns.Add(myDataColumn);

// Create Make column and add to table.
myDataColumn = new DataColumn();
myDataColumn.DataType = Type.GetType("System.String");
myDataColumn.ColumnName = "Make";
inventoryTable.Columns.Add(myDataColumn);

// Create Color column and add to table.
myDataColumn = new DataColumn();
myDataColumn.DataType = Type.GetType("System.String");
myDataColumn.ColumnName = "Color";
inventoryTable.Columns.Add(myDataColumn);

// Create PetName column and add to table.
myDataColumn = new DataColumn();
myDataColumn.DataType = Type.GetType("System.String");
myDataColumn.ColumnName = "PetName";
myDataColumn.AllowDBNull = true;
inventoryTable.Columns.Add(myDataColumn);
```

Before you add the rows, take the time to set the table's primary key. To do so, set the DataTable.PrimaryKey property to whichever column necessary. Because more than a single column can function as a table's primary key, be aware that the PrimaryKey property requires an array of DataColumn types. For the Inventory table, assume the CarID column is the only aspect of the primary key, as shown here:

```
// Make the ID column the primary key column.
DataColumn[] PK = new DataColumn[1];
PK[0] = inventoryTable.Columns["CarID"];
inventoryTable.PrimaryKey = PK;
```

Last but not least, you need to add valid data to the table. Assuming you have an appropriate ArrayList maintaining Car types, you can fill the table as shown here:

```
// Iterate over the array list to make rows (remember, the ID is
// autoincremented).
foreach(Car c in arTheCars)
```

```
{
    DataRow newRow;
    newRow = inventoryTable.NewRow();
    newRow["Make"] = c.make;
    newRow["Color"] = c.color;
    newRow["PetName"] = c.petName;
    inventoryTable.Rows.Add(newRow);
}
```

To display your new local in-memory table, assume you have a Windows Forms application with a main Form displaying a DataGrid. As you saw in Chapter 11, the DataSource property is used to bind a DataTable to the GUI. The output is shown in Figure 13-9.

Figure 13-9. Binding the DataTable to a DataGrid

Here, you added rows by specifying the string name of the column to modify. However, you may also specify the numerical index of the column, which can be very helpful when you need to iterate over each column. Thus, the previous code could be updated as shown here (and still achieve the same end result):

```
foreach(Car c in arTheCars)
{
    // Specify columns by index.
    DataRow newRow;
    newRow = inventoryTable.NewRow();
    newRow[1] = c.make;
    newRow[2] = c.color;
    newRow[3] = c.petName;
    inventoryTable.Rows.Add(newRow);
}
```

Manipulating a DataTable: Deleting Rows

What if you wish to remove a row from a data table? One approach is to call the Delete() method of the DataRowCollection type. Simply specify the index (or DataRow) representing the row to remove. Assume you update your GUI as shown in Figure 13-10.

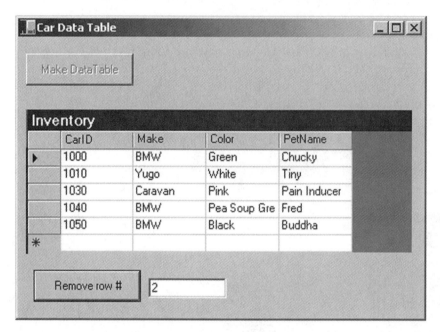

Figure 13-10. Removing rows from a DataTable

If you look at the previous screen shot, you will notice that you specified the second row in the DataTable, and therefore CarID 1020 has been blown away. The following logic behind the new Button's Click event handler removes the specified row from your in-memory DataTable:

```
// Remove this row from the DataRowCollection.
protected void btnRemoveRow_Click (object sender, System.EventArgs e)
{
    try
    {
        inventoryTable.Rows[(int.Parse(txtRemove.Text))].Delete();
        inventoryTable.AcceptChanges();
    }
    catch(Exception ex)
```

```
    {
        MessageBox.Show(ex.Message);
    }
}
```

The Delete() method might have been better named MarkedAsDeletable()
given that the row is typically not removed until the DataTable.AcceptChanges()
method has been called. In effect, the Delete() method simply sets a flag that says
"I am ready to die when my table tells me." Also understand that if a row has
been marked for deletion, a DataTable may reject those changes before calling
AcceptChanges(), as shown here:

```
// Mark a row as deleted, but reject the changes.
protected void btnRemoveRow_Click (object sender, System.EventArgs e)
{
    inventoryTable.Rows[txtRemove.Text.ToInt32()].Delete();

    // Do more work. . .

    inventoryTable.RejectChanges();      // Restore RowState.
}
```

Manipulating a DataTable: Applying Filters and Sort Orders

You may wish to see a small subset of a DataTable's data, as specified by some
sort of filtering criteria. For example, what if you wish to only see a certain make
of automobile from the in-memory Inventory table? The Select() method of the
DataTable class provides this very functionality. Update your GUI once again, this
time allowing users to specify a string that represents the make of the automobile
they are interested in viewing (Figure 13-11).

The Select() method has been overloaded a number of times to provide different selection semantics. At its most basic level, the parameter sent to Select() is
a string that contains some conditional operation. To begin, observe the following logic for the Click event handler of your new Button:

```
protected void btnGetMakes_Click (object sender, System.EventArgs e)
{
    // Build a filter based on user input.
    string filterStr = "Make='" + txtMake.Text + "'";

    // Find all rows matching the filter.
    DataRow[] makes = inventoryTable.Select(filterStr);
```

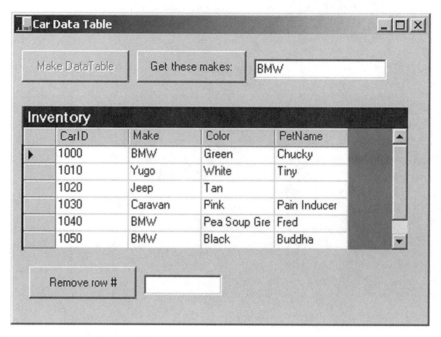

Figure 13-11. Specifying a filter

```
// Show what we got!
if(makes.Length = = 0)
    MessageBox.Show("Sorry, no cars...", "Selection error!");
else
{
    string strMake = null;
    for(int i = 0; i < makes.Length; i++)
    {
        DataRow temp = makes[i];
        strMake += temp["PetName"].ToString() + "\n";

    }
    MessageBox.Show(strMake, txtMake.Text + " type(s):");
}
}
```

Here, you first build a simple filter criteria based on the value in the associated TextBox. If you specify BMW, your filter is Make = 'BMW'. When you send this filter to the Select() method, you get back an array of DataRow types, which represent each row that matches the filter criteria (Figure 13-12).

Figure 13-12. Filtered data

A filter string can be composed of any number of relational operators. For example, what if you wanted to find all cars with an ID greater than 1030? You could write the following (see Figure 13-13 for output):

```
// Now show the pet names of all cars with ID greater than 1030.
DataRow[] properIDs;
string newFilterStr = "ID > '1030'";
properIDs = inventoryTable.Select(newFilterStr);
string strIDs = null;

for(int i = 0; i < properIDs.Length; i++)
{
    DataRow temp = properIDs[i];
    strIDs += temp["PetName"].ToString()
            + " is ID " + temp["ID"] + "\n";
}
MessageBox.Show(strIDs, "Pet names of cars where ID > 1030");
```

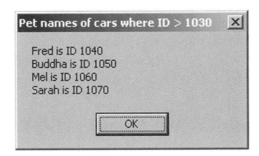

Figure 13-13. Specifying a range of data

Filtering logic is modeled after standard SQL syntax. To prove the point, assume you wish to obtain the results of the previous Select() command alphabetically based on pet name. In terms of SQL, this translates into a sort based on the PetName column. Luckily the Select() method has been overloaded to send in a sort criterion, as shown here:

```
makes = inventoryTable.Select(filterStr, "PetName");
```

This returns something like what is shown in Figure 13-14.

Figure 13-14. Ordered data

If you want the results in descending order, call Select(), as shown here:

```
// Return results in descending order.
makes = inventoryTable.Select(filterStr, "PetName DESC");
```

In general, the sort string contains the column name followed by "ASC" (ascending, which is the default) or "DESC" (descending). If need be, multiple columns can be separated by commas.

Manipulating a DataTable: Updating Rows

The final aspect of the DataTable you should be aware of is the process of updating an exiting row with new values. One approach is to first obtain the row(s) that match a given filter criterion using the Select() method. Once you have the DataRow(s) in question, modify them accordingly. For example, assume you have a new Button that (when clicked) searches the DataTable for all rows where Make is equal to BMW. Once you identify these items, you change the Make from 'BMW' to 'Colt':

```
// Find the rows you want to edit with a filter.
protected void btnChange_Click (object sender, System.EventArgs e)
{
    // Build a filter.
    string filterStr = "Make='BMW'";
    string strMake = null;
```

```
// Find all rows matching the filter.
DataRow[] makes = inventoryTable.Select(filterStr);

// Change all Beemers to Colts!
for(int i = 0; i < makes.Length; i++)
{
    DataRow temp = makes[i];
    strMake += temp["Make"] = "Colt";
    makes[i] = temp;
}
}
```

The DataRow class also provides the BeginEdit(), EndEdit(), and CancelEdit() methods, which allow you to edit the content of a row while temporarily suspending any associated validation rules. In the previous logic, each row was validated with each assignment. (Also, if you capture any events from the DataRow, they fire with each modification.) When you call BeginEdit() on a given DataRow, the row is placed in edit mode. At this point you can make your changes as necessary and call either EndEdit() to commit these changes or CancelEdit() to roll back the changes to the original version. For example:

```
// Assume you have obtained a row to edit.
// Now place this row in edit mode'.
rowToUpdate.BeginEdit();

// Send the row to a helper function, which returns a Boolean.
if( ChangeValuesForThisRow( rowToUpdate) )
{
    rowToUpdate.EndEdit();      // OK!
}
else
{
    rowToUpdate.CancelEdit();  // Forget it.
}
```

Although you are free to manually call these methods on a given DataRow, these members are automatically called when you edit a DataGrid widget that has been bound to a DataTable. For example, when you select a row to edit from a DataGrid, that row is automatically placed in edit mode. When you shift focus to a new row, EndEdit() is called automatically. To test this behavior, assume you have manually updated each car to be of a given Make using the DataGrid (Figure 13-15).

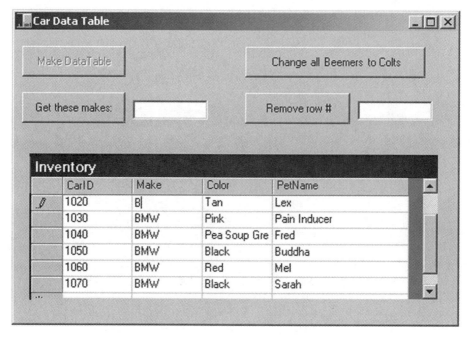

Figure 13-15. Editing rows in a DataGrid

If you now request all BMWs, the message box correctly returns *all* rows, as the underlying DataTable associated to the DataGrid has been automatically updated (Figure 13-16).

Figure 13-16. The Inventory DataTable

Understanding the DataView Type

In database nomenclature, a *view object* is a stylized representation of a table. For example, using Microsoft SQL Server, you could create a view for your current

Inventory table that returns a new table only containing automobiles of a given color. In ADO.NET, the DataView type allows you to programmatically extract a subset of data from the DataTable.

One great advantage of holding multiple views of the same table is that you can bind these views to various GUI widgets (such as the DataGrid). For example, one DataGrid might be bound to a DataView showing all autos in the Inventory, while another may be configured to display only green automobiles. On a related note, the DataTable type provides the DefaultView property that returns the default DataView for the table.

Here is an example. Your goal is to update the user interface of the current Windows Forms application to support two additional DataGrid types. One of these grids only shows the rows from the Inventory that match the filter Make='Colt'. The other grid only shows red automobiles (i.e., Color='Red'). Figure 13-17 shows the GUI update.

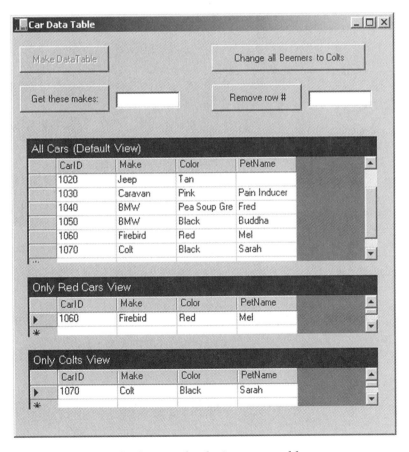

Figure 13-17. Creating multiple views for the Inventory table

To begin, you need to create two member variables of type DataView:

```
public class mainForm : System.Windows.Forms.Form
{
    // Views of the DataTable.
    DataView redCarsView;        // I only show red cars.
    DataView coltsView;          // I only show Colts.
...
}
```

Next, assume you have a new helper function named CreateViews(), which is called directly after the DataTable has been fully constructed, as shown here:

```
protected void btnMakeDataTable_Click (object sender, System.EventArgs e)
{
    // Make the data table.
    MakeTable();

    // Make views.
    CreateViews();
    ...
}
```

Here is the implementation of this new helper function. Notice that the constructor of each DataView has been passed the DataTable that will be used to build the custom set of data rows:

```
private void CreateViews()
{
    // Set the table that is used to construct these views.
    redCarsView = new DataView(inventoryTable);
    coltsView = new DataView(inventoryTable);

    // Now configure the views using a filter.
    redCarsView.RowFilter = "Color = 'red'";
    coltsView.RowFilter = "Make = 'colt'";

    // Bind to grids.
    RedCarViewGrid.DataSource = redCarsView;
    ColtsViewGrid.DataSource = coltsView;
}
```

As you can see, the DataView class supports a property named RowFilter, which contains the string representing the filtering criteria used to extract matching rows. Once you have your view established, set the grid's DataSource property accordingly. That's it! Because DataGrids are smart enough to detect changes to their underlying data source, if you click the Make Beemers Colts button, the ColtsViewGrid is updated automatically.

In addition to the RowFilter property, Table 13-8 describes some additional members of the DataView class.

Table 13-8. Members of the DataView Type

DATAVIEW MEMBER	MEANING IN LIFE
AddNew()	Adds a new row to the DataView.
AllowDelete AllowEdit AllowNew	Configure whether the DataView allows deleting, inserting, or updating of its rows.
Delete()	Deletes a row at the specified index.
RowFilter	Gets or sets the expression used to filter which rows are viewed in the DataView.
Sort	Gets or sets the sort column or columns and sort order for the table.
Table	Gets or sets the source DataTable.

SOURCE CODE   *The complete CarDataTable project is included under the Chapter 13 subdirectory.*

Understanding the Role of the DataSet

You have been examining how to build a DataTable to represent a single table of data held in memory. Although DataTables can be used as stand-alone entities, they are more typically contained in a DataSet. In fact, most data access types supplied by ADO.NET only return a populated DataSet, not an individual DataTable.

Simply put, a DataSet is an in-memory representation of any number of tables (which may be just a single DataTable) as well as any (optional) relationships between these tables and any (optional) constraints. To gain a better understanding of the relationship among these core types, consider the logical hierarchy shown in Figure 13-18.

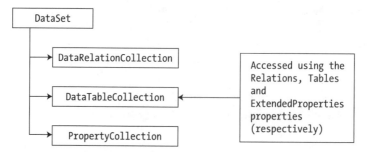

Figure 13-18. Collections of the DataSet

The Tables property of the DataSet allows you to access the DataTableCollection that contains the individual DataTables. Another important collection used by the DataSet is the DataRelationCollection. Given that a DataSet is a disconnected version of a database schema, it can programmatically represent the parent/child relationships between its tables.

For example, a relation can be created between two tables to model a foreign key constraint using the DataRelation type. This object can then be added to the DataRelationCollection through the Relations property. At this point, you can navigate between the connected tables as you search for data. You will see how this is done a bit later in the chapter.

The ExtendedProperties property provides access to the PropertyCollection type, which allows you to associate any extra information to the DataSet as name/value pairs. This information can literally be anything at all, even if it has no bearing on the data itself. For example, you can associate your company's name to a DataSet, which can then function as in-memory metadata, as shown here:

```
// Make a DataSet and add some metadata.
DataSet ds = new DataSet("MyDataSet");
ds.ExtendedProperties.Add("CompanyName", "Intertech, Inc");

// Print out the metadata.
Console.WriteLine(ds.ExtendedProperties["CompanyName"].ToString());
```

Other examples of extended properties might include an internal password that must be supplied to access the contents of the DataSet, a number representing a data refresh rate, and so forth. Be aware that the DataTable itself also supports the ExtendedProperties property.

Members of the DataSet

Before exploring too many other programmatic details, take a look at the public interface of the DataSet. The properties defined by the DataSet are centered on providing access to the internal collections, producing XML data representations and providing detailed error information. Table 13-9 describes some core properties of interest.

Table 13-9. Properties of the Mighty DataSet

DATASET PROPERTY	MEANING IN LIFE
CaseSensitive	Indicates whether string comparisons in DataTable objects are case-sensitive (or not).
DataSetName	Gets or sets the name of this DataSet. Typically this value is established as a constructor parameter.
DefaultViewManager	Establishes a custom view of the data in the DataSet.
EnforceConstraints	Gets or sets a value indicating whether constraint rules are followed when attempting any update operation.
HasErrors	Gets a value indicating whether there are errors in any of the rows in any of the tables of this DataSet.
Relations	Get the collection of relations that link tables and allow navigation from parent tables to child tables.
Tables	Provides access to the collection of tables maintained by the DataSet.

The methods of the DataSet mimic some of the functionality provided by the aforementioned properties. In addition to interacting with XML streams, other methods exist to allow you to copy the contents of your DataSet, as well as establish the beginning and ending points of a batch of updates. Table 13-10 describes some core methods.

Now that you have a better understanding of the role of the DataSet (and some idea what you can do with one), let's run through some specifics. Once this discussion of the ADO.NET DataSet is complete, the remainder of this chapter will focus on how to obtain DataSet types from external sources (such as a relational database) using the types defined by the System.Data.SqlClient and System.Data.OleDb namespaces.

Building an In-Memory DataSet

To illustrate the use of a DataSet, create a new Windows Forms application that maintains a single DataSet, containing three DataTable objects named Inventory,

Table 13-10. Methods of the Mighty DataSet

DATASET METHOD	MEANING IN LIFE
AcceptChanges()	Commits all the changes made to this DataSet since it was loaded or the last time AcceptChanges() was called.
Clear()	Completely clears the DataSet data by removing every row in each table.
Clone()	Clones the structure of the DataSet, including all DataTables, as well as all relations and any constraints.
Copy()	Copies both the structure and data for this DataSet.
GetChanges()	Returns a copy of the DataSet containing all changes made to it since it was last loaded or since AcceptChanges() was called.
GetChildRelations()	Returns the collection of child relations that belong to a specified table.
GetParentRelations()	Gets the collection of parent relations that belong to a specified table.
HasChanges()	Overloaded. Gets a value indicating whether the DataSet has changes, including new, deleted, or modified rows.
Merge()	Overloaded. Merges this DataSet with a specified DataSet.
ReadXml() ReadXmlSchema()	Allow you to read XML data from a valid stream (file based, memory based, or network based) to the DataSet.
RejectChanges()	Rolls back all the changes made to this DataSet since it was created or the last time DataSet.AcceptChanges was called.
WriteXml() WriteXmlSchema()	Allow you to write the contents of a DataSet to a valid stream.

Customers, and Orders. The columns for each table will be minimal but complete, with one column marking the primary key for each table. Most importantly, you can model the parent/child relationships between the tables using the DataRelation type. Your goal is to build the database shown in Figure 13-19 in memory.

Here, the Inventory table is the parent table to the Orders table, which maintains a foreign key (CarID) column. Also, the Customers table is the parent table to the Orders table. (Again note the foreign key, CustID.) As you will soon see, when you add DataRelation types to your DataSet, they may be used to navigate between the tables to obtain and manipulate the related data.

To begin, assume you have added a set of member variables to your main Form, representing the individual DataTables and containing DataSet, as shown here:

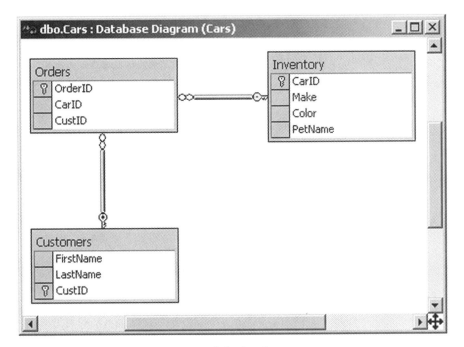

Figure 13-19. The In-Memory Automobile database

```
public class mainForm : System.Windows.Forms.Form
{
    // Inventory DataTable.
    private DataTable inventoryTable = new DataTable("Inventory");

    // Customers DataTable.
    private DataTable customersTable = new DataTable("Customers");

    // Orders DataTable.
    private DataTable ordersTable = new DataTable("Orders");

    // Our DataSet!
    private DataSet carsDataSet = new DataSet("CarDataSet");
...
}
```

Now, to keep things as OO as possible, build some (very) simple wrapper classes to represent a Car and Customer in the system. Note that the Customer class maintains a field that identifies the car a customer is interested in buying, as shown here:

```
public class Car
{
    // Make public for easy access.
    public string petName, make, color;
    public Car(string petName, string make, string color)
    {
        this.petName = petName;
        this.color = color;
        this.make = make;
    }
}

public class Customer
{
    public Customer(string fName, string lName, int currentOrder)
    {
        this.firstName= fName;
        this.lastName = lName;
        this.currCarOrder = currentOrder;
    }
    public string firstName, lastName;
    public int currCarOrder;
}
```

The main Form maintains two ArrayList types that hold a set of cars and customers, which are populated with some sample data in the scope of the Form's
constructor. Next, the constructor calls a number of private helper functions to
build the tables and their relationships. Finally, this method binds the Inventory
and Customer DataTables to their corresponding DataGrid widgets. Notice that
the following code binds a given DataTable in the DataSet using the
SetDataBinding() method:

```
// Your list of Cars and Customers.
private ArrayList arTheCars, arTheCustomers;

public mainForm()
{
    // Fill the car array list with some cars.
    arTheCars = new ArrayList();
    arTheCars.Add(new Car("Chucky", "BMW", "Green"));
    . . .
```

```
// Fill the other array list with some customers.
arTheCustomers = new ArrayList();
arTheCustomers.Add(new Customer("Dave", "Brenner", 1020));
. . .


// Make data tables (using the same techniques seen previously).
MakeInventoryTable();
MakeCustomerTable();
MakeOrderTable();
// Add relation (seen in just a moment).
BuildTableRelationship();


// Bind to grids (Param1 = DataSet, Param2 = name of table in DataSet).
CarDataGrid.SetDataBinding(carsDataSet, "Inventory");
CustomerDataGrid.SetDataBinding(carsDataSet, "Customers");
}
```

Each DataTables is constructed using the techniques examined earlier in this chapter. To keep focused on the DataSet logic, I will not repeat every detail of the table-building logic here. However, be aware that each table is assigned a primary key that is autoincremented. Here is some partial table-building logic (check out same code for complete details):

```
private void MakeOrderTable()
{
. . .
    // Add table to the DataSet.
    carsDataSet.Tables.Add(customersTable);

    // Create OrderID, CustID, CarID columns and add to table. . .
    // Make the ID column the primary key column. . .
    // Add some orders.
    for(int i = 0; i < arTheCustomers.Count; i++)
    {
        DataRow newRow;
        newRow = ordersTable.NewRow();
        Customer c = (Customer)arTheCustomers[i];
        newRow["CustID"] = i;
        newRow["CarID"] = c.currCarOrder;
        carsDataSet.Tables["Orders"].Rows.Add(newRow);
    }
}
```

The MakeInventoryTable() and MakeCustomerTable() helper functions behave almost identically.

Expressing Relations Using the DataRelation Type

The really interesting work happens in the BuildTableRelationship() helper function. Once a DataSet has been populated with a number of tables, you can *optionally* choose to programmatically model their parent/child relationships. Be aware that this is not mandatory. You can have a DataSet that does little else than hold a collection of DataTables in memory (even a single DataTable). However, when you do establish the interplay between your DataTables, you can navigate between them on the fly and collect any sort of information you may be interested in obtaining, all while disconnected from the data source.

The System.Data.DataRelation type is an OO wrapper around a table-to-table relationship. When you create a new DataRelation type, specify a friendly name, followed by the parent table (for example, Inventory) and the related child table (Orders). For a relationship to be established, each table must have an identically named column (CarID) of the same data type (Int32 in this case). In this light, a DataRelation is basically bound by the same rules as a relational database. Here is the complete implementation of the BuildTableRelationship() helper function:

```
private void BuildTableRelationship()
{
    // Create a DR obj.
    DataRelation dr = new DataRelation("CustomerOrder",
        carsDataSet.Tables["Customers"].Columns["CustID"],      // Parent.
        carsDataSet.Tables["Orders"].Columns["CustID"]);        // Child.

    // Add to the DataSet.
    carsDataSet.Relations.Add(dr);

    // Create another DR obj.
    dr = new DataRelation("InventoryOrder",
        carsDataSet.Tables["Inventory"].Columns["CarID"],       // Parent.
        carsDataSet.Tables["Orders"].Columns["CarID"]);         // Child.

    // Add to the DataSet.
    carsDataSet.Relations.Add(dr);
}
```

As you can see, a given DataRelation is held in the DataRelationCollection maintained by the DataSet. The DataRelation type offers a number of properties that allow you to obtain a reference to the child and/or parent table that is participating in the relationship, specify the name of the relationship, and so on. (See Table 13-11.)

Table 13-11. Properties of the DataRelation Type

DATARELATION PROPERTY	MEANING IN LIFE
ChildColumns ChildKeyConstraint ChildTable	Obtain information about the child table in this relationship as well as the table itself.
DataSet	Gets the DataSet to which the relations' collection belongs.
ParentColumns ParentKeyConstraint ParentTable	Obtain information about the parent table in this relationship as well as the table itself.
RelationName	Gets or sets the name used to look up this relation in the parent data set's DataRelationCollection.

Navigating Between Related Tables

To illustrate how a DataRelation allows you to move between related tables, extend your GUI to include a new Button type and a related TextBox. The end user is able to enter the ID of a customer and obtain all the information about that customer's order, which is placed in a simple message box (Figure 13-20).

Figure 13-20. Navigating data relations

The Button's Click event handler is as shown here (error checking removed for clarity):

```
protected void btnGetInfo_Click (object sender, System.EventArgs e)
{
    string strInfo = "";
    DataRow drCust = null;
    DataRow[] drsOrder = null;

    // Get the specified CustID from the TextBox.
    int theCust = int.Parse(this.txtCustID.Text);

    // Now based on CustID, get the correct row in Customers table.
    drCust = carsDataSet.Tables["Customers"].Rows[theCust];
    strInfo += "Cust #" + drCust["CustID"].ToString() + "\n";

    // Navigate from customer table to order table.
    drsOrder =   drCust.GetChildRows(carsDataSet.Relations["CustomerOrder"]);

    // Get customer name.
    foreach(DataRow r in drsOrder)
        strInfo += "Order Number: " + r["OrderID"] + "\n";

    // Now navigate from order table to inventory table.
    DataRow[] drsInv =
        drsOrder[0].GetParentRows(carsDataSet.Relations["InventoryOrder"]);

    // Get Car info.
    foreach(DataRow r in drsInv)
    {
        strInfo += "Make: " + r["Make"] + "\n";
        strInfo += "Color: " + r["Color"] + "\n";
        strInfo += "Pet Name: " + r["PetName"] + "\n";
    }
    MessageBox.Show(strInfo, "Info based on cust ID");
}
```

As you can see, the key to moving between data tables is to use a handful of methods defined by the DataRow type. Let's break this code down step by step. First, you obtain the correct customer ID from the text box and use it to grab the correct row in the Customers table (using the Rows property, of course), as shown here:

```
// Get the specified CustID from the TextBox.
int theCust = int.Parse(this.txtCustID.Text);
```

```
// Now based on CustID, get the correct row in Customers table.
DataRow drCust = null;
drCust = carsDataSet.Tables["Customers"].Rows[theCust];
strInfo += "Cust #" + drCust["CustID"].ToString() + "\n";
```

Next, you navigate from the Customers table to the Orders table, using the CustomerOrder data relation. Notice that the DataRow.GetChildRows() method allows you to grab rows from your child table, and once you do, you can read information out of the table, as shown here:

```
// Navigate from customer table to order table.
DataRow[] drsOrder = null;
drsOrder =   drCust.GetChildRows(carsDataSet.Relations["CustomerOrder"]);

// Get customer name.
foreach(DataRow r in drsOrder)
strInfo += "Order Number: " + r["OrderID"] + "\n";
```

Your final step is to navigate from the Orders table to its parent table (Inventory), using the GetParentRows() method. At this point, you can read information from the Inventory table using the Make, PetName, and Color columns, as shown here:

```
// Now navigate from order table to inventory table.
DataRow[] drsInv =
    drsOrder[0].GetParentRows(carsDataSet.Relations["InventoryOrder"]);

foreach(DataRow r in drsInv)
{
    strInfo += "Make: " + r["Make"] + "\n";
    strInfo += "Color: " + r["Color"] + "\n";
    strInfo += "Pet Name: " + r["PetName"] + "\n";
}
```

As a final example of navigating relations programmatically, the following code prints out the values in the Orders table that is obtained indirectly using the InventoryOrders relationship:

```
protected void btnGetChildRels_Click (object sender, System.EventArgs e)
{
    // Ask the CarsDataSet for the child relations of the inv. table.
    DataRelationCollection relCol;
    DataRow[] arrRows;
```

```
string info = "";
relCol = carsDataSet.Tables["inventory"].ChildRelations;

info += "\tRelation is called: " + relCol[0].RelationName + "\n\n";
// Now loop over each relation and print out info.
foreach(DataRelation dr in relCol)
{
    foreach(DataRow r in inventoryTable.Rows)
    {
        arrRows = r.GetChildRows(dr);

        // Print out the value of each column in the row.
        for (int i = 0; i < arrRows.Length; i++)
        {
            foreach(DataColumn dc in arrRows[i].Table.Columns )
            {
                info += "\t" + arrRows[i][dc];
            }
            info += "\n";
        }
    }
    MessageBox.Show(info,
            "Data in Orders Table obtained by child relations");
}
}
```

Figure 13-21 shows the output.

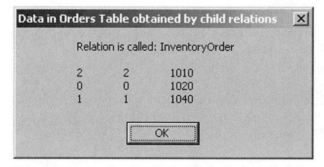

Figure 13-21. Navigating parent/child relations

Hopefully this last example has you convinced of the usefulness of the DataSet type. Given that a DataSet is completely disconnected from the underlying data source, you can work with an in-memory copy of data and navigate around each table to make any necessary updates, deletes, or inserts. Once this is done, you can submit your changes to the data store for processing. Of course you don't yet know how to get connected! There is one final item of interest regarding the DataSet before addressing this issue.

Reading and Writing XML-Based DataSets

A major design goal of ADO.NET was to apply a liberal use of XML infrastructure. Using the DataSet type, you can write an XML representation of the contents of your tables, relations, and other schematic details to a given stream (such as a file). To do so, simply call the WriteXml() method, as shown here:

```
protected void btnToXML_Click (object sender, System.EventArgs e)
{
    // Write your entire DataSet to a file in the app directory.
    carsDataSet.WriteXml("cars.xml");
    MessageBox.Show("Wrote CarDataSet to XML file in app directory");
    btnReadXML.Enabled = true;
}
```

If you now open your new file in the Visual Studio.NET IDE (Figure 13-22), you will see that the entire DataSet has been transformed to XML. (If you are not comfortable with XML syntax, don't sweat it. The DataSet understands XML just fine.)

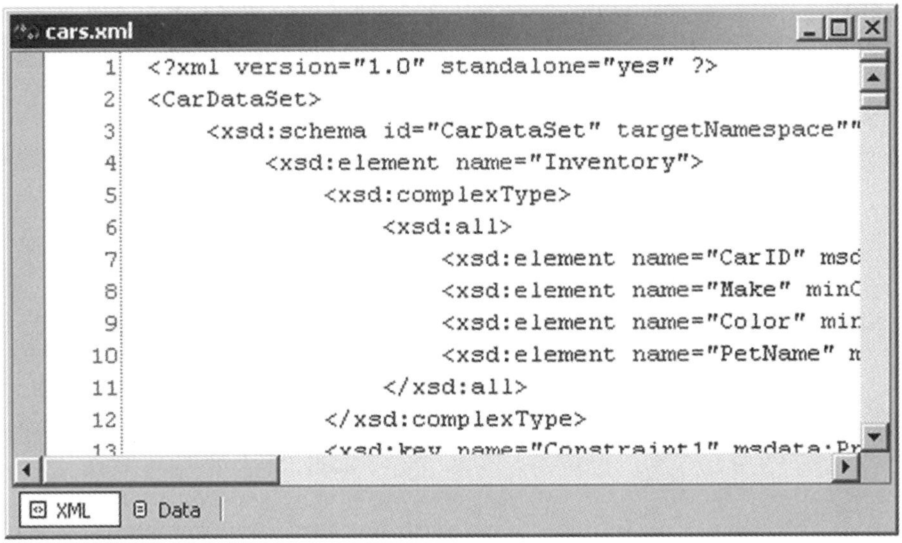

Figure 13-22. The DataSet as XML

To test the ReadXml() method of the DataSet, perform a little experiment. The CarDataSet application has a Button that will clear out the current DataSet completely (including all tables and relations). After the in-memory representation has been gutted, instruct the DataSet to read in the cars.xml file, which as you would guess restores the entire DataSet, as shown here:

```
protected void btnReadXML_Click (object sender, System.EventArgs e)
{
    // Kill current DataSet.
    carsDataSet.Clear();
    carsDataSet.Dispose();
    MessageBox.Show("Just cleared data set...");
    carsDataSet = new DataSet("CarDataSet");

    carsDataSet.ReadXml( "cars.xml" );

    MessageBox.Show("Reconstructed data set from XML file...");
    btnReadXML.Enabled = false;

    // Bind to grids.
    CarDataGrid.SetDataBinding(carsDataSet, "Inventory");
    CustomerDataGrid.SetDataBinding(carsDataSet, "Customers");
}
```

Be aware that under the hood, these XML-centric methods are using types defined in the System.Xml.dll assembly (specifically the XmlReader and XmlWriter classes). Therefore, in addition to setting a reference to this binary, you also need to make explicit reference to its types, as shown here:

```
// Need this namespace to call ReadXml() or WriteXml()!
using System.Xml;
```

Figure 13-23 shows your final product.

SOURCE CODE   *The CarDataSet application is included under the Chapter 13 subdirectory.*

Building a Simple Test Database

Now that you understand how to create and manipulate a DataSet in memory, you can get down to the business of making a data connection and seeing how to obtain a populated DataSet. In keeping with the automotive theme used

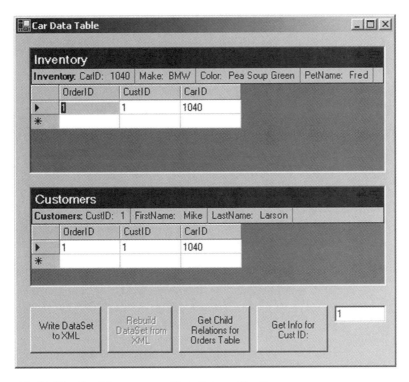

Figure 13-23. The final in-memory DataSet application

throughout this text, I have included two versions of a sample Cars database
(available for download at www.apress.com) that models the Inventory, Orders,
and Customers tables examined during the chapter.

The first version is a SQL script that builds the tables (including their rela-
tionships) and is intended for users of SQL Server 7.0 (and greater). To create the
Cars database, begin by opening the Query Analyzer utility that ships with SQL
Server. Next, connect to your machine and open the cars.sql file. Before you run
the script, be sure that the path listed in the SQL file points to *your installation* of
MS SQL Server. Thus, be sure you edit the following DDL (in bold) as necessary:

```
CREATE DATABASE [Cars]  ON (NAME = N'Cars_Data', FILENAME
=N' D:\MSSQL7\Data \Cars_Data.MDF' ,
SIZE = 2, FILEGROWTH = 10%)

LOG ON (NAME = N'Cars_Log', FILENAME
= N' D:\MSSQL7\Data\Cars_Log.LDF' ,
SIZE = 1, FILEGROWTH = 10%)
GO
```

Now run your script. Once you do, open up the SQL Server Enterprise Manager (Figure 13-24). You should see the Cars database with all three interrelated tables (with some sample data to boot).

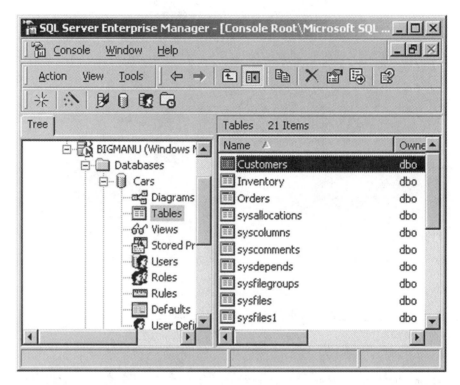

Figure 13-24. The SQL Server Cars database

The second version of the Cars database is for users of MS Access. Under the Access DB folder you will find the cars.mdb file, which contains the same information and underlying structure as the SQL Server version. During the remainder of this chapter, I will assume that you are connecting to the SQL Server Cars database rather than the Access equivalent. In just a bit, however, you will see how to configure an ADO.NET connection string to hook into an *.mdb file.

ADO.NET Managed Providers

If you are coming to ADO.NET from a classic ADO background, you can assume that a managed provider is the .NET equivalent of an OLE DB provider. In other words, the managed provider is your gateway between a raw data store and a populated DataSet.

As mentioned earlier in this chapter, ADO.NET ships with two canned managed providers. The first of these is the OleDb managed provider, which is composed of the types defined in the System.Data.OleDb namespace. The OleDb provider allows you to access data located in any data store that supports the OLE DB protocol. Thus, like with classic ADO, you may use the ADO.NET managed provider to access SQL Server, Oracle, or MS Access databases. Because the types in the System.Data.OleDb namespace must communicate with unmanaged code (e.g., the OLE DB providers), you need to be aware that a number of .NET to COM translations occur behind the scenes, which can affect performance.

The other managed provider (the SQL provider) offers direct access to MS SQL Server data stores, and *only* SQL Server data stores (version 7.0 and greater). The System.Data.SqlClient namespace contains the types used by the SQL provider and provides the same functionality as the OleDb provider. In fact, for the most part, both namespaces have similarly named items. The key difference is that the SQL provider does not use the OLE DB or classic ADO protocols and thus offers numerous performance benefits.

Recall that the System.Data.Common namespace defines a number of abstract types that provide a common interface for each managed provider. First, each defines an implementation of the IDbConnection interface, which is used to configure and open a session with the data store. Objects that implement the IDbCommand interface are used to issue SQL queries against the database. Next is IDataReader, which allows you to read data using a forward-only, read-only cursor. Last but not least are types that implement IDbDataAdapter, which are responsible for populating a DataSet on behalf of the interested client.

For the most part you will not need to interact with the System.Data.Common namespace directly. However, to use either provider requires that you specify the proper using directive, as shown here:

```
// Going to access an OLE DB compliant data source.
using System.Data;
using System.Data.OleDb;

// Going to access SQL Server (7.0 or greater).
using System.Data;
using System.Data.SqlClient;
```

Working with the OleDb Managed Provider

Once you are comfortable with one managed provider, you can easily manipulate other providers. Begin by examining how to connect using the OleDb managed provider. When you need to connect to any data source other than MS SQL Server, you will use the types defined in System.Data.OleDb. Table 13-12 provides a walkthrough of the core types.

Table 13-12. Types of the System.Data.OleDb Namespace

SYSTEM.DATA.OLEDB TYPE	MEANING IN LIFE
OleDbCommand	Represents a SQL query command to be made to a data source.
OleDbConnection	Represents an open connection to a data source.
OleDbDataAdapter	Represents a set of data commands and a database connection are used to fill the DataSet and update the data source.
OleDbDataReader	Provides a way of reading a forward-only stream of data records from a data source.
OleDbErrorCollection OleDbError OleDbException	OleDbErrorCollection maintains a collection of warnings or errors returned by the data source, each of which is represented by an OleDbError type. When an error is encountered, an exception of type OleDbException is thrown.
OleDbParameterCollection OleDbParameter	Much like classic ADO, the OleDbParameterCollection collection holds onto the parameters sent to a stored procedure in the database. Each parameter is of type OleDbParameter.

Establishing a Connection Using the OleDbConnection Type

The first step to take when working with the OleDb managed provider is to establish a session with the data source using the OleDbConnection type. Much like the classic ADO Connection object, OleDbConnection types are provided with a formatted connection string, containing a number of name/value pairs. This information is used to identify the name of the machine you wish to connect to, required security settings, the name of the database on that machine, and, most importantly, the name of the OLE DB provider. (See online help for a full description of each name/value pair.)

The connection string may be set using the OleDbConnection. ConnectionString property or as a constructor argument. Assume you wish to connect to the Cars database on a machine named BIGMANU using the SQL OLE DB provider. The following logic does the trick:

```
// Build a connection string.
OleDbConnection cn = new OleDbConnection();
```

```
cn.ConnectionString = "Provider=SQLOLEDB.1;" +        // Which provider?
                      "Integrated Security=SSPI;" +
                      "Persist Security Info=False;" +  // Persist security?
                      "Initial Catalog=Cars;" +         // Name of database.
                      "Data Source=BIGMANU;";           // Name of machine.
```

As you can infer from the preceding code comments, the Initial Catalog name refers to the database you are attempting to establish a session with (Pubs, Northwind, Cars, and so on). The Data Source name identifies the name of the machine that maintains the database. The final point of interest is the Provider segment, which specifies the name of the OLE DB provider that will be used to access the data store. Table 13-13 describes some possible values.

Table 13-13. Core OLE DB providers

PROVIDER SEGMENT VALUE	MEANING IN LIFE
Microsoft.JET.OLEDB.4.0	You want to use the Jet OLE DB provider to connect to an Access database.
MSDAORA	You want to use the OLE DB provider for Oracle.
SQLOLEDB	You want to use the OLE DB provider for MS SQL Server.

Once you have configured the connection string, the next step is to open a session with the data source, do some work, and release your connection to the data source, as shown here:

```
// Build a connection string (can specify User ID and Password if needed).
OleDbConnection cn = new OleDbConnection();
cn.ConnectionString =   "Provider=SQLOLEDB.1;" +         // Which provider?
                        "Integrated Security=SSPI;" +
                        "Persist Security Info=False;" + // Persist security?
                        "Initial Catalog=Cars;" +        // Name of database.
                        "Data Source=BIGMANU;";          // Name of machine.
cn.Open();
    // Do some interesting work here.
cn.Close();
```

In addition to the ConnectionString, Open(), and Close() members, the OleDbConnection class provides a number of members that let you configure attritional settings regarding your connection, such as timeout settings and transactional information. Table 13-14 gives a partial rundown.

Table 13-14. Members of the OleDbConnection Type

OLEDBCONNECTION MEMBER	MEANING IN LIFE
BeginTransaction() CommitTransaction() RollbackTransaction()	Used to programmatically commit, abort, or roll back a current transaction.
Close()	Closes the connection to the data source. This is the preferred method.
ConnectionString	Gets or sets the string used to open a session with a data store.
ConnectionTimeout	Gets or sets the time to wait while establishing a connection before terminating the attempt and generating an error. The default value is 15 seconds.
Database	Gets or sets the name of the current database or the database to be used once a connection is open.
DataSource	Gets or sets the name of the database to connect to.
Open()	Opens a database connection with the current property settings.
Provider	Gets or sets the name of the provider.
State	Gets the current state of the connection.

Building a SQL Command

The OleDbCommand class is an OO representation of a SQL query, which is manipulated using the CommandText property. Many types in the ADO.NET namespace require an OleDbCommand as a method parameter to send the request to the data source. In addition to holding the raw SQL query, the OleDbCommand type defines other members that allow you to configure various characteristics of the query (Table 13-15).

Working with the OleDbCommand type is very simple, and like with the OleDbConnection object, there are numerous ways to achieve the same end result. As an example, note the following (semantically identical) ways to configure a SQL query using an active OleDbConnection object. In each case, assume you already have an OleDbConnection named cn:

```
// Specify a SQL command (take one).
string strSQL1 = "Select Make from Inventory where Color='Red'";
OleDbCommand myCommand1 = new OleDbCommand(strSQL1, cn);
```

```
// Specify SQL command (take two).
string strSQL2 = "Select Make from Inventory where Color='Red'";
OleDbCommand myCommand2 = new OleDbCommand();
myCommand.Connection = cn;
myCommand.CommandText = strSQL2;
```

Table 13-15. Members of the OleDbCommand Type

OLEDBCOMMAND MEMBER	MEANING IN LIFE
Cancel()	Cancels the execution of a command.
CommandText	Gets or sets the SQL command text or the provider-specific syntax to run against the data source.
CommandTimeout	Gets or sets the time to wait while executing the command before terminating the attempt and generating an error. The default is 30 seconds.
CommandType	Gets or sets how the CommandText property is interpreted.
Connection	Gets or sets the OleDbConnection used by this instance of the OleDbCommand.
ExecuteReader()	Returns an instance of an OleDbDataReader.
Parameters	Gets the collection of OleDbParameterCollection.
Prepare()	Creates a prepared (or compiled) version of the command on the data source.

Working with the OleDbDataReader

Once you have established the active connection and SQL command, the next step is to submit the query to the data source. There are a number of ways to do so. The OleDbDataReader type is the simplest, fastest, but least flexible way to obtain information from a data store. This class represents a read-only, forward-only stream of data returned one record at a time as a result of a SQL command.

The OleDbDataReader is useful when you need to iterate over large amounts of data very quickly and have no need to work an in-memory DataSet representation. For example, if you request 20,000 records from a table to store in a text file, it would be rather memory intensive to hold this information in a DataSet. A better approach would be to create a data reader that spins over each record as rapidly as possible. Be aware however, that DataReaders (unlike DataSets) maintain a connection to their data source until you explicitly close the session.

To illustrate, the following class issues a simple SQL query against the Cars database, using the ExecuteReader() method of the OleDbCommand type. Using the Read() method of the returned OleDbDataReader, we dump each member to the standard IO stream:

```
public class OleDbDR
{
    static void Main(string[] args)
    {
        // Step 1: Make a connection.
        OleDbConnection cn = new OleDbConnection();
        cn.ConnectionString = "Provider=SQLOLEDB.1;" +
            "Integrated Security=SSPI;" +
            "Persist Security Info=False;" +
            "Initial Catalog=Cars;" +
            "Data Source=BIGMANU;";
        cn.Open();

        // Step 2: Create a SQL command.
        string strSQL = "SELECT Make FROM Inventory WHERE Color='Red'";
        OleDbCommand myCommand = new OleDbCommand(strSQL, cn);

        // Step 3: Obtain a data reader ala ExecuteReader().
        OleDbDataReader myDataReader;
        myDataReader = myCommand.ExecuteReader();

        // Step 4: Loop over the results.
        while (myDataReader.Read())
        {
            Console.WriteLine("Red car: " +
                myDataReader["Make"].ToString());
        }

        myDataReader.Close();
        cn.Close();
    }
}
```

The result is the listing of all red automobiles in the Cars database (Figure 13-25).

Recall that DataReaders are forward-only, read-only streams of data. Therefore, there is no way to navigate around the contents of the OleDbDataReader. All you can do is read each record and use it in your application:

```
// Get the value in the 'Make' column.
Console.WriteLine("Red car: {0}", myDataReader["Make"].ToString());
```

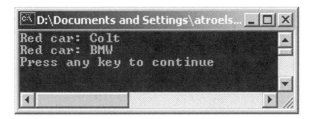

Figure 13-25. The OleDbDataReader in action

When you are finished using the DataReader, make sure to terminate the session using the appropriately named method, Close(). In addition to the Read() and Close() methods, there are a number of other methods that allow you to obtain a value from a specified column in a given format (e.g., GetBoolean(), GetByte(), and so forth). Also, the FieldCount property returns the number of columns in the current record, and so forth.

SOURCE CODE   *The OleDbDataReader application is included under the Chapter 13 subdirectory.*

Connecting to an Access Database

Now that you know how to pull data from SQL Server, let's take a moment to see how to obtain data from an Access database. To illustrate, let's modify the previous OleDbDataReader application to read from the cars.mdb file.

Much like classic ADO, the process of connecting to an Access database using ADO.NET requires little more than retrofitting your construction string. First, set the Provider segment to the JET engine, rather than SQLOLEDB. Beyond this adjustment, set the data source segment to point to the path of your *.mdb file, as shown here:

```
// Be sure to update the data source segment if necessary!
OleDbConnection cn = new OleDbConnection();
cn.ConnectionString = "Provider=Microsoft.JET.OLEDB.4.0;" +
                    @"data source = D:\Chapter 13\Access DB\cars.mdb";
 cn.Open();
```

Once the connection has been made, you can read and manipulate the contents of your data table. The only other point to be aware of is that, given that the use of the JET engine requires OLEDB, you must use the types defined in the System.Data.OleDb namespace (e.g., the OleDb managed provider). Remember, the SQL provider only allows you to access MS SQL Server data stores!

Executing a Stored Procedure

When you are constructing a distributed application, one of the design choices you face is where to store the business logic. One approach is to build reusable binary code libraries, which can be managed by a surrogate process such as the Windows 2000 Component Services manager. Another approach is to place the system's business logic on the data layer in the form of stored procedures. Yet another approach is to supply a blend of each technique.

A stored procedure is a named block of SQL code stored at the database. Stored procedures can be constructed to return a set of rows (or native data types) to the calling component and may take any number of optional parameters. The end result is a unit of work that behaves like a typical function, with the obvious differences of being located on a data store rather than a binary business object.

Let's add a simple stored procedure to the existing Cars database called GetPetName, which takes an input parameter of type integer. (If you ran the supplied SQL script, this stored proc is already defined.) This is the numerical ID of the car for which you are interested in obtaining the pet name, which is returned as an output parameter of type char. Here is the syntax:

```
CREATE PROCEDURE GetPetName
     @carID int,
     @petName char(20) output
AS
SELECT @petName = PetName from Inventory where CarID = @carID
```

Now that you have a stored procedure in place, let's see the code necessary to execute it. Begin as always by creating a new OleDbConnection, configure your connection string, and open the session. Next, create a new OleDbCommand type, making sure to specify the name of the stored procedure and setting the CommandType property accordingly, as shown here:

```
// Open connection to data store.
OleDbConnection cn = new OleDbConnection();
cn.ConnectionString = "Provider=SQLOLEDB.1;" + "Integrated Security=SSPI;" +
                      "Persist Security Info=False;" + "Initial Catalog=Cars;" +
                      "Data Source=BIGMANU;";
cn.Open();



// Make a command object for the stored proc.
OleDbCommand myCommand = new OleDbCommand("GetPetName", cn);
myCommand.CommandType = CommandType.StoredProcedure;
```

The CommandType property of the OleDbCommand class can be set using any of the values specified in the related CommandType enumeration (Table 13-16).

Table 13-16. Values of the CommandType Enumeration

COMMANDTYPE ENUMERATION VALUE	MEANING IN LIFE
StoredProcedure	Used to configure an OleDbCommand that triggers a stored procedure.
TableDirect	The OleDbCommand represents a table name whose columns are all returned.
Text	The OleDbCommand type contains a standard SQL text command. This is the default value.

When you issue basic SQL queries (e.g., "SELECT * FROM Inventory") to the data source, the default CommandType.Text setting is appropriate. However, to issue a command to hit a stored procedure, specify CommandType. StoredProcedure.

Specifying Parameters Using the OleDbParameter Type

The next task is to establish the parameters used for the call. The OleDbParameter type is an OO wrapper around a particular parameter passed to (or received from) the stored procedure. This class maintains a number of properties that allow you to configure the name, size, and data type of the parameter, as well as its direction of travel. Table 13-17 describes some key properties of the OleDbParameter type.

Given that you have one input and one output parameter, you can configure your types as so. Note that you then add these items to the OleDbCommand type's ParametersCollection (which is, of course, accessed via the Parameters property):

```
// Create the parameters for the call.
OleDbParameter theParam = new OleDbParameter();

// Input.
theParam.ParameterName = "@carID";
theParam.DbType = OleDbType.Integer;
theParam.Direction = ParameterDirection.Input;
theParam.Value = 1;                          // Car ID = 1.
myCommand.Parameters.Add(theParam);
```

```
// Output.
theParam = new OleDbParameter();
theParam.ParameterName = "@petName";
theParam.DbType = OleDbType.Char;
theParam.Size = 20;
theParam.Direction = ParameterDirection.Output;
myCommand.Parameters.Add(theParam);
```

The final step is to execute the command using
OleDbCommand.ExecuteNonQuery(). Notice that the Value property of the
OleDbParameter type is accessed to obtain the returned pet name, as shown here:

```
// Execute the stored procedure!
myCommand.ExecuteNonQuery();
```

```
// Display the result.
Console.WriteLine("Stored Proc Info:");
Console.WriteLine("Car ID: " + myCommand.Parameters["@carID"].Value);
Console.WriteLine("PetName: " + myCommand.Parameters["@petName"].Value);
```

Table 13-17. Members of the OleDbParameter Type

OLEDBPARAMETER PROPERTY	MEANING IN LIFE
DataType	Establishes the type of the parameter, in terms of .NET.
DbType	Gets or sets the native data type from the data source, using the OleDbType enumeration.
Direction	Gets or sets whether the parameter is input only, output only, bidirectional, or a return value parameter.
IsNullable	Gets or sets whether the parameter accepts null values.
ParameterName	Gets or sets the name of the OleDbParameter.
Precision	Gets or sets the maximum number of digits used to represent the Value.
Scale	Gets or sets the number of decimal places to which Value is resolved.
Size	Gets or sets the maximum parameter size of the data.
Value	Gets or sets the value of the parameter.

Figure 13-26 shows the output.

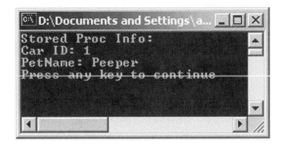

Figure 13-26. Triggering the stored procedure

SOURCE CODE   *The OleDbStoredProc project is included under the Chapter 13 subdirectory.*

The Role of the OleDbDataAdapter Type

At this point you should understand how to connect to a data source using the OleDbConnection type, issue a command (using the OleDbCommand and OleDbParameter types), and work with the OleDbDataReader. This is just fine when you want to iterate over a batch of data very quickly or trigger a stored procedure. However, the most flexible way to obtain a complete DataSet from the data store is through the use of the OleDbDataAdapter.

In a nutshell, this type pulls information from a data store and populates a DataTable in a DataSet using the OleDbDataAdapter.Fill() method, which has been overloaded a number of times. Here are a few possibilities (FYI, the integer return type holds the number of records returned):

```
// Fills the data set with records from a given source table.
public int Fill(DataSet yourDS, string tableName);

// Fills the data set with the records located between
// the given bounds from a given source table.
public int Fill(DataSet yourDS, string tableName,
                int startRecord, int maxRecord);
```

Before you can call this method, you need a valid OleDbDataAdapter object reference. The constructor has also been overloaded a number of times, but in general you need to supply the connection information and the SQL SELECT statement used to fill the DataTable.

The OleDbDataAdapter type not only is the entity that fills the tables of a DataSet on your behalf, but also is in charge of maintaining a set of core SQL statements used to push updates back to the data store. Table 13-18 describes some core members of the OleDbDataAdapter type.

Table 13-18. Core Members of the OleDbDataAdapter

OLEDBDATAADAPTER MEMBER	MEANING IN LIFE
DeleteCommand InsertCommand SelectCommand UpdateCommand	Used to establish SQL commands that will be issued to the data store when the Update() method is called. Each of these properties is set using an OleDbCommand type.
Fill()	Fills a given table in the DataSet with some number of records.
GetFillParameters()	Returns all parameters used when performing the select command.
Update()	Calls the respective INSERT, UPDATE, or DELETE statements for each inserted, updated, or deleted row for a given table in the DataSet.

The key properties of the OleDbDataAdapter (as well as the SqlDataAdapter) are DeleteCommand, InsertCommand, SelectCommand, and UpdateCommand. A data adapter understands how to submit changes on behalf of a given command. For example, when you call Update(), the data adapter uses the SQL commands stored in each of these properties automatically. As you will see, the amount of code required to configure these properties is a bit on the verbose side. Before you check these properties out firsthand, let's begin by learning how to use a data adapter to fill a DataSet programmatically.

Filling a DataSet Using the OleDbDataAdapter Type

The following code populates a DataSet (containing a single table) using an OleDbDataAdapter:

```
public class MyOleDbDataAdapter
{
    // Step 1: Open a connection to Cars db.
    OleDbConnection cn = new OleDbConnection();
    cn.ConnectionString = "Provider=SQLOLEDB.1;" +
                        "Integrated Security=SSPI;" +
                        "Persist Security Info=False;" +
                        "Initial Catalog=Cars;" +
                        "Data Source=BIGMANU;";
    cn.Open();
```

```
// Step 2: Create data adapter using the following SELECT.
string sqlSELECT = "SELECT * FROM Inventory";
OleDbDataAdapter dAdapt = new OleDbDataAdapter(sqlSELECT, cn);

// Step 3: Create and fill the DataSet, close connection.
DataSet myDS = new DataSet("CarsDataSet");
try
{
    dAdapt.Fill(myDS, "Inventory");
}
catch(Exception ex)
{
    Console.WriteLine(ex.Message);
}
finally
{
    cn.Close();
}

// Private helper function.
PrintTable(myDS);
return 0;
}
```

Notice that unlike your work during the first half of this chapter, you did *not* manually direct a DataTable type and add it to the DataSet. Rather, you specified the Inventory table as the second parameter to the Fill() method. Internally, Fill() builds the DataTable given the name of the table in the data store using the SELECT command. In this iteration, the connection between the given SQL SELECT statement and the OleDbDataAdapter was established as a constructor parameter:

```
// Create a SELECT command as string type.
string sqlSELECT = "SELECT * FROM Inventory";
OleDbDataAdapter dAdapt = new OleDbDataAdapter(sqlSELECT, cn);
```

As a more OO-aware alternative, you can use the OleDbCommand type to hold onto the SELECT statement. To associate the OleDbCommand to the OleDbDataAdapter, use the SelectCommand property, as shown here:

```
// Create a SELECT command object.
OleDbCommand selectCmd = new OleDbCommand("SELECT * FROM Inventory", cn);
```

```
// Make a data adapter and associate commands.
OleDbDataAdapter dAdapt = new OleDbDataAdapter();
dAdapt.SelectCommand = selectCmd;
```

Notice that in this case, you attach the active OleDbConnection as a parameter to the OleDbCommand. Figure 13-27 shows the end result.

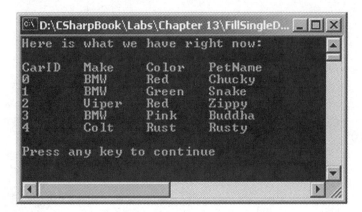

Figure 13-27. The OleDbDataAdapter in action

The PrintTable() method is little more than some formatting razzle-dazzle:

```
public static void PrintTable(DataSet ds)
{
    // Get Inventory table from DataSet.
    Console.WriteLine("Here is what we have right now:\n");
    DataTable invTable = ds.Tables["Inventory"];

    // Print the Column names.
    for(int curCol= 0; curCol< invTable.Columns.Count; curCol++)
    {
        Console.Write(invTable.Columns[curCol].ColumnName.Trim() + "\t");
    }
    Console.WriteLine();

    // Print each cell.
    for(int curRow = 0; curRow < invTable.Rows.Count; curRow++)
    {
        for(int curCol= 0; curCol< invTable.Columns.Count; curCol++)
        {
            Console.Write(invTable.Rows[curRow][curCol].ToString().Trim()
                    + "\t");
        }
```

```
        Console.WriteLine();
    }
}
```

SOURCE CODE   *The FillSingleDSWithAdapter project is under the Chapter 13 subdirectory.*

Working with the SQL Managed Provider

Before you see the details of inserting, updating, and removing records using a data adapter, I would like to introduce the SQL managed provider. As you recall, the OleDb provider allows you to access any OLE DB compliant data store, but is less optimized than the SQL provider.

When you know that the data source you need to manipulate is MS SQL Server, you will find performance gains if you use the System.Data.SqlClient namespace directly. Collectively, these classes constitute the functionality of the SQL managed provider, which should look very familiar given your work with the OleDb provider (Table 13-19).

Table 13-19. Core Types of the System.Data.SqlClient Namespace

SYSTEM.DATA.SQLCLIENT TYPE	MEANING IN LIFE
SqlCommand	Represents a Transact-SQL query to execute at a SQL Server data source.
SqlConnection	Represents an open connection to a SQL Server data source.
SqlDataAdapter	Represents a set of data commands and a database connection used to fill the DataSet and update the SQL Server data source.
SqlDataReader	Provides a way of reading a forward-only stream of data records from a SQL Server data source.
SqlErrors SqlError SqlException	SqlErrors maintains a collection of warnings or errors returned by SQL Server, each of which is represented by a SQLError type. When an error is encountered, an exception of type SQLException is thrown.
SqlParameterCollection SqlParameter	SqlParametersCollection holds onto the parameters sent to a stored procedure held in the database. Each parameter is of type SQLParameter.

Given that working with these types is almost identical to working with the OleDb managed provider, you should already know what to do with these types, as they have the same public interface. To help you get comfortable with this new set of types, the remainder of the examples use the SQL managed provider.

The *System.Data.SqlTypes* Namespace

On a quick related note, when you use the SQL managed provider, you also have the luxury of using a number of managed types that represent native SQL server data types. Table 13-20 gives a quick rundown.

Table 13-20. Types of the System.Data.SqlTypes Namespace

SYSTEM.DATA.SQLTYPES WRAPPER	NATIVE SQL SERVER
SqlBinary	binary, varbinary, timestamp, image
SqlInt64	bigint
SqlBit	bit
SqlDateTime	datetime, smalldatetime
SqlNumeric	decimal
SqlDouble	float
SqlInt32	int
SqlMoney	money, smallmoney
SqlString	nchar, ntext, nvarchar, sysname, text, varchar, char
SqlNumeric	numeric
SqlSingle	real
SqlInt16	smallint
System.Object	sql_variant
SqlByte	tinyint
SqlGuid	uniqueidentifier

Inserting New Records Using the *SqlDataAdapter*

Now that you have flipped from the OleDb provider to the realm of the SQL provider, you can return to the task of understanding the role of data adapters. Let's examine how to insert new records in a given table using the SqlDataAdapter (which would be nearly identical to using the OleDbDataAdapter). As always, begin by creating an active connection, as shown here:

```
public class MySqlDataAdapter
{
    public static void Main()
```

```
    {
        // Step 1: Create a connection and adapter (with select command).
        SqlConnection cn = new
            SqlConnection("server=(local);uid=sa;pwd=;database=Cars");

        SqlDataAdapter dAdapt = new
            SqlDataAdapter("Select * from Inventory", cn);

        // Step 2: Kill record you inserted.
        cn.Open();
        SqlCommand killCmd = new
            SqlCommand("Delete from Inventory where CarID = '1111'", cn);
        killCmd.ExecuteNonQuery();
        cn.Close();
    }
}
```

You can see that the connection string has cleaned up quite a bit. In particular, notice that you do not need to define a Provider segment (as the SQL types only talk to a SQL server!). Next, create a new SqlDataAdapter and specify the value of the SelectCommand property as a constructor parameter (just like with the OleDbDataAdapter).

The second step is really more of a good housekeeping chore. Here, you create a new SqlCommand type that will destroy the record you are about to enter (to avoid a primary key violation). The next step is a bit more involved. Your goal is to create a new SQL statement that will function as the SqlDataAdapter's InsertCommand. First, create the new SqlCommand and specify a standard SQL insert, followed by SqlParameter types describing each column in the Inventory table, as shown here:

```
public static void Main()
{
    . . .
    // Step 3: Build the insert Command!
    dAdapt.InsertCommand = new SqlCommand("INSERT INTO Inventory" +
        "(CarID, Make, Color, PetName) VALUES" +
        "(@CarID, @Make, @Color, @PetName)", cn)";

    // Step 4: Build parameters for each column in Inventory table.
    SqlParameter workParam = null;
```

```
// CarID.
workParam = dAdapt.InsertCommand.Parameters.Add(new
    SqlParameter("@CarID", SqlDbType.Int));
workParam.SourceColumn = "CarID";
workParam.SourceVersion = DataRowVersion.Current;

// Make.
workParam = dAdapt.InsertCommand.Parameters.Add(new
    SqlParameter("@Make", SqlDbType.VarChar));
workParam.SourceColumn = "Make";
workParam.SourceVersion = DataRowVersion.Current;

// Color.
workParam = dAdapt.InsertCommand.Parameters.Add(new
    SqlParameter("@Color", SqlDbType.VarChar));
workParam.SourceColumn = "Color";
workParam.SourceVersion = DataRowVersion.Current;
// PetName.
workParam = dAdapt.InsertCommand.Parameters.Add(new
    SqlParameter("@PetName", SqlDbType.VarChar));
workParam.SourceColumn = "PetName";
workParam.SourceVersion = DataRowVersion.Current;
}
```

Now that you have formatted each of the parameters, the final step is to fill the DataSet and add your new row (note that the PrintTable() helper function has carried over to this example):

```
public static void Main()
{
    ...
    // Step 5: Fill data set.
    DataSet myDS = new DataSet();
    dAdapt.Fill(myDS, "Inventory");
    PrintTable(myDS);

    // Step 6: Add new row.
    DataRow newRow = myDS.Tables["Inventory"].NewRow();
    newRow["CarID"] = 1111;
    newRow["Make"] = "SlugBug";
    newRow["Color"] = "Pink";
    newRow["PetName"] = "Cranky";
    myDS.Tables["Inventory"].Rows.Add(newRow);
```

```
// Step 7: Send back to database and reprint.
try
{
    dAdapt.Update(myDS, "Inventory");
    myDS.Dispose();
    myDS = new DataSet();
    dAdapt.Fill(myDS, "Inventory");
    PrintTable(myDS);
}
catch(Exception e){ Console.Write(e.ToString()); }
}
```

When you run the application, you see the output shown in Figure 13-28.

```
D:\CSharpBook\Labs\Chapter 13\InsertRo...

Here is what we have right now:

CarID    Make     Color    PetName
0        BMW      Red      Chucky
1        BMW      Green    Snake
2        Viper    Red      Zippy
3        BMW      Pink     Buddha
4        Colt     Rust     Rusty

Here is what we have right now:

CarID    Make     Color    PetName
0        BMW      Red      Chucky
1        BMW      Green    Snake
2        Viper    Red      Zippy
3        BMW      Pink     Buddha
4        Colt     Rust     Rusty
1111     SlugBug  Pink     Cranky

Press any key to continue
```

Figure 13-28. The InsertCommand Property in action

SOURCE CODE *The InsertRowsWithSqlAdapter project can be found under the Chapter 13 subdirectory.*

Updating Existing Records Using the SqlDataAdapter

Now that you can insert new rows, look at how you can update existing rows. Again, start the process by obtaining a connection (using the SqlConnection type) and creating a new SqlDataAdapter. Next set the value of the

UpdateCommand property, using the same general approach as when setting the value of the InsertCommand. Here is the relevant code in Main():

```
public static void Main()
{
    // Step 1: Create a connection and adapter (same as previous code)
    . . .

    // Step 2: Establish the UpdateCommand.
    dAdapt.UpdateCommand = new SqlCommand
        ("UPDATE Inventory SET Make = @Make, Color = " +
        "@Color, PetName = @PetName " +
        "WHERE CarID = @CarID" , cn);

    // Step 3: Build parameters for each column in Inventory table.
    // Same as before, but now you are populating the ParameterCollection
    // of the UpdateCommand.  For example:
    SqlParameter workParam = null;
    workParam = dAdapt.UpdateCommand.Parameters.Add(new
        SqlParameter("@CarID", SqlDbType.Int));
    workParam.SourceColumn = "CarID";
    workParam.SourceVersion = DataRowVersion.Current;

    // Do the same for PetName, Make, and Color params.

    // Step 4: Fill data set.
    DataSet myDS = new DataSet();
    dAdapt.Fill(myDS, "Inventory");
    PrintTable(myDS);

    // Step 5: Change columns in second row to 'FooFoo'.
    DataRow changeRow = myDS.Tables["Inventory"].Rows[1];
    changeRow["Make"] = "FooFoo";
    changeRow["Color"] = "FooFoo";
    changeRow["PetName"] = "FooFoo";

    // Step 6: Send back to database and reprint.
    try
    {
        dAdapt.Update(myDS, "Inventory");
        myDS.Dispose();
        myDS = new DataSet();
        dAdapt.Fill(myDS, "Inventory");
        PrintTable(myDS);
    }
```

```
        catch(Exception e)
        { Console.Write(e.ToString()); }
}
```

Figure 13-29 shows the output.

Figure 13-29. Updating existing rows

SOURCE CODE   *The UpdateRowsWithSqlAdapter project is found under the Chapter 13 subdirectory.*

Autogenerated SQL Commands

At this point you can use the data adapter types (OleDbDataAdapter and SqlDataAdapter) to select, delete, insert, and update records from a given data source. Although the general process is not rocket science, it is a bit of a bother to build up all the parameter types and configure the InsertCommand, UpdateCommand, and DeleteCommand properties by hand. As you would expect, some help is available.

One approach is to use the SqlCommandBuilder type. If you have a DataTable composed from a single table (not from multiple joined tables), the SqlCommandBuilder automatically sets the InsertCommand, UpdateCommand, and DeleteCommand properties based on the initial SelectCommand! In addition to the no-join restriction, the single table must have been assigned a primary key, and this column must be specified in the initial SELECT statement. The benefit is that you have no need to build all those SqlParameter types by hand.

To illustrate, assume you have a new Windows Forms example, which allows the user to edit the values in a DataGrid. When finished, the user may submit changes back to the database using a Button type. First, assume the following constructor logic:

```
public class mainForm : System.Windows.Forms.Form
{
    private SqlConnection cn = new
        SqlConnection("server=(local);uid=sa;pwd=;database=Cars");

    private SqlDataAdapter dAdapt;

    private SqlCommandBuilder invBuilder;
    private DataSet myDS = new DataSet();

    private System.Windows.Forms.DataGrid dataGrid1;
    private System.Windows.Forms.Button btnUpdateData;
    private System.ComponentModel.Container components;

    public mainForm()
    {
        InitializeComponent();

        // Create the initial SELECT SQL statement.
        dAdapt = new SqlDataAdapter("Select * from Inventory", cn);

        // Autogenerate the INSERT, UPDATE,
        // and DELETE statements.
        invBuilder = new SqlCommandBuilder(dAdapt);

        // Fill and bind.
        dAdapt.Fill(myDS, "Inventory");
        dataGrid1.DataSource = myDS.Tables["Inventory"].DefaultView;
    }
...
}
```

Beyond closing the connection upon exiting, that's it! At this point the SqlDataAdapter has all the information it needs to submit changes back to the data store. Now assume that you have the following logic behind the Button's Click event:

```
private void btnUpdateData_Click(object sender, System.EventArgs e)
{
    try
    {
        dataGrid1.Refresh();
        dAdapt.Update(myDS, "Inventory");
    }
    catch(Exception ex)
    {
        MessageBox.Show(ex.ToString());
    }
}
```

As usual, you call Update() and specify the DataSet and table to update. If you take this out for a test run, you see something like Figure 13-30 (be sure you exit out of edit more on the DataTable before you submit your results!).

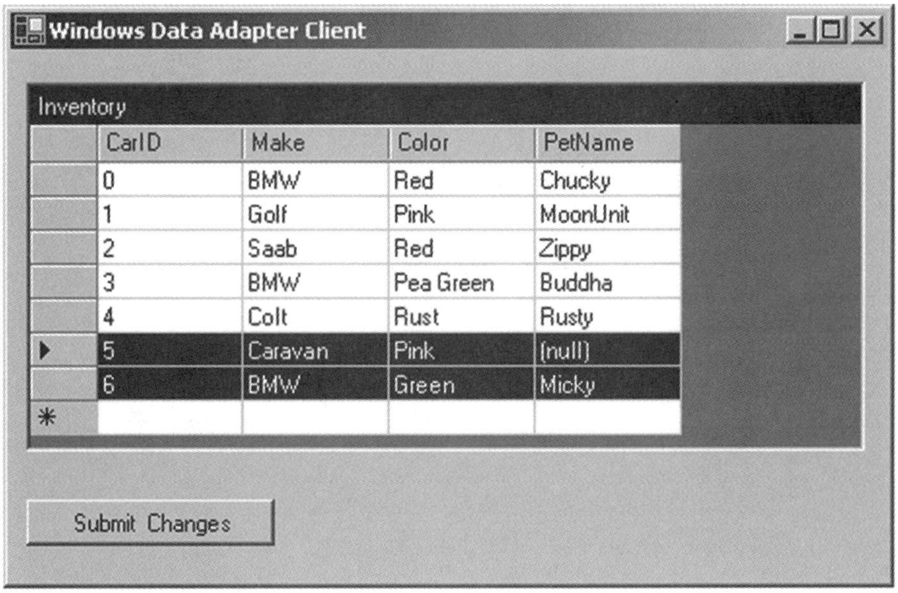

	CarID	Make	Color	PetName
	0	BMW	Red	Chucky
	1	Golf	Pink	MoonUnit
	2	Saab	Red	Zippy
	3	BMW	Pea Green	Buddha
	4	Colt	Rust	Rusty
▶	5	Caravan	Pink	(null)
	6	BMW	Green	Micky
*				

Figure 13-30. Extending the DataSet with new DataRows

Excellent! I am sure you agree that autogenerated commands are far simpler than working with the raw parameters. Like all things, of course, there are trade-offs. Specifically, if you have a DataTable composed from a joint operation, you cannot use this technique. Also, as you have seen, when you work with parameters in the raw, you have a much finer level of granularity.

SOURCE CODE *The WinFormSqlAdapter project is included under the Chapter 13 subdirectory.*

Filling a Multitabled DataSet (and Adding DataRelations)

To wrap things up, let's come full circle and build a final Windows Forms example that mimics the application you created during the first half of this chapter. The GUI is simple enough. In Figure 13-31 you can see three DataGrid types that hold the data retrieved from the Inventory, Orders, and Customers tables of the Cars database. In addition, the single Button pushes any and all changes back to the data store:

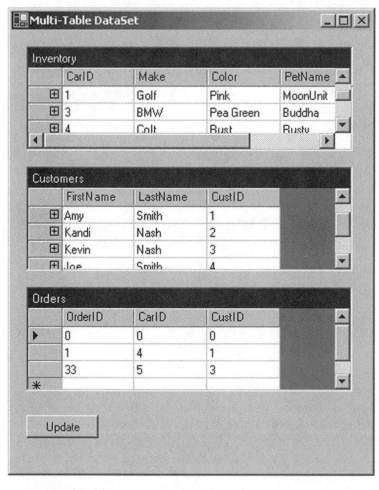

Figure 13-31. A multitable DataSet on display

To keep things even simpler, we will use autogenerated commands for each of the three SqlDataAdapters (one for each table). First, here is the Form's state data:

```
public class mainForm : System.Windows.Forms.Form
{
    private System.Windows.Forms.DataGrid custGrid;
    private System.Windows.Forms.DataGrid inventoryGrid;
    private System.Windows.Forms.Button btnUpdate;
    private System.Windows.Forms.DataGrid OrdersGrid;
    private System.ComponentModel.Container components;

    // Here is the connection.
    private SqlConnection cn = new
            SqlConnection("server=(local);uid=sa;pwd=;database=Cars");

    // Our data adapters (for each table).
    private SqlDataAdapter invTableAdapter;
    private SqlDataAdapter custTableAdapter;
    private SqlDataAdapter ordersTableAdapter;

    // Command builders (for each table).
    private SqlCommandBuilder invBuilder = new SqlCommandBuilder();
    private SqlCommandBuilder orderBuilder = new SqlCommandBuilder();
    private SqlCommandBuilder custBuilder = new SqlCommandBuilder();

    // The dataset.
    DataSet carsDS = new DataSet();
...
}
```

The Form's constructor does the grunge work of creating your data-centric member variables and filling the DataSet. Also note that there is a call to a private helper function, BuildTableRelationship(), as shown here:

```
public mainForm()
{
    InitializeComponent();

    // Create adapters.
    invTableAdapter = new SqlDataAdapter("Select * from Inventory", cn);
    custTableAdapter = new SqlDataAdapter("Select * from Customers", cn);
    ordersTableAdapter = new SqlDataAdapter("Select * from Orders", cn);
```

```
        // Autogenerate commands.
        invBuilder = new SqlCommandBuilder(invTableAdapter);
        orderBuilder = new SqlCommandBuilder(ordersTableAdapter);
        custBuilder = new SqlCommandBuilder(custTableAdapter);

        // Add tables to DS.
        invTableAdapter.Fill(carsDS, "Inventory");
        custTableAdapter.Fill(carsDS, "Customers");
        ordersTableAdapter.Fill(carsDS, "Orders");

        // Build relations between tables.
        BuildTableRelationship();
    }
```

The BuildTableRelationship() helper function does just what you would expect. Recall that the Cars database expresses a number of parent/child relationships. The code looks identical to the logic seen earlier in this chapter, as shown here:

```
private void BuildTableRelationship()
{
    // Create a DR obj.
    DataRelation dr = new DataRelation("CustomerOrder",
        carsDS.Tables["Customers"].Columns["CustID"],
        carsDS.Tables["Orders"].Columns["CustID"]);

    // Add relation to the DataSet.
    carsDS.Relations.Add(dr);

    // Create another DR obj.
    dr = new DataRelation("InventoryOrder",
        carsDS.Tables["Inventory"].Columns["CarID"],
        carsDS.Tables["Orders"].Columns["CarID"]);
    // Add relation to the DataSet.
    carsDS.Relations.Add(dr);

    // Fill the grids!
    inventoryGrid.SetDataBinding(carsDS, "Inventory");
    custGrid.SetDataBinding(carsDS, "Customers");
    OrdersGrid.SetDataBinding(carsDS, "Orders");
}
```

Now that the DataSet has been filled and disconnected from the data source, you can manipulate each table locally. To do so, simply insert, update, or delete values from any of the three DataGrids. When you are ready to submit the data back for processing, click the Form's Update Button. The code behind the Click event should be clear at this point, as shown here:

```
private void btnUpdate_Click(object sender, System.EventArgs e)
{
    try
    {
        invTableAdapter.Update(carsDS, "Inventory");
        custTableAdapter.Update(carsDS, "Customers");
        ordersTableAdapter.Update(carsDS, "Orders");
    }
    catch(Exception ex)
    {
        MessageBox.Show(ex.Message);
    }
}
```

Once you update, you can find each table in the Cars database correctly altered.

At this point you should feel comfortable working with both the OleDb and SQL managed providers and understand how to manipulate and update the resulting DataSet. Obviously there are many other additional facets of ADO.NET, such as transactional programming, security issues, and so forth. I assume you will keep exploring as you see fit.

One other aspect of ADO.NET you have not investigated are the numerous VS.NET data Wizards. Suffice it to say, when you drag a Data widget (from the Toolbox Window) onto a design time template, you can launch a number of wizards that create connection strings for SqlConnection and OleDbConnection types; automatically build the SELECT, INSERT, DELETE, and UPDATE command for a given data adapter; and so forth. After your hard work in this chapter, learning how to interact with these tools should be a cakewalk.

SOURCE CODE   *The MultiTableDataSet project is included under the Chapter 13 subdirectory.*

Summary

ADO.NET is a new data access technology developed with the disconnected *n*-tier application firmly in mind. The System.Data namespace contains most of the core types you need to programmatically interact with rows, columns, tables, and views. As you have seen, the System.Data.SqlClient and System.Data.OleDb namespaces define the types you need to establish an active connection.

The centerpiece of ADO.NET is the DataSet. This type represents an in-memory representation of any number of tables and any number of optional interrelationships, constraints, and expressions. The beauty of establishing relations on your local tables is that you are able to programmatically navigate between them while disconnected from the remote data store.

Finally, this chapter examined the role of the data adapter (OleDbDataAdapter and SqlDataAdapter). Using this type (and the related SelectCommand, InsertCommand, UpdateCommand, and DeleteCommand properties), the adapter can resolve changes in the DataSet with the original data store. While there is more to the ADO.NET namespaces than I had time to cover in this single chapter, you should now have a strong foundation on which to build.

CHAPTER 14

Web Development
and ASP.NET

Until now all of your example applications have used Windows Forms or console-based front ends. In this chapter, you begin to explore how the .NET platform facilitates the construction of browser-based presentation layers. To begin, you will review some basic Web atoms, including HTML, HTTP requests (POST and GET), the role of client-side scripting (using JavaScript), and classic ASP. Of course, if you are already "Web aware," feel free to skim or skip this section entirely.

As you will see, ASP.NET supports a far more robust programming model than does classic ASP. For example, you can now partition your HTML presentation logic and business logic into discrete locations using a technique called *Codebehind*. Also, building Web applications with ASP.NET enables you to use "real" programming languages such as C# and VB.NET, rather than interpreted scripting languages. As you examine the architecture of an ASP.NET Web application, you will learn about the almighty Page type and the classic ASP-like Request, Response, Session, and Application properties.

To wrap up, the chapter shifts focus to examine the role of server-side controls (e.g., WebForm Controls), control validation, and server-side events. Once you have absorbed this material, you will be ready to examine the topic of ASP.NET Web services in Chapter 15.

Web Applications and Web Servers

Before diving into the ASP.NET framework, let's take some time to review the basic architecture of a simple Web application and check out some core Web-centric technologies in the process. To begin, a *Web application* can be understood as a collection of related files (*.htm, *.asp, *.aspx, image files, and so on) and related components (.NET or classic COM binaries) stored on a Web server.

A *Web server* is a software product in charge of hosting your Web applications and typically provides a number of related services such as integrated security, FTP (File Transfer Protocol) support, mail exchange services, and so forth. Internet Information Server (IIS) is Microsoft's enterprise-level Web server product.

Currently, IIS is in its fifth version (IIS 5.0) and has been integrated as part of the Windows 2000 operating system.

When you create classic ASP and ASP.NET Web applications, you will be required to (directly or indirectly) interact with IIS. Be aware, however, that IIS is *not* automatically selected when you install Windows 2000 Professional Edition. Therefore, you may be required to manually install IIS before proceeding through this chapter. To install IIS, simply access the Add/Remove Program applet from the Control Panel folder and select "Add/Remove Windows Components."

Assuming you have IIS properly installed on your workstation, you can interact with IIS from the Administrative Tools folder (again located in the Control Panel folder). For this chapter you are only concerned with the Default Web Site node (Figure 14-1).

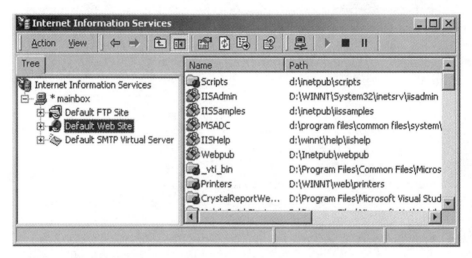

Figure 14-1. The IIS applet

Understanding Virtual Directories

A given IIS installation is able to host numerous Web applications, each of which reside in a *virtual directory*. Each virtual directory is mapped to a physical directory on the local hard drive. Therefore, if you create a new Web application named FrogsAreUs, the outside world navigates to your site using a Universal Resource Locator (URL) such as http://www.FrogsAreUs.com (assuming your site's IP address has been registered with the world at large). Internally however, the Cars Web application may map to a physical directory such as "C:\FrogsSite," which contains the set of files that constitute the Web application.

To illustrate the process, you will create a simple Web application named Cars. The first step is to create a new folder on your machine to hold the collection of files that constitute this new site (C:\CarsWebSite). Once this is done, you need to create a new virtual directory to host the Cars site. There are many ways to accomplish this using the IIS applet, one of which is to simply right-click the Default Web Site node and select New|Virtual Directory from the context menu (Figure 14-2).

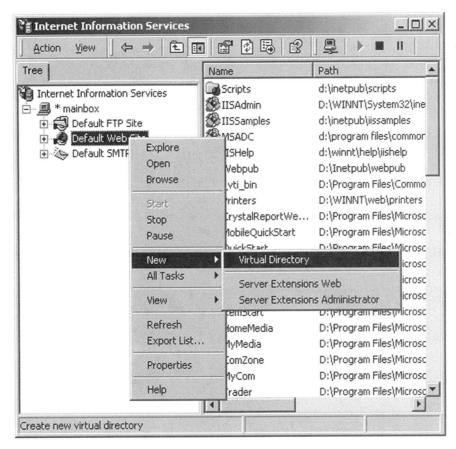

Figure 14-2. Creating a virtual directory

This menu selection launches an integrated wizard. Skip past the welcome screen and give your Web site a name (Cars). Next, you are asked to specify the physical folder on your hard drive that contains the various files and images that represent this site (in this case, C:\CarsWebSite).

The final step of the wizard prompts you for some basic traits about your new virtual directory (such as read/write access to the files it contains, the ability to view these files from a Web browser, the ability to launch executables [e.g., CGI applications], and so on). For this endeavor, the default selections are just fine. (As you would hope, you can always modify your selections after running this tool using the Properties window.) Once you are finished, you will see that your new virtual directory has been registered with IIS (Figure 14-3).

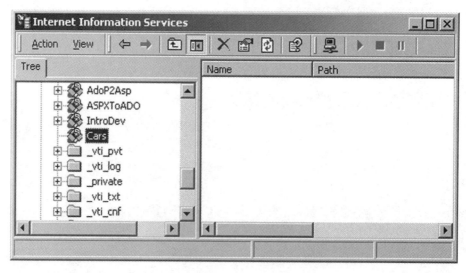

Figure 14-3. Your new virtual directory

The Basic Structure of an HTML Document

Now that you have a virtual directory, you need to create the Web application itself. When you build Web applications, you cannot escape the use of the Hypertext Markup Language (HTML). As you know, HTML is a standard markup language used to describe how text, images, links, and various HTML GUI widgets are rendered by the hosting Web browser. While it is true that modern IDEs (including Visual Studio.NET) have numerous built-in tools that hide most of the raw HTML from view, you still need to feel comfortable with HTML as you work with ASP.NET.

A given HTML file consists of a core set of HTML tags, used to specify the fact that it is an HTML file, general document information (title, file metadata, and so forth), and the body of the document (i.e., the collection of text, images, tables, links, and so on). Keep in mind that HTML tags are not case sensitive. Therefore, in the eyes of the hosting browser, <HTML>, <html>, and <Html> are identical.

To get started, open the Visual Studio.NET IDE and insert an empty HTML file using the File|Miscellaneous Files|New File. . . menu selection and save this file under your physical directory as default.htm. If you examine the new *.htm file created by the IDE, you will find the following skeleton markup tags:

```
<HTML>
<HEAD>
<TITLE></TITLE>
<META NAME="GENERATOR" Content="Microsoft Visual Studio">
```

```
<META HTTP-EQUIV="Content-Type" content="text/html">
</HEAD>
<BODY>

<!- Insert HTML here ->

</BODY>
</HTML>
```

A given HTML tag is opened using the *<X>* notation and closed with a corresponding *</X>* (slash) tag. Although the syntax of HTML does allow for a degree of laziness (closing end tags are not absolutely required in many cases), it is good practice to always close a tag with the *</X>* syntax. The <HTML> and </HTML> tags are used to mark the beginning and end of your document. As you may guess, Web browsers use these tags to understand where to begin applying the rendering formats specified in the body of the document.

The <HEAD> tags are used to hold any metadata about the document itself. Here the HTML header uses some <META> tags that describe the origin of this file (MS Visual Studio) and file content. Currently our page has no title, so let's modify this HTML file to look like the following:

```
<HTML>

<HEAD>
<TITLE>HTML is unavoidable</TITLE>
<META NAME="GENERATOR" Content="Microsoft Visual Studio">
<META HTTP-EQUIV="Content-Type" content="text/html">
</HEAD>
<BODY>

<!- Insert HTML here ->

</BODY>
</HTML>
```

The <TITLE> tag is used to specify the text string that should be placed in the title bar of the hosting Web browser. Once you save this file and open it in a browser, you will see something like Figure 14-4. (Note the caption of the window.)

The real action behind an HTML file takes place in the <BODY> tag set. Nestled within these tags are any number of additional tags used to render and format textual or graphical information. While an exhaustive examination of

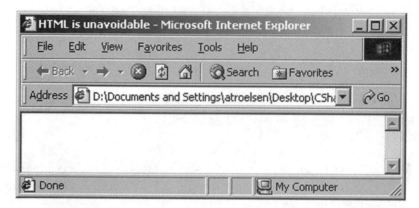

Figure 14-4. The <TITLE> tag in action

every HTML tag is (way) beyond the scope of this book, the next several pages document some of the core tags you are bound to run into when working with ASP.NET Web applications.

Basic HTML Text Formatting

One obvious use of an HTML file is to display textual messages. In HTML, text elements are typically placed within the <BODY> tag set. For example, assume that you are building a login page for a given Web application (note the HTML comment syntax), as shown here:

```
<BODY>
     <!- Prompt for user ->
     The Cars Login Page
</BODY>
```

Notice that in this case, you did not surround the text block with corresponding tags. When the browser finds a line of untagged text, it pumps out the textual information exactly as written. Thus, if you update the <BODY> as shown here:

```
<BODY>
     <!- Prompt for user ->
     The Cars Login Page
     Please enter your user name and password.
</BODY>
```

you see that the browser does not add the expected line break (Figure 14-5).

Figure 14-5. Untagged textual information omits line breaks

To flow text over multiple lines, you need to use the <P> and </P> (Paragraph) tags, which instruct the browser to begin a new paragraph, as shown here:

```
<BODY>
    <!- Technically, you do not need to close a paragraph with </p> ->
    The Cars Login Page
    <p>Please enter your user name and password.</p>
</BODY>
```

Figure 14-6 shows the new output.

Figure 14-6. The <P> tag begins a new paragraph

To insert a new blank line (rather than begin a new paragraph), use the
 (BReak) tags instead. (See Figure 14-7.)

```
<BODY>
    <!- Insert a break without a blank line ->
    The Cars Login Page
    <br>Please enter your user name and password.</br>
</BODY>
```

Figure 14-7. The <br> tag simply starts a new line

Now that you can add multiple lines of text (with carriage returns), you may wish to add some bold or italic formatting, using the <B> and <I> tags. For example, to apply bold formatting to the first line of text and italicize specific words in the second line, you could write the following (see Figure 14-8 for output):

```
<BODY>
    <!- Bold and italic formatting ->
    <b>The Cars Login Page</b>
    <br>Please enter your <i>user name</i> and <i>password</i>.
</BODY>
```

Working with Format Headers

The final textual formatting issue you will examine is the use of the various heading tags. Using <h1>, <h2>, <h3>, <h4>, <h5>, and <h6> tags, you can alter the size of the rendered text. The <h1> tag is your largest possible option, while <h6> marks the smallest format. Here is an example:

Figure 14-8. Bold and italic text

```
<BODY>
    <!- Prompt for user ->
    <h1>The Cars Login Page</h1>
    <br><h3>Please enter your <i>user name</i> and <i>password</i>.</h3>
</BODY>
```

Finally, you can apply the <center> tag (also as left, right, and justify) to force a block of text to be centered in the browser's client area, as shown here:

```
<BODY>
    <!- Prompt for user ->
    <center>
    <h1>The Cars Login Page</h1>
    <br><h3>Please enter your <i>user name</i> and <i>password</i>.</h3>
    </center>
</BODY>
```

Figure 14-9 shows the end result. (Note as you resize the browser, the text remains centered.)

Visual Studio.NET HTML Editors

So far, your simple HTML page is rather bland. To help spruce things up, let's take a moment to check out some of the design time tools supplied by the VS.NET IDE. First and foremost, you may configure various aspects of the page itself using the Properties window. To do so, select the DOCUMENT object and hack away (Figure 14-10).

Figure 14-9. Working with HTML header tags

Figure 14-10. Visual editing of an HTML document begins here

For example, if you modify the bgColor property (which sets the background color of the page), the underlying HTML file is updated automatically (Figure 14-11).

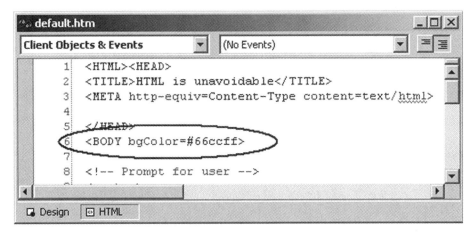

Figure 14-11. Design time modifications are recorded as HTML

The IDE also provides an HTML Formatting toolbar (Figure 14-12), which allows you to modify the appearance of your text (color, font, header size, bullet points, and so on).

Figure 14-12. The HTML formatting toolbar

Thus, you can build up the verbiage of your page using a word-processor–like approach. The difference is that raw HTML is generated under the hood. As you build your pages, I assume you will take the time to play around with various formatting scenarios and examine the underlying HTML tags.

HTML Form Development

Now that you have had an initial look at the layout of a basic HTML page, you can explore how to facilitate some user interaction. As you will see later in this chapter, the ASP.NET framework supplies a number of WebForm controls, which are responsible for generating HTML tags automatically. The beauty of using the WebForm control set is the fact that you (as a Web developer) can build the UI of the returned page without concern for the underlying HTML. The controls you are about to briefly examine are *not* .NET WebForm controls but simply a set of built-in widgets used during HTML form development.

An HTML form is simply a named group of related UI elements used to gather user input, which is then transmitted to the Web application via HTTP. (You will see exactly how in just a bit.) Do not confuse an HTML form with the literal client area displayed in a browser. In reality, an HTML form is more of a *logical grouping* of widgets placed in the <form> and </form> tag pairs, as shown here:

```
<form name = MainForm id = MainForm>
    <!-Add UI elements here ->
</form>
```

Here you have created a form and assigned the ID and friendly name to MainForm. While this is technically optional, get in the habit of doing so. Later in this chapter, you will find this useful when working with client-side scripting, where you frequently need to identify controls by name.

Typically, the opening <form> tag supplies an action attribute, which specifies the URL to which to submit the form data, as well as the method of transmitting that data itself (posting or getting). You will examine this aspect of the <form> tag in just a bit. For the time being, let's look at the sort of items that can be placed in an HTML form. The Visual Studio.NET IDE provides an HTML toolbar that allows you to select each HTML-based UI widget (Figure 14-13).

Figure 14-13. The HTML controls

Table 14-1 gives a rundown of some the more common items.

Table 14-1. Common HTML GUI Types

HTML GUI WIDGET	MEANING IN LIFE
Button	A button that does not support the type attribute used to trigger a SUBMIT or RESET. This sort of button can be used to hit a block of client-side script code or any other logic that does not require a trip to the Web server.
Checkbox Radio Button Listbox Dropdown	Standard UI selection elements.
Image	Allows you to specify an image to render onto the form.
Reset Button	This button element has its type attribute set to RESET. This instructs the browser to clear out the values in each UI element on the page to their default values.
Submit Button	This button element has its type attribute set to SUBMIT, which sends the form data to the recipient of a request.
Text Field Text Area Password Field	These UI elements are used to hold a single line (or multiple lines) of text. The Password Field renders input data using an asterisk (*) character mask.

As an interesting side note, be aware that the .NET base class libraries supply a number of managed types that correspond to these raw HTML widgets. For further information, check out the System.Web.UI.HtmlControls namespace.

Building the User Interface

The first step in building a user interface using HTML form widgets is to declare a <form> segment of the HTML document. Thus, add the following markup:

```
<HTML>
<HEAD>
<TITLE>HTML is unavoidable</TITLE>
<META NAME="GENERATOR" Content="Microsoft Visual Studio">
<META HTTP-EQUIV="Content-Type" content="text/html">
</HEAD>
<BODY BGCOLOR="#66ccff">
```

```
<!- Prompt for user ->
<center>
<h1>The Cars Login Page</h1>
<br><h3>Please enter your <i>user name</i> and <i>password</i>.</h3>

<!- Build a form to get user info ->
<form name=MainForm >
</form>

</center>
</BODY>
</HTML>
```

At this point, you can either flip back to design mode and drag and drop the HTML widgets onto the form or add HTML tags by hand. In general, each HTML widget is described using a name attribute (used to identify the item programmatically) and a type attribute (used to specify which UI element you are interested in placing in the <form> declaration). Depending which UI widget you manipulate, you will find additional attributes specific to that particular item. As you would expect, each UI element and its attributes can be modified using the Property window.

The UI you will build will contain two text fields (one of which is a Password widget), as well as two button types (one for submitting the form data and the other to reset the form data to the default values). Here is the associated HTML (by the way, " " identifies a single blank space):

```
<form name=MainForm >
    <p>User Name:  
    <input id = txtUserName type = text></p>
    <p>Password:   
    <input name = txtPassword type = password></p>
    <input name = btnSubmit type = submit value = Submit>  
    <input name = btnReset type = reset value = Reset>
</form>
```

Notice that you have assigned relevant names to each widget (txtUserName, txtPassword, btnSubmit, and btnReset). Of greater importance, note that each input button has an extra attribute named value, which marks these buttons as UI items that automatically clear all fields to their initial values (value = Reset) or send the form data to the recipient (value = Submit).

Other UI elements may also take a value attribute. For example, you can set the value of the txtUserName text box as shown in Figure 14-14.

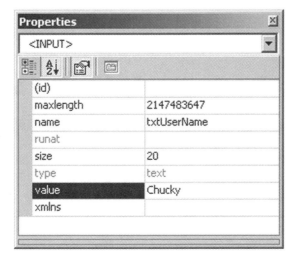

Figure 14-14. Setting a widget's value

The string "Chucky" is now the default value of the txtUserName UI widget.
To test out your application thus far, save your changes and open the *htm file.
Notice that when you enter values into the Text Box items and click the Reset but-
ton, the UI elements are reassigned their default values.

Figure 14-15, then, is your creation thus far.

Figure 14-15. An extremely boring Web page

Adding an Image

The final raw HTML UI topic here is how to incorporate images into your HTML documents. Like other aspects of HTML, images are marked using tags, specifically, <img>, as shown here:

```
<img alt="You gotta log in to see this!" src="car.gif" border=4>
```

The alt (alternative) attribute is used to specify a textual equivalent to the graphic image specified by the src (source) attribute. This text blurb is used as pop-up text when the cursor is placed over the image or, in browsers that do not support graphical images, as a textual alternative. The border attribute is optional, but is used here to render an outline around your image. Be aware that the value assigned to the alt attribute may be a hard-coded path or (as you have here) without a specified path. This approach assumes that the images used are in the same folder as the *.htm files using them. Figure 14-16 shows the update.

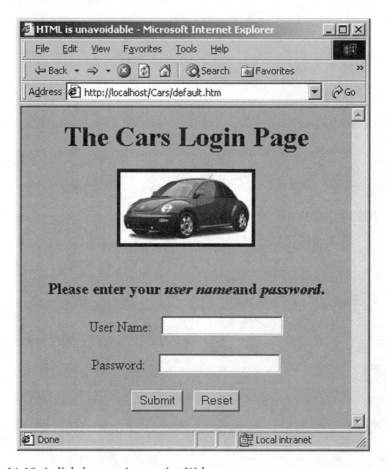

Figure 14-16. A slightly more interesting Web page

The Role of Client-Side Scripting

Now that you have a better understanding of how to construct an HTML form, the next issue is to examine the role of client-side scripting. The inherit evil of a Web application is the need to make frequent calls to the server machine to update the HTML rendered into the browser. Of course, while round trips are unavoidable, you should always be aware of ways to minimize travel across the wire. One technique that saves round trips is using client-side scripting to validate user input before submitting the form data to the recipient.

For example, currently you require the end user to enter a password and user name. If either field is blank, you do not allow a submission of the form's data to occur. Of course, HTML cannot help in this endeavor, as HTML is only concerned with the display of content. To augment the functionality of standard HTML, you must use a given scripting language (or if necessary any number of scripting languages).

There are many scripting languages. Two of the more popular are VBScript and JavaScript. VBScript is a subset of the Visual Basic 6.0 programming language. Be aware that Microsoft Internet Explorer (IE) is the only Web browser that has built-in support for client-side VBScript support. Thus, if you wish your HTML pages to work correctly in any commercial Web browser, do *not* use VBScript for your client-side scripting logic.

The truth is that VBScript is effectively dead as of the release of the .NET platform. The reason is simple. Unlike classic ASP, ASP.NET does not use scripting languages at all. Rather, ASP.NET pages use full-fledged programming languages (VB.NET, C#, and so on) to perform server-side logic.

The other popular scripting language is JavaScript. Be very aware that JavaScript is in no way, shape, or form a subset of the Java language. While JavaScript and Java have a somewhat similar syntax, JavaScript is not a full-fledged programming language and thus is far less powerful than Java itself. The good news is that all Web browsers support JavaScript, which makes it a natural candidate for client-side validation. (As an interesting side note, understand that JavaScript is standardized as ECMAScript, whereas JScript is the Microsoft implementation of JavaScript.)

A Client-Side Scripting Example

To begin understanding client-side scripting, you first need to examine how to intercept events from HTML GUI widgets. Assume you have a new and very simple HTML page that looks like Figure 14-17.

Next, you need to assign a valid ID and name to the button using the Properties window (testBtn will do the trick). To capture the click event for this button, activate the HTML view and select your button from the left drop-down list. Using the right drop-down list box, select the onclick event (Figure 14-18).

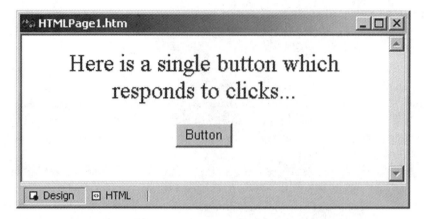

Figure 14-17. A new HTML page

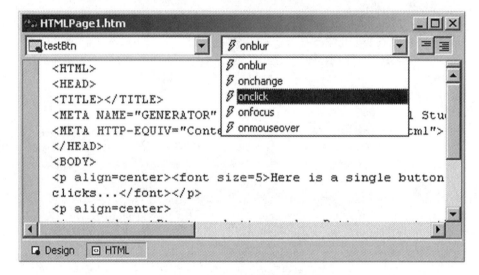

Figure 14-18. Capturing HTML widget events

Once you do this, you will find two major HTML updates (shown in bold):

```
<HTML>
<HEAD>
<TITLE></TITLE>
<META NAME="GENERATOR" Content="Microsoft Visual Studio">
<META HTTP-EQUIV="Content-Type" content="text/html">
```

```
<script id=clientEventHandlersJS language=javascript>
<!-
function testBtn_onclick() {
}
//->
</script>

</HEAD>
<BODY>
<p align = center>
<font size = 5>Here is a single button which responds to clicks. . .</font></p>
<p align = center>
<input id =testBtn type=button value=Button name=testBtn
  language=javascript onclick="return testBtn_onclick()">
</p>

</BODY>
</HTML>
```

As you can see, a new <script> block has been added to your HTML header, with JavaScript specified as the language of choice. Note that the scripting block has been placed with HTML style comments. The reason is simple. If your page ends up on a browser that does not support JavaScript, the code will be treated as a comment block and ignored. Of course your page may be less functional, but the up side is that your page will not blow up when rendered into the browser.

Next, notice that the attribute set for the HTML button has a new member named onclick, which is assigned the new JavaScript function. Thus, when the button is clicked, this method is called automatically. By way of a simple test, if you update the function as shown here:

```
<script id = clientEventHandlersJS language = javascript>
<!-
function testBtn_onclick()
{
    // JavaScript function call (a message box).
    alert("Hey, stop clicking me. . .");
}
//->
</script>
```

you will see a message box pop up when you click the button (Figure 14-19).

Figure 14-19. IE alert

Validating the default.htm HTML Page

Now, update your current default.htm page to support some client-side validation. The goal is to ensure that when the user clicks the Submit button, you call a
JavaScript function that checks each text box for empty entries. If this is the case,
you pop up an alert that instructs the user to reenter the required data. First,
assign an onclick event for the Submit button to a JavaScript method named
ValidateData(). Within the logic of this method, check each text box for empty
strings, as shown here:

```
<script language = javascript>
<!- Scope the names of the text boxes with the name of the form!
function ValidateData()
{
    // If they forget either item, popup a message box.
    if((MainForm.txtUserName.value = = "") ||
    (MainForm.txtPassword.value = = ""))
    {
        alert("You must supply a user name and password!");
        return false;
    }
    return true;
}
->
</script>
. . .
<input id = btnSubmit onclick = "return ValidateData()" type = submit
  value = Submit name = btnSubmit>
```

While you're at it, add another JavaScript method named GetTheDate(),
which will be called when the page is loaded to display the time and date when
the user logs on. To call this function requires a separate <script> tag, which uses

the write() method of the Internet Explorer Document object to pump out a block of text, as shown here:

```
<HTML>
<HEAD>
<TITLE>HTML is unavoidable</TITLE>

<script language = javascript>
<!- Here are the JavaScript methods for this form.
function ValidateData()
{
    if((MainForm.txtUserName.value = = "") ||
       (MainForm.txtPassword.value = = ""))
    {
        alert("You must supply a user name and password!");
        return false;
    }
    return true;
}
function GetTheDate() { return Date(); }
->
</script>

</HEAD>
<BODY bgColor=#66ccff>

<!- Prompt for user ->
<center>
<h1>The Cars Login Page</h1>
<h2>Today is: </h2>
<script language=javascript>
    // document.write() is part of the IE object model.
    document.write(GetTheDate());
</script>
<br>
<h3>Please enter your <i>user name</i>and <i>password</i>.</h3>

<!- Build a form to get user info ->
<form name=MainForm>
    <p>User Name:   <input type=text name=txtUserName></p>
    <p>Password:   
    <input type=password name=txtPassword></p>
    <input id=btnSubmit onclick=ValidateData() type=submit
    value=Submit name=btnSubmit>  
```

```
        <input type=reset value=Reset name=btnReset>
</form>
</center>
</BODY>
</HTML>
```

Submitting the Form Data (GET and POST)

At this point you have been exposed to a number of Web-centric design techniques. Now that you have a simple Web front end, you need to examine the very
important topic of submitting this data to a Web application. When you build an
HTML form, you typically supply an action attribute to specify the recipient of
the incoming data. Possible receivers include mail servers, other HTML files, an
Active Server Page (classic or .NET), and so forth. For this example, you use a
classic ASP file (which you will build in just a moment). Update your HTML file
by specifying the following attribute in the opening <form> tag, as shown here:

```
<form name=MainForm
action="http://localhost/Cars/ClassicASPPage.asp" method = "GET">
    . . .
</form>
```

This extra attribute specifies that when the Submit button for this form is
clicked, the form data should be sent to an ASP page (named
ClassicASPPage.asp) located under the Cars virtual directory located on the current machine (i.e., localhost). When you specify method = GET as the mode of
transmission, the form data is appended to the query string as a set of
name/value pairs. The other method of transmitting form data to the Web server
is to specify method = POST, as shown here:

```
<form name=MainForm
action="http://localhost/Cars/ClassicASPPage.asp" method = "POST">
    . . .
</form>
```

In this case, the form data is not appended to the query string, but instead is
written to a separate line sent with the HTTP header. In this way, the form data is
not directly visible to the outside world and is therefore a bit more secure. (More
importantly, POST is not limited by character length.) For the time being, assume
you have specified the GET method of form data transfer.

Parsing a Query String

To understand exactly how the receiving ASP file can extract out the form's data, you need to examine the query string. When you submit form data using the GET action, you see a slightly mangled text string appearing in your browser's Address box. Here is an example:

```
http://localhost/Cars/ClassicASPPage.asp?
txtUserName=Chucky&txtPassword=somepassword&btnSubmit=Submit
```

One core feature of this (and any) query string is the question mark delimiter (?). On the left side of the ? is the address of the recipient (your ASP page). On the right side is a string composed of any number of name/value pairs (such as txtUserName=Chucky).

As you can see, each name/value pair is separated by an ampersand (&). This particular query string was quite simple to parse, given that you have not injected any blank spaces in the process. However, if the user name is changed from Chucky to Chucky Chuckles, you find the following query string:

```
http://localhost/Cars/ClassicASPPage.asp?txtUserName=
Chucky+Chuckles&txtPassword=somepasswork&btnSubmit=Submit
```

Notice how extra spaces are marked with a + marker. Thus, if you have five spaces between Chucky and Chuckles, you find:

```
http://localhost/Cars/ClassicASPPage.asp?txtUserName=
Chucky+++++Chuckles&txtPassword=somepassword&btnSubmit=Submit
```

In addition to handling spaces, query strings represent various oddball characters (e.g., nonalphanumeric characters such as ^ and ~) as their hexadecimal ASCII equivalents. Thus, if you resubmit to the ASP page using Hello^77 as the password, you find this:

```
http://localhost/Cars/ClassicASPPage.asp?txtUserName=
Chucky++++Chuckles&txtPassword=Hello%5E77&btnSubmit=Submit
```

Building a Classic Active Server Page

To receive the form data you need to build the ClassicASPPage.asp file, insert a new Active Server Page file using Visual Studio.NET (Figure 14-20). Be sure the file name you assign to this new item is the same name as specified in your form's action attribute (and also be sure to save this file into the folder to which your virtual directory has been mapped).

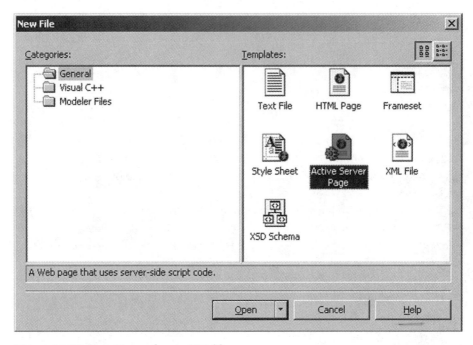

Figure 14-20. Inserting a classic ASP file

An Active Server Page is a hodgepodge of HTML code and server-side script. If you have never worked with classic ASP, understand that the goal of ASP is to dynamically build HTML on the fly using server-side scripting. For example, you may have a scripting block that reads a table from a data source (using ADO) and returns the rows as generic HTML.

For this example, the ASP page uses the intrinsic ASP Request object to read the values of the incoming query string and render them as HTML (thus just echoing the input). Here is the relevant script (note the use of <% . . . %> to mark a block of script):

```
<%@ Language=VBScript %>      <!- VBScript A-OK on the server side ->
<HTML>
<HEAD>
<META NAME="GENERATOR" Content="Microsoft Visual Studio 7.0">
</HEAD>
<BODY>
```

```
<!- Send back the info they gave us ->
<center>
    <h1>You said: </h1>
    <b>User Name: </b><%= Request.QueryString("txtUserName") %><br>
    <b>Password: </b><%= Request.QueryString("txtPassword") %><br>
</center>
</BODY>
</HTML>
```

The first thing to be aware of is that an *.asp file begins and ends with the standard <html>, <head>, and <body> tag pairs. Here you use the Request object, which like any classic COM type supports a number of properties, methods, and events. You call the QueryString() method to examine the values contained in each HTML widget (submitted via "method = GET"). Also note that the <%= . . .%> notation is a shorthand way of saying "Insert the following into the HTTP response." To gain a finer level of flexibility, you could use the ASP Response object directly. Here is an example:

```
<!- Send back the info they gave us ->
<center>
    <h1>You said:</h1>
    <b>User Name: </b><%= Request.QueryString("txtUserName") %><br>
    <b>Password: </b>
    <%
        dim pwd
        pwd = Request.QueryString("txtPassword")
        Response.Write (pwd)
    %>
</center>
```

The Request and Response objects of classic ASP provide a number of additional members. Furthermore, class ASP also defines a small number of additional objects (Session, Server, Application, and ObjectContext) that you can use while constructing your Web application. You will not examine the functionality of these classic ASP items here. However, later in this chapter you will find that the same behavior is supplied using properties of the ASP.NET Page type.

In any case, to trigger the ASP logic, simply launch your default.htm page from a browser and submit the information. After the script is processed, you are returned a brand new (dynamically generated) HTML file (Figure 14-21).

Granted, this current example is not very sexy. Nevertheless, you should be able to understand the key principle behind ASP (and thus ASP.NET) programming: Given some data submitted by an HTML form, you can use code to dynamically return content to the user.

Figure 14-21. The dynamically generated HTML

Responding to POST Submissions

Currently, your default.htm file specifies GET as the method of sending your form's data to the receiving *.asp page. Using this approach, the values contained in the various GUI widgets are appended to the end of the query string. It is important to note that the ASP Request.QueryString() method is *only* able to extract data submitted via the GET method. If you change your method of data transfer to action = POST and rerun your Web application, you will be saddened to find an empty response (Figure 14-22).

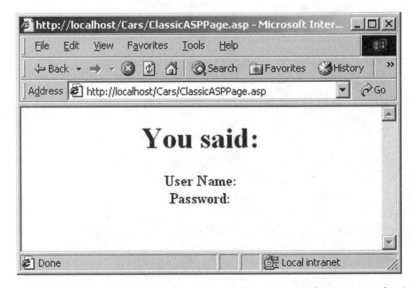

Figure 14-22. The QueryString() method can only proceess information submitted using HTTP GET

This is because the form data has now been sent as part of the HTTP header, rather than as appended textual information. The good news is that this same information can obtained using the Request.Form collection. To submit your data using the POST technique, you can update your *.asp file as shown here:

```
<BODY>
<!- Send back the info they gave us ->
<center>
    <h1>You said:</h1>
    <b>User Name: </b><%= Request.Form("txtUserName") %><br>
    <b>Password: </b>
    <%
        dim pwd
        pwd = Request.Form("txtPassword")
        Response.Write (pwd)
    %>
</center>
</BODY>
```

Once you do, you see that you can read the incoming data once again. This time, however, the values are not appended to the URL (Figure 14-23).

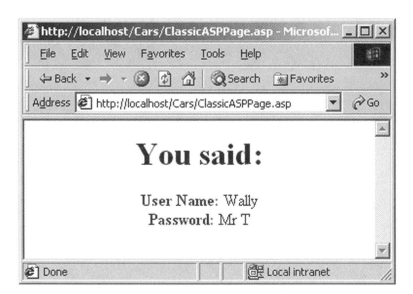

Figure 14-23. POSTed data can be processed using Request.Form

Figure 14-24 illustrates each technique used to submit form data to a recipient and the corresponding technique to obtain this data from a classic ASP Web application.

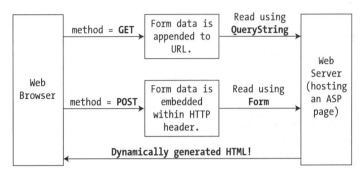

Figure 14-24. Submitting data to an ASP page using HTTP GET and POST

Building Your First Official ASP.NET Application

Before ending this review of Web basics, open the default.htm file and update the opening <form> tag as shown here (note the aspx file extension):

```
<form name=MainForm
action="http://localhost/Cars/ClassicASPPage.aspx"
method=post ID=Form1>
```

Then change the file extension of your classic ASP file to *.aspx and rerun the application. You should see no difference at all (Figure 14-25).

Figure 14-25. An ASP.NET application

Congratulations! You have just created your first ASP.NET application (by virtue of the *.aspx file extension). As you can see, all of the techniques presented thus far are valid in the world of ASP.NET. At this point you should (hopefully) feel more comfortable working with Web-based applications and understand how each of these building blocks interrelate. With this review out of the way, you can now spend the remainder of this chapter examining the framework of ASP.NET.

SOURCE CODE   *The Cars project is included under the Chapter 14 subdirectory.*

Some Problems with Classic ASP

While many successful Web applications have been created using classic ASP, this architecture is not without its down side. Perhaps the biggest downfall of ASP proper is the very point that makes it a powerful platform: scripting languages. While it is true that the ASP scripting parser is sophisticated enough to cache the compiled script after the first use, scripting languages such as VBScript and JavaScript are interpreted, typeless entities that do not really lend themselves to robust OO programming techniques.

Another problem with classic ASP is the fact that an *.asp page does not yield very modularized code. Given that ASP is a blend of HTML and script in a *single* page, most ASP Web applications are a confused mix of two very different programming techniques. While it is true that classic ASP allows you to partition related code into distinct files, the underlying object model does not support true separation of concerns. In an ideal world, a Web framework would allow the presentation logic (i.e., HTML code) to remain separate from the business logic (i.e., functional code).

One final issue is the fact that classic ASP demands a good deal of boilerplate, redundant script that tends to repeat between projects. Almost all Web applications need to validate user input, render rich HTML content, and so on. In classic ASP, you are the one in charge of adding the appropriate server-side scripting code. Ideally, a Web framework (rather than a human) is in charge of these details.

Some Benefits of ASP.NET

ASP.NET addresses each of the limitations of classic ASP. First and foremost, ASP.NET files (*.aspx) do not use scripting languages. As mentioned earlier, ASP.NET allows you to use real programming languages such as C#, JScript.NET, and Visual Basic.NET. Because of this, you can apply each technique you have learned throughout this book directly to your Web development efforts. As you would expect, *.aspx pages can make programmatic use of the .NET class libraries as well as access the functionality provided by custom assemblies.

Next, ASP.NET applications provide numerous ways to decrease the amount of code you need to write to begin with. For example, through the use of server-side Web controls, you can build a browser-based front end using various GUI widgets that emit raw HTML under the hood. Other Web controls are used to perform automatic validation of your GUI items (which decreases the amount of client-side script you are responsible for authoring).

Beyond the simplification of your coding efforts, ASP.NET offers numerous practical bells and whistles. For example, all ASP.NET Web applications use the integrated Visual Studio.NET IDE (a huge improvement from debugging scripting logic using Visual Interdev). To begin seeing these and other benefits in action, let's begin by examining the core ASP.NET namespaces.

The ASP.NET Namespaces

The .NET class libraries contain numerous namespaces that represent Web-based technologies. Generally speaking, these namespaces can be grouped into three major categories: core Web atoms (e.g., HTTP types, configuration types, and security types), UI (WebForm controls), and Web services (described in Chapter 15). While a full examination of each item would require a book on its own, you can certainly come to terms with the functionality offered by the core namespaces described in Table 14-2.

Table 14-2. ASP.NET Namespaces

WEB CENTRIC NAMESPACE	MEANING IN LIFE
System.Web	System.Web defines core types that enable browser/Web server communication (such as request and response capabilities, cookie manipulation, and file transfer).
System.Web.Caching	This namespace contains types that facilitate caching support for a Web application.
System.Web.Configuration	This namespace contains types that allow you to configure your Web application in conjunction with the project's Web configuration file.
System.Web.Security	Security support for a Web application.
System.Web.Services System.Web.Services.Description System.Web.Services.Discovery System.Web.Services.Protocols	These namespaces provide the types that allow you to build Web services, examined in Chapter 15.
System.Web.UI System.Web.UI.WebControls System.Web.UI.HtmlControls	These namespaces define a number of types that allow you to build a GUI front end for your Web application.

The Core Types of System.Web

The System.Web namespace defines the minimal and complete set of types that allow a browser-based client to communicate and interact with the Web server. Table 14-3 is a quick rundown of some items of interest, many of which are examined in greater detail throughout this chapter.

Table 14-3. Core Types of the System.Web Namespace

SYSTEM.WEB TYPE	MEANING IN LIFE
HttpApplication	The HttpApplication class defines the members common to all ASP.NET applications. As you will see, the global.asax file defines a class derived from HttpApplication.
HttpApplicationState	The HttpApplicationState class enables developers to share global information across multiple requests, sessions, and pipelines in an ASP.NET application.
HttpBrowserCapabilities	Enables the server to compile information on the capabilities of the browser running on the client.
HttpCookie	Provides a type-safe way to access multiple HTTP cookies.
HttpRequest	Provides an object-oriented way to enable browser-to-server communication (e.g., used to gain access to the HTTP request data supplied by a client).
HttpResponse	Provides an object-oriented way to enable server-to-browser communication (e.g., used to send output to a client).

Understanding the Application/Session Distinction

One aspect of Web-based programming that may be new to desktop application developers is the distinction between application and session state. Recall that a Web application can be understood as a collection of all related files located under a virtual directory. ASP.NET provides the HttpApplication type to represent the common methods, properties, and events for a given Web application. As you will see, the globals.asax file defines a single type (named Global) that derives from the HttpApplication base class.

Closely related to the HttpApplication type is HttpApplicationState type. This class enables you to share global information across multiple sessions in an ASP.NET application. A Web session expresses one user's interaction with the Web application. For example, if 20,000 users are logged onto the Cars site, 20,000 sessions are in process.

In ASP.NET, each session retains stateful information for a given user, programmatically represented by the HttpSessionState type. In this way, each user has an allocated block of memory that represents the user's interaction unique with the Web application. (After all, if two users have logged onto the Cars site, user A may want a brand new BMW while user B may want a 1970 Colt.) The relationship between a Web application and Web sessions is shown in Figure 14-26.

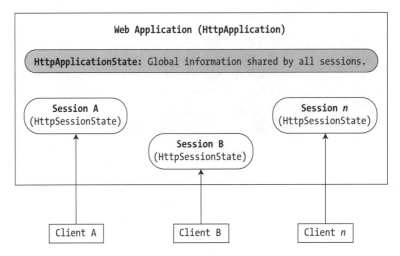

Figure 14-26. Application and session state

Under classic ASP, the notions of application and session state are represented using distinct object types (Application and Session). Under ASP.NET, a Page-derived type defines identically named *properties* (also named Application and Session), which expose the underlying HttpApplicationState and HttpSessionState types. You will learn more details in just a bit.

Creating a Simple C# Web Application

To get the ball rolling, let's build a small test project and examine the overall structure of the ASP.NET framework. First, create a new C# Web Application project workspace named FirstWebApplication (Figure 14-27).

Before you click the OK button, take a minute to notice that the Location text box maps not to a specific folder on your hard drive, but rather to the URL of the machine hosting this Web application. The Visual Studio.NET solution files (*.sln and *.suo) are stored under the "My Documents\Visual Studio Projects" subfolder.

Once the new project workspace has been created, you will notice that a design time template has been opened automatically (Figure 14-28).

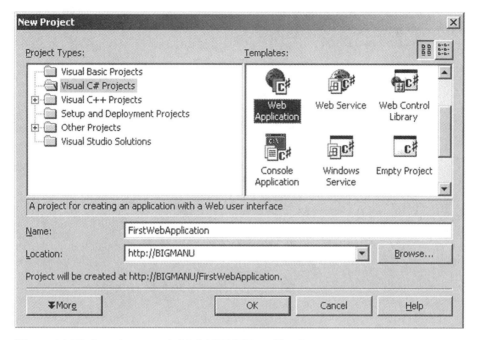

Figure 14-27. Creating your initial ASP.NET application

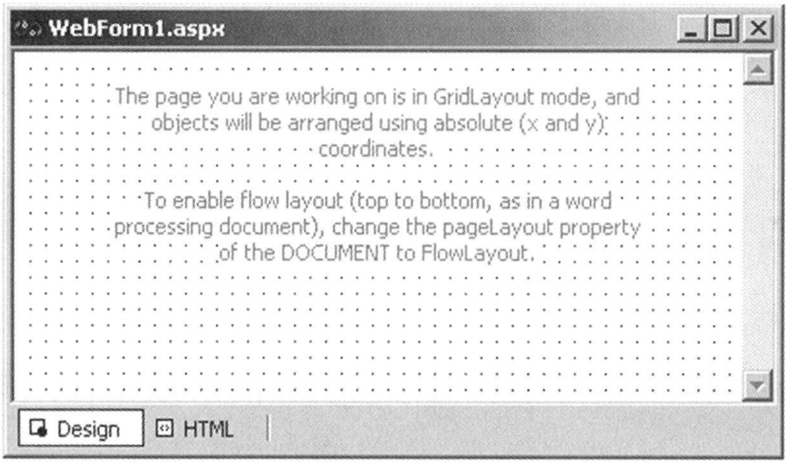

Figure 14-28. Your design time template

Much like a Windows Forms application, this template represents the visual appearance of the *.aspx file you are constructing. The difference, of course, is that you are using HTML-based WebForm controls rather than Win32-based Windows Forms controls. Note that the default name for this page is WebForm1.

Given that this will be the page requested by the outside world, let's rename it to the more appropriate default.aspx.

Next, look at your Solution Explorer window (Figure 14-29). You have been given a number of new files and external assembly references.

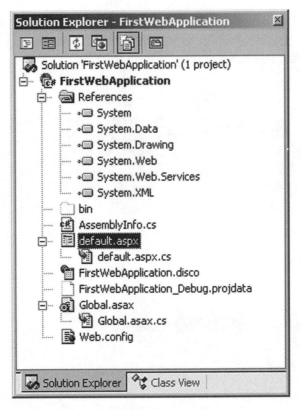

Figure 14-29. Initial files of an ASP.NET application

If you open IIS, you see that a new virtual directory (FirstWebApplication) has been automatically created on your behalf (Figure 14-30).

As you can see, each file in the workspace has been included in this virtual directory. The physical folder to which this virtual directory is mapped can be located under a subdirectory under <drive>:\Inetpub\wwwroot (Figure 14-31).

Examining the Initial *.aspx File

If you examine the HTML behind your *.aspx file, you see that you have been given the minimal set of tags that establish a basic HTML form. The first point of

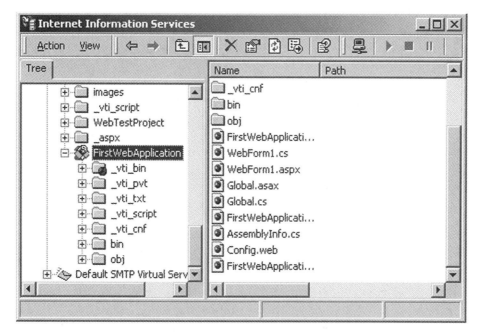

Figure 14-30. The new (automatically created) virtual directory

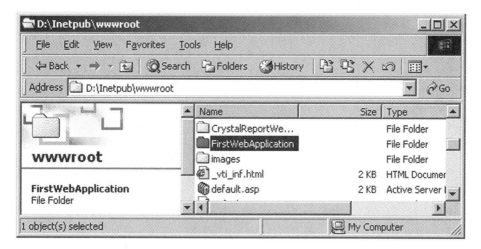

Figure 14-31. The physical file containing your project files

interest is the runat attribute appearing in the opening <form> tag. This attribute is the heart and sole of ASP.NET and is used to mark an item as a candidate for processing by the ASP.NET runtime to generate HTML to return to the browser, as shown here:

```
<%@ Page language="c#" Codebehind="default.aspx.cs"

AutoEventWireup="false" Inherits="FirstWebApplication.WebForm1" %>
<HTML>
    <HEAD>
        <meta name=vs_targetSchema content="Internet Explorer 5.0">
        <meta name="GENERATOR" Content="Microsoft Visual Studio 7.0">
        <meta name="CODE_LANGUAGE" Content="C#">
    </HEAD>
    <body MS_POSITIONING="GridLayout">
        <form method="post" runat="server">
        </form>
    </body>
</HTML>
```

The initial code block establishes a number of traits regarding the current page. First, you can see the name of the language used behind the scenes to construct your page (C#). The Codebehind attribute names the C# file that represents the behind the scenes processing. The Inherits attribute is used to specify the name of the class that represents the class defined in the file specified by Codebehind. (You will examine these topics further in just a bit.)

Examining the Web.config File

The web.config file contains XML data used to control various aspects of your Web application's configuration. Typically speaking, this file is located in the root of the associated virtual directory of the Web application and applies to each subdirectory. By default, this file contains compilation, error, security, debugging, session, and globalization centric information (Figure 14-32).

In addition, the web.config file may be extended with various other tags beyond the default. I leave it to you to check out the remaining variations.

Examining the Global.asax File

Similar to classic ASP, ASP.NET applications define a global file (global.asax) that allows you to interact with application-level (and session-level) events as well as to share common state data. If you right-click your application's global.asax file and select View Code, you see that this information is represented by a class named Global that derives from the HttpApplication base class, as shown here:

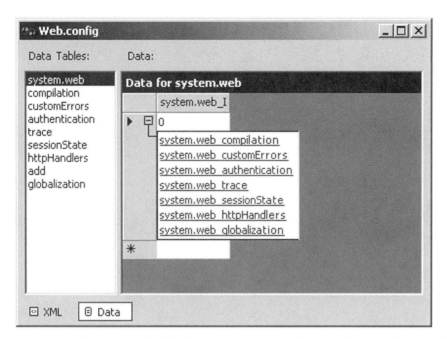

Figure 14-32. The web.config file allows you to adjust the core behavior of your Web application using XML tags

```
public class Global : System.Web.HttpApplication
{
    protected void Application_Start(Object sender, EventArgs e){}

    protected void Session_Start(Object sender, EventArgs e){}

    protected void Application_BeginRequest(Object sender, EventArgs e){}

    protected void Application_EndRequest(Object sender, EventArgs e){}

    protected void Session_End(Object sender, EventArgs e){}

    protected void Application_End(Object sender, EventArgs e){}
}
```

In some respects, the Global class acts as the intermediary between the external client and your Web Form. If you have a background in classic ASP, some of these events may already be familiar to you. In general, these events allow you to respond to the initialization (and termination) of the Web application and the individual sessions.

Adding Some Simple C# Logic

If you specify the Web address of your new Web application at this point, the ASP.NET engine will return an empty page. To remedy this situation, let's modify the body of your *.aspx file to return some textual information that specifies various aspects regarding the incoming HTTP request (the System.Web.UI.Page.Response property will be investigated in more detail later in this chapter):

```
<body MS_POSITIONING="GridLayout">
    <h1>
            <b>I am:</b>
    </h1>
    <%=this.ToString() %>
    <h1>
            <b>You are:</b>
    </h1>
    <%= Request.ServerVariables["HTTP_USER_AGENT"] %>

    <form method="post" runat="server" ID="Form1">
    </form>
</body>
```

Once you are done, compile and run the project. An HTML page is returned (Figure 14-33) that documents the agent who sent this request, as well as the string name of the entity receiving the request (the name of your page).

So far, it looks like ASP.NET is functionally identical to classic ASP. In fact, if you worked through the sample classic ASP application earlier in this chapter, things should look quite familiar. The only difference thus far is the fact that what you used to regard as the Request *object* is now a *property* of the Page base class. Also, as you can see, you are *not* writing script code in our <%. . .%> tags, but full-fledged C# code, as shown here:

```
<h1><b>I am: </b> <%=this.ToString() %></h1>
```

The Architecture of an ASP.NET Web Application

Now that you have had a chance to build a simple Web application, you can begin digging a bit deeper into the architecture itself. The first major point of interest is the mysterious Codebehind attribute in the initial script block, as shown here:

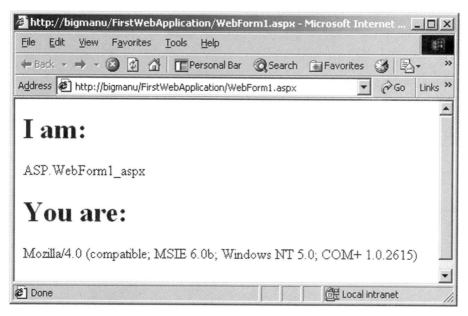

Figure 14-33. Documenting who's who

```
<%@ Page language="c#" Codebehind="WebForm1.aspx.cs"
AutoEventWireup="false" Inherits="FirstWebApplication.WebForm1" %>
```

The major difference between classic ASP and ASP.NET is that the *.aspx page, which is requested by an external client, is represented by a unique C# class, identified by the Codebehind attribute. When the client requests a particular *.aspx page, an object of this class is instantiated (and manipulated) by the ASP.NET runtime. Notice, however, that this C# file is not shown in the Solution Explorer. To access the Codebehind file, simply right-click an open *.aspx file and select View Code. Here is the initial code block:

```
namespace FirstWebApplication
{
    using System;
    using System.Collections;
    using System.ComponentModel;
    using System.Data;
    using System.Drawing;
    using System.Web;
    using System.Web.SessionState;
    using System.Web.UI;
    using System.Web.UI.WebControls;
    using System.Web.UI.HtmlControls;
```

```
public class WebForm1 : System.Web.UI.Page
{

    public WebForm1()
    {
        Page.Init += new System.EventHandler(Page_Init);
    }

    protected void Page_Load(object sender, System.EventArgs e)
    {
        // Put user code to initialize the page here.
    }

    protected void Page_Init(object sender, EventArgs e)
    {
        InitializeComponent();
    }

    private void InitializeComponent()
    {
        this.Load += new System.EventHandler(this.Page_Load);
    }
}
}
```

The default skeleton code is not too complicated. The constructor of the Page-derived class establishes an event handler for the Init event. The implementation of this handler calls InitializeComponents(), which establishes another event handler for the Load event.

The System.Web.UI.Page Type

To understand the purpose of this autogenerated class, let's begin by examining the System.Web.UI.Page base class. The Page class defines the properties, methods, and events common to all pages processed on the server by the ASP.NET runtime. Table 14-4 describes some (but by no means all) of the core properties.

As you can see, the Page type defines properties that correlate to the intrinsic object model of classic ASP. In addition to defining a number of inherited methods (which you typically do not need to interact with directly), Page also supplies the critical events described in Table 14-5.

Table 14-4. Properties of the Page Type

SYSTEM.WEB.UI.PAGE PROPERTY	MEANING IN LIFE
Application	Gets the HttpApplicationState object provided by the runtime.
Cache	Indicates the Cache object in which to store data for the page's application.
IsPostBack	Gets a value indicating whether the page is being loaded in response to a client postback, or if it is being loaded and accessed for the first time.
Request	Gets the HttpRequest object that provides access data from incoming HTTP requests.
Response	Gets the HttpResponse object that allows you to send HTTP response data back to a client browser.
Server	Gets the HttpServerUtility object supplied by the HTTP runtime.
Session	Gets the System.Web.SessionState.HttpSessionState object, which provides information about the current request's session.

Table 14-5. Events of the Page Type

SYSTEM.WEB.UI.PAGE EVENT	MEANING IN LIFE
Init	This event is fired when the page is initialized and is the first step in the page's life cycle.
Load	Once initialized, the Load event is fired. Here, you can configure any WebForm controls with an initial look and feel.
Unload	Occurs when the control is unloaded from memory. Controls should perform any final cleanup before termination.

The event handler for the Load event is a perfect place to connect to a data source (to populate a given WebForm DataGrid) and perform any necessary prep work. The Unload handler is a perfect place to clean up any allocated resources.

The *.aspx/Codebehind Connection

In addition to this boilerplate code, the C# class represented by the Codebehind tag can be extended with any number of custom properties and methods that can be called (indirectly) by the <%. . .%> code blocks in your *.aspx file. As you

recall, classic ASP requires you to define your custom functionality directly in the
*.asp file. Thus, your pages were a jumble of HTML tags and VBScript (or
JavaScript) code. Because of this the *.asp files were hard to read and even harder
to maintain and reuse.

Furthermore, recall that the whole approach of classic ASP was not terribly
object oriented. ASP.NET has resolved these problems by providing a way for you
to truly separate the logic that dynamically generates the returned HTML (the
*.aspx) file from the implantation of your page's logic (e.g., the *.aspx.cs file).

Now, one slightly odd concept is that when you are writing code in the *.aspx
file, you can reference the custom methods and properties defined in the
*.aspx.cs file. Let's see a simple example.

Assume you wish to build a simple function that obtains the current time
and date. You may do so directly in your Page-derived class as shown here:

```
public class WebForm1 : System.Web.UI.Page
{
    // Generated code. . .

    public string GetDateTime()
    {
        return DateTime.Now.ToString();
    }
}
```

To reference this method in your *.aspx code, you can simply write:

```
<body>
    <!- Get the time from the C# class ->
    <% Response.Write(GetDateTime()); %>
. . .
    <form method="post" runat="server" ID=Form1>
    </form>
</body>
```

You can also make reference to the inherited Page members directly in your
C# class. Thus, you could also write:

```
public class WebForm1 : System.Web.UI.Page
{
    // Generated code.
```

```
    public void GetDateTime()
    {
        Response.Write("It is now " + DateTime.Now.ToString());
    }
}
```

And then simply call:

```
<!- Get the time ->
<% GetDateTime(); %>
```

Working with the Page.Request Property

As you have seen earlier in this chapter, the basic flow of a Web session begins with a client logging onto a site, filling in user information, and clicking a Submit button maintained by an HTML form. In most cases, the opening tag of the form statement specifies an action and method attribute, which specifies the file on the Web server that will be sent the data in the various HTML widgets, and the method of sending this data (GET or POST). Here is an example:

```
<form name=MainForm action="http://localhost/default.aspx" method=get ID=Form1>
```

In ASP.NET, the Page.Request property provides access to the data sent by the HTTP request. Under the hood, this property manipulates an instance of the HttpRequest type. Table 14-6 lists some core members (which should look strangely familiar to you if you are coming from a classic ASP background).

You saw the members of the HttpRequest type earlier in this chapter. For example, when you spit out various characteristics of the incoming HTTP request, you used what looked to be an object named Request, as shown here:

```
<b>You Are: </b><%= Request.ServerVariables["HTTP_USER_AGENT"] %>
```

What you are really doing is accessing a property on the returned HttpRequest type, as shown here:

```
<b>You Are: </b>
<%
    HttpRequest r;
    r = this.Request;
    Response.Write(r.ServerVariables["HTTP_USER_AGENT"]);
%>
```

Table 14-6. Members of the HttpRequest Type

SYSTEM.WEB.HTTPREQUEST MEMBER	MEANING IN LIFE
ApplicationPath	Gets the virtual path to the currently executing server application.
Browser	Provides information about incoming client's browser capabilities.
ContentType	Indicates the MIME content type of an incoming request. This property is read only.
Cookies	Gets a collection of client's cookie variables.
FilePath	Indicates the virtual path of the current request. This property is read only.
Files	Gets the collection of client-uploaded files (multipart MIME format).
Filter	Gets or sets a filter to use when reading the current input stream.
Form	Gets a collection of Form variables.
Headers	Gets a collection of HTTP headers.
HttpMethod	Indicates the HTTP data transfer method used by the client (GET, POST). This property is read only.
IsSecureConnection	Indicates whether the HTTP connection is secure (that is, HTTPS). This property is read only.
Params	Gets a combined collection of QueryString + Form+ ServerVariable + Cookies.
QueryString	Gets the collection of QueryString variables.
RawUrl	Gets the current request's raw URL.
RequestType	Indicates the HTTP data transfer method used by the client (GET, POST).
ServerVariables	Gets a collection of Web server variables.
UserHostAddress	Gets the IP host address of the remote client.
UserHostName	Gets the DNS name of the remote client.

See the connection? Now, let's check out the Request.Response property (and the related HttpResponse type).

Working with the Page.Response Property

The Response property of the Page class provides access to an internal HttpResponse type. This type defines a number of properties that allow you to format the HTTP response sent back to the client browser. Table 14-7 lists some core properties (which again should look familiar if you have a classic ASP background).

Table 14-7. Properties of the HttpResponse Type

SYSTEM.WEB.HTTPRESPONSE PROPERTY	MEANING IN LIFE
Cache	Returns the caching semantics of the Web page (e.g., expiration time, privacy, vary clauses).
ContentEncoding	Gets or sets the HTTP character set of output.
ContentType	Gets or sets the HTTP MIME type of output.
Cookies	Gets the HttpCookie collection sent by the current request.
Filter	Specifies a wrapping filter object to modify the HTTP entity body before transmission.
IsClientConnected	Gets a value indicating whether the client is still connected to the server.
Output	Enables custom output to the outgoing HTTP content body.
OutputStream	Enables binary output to the outgoing HTTP content body.
StatusCode	Gets or sets the HTTP status code of output returned to the client.
StatusDescription	Gets or sets the HTTP status string of output returned to the client.
SuppressContent	Gets or sets a value indicating that HTTP content will not be sent to the client.

Also, consider the methods of the HttpResponse type described in Table 14-8.

Perhaps the most important aspect of the HttpResponse type is the ability to write to the HTTP output stream. As you have seen, you may directly call the Write() method or inline an output request using the <%= . . . %> notation (like

Table 14-8. Methods of the HttpResponse Type

SYSTEM.WEB.HTTPREQUEST METHOD	MEANING IN LIFE
AppendHeader()	Adds an HTTP header to the output stream.
AppendToLog()	Adds custom log information to the IIS log file.
Clear()	Clears all headers and content output from the buffer stream.
Close()	Closes the socket connection to a client.
End()	Sends all currently buffered output to the client, then closes the socket connection.
Flush()	Sends all currently buffered output to the client.
Redirect()	Redirects a client to a new URL.
Write()	Writes values to an HTTP output content stream.
WriteFile()	Overloaded. Writes a file directly to an HTTP content output stream.

classic ASP). Thus, you can manipulate this object from your *.aspx file as shown here:

```
<b>You are: </b>
<%
    HttpRequest r;
    r = this.Request;

    HttpResponse rs;
    rs = this.Response;

    rs.Write(r.ServerVariables["HTTP_USER_AGENT"]);
%>
```

The preceding code is exactly equivalent to the following:

```
<%= Request.ServerVariables["HTTP_USER_AGENT"] %>
```

Working with the Page.Application Property

The Application property of the Page class provides access to the underlying HttpApplicationState type. As mentioned earlier, HttpApplicationState enables developers to share global information across multiple sessions in an ASP.NET application. Table 14-9 describes some core properties.

Table 14-9. Properties of the HttpApplicationState Type

HTTPAPPLICATIONSTATE PROPERTY	MEANING IN LIFE
AllKeys	Enables user to retrieve all application state object names in a collection.
Count	Gets the number of item objects in the application state collection.
Keys	Returns a NameObjectCollectionBase.KeysCollection instance containing all the keys in the NameObjectCollectionBase instance.
StaticObjects	Exposes all objects declared via an <x runat=server></x> tag in the ASP.NET application file.

When you need to create data members that can be shared among all active sessions, you need to establish a simple name/value pair (e.g., firstUser = "chuck") and insert it to the internally maintained KeysCollection. To do so, use the class indexer, as shown here:

```
public class WebForm1 : System.Web.UI.Page
{
    protected void Page_Load(object sender, EventArgs e)
    {
        if (!IsPostBack)
        {
            // Create an application-level data member.
            Application["AppString"] = "Initial App Value";
        }
    }
...
}
```

Later, when you need to reference this value, simply extract it using the same property, as shown here:

```
string appVar = "App: " + Application["AppString"];
```

Working with the Page.Session Property

As mentioned earlier, a *session* is little more than a given user's interaction with a Web application. To maintain stateful information for a particular end user, use the Session property (which as luck would have it works just like the Application property). I'll assume you will check out this property at your leisure.

SOURCE CODE *The WebForm1.aspx and WebForm1.aspx.cs files can be found under the Chapter 14 subdirectory.*

Debugging and Tracing ASP.NET Applications

If you have worked with Visual Interdev, you understand the pain associated with debugging classic ASP applications. The good news is that when you are building ASP.NET Web projects, you can use the same debugging techniques as you would with any other sort of Visual Studio.NET project type. Thus, you can set break-points in script blocks (as well as any C# class files), start a debug session (press F5), and step through your code (Figure 14-34).

```
Default.aspx                                            _ □ ×

Client Objects & Events          ▼   (No Events)              ▼   = ≡

   13        <h1><b>You are: </b></h1>
   14
   15      <%
   16          HttpRequest r;
   17          r = this.Request;
   18
●  19          HttpResponse rs;
⟳  20 |        rs = this.Response;
○  21
●  22          rs.Write(r.ServerVariables["HTTP_USER_AGENT"]);
○  23      %>
   24
   25      <form method="post" runat="server" ID=Form1>

  Design    HTML
```

Figure 14-34. Establishing break points

Also, you can enable tracing support for your *.aspx files by specifying the trace attribute in your opening script block, as shown here:

```
<%@ Page language="c#" Codebehind="WebForm1.aspx.cs"
AutoEventWireup="false" Inherits="FirstWebApplication.WebForm1" trace = "true"
%>
```

When you do so, the returned HTML contains trace information regarding the previous HTTP response (Figure 14-35).

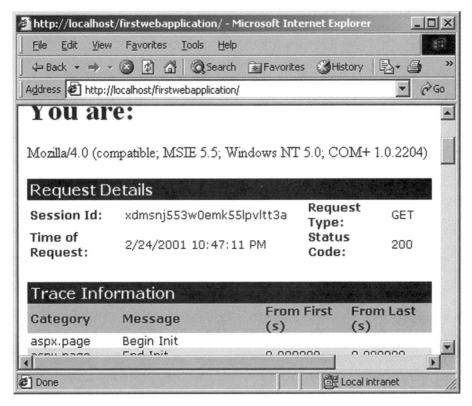

Figure 14-35. Enabling trace information

To insert your own trace messages into the mix, you can use the Trace type. Any time you wish to log a custom message (from a script block or C# source code file), simply call the Write() method (Figure 14-36), as shown here:

```
<%
    Trace.Write("App Category", "About to determine agent...");
    HttpRequest r;
    r = this.Request;

    HttpResponse rs;
    rs = this.Response;

    rs.Write(r.ServerVariables["HTTP_USER_AGENT"]);
%>
```

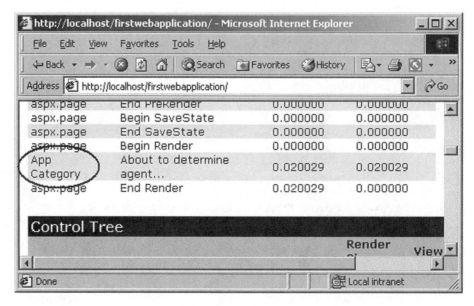

Figure 14-36. Logging custom trace messages

While working with the HttpRequest and HttpResponse types are a step in the right direction, your first crack at a feature-rich thin client leaves much to be desired. Next, let's take a tour of the Web-centric GUI widgets.

Understanding the Benefits of WebForm Controls

One major benefit of ASP.NET is the ability to assemble the user interface of your Web pages using the GUI types defined in the System.Web.UI.WebControls namespace. These controls (which go by the name server controls, Web controls, or Web form controls) are *extremely* helpful in that they automatically generate the necessary HTML tags required by the browser.

For example, in classic ASP, if you author a Web page that needs to display a series of text boxes, you basically needed to type the HTML tags directly into the ASP page. However, in ASP.NET, you simply design your Web form using the design time template and intrinsic WebForm controls. Here is an example:

```
<form method="post" runat="server">
    <asp:TextBox id=TextBox1 style="Z-INDEX: 101; LEFT: 27px; POSITION:
    absolute; TOP: 30px" runat="server">
    </asp:TextBox>
</form>
```

When the ASP.NET runtime encounters widgets with this attribute, the correct HTML is inserted into the response stream automatically, as shown here:

```
<input name="TextBox1" type="text" id="TextBox1" style="Z-INDEX: 101;
LEFT: 27px; POSITION: absolute; TOP: 30px" />
```

Granted, in this situation, it looks as if the WebForm controls required more markup than the raw HTML widget definition. However, not all controls are as trivial as a simple TextBox. For example, some Web controls encapsulate full-blown calendars, ad rotators, HTML tables, data grids, and so forth. In such a case, the WebForm controls can save you dozens of lines of raw HTML code.

Another benefit is that each ASP.NET control has a corresponding class in the System.Web.UI.WebControls namespace and can therefore be programmatically manipulated from your *.aspx file as well as the associated Page-derived class (e.g., the C# class marked by the Codebehind attribute). On a related note, Web controls also host a number of events that can be processed on the *server* (more later).

The final core benefit of using WebForm controls (rather than raw HTML controls) is the fact that ASP.NET provides a whole set of controls to validate the user-supplied data. Therefore, you do not need to generate client-side JavaScript routines to validate the data (although you are still free to do so).

Working with WebForm Controls

When you build Web Application projects, you will notice that your Toolbox window has an active tab named Web Forms (Figure 14-37).

Understand that each server control can be configured using the Property window of the Visual Studio.NET IDE. Given your work with Windows Forms earlier, you should have no problems understanding the build of a given widget's property set. For example, if you have a textbox control (which I have assigned the ID of txtEMail), you will find the choices shown in Figure 14-38.

As you configure a given WebControl using the Property window, your changes are written directly to the *.aspx file. As an example, if you select the txtEMail text box and modify the BorderStyle, BorderWidth, BackColor, BorderColor, and ToolTip properties, the opening <asp:textbox> tag has a number of new name/value pairs representing your selections, as shown here:

```
<asp:textbox id=txtEMail runat="server" BorderStyle="Ridge" BorderWidth="5px"
BackColor="PaleGreen" BorderColor="DarkOliveGreen"
ToolTip="Enter your e-mail here. . .">
</asp:TextBox>
```

Figure 14-37. The Web controls

Figure 14-38. Like Windows Forms Controls, Web Form Controls are configured using the Property window

Again, the result is plain old HTML:

```
<input name="txtEMail" type="text" value="fdfdf" id="txtEMail"
title="Enter your e-mail here..."
style="background-color:PaleGreen;border-color:DarkOliveGreen;
border-width:5px;border-style:Ridge;" />
```

Now let's examine exactly how these server controls are represented in the *.aspx file. A given WebControl is defined using an XML-like syntax in which the opening element tag is always <asp: *controlType* runat="server">. The closing tag is simply </asp: *controlType*>. Thus, you will find that each control is represented in the *.aspx file using syntax such as the following:

```
<asp:TextBox id=TextBox1 style="Z-INDEX: 101; LEFT: 27px;
POSITION: absolute; TOP: 30px" runat="server">
</asp:TextBox>

<asp:Button id=Button1 style="Z-INDEX: 102; LEFT: 26px;
POSITION: absolute; TOP: 66px" runat="server"
 DESIGNTIMEDRAGDROP="21" Text="Button">
</asp:Button>
```

The runat="server" attribute marks this item as a server-side control and informs the ASP.NET runtime that this item needs to be processed before returning the response stream to the browser, to generate the necessary HTML. Now, open the Codebehind class. You will notice that you now have a number of new member variables that represent each server control. As you can see, the names of these variables are the same as those of the ID element defined in the *.aspx file:

```
public class WebForm1 : System.Web.UI.Page
{
    protected System.Web.UI.WebControls.Button btnSubmit;
    protected System.Web.UI.WebControls.CheckBox ckBoxNewsLetter;
    protected System.Web.UI.WebControls.TextBox txtEMail;
    protected System.Web.UI.WebControls.TextBox txtLName;
    protected System.Web.UI.WebControls.TextBox txtFName;
...
}
```

In this way, you can programmatically manipulate your items using C# code in the *.aspx file or in your custom-defined routines in the Page-derived class.

The Derivation of WebForm Controls

All of the ASP.NET server-side controls ultimately derive from a common base class named System.Web.UI.WebControls.WebControl. WebContol in turn derives from System.Web.UI.WebControls.Control, which in turn derives from System.Object. For example, the derivation of the WebForm Button type would be understood as shown in Figure 14-39.

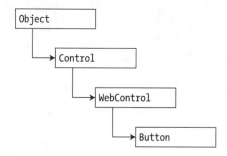

Figure 14-39. Base classes of a Web Control

Control and WebControl each define a number of properties common to all server-side controls. To help gain an understanding of your inherited functionality, consider the partial set of Control properties described in Table 14-10.

Table 14-10. Properties of the Control Base Class

CONTROL PROPERTY	MEANING IN LIFE
ID	Gets or sets the identifier for the control. Setting the property on a control allows programmatic access to the control's properties as well as the chance to respond to events sent by the control.
MaintainState	Gets or sets a value indicating whether the control should maintain its view state, and the view state of any child control in contains, when the current page request ends (more later).
Page	Gets the Page object that contains the current control.
Visible	Gets or sets a value that indicates whether a control should be rendered on the page.

As you can tell, the Control type provides a number of non-GUI-related behaviors. WebControl also defines some additional properties that allow you to configure the look and feel of the server-side widget (Table 14-11).

Table 14-11. Properties of the Control Base Class

WEBCONTROL PROPERTY	MEANING IN LIFE
BackColor	Gets or sets the background color of the Web control.
BorderColor	Gets or sets the border color of the Web control.
BorderStyle	Gets or sets the border style of the Web control.
BorderWidth	Gets or sets the border width of the Web control.
Enabled	Gets or sets a value indicating whether the Web control is enabled.
Font	Gets font information for the Web control.
ForeColor	Gets or sets the foreground color (typically the color of the text) of the Web control.
Height Width	Gets or sets the height and width of the Web control.
TabIndex	Gets or sets the tab index of the Web control.
ToolTip	Gets or sets the tool tip for the Web control to be displayed when the cursor is over the control.

Categories of WebForm Controls

While all the types in the System.Web.UI.WebControls namespace are GUI related, you can break down their functionality into four broad categories:

- Intrinsic controls

- Rich controls

- Data-centric controls

- Input validation controls

Given your work with Windows Forms controls earlier in this book, you should feel right at home. Just remember that while Windows Forms types encapsulate the raw Win32 API from view, WebForm controls encapsulate the generation of raw HTML tags.

Working with the Intrinsic WebForm Controls

To begin, let's examine some of the intrinsic controls. These types are basically .NET components that have a direct HTML widget counterpart. (If there is no direct counterpart, the WebForm control sends back HTML tags that simulate one.) For example, to display a list of items for the end user (see Figure 14-40), you can construct a WebForm ListBox (and the related ListItems), as shown here:

```
<asp:ListBox id=ListBox1 runat="server" Width="86" Height="69">
    <asp:ListItem Value="BMW">BMW</asp:ListItem>
    <asp:ListItem Value="Jetta">Jetta</asp:ListItem>
    <asp:ListItem Value="Colt">Colt</asp:ListItem>
    <asp:ListItem Value="Grand Am">Grand Am</asp:ListItem>
</asp:ListBox>
```

Figure 14-40. Building a ListBox

When the controls are processed by the ASP.NET runtime, the resulting HTML (which is of course displayed in the browser) looks something like this:

```
<select name="ListBox1" id="ListBox1" size="5" style="height:69px;width:86px;">
    <option value="BMW">BMW</option>
    <option value="Jetta">Jetta</option>
    <option value="Colt">Colt</option>
    <option value="Grand Am">Grand Am</option>
</select>
```

Table 14-12 describes some of the core intrinsic WebForm controls.

Working with these intrinsic controls is more or less just like working with their Windows Forms equivalents. Given that the Visual Studio.NET IDE provides the Property window to configure a selected widget, your task is even simpler. Therefore, rather than walking through each and every intrinsic control, let's spend time looking at a few common configurations.

Table 14-12. A Sampling of Intrinsic Web Controls

WEBFORM INTRINSIC CONTROL	MEANING IN LIFE
Button ImageButton	Various button types.
CheckBox CheckBoxList	A basic check box (CheckBox) or a list box containing a set of check boxes (CheckBoxList).
DropDownList ListBox ListItem	These types allow you to construct standard list box items.
Image Panel Label	These types represent containers for static text and images (as well as a way to group them).
RadioButton RadioButtonList	A basic radio button type (RadioButton) or a list box containing a set of radio buttons (RadioButtonList).
TextBox	Text box for user input. May be configured as a single-line or multiline text box.

Creating a Group of Radio Buttons

Radio button types tend to work as a group in which only one item in the group can be selected at a given time. For example, if you are interested in the UI shown in Figure 14-41, you can write the following script in the body of your form:

```
<body>
<p><font size=5><em>How shall we contact you?</em></font></p>

<p><asp:RadioButton id=RadioHome runat="server"
Text="Contact me at home" GroupName="ContactGroup">
</asp:RadioButton></p>

<p><asp:RadioButton id=RadioWork runat="server"
 Text="Contact me at work" GroupName="ContactGroup">
</asp:RadioButton></p>

<p><asp:RadioButton id=RadioDontBother runat="server"
Text="Don't bother me..." GroupName="ContactGroup">
</asp:RadioButton></p>
</body>
```

Figure 14-41. Building a set of related radio buttons

Notice that each RadioButton type has a GroupName attribute. Given that each items has been mapped to the same group (ContactGroup), each is mutually exclusive.

Creating a Scrollable, Multiline TextBox

Another common widget is a multiline text box (Figure 14-42).

Figure 14-42. A multiline TextBox

As you would expect, configuring a text box to function in this way is simply a matter of adding the correct attribute set to the opening <asp:TextBox> tag. Consider this example:

```
<p><asp:TextBox id=TextBox1 runat="server" Width="183" Height="96"
TextMode="MultiLine" BorderStyle="Ridge">
</asp:TextBox></p>
```

When you set the TextMode attribute to MultiLine, the TextBox automatically displays a vertical scroll bar when the content is larger than the display area. The remaining intrinsic controls are rather self-explanatory, so take the time to check out their property set.

The Rich Controls

Rich controls are also widgets that emit HTML to the HTTP response stream. The difference between these types and the set of intrinsic controls is that they have no direct HTML counterpart. Table 14-13 describes two rich controls.

Table 14-13. Rich WebControl Widgets

WEBFORM RICH CONTROL	MEANING IN LIFE
AdRotator	This control allows you to randomly display text/images using a corresponding XML configuration file.
Calendar	This control returns HTML that represents a GUI-based calendar.

Working with the Calendar Control

The Calendar control is a widget for which there is no direct HTML equivalent. Nevertheless, this type has been designed to return a batch of HTML tags that simulate such an entity. For example, suppose you place a Calendar control on your WebForm as shown here:

```
<asp:Calendar id=Calendar1 runat="server"></asp:Calendar></p>
```

You find that a *huge* amount of raw HTML has been generated automatically! To test things for yourself, place a Calendar type on your design time template, save the *.aspx file, and navigate to the correct virtual directory. Once you get back the response, right-click the browser and select View Source (Figure 14-43).

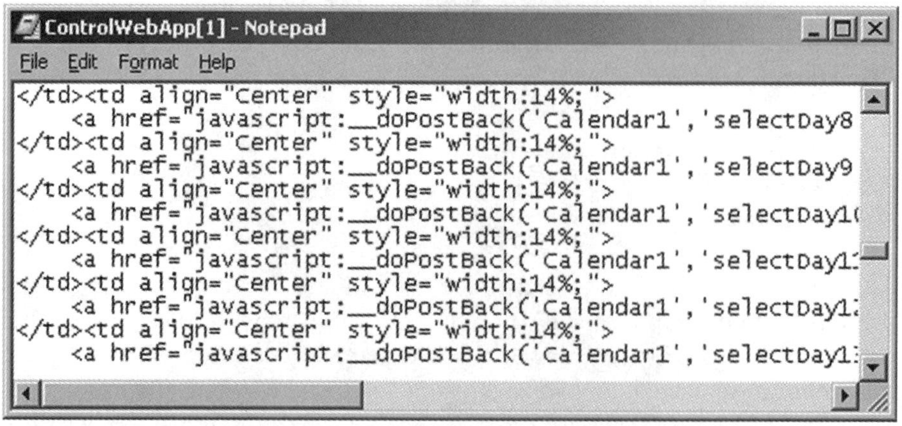

Figure 14-43. The Calendar Web control emits complex HTML

Like its Windows Forms counterpart, the server-side Calendar control is highly customizable. One member of interest is the SelectionMode property. By default, the Calendar control only allows the end user to select a single day (e.g., SelectionMode = Day). You can change this behavior by assigning this property to any of the following alternatives:

- None: No selection can be made (e.g., the Calendar is just for display purposes).

- DayWeek: User may select a single day or an entire week.

- DayWeekMonth: User may select a single day, an entire week, or an entire month.

For example, if you choose DayWeekMonth, the returned HTML renders an additional leftmost column (to allow the end user to select a given week) as well as a selector in the upper left (to allow the end user to select the entire month). Here is the full configuration, which is shocking until you recall that each attribute was configured using the VS.NET IDE's Property window:

```
<asp:Calendar id=Calendar1 runat="server" SelectionMode="DayWeekMonth"
DayNameFormat="FirstLetter" BackColor="White"
SelectorStyle-ForeColor="#336666" SelectorStyle-BackColor="#99CCCC"
NextPrevStyle-Font-Size="8pt" NextPrevStyle-ForeColor="#CCFF99"
TodayDayStyle-BackColor="#99CCCC" DayHeaderStyle-Height="1px"
DayHeaderStyle-ForeColor="#336666" DayHeaderStyle-BackColor="#99CCCC"
Font-Size="8pt" Font-Names="Verdana" Height="200"
OtherMonthDayStyle-ForeColor="#999999" TitleStyle-Font-Size="11pt"
```

```
TitleStyle-Font-Bold="True" TitleStyle-ForeColor="#CCFF99"
TitleStyle-BackColor="#003399" ForeColor="#003399" BorderColor="#3366CC"
 Width="221" SelectedDayStyle-ForeColor="#CCFF99"
SelectedDayStyle-BackColor="#009999"
TodayDayStyle-ForeColor="White" BorderWidth="1px"
TitleStyle-BorderStyle="Solid" TitleStyle-BorderWidth="1px"
TitleStyle-BorderColor="#3366CC" WeekendDayStyle-BackColor="#CCCCFF"
SelectedDayStyle-Font-Bold="True" CellPadding="1">
</asp:Calendar>
```

Figure 14-44 shows output as rendered in Microsoft Internet Explorer.

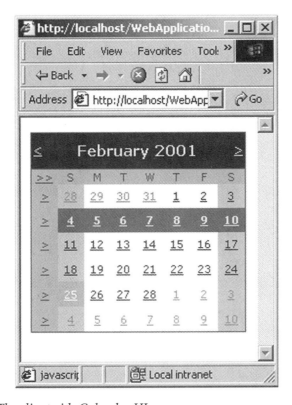

Figure 14-44. The client-side Calendar UI

Working with the AdRotator

Although classic ASP also provided an AdRotator control, the ASP.NET variation
has been substantially upgraded. The role of this widget is to randomly display a

given advertisement at some position in the browser. When you place a server-side AdRotator widget on your design time template, the display is a simple placeholder. Functionally, this control cannot do its magic until you set the AdvertisementFile property to point to the XML file that describes each ad.

The format of the advertisement file is quite simple. For each ad you wish to show, create a unique <Ad> element. At minimum, each <Ad> element specifies the image to display (ImageUrl), the URL to navigate to if the image is selected (TargetUrl), mouseover text (AlternateText), and the weighing for the ad (Impressions). For example, assume you have a file (ads.xml) that defines two possible ads, as shown here:

```
<Advertisements>
    <Ad>
        <ImageUrl>SlugBug.jpg</ImageUrl>
        <TargetUrl>http://www.Cars.com</TargetUrl>
        <AlternateText>Your new Car?</AlternateText>
        <Impressions>80</Impressions>
    </Ad>

    <Ad>
        <ImageUrl>car.gif</ImageUrl>
        <TargetUrl>http://www.CarSuperSite.com</TargetUrl>
        <AlternateText>Like this Car?</AlternateText>
        <Impressions>80</Impressions>
    </Ad>
</Advertisements>
```

Once you set the AdvertisementFile property correctly (and insure that the images and XML file are in the correct virtual directory), one of these two ads is randomly displayed when users navigate to the site, as shown here:

```
<asp:AdRotator id=AdRotator1 runat="server" Width="470"
 Height="60" AdvertisementFile="ads.xml">
</asp:AdRotator>
```

Thus you might find the output as seen in Figure 14-45.

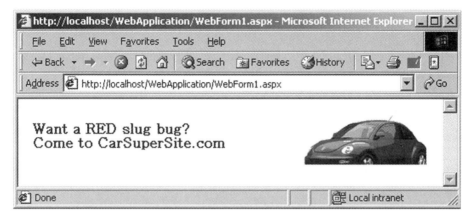

Figure 14-45. One possible ad

Or perhaps you might find something like Figure 14-46.

Figure 14-46. Another possible ad

Be aware that the Height and Width properties of the AdRotator are used to establish the size of your ads. In this example, each ad is the default 60 by 470 pixels. If your ads are larger (or smaller) than the AdRotator's size, you will find skewed images.

SOURCE CODE   *The files for the Controls project are included under the Chapter 14 subdirectory.*

Datacentric Controls

WebForm defines a number of widgets that generate HTML based (in part) on a connection to a data store. As you would expect, these controls can be fed in ADO.NET DataSets, just like their Windows Forms counterparts. Table 14-14 gives a partial list.

Table 14-14. Web Form Data Controls

WEBFORM DATA CONTROL	MEANING IN LIFE
DataGrid	A widget that displays ADO.NET DataSets in a grid.
DataList	A widget bound to a given data source.

In addition to these core datacentric WebForm types, be aware that most intrinsic controls can be configured to display information obtained from a data store or UDT (user-defined type). You will examine how to bind to custom types in just a moment, but first let's check out the process of binding a DataSet to the Web-centric DataGrid widget.

Filling a DataGrid

Far and away one of the most common tasks in Web development is reading a data source for information and returning said data in a tabular format. Using classic ASP this was accomplished by obtaining an ADO Recordset and building an HTML table on the fly using various HTML tags. The same end result can be achieved using the WebForm DataGrid with minimal fuss and bother.

To illustrate, let's assume that when a user navigates to a given *.aspx page, you wish to read the Cars database (developed in Chapter 13) and return the results. Your first task is to write an event handler for the Load event of the page class. Once you do, you can then create a DataSet object and bind it directly to the DataGrid. Here is the corresponding C# code (understand that DataGrid1 is the name of the server-side widget you dropped onto your design time form):

```
// Don't forget to specify a using directive for System.Data.SQL!
protected void Page_Load(object sender, EventArgs e)
{
    if (!IsPostBack)
    {
        // Fill the DataGrid with the Inventory table.
        SqlConnection sqlConn = new SqlConnection();
        sqlConn.ConnectionString = "data source=.; initial catalog=Cars;" +
            "integrated security=sspi;";
```

```
    SqlDataAdapter dsc =
        new SqlDataAdapter("Select * from Inventory", sqlConn);
    DataSet ds = new DataSet();
    dsc.Fill(ds, "Inventory");

    DataGrid1.DataSource = ds.Tables["Inventory"].DefaultView;
    DataGrid1.DataBind();
  }
}
```

The output is very satisfying (Figure 14-47).

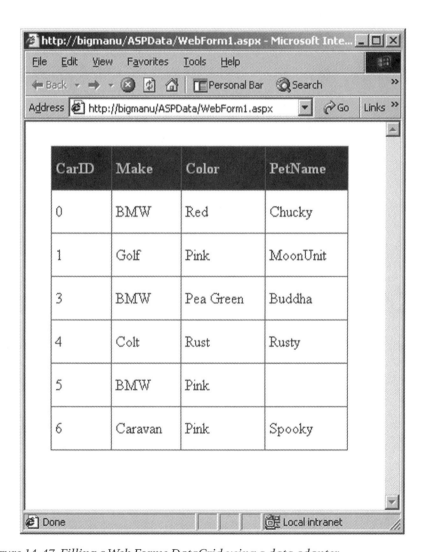

Figure 14-47. Filling a Web Forms DataGrid using a data adapter

More on Data Binding

As you have seen, the DataGrid control provides the DataSource and DataBind() members to allow you to render the contents of a given DataTable. This is obviously a great boon to the enterprise developer. However, WebForm controls (as well as Windows Forms controls) also allow you to bind other sources of data to a given widget.

For example, assume that you have a well-known set of values represented by a simple string array. Using the same technique as for binding to DataGrid types, you can attach an array to a GUI type. For example, if you place an ASP.NET List-Box control (with the ID of petNameList) on your *.aspx page, you can update the Page_Load() event handler as shown here:

```
protected void Page_Load(object sender, EventArgs e)
{
    if (!IsPostBack)
    {
        // Create an array of data to bind to the list box.
        string[] carPetNames =
        {
            "Viper", "Hank", "Ottis", "Alphonzo", "Cage", "TB"
        };
        petNameList.DataSource = carPetNames;
        petNameList.DataBind();
    }
}
```

As you would expect, the output is as shown in Figure 14-48.

Recall that all .NET arrays map to the System.Array type. Also recall that System.Array implements the IEnumerable interface. The fact is that any type that implements IEnumerable can be bound to a GUI widget. Therefore, if you update your simple string array to an instance of the ArrayList type, the output is identical, as shown here:

```
protected void Page_Load(object sender, EventArgs e)
{
    if (!IsPostBack)
    {
        // Now use an array list.
        ArrayList carPetNames = new ArrayList();
        carPetNames.Add("Viper");
        carPetNames.Add("Ottis");
        carPetNames.Add("Alphonzo");
```

```
        carPetNames.Add("Cage");
        carPetNames.Add("TB");
        petNameList.DataSource = carPetNames;
        petNameList.DataBind();
    }
}
```

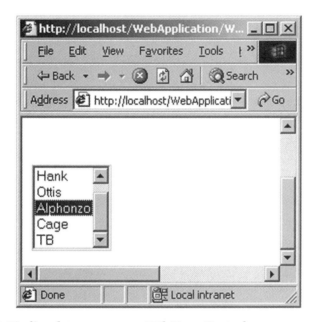

Figure 14-48. Binding data to common Web Form Controls

SOURCE CODE *The files for the ASPData Web application can be found under the Chapter 14 subdirectory.*

Validation Controls

The final conceptual set of WebForm controls are termed *validation controls.* Like their Windows Forms equivalents, these types are used to ensure that the data submitted by the user is well formatted based on your application logic. Table 14-15 gives a rundown of the core validation controls.

To illustrate the basics of working with validation controls, let's create a new C# Web Application project workspace named ValidateWebApp. Change the name of your *.aspx file to default.aspx and then open the design time template. Now, create the simple UI shown in Figure 14-49 using standard drag-and-drop techniques. Be aware that the text items can be assembled using raw HTML tags and do not need to be represented by a Label object.

Table 14-15. Validation Controls

WEBFORM VALIDATION CONTROL	MEANING IN LIFE
CompareValidator	Validates that the value of an input control is equal to a given value of another input control.
CustomValidator	Allows you to build a custom validation function that validates a given control.
RangeValidator	Determines that a given value is in a predetermined range.
RegularExpressionValidator	Checks if the value of the associated input control matches the pattern of a regular expression.
RequiredFieldValidator	Ensures that a given input control contains a value (and is thus not empty).
ValidationSummary	Displays a summary of all validation errors of a page in a list, bulleted list, or single paragraph format. The errors can be displayed inline and/or in a popup message box.

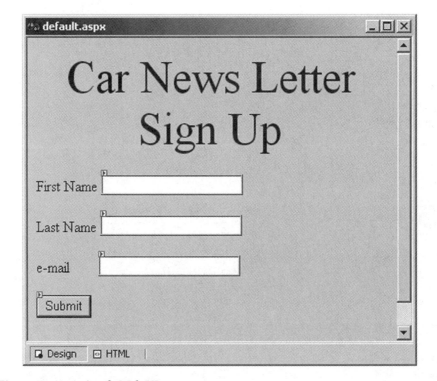

Figure 14-49. A simple Web UI

Next let's examine how to use the WebForm validation controls. To illustrate, assume that you wish to ensure that the txtEMail text box contains information (before you submit the form to the Web server). At design time, you can simply place a RequiredFieldValidator widget on your form.

Using the Properties window, you can set the ErrorMessage property to a given value (which is displayed when the validation fails), as well as establish the ID of the control this widget is in charge of validating using the ControlToValidate property (Figure 14-50).

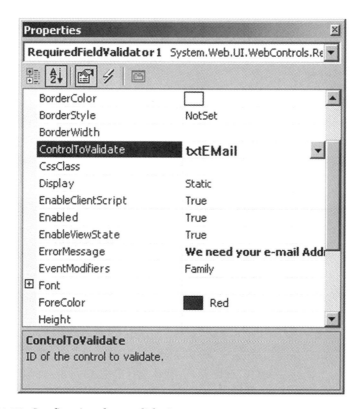

Figure 14-50. Configuring data validation

Under the hood, the *.aspx logic can be seen as follows:

```
<asp:RequiredFieldValidator id=RequiredFieldValidator1 style="Z-INDEX: 109;
LEFT: 351px; POSITION: absolute; TOP: 204px"
runat="server"
ErrorMessage="We need your e-mail Address!"
ControlToValidate="txtEMail">
</asp:RequiredFieldValidator>
```

In addition, you have the Page-derived C# class (as specified by the Codebehind attribute) as a new (appropriately typed) member variable, as shown here:

```
public class WebForm1 : System.Web.UI.Page
{
    protected System.Web.UI.WebControls.Button btnSubmit;
    protected System.Web.UI.WebControls.RequiredFieldValidator
            RequiredFieldValidator1;
    protected System.Web.UI.WebControls.TextBox txtEMail;
    protected System.Web.UI.WebControls.TextBox txtLName;
    protected System.Web.UI.WebControls.TextBox txtFName;
...
}
```

Now, save your page and refresh your browser. At this point, you should not see any noticeable changes. However, when you attempt to click the Submit button before you fill the txtEMail text box, your error message is suddenly visible, as shown in Figure 14-51.

Figure 14-51. The RequiredFieldValidator in action

Once you enter data in the txtEMail text box, the error message is removed. If you look at the HTML rendered by the browser, you see that the RequiredFieldValidator control generated a client-side JavaScript function free of charge. However, if the validation control determines that the browser that submitted the HTTP request is unable to support such logic, the returned HTML page redirects the error processing back to the Web server.

SOURCE CODE   *The ValidateWebApp project is included under the Chapter 14 subdirectory.*

Handling WebForm Control Events

As you have seen, one common approach to handling events fired by HTML GUI widgets is through the use of client-side JavaScript. In any case where your event handling requires any rendering logic, browser alerts (e.g., message boxes), or other direct interaction with the browser's object model, this is the way to go. However, other times you have a particular ASP.NET widget that performs non-GUI processing (such as performing a numerical calculation, editing a data table, and so on).

While you are still free to use client-side scripting for these purposes, ASP.NET does offer another alternative. Each WebForm control responds to its own set of events, which can be configured to process event handlers *on the server.* To configure a control to do so, simply add an event handler using the Property window.

For example, assume you need to determine which day has been selected on a Calendar control. You can capture the SelectionChanged event and act accordingly, as shown here:

```
protected void Calendar1_SelectionChanged (object sender, System.EventArgs e)
{
    Response.Write("<h5>Your car will be delivered on:" +
                Calendar1.SelectedDate.Date + "</h5>");
}
```

Now when the user triggers the SelectionChanged event, the browser makes a post back to the server to call the correct event handler. Figure 14-52 shows the end result.

Even though ASP.NET provides the ability to handle GUI widget events on the Web server, you need to be aware of the obvious drawback: This will increase the number of postbacks to the remote machine and therefore degrade the performance of your Web application. However, on the up side, when used prudently server-side event handling leads to more modular and maintainable code.

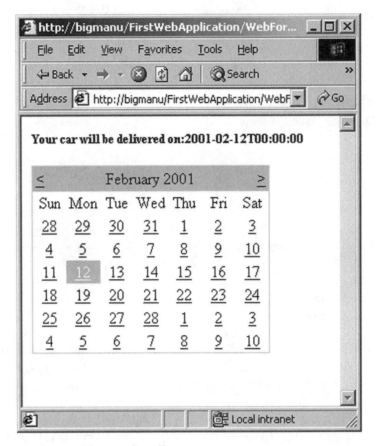

Figure 14-52. Server-side event handling

Summary

Building Web applications requires a different frame of mind than is used to assemble traditional desktop applications. In this chapter, you began with a quick and painless review of some core Web atoms, including HTML, HTTP, the role of client-side scripting, and server-side scripts using classic ASP.

The bulk of this chapter was spent examining the architecture of an ASP.NET application. As you have seen, each *.aspx file in your project has an associated System.Web.UI.Page derived class. Using this code behind approach, ASP.NET allows you to build more reusable and OO-aware systems. Furthermore, you have seen that the core properties defined by the Page type (Session, Application, Request, and Response) provide access to an underlying object instance. This chapter concluded by examining the use of WebForm types. These GUI widgets are in charge of emitting HTML tags to the client side.

CHAPTER 15

Building (and Understanding) Web Services

In many ways, this chapter represents the summation of all the topics you have explored over the course of this book. Here you will examine the construction and consumption of ASP.NET Web services. Simply put, a Web service is a unit of managed code (typically installed under IIS) that can be remotely invoked using HTTP.

As you will see, Web services consist of three supporting technologies: the Web Service Description Language (WSDL), a wire protocol (HTTP GET, HTTP POST, or SOAP), and a discovery service (*.disco files). You will begin by building a simple Calculator Web service and from there create an automobile centric Web service that can return ADO.NET DataSets, ArrayLists, and custom types.

Once you have been exposed to the core building blocks of .NET Web services, the chapter concludes by showing how to build a proxy class (using VS.NET as well as the wsdl.exe utility) that can be consumed by Web-based, console-based, and Windows Forms clients.

Understanding the Role of Web Services

From a high level, one can define a Web service as a unit of code that can be activated using HTTP requests. Now, let's think this one through a bit. Historically speaking, remote access to binary units required platform-specific (and sometimes language-specific) protocols. A classic example of this approach would be DCOM. DCOM clients access remote COM types using tightly coupled RPC calls. CORBA also requires the use of a tightly coupled protocol to activate remote types. EJB (Enterprise Java Beans) requires a specific protocol and (by and large) a specific language (Java). The problem with each of these remoting architectures is that they are proprietary protocols, which typically require a tight connection to the remote source.

As you already know, .NET is extremely language agnostic. Using C#, VB.NET, or any other .NET-aware language, you can build types that can be consumed and extended across language boundaries. Using Web services, you can access your language-neutral assemblies using nothing but HTTP. Of all the protocols in existence today, HTTP is the one specific wire protocol that all platforms tend to agree on.

Thus, using Web services, you (as a Web service developer) can use any language you wish. You (as a Web service consumer) can use standard HTTP to invoke methods on the types defined in the Web service. The bottom line is that you suddenly have true language and platform integration. It is not about COM or Java or CORBA anymore. It is all about HTTP and your programming language of choice (which is of course C#). As you will see, SOAP (Simple Object Access Protocol) and XML are also two key pieces of the Web service architecture, which are used in conjunction with standard HTTP.

Like any .NET assembly, a Web service contains some number of classes, interfaces, enumerations, and structures that provide black box functionality to remote clients. The only real restriction to be aware of is that because Web services are designed to facilitate *remote* invocations, you should avoid the use of any GUI-centric logic. Web services typically define business objects that execute a unit of work (e.g., perform a calculation, read a data source, or whatnot) for the consumer and wait for the next request.

One aspect of Web services that might not be readily understood is the fact that the Web service consumer does not necessarily need to be a browser-based client. As you will see, console-based and Windows Forms–based clients can consume a Web service just as easily. In each case the client indirectly interacts with the Web service through an intervening proxy. The proxy (which will be described in detail later in the chapter) looks and feels like the real remote type and exposes the same set of members. Under the hood, however, the proxy code really forwards the request to the Web service using standard HTTP or optionally, SOAP messages.

The Anatomy of a Web Service

Web services are typically hosted by IIS under a unique virtual directory, much like a standard ASP.NET Web application. However, in addition to the managed code that constitutes the exported functionality, a Web service requires some supporting infrastructure. In a nutshell, a Web service requires the following:

- A wire protocol (e.g., HTTP GET / HTTP POST or SOAP)

- A description service (so that clients know what the Web service can do)

- A discovery service (so that clients know the Web service exists)

You will examine the details behind each requirement in this chapter. However, just to get into the correct frame of mind, here is a brief overview of each supporting technology.

Previewing the Wire Protocol

Much like an ADO.NET DataSet, information is transmitted between a Web service consumer and Web service as XML. As mentioned, HTTP is the protocol that transmits this data. More specifically, you can use HTTP GET, HTTP POST, or SOAP to move information between consumers and Web services. By and large, SOAP will be your first choice, for as you will see, SOAP messages can contain XML descriptions of very complex types (custom classes, ADO.NET DataSets, arrays of objects, and so forth).

Previewing Web Service Description Services

For a Web service consumer to use a remote Web service, it must fully understand the exposed members. For example, the client must know that there is a method named Foo() that takes three parameters of type {string, bool, int} and returns a type named Bar before it can invoke it. Again, XML steps up to the plate to offer a generic way to describe the Web service. Formally, the XML schema used to describe a Web service is termed the Web Service Description Language, or WSDL.

Previewing Discovery Services

In the previous chapter, you briefly studied *.disco (an abbreviation for DISCOvery of Web Services) files. These XML based files allow a client to dynamically discover the Web services exposed from a given URL. Understand that a client in this sense could be a block of code you are currently authoring or a design time wizard. You will see the syntax of a *.disco file at the end of this chapter.

An Overview of the Web Service Namespaces

As you would imagine, each of these requirements is supported by various .NET types, contained in the namespaces described in Table 15-1.

Table 15-1. Web Service Namespaces

WEB SERVICE CENTRIC NAMESPACE	MEANING IN LIFE
System.Web.Services	This namespace contains the minimal and complete set of types needed to build a Web service.
System.Web.Services.Description	These types allow you to programmatically interact with WSDL.
System.Web.Services.Discovery	These types (used in conjunction with a *.disco file) allow a Web consumer to programmatically discover the Web services installed on a given machine.
System.Web.Services.Protocols	The XML-based data that is exchanged between a Web consumer and a Web service may be transmitted using one of three protocols (HTTP GET, HTTP POST, and SOAP). This namespace defines a number of types that represent these wire protocols.

Examining the System.Web.Services Namespace

Despite the rich functionality provided by the .NET Web services namespaces, for most projects the only types you will need to directly interact with are defined in the System.Web.Services namespace. As you can see from Table 15-2, the number of types is quite small.

Table 15-2. Members of the System.Web.Services Namespace

SYSTEM.WEB.SERVICES TYPE	MEANING IN LIFE
WebMethodAttribute	Adding the [WebMethod] attribute to a method in a Web service makes the method callable from a remote client using HTTP.
WebService	Defines the optional base class for Web services.
WebServiceAttribute	The WebService attribute may be used to add information to a Web service, such as a string describing its functionality. The attribute is not required for a Web service to be published and executed.
WebServiceBindingAttribute	Declares the binding protocol a given Web service method is implementing.

Building a Simple Web Service

Before diving much further into the details, let's build a simple example. (Don't worry, you will construct a more exotic Web service later). Fire up Visual Studio.NET and create a new C# Web service project named CalcWebService (Figure 15-1).

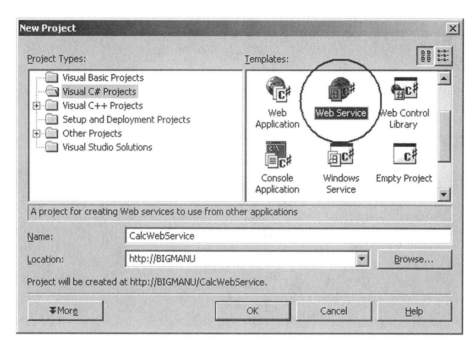

Figure 15-1. Creating a Web service project workspace

Like an ASP.NET application, Web service projects automatically create a new virtual directory under IIS (Figure 15-2) and store your project files under the \My Documents\Visual Studio Projects subdirectory.

Because of the configuration of a Web service project, if you wish to use the downloadable source code during this chapter, begin by creating a new project workspace and simply import the predefined class. In any case, when you examine the Solution Explorer (Figure 15-3), you should feel right at home with these new project files, given the material presented in Chapter 14.

The Global.asax and Web.config files serve the same purpose as (and look identical to) an ASP.NET application. As you recall from the Chapter 14, the Global.asax file allows you to respond to global-level events. Web.config allows you to declaratively configure your new Web service (again using XML notation). The items of interest to us at this point are the *.asmx, *.asmx.cs, and *.disco files as described in Table 15-3.

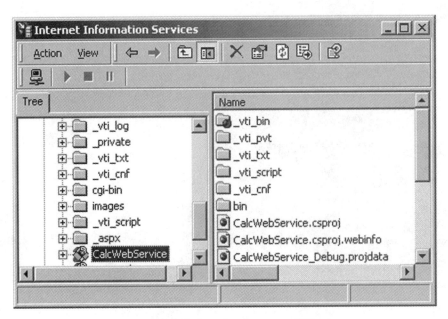

Figure 15-2. Web services are installed under the care of IIS

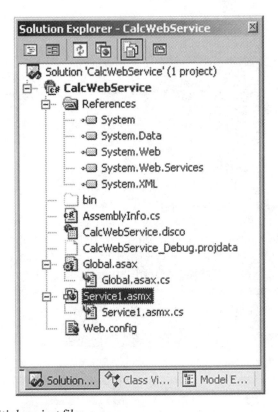

Figure 15-3. Initial project files

Table 15-3. Core Files of a VS.NET Web Service Project

WEB SERVICE PROJECT FILE	MEANING IN LIFE
*.asmx *.asmx.cs	These files define the methods of your Web service. Like an *.aspx file, each *.asmx file has a corresponding *.cs file to hold the code behind.
*.disco	Again, this file extension is short for "DISCOvery of Web Services" and contains an XML description of the Web services at a given URL.

The Codebehind File (*.asmx.cs)

A *.asmx file represents a given Web service in your current project workspace. To view the code behind the design time template, select the View Code option to check out the corresponding *.asmx.cs class definition, as shown here:

```
public class Service1 : System.Web.Services.WebService
{
    public Service1(){ InitializeComponent(); }

    private void InitializeComponent() {}

    public override void Dispose() {}
};
```

As you can see, the only real point of interest is the fact that you derive from a new base class: WebService. You will examine the members defined by this type in just a moment. For the time being, just understand that Web services have the *option* of deriving from this base class type. In fact, if you comment out the over-ridden Dispose() method and derive directly from System.Object, the Web service still functions correctly, as shown here:

```
// I'm still a Web service!
public class Service1
{
    public Service1() { InitializeComponent(); }

    private void InitializeComponent() {}

    // public override void Dispose() {}
};
```

Adding Some Simple Functionality

For this initial Web service, let's keep things short and sweet and add four methods that allow the outside world to add, subtract, multiply, and divide two integers. As you would expect, methods that you wish to make available via HTTP requests must be declared as public. In addition to this (obvious) fact, each method must support the [WebMethod] attribute. Therefore, you can update your initial class as shown here:

```
public class Service1 : System.Web.Services.WebService
{
    public Service1() { InitializeComponent(); }

    private void InitializeComponent(){}

    public override void Dispose(){}

    [WebMethod]
    public int Add(int x, int y){ return x + y; }

    [WebMethod]
    public int Subtract(int x, int y){ return x - y; }

    [WebMethod]
    public int Multiply(int x, int y){ return x * y; }

    [WebMethod]
    public int Divide(int x, int y)
    {
        if(y = = 0)
        {
            throw new DivideByZeroException("Dude, can't divide by zero!");
        }
        return x / y;
    }
}
```

Testing Your Web Service

Once you compile your Web service, you can execute it using the Visual Studio.NET IDE (Simply run or debug the application.) By default, your machine's active browser functions as a makeshift client, showing an HTML view of the methods marked with the [WebMethod] attribute. See Figure 15-4 for a test run.

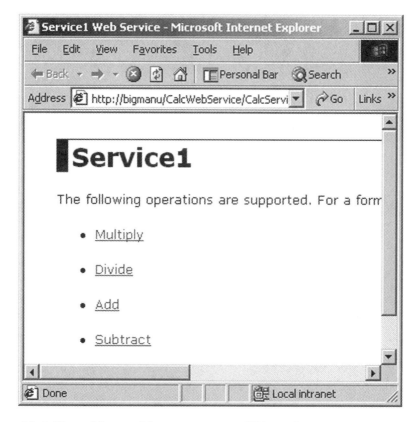

Figure 15-4. IE provides a quick way to test your Web services

In addition to listing each method defined in a given Web service, you can also invoke each method directly from within the browser. For example, click the Add link and enter some text values (Figure 15-5). As you can see, the rendered HTML provides TextBox types to allow user input.

When you invoke the method, the result (490) is returned via an XML attribute (Figure 15-6).

One point of interest is how the information is sent to the Web service. If you check out the generated query string, you will find the following:

```
http://bigmanu/CalcWebService/CalcService.asmx/Add?x=44&y=446
```

Notice that the URL is composed of the name of the method to be called (Add) followed by the incoming parameter names (and values).

As you can see, it is relatively simple to build and test a Web service. Later in this chapter you will build some more exotic Web service clients. Before you do, let's examine some further details behind the Web service architecture.

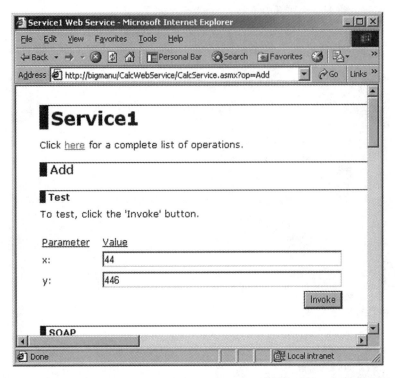

Figure 15-5. IE allows you to invoke a Web method with specific parameters

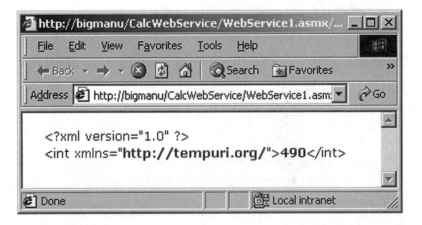

Figure 15-6. The end result

The WebMethodAttribute Type

The WebMethod attribute must be applied to each method you wish to expose to the outside world through HTTP. Like most attributes, the WebMethod type may take a number of optional constructor parameters. For example, to describe the functionality of a particular Web method, you can use the following syntax:

```
[WebMethod(Description = "Yet another way to add numbers!")]
public int Add(int x, int y){ return x + y; }
```

In some respects, setting the Description aspect of the WebMethod attribute is analogous to the IDL [helpstring] attribute. If you compile and test once again, you see something like Figure 15-7.

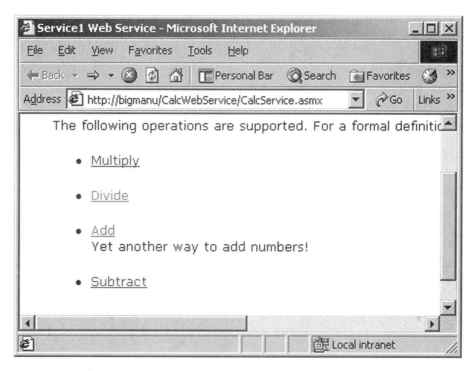

Figure 15-7. The end result of setting the WebMethod.Description property

Under the hood, the WSDL contract has been updated with a new <documentation> attribute (more on WSDL in just a bit), as shown here:

```
<operation name="Add">
    <input message="s0:AddSoapIn" />
    <output message="s0:AddSoapOut" />
    <documentation>Yet another way to add numbers!</documentation>
</operation>
```

In addition to the Description aspect, you can also configure the WebService attribute type using any of the core properties described in Table 15-4.

Table 15-4. The WebServiceAttribute

WEBSERVICEATTRIBUTE PROPERTY	MEANING IN LIFE
Description	Used to add a friendly text description of your Web method.
EnableSession	By default, this property is set to true, which configures this method to maintain session state (as discussed in Chapter 14). You may disable this behavior if you set it to false.
MessageName	This property can be used to configure how a Web method is represented in WSDL, to avoid name clashes.
TransactionOption	Web methods can function as the root of a COM+ transaction. This property may be assigned any value from the System.EnterpriseServices.TransactionOption enumeration.

One item of special interest is the MessageName property. To illustrate, assume your Web calculator now defines an additional method that can add two floats, as shown here:

```
[WebMethod(Description = "Add 2 integers.")]
public int Add(int x, int y){ return x + y; }


[WebMethod(Description = "Add 2 floats.")]
public float Add(float x, float y){ return x + y; }
```

If you were to compile your updated class, you would be happy to find no generated errors. However, when you request access to the Web service, you find the following complaint:

```
System.Exception: Both Single Add(Single, Single) and Int32 Add(Int32, Int32)
use the message name 'Add'.
```

One requirement of WSDL is that each < soap:operation soapAction > attribute (used to define the name of a given Web method) must be uniquely named. However, the default behavior of the WSDL generator is to generate the < soap:operation soapAction > name *exactly* as it appears in the source code definition. (That's why you ended up with two Web methods named Add().) To resolve the name clash, you can either rename your method or simply use the MessageName property to establish a unique name, as shown here:

```
[WebMethod(Description = "Add 2 integers.")]
public int Add(int x, int y){ return x + y; }


[WebMethod(Description = "Add 2 floats.", MessageName = "AddFloats")]
public float Add(float x, float y){ return x + y; }
```

With this, you can see that each WSDL description is now unique:

```
<operation name="Add">
<soap:operation soapAction="http://tempuri.org/AddFloats" style="document" />
    <input name="AddFloats">
        <soap:body use="literal" />
    </input>
    <output name=" AddFloats">
        <soap:body use="literal" />
    </output>
</operation>

<operation name="Add">
<soap:operation soapAction="http://tempuri.org/Add" style="document" />
    <input>
        <soap:body use="literal" />
    </input>
    <output>
        <soap:body use="literal" />
    </output>
</operation>
```

On a related note, the WebServiceAttribute also provides a Description property to allow you to document the overall functionality of the Web service itself, as shown here:

```
[WebService( Description = "The painfully simple web service" )]
public class Service1 : System.Web.Services.WebService
{
...
}
```

If you rerun the application, you see something like Figure 15-8.

Figure 15-8. The WebServiceAttribute describes the nature of your creation

The System.Web.Services.WebService Base Class

As mentioned earlier in this chapter, .NET Web services are free to derive directly from System.Object. However, by default, Web services developed using Visual Studio.NET automatically derive from the WebService base class. The functionality provided by this type equips your Web service to interact with the same types used by the ASP.NET object model (Table 15-5).

As you recall from Chapter 14, the Application and Session properties allow you to maintain stateful data during the execution of your ASP.NET Web applications. Web services provide the exact same functionality. For example, assume your CalcWebService maintains an application-level variable (and is thus available to each session) that holds the value of PI, as shown here:

```
public class Service1 : System.Web.Services.WebService
{
    public Service1()
    {
        InitializeComponent();
        Application["SimplePI"] = 3.14F;
    }
}
```

```
[WebMethod]
public float GetSimplePI()
{ return (float)Application["SimplePI"]; }
...
}
```

Table 15-5. Core Properties of the WebService Base Type

SYSTEM.WEB.SERVICES.WEBSERVICE PROPERTY	MEANING IN LIFE
Application	Gets a reference to the application object for the current HTTP request.
Context	Gets the ASP.NET Context object for the current request, which encapsulates all HTTP-specific context used by the HTTP server to process Web requests.
Server	Gets a reference to the HttpServerUtility for the current request.
Session	Gets a reference to the SessionState.HttpSessionState instance for the current request.
User	Gets the ASP.NET server User object, which can be used to authenticate a given user.

Understanding the Web Service Description Language (WSDL)

Now that you have seen a simple Web service in action, let's talk a bit about how your Web methods are described under the hood. COM programmers understand that IDL is a metalanguage used to define each aspect of a COM item. .NET programmers understand that compilers that produce managed code also emit full and complete metadata that completely describes all types in the assembly. When a binary image (COM or .NET) is described in language-neutral terms, you essentially establish a contract that the client can read to understand method-calling conventions, type names, base types, supported interfaces, and so on.

In the same spirit of IDL and .NET metadata, Web services are also described using the metalanguage WSDL. WSDL is a block of XML that fully describes how external clients can interact with the Web services on a given machine, the methods they support, and the syntax of the various wire protocols (GET, POST, and SOAP).

When you test your Web services from your browser of choice, you will see a link entitled Service Description (Figure 15-9).

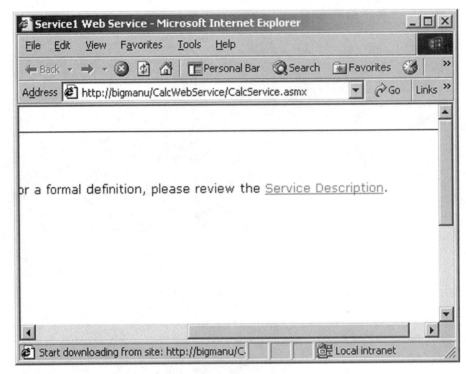

Figure 15-9. This link allows you to view the underlying WSDL

When you select this link, a separate window opens that describes the contract defined by the current Web service (Figure 15-10).

Although you can always choose to remain blissfully unaware of the exact WSDL syntax, let's run through some basics. First of all, a WSDL contract is opened and closed using the <definitions> tag. After the opening tag comes a set of nodes that define the various wire protocols, as shown here:

```
<?xml version="1.0" ?>
<definitions xmlns:s="http://www.w3.org/2000/10/XMLSchema"
xmlns:http="http://schemas.xmlsoap.org/wsdl/http/"
        xmlns:mime="http://schemas.xmlsoap.org/wsdl/mime/"
        xmlns:urt="http://microsoft.com/urt/wsdl/text/"
        xmlns:soap="http://schemas.xmlsoap.org/wsdl/soap/"
        xmlns:soapenc="http://schemas.xmlsoap.org/soap/encoding/" xmlns
        xmlns:s0="http://tempuri.org/" targetNamespace="http://tempuri.org/"
        xmlns="http://schemas.xmlsoap.org/wsdl/">
    . . .
```

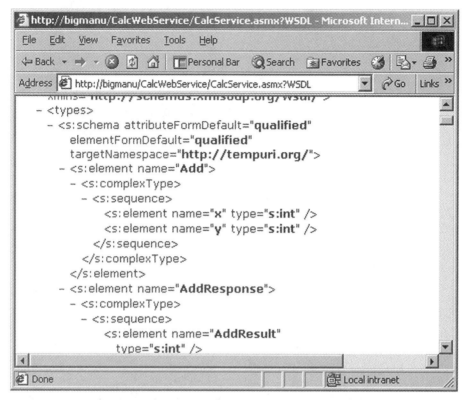

Figure 15-10. The raw WSDL

Next you will find the WSDL definition for each Web method defined by the Web service in terms of the GET, POST, and SOAP wire protocols (Figure 15-11).

As you can see, each Web method has an In and Out variation. Therefore, the Subtract() Web method has six unique <message name> tags: one In/Out pair for HTTP POST, one pair for HTTP GET, and another pair for SOAP. For example, here is the WSDL definition for Subtract when using the HTTP POST protocol:

```
<message name="SubtractHttpPostIn">
    <part name="x" type="s:string" />
    <part name="y" type="s:string" />
</message>

<message name="SubtractHttpPostOut">
    <part name="Body" element="s0:int" />
</message>
```

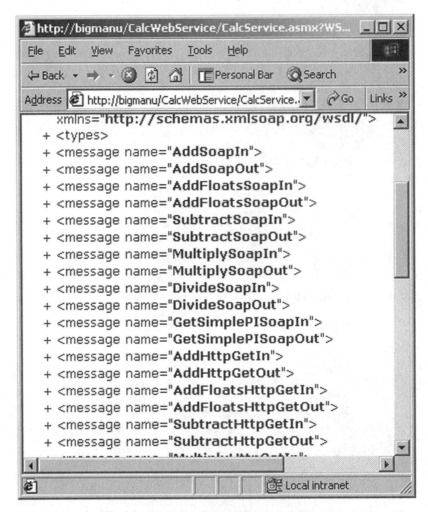

Figure 15-11. Each Web method has a GET, POST, and SOAP pair

If you examine the SOAP description of the same method, you find the following:

```
<message name="SubtractSoapIn">
    <part name="parameters" element="s0:Subtract" />
</message>

<message name="SubtractSoapOut">
    <part name="parameters" element="s0:SubtractResponse" />
</message>
```

Again, much like other metalanguages, WSDL is typically of direct interest only if you are building something custom parsers or type viewers. If this is your lot in life (or if you are just interested in playing with some new toys), you should take the time to explore the System.Web.Services.Description namespace. Here you will find a plethora of types that allow you to programmatically manipulate WSDL. If you are not interested in this endeavor, simply understand that WSDL fully describes the calling conventions (and transport protocols) that enable an external client to call the Web methods defined by a given Web service.

Web Service Wire Protocols

As you know, the purpose of a Web service is to return XML-based data to a consumer, using the HTTP protocol. Specifically, a Web server bundles this data into the body of an HTTP message and transmit it to the consumer using one of three specific techniques (Table 15-6).

Table 15-6. Web Service Wire Protocols

TRANSMISSION PROTOCOL	MEANING IN LIFE
HTTP GET	GET submissions append parameters to the query string of the current URL.
HTTP POST	POST transmissions embed the data points into the header of the HTTP message rather than appending them to the query string.
SOAP	SOAP is a wire protocol that specifies how to submit data across the wire using XML.

While each approach leads to the same end result (calling a remote method using HTTP), your choice of wire protocol will determine the types of parameters (and return types) that can be sent between each interested party. The SOAP protocol will offer you the greatest form of flexibility. However, for completion let's begin by examining the use of standard GET and POST encoding.

Transmitting Data Using HTTP GET and POST

As described in Chapter 14, HTTP GET transmissions are sent to the recipient by appending name/value pairs to the end of the receiving URL. Recall that a question mark (?) is the character that signifies the separation of the page from the named set of parameters. HTTP POST transmissions also represent incoming data as a set of name/value pairs, which are placed in the body of the HTTP message. When you use GET or POST transmissions, the end result looks identical. The returned data is expressed in simple XML notation, taking the form *<type>*VALUE *</type>*.

Although GET and POST verbs may be familiar constructs, you must be aware that this method of transportation is not rich enough to represent such complex items as structures or object instances. When you use GET and POST verbs, you can only interact with Web methods using the types listed in Table 15-7.

Table 15-7. Supported POST and GET Data Types

SUPPORTED GET/POST DATA TYPES	MEANING IN LIFE
Enumerations	GET and POST verbs support the transmission of System.Enum types. These are represented as a static constant string.
Simple Arrays	You can construct arrays of any primitive type.
Strings	GET and POST transmit all numerical data as a string token. *String* really refers to the string representation of CLR primitives such as Int16, Int32, Int64, Boolean, Single, Double, Decimal, DateTime, and so forth.

To build an HTML form that submits data using GET or POST semantics, you specify the *.asmx file as the recipient of the form data. As a simple example, assume the following *.htm file creates a UI that allows the end user to enter two numbers to send to the Subtract() method of the CalcWebService, using the GET protocol:

```
<HTML>
<HEAD>
<TITLE></TITLE>
<META NAME="GENERATOR" Content="Microsoft Visual Studio 7.0">
</HEAD>
<BODY>

<form method = 'GET' action =
'http://localhost/CalcWebService/CalcService.asmx/Subtract'>
    <p>First Number:
    <input id=Text1 name = x type=text> </p>
    <p>Second Number
    <input id=Text2 name = y type=text></p>
    <p>
    <input id=Submit1 type=submit value=Submit></p>
</form>

</BODY>
</HTML>
```

A few points of interest. First, the action attribute points to not only the *.asmx file, but also the name of the method to invoke. Next, notice that the name attribute is used to identify the name of each parameter. (Recall that Subtract() takes two integers named x and y.)

Figure 15-12 shows the result of entering 300 and 3 as input data.

Figure 15-12. Subtracting numbers ala HTTP GET

Figure 15-13 shows the result.

```
<?xml version="1.0" ?>
<int xmlns="http://tempuri.org/">297</int>
```

Figure 15-13. Note the query string

SOURCE CODE   *The CalcGET HTML page is included under the Chapter 15 subdirectory.*

Transmitting Data Using SOAP

A far sexier alternative to moving information between a consumer and Web service is to use SOAP, which can represent complex types (in XML notation) as shown in Table 15-8.

Table 15-8. SOAP Types

ADDITIONAL SOAP DATA TYPES	MEANING IN LIFE
ADO.NET DataSets	Although the DataSet is just another class, it is important to point out that this type is supported.
Complex Arrays	You may build arrays of classes, structures, and XML nodes.
Custom Types	Using SOAP, you can build Web methods that expose custom types.
XML Nodes	Your Web methods may expose XML nodes that are transported as XML!

Although a complete examination of SOAP is outside the scope of this text, understand that SOAP was designed to be as simple as possible. Given this, SOAP itself does not define a specific protocol and can thus be used with any number of existing Internet protocols (HTTP, SMTP, and others).

In a nutshell, the SOAP specification contains two aspects. First is the envelope (which can conceptually be understood as the box containing the relevant information). Second, we have the rules that are used to describe the information in that message.

Recall that when you use SOAP to call your Add() method, the SOAP definition looks like this:

```
<message name="AddFloatsSoapIn">
    <part name="parameters" element="s0:AddFloats" />
</message>
<message name="AddFloatsSoapOut">
    <part name="parameters" element="s0:AddFloatsResponse" />
</message>
```

Open the WSDL window for your CalcWebService. Toward the end of the page, you will find three XML nodes describing the GET, POST and SOAP bindings, as shown in Figure 15-14.

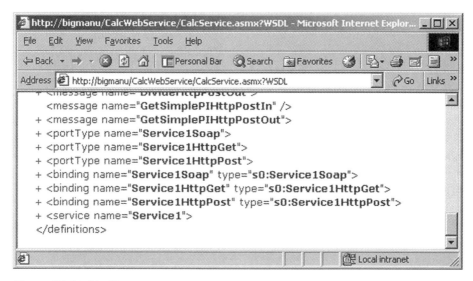

Figure 15-14. Bindings

If you expand the SOAP binding for you Web service, you find the following description for the Add() method (note the input and output tags):

```
<operation name="Add">
<soap:operation soapAction="http://tempuri.org/AddFloats" style="document" />
    <input name="AddFloats">
        <soap:body use="literal" />
    </input>
    <output name="AddFloats">
        <soap:body use="literal" />
    </output>
</operation>
```

While it is edifying to understand what is being sent back and forth across the wire, the good news is that the internals of a SOAP message are hidden from view (as you will notice during the remainder of this chapter).

SOURCE CODE   *The CalcService.asmx.cs file can be found under the Chapter 15 subdirectory.*

WSDL into C# Code (Generating a Proxy)

At this point, you should feel fairly comfortable with the composition of a .NET Web service. The next step is to understand how to build clients that can consume these services. As you have seen, WSDL is used to describe Web methods in

XML syntax. However, it would undesirable to construct clients that *manually* request a WSDL definition and *manually* parse each node to establish a connection to the remote service. A much-preferred approach is to leverage a tool that can generate a proxy to the Web method.

Proxies can be simply defined as types (classes in this case) that look and feel exactly like the remote entity they pretend to be. If you have a background in classic COM, this should sound familiar. When you send an IDL file to the MIDL compiler, one of the generated files (*_p.c) contains C-based stub and proxy code that can be compiled into a binary DLL. The COM client makes calls on the proxy class, which packages up the incoming parameters and sends them to the receiving stub (using the ORPC protocol). The stub in turn unpackages the request and hands off the request to the real COM object.

The same general behavior takes place when a consumer uses a remote Web service. The key difference is that accessing a Web service does *not* depend on a propriety binary format, specific platform, or given programming language. All that is required is an understanding of HTTP and XML.

Generating a Web service proxy is quite simple. First, you can use a stand-alone command-line tool named wsdl.exe. As an attractive alternative, the Visual Studio.NET IDE allows you to reference a Web service using a friendly wizard. Let's examine each approach.

Building a Proxy Using wsdl.exe

The wsdl.exe command-line tool generates a code file that represents the proxy to the remote Web service. At a minimum, you need to specify the name of proxy file to be generated and the URL where the WSDL can be obtained, as shown here:

```
wsdl.exe /out:c:\calcproxy.cs
http://localhost/calcwebservice/calcservice.asmx?WSDL
```

The wsdl.exe utility generates C# code by default. If you choose to have your proxy written in VB.NET or JScript.NET syntax, you can use the optional /l: (Language) flag. Table 15-9 lists some of the more interesting command-line options

Examining the Proxy Code

If you have ever examined the underlying stub and proxy code for classic ORPC (DCOM) request/response, you will be extremely happy to find a simple, readable C# class file. First comes the class definition (note the use of the WebServiceBinding attribute), as shown here:

Table 15-9. Various Flags of the wsdl.exe Utility

WSDL.EXE FLAG	MEANING IN LIFE
/l[anguage]:	Specifies the language to use for the generated proxy class. You can specify CS (default), VB, or JS as the language argument.
/n[amespace]:	Specifies the namespace for the generated proxy or template. The default namespace is the global namespace.
/out:	Specifies the file in which to save the generated proxy code. The tool derives the default file name from the service name. The tool saves generated datasets in different files.
/protocol:	Specifies the protocol to implement. (The default is SOAP.) You can specify SOAP, HttpGet, HttpPost, or a custom protocol specified in the configuration file.

```
using System.Xml.Serialization;
using System;
using System.Web.Services.Protocols;
using System.Web.Services;

[System.Web.Services.WebServiceBindingAttribute(Name="Service1Soap",
Namespace="http://tempuri.org/")]
public class Service1 : System.Web.Services.Protocols.SoapHttpClientProtocol
{
    public Service1()
    {
        this.Url = "http://localhost/calcwebservice/calcservice.asmx";
    }
...
}
```

As you can see, the constructor of this proxy class maintains the URL of the remote Web service and stores it in the inherited Url property. Also notice that your immediate base class is of type SoapHttpClientProtocol. This type specifies most of the implementation for communicating with a SOAP Web service over HTTP. (The remaining functionality comes from numerous base classes.) Table 15-10 describes some interesting inherited members.

Table 15-10. Core Inherited Properties

INHERITED MEMBERS	MEANING IN LIFE
BeginInvoke()	Starts an asynchronous invocation of a method of a SOAP Web service.
EndInvoke()	Ends an asynchronous invocation of a method of a remote SOAP Web service.
Invoke()	Synchronously invokes a method of a SOAP Web service.
Proxy	Gets or sets proxy information for making a Web service request through a firewall.
Timeout	Gets or sets the timeout (in milliseconds) used for synchronous calls.
Url	Gets or sets the base URL to the server to use for requests.
UserAgent	Gets or sets the value for the user agent header sent with each request.

Of course the real meat of the generated proxy is the method implementations themselves. The generated proxy code defines synchronous and asynchronous members for each Web method defined in the Web service. As you are aware, synchronous method invocations are blocked until the call returns. Asynchronous method inoculations return control to the calling client immediately after receiving the invocation request. When the processing has finished, the runtime makes a callback to the client. Here is the synchronous Add() implementation:

```
[System.Web.Services.Protocols.SoapMethodAttribute("http://tempuri.org/Add",
MessageStyle=
    System.Web.Services.Protocols.SoapMessageStyle.ParametersInDocument)]
public int Add(int x, int y)
{
    object[] results = this.Invoke("Add", new object[] {x, y});
    return ((int)(results[0]));
}
```

Each Web method is marked with the SoapMethod attribute. Also, notice that the Add() method has the same signature as the original Web method. As far as clients are concerned, when they call the Add() method, the logic is executed directly. Of course in reality the incoming parameters (along with the named method) are sent to SoapHttpClientProtocol.Invoke(). At this point, the HTTP request is sent to the correct URL.

One update you will want to make for the generated proxy file is to wrap the class in a namespace definition, as shown here, as this is not done on your behalf unless you explicitly specify the /n flag:

```
namespace TheCalcProxy
{
public class Service1 : System.Web.Services.Protocols.SoapHttpClientProtocol
{
    . . .
}
}
```

Building the Assembly

Before you can create clients that use your Web service, you need to build an assembly to contain the proxy type. You can use the C# compiler directly or select a new C# Code Library using Visual Studio.NET. Either way, be sure to add references to the System.Web.Services.dll and System.Xml.dll references, as shown here:

```
csc /r:system.web.services.dll /r:system.xml.dll /out:C:\CalcProxy.dll
/t:library calcproxy.cs
```

The end result is a new library that contains your proxy class (Figure 15-15).

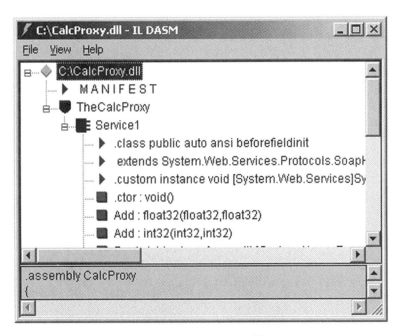

Figure 15-15. Your proxy, wrapped in a .NET assembly

Building a Client

At this point, you can create a new Form-based, ASP.NET, or Console-based application; add a reference to your assembly; and write some code. (In each case you need to ensure that a reference to System.Web.Services.dll is included.) To keep things simple, here is a Console-based client:

```csharp
// Don't forget to set a reference to
// System.Web.Services.dll!
namespace WebServiceConsumer
{
    using System;

    using TheCalcProxy;      // Specify the namespace.

    public class WebConsumer
    {
        public static int Main(string[] args)
        {
            // Work with the Web service.
            Service1 w = new Service1();
            Console.WriteLine("100 + 100 is {0}",
                                w.Add(100 , 100));
            try
            {
                w.Divide(0, 0);
            }
            catch(DivideByZeroException e)
            {
                Console.WriteLine(e.Message);
            }
            return 0;
        }
    }
}
```

Figure 15-16 shows the output. (Notice that your custom exception message has been passed along as an inner exception.)

SOURCE CODE   *The CalcClient project can be found under the Chapter 15 subdirectory.*

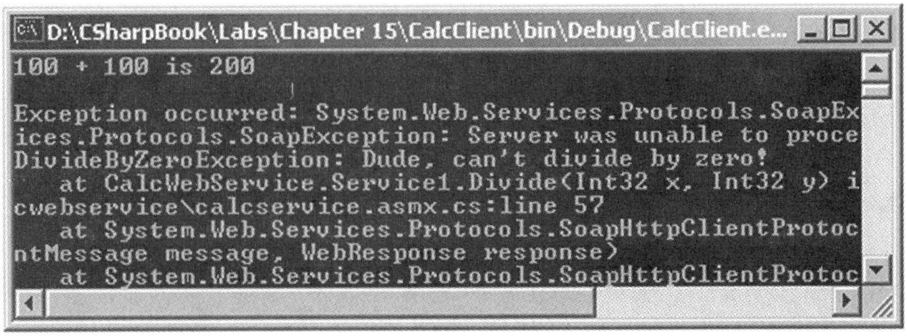

Figure 15-16. A console Web service consumer

Generating a Proxy with VS.NET

Working with the wsdl.exe utility and C# compiler is a bit clumsy. The only real benefit of using the wsdl.exe command-line tool is that it allows you to directly specify a given wire protocol (GET, POST, or SOAP) using the /protocol flag. In contrast, Visual Studio.NET only creates proxies that respond to the SOAP protocol (which is typically what you want anyway).

To illustrate, let's build a Windows Forms client application. Assume you have a simple user interface that allows the user to define two values passed to the various methods (Add(), Subtract(), and so on). Once your GUI has been established, you can add a Web reference to your project (Figure 15-17).

You can then type in the URL that points to a given *.asmx file and view the WSDL contract as well as the set of Web methods (Figure 15-18).

Now, select View Contract and add the reference. A new Web References node has been added to your Solution Explorer window (Figure 15-19).

At this point, you are ready to specify work with the Service1 type directly (note that the name of the generated namespace is the name of the machine hosting the Web service), as shown here:

```csharp
using localhost;
public class mainForm : System.Windows.Forms.Form
{
    protected void btnAdd_Click (object sender, System.EventArgs e)
    {
        localhost.Service1 w = new localhost.Service1();
        int ans = w.Add(int.Parse(txtNumb1.Text), int.Parse(txtNumb2.Text));
        lblAns.Text = ans.ToString();
    }
...
}
```

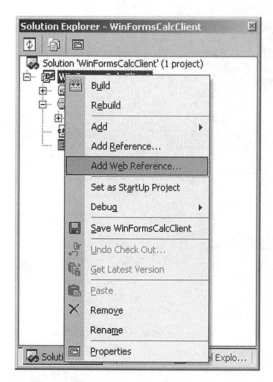

Figure 15-17. Adding a Web reference automatically generates the proxy file

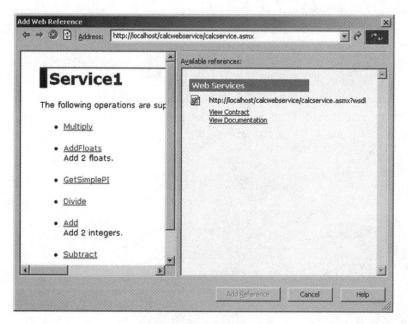

Figure 15-18. The Add Reference dialog box allows you to view Web methods and the raw WSDL

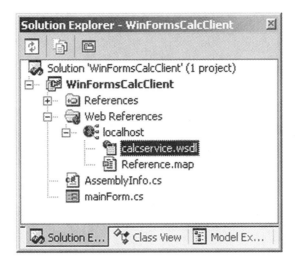

Figure 15-19. The Web References node

SOURCE CODE *The WinFormsCalcClient can be found under the Chapter 15 subdirectory.*

A More Interesting Web Service (and Web Client)

So much for Math 101. The real power of Web services becomes much more evident when you build Web methods that return complex types, unlike the very simple CalcWebService example you have been examining. Thus, you need to build a more interesting Web service that can return ADO.NET DataSets, custom types, and arrays of types. As you recall, this demands the use of SOAP.

Create a new C# Web service project workspace named CarsWebService. Your first goal is to create a Web method that returns an ADO.NET DataSet, containing the full set of records in the Inventory table. Let's call this Web method GetAllCars(). The return value is (of course) a DataSet. The implementation logic fills the DataSet using an SqlDataAdapter type, as shown here:

```
// Return all cars in inventory table.
public DataSet GetAllCars()
{
    // Fill the DataGrid with the Inventory table.
    SqlConnection sqlConn = new SqlConnection();
    sqlConn.ConnectionString = "data source=.; initial catalog=Cars;" +
                               "user id=sa; password=";
    SqlDataAdapter dsc =
        new SqlDataAdapter("Select * from Inventory", sqlConn);
```

```
        DataSet ds = new DataSet();
        dsc.Fill(ds, "Inventory");
        return ds;
}
```

If you now create a Windows Forms client (and add a reference to this Web service), you can call the GetAllCars() method in the Form's Load event and attach the Inventory table to a DataGrid widget (Figure 15-20), as shown here:

```
private void mainForm_Load(object sender, System.EventArgs e)
{
    bigmanu.Service1 s = new bigmanu.Service1();
    DataSet ds = s.GetAllCars();
    dataGrid1.DataSource = ds.Tables["Inventory"];
}
```

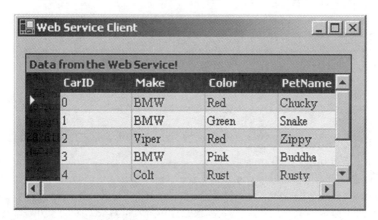

Figure 15-20. Obtaining a DataSet from the Car Web service

Serializing Custom Types

The SOAP protocol is also able to transport XML representations of custom data types. To illustrate, let's build the *final* Car type of the book (thank me later). Insert a new class named Car in your current CarsWebService application. This iteration is simple: You have two public fields (to represent the pet name and max speed) and an overloaded constructor to set the data. Also notice the very important extra detail, the use of the XmlInclude attribute (defined in the System.Xml.Serialization namespace), as shown here:

```
namespace CarsWebService
{
    using System;
    using System.Xml.Serialization;

    [XmlInclude(typeof(Car))]
    public class Car
    {
        public Car(){}
        public Car(string n, int s)
        {petName = n; maxSpeed = s;}

        public string petName;
        public int maxSpeed;
    }
}
```

Technically speaking, the process of transforming the stateful data of an object into an XML representation is termed *serialization*. Given that XML itself has no clue what a car type is, you must mark each custom type to be serialized as XML includable using the XmlIncludeAttribute type.

Next, define as private an ArrayList data member (carList) and fill it with some initial cars in the constructor of your Web service, as shown here:

```
public Service1()
{
    InitializeComponent();

    // Add cars.
    carList.Add(new Car("Zippy", 170));
    carList.Add(new Car("Fred", 80));
    carList.Add(new Car("Sally", 40));
}
```

Now let's add two additional Web methods. GetCarList() returns the entire array of autos. GetACarFromList() returns a specific car from the array list based on a numerical index. The implementation of each method is simple, as shown here:

```
// Return a given car from the list.
[WebMethod]
public Car GetACarFromList(int carToGet)
```

```
    {
        if(carToGet <= carList.Count)
        {
            return (Car) carList[carToGet];
        }
        throw new IndexOutOfRangeException();
    }


    // Return the entire set of cars.
    [WebMethod]
    public ArrayList GetCarList()
    {
        return carList;
    }
```

Enhancing Your Windows Forms Client

The next task is exercising the GetACarFromList() and GetCarList() members from our client application. Given that your Web service is a .NET assembly at heart, understand that the definition of the car type has been described in the assembly's metadata. (You may need to refresh the Web reference using the Solution Explorer.) To illustrate, you can create a given car as shown here:

```
protected void btnGetCar_Click (object sender, System.EventArgs e)
{
    try
    {
        bigmanu.Car c;
        bigmanu.Service1 cws = new bigmanu.Service1();
        c = cws.GetACarFromList(int.Parse(txtCarToGet.Text));
        MessageBox.Show(c.petName, "Car " + txtCarToGet.Text
                    + " is named:");
        cws.Dispose();
    }
    catch
    {
        MessageBox.Show("No car with that number. . .");
    }
}
```

Figure 15-21 shows a test run. (Remember that you are referencing the ID of the car in the ArrayList, not the Inventory table!)

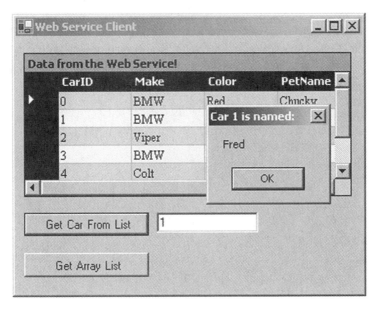

Figure 15-21. Grabbing a car from the ArrayList

As far as the ArrayList returned from GetCarList() is concerned, you can hold the entire set of items in an object array and cast accordingly, as shown here:

```
private void btnArrayList_Click(object sender, System.EventArgs e)
{
    bigmanu.Service1 cws = new bigmanu.Service1();
    object[] objs = cws.GetCarList();
    string petNames = "";

    // Print out pet name of each item in array.
    for(int i = 0; i< objs.Length; i++)
    {
        // Extract next car!
        bigmanu.Car c = (bigmanu.Car)objs[i];
        petNames += c.petName + "\n";
    }
    MessageBox.Show(petNames, "Pet names for cars in array list:");
    cws.Dispose();
}
```

Building Serializable Types (Further Details)

When a custom type is serialized into XML, you are essentially storing the stateful data from the object for later use. Therefore, for the runtime to serialize a given member of a custom type, it must somehow have *access* to the underlying value. As you recall, the car you previously created supported two public fields, as shown here:

```
[XmlInclude(typeof(Car))]
public class Car
{

    public string petName;
    public int maxSpeed;
}
```

You can change each of these members to private as shown here:

```
[XmlInclude(typeof(Car))]
public class Car
{
    public Car(){}
    public Car(string n, int s)
    {petName = n; maxSpeed = s;}

    // Serialize me?
    private string petName;
    private int maxSpeed;
}
```

When you test the GetCarList() method once again, you find an ArrayList with three cars. However, each item would have *no state data* expressed in the XML. The reason is simple enough. The runtime could not access this private data! The short answer is, if you wish the state of your types to be serialized into an equivalent XML representation, you must either supply public fields or provide access to private data using a corresponding property, as shown here:

```
[XmlInclude(typeof(Car))]
public class Car
{
...
    private string petName;
    private int maxSpeed;
    public string PetName
```

```
    {
        get{ return petName;}
        set{ petName = value;}
    }
    public int MaxSpeed
    {
        get{ return maxSpeed;}
        set{ maxSpeed = value;}
    }
}
```

In summary, building types that are available through a Web service is more or less just like building any C# data type. The only real points to be aware of are that you need to mark the type with the [XmlInclude] attribute and only publicly accessible points of data can be represented in the underlying XML.

SOURCE CODE *The CarsWebService.asmx.cs file and CarClient project can be found under the Chapter 15 subdirectory.*

Understanding the Discovery Service Protocol

The final topic of this chapter is to address the cleverly named *.disco file (which you recall is an abbreviated form of DISCOvery of Web Services). Whenever a remote (or local) client is interested in using a Web service, the first step is to determine which Web services exist on a given machine. While the .NET class library defines the types that allow you to examine registered Web services programmatically, discovery services are also required by numerous design time CASE tools (such as the Add Web Reference Wizard).

The *.disco file is used to describe each Web service in a given virtual directory and any related subfolders. When you create a new Visual Studio.NET Web project, you automatically receive a *.disco file that looks like this:

```
<?xml version="1.0" ?>
<dynamicDiscovery xmlns="urn:schemas-dynamicdiscovery:disco.2000-03-17">
<exclude path="_vti_cnf" />
<exclude path="_vti_pvt" />
<exclude path="_vti_log" />
<exclude path="_vti_script" />
<exclude path="_vti_txt" />
<exclude path="Web References" />
</dynamicDiscovery>
```

The <dynamicDiscover> tag signifies that the *.disco file is to be processed on the server to return an XML description for each Web service in a given virtual directory. In addition to the <dynamicDiscovery> tags, you can also see that a number of irrelevant paths have been excluded from this search. To illustrate, launch IE and navigate to the CarsWebService.disco file (Figure 15-22).

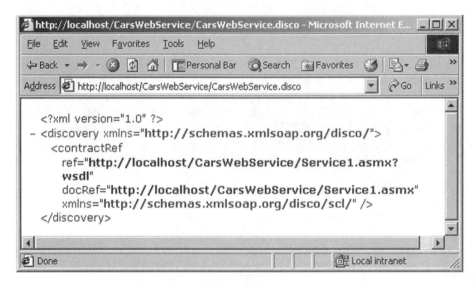

Figure 15-22. The *.disco file provides discovery services

Adding a New Web Service

Understand that a single *.disco file describes each and every Web service installed under a given virtual directory. Assume you have added another Web service to your current CarWebService project using the Project|Add Web Service. . . menu selection named MotorBikes.asmx (Figure 15-23).

The MotorBikes class defines a single Web method, as shown here:

```csharp
[WebMethod]
public string GetBikerDesc()
{
    return "Name: Tiny. Weight: 374 pounds.";
}
```

If you recompile the application and once again specify the *.disco file from IE, you have Figure 15-24.

As you can see, you now have two <contractRef> nodes, one for automobiles and one for motorcycles. Granted, viewing the results of a disco query from within IE is not all that fascinating. Recall however that this same file is used with

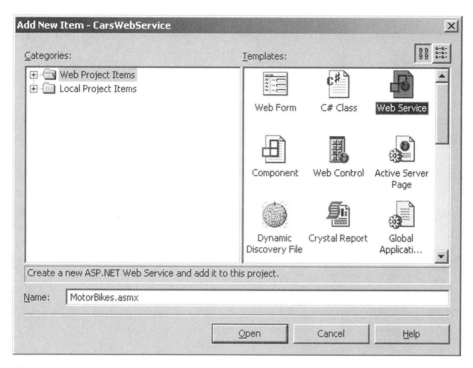

Figure 15-23. A single Web service project may contain multiple Web classes

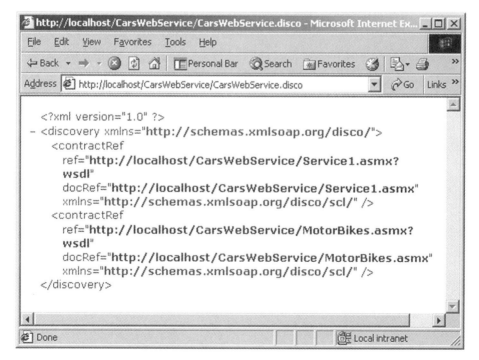

Figure 15-24. *.disco files describe all Web services under a given virtual directory

the Add Web Reference Wizard. Furthermore, you could also programmatically obtain this same information using various WSDL-centric .NET types. However, I will leave this task as an exercise for any interested readers.

Summary

This chapter has exposed you to the core building blocks of .NET Web services. The chapter began by examining the core namespaces (and core types in these namespaces) used during Web service development. As you have seen, Web services require three interrelated technologies: a lookup mechanism (*disco files), a description language (WSDL), and a wire protocol (GET, POST, or SOAP).

Once you have created any number of [WebMethod]-enabled members, you can interact with a Web service through an intervening proxy. The wsdl.exe utility generates such a proxy, which can be used by the client like any other C# type. As you have seen, by default wsdl.exe generated C# code using SOAP as the method of transport. This can be adjusted using various command-line switches. Finally, this chapter (as well as the book itself!) concluded by exploring how you can expose custom types from a Web service using the XmlInclude attribute.

Index

About Apress

Apress, located in Berkeley, CA, is an innovative publishing company devoted to meeting the needs of existing and potential programming professionals. Simply put, the "A" in Apress stands for the "Author's Press™." Apress' unique author-centric approach to publishing grew from conversations between Dan Appleman and Gary Cornell, authors of best-selling, highly regarded computer books. In 1998, they set out to create a publishing company that emphasized quality above all else, a company with books that would be considered the best in their market. Dan and Gary's vision has resulted in over 30 widely acclaimed titles by some of the industry's leading software professionals.

Do You Have What It Takes to Write for Apress?

Apress is rapidly expanding its publishing program. If you can write and refuse to compromise on the quality of your work, if you believe in doing more then rehashing existing documentation, and if you're looking for opportunities and rewards that go far beyond those offered by traditional publishing houses, we want to hear from you!

Consider these innovations that we offer all of our authors:

- **Top royalties with *no* hidden switch statements**
  Authors typically receive only half of their normal royalty rate on foreign sales. In contrast, Apress' royalty rate remains the same for both foreign and domestic sales.
- **A mechanism for authors to obtain equity in Apress**
  Unlike the software industry, where stock options are essential to motivate and retain software professionals, the publishing industry has adhered to an outdated compensation model based on royalties alone. In the spirit of most software companies, Apress reserves a significant portion of its equity for authors.
- **Serious treatment of the technical review process**
  Each Apress book has a technical reviewing team whose remuneration depends in part on the success of the book, since they too receive royalties.

Moreover, through a partnership with Springer-Verlag, one of the world's major publishing houses, Apress has significant venture capital behind it. Thus, we have the resources to produce the highest quality books *and* market them aggressively.

If you fit the model of the Apress author who can write a book that gives the "professional what he or she needs to know™," then please contact one of our Editorial Directors, Gary Cornell (gary_cornell@apress.com), Dan Appleman (dan_appleman@apress.com), Karen Watterson (karen_watterson@apress.com), or Jason Gilmore (jason_gilmore@apress.com) for more information.

Apress Titles

ISBN	LIST PRICE	AUTHOR	TITLE
1-893115-01-1	$39.95	Appleman	Dan Appleman's Win32 API Puzzle Book and Tutorial for Visual Basic Programmers
1-893115-23-2	$29.95	Appleman	How Computer Programming Works
1-893115-97-6	$39.95	Appleman	Moving to VB.NET: Strategies, Concepts and Code
1-893115-09-7	$29.95	Baum	Dave Baum's Definitive Guide to LEGO MINDSTORMS
1-893115-84-4	$29.95	Baum, Gasperi, Hempel, and Villa	Extreme MINDSTORMS
1-893115-82-8	$59.95	Ben-Gan/Moreau	Advanced Transact-SQL for SQL Server 2000
1-893115-99-2	$39.95	Cornell/Morrison	Programming VB.NET: A Guide for Experienced Programmers
1-893115-85-2	$34.95	Gilmore	A Programmer's Introduction to PHP 4.0
1-893115-17-8	$59.95	Gross	A Programmer's Introduction to Windows DNA
1-893115-62-3	$39.95	Gunnerson	A Programmer's Introduction to C#, Second Edition
1-893115-10-0	$34.95	Holub	Taming Java Threads
1-893115-04-6	$34.95	Hyman/Vaddadi	Mike and Phani's Essential C++ Techniques
1-893115-79-8	$49.95	Kofler	Definitive Guide to Excel VBA
1-893115-50-X	$34.95	Knudsen	Wireless Java: Developing with Java 2, Micro Edition
1-893115-75-5	$44.95	Kurniawan	Internet Programming with VB
1-893115-19-4	$49.95	Macdonald	Serious ADO: Universal Data Access with Visual Basic

ISBN	LIST PRICE	AUTHOR	TITLE
1-893115-06-2	$39.95	Marquis/Smith	A Visual Basic 6.0 Programmer's Toolkit
1-893115-22-4	$27.95	McCarter	David McCarter's VB Tips and Techniques
1-893115-76-3	$49.95	Morrison	C++ For VB Programmers
1-893115-80-1	$39.95	Newmarch	A Programmer's Guide to Jini Technology
1-893115-81-X	$39.95	Pike	SQL Server: Common Problems, Tested Solutions
1-893115-20-8	$34.95	Rischpater	Wireless Web Development
1-893115-93-3	$34.95	Rischpater	Wireless Web Development with PHP and WAP
1-893115-24-0	$49.95	Sinclair	From Access to SQL Server
1-893115-94-1	$29.95	Spolsky	User Interface Design for Programmers
1-893115-59-3	$59.95	Troelsen	C# and the .Net Platform
1-893115-16-X	$49.95	Vaughn	ADO Examples and Best Practices
1-893115-83-6	$44.95	Wells	Code Centric: T-SQL Programming with Stored Procedures and Triggers
1-893115-95-X	$49.95	Welschenbach	Cryptography in C and C++
1-893115-05-4	$39.95	Williamson	Writing Cross-Browser Dynamic HTML
1-893115-78-X	$49.95	Zukowski	Definitive Guide to Swing for Java 2, Second Edition
1-893115-92-5	$49.95	Zukowski	Java Collections

Available at bookstores nationwide or from Springer Verlag New York, Inc. at 1-800-777-4643; fax 1-212-533-3503. Contact us for more information at sales@apress.com.

Apress Titles Publishing SOON!

ISBN	AUTHOR	TITLE
1-893115-96-8	Jorelid	Architecting a Servlet and JSP Based Application
1-893115-56-9	Kofler/Kramer	MySQL
1-893115-87-9	Kurata	Doing Web Development: Client-Side Techniques
1-893115-54-2	Trueblood/Lovett	Data Mining and Statistical Analysis Using SQL

To order, call (800) 777-4643 or email sales@apress.com.